GREAT PUBS *of* ENGLAND

THIRTY-THREE OF ENGLAND'S BEST
HOSTELRIES FROM THE HOME COUNTIES TO THE NORTH

— HORST A. FRIEDRICHS — STUART HUSBAND —

PRESTEL
MUNICH · LONDON · NEW YORK

CONTENTS

LONDON / SOUTH-EAST

SOUTH-WEST

NORTH

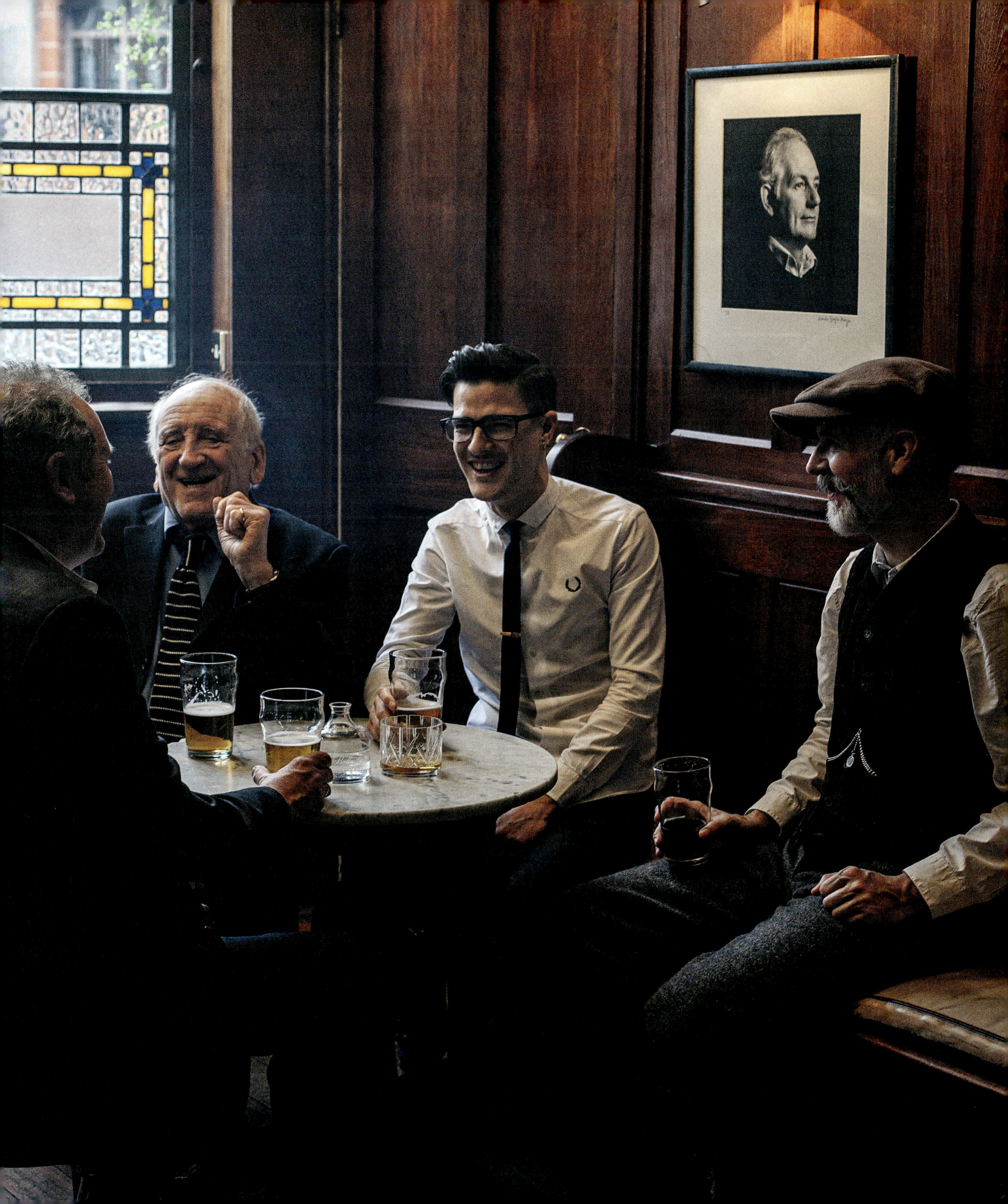

PUBS ARE FOR PEOPLE

BY JOHN WARLAND

For all the sumptuous photography and evocative prose you'll find within these pages, it's the enduring sense of community and celebration of humanity embodied by the public house that rings out loud and clear. The landlords and ladies and patrons featured here are wonderfully diverse, offering a perfect mirror to the richness of British society. Pubs are, above all else, melting pots; places where all and sundry can enter and engage in spirited conversation or partake of the general bonhomie, irrespective of class, wealth or other such markers.

Since time immemorial, the public house has offered a place of shelter, liquid refreshment, sustenance and occasional lodging. But it's much more than the sum of these parts. It's often the very heart of a community, raising funds for its patrons, providing ad-lib counselling services, and offering a sociable antidote to the prevalent plague of loneliness. The pub is the backdrop for first dates, mending broken hearts, or toasting hatches, matches and dispatches. It's the hub of local life, as any self-respecting soap opera scriptwriter who has set a key scene in The Bull, The Queen Vic or The Rover's Return will tell you. At its best a great pub feels like home, or makes you feel like you're at home; it's not always the closest to where you are, but it's a perfect fit with who you are.

This wonderfully curated selection of eclectic and often eccentric hostelries across the breadth of England will certainly provoke a thirsty wanderlust. From rural retreats serving up ribs of beef over an open fire to urban oases and ultimate locals, there is a pub for all persuasions here. A punter once wrote, of Ye Olde Cheshire Cheese – a pub that's lived up to its name by enduring for at least 500 years – "A push at the door, and I have passed into another world." That's as true for its peers today, whether you're looking for the eternal verities – low light, warm hearths, the buzz of chinwaggery – or more modern and specialised forms of communality, such as digital detox, haute-hearty gastro-fare, or late-night music and cabaret.

The post-pandemic landscape has forced many a pub to pivot to serve the changing world around them. From working out whether a Scotch Egg could be classified as a "substantial meal", to guessing if their doors would be open long enough to tap their cask ale, it's been a rough rollercoaster ride. And, given that over 25 per cent of pubs in England shut their doors in the decade before Covid hit, you'd be forgiven for thinking that they're hovering dangerously close to the "endangered species" list. But good pubs will always serve good beer to good people. They might have to throw some artisanal gins or Korean BBQ chicken wings into the mix to broaden their church, but the fluid fundamentals remain unchanged.

As the creator of London's finest pub walks, I do have some skin in this game. We're regularly joined by people from across the world, and from all ages and backgrounds, eager to follow in the footsteps of Pepys, Johnson, Dickens and Shakespeare. I'm sure that this book will inspire them, as it has me, to go forth and explore England's liquid history anew. It's the perfect snapshot of where pubs have been, where they are now, and where they might be headed. The pub has never needed our support more, so please indulge your ancient and inalienable right to push open that brass-handled door and enjoy some elbow-bending activity whenever and wherever possible.

The pub is dead. Long live the pub.

JOHN WARLAND is the founder of Liquid History Tours, guided walking itineraries that explore London's rich hostelry heritage, and author of the *Liquid History* book. He's also a noted garden designer, winning six RHS Gold medals at the Chelsea and Hampton Court flower shows. Little wonder that a beer garden is his happy place.

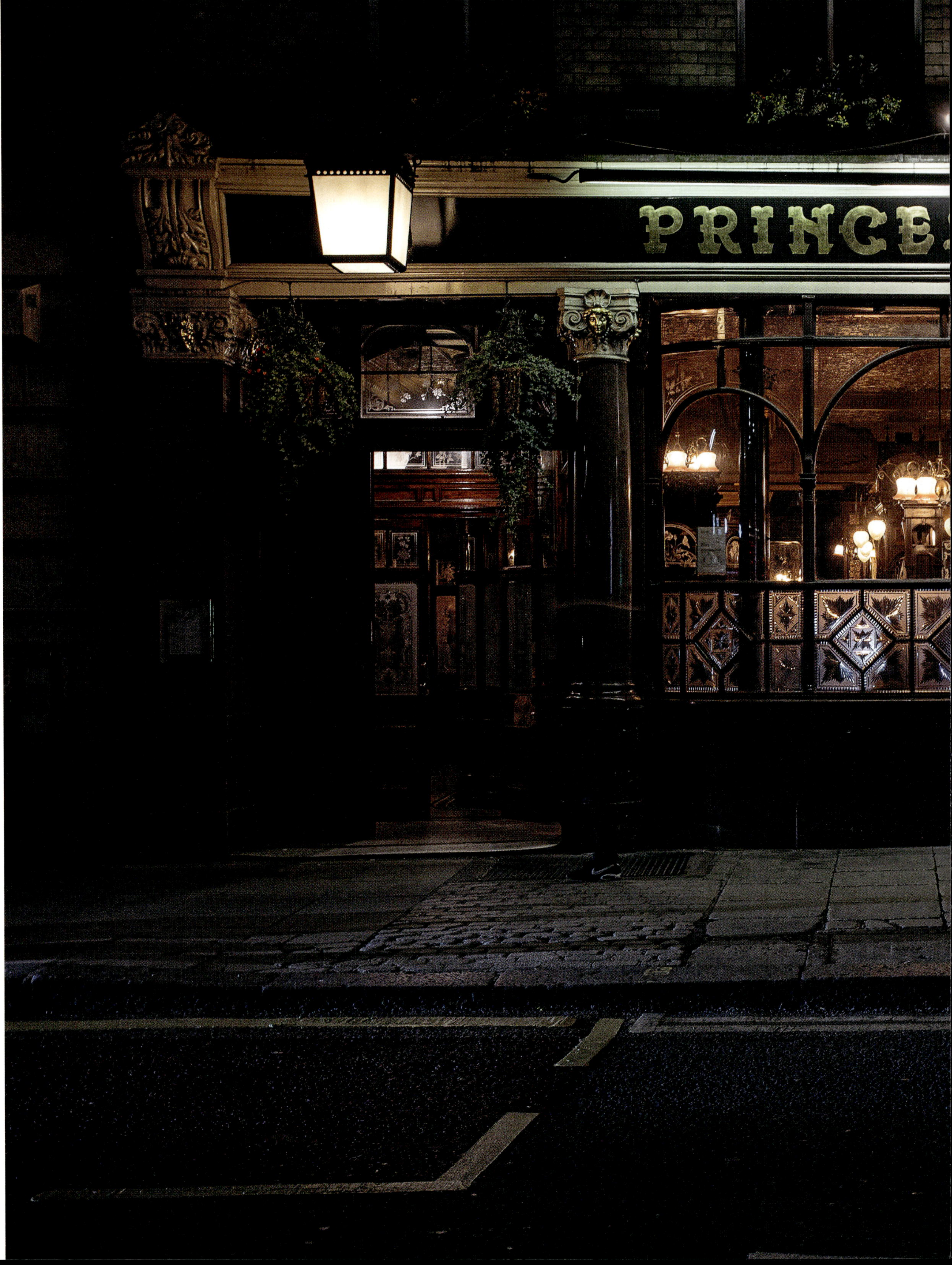
PRINCE

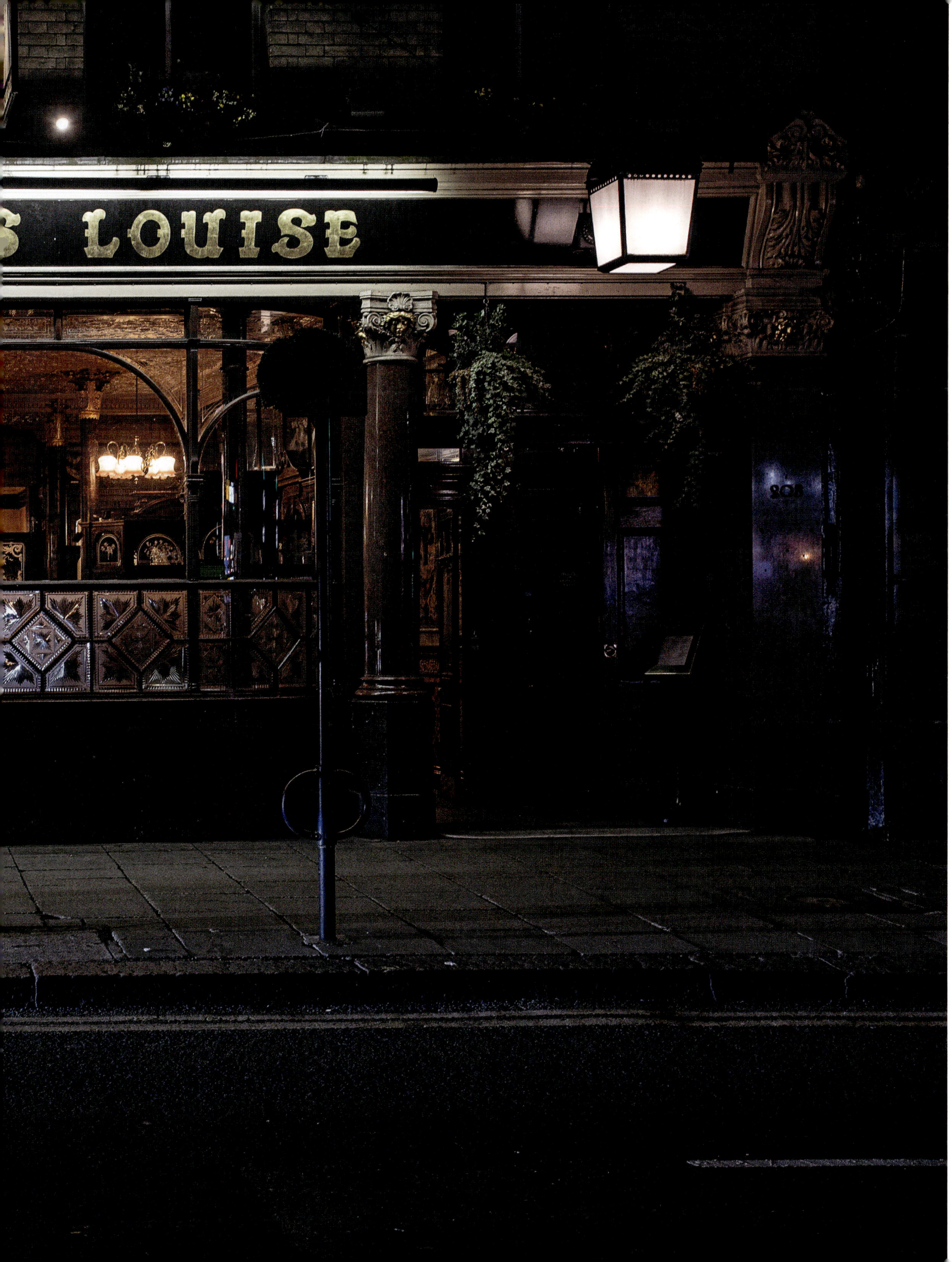

208 HIGH HOLBORN, LONDON

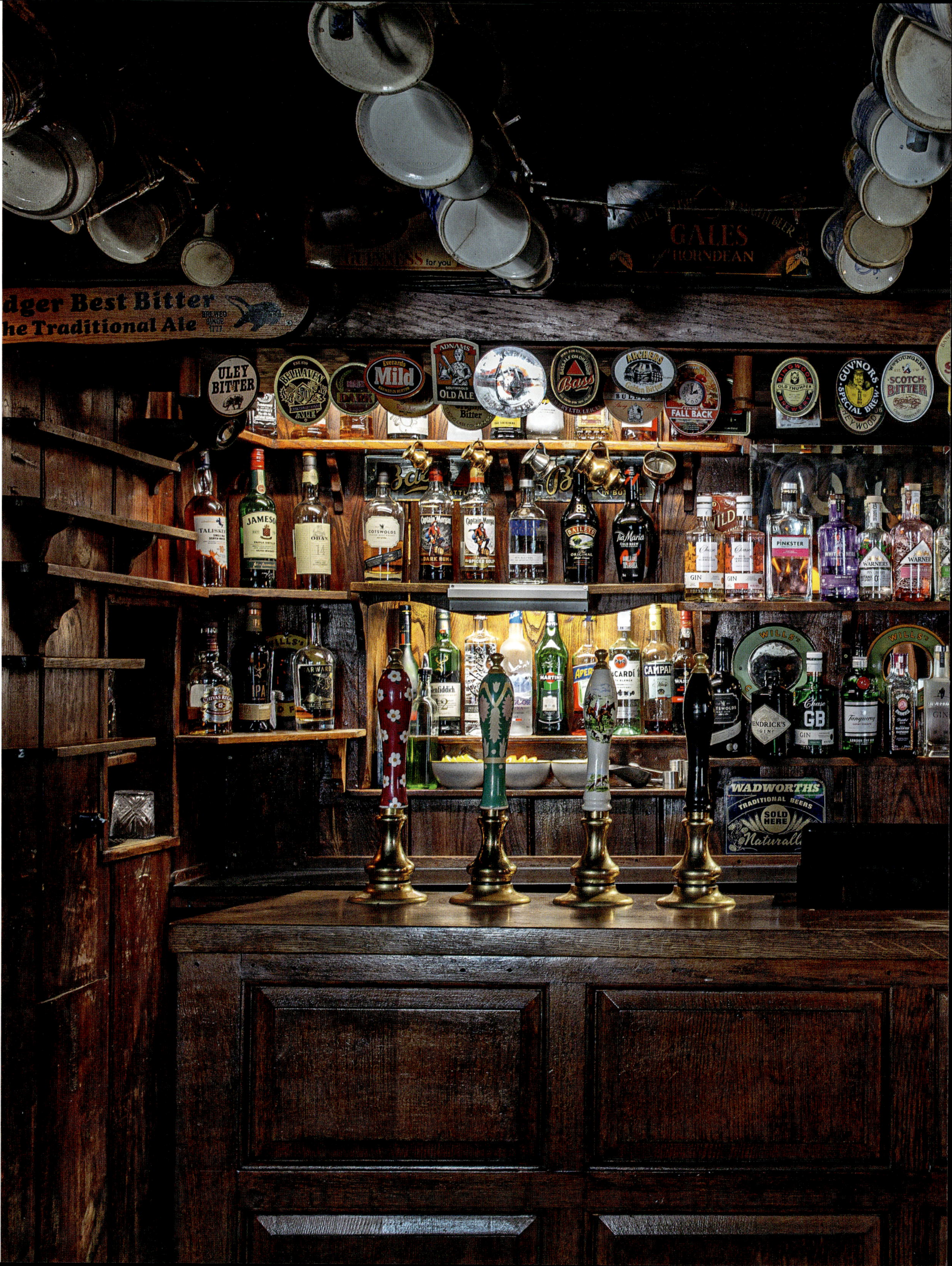
GALES
HORNDEAN
ULEY BITTER
Mild
ADNAMS
OLD ALE
Bass
ARCHERS
FALL BACK
GUV'NORS SPECIAL BREW
SCOTCH BITTER
PINKSTER
Tia Maria
WADWORTHS
TRADITIONAL BEERS
SOLD HERE

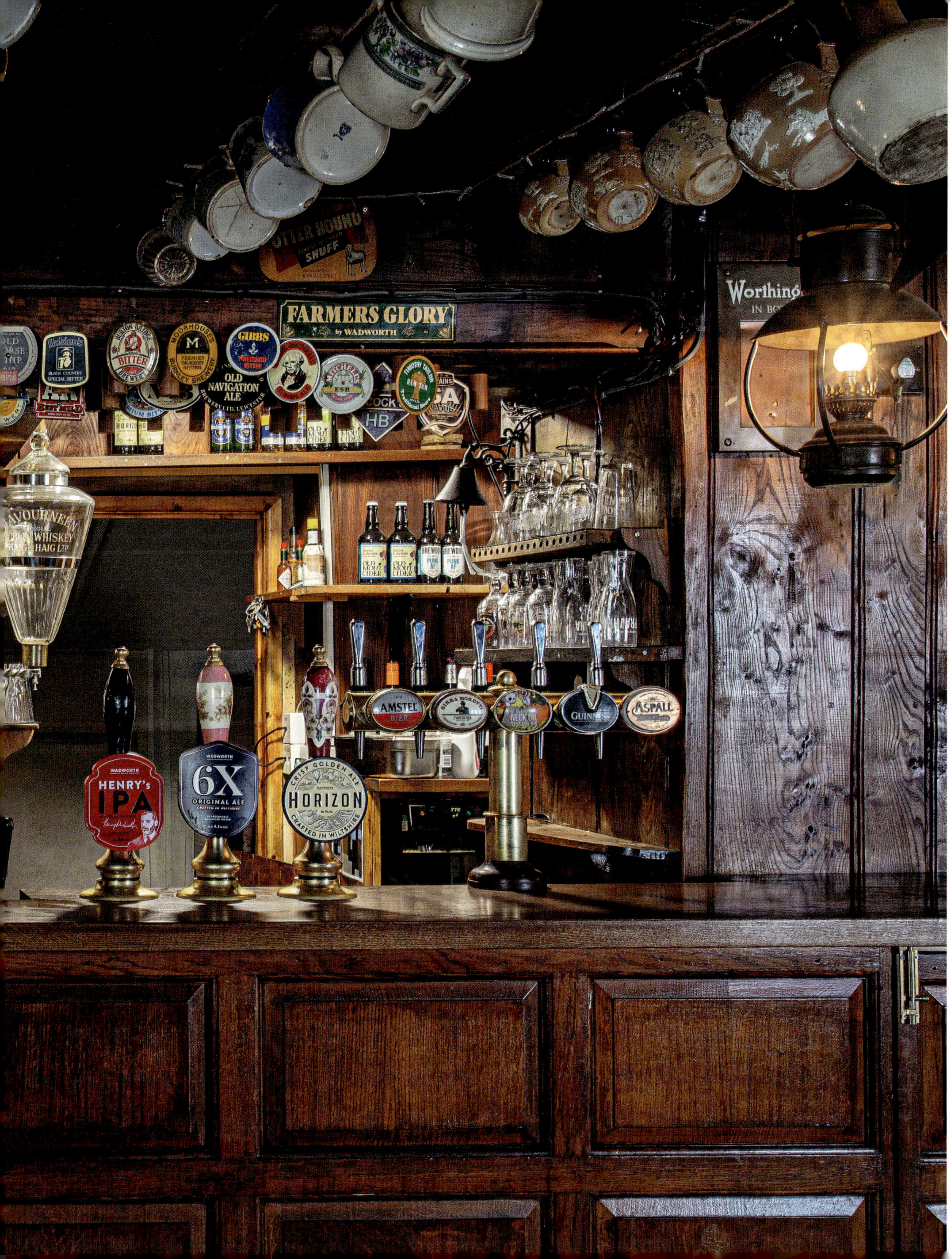

1 MINSTER ST, SALISBURY

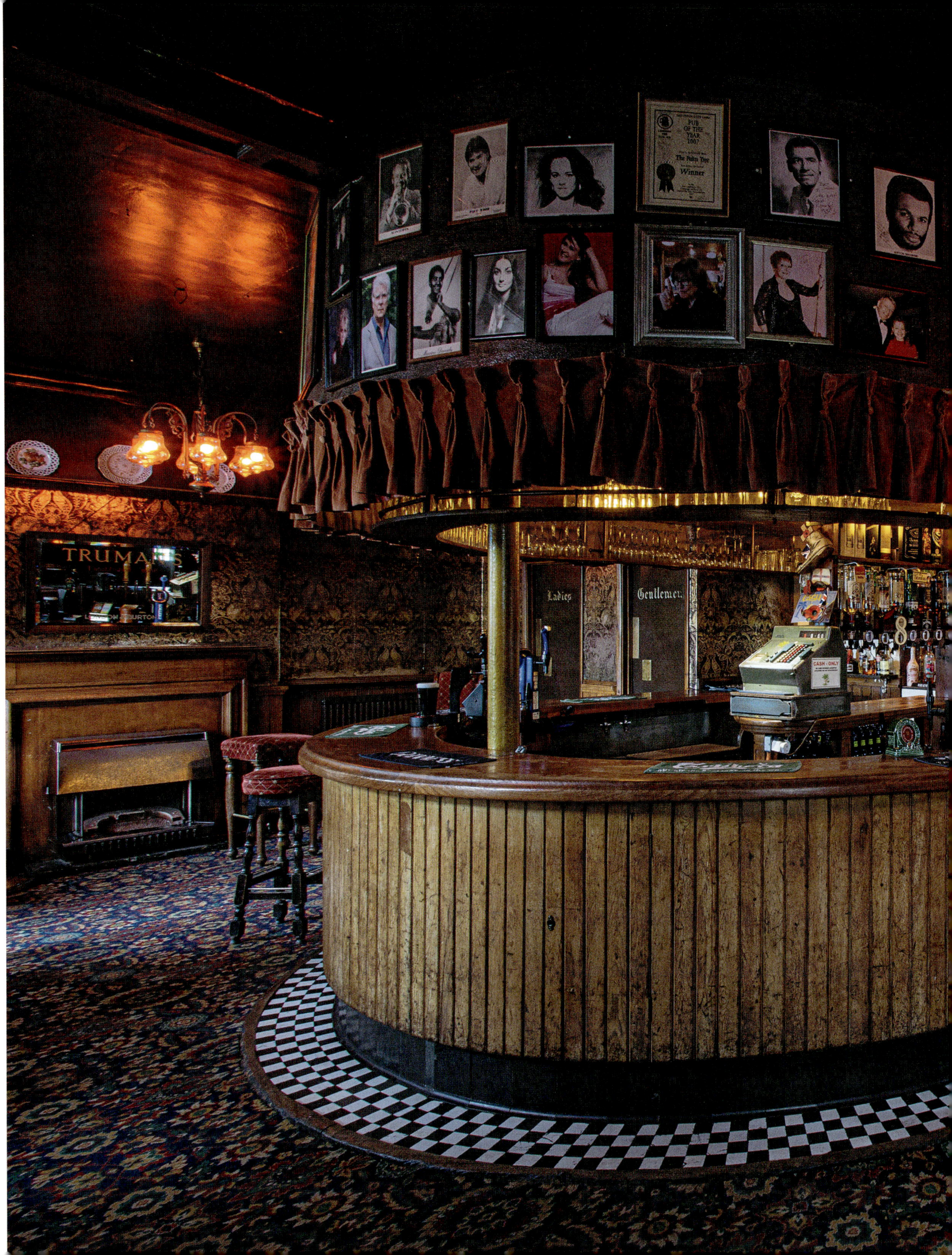
Ladies
Gentlemen

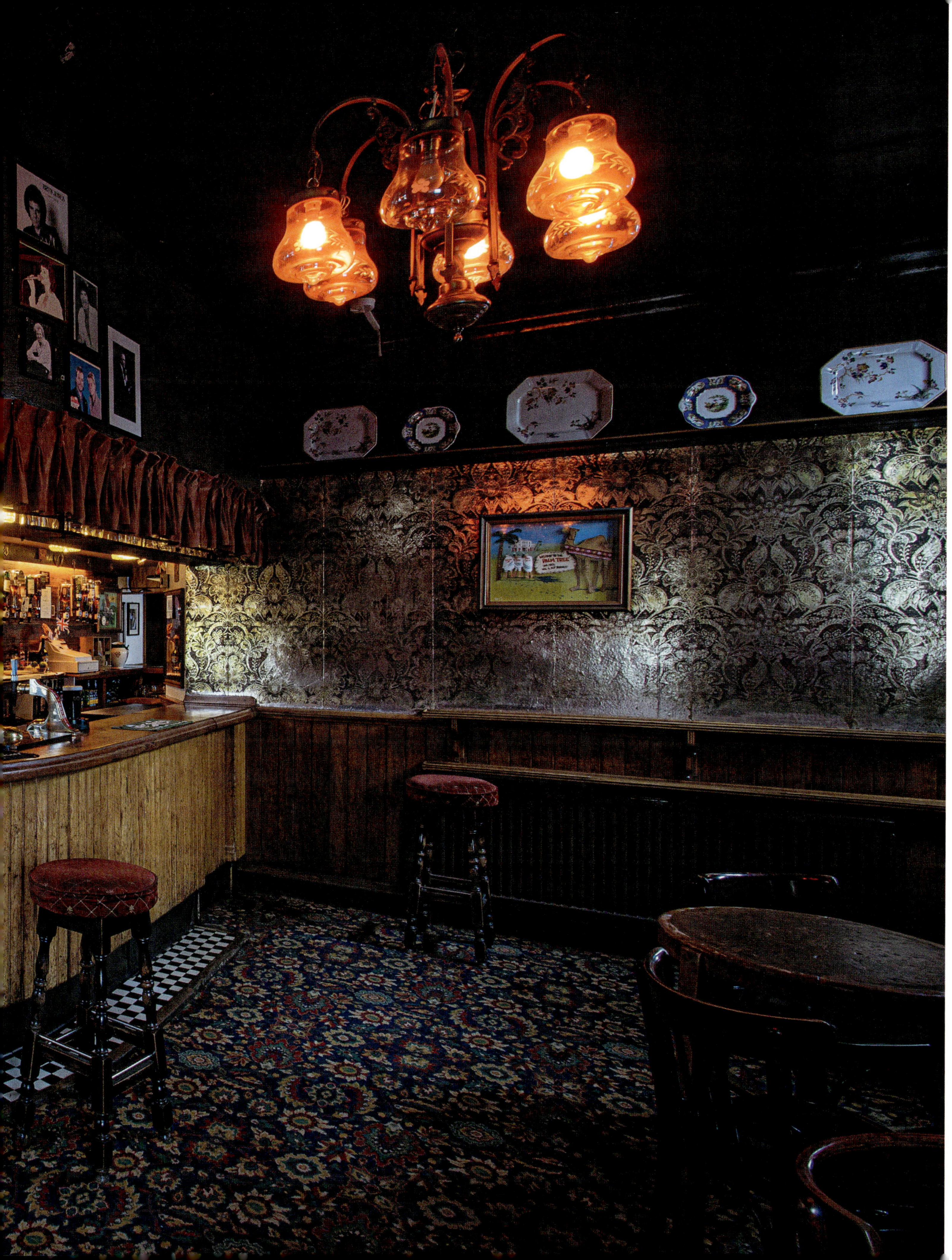

127 GROVE RD, LONDON

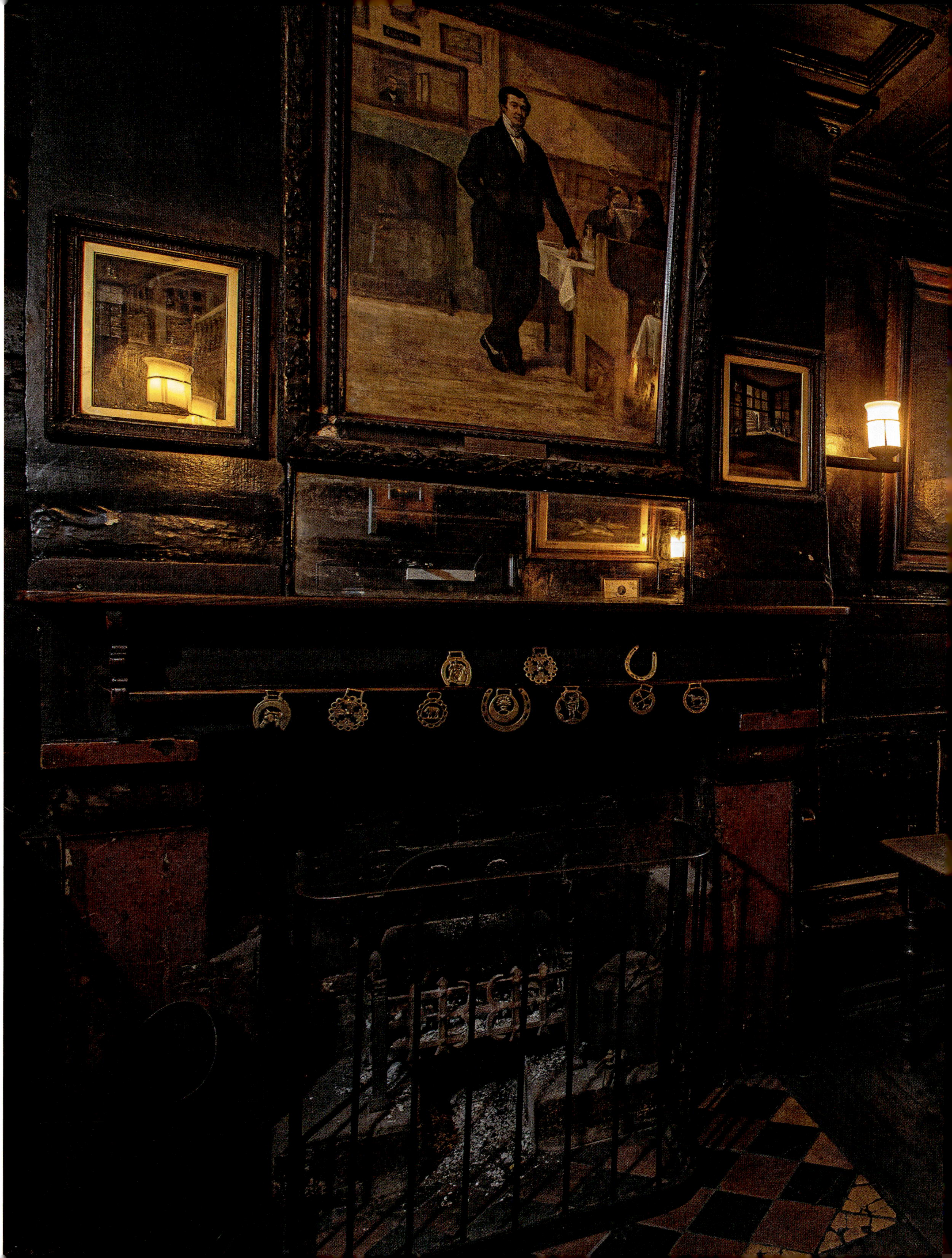

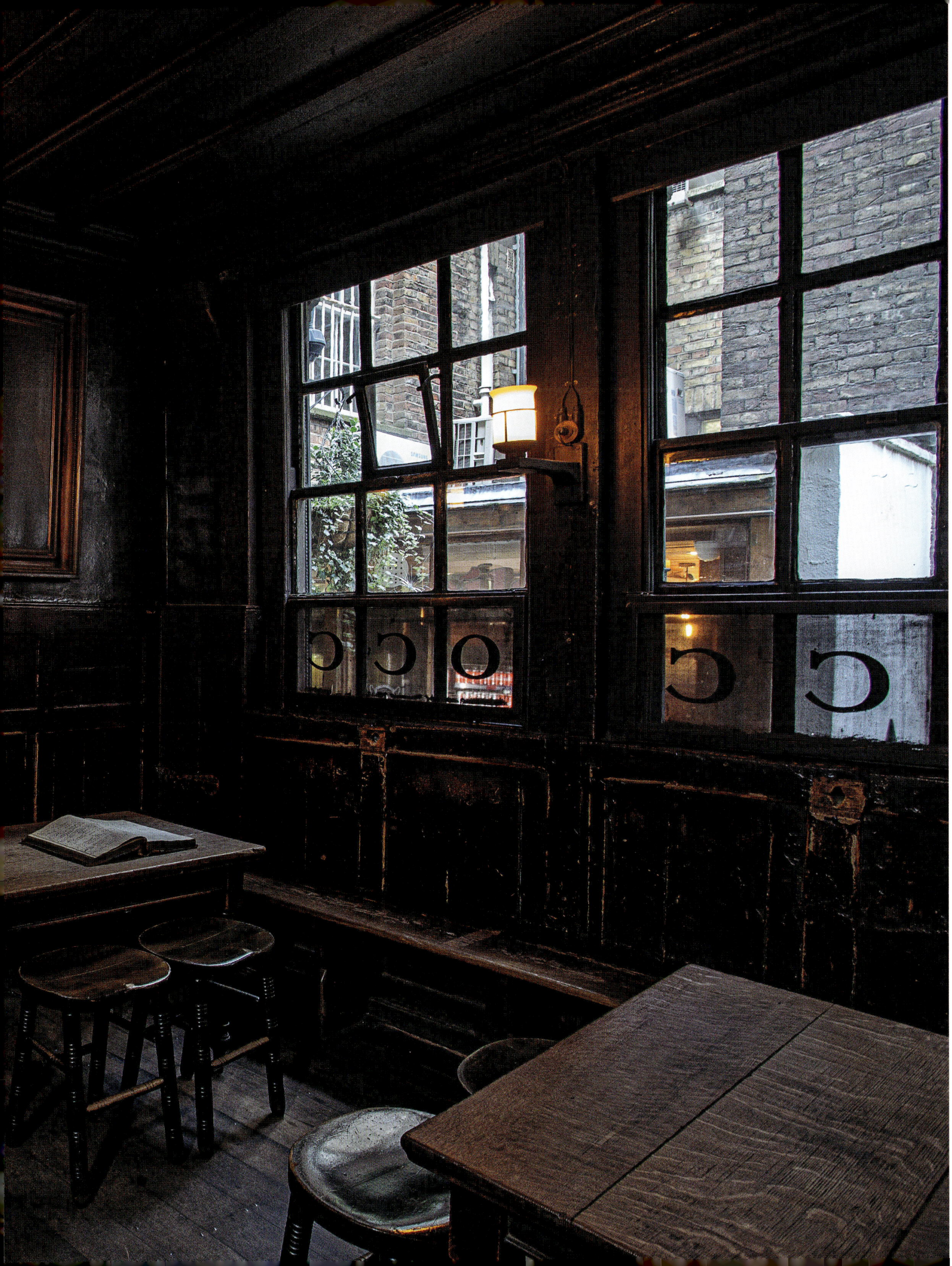

145 FLEET ST, LONDON

THE GUNTON ARMS

NORTH NORFOLK CROMER RD, THORPE MARKET, NORWICH

Ivor Braka is expounding on his vision as a pub landlord. "I wanted to create a pub that I'd be happy to patronise," he says. "I was told very forcibly that I had to design it with the public in mind." A beat, and a wry grin. "But I've always been of the opinion that one should do exactly the opposite. I resisted the idea that the customer is always right."

Braka is known as the "rock 'n' roll art dealer", not only for his cutting-edge sensibilities – he started trading Bacons, Freuds and Auerbachs very early, and his collection now encompasses choice YBA pieces (Hirst butterflies, Emin neons) alongside Vorticist drawings and Spanish old masters – but also for his elegantly wasted look: long grey hair, leather waistcoat, skinny jeans and – on special occasions – full Alice Cooper make-up. He's never had a gallery, but in many ways The Gunton Arms, the pub he opened in Thorpe Market near the tip of north Norfolk in 2011, is his Gesamtkunstwerk – a country inn given a very "Brakish" spin, from food to ambience to décor.

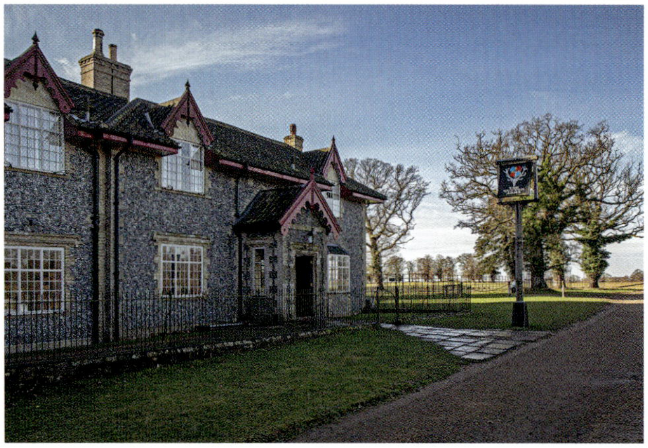

The Gunton sits on the edge of the thousand-acre Gunton Park estate, which Braka, who lives in a former observatory just down the road, has been helping restore to its Georgian splendour (planting 800,000 trees, reintroducing a deer herd) for some years; the pebble-dashed, leaded-windowed building was originally the estate manager's house, then a slightly chintzy country-house hotel called the Elderton Lodge. When Braka acquired it, "I stripped everything back to its bones," he says. "I wanted people to feel like they were walking into another world."

That world has been painstakingly crafted to be a little darker, more mysterious, more romantic, and a tad more subversive than our own. The roaring hearths and chunky cabinets are offset by burnt-orange walls (dirt was rubbed in to create the artfully scuffed look) and subdued lighting. The Elk Room is dominated by an imposing skull and antlers of the titular mammal above a massive fireplace, where lumps of prime rib are theatrically seared on a thick slab of steel (Simone Tattersall and her husband Stuart, Braka's general manager and head chef respectively, were recruited from the empire of Mark Hix, caterer-in-chief to the YBAs and pioneer of the painstakingly sourced, seasonally adjusted, haute barnyard style of cuisine that the Gunton has refined). And then there's the art.

It starts innocuously enough, with hunting prints and paintings of complacently plump cows in the lobby lounge; but penetrate further and things take a more disconcerting turn, with a room of Tracey Emin neons ("I said don't practise on me"), and, in a banquette-heavy snug, a suite of homoerotic drawings by Tom of Finland. There's an oil by Jonathan Yeo of fallen leaves, serenely autumnal until you notice the images of genitalia concealed within ("the young farmers like that one", says Simone), there's a crab wrapped in a doily by the Portuguese sculptor Joana Vasconcelos (which unfailingly gives rise to lots of quips about "dressed crab"), and there are photos of Mrs Braka, aka the supermodel Kristen McMenamy, in various states of artistic deshabille. "I really wanted to have interesting world-class art in a place where you normally wouldn't expect to see it," says Braka. "I like that I'm showing it to people who might ordinarily dislike modern art or who've never engaged with it."

But beyond the art, says Braka, the Gunton serves a wider purpose: "The primary reason for doing this was to create a place where people can gather. Here, we get everyone from lords and ladies to estate workers and local villagers, and, whether you're just here for a drink or staying in the guest rooms, you can strike up a conversation with someone at the bar, which is something that's really diminishing in England." The contented buzz of the postprandial crowd – fed, watered and even, possibly, cultured – bears him out. "Besides," he says, "if I'm going to have a pub at the end of my garden, why shouldn't it be the best one I can possibly devise?"

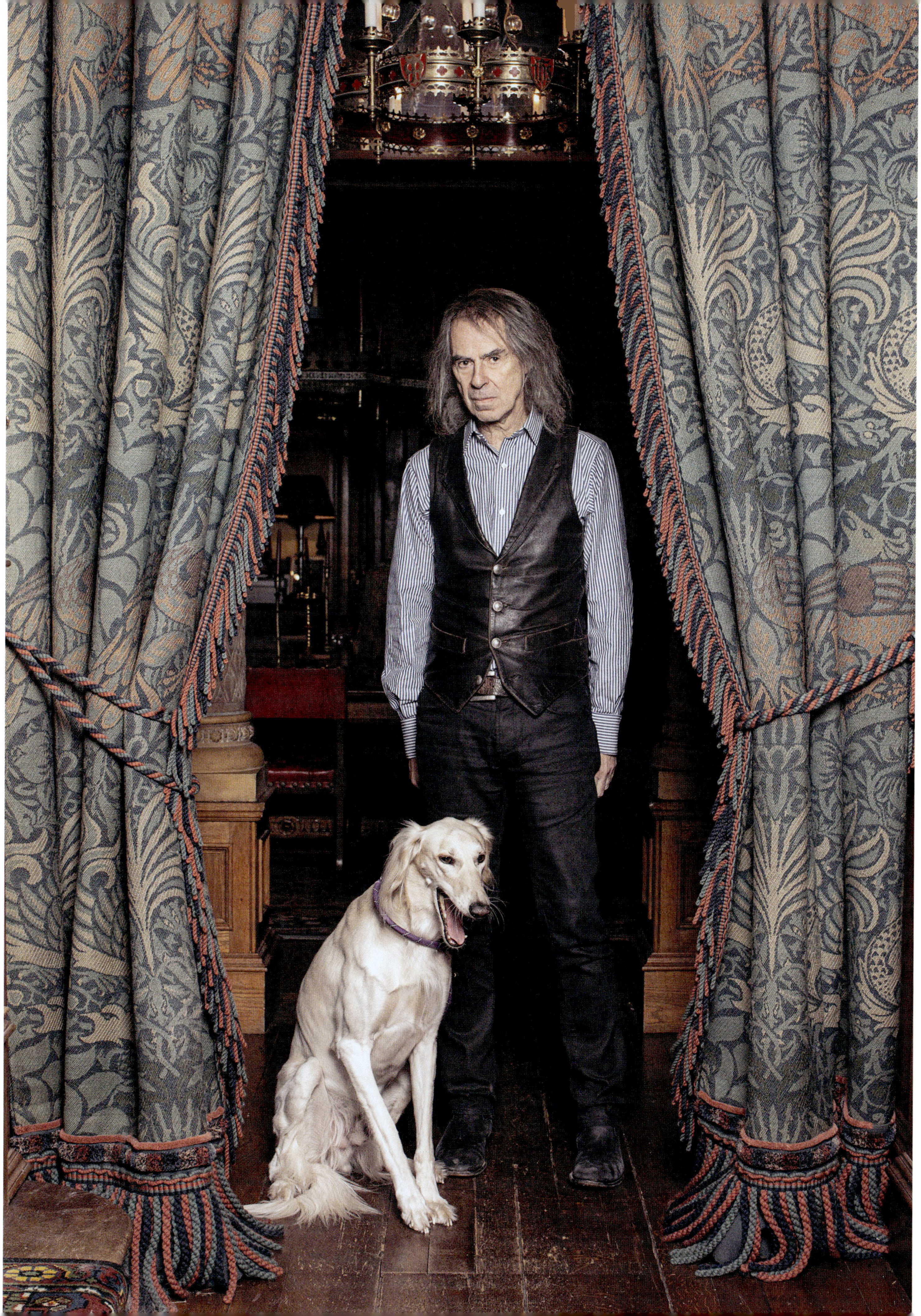

"PEOPLE WILL BUY INTO A STRONG VISION"

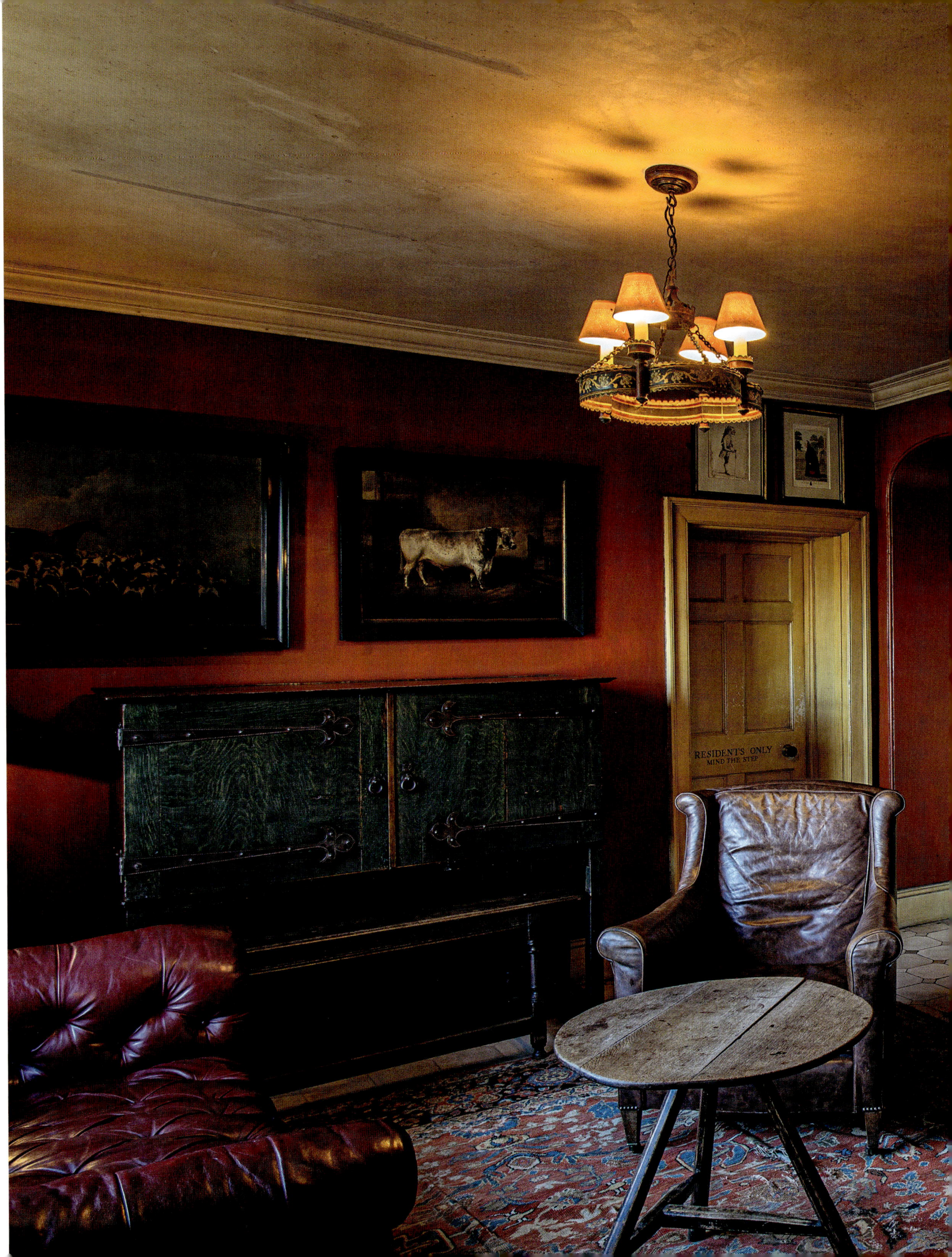
RESIDENT'S ONLY
MIND THE STEP

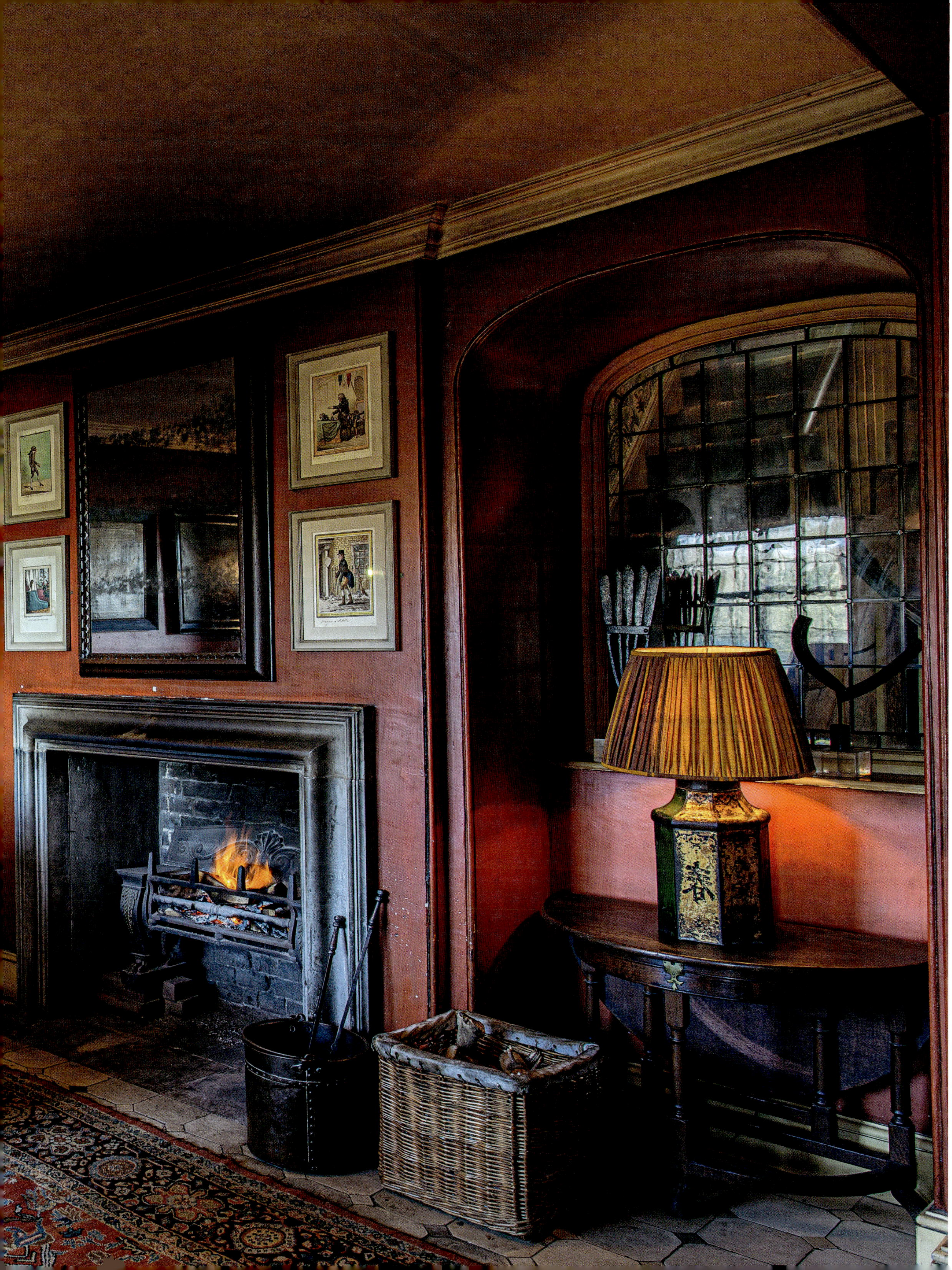

“SHADY CORNERS ARE MORE ROMANTIC”

"WE GET A GREAT MIX OF LOCALS AND VISITORS"

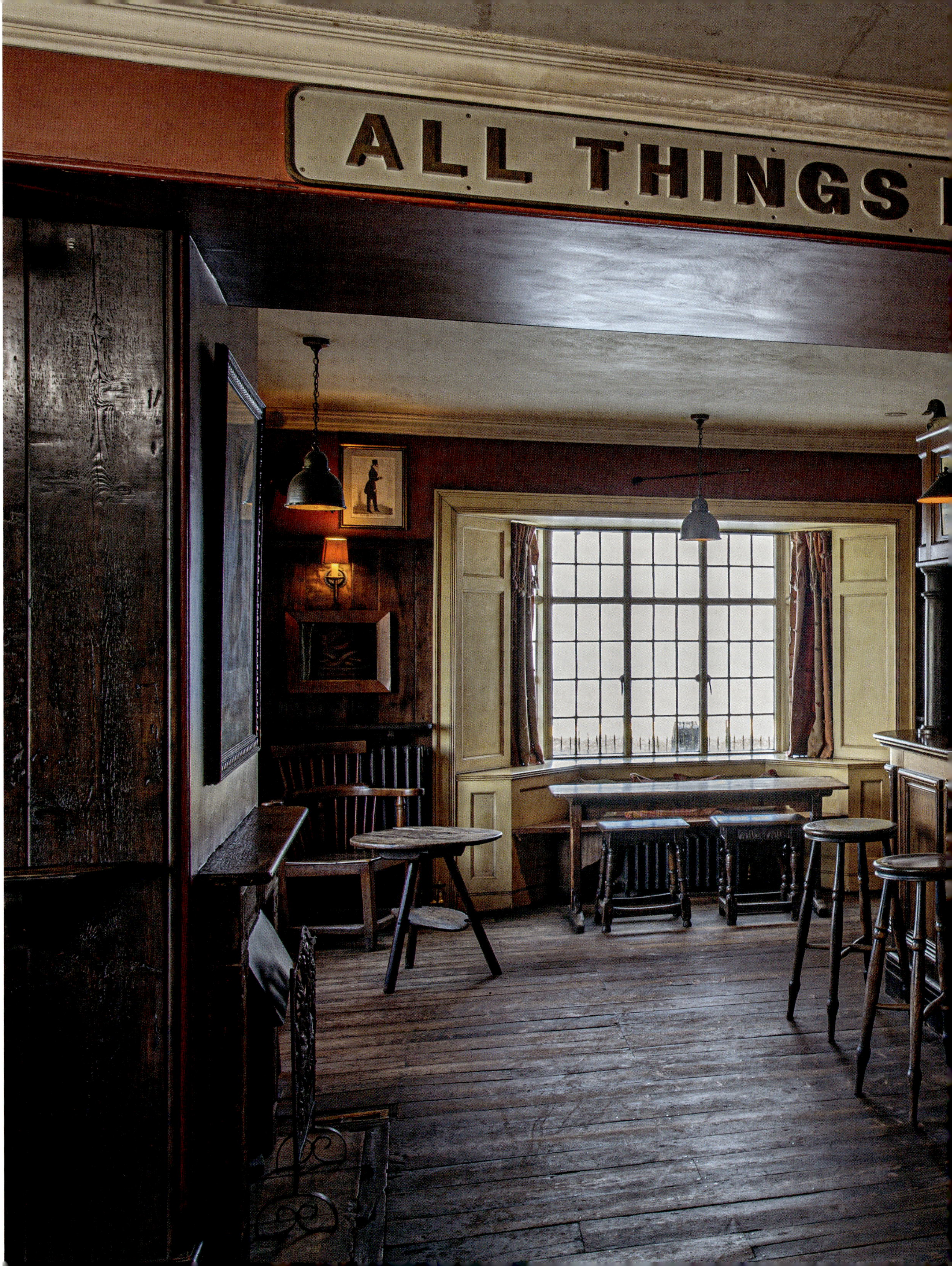

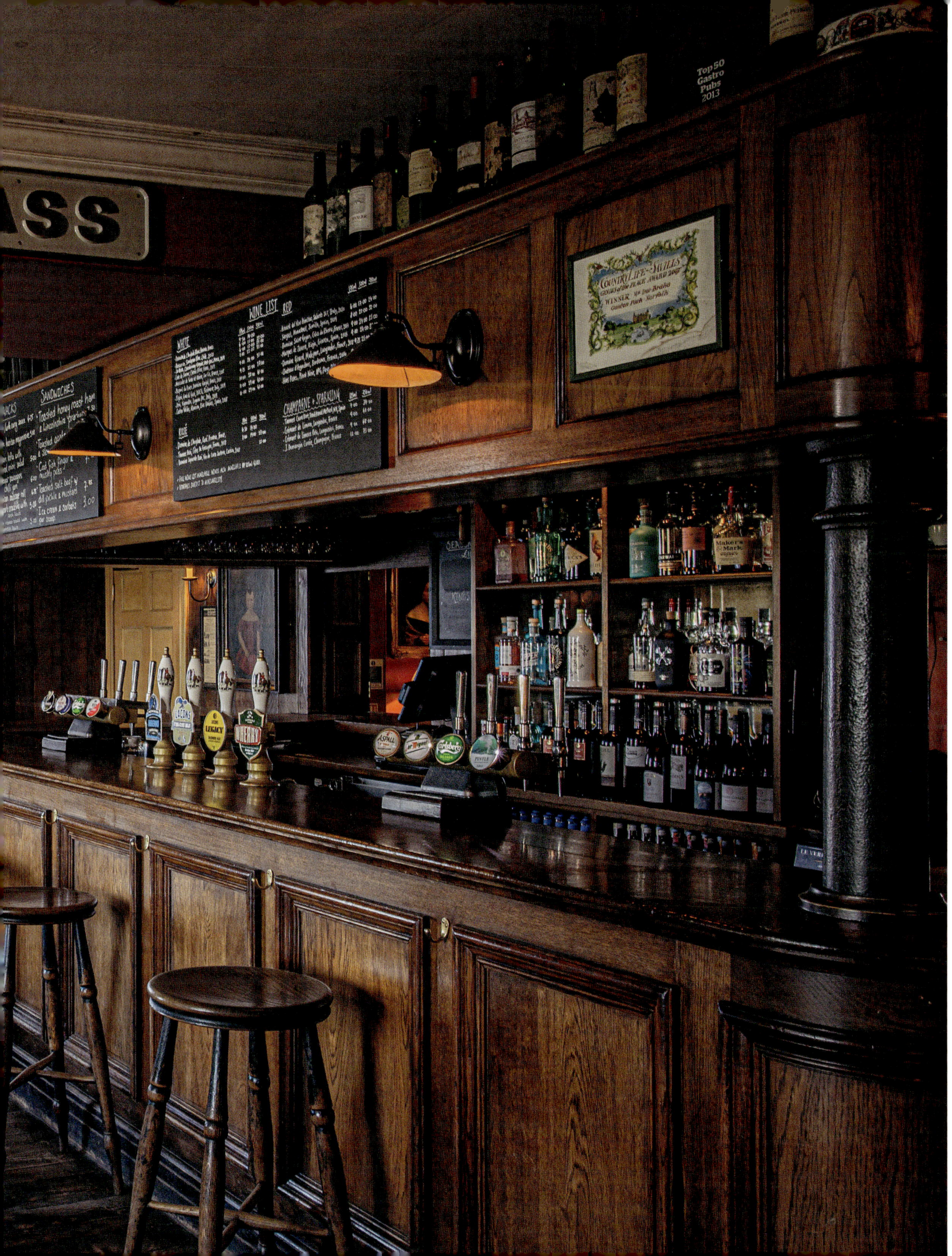

"A PLACE WHERE PEOPLE CAN GATHER"

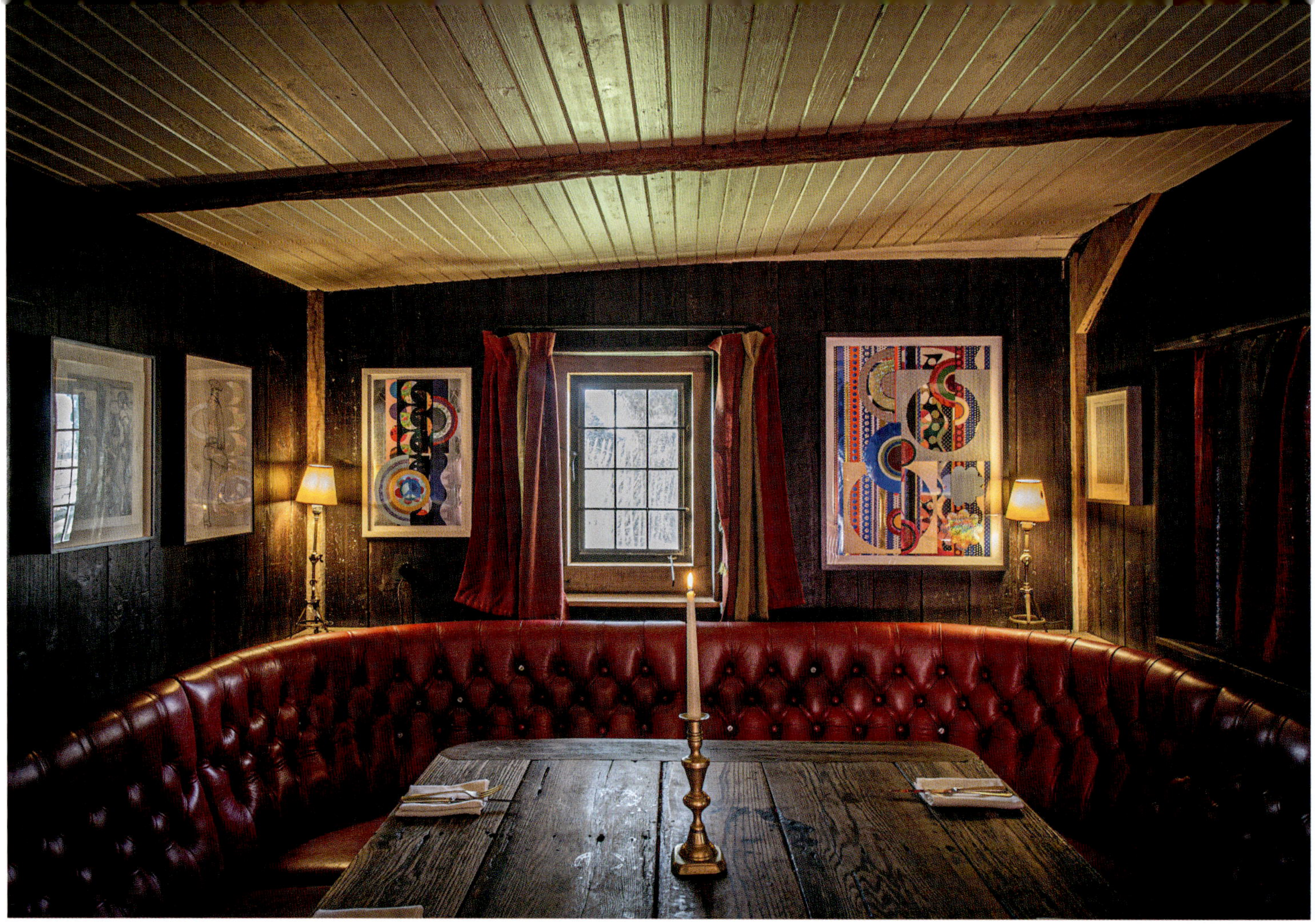

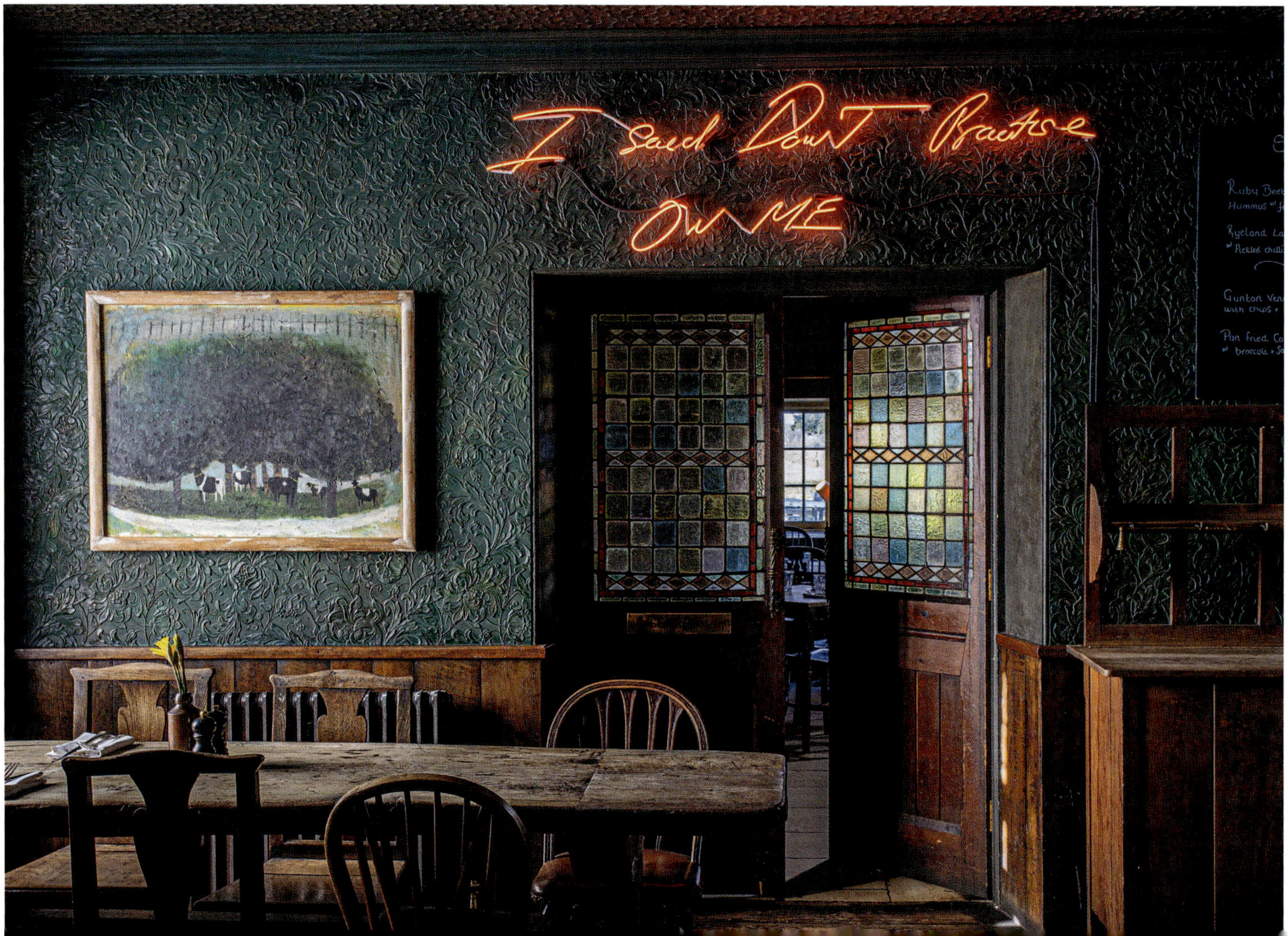
I said Don't Practise
ON ME

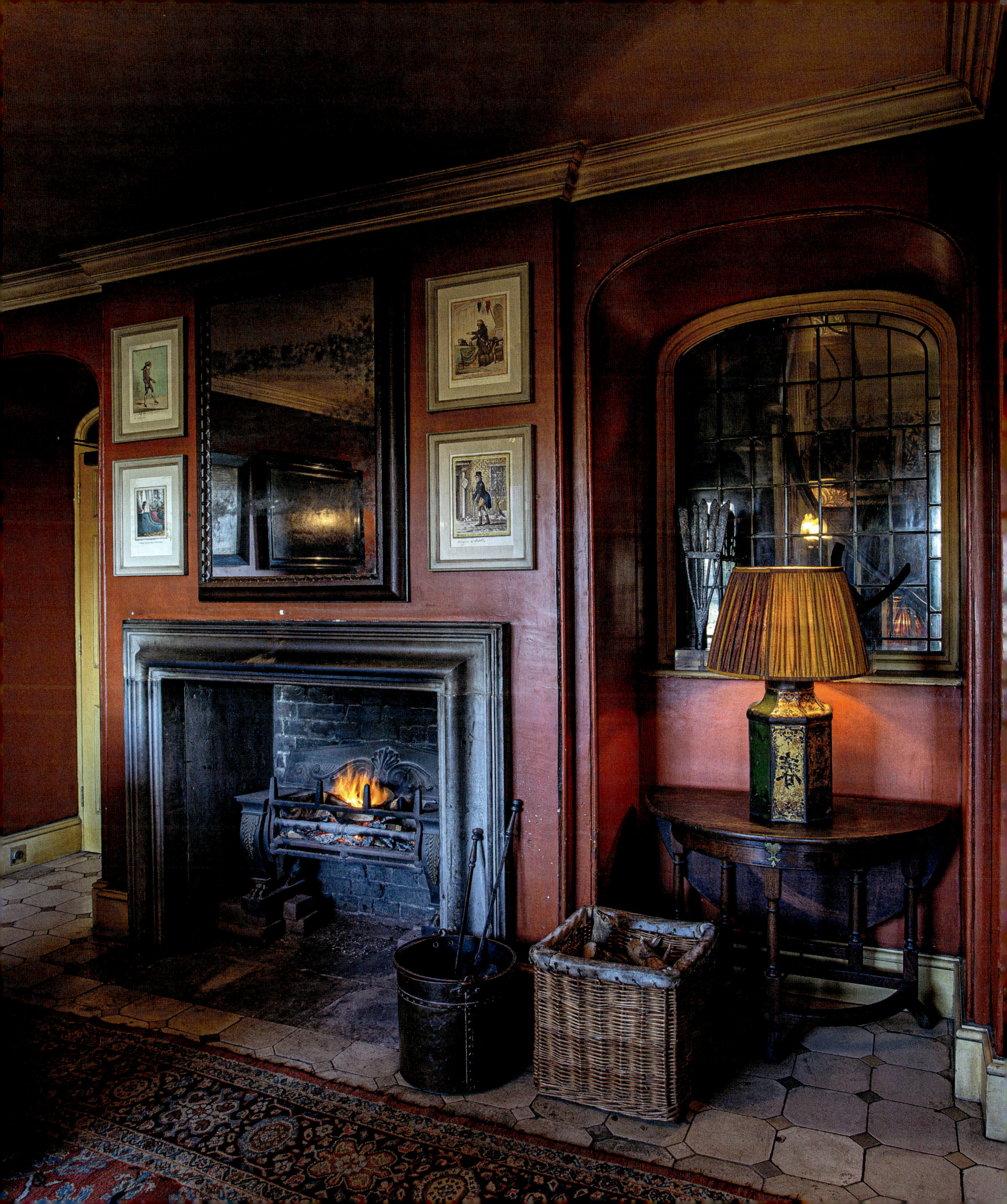

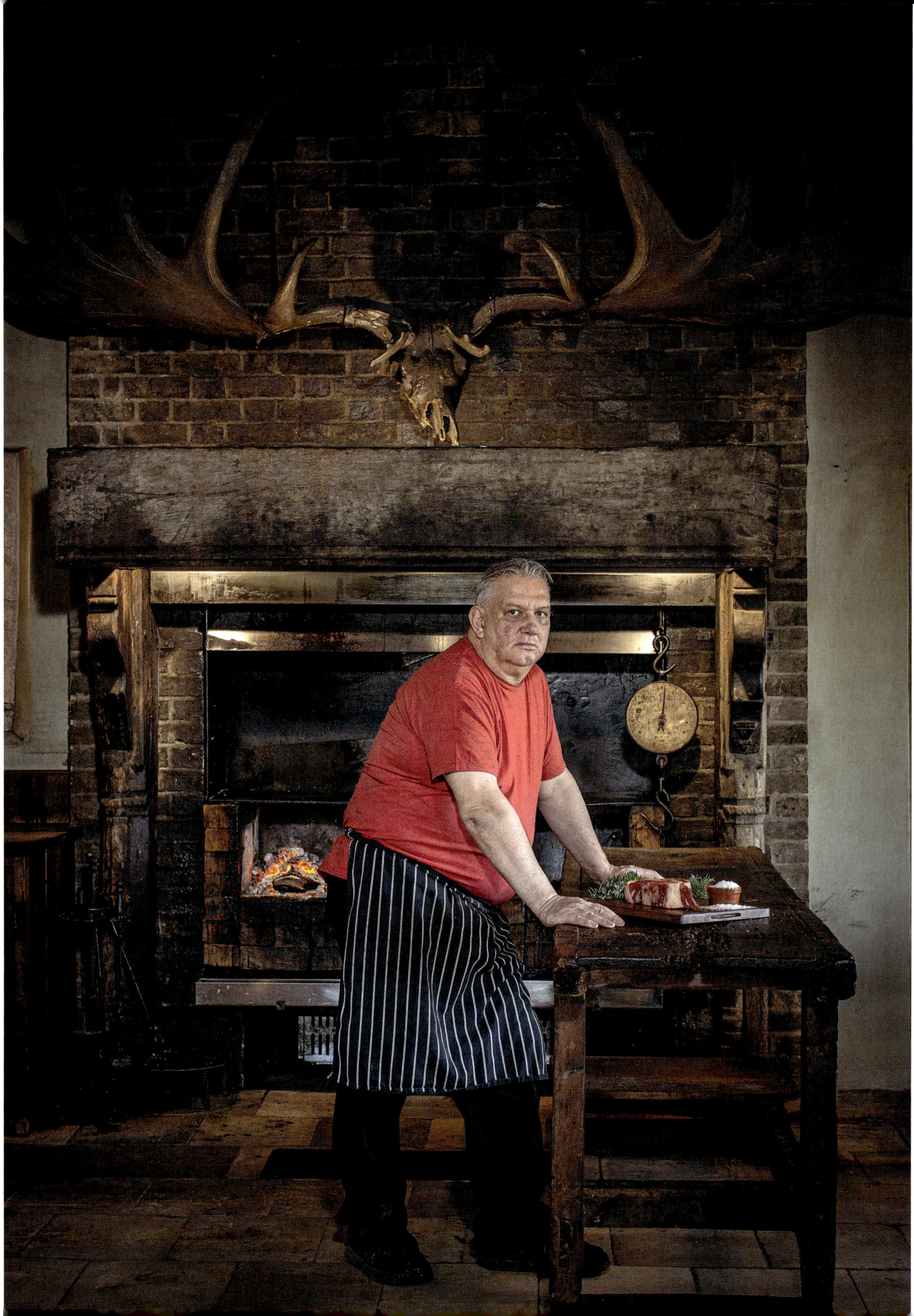

"THE FOOD IS HONEST, AND LED BY ITS INGREDIENTS"

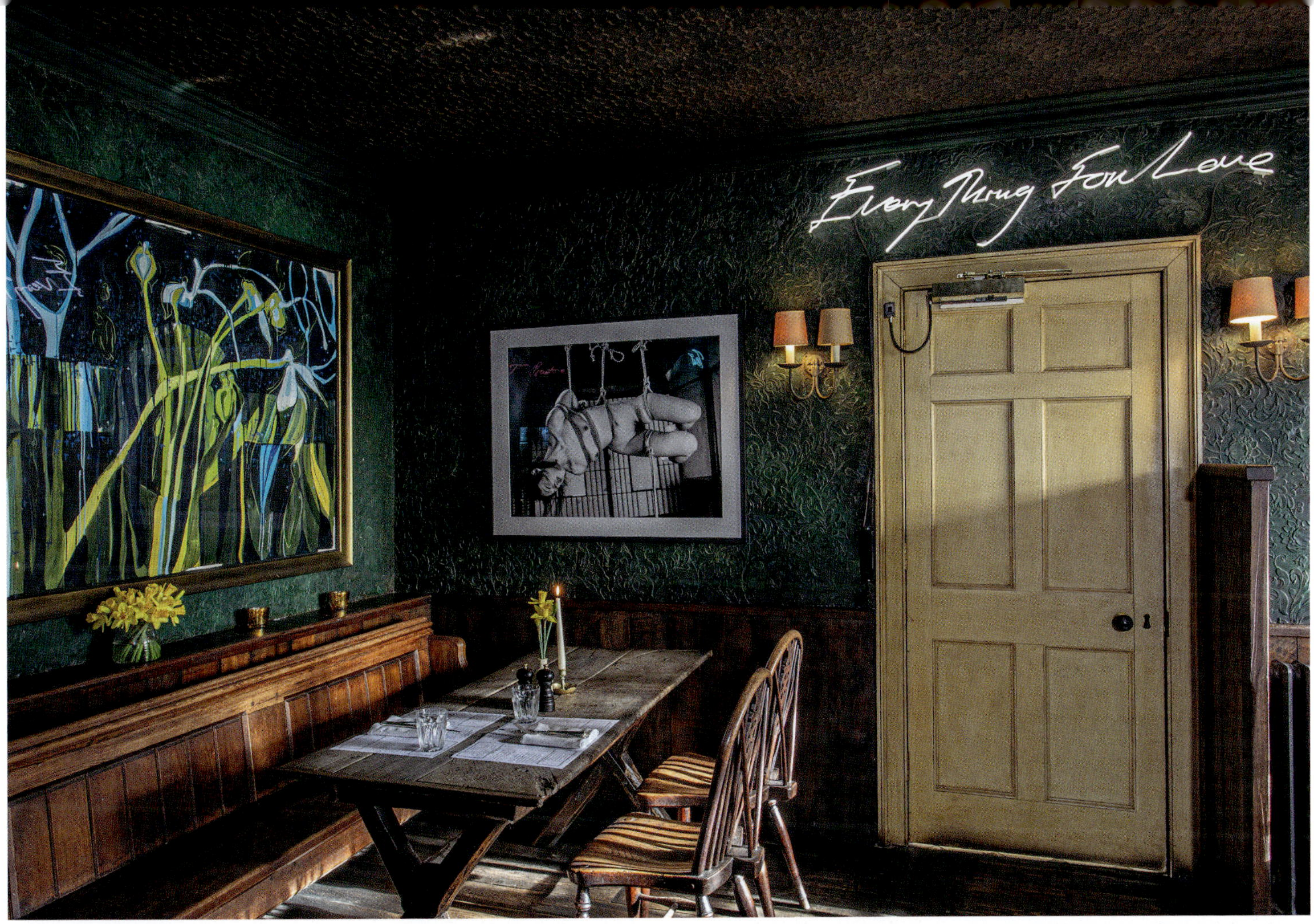

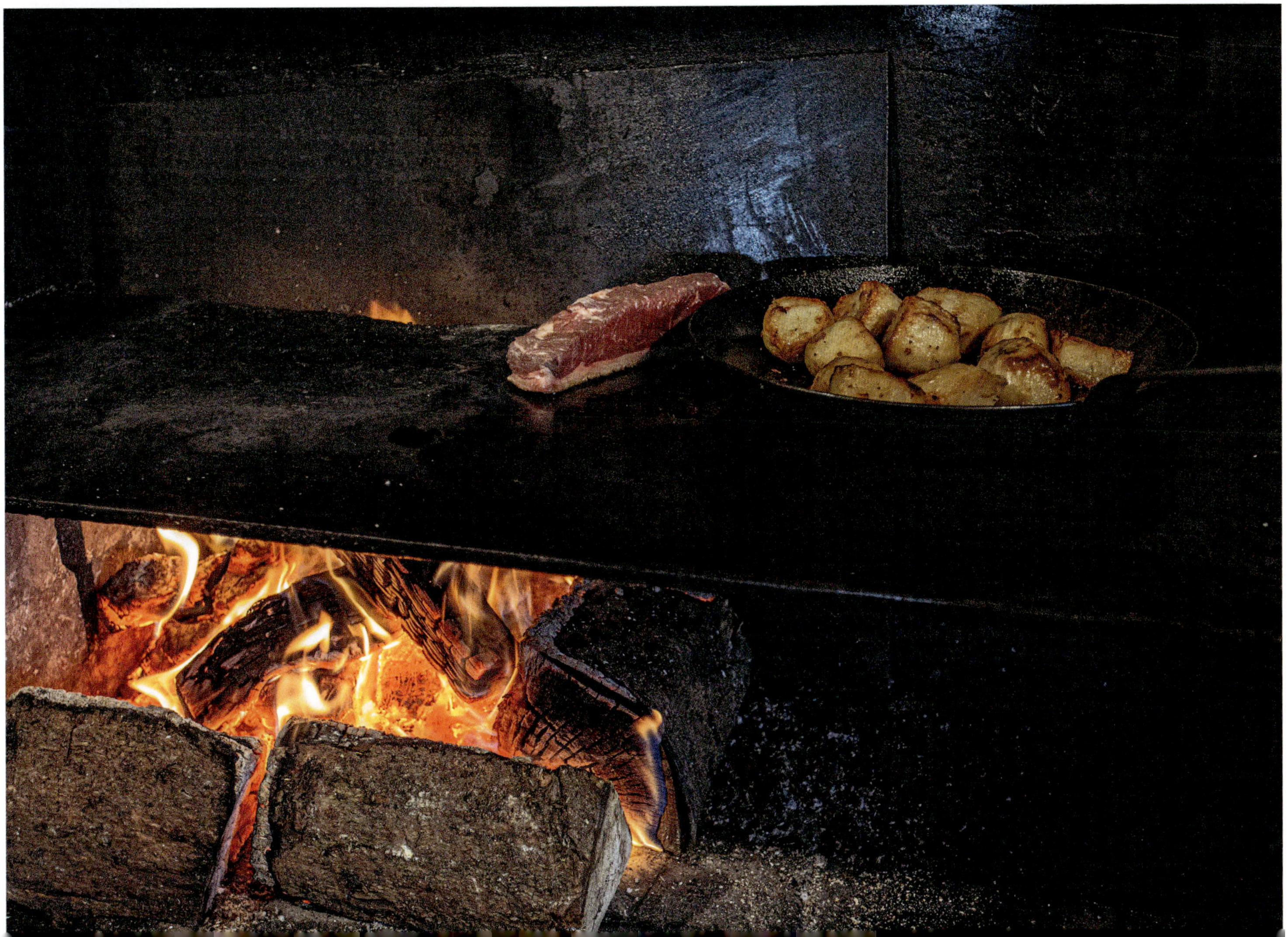

"YOUR IMAGINATION CAN TAKE FLIGHT"

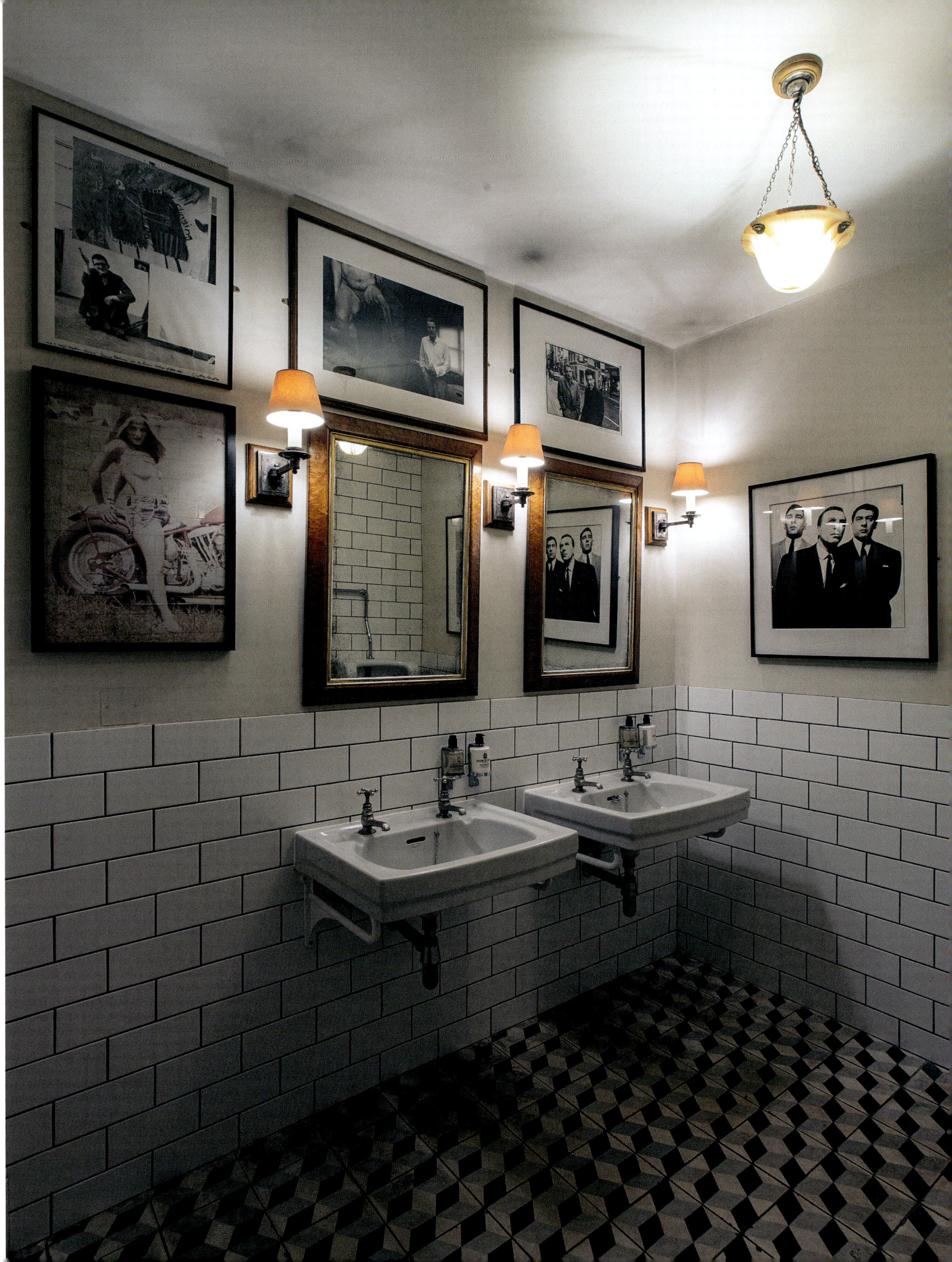

"THERE'S A SENSE OF THEATRE, OF FANTASY"

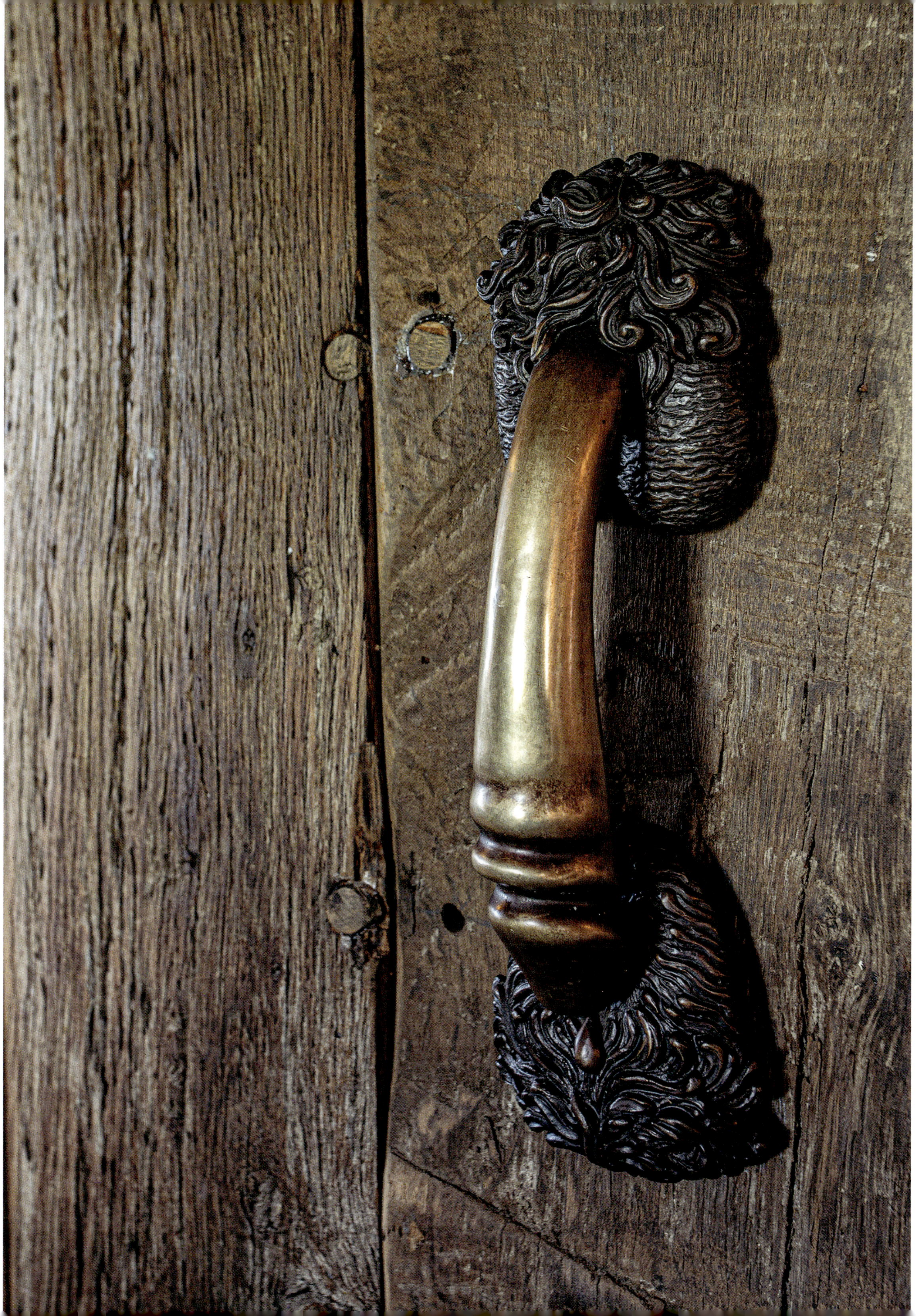

"IT'S ABOUT THE BIG THEMES – LIFE, SEX AND DEATH"

THE BOLEYN TAVERN

1 BARKING RD, LONDON

London's pubs offer a wealth of eclectic experiences, but it's only at The Boleyn Tavern that you can sit in a curtained booth to eat your fish, chips and mushy peas with the etched-glass likenesses of footballing legends Bobby Moore, Trevor Brooking or Geoff Hurst looking down on you, maybe offering their benign benediction as you succumb to a second helping of chocolate stout cake.

The linking of this beautiful pub with the beautiful game is by no means random. The Boleyn Tavern sits on a busy junction in Upton Park, London E6, just a few yards from what was once the Boleyn Ground, the home of West Ham United football team. On match days, as old hands attest, the surrounding streets were closed off, and The Boleyn was packed to the gunnels with home supporters (clutching their £3 pints in genuine glasses) and away supporters (who were charged £4 for the same pint in a plastic glass). The pub has now been restored to its Victorian splendour thanks to the independent Remarkable Pubs chain, with seven snugs divided by ornate panels, Carrara marble floors, and a massive stained-glass skylight dominating what was once a dingy billiards room and is now an open kitchen serving elevated pub grub such as gochujang-glazed chicken wings. Regulars will happily scroll through their phones to find old sepia-tinted shots of The Boleyn, taken by their grandparents, with tram tracks running alongside; they're equally happy settling in with a hand-pumped real ale and basking in the glory of a place that's once again an expansive temple to relaxation, pleasure, company and enjoyment. To sum up, in four words: Back. Of. The. Net.

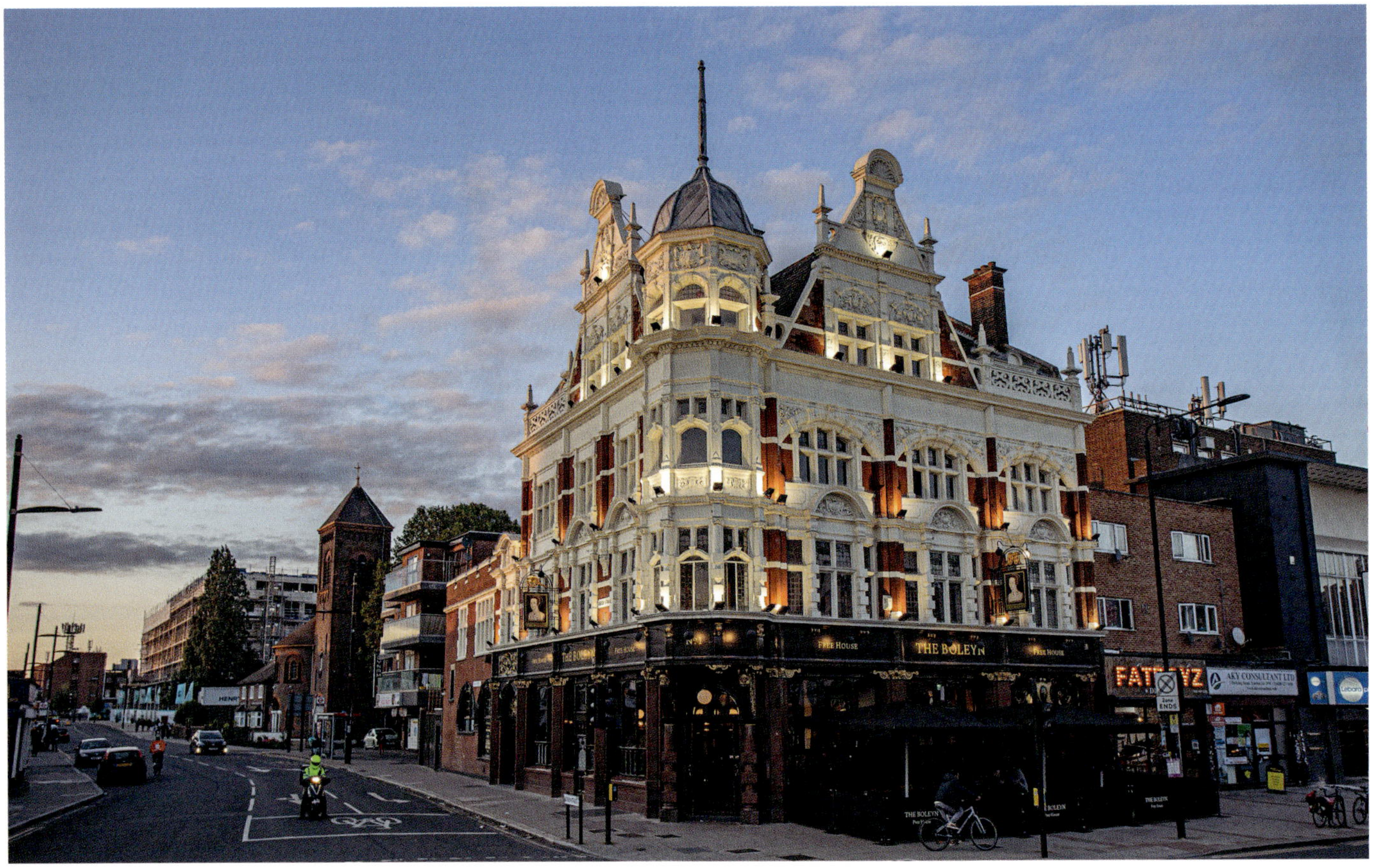

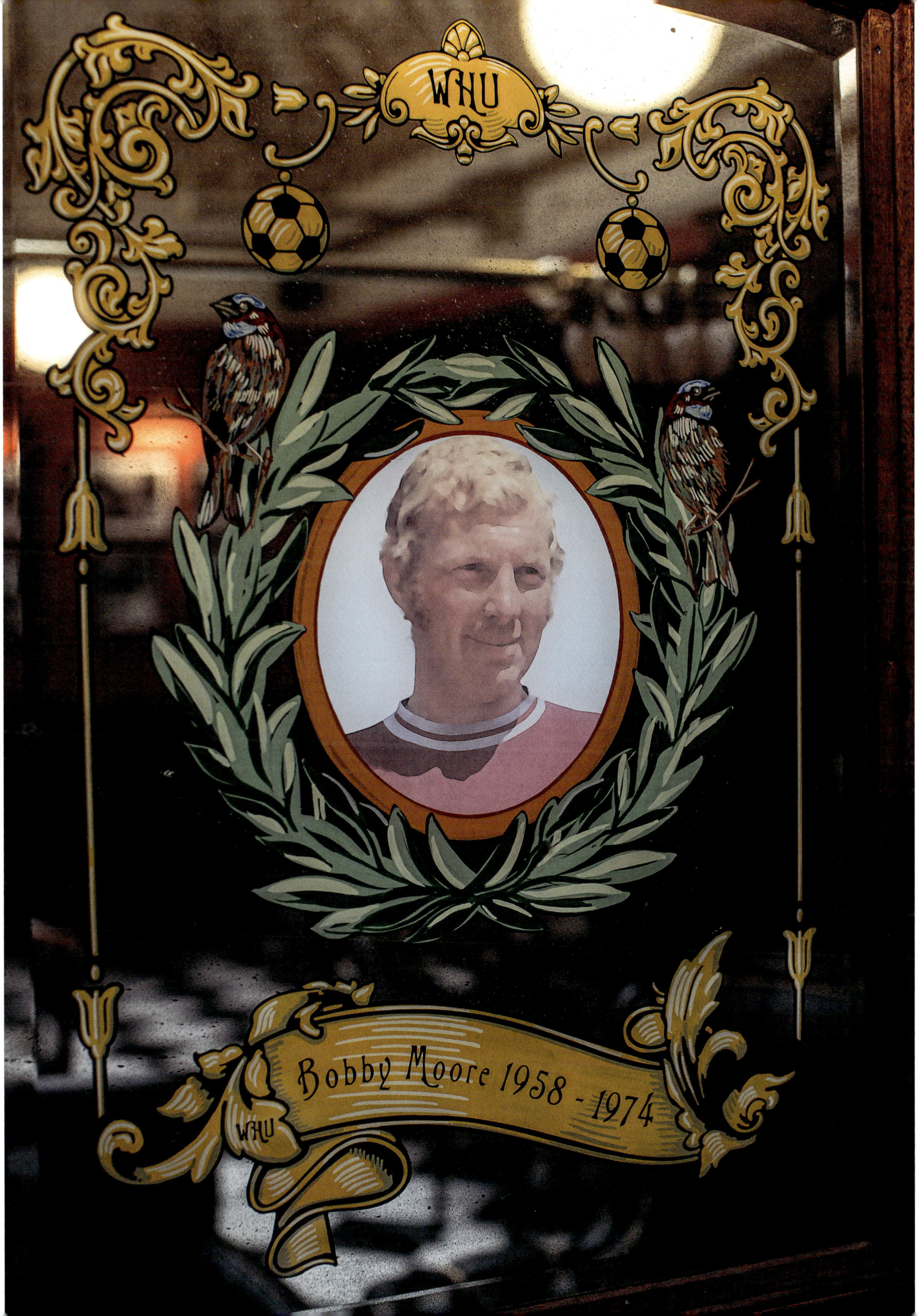
WHU
Bobby Moore 1958 - 1974
WHU

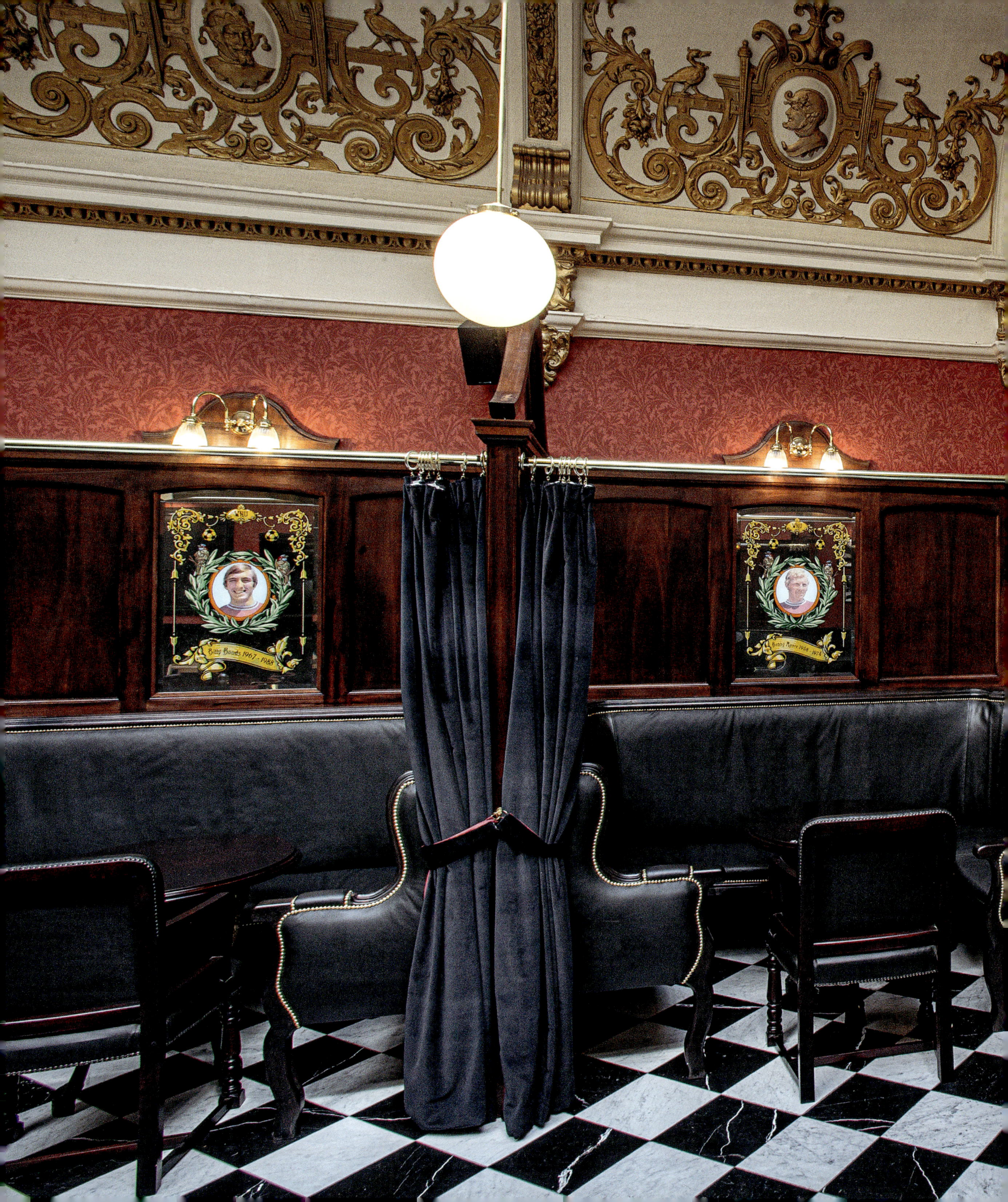
Billy Bonds 1967 - 1988
Bobby Moore 1958 - 1974

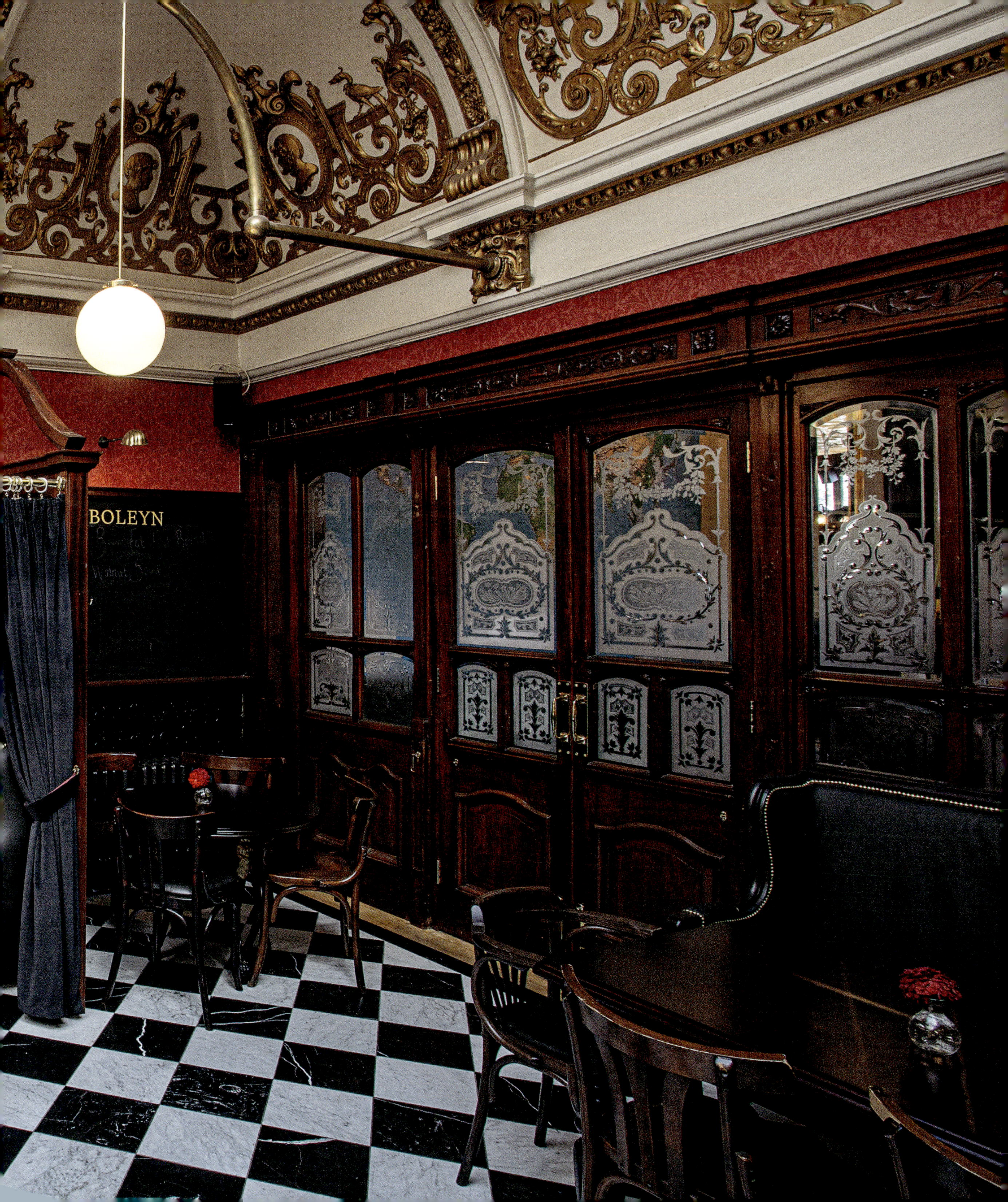
BOLEYN

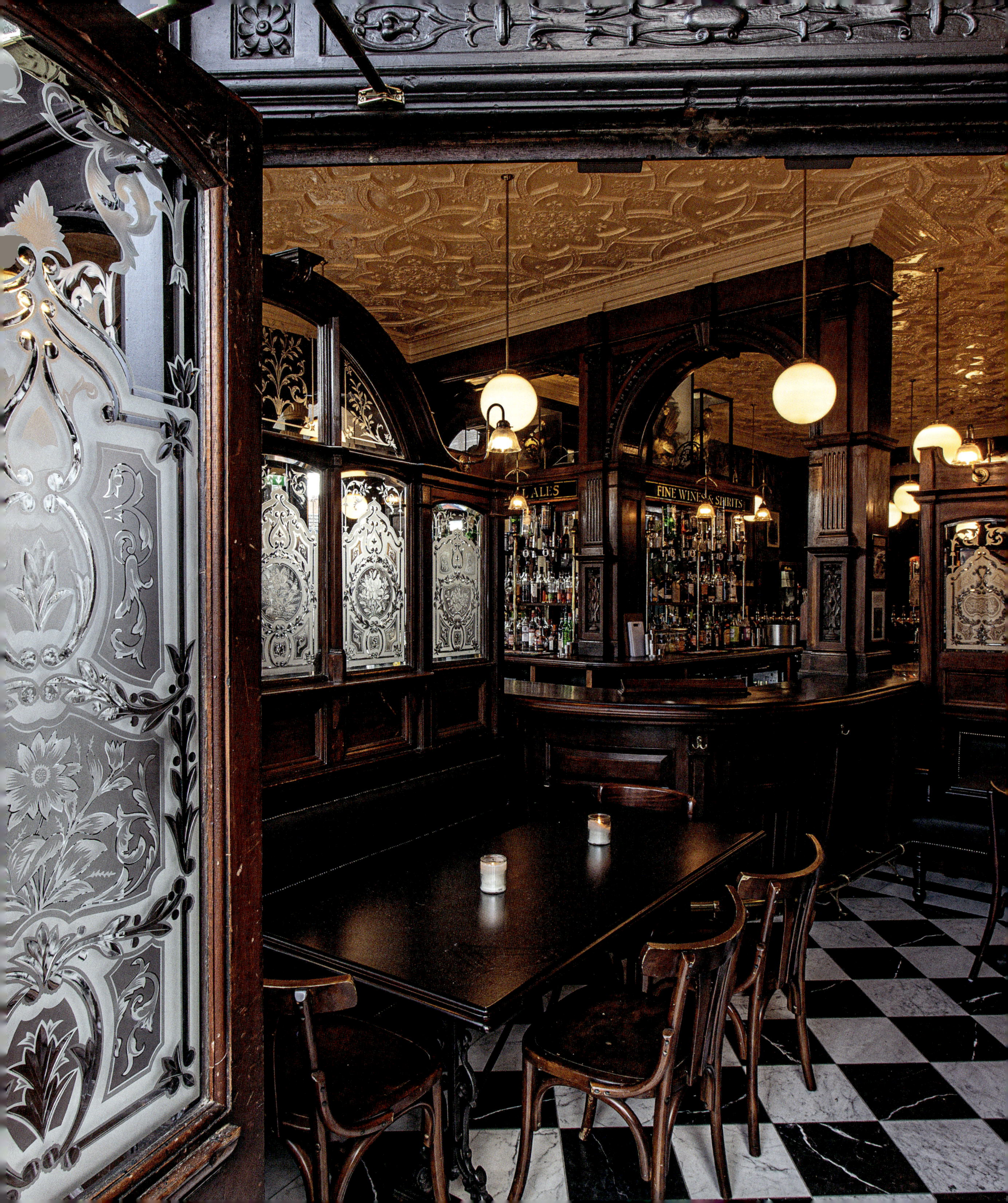
ALES
FINE WINES & SPIRITS

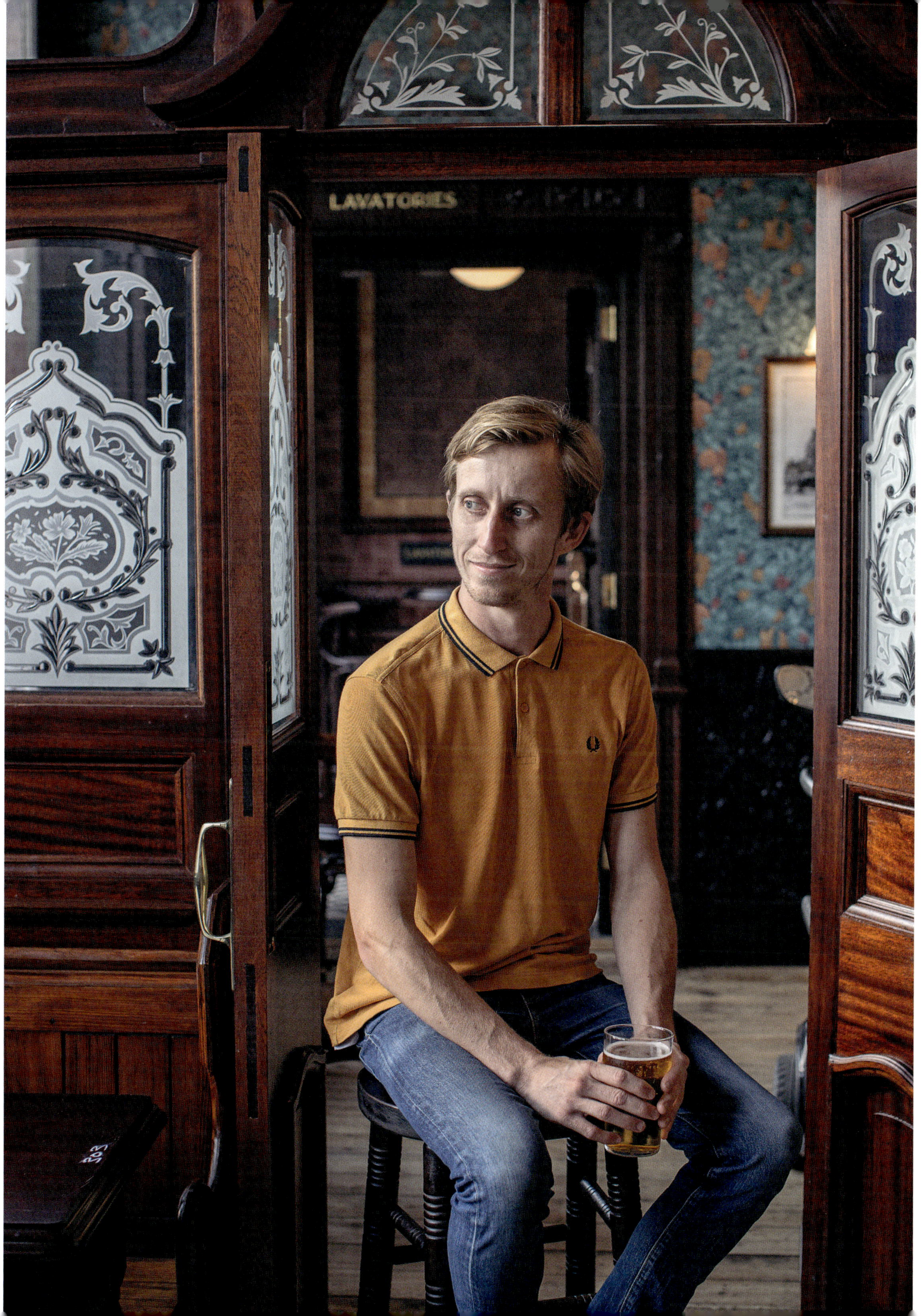
LAVATORIES

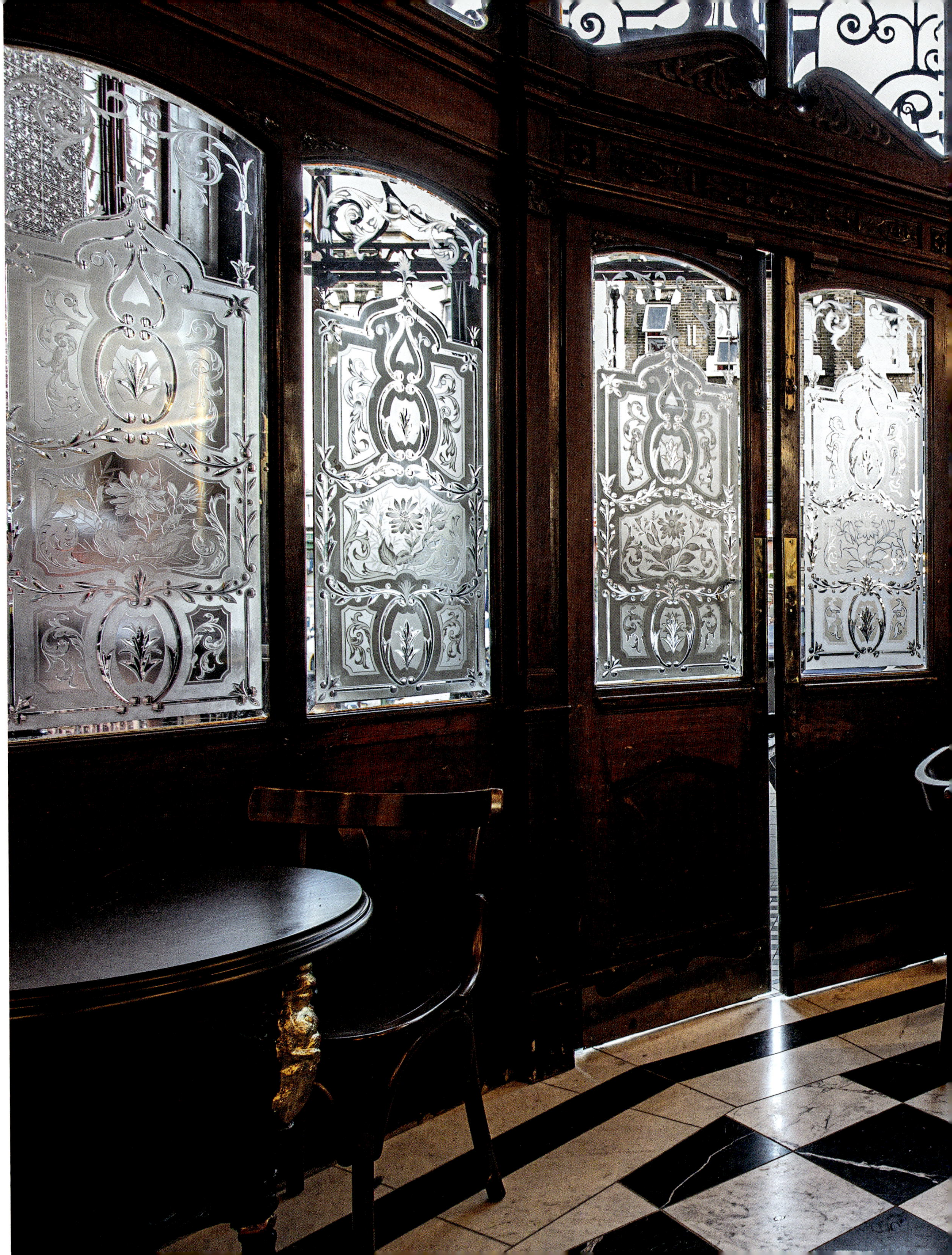

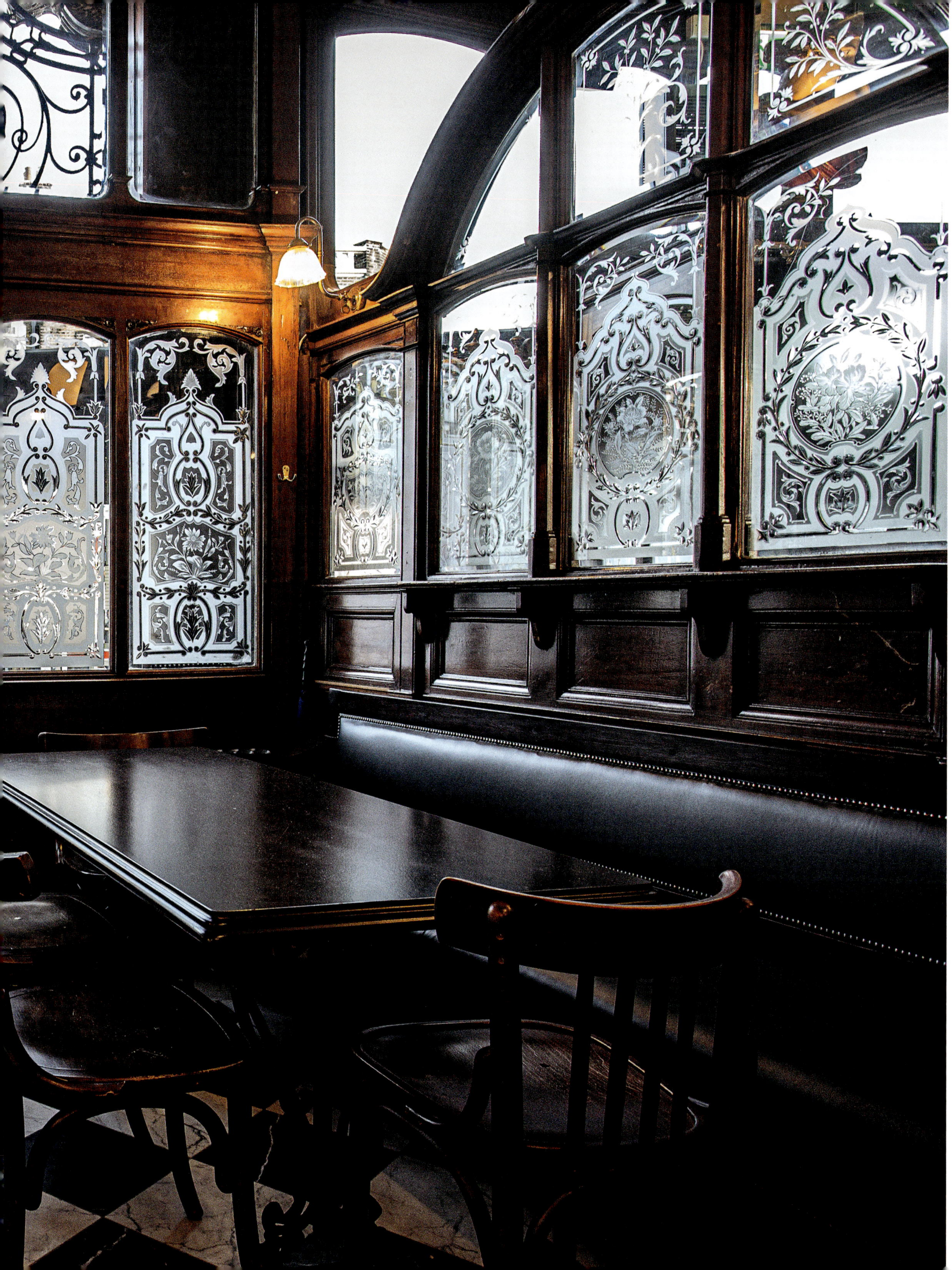

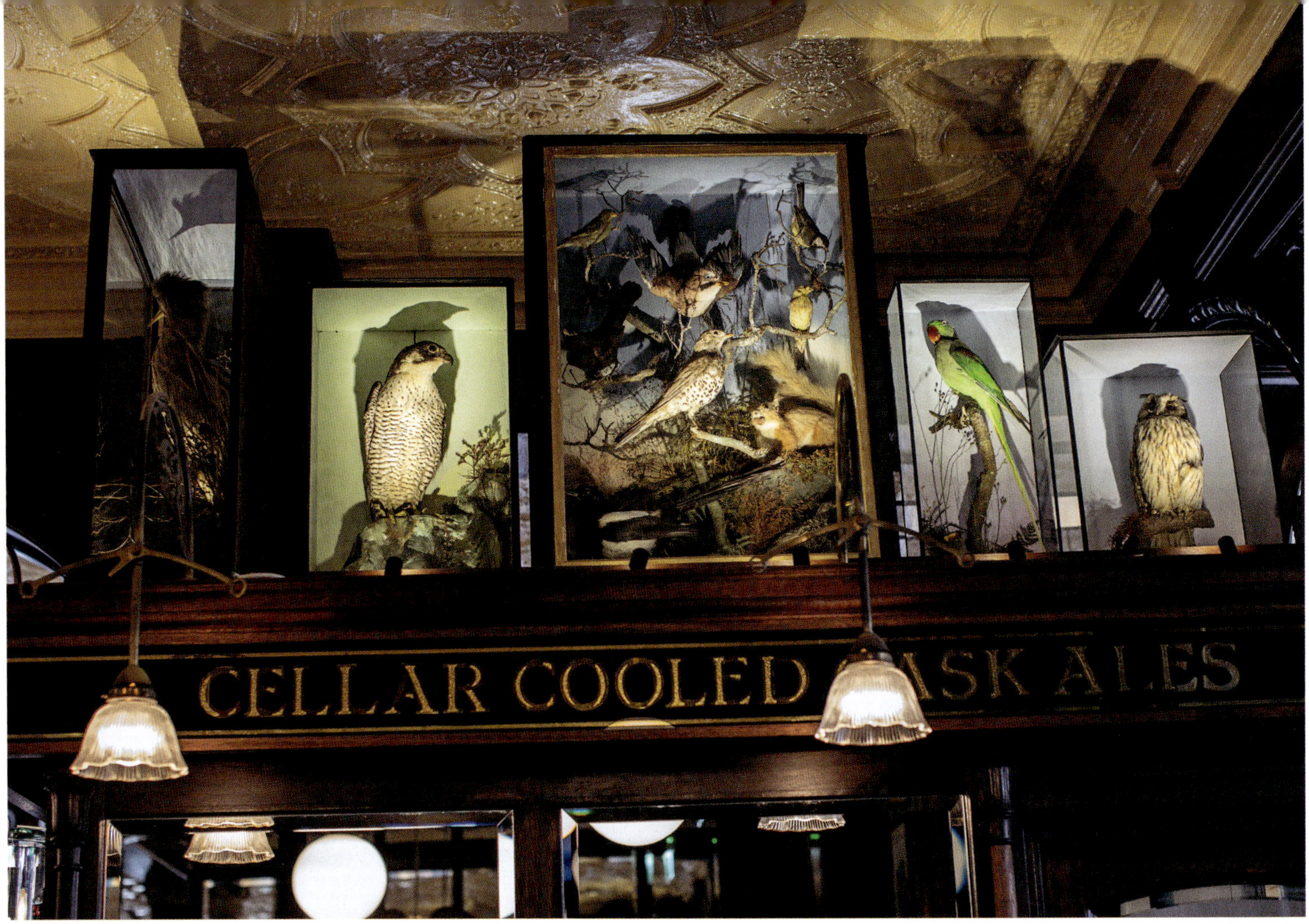
CELLAR COOLED
ASK ALES

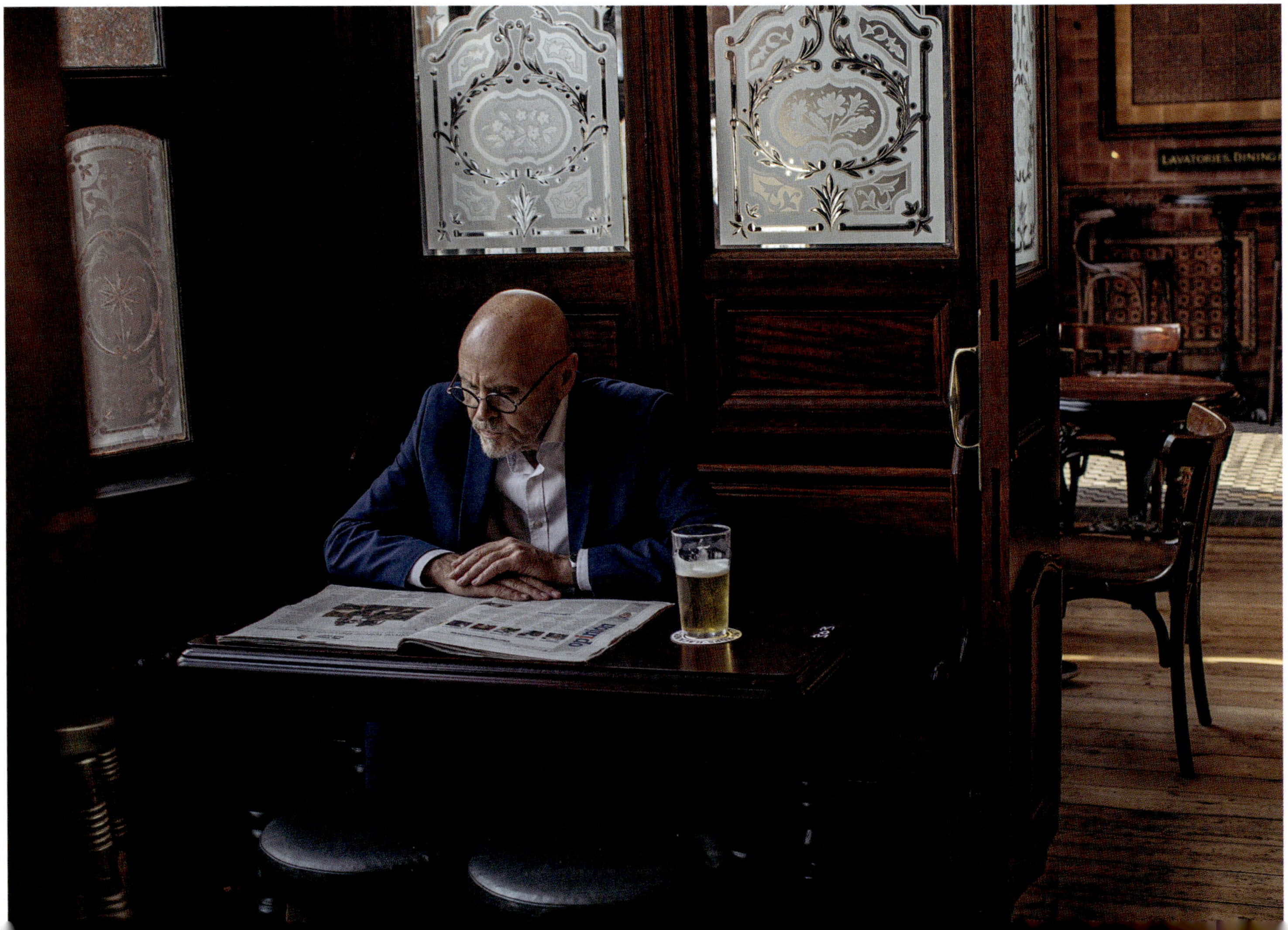

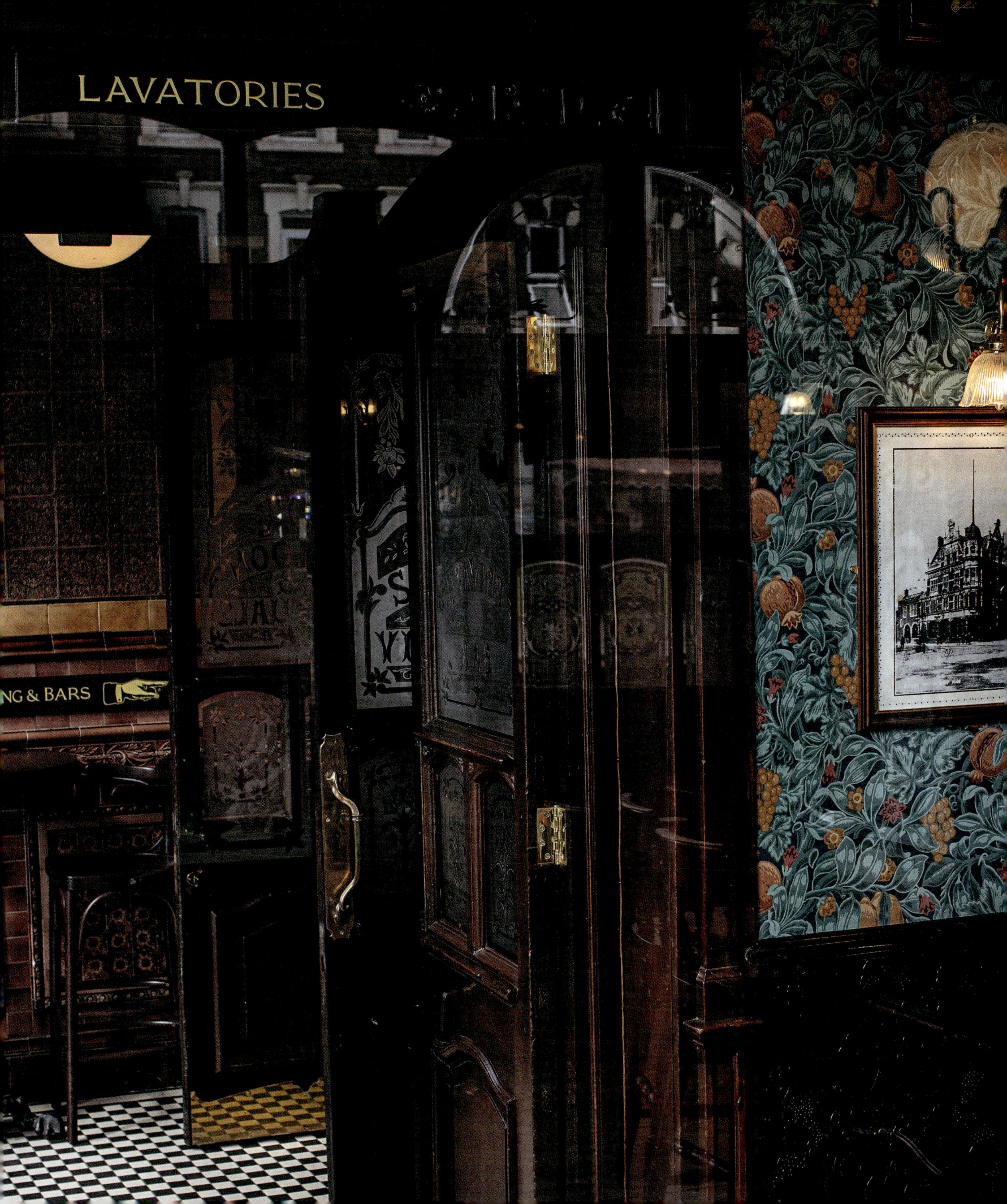
LAVATORIES
NG & BARS

YE OLDE CHESHIRE CHEESE

145 FLEET ST, LONDON

Fittingly, for a pub in the heart of Fleet Street – once the centre of the tabloid newspaper industry, whose hacks would never let the truth stand in the way of a good story – Ye Olde Cheshire Cheese is a repository of tales that may have grown in the telling. Was this Samuel Johnson's favoured pub? Well, there's no actual record of the seventeenth-century polymath's ever visiting the place, but his "favourite chair" is nonetheless installed in a corner, beneath a slightly dyspeptic portrait of the man. Did the establishment once boast a grey parrot named Polly who could swear like a navvy? Yes – he was a fixture for four decades before dying in 1926, and his taxidermic figure now watches over the Chop Room – but whether he could also imitate the popping of a cork, followed by the "glug glug glug" as the wine was poured, and whether he repeated this feat so many times during Armistice Day in 1918 that he fainted from the exertion, are matters of purest conjecture.

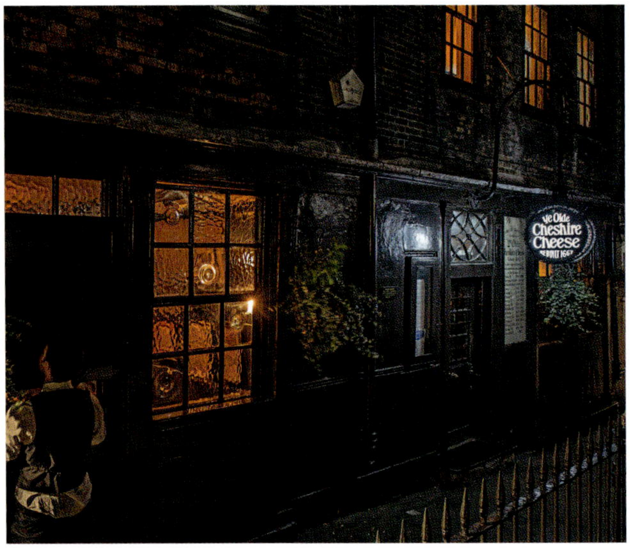

What's indisputable is that the "Ye Olde" bit of the pub's name is more than mere hyperbole; witness the "rebuilt 1667" legend on its sign (the original wooden sixteenth-century structure having succumbed to the Great Fire) or the list of sixteen monarchs who've reigned in England since the pub's existence, displayed to the right of the entrance. But witness, also, the labyrinth within. Authentically scuffed corridors and precipitous stairwells lead up, down, right and left, anterooms are nestled within larger salons, and lowering ceilings lead to echoing caverns. You can work here for months, as the current barman has done, and still not be sure that you've ventured into every nook and cranny. The vaulted heights of the Cellar Bar indicate its previous use as a thirteenth-century Carmelite monastery, while the series of bawdy seventeenth-century tiles that once adorned an upstairs fireplace, and have now been packed off to the Museum of London ("they were more saucy postcard than dark web", according to one of those who got an eyeful) suggest that part of the building may once have been a brothel. A heritage of contemplation and/or sensual pleasure; no wonder that the Cheshire Cheese has proved so congenial for writers, from Dickens ("he took him down Ludgate-hill to Fleet Street, and so, up a covered way, into a tavern ... with a good plain dinner and good wine", from *A Tale of Two Cities*) to P. G. Wodehouse ("Yesterday, I looked in at the Garrick at lunch time, took one glance of loathing at the mob, and went off to lunch by myself at the Cheshire Cheese," from *A Life in Letters*), not to mention the less celebrated contributors to the pub's collection of leather-bound visitors' books, which date back to the Victorian era, and feature many poems that venture to rhyme "Cheese" with "ease".

The Cheshire Cheese exhibits all the creaks, groans, crackles and booms of a venerable chunk of living history, right down to the basement chills (the recent removal of a manhole cover revealed a gurgling remnant of the River Fleet, one of London's legendary lost rivers) and up to the roaring hearths (the fires have been known to be lit right through the tepid English summer). What saves it from becoming a kind of pewter-tankard museum piece is the singular sense of refuge it continues to offer. "A push at the door, and I have passed into another world," wrote the artist Joseph Pennell in *Harper's Weekly* in 1887. You'll no longer be provided with a free pipe and tobacco on entering, and you'll be nursing a pint of Samuel Smith's Organic Lager rather than a jug of mead. Even the hacks have long since departed the area. But the Cheshire Cheese rolls on, its assortment of walls absorbing yet more gossip and debate, concord and dispute, as successive waves of patrons put the outside world to rights. After all, there are always new stories to tell.

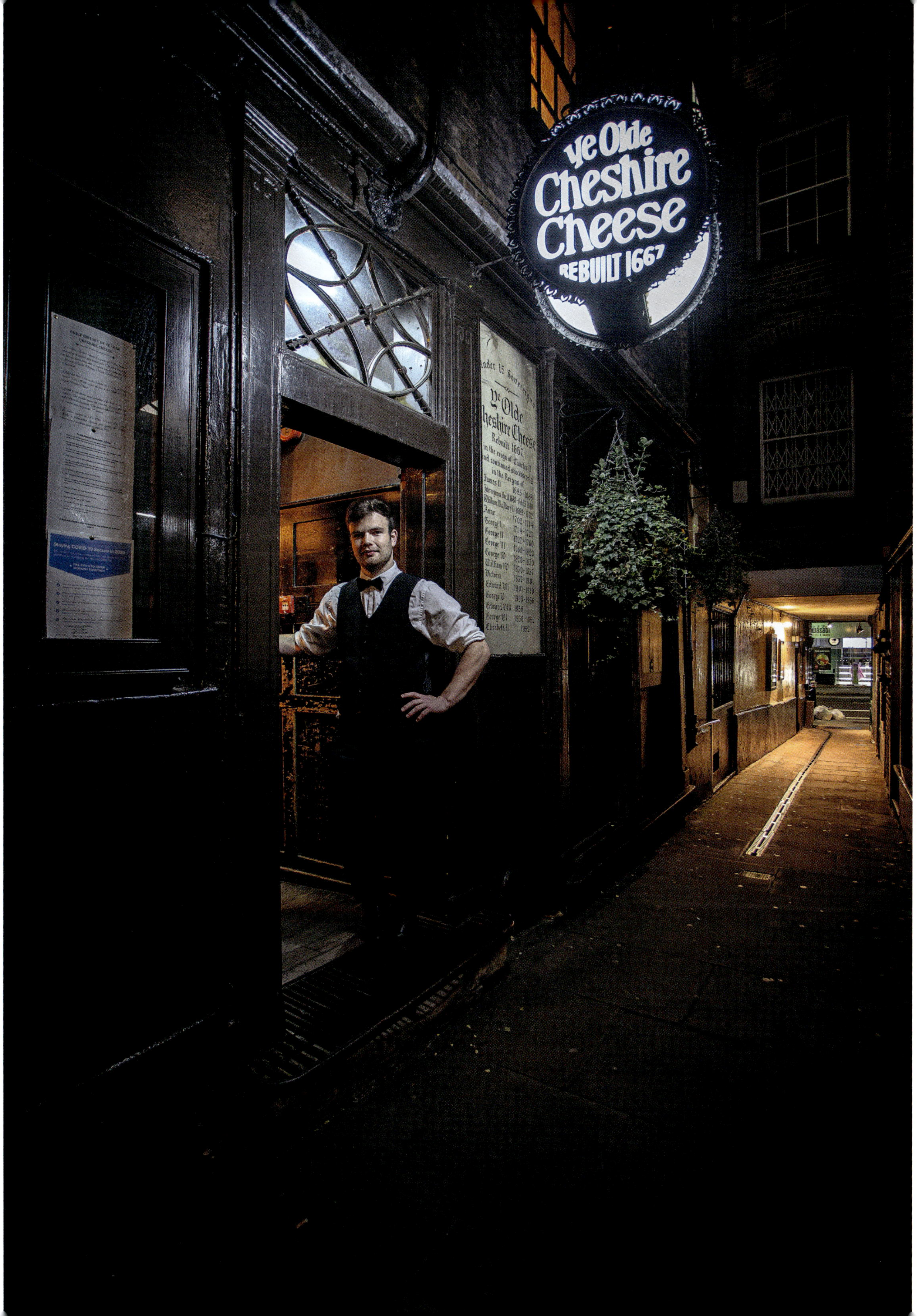

"UP A COVERED WAY, INTO A TAVERN ..."

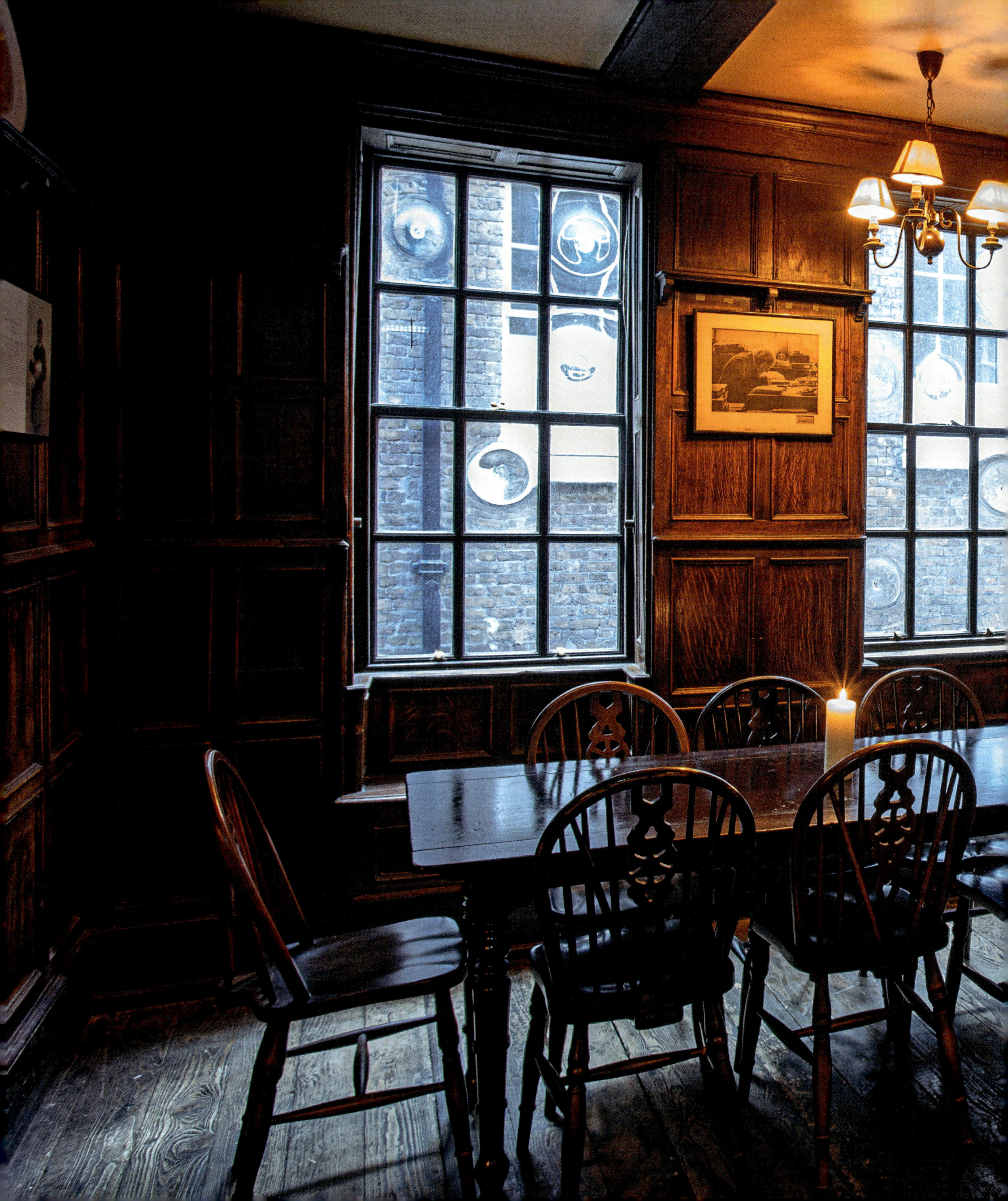

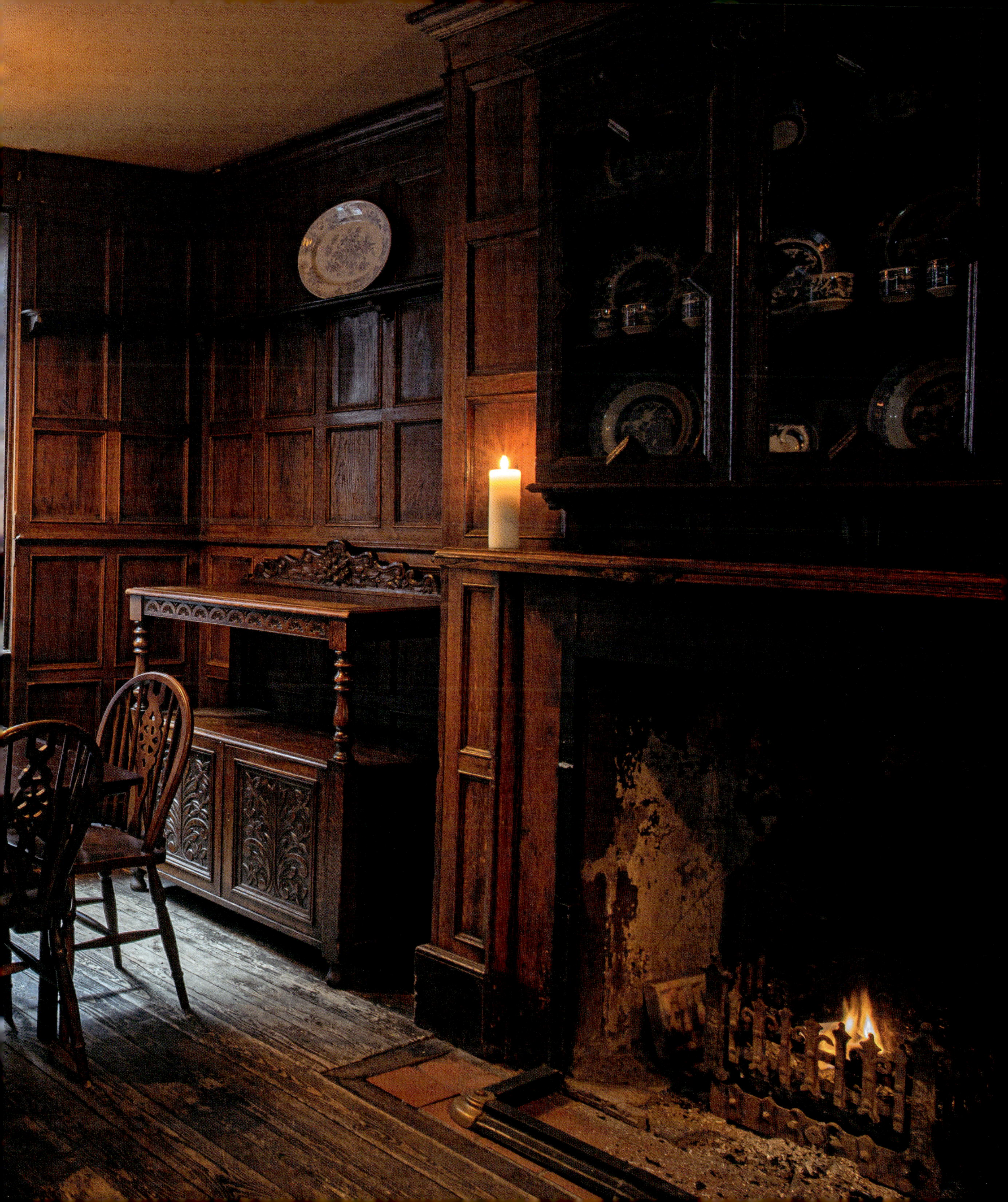

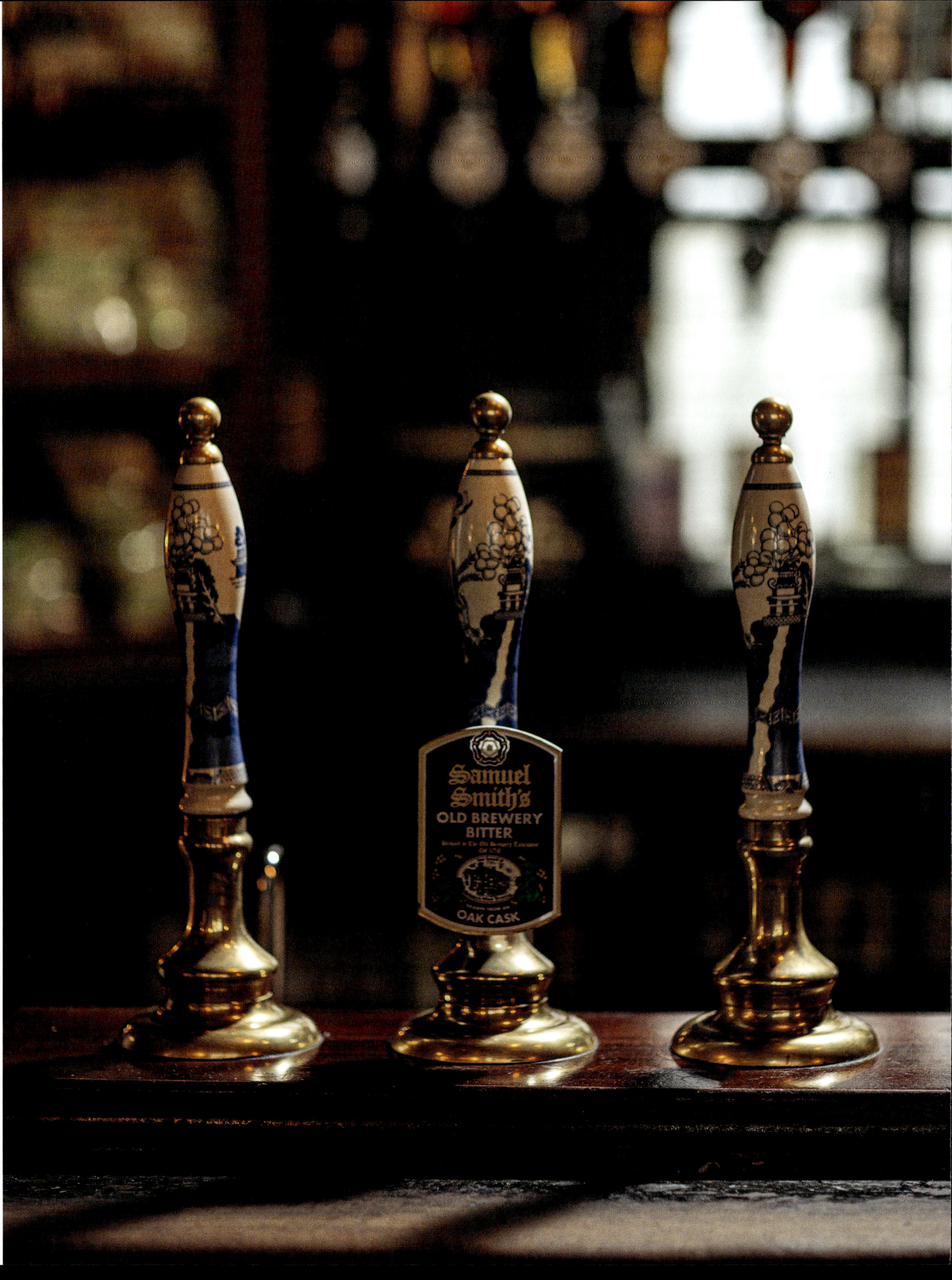
Samuel Smith's
OLD BREWERY
BITTER
OAK CASK

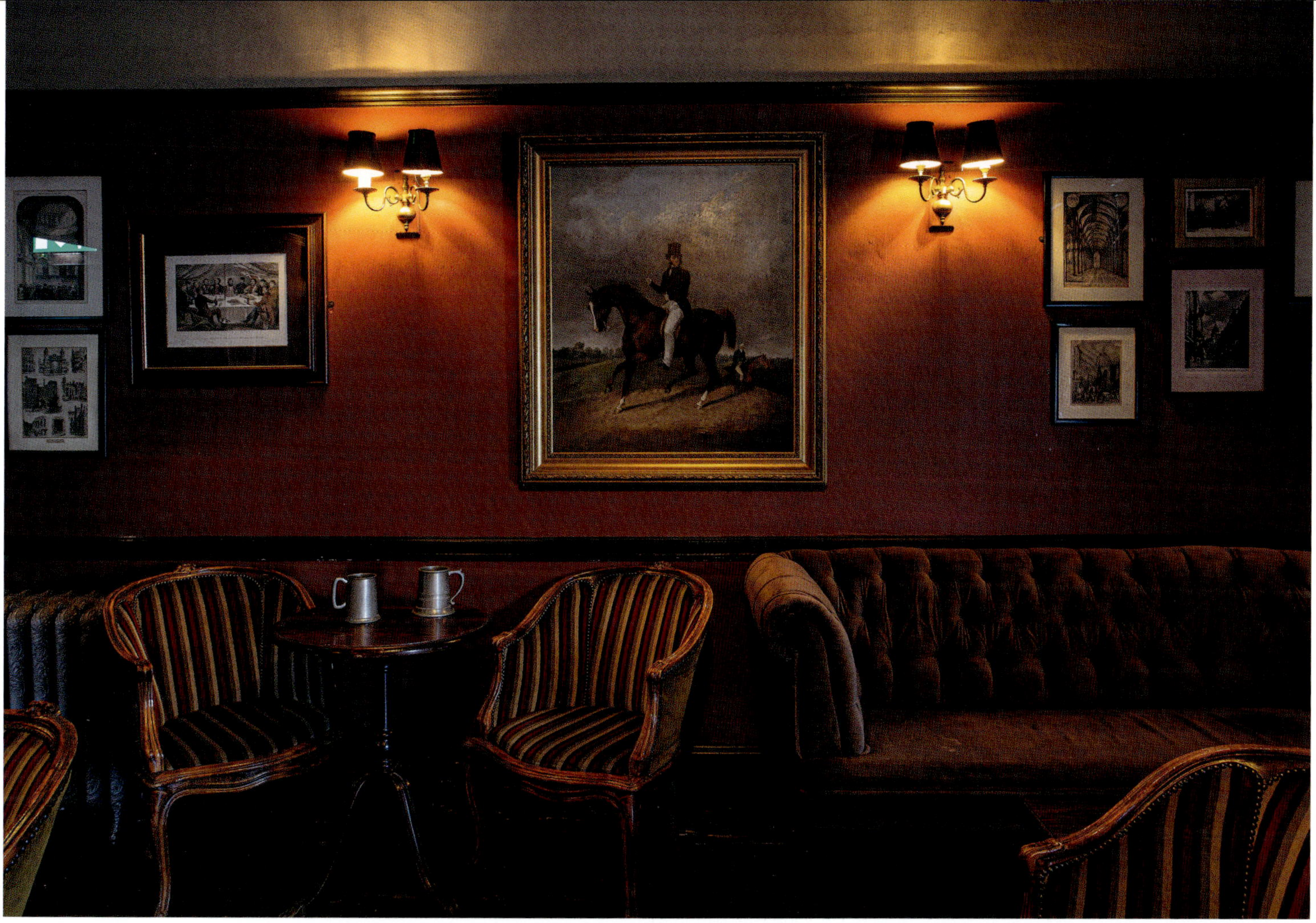

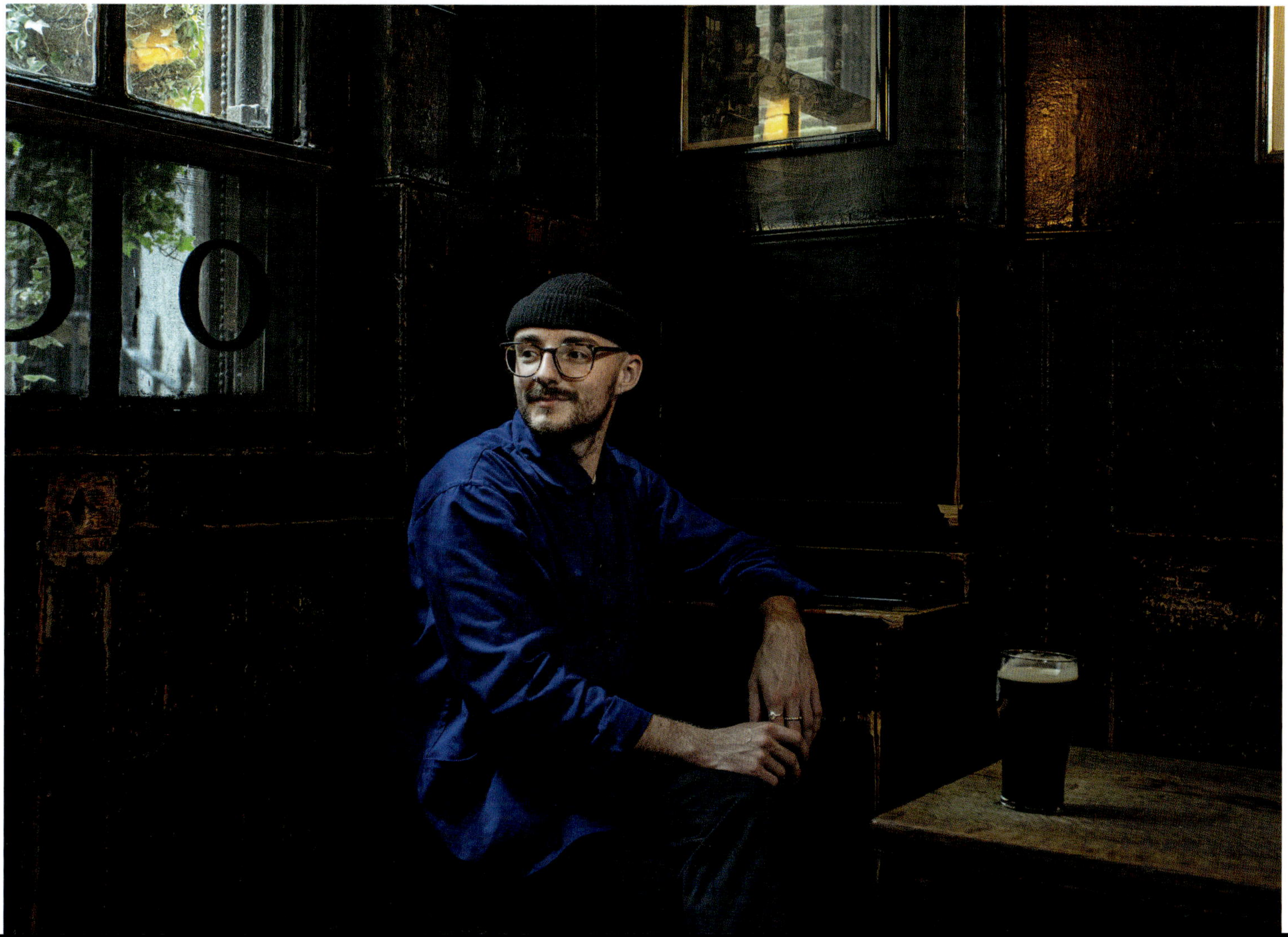

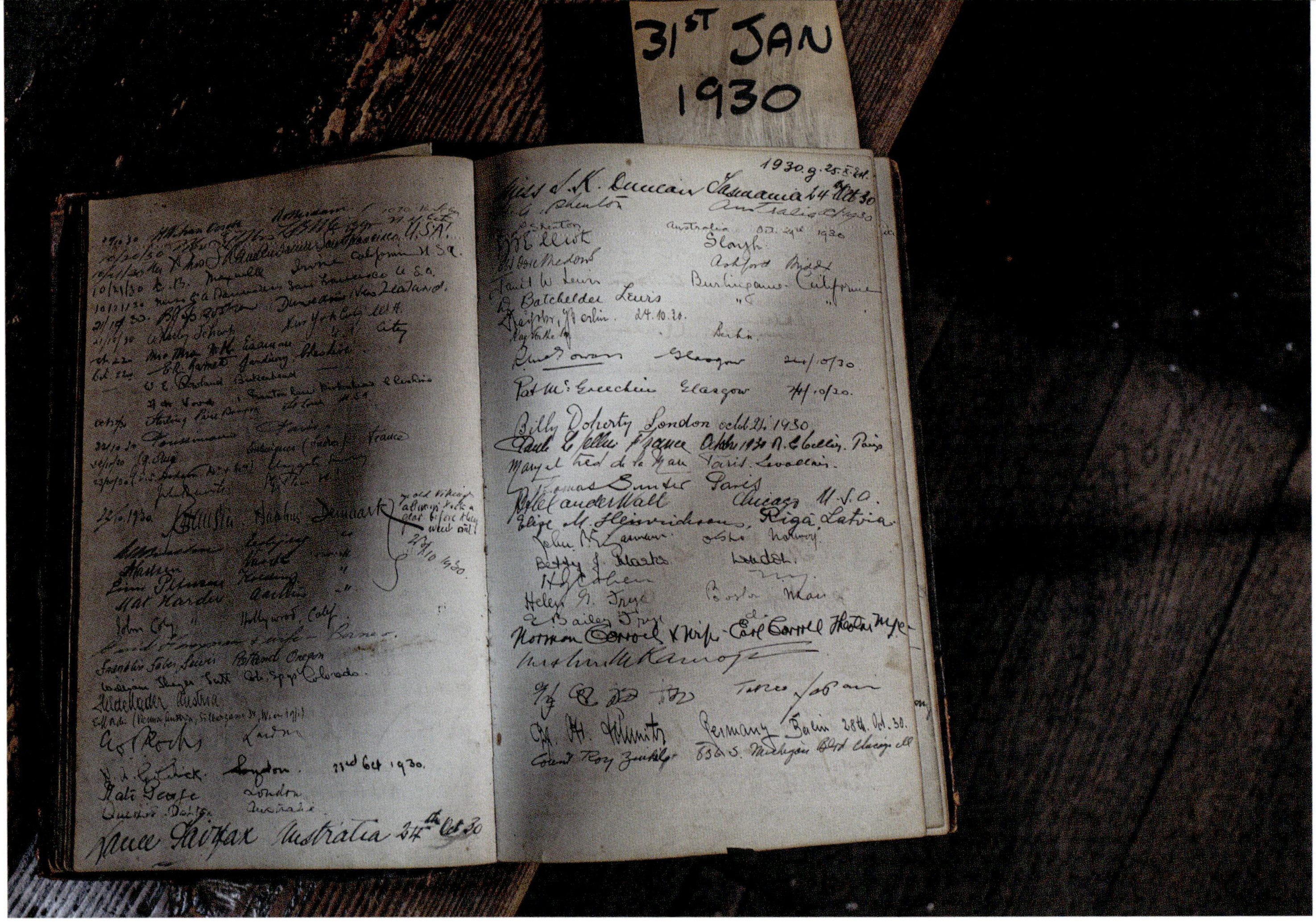
31ST JAN
1930

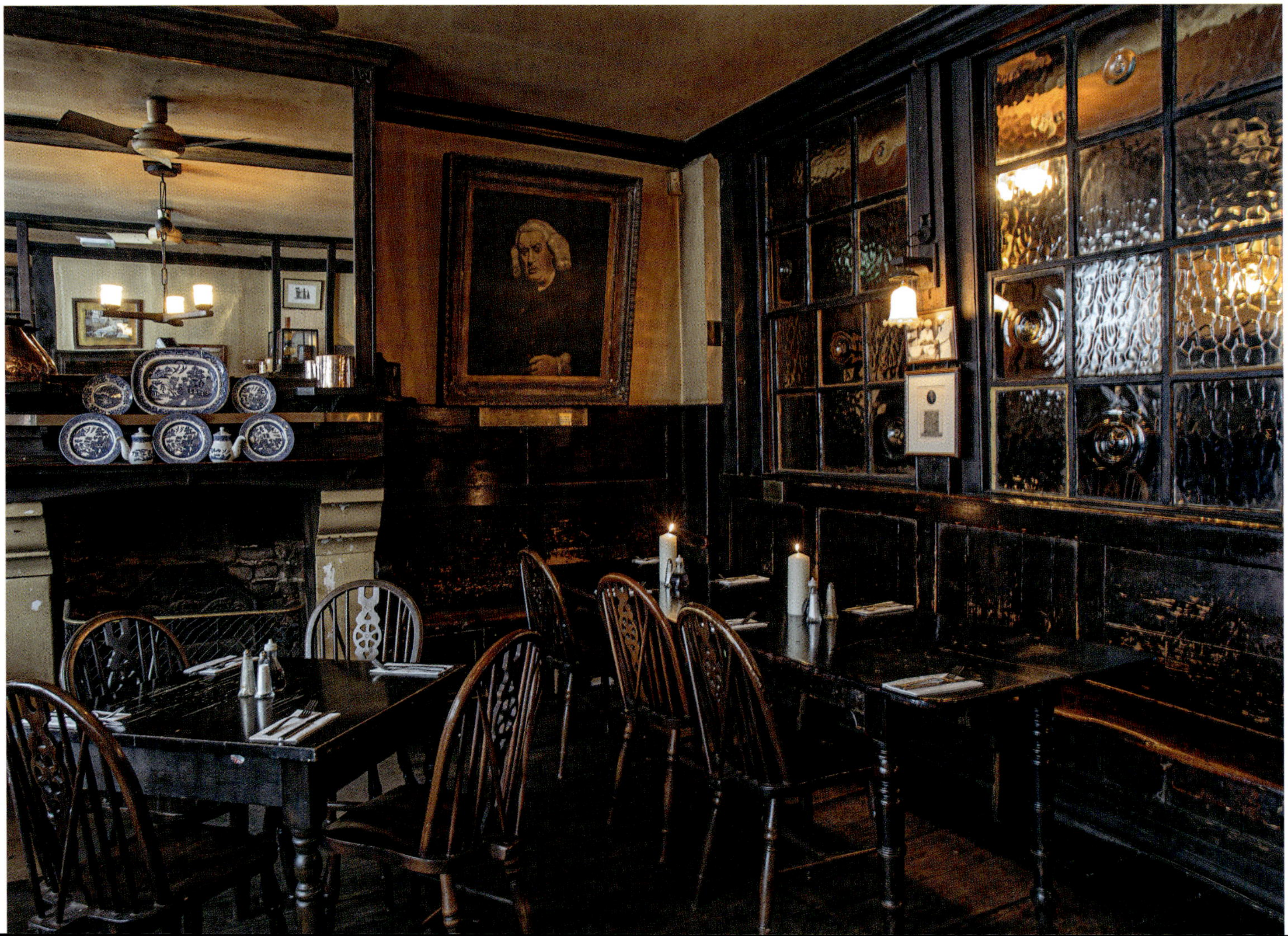

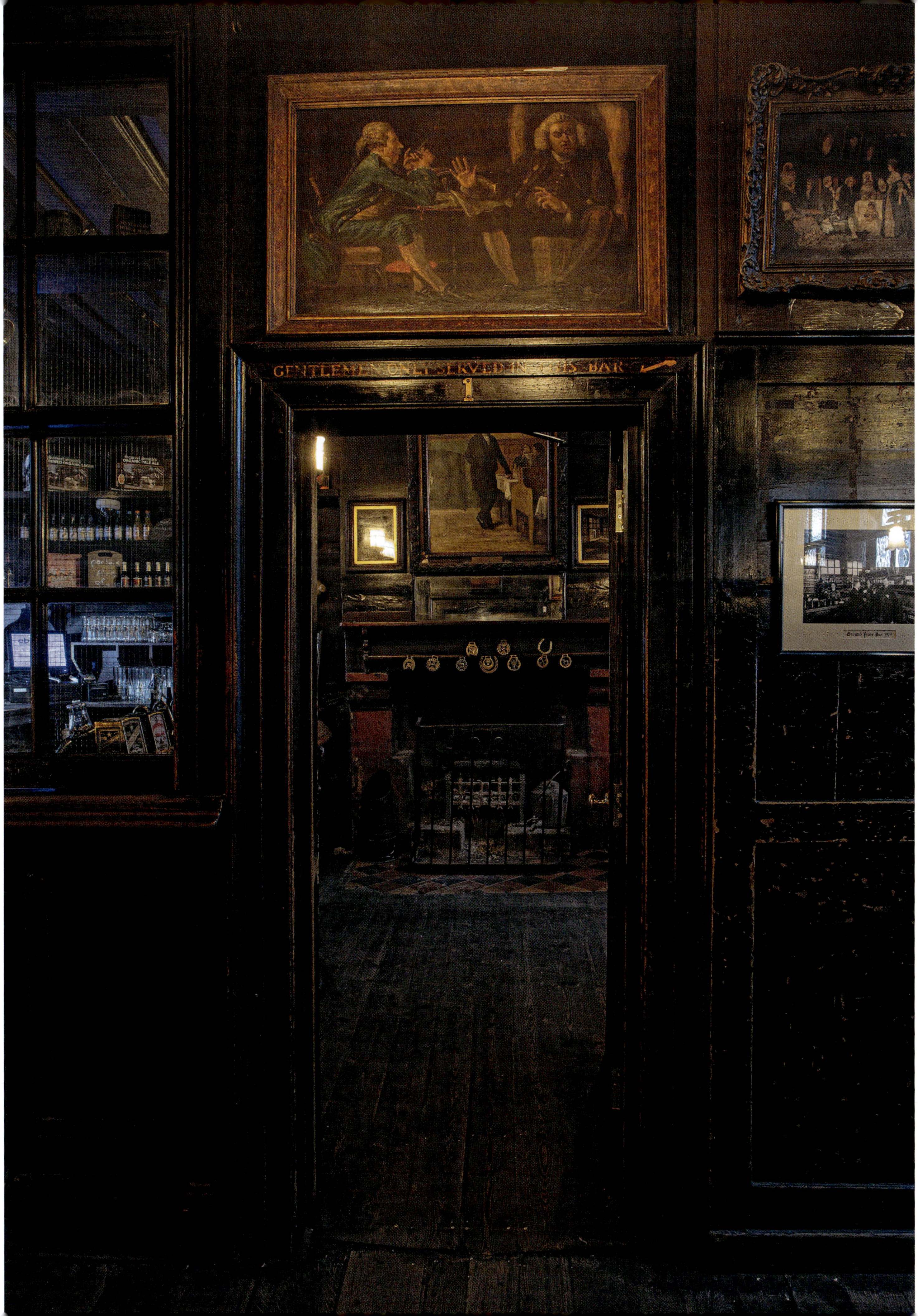

"A PUSH AT THE DOOR, AND I HAVE PASSED INTO ANOTHER WORLD"

THE GUINEA GRILL

30 BRUTON PL, LONDON

The definition of "conviviality", according to the *New Oxford Dictionary*, is "fit for a feast, or festive". The Guinea Grill actually predates the word – there's been a pub on this Mayfair site since the fifteenth century, and "conviviality" wasn't coined until the mid-1700s – but it's not hard to imagine this eminently congenial establishment being its inspiration. Because here, a stone's throw from the bustle of Bond Street and Berkeley Square, is a place where time seems to slow down, and the eternal verities – a medium-rare porterhouse, a fine claret, a sharp Stilton – can be lingered over and thoroughly savoured.

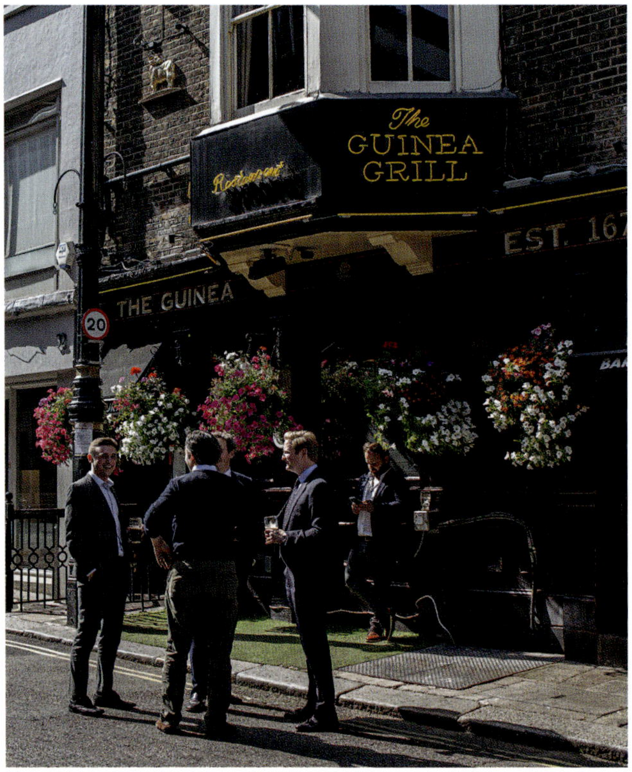

If The Guinea fosters a strong sense of loyalty among its patrons, from Mayfair residents and local office workers to returning American and European visitors, that's because of its perception as a hidden gem. Tucked away in Bruton Place – a street of mews dwellings that once held the carriages and servants of Mayfair's swells, who fled the City of London after the seventeenth-century ravages of the Great Fire and Great Plague – it's the kind of place you stumble upon, your interest piqued by a compact, wood-panelled, warm-hued bar peopled with patrons nursing pints of ale and tucking into Welsh Rarebit much as the coachmen and ladies' maids would have done nearly half a millennium ago. Royal patronage is inferred by a photo of the Queen Mother pulling a pint on a visit from nearby Clarence House (with a tumbler of gin, her tipple of choice, presumably just out of shot), while the crowd good-naturedly spills into the street during the warmer months.

But the delightful sense of discovery doesn't end with the bar. Through a separate entrance, and past a tilted, smoking-hot grill and a cabinet of choice meat cuts (dry-aged and supplied by master butcher Frank Godfrey of Islington, who maintains a dedicated fridge for The Guinea), you're shown into a secluded dining room, where, as food critic Giles Coren wrote in *The Times*, "well-dressed gentlemen and the odd lady are rammed hugger-mugger, as in the chophouses of the Victorian Golden Age." Portraits of Mayfair eminences look on from the walls as a menu of imperishable British classics – prawn cocktail with Marie Rose sauce, rock oysters, steak and kidney pie, beef Wellington – is served. Here, as afternoon elides into evening and lunch elides into dinner, buttons are undone, friendships are cemented or created, and the old-school ambience is relished.

Mayfair, for all its conspicuous wealth – this is, after all, the most expensive spot on the London Monopoly board, with as many private members' clubs and blue-chip galleries as public bars – still retains a somewhat raffish air, which The Guinea personifies. You might find Madonna, Mick Jagger or Henry Cavill here (and one-time Mayfair resident Jimi Hendrix was a regular), but they'll be hanging out at the bar, or wolfing down a pie, alongside the disparate cast of art dealers, hedge fund CEOs, politicians, impeccably accessorised local residents, and MI5 spooks (who, of all people, appreciate the establishment's discretion) that regard The Guinea as their own. The variety of "Ests" it displays mark key moments in its evolution – 1423, when it was established; 1675, when it became The Guinea; 1851, when it became a Young's pub; and even 2021, as it expands into a building across the street – but, at its heart, The Guinea is simply a fail-safe staple, a trusted friend to those in the know; a place that was around before the notion of conviviality officially existed, but where it came to reign supreme.

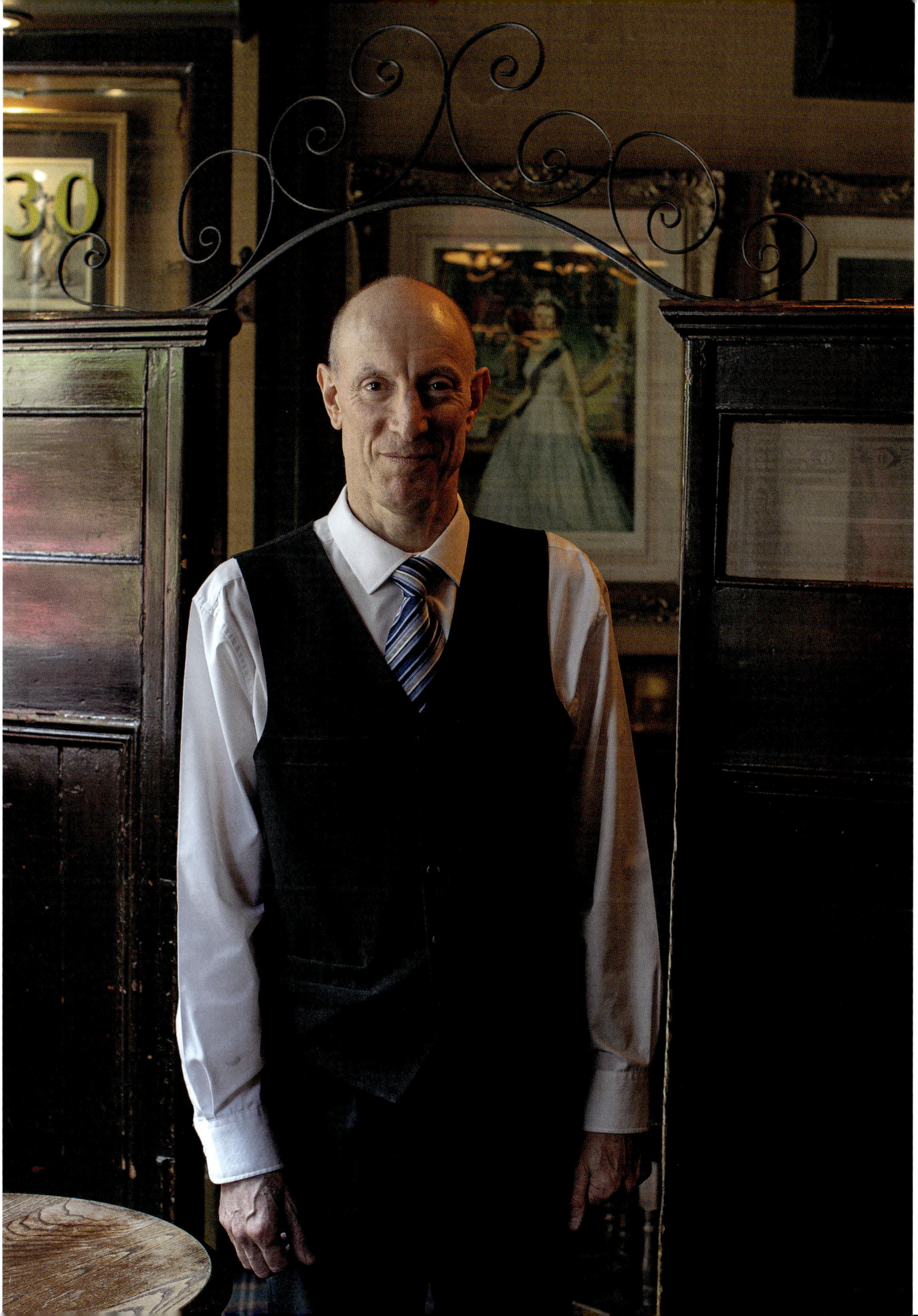

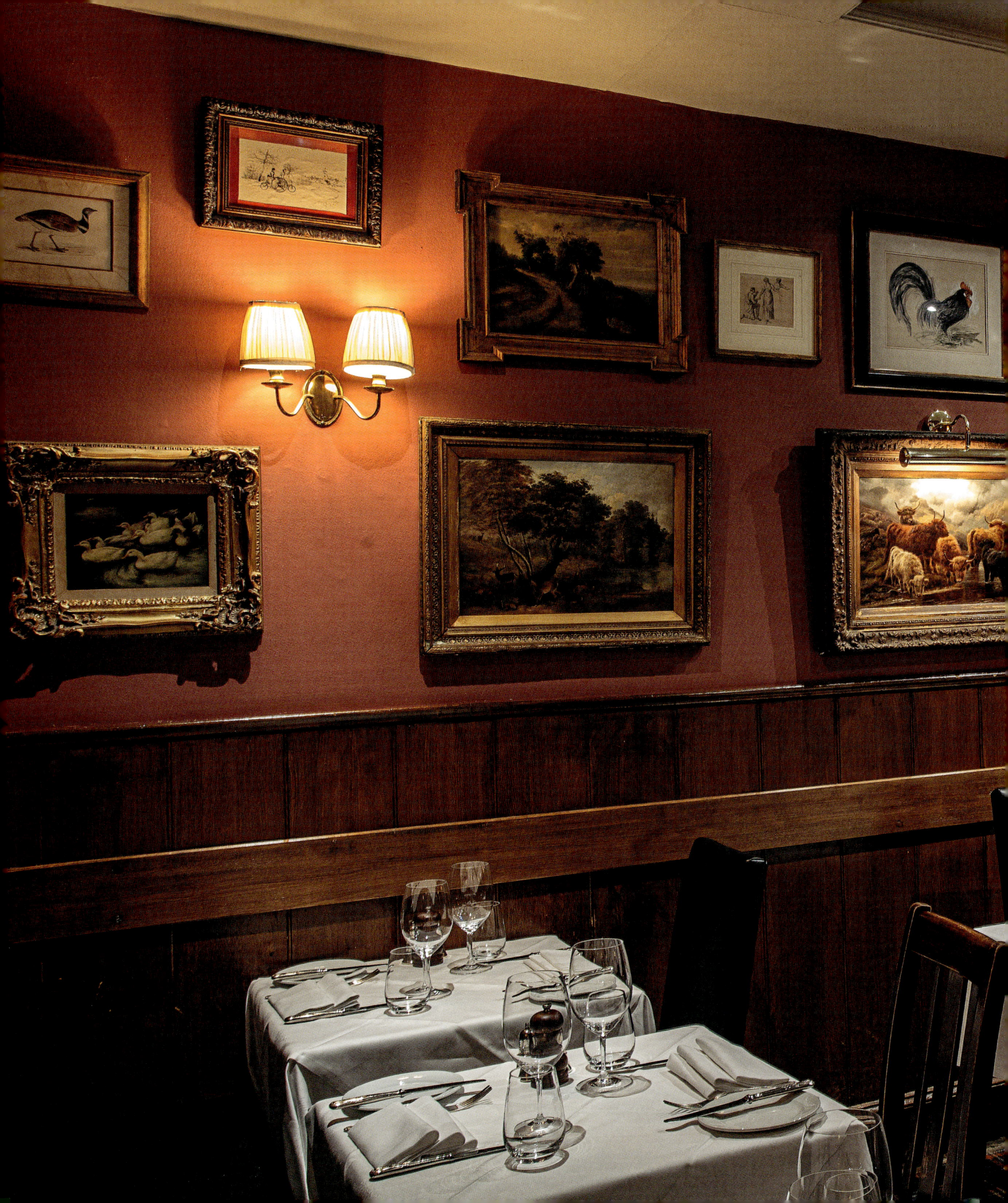

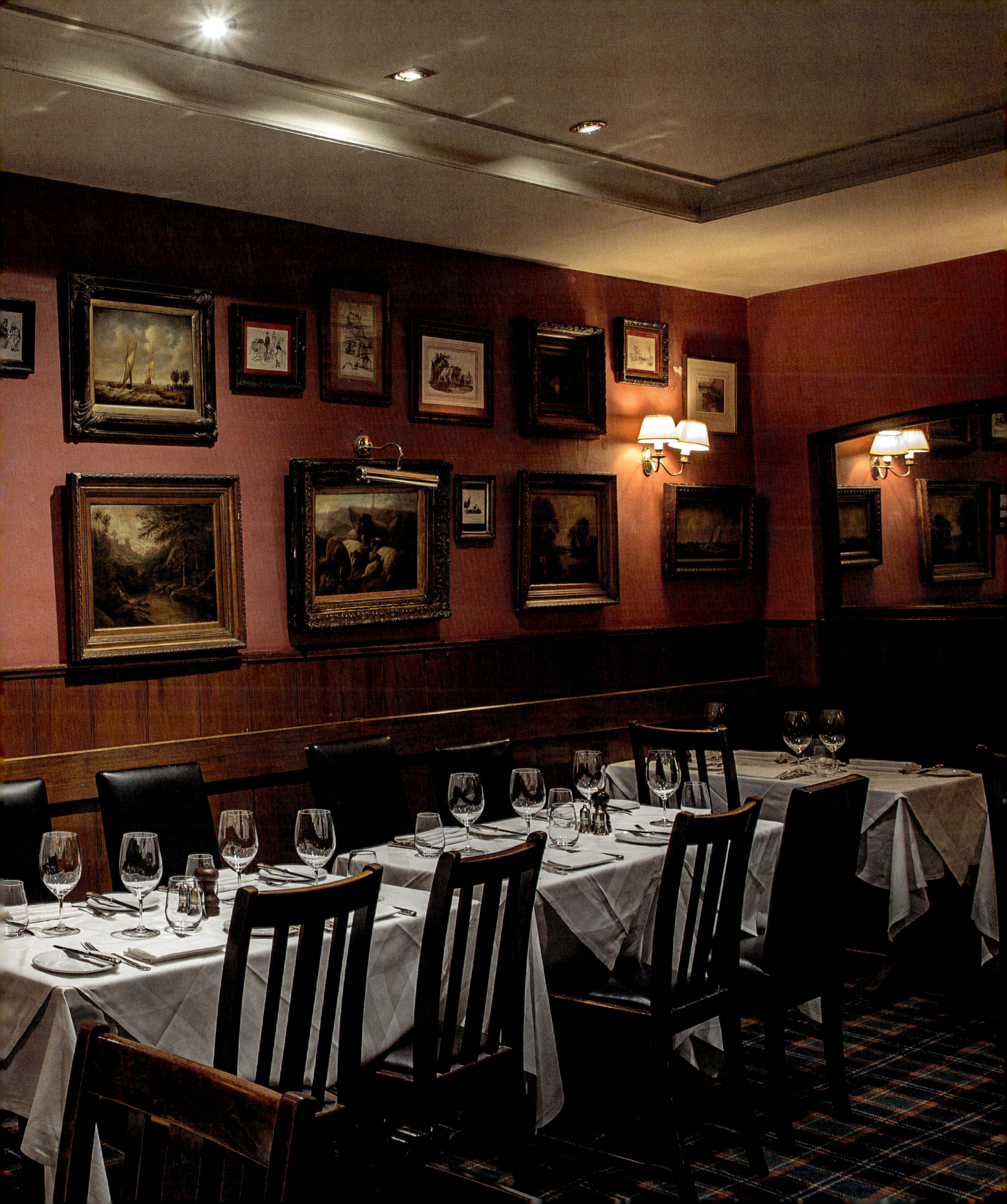

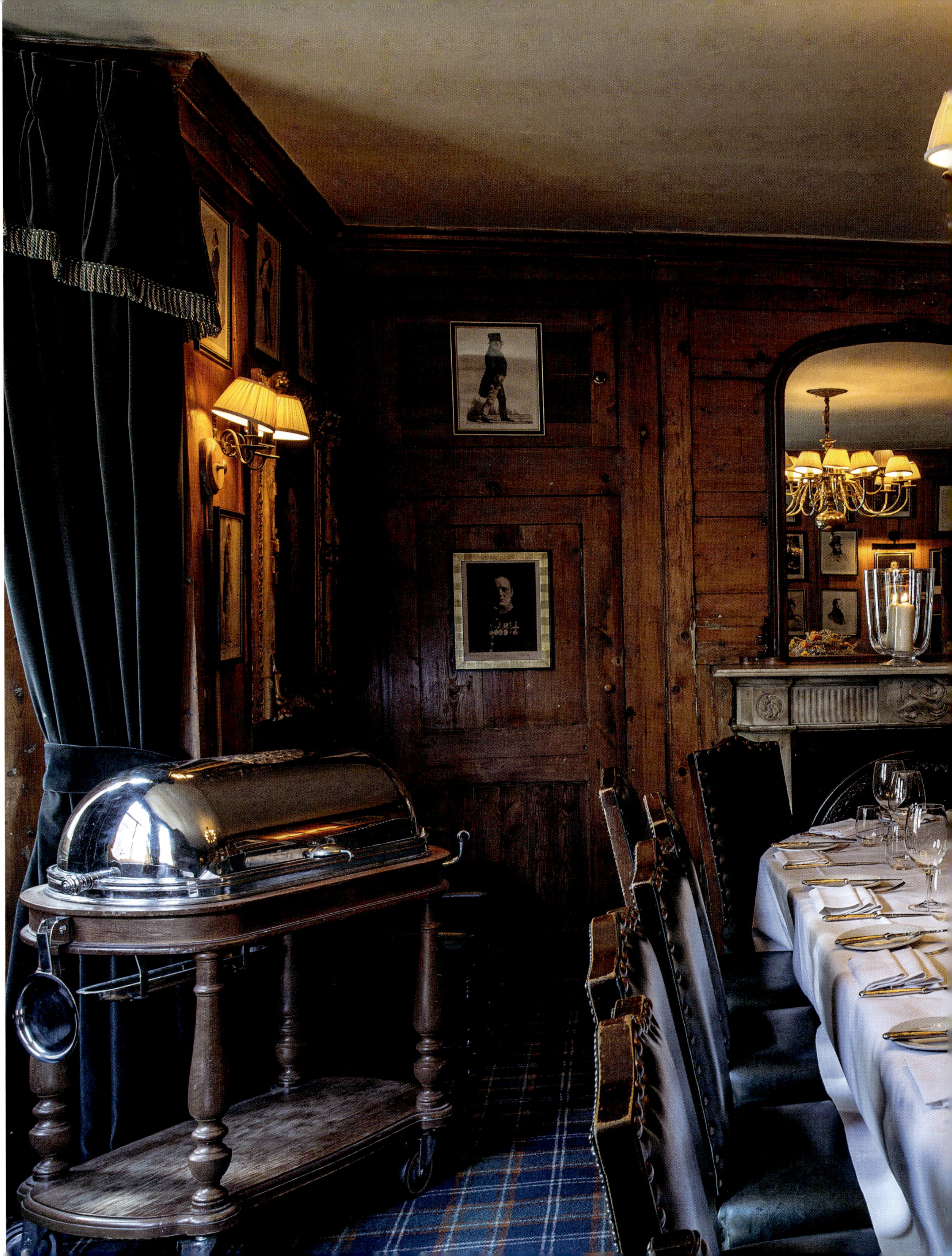

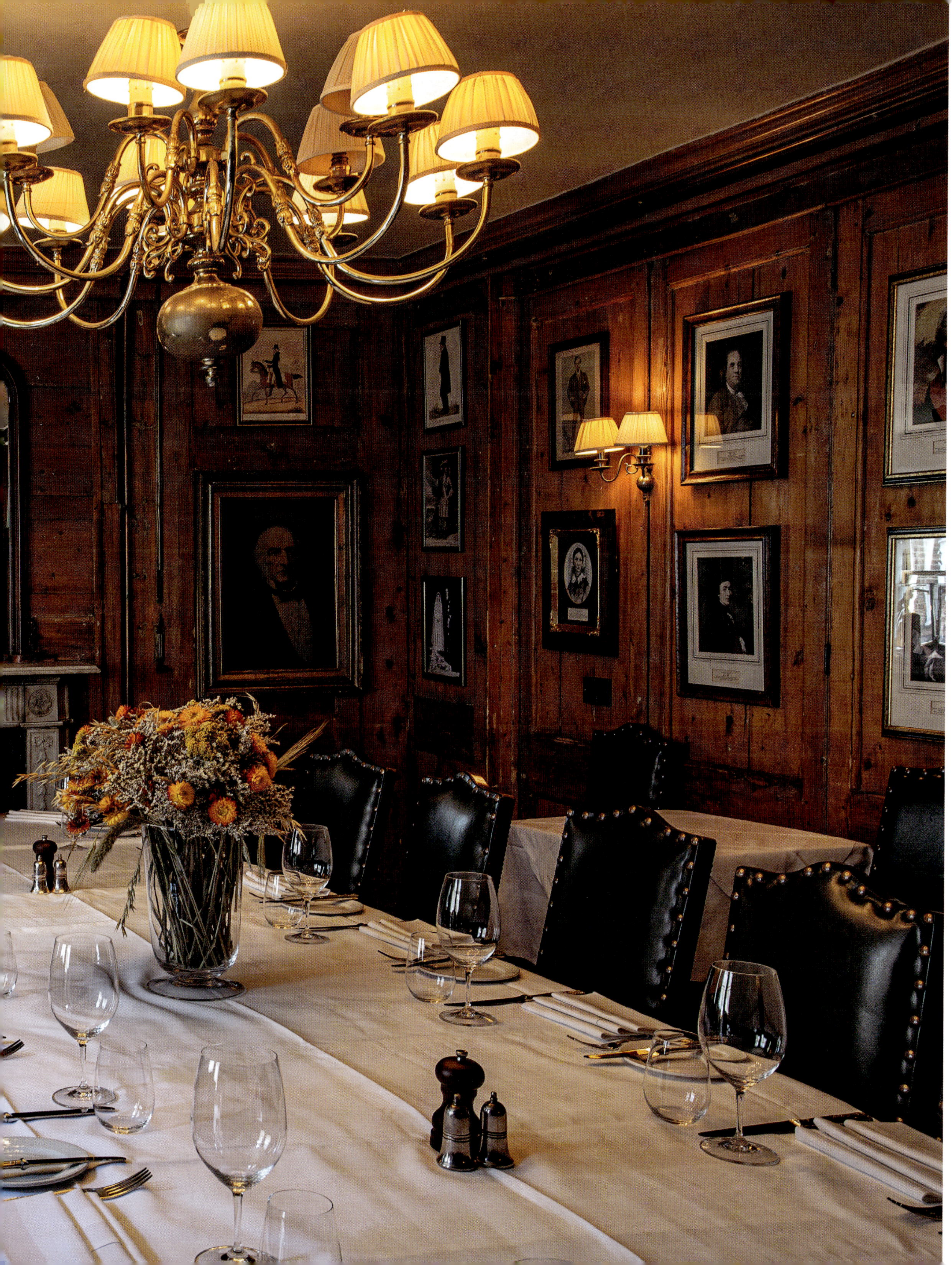

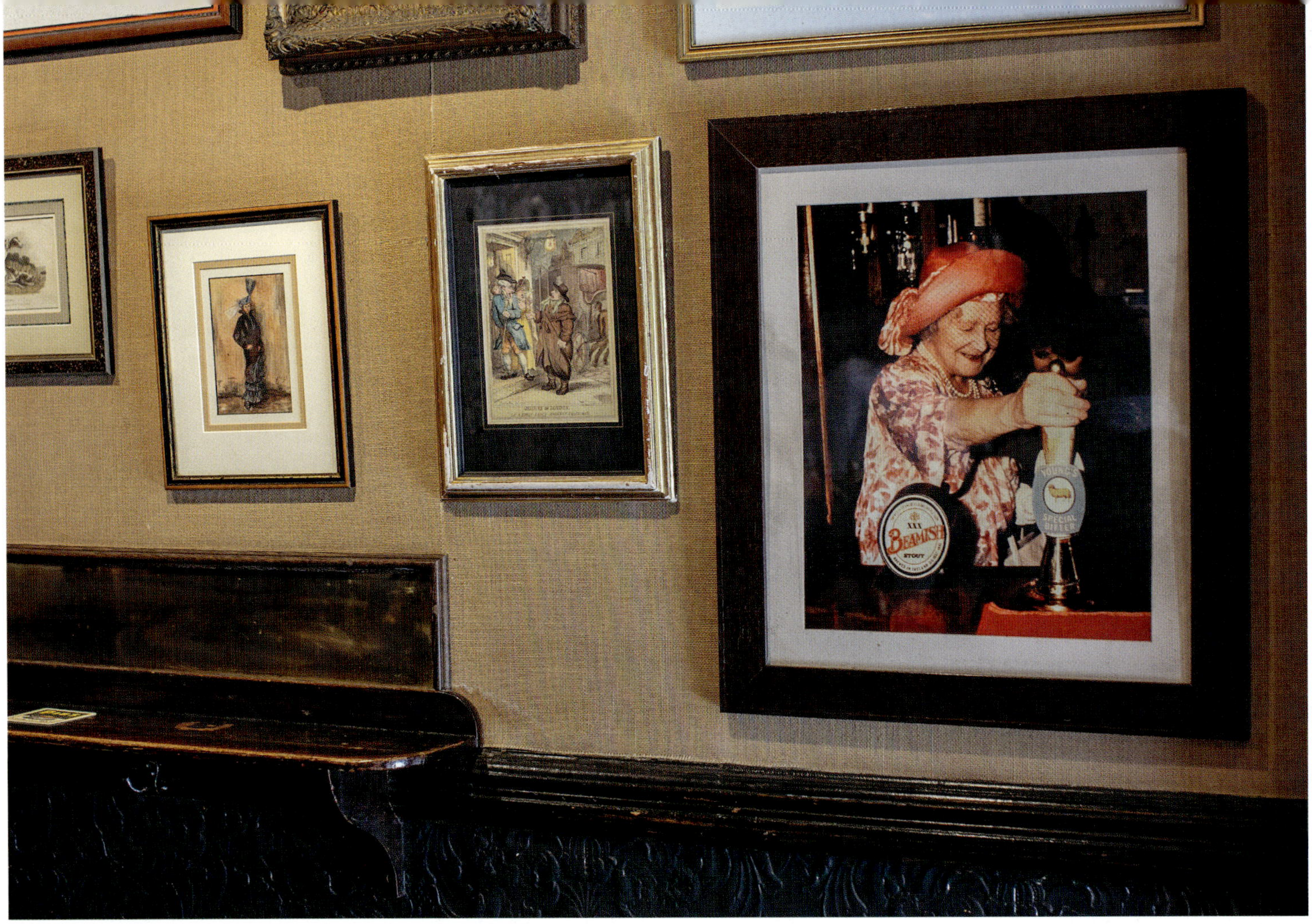
XXX
BEAMISH
STOUT

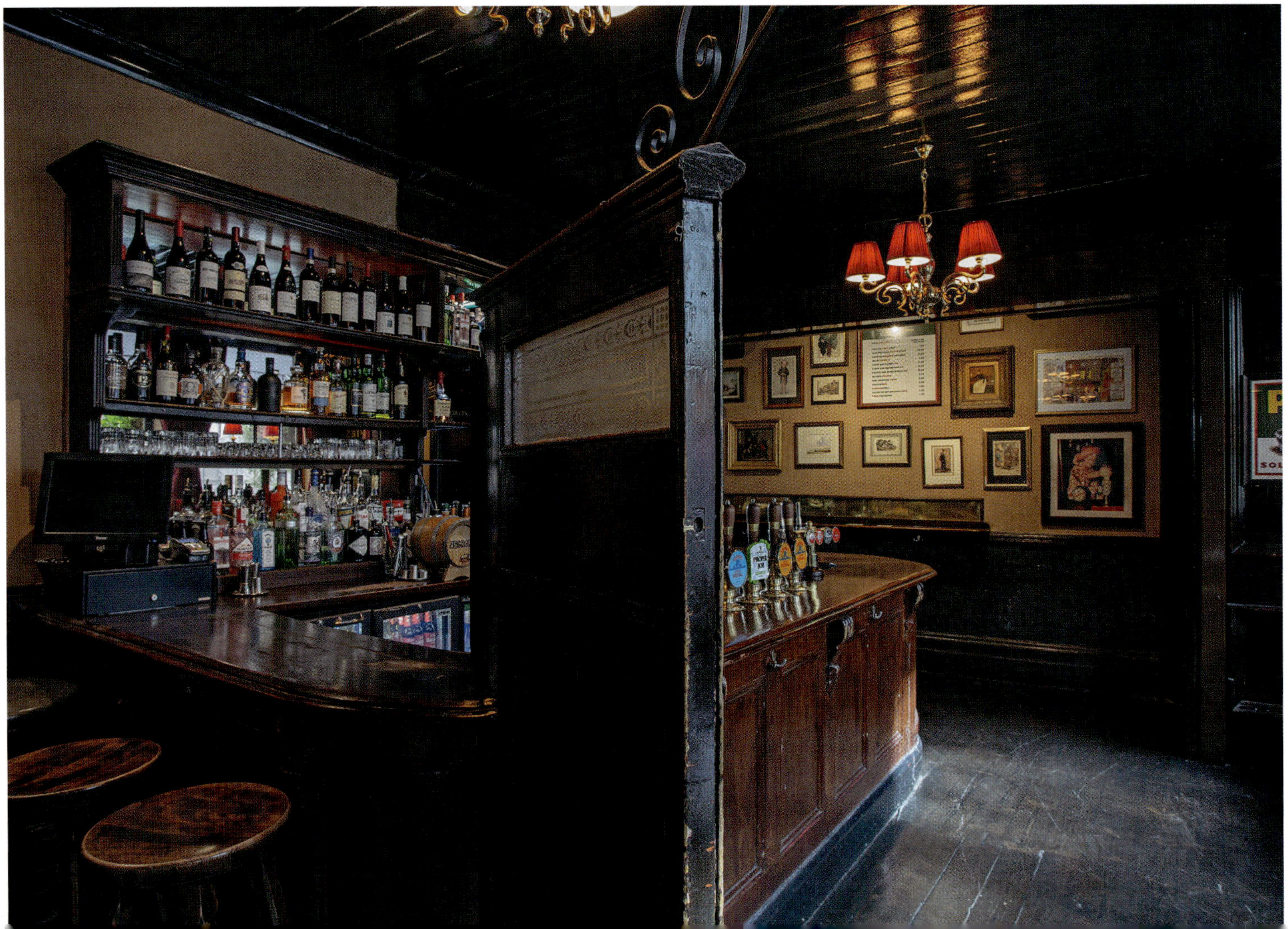

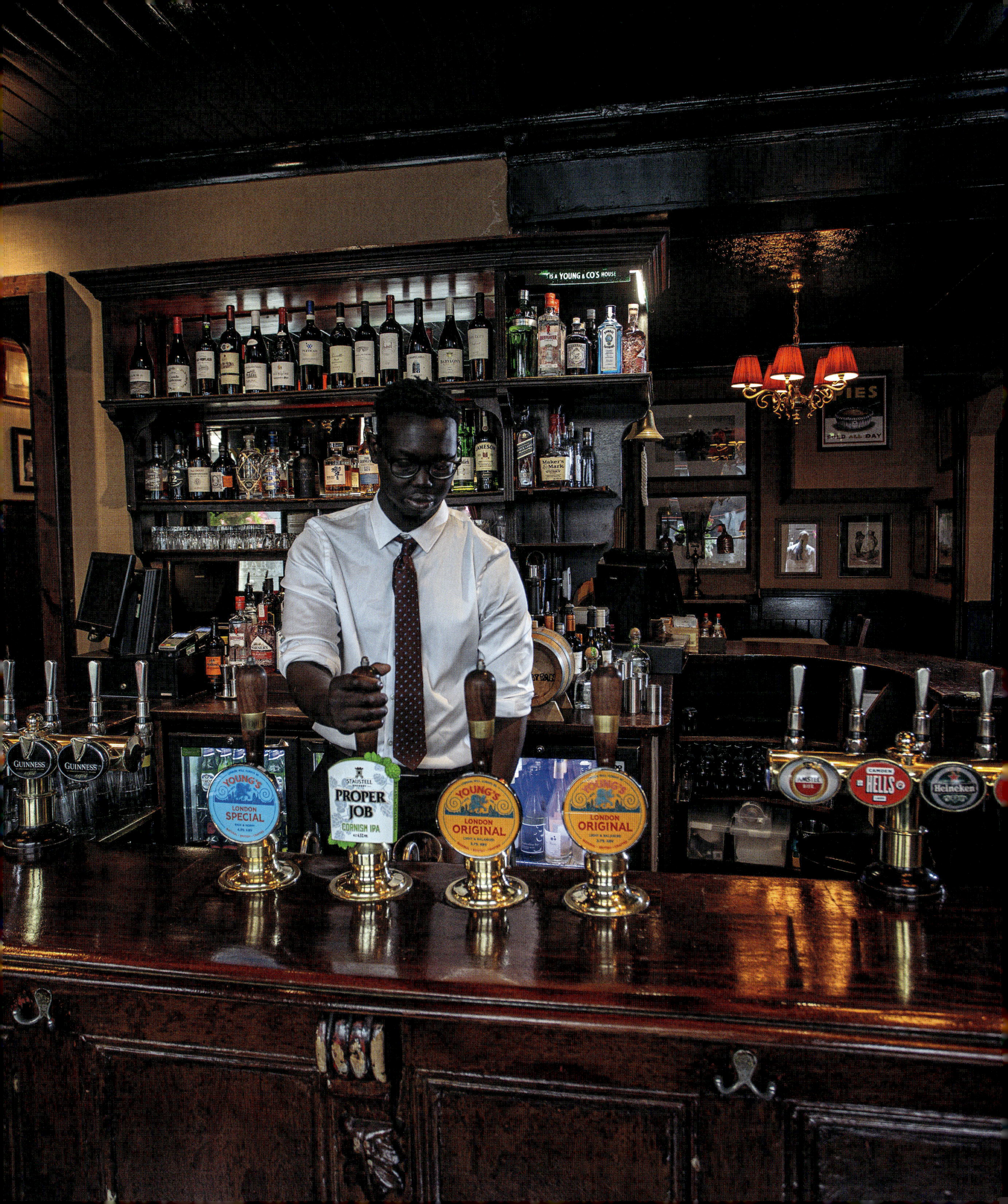

'TIS A YOUNG & CO'S HOUSE
SOLD ALL DAY
GUINNESS
GUINNESS
YOUNG'S
LONDON
SPECIAL
ST AUSTELL
PROPER
JOB
CORNISH IPA
YOUNG'S
LONDON
ORIGINAL
YOUNG'S
LONDON
ORIGINAL
AMSTEL
CAMDEN
HELLS
Heineken

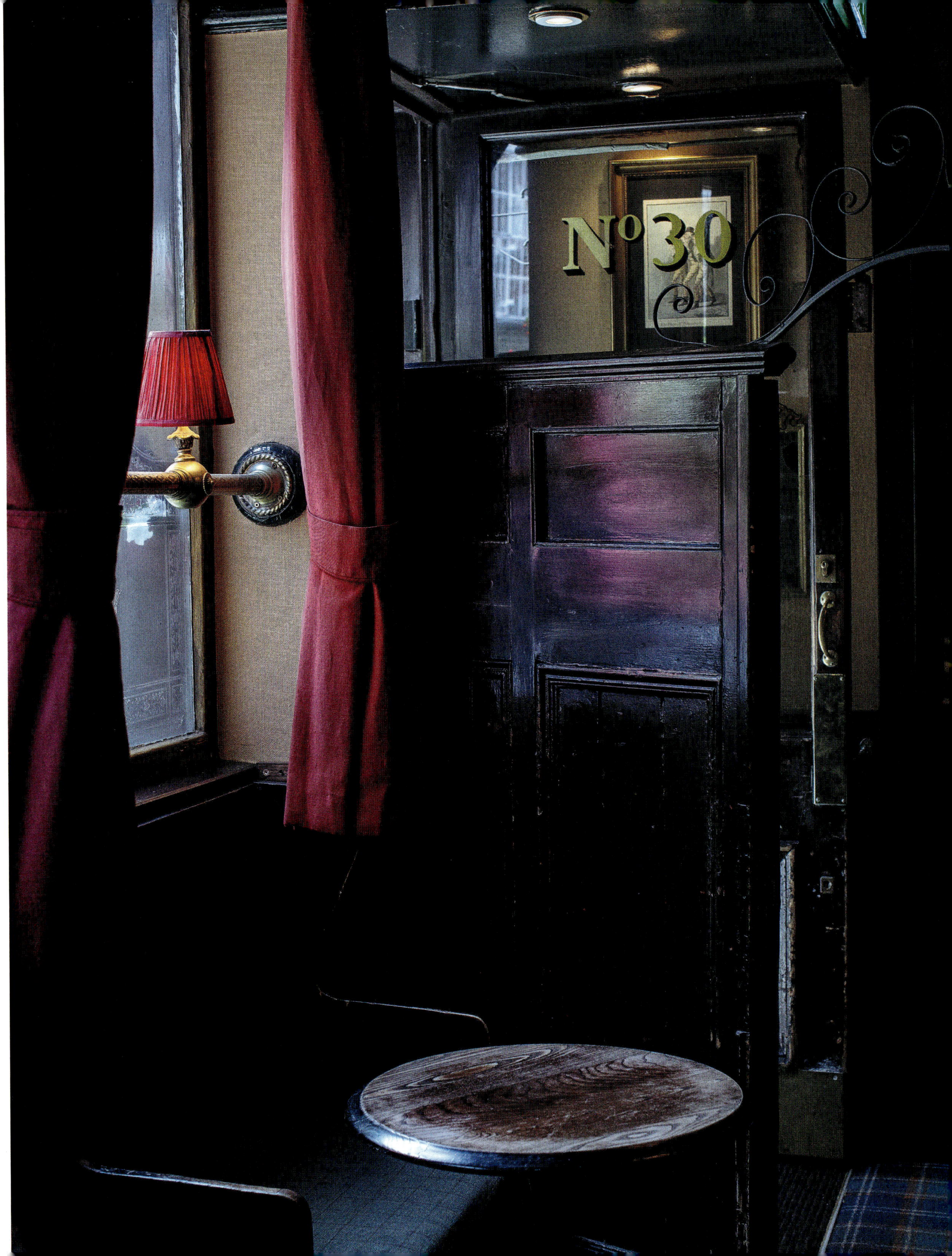
Nº30

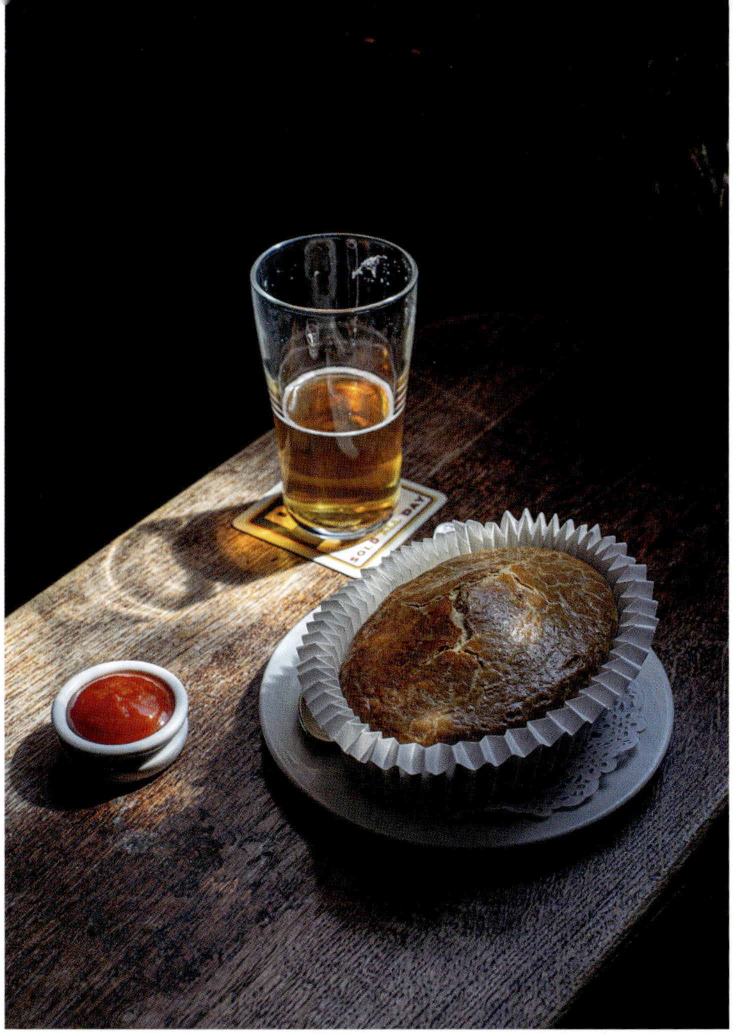

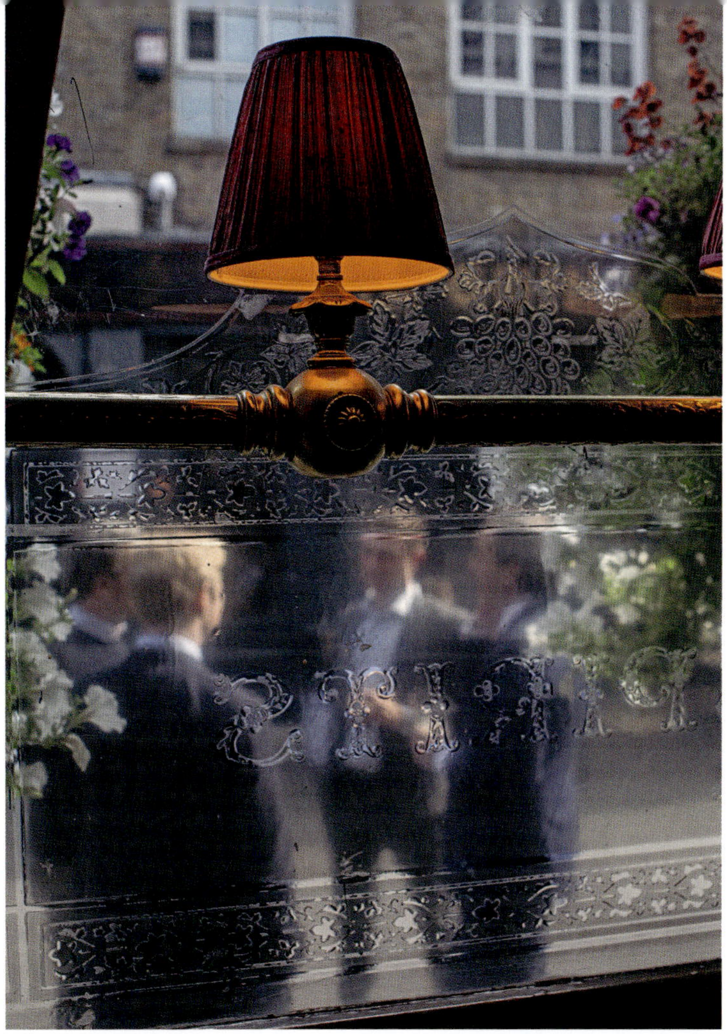

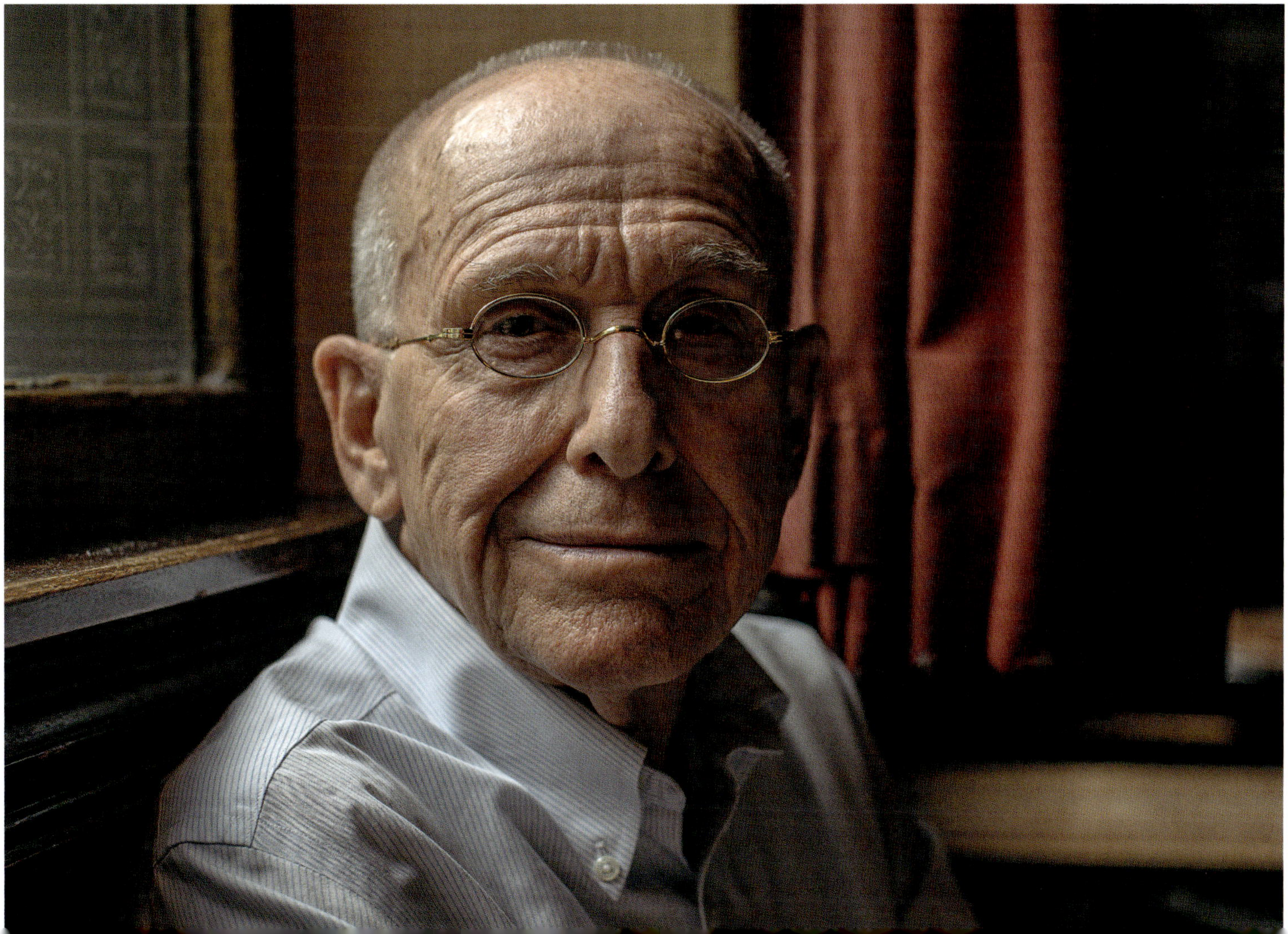

MARKSMAN PUBLIC HOUSE

254 HACKNEY RD, LONDON

Let's get one thing straight from the start. The Marksman is not a restaurant with a bar attached; it's a pub with an upstairs dining room. This much should be plain as you enter from the Hackney Road to discover what amounts to the Platonic ideal of a cosy Victorian-style local; warm wood panelling, contentedly creaking floorboards, bottle-green leather banquettes, a horseshoe-shaped bar with brass taps, a smattering of locals chewing the fat. But take a closer look at what's actually being chewed; rather than the gastropub staples of burgers and ploughman's, you've got modern British classics-in-the-making like beef and barley buns ("a glazed dome of soft bread roll containing a filling of finely diced braised beef", according to *Observer* food critic Jay Rayner), fried potatoes with burnt onion mayonnaise ("like a dozen of the best chips ever, pressed together"), and brown butter and honey tart ("all the wobble and softness of a newborn's thigh"). Seafood platters are served alongside chicken and girolle pies, and even the Sunday roasts – mallard, say, with damson jelly and bread sauce – go above and beyond. "The joy is not simply in the cooking," wrote Rayner. "It's in the simplicity of the offering, the resolute lack of flimflam and hauteur."

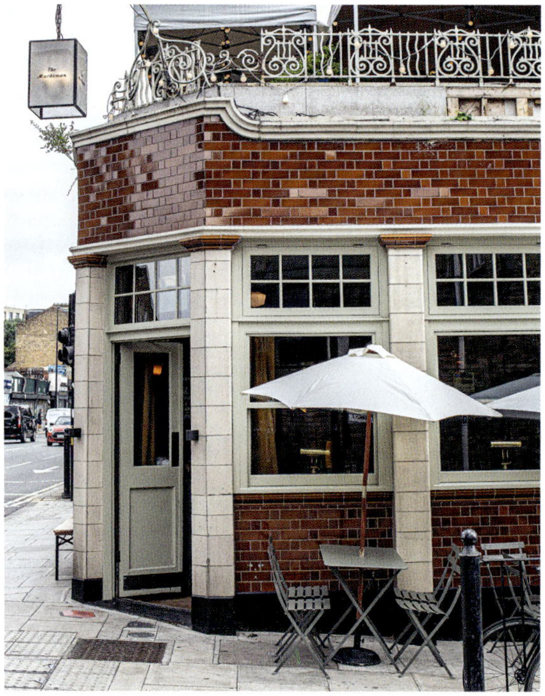

That attitude is embodied in the Marksman's owner-chefs, Tom Harris and Jon Rotheram. Both cut their teeth in restaurants – St John and Jamie Oliver's Fifteen, respectively – but set their sights on a pub for their own venture. "By their nature, pubs are more democratic than restaurants," says Harris. "You just walk in off the street, and no one's intimidated or thinks it's not for them. We knew this place, because we're locals ourselves – we both live just down the road. So when we took it over in 2015, we worked very hard on keeping it looking as unassuming as it's always done."

Rotheram: "But so many times when you walk into a pub, your first thought is, if only they had a great wine list, or decent craft beers, or native spirits, or a nice vermouth, or something a bit more ambitious on the menu. So the focus for us was on raising the bar, as it were, and on the quality of the offer, while keeping the whole feel very down to earth."

Harris: "We also wanted to promote British food, because those were the kinds of kitchens we came from. And where's the best place to serve that kind of hearty, yeoman fare? A pub. We're showcasing the best of British, from our shores and farms, from Hereford wing rib to crabs and langoustines. And that sense of place finds its perfect setting here."

The bar provides the Marksman's beating heart, around which the other spaces – the cool, contemporary upstairs dining room, designed by Martino Gamper, whose studio is nearby, plus a small outdoor terrace and a kitchen-adjacent cellar room for private dining – revolve. Thus Harris and Rotheram can cater to everyone from the "old boys" who've been dropping in for decades to the fashion and gallery crowds that helped refashion Hackney into hipster central. "We love that attitude of coming in, having a drink, then maybe going to another room for something to eat, or just having a few snacks or small plates at the bar," says Harris. "The quality is the same down or up," adds Rotheram. "We don't have any cheap seats."

The Marksman carried off Michelin's Best Pub in Britain award in 2017, and, sipping a glass of Buriana (from the reassuringly great wine list) at a corner table on a sunny Friday afternoon, it's not hard to see why – Harris and Rotheram's establishment, like their beef and barley bun, is a simple enough proposition, on which an uncommon amount of thought, attention and care has been lavished.

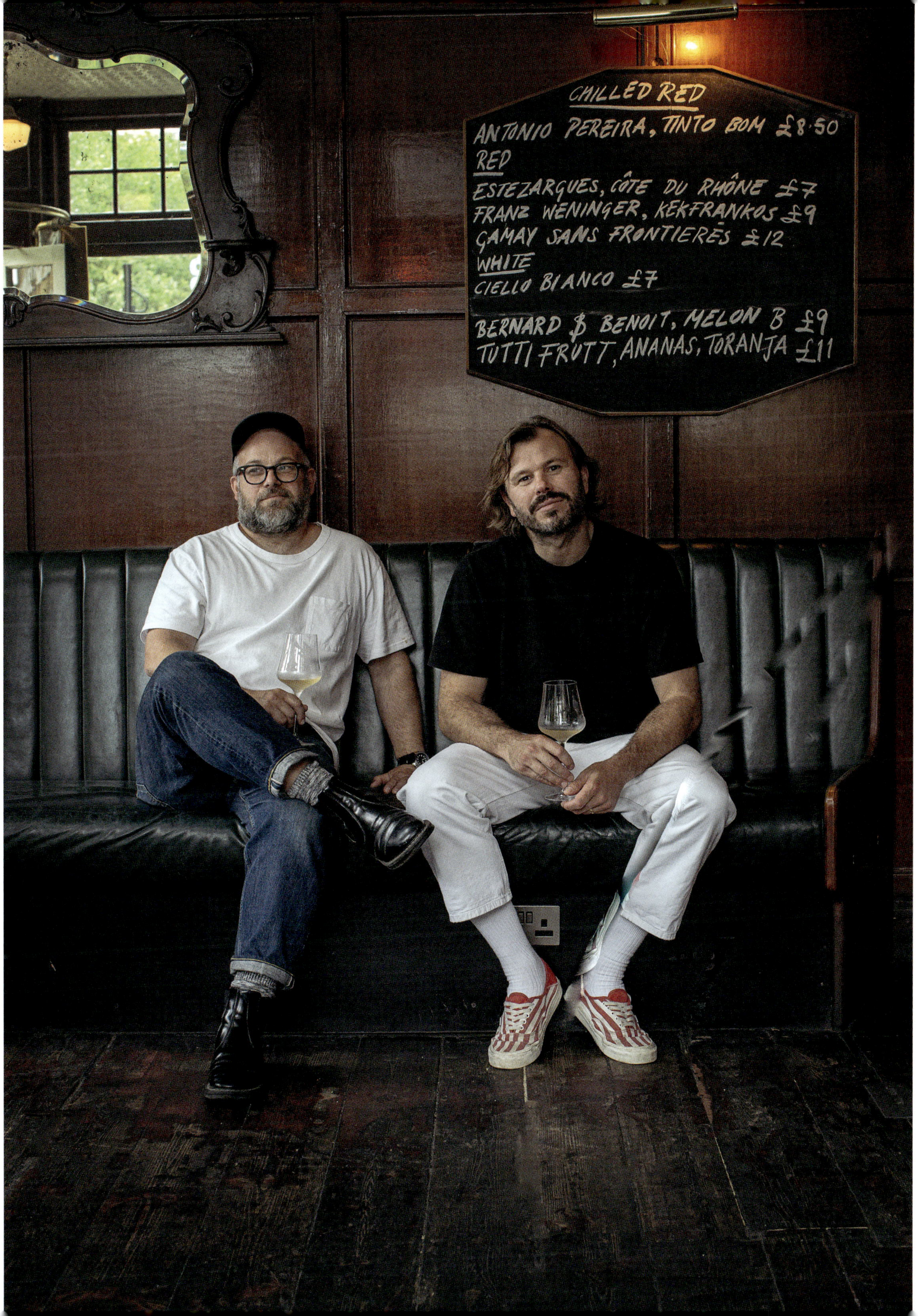

"THE FOCUS FOR US IS ON RAISING THE BAR"

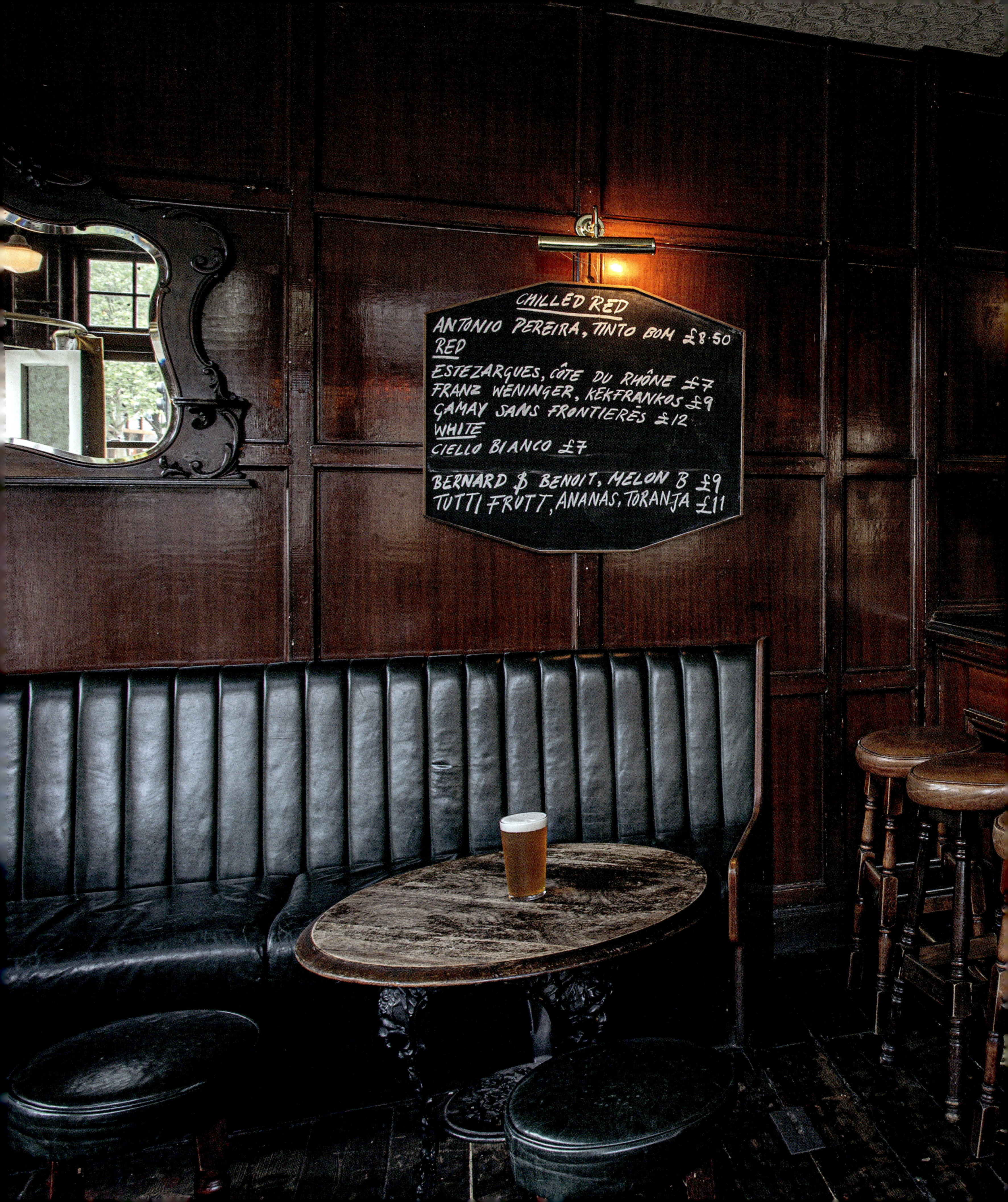
CHILLED RED
ANTONIO PEREIRA, TINTO BOM £8.50
RED
ESTEZARGUES, CÔTE DU RHÔNE £7
FRANZ WENINGER, KEKFRANKOS £9
GAMAY SANS FRONTIERÈS £12
WHITE
CIELLO BIANCO £7
BERNARD $ BENOIT, MELON B £9
TUTTI FRUTT, ANANAS, TORANJA £11

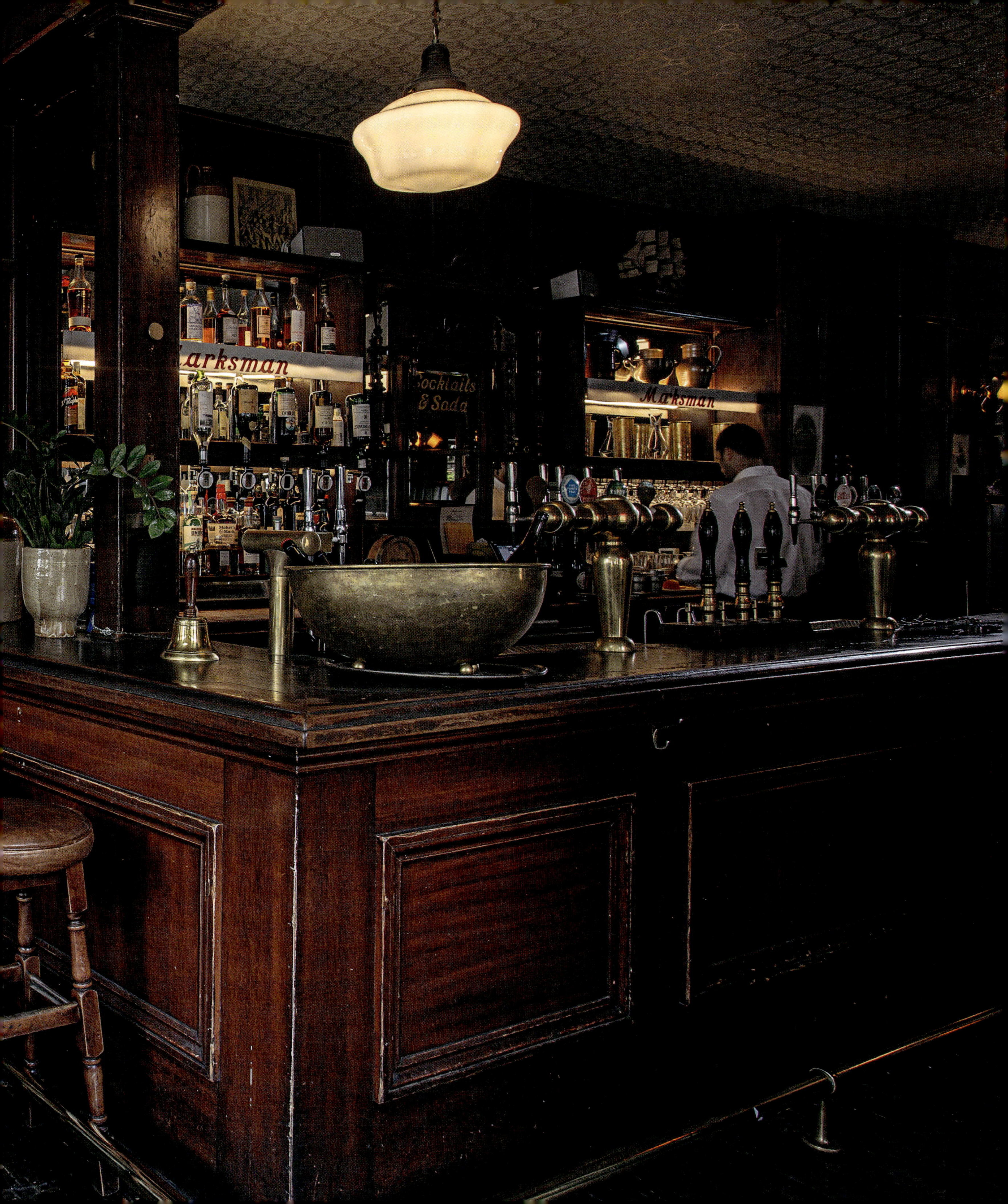
arksman
Cocktails
& Soda
Marksman

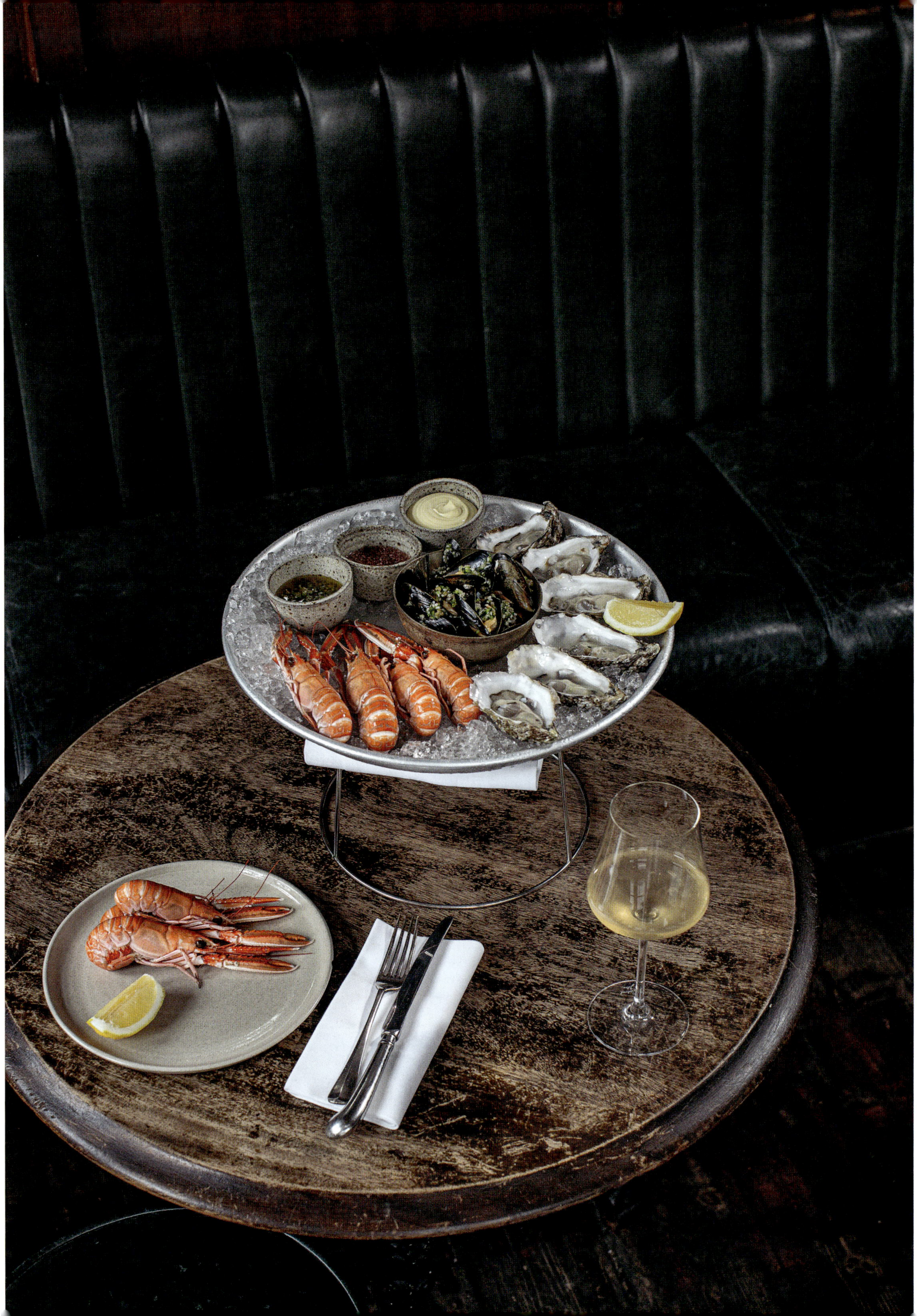

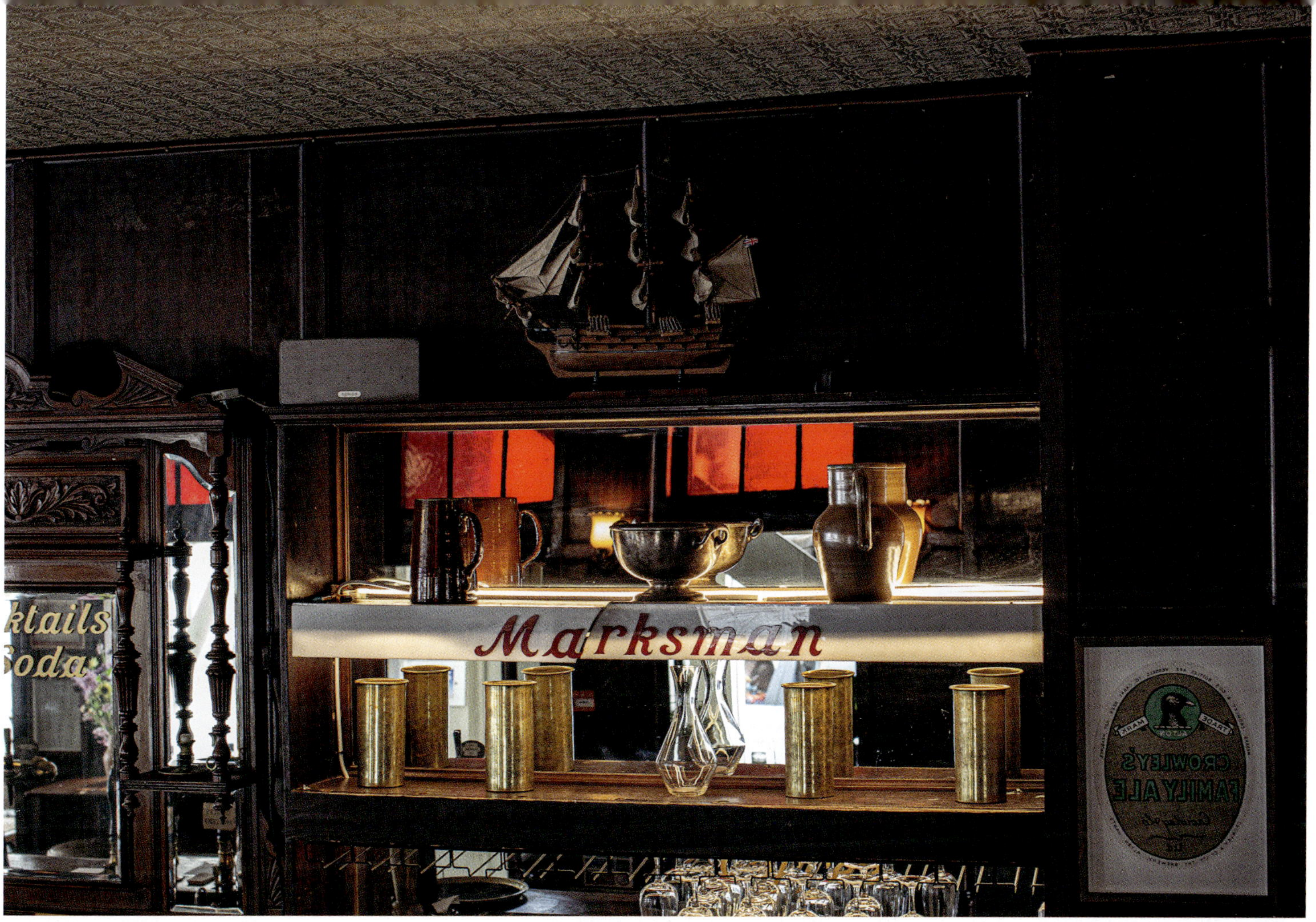
ktails
Soda
Marksman

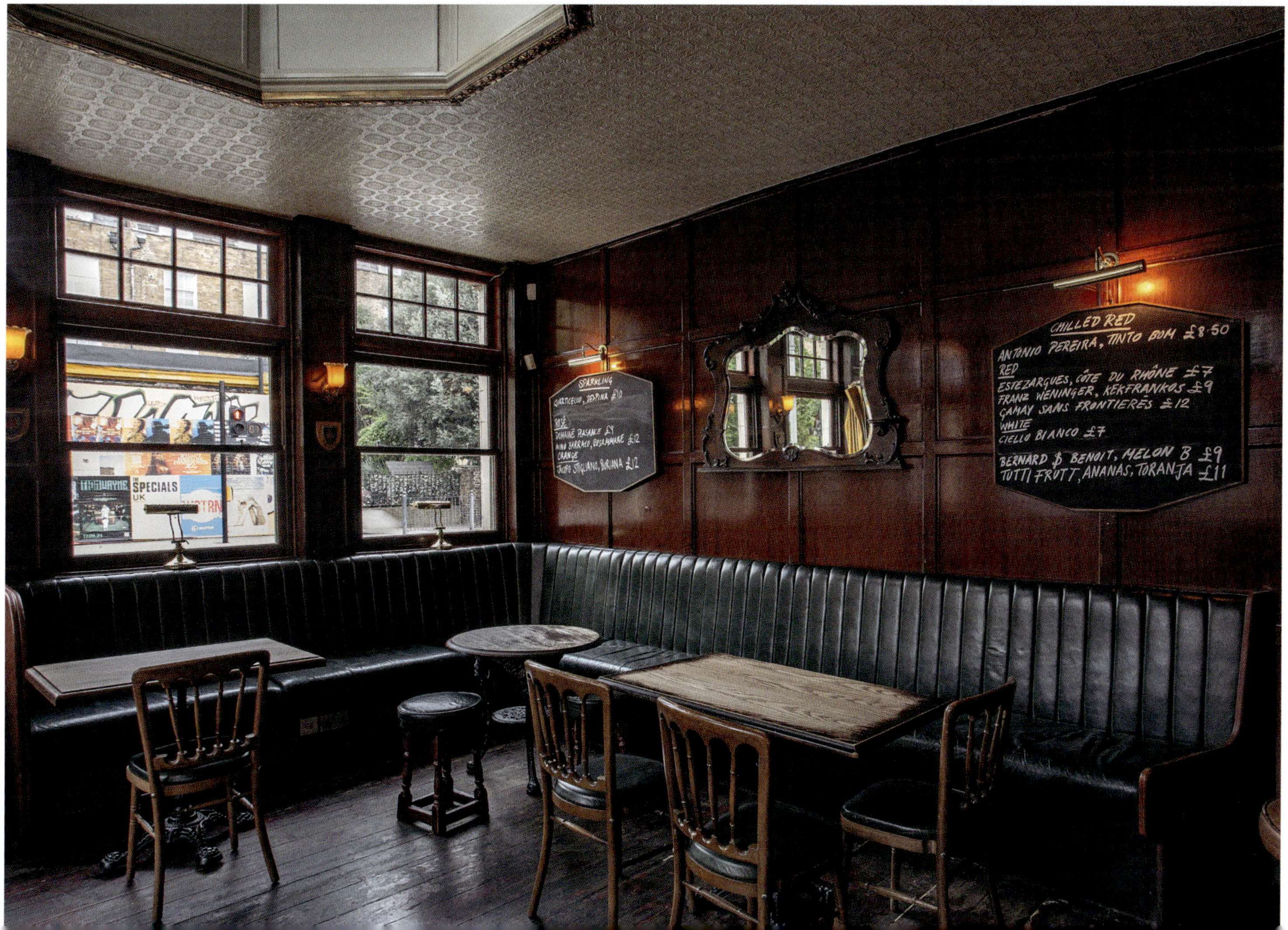
SPECIALS
CHILLED RED
ANTONIO PEREIRA, TINTO BOM £8·50
RED
ESTEZARGUES, CÔTE DU RHÔNE £7
FRANZ WENINGER, KEKFRANKOS £9
GAMAY SANS FRONTIÈRES £12
WHITE
CIELLO BIANCO £7
BERNARD & BENOIT, MELON B £9
TUTTI FRUTT, ANANAS, TORANJA £11

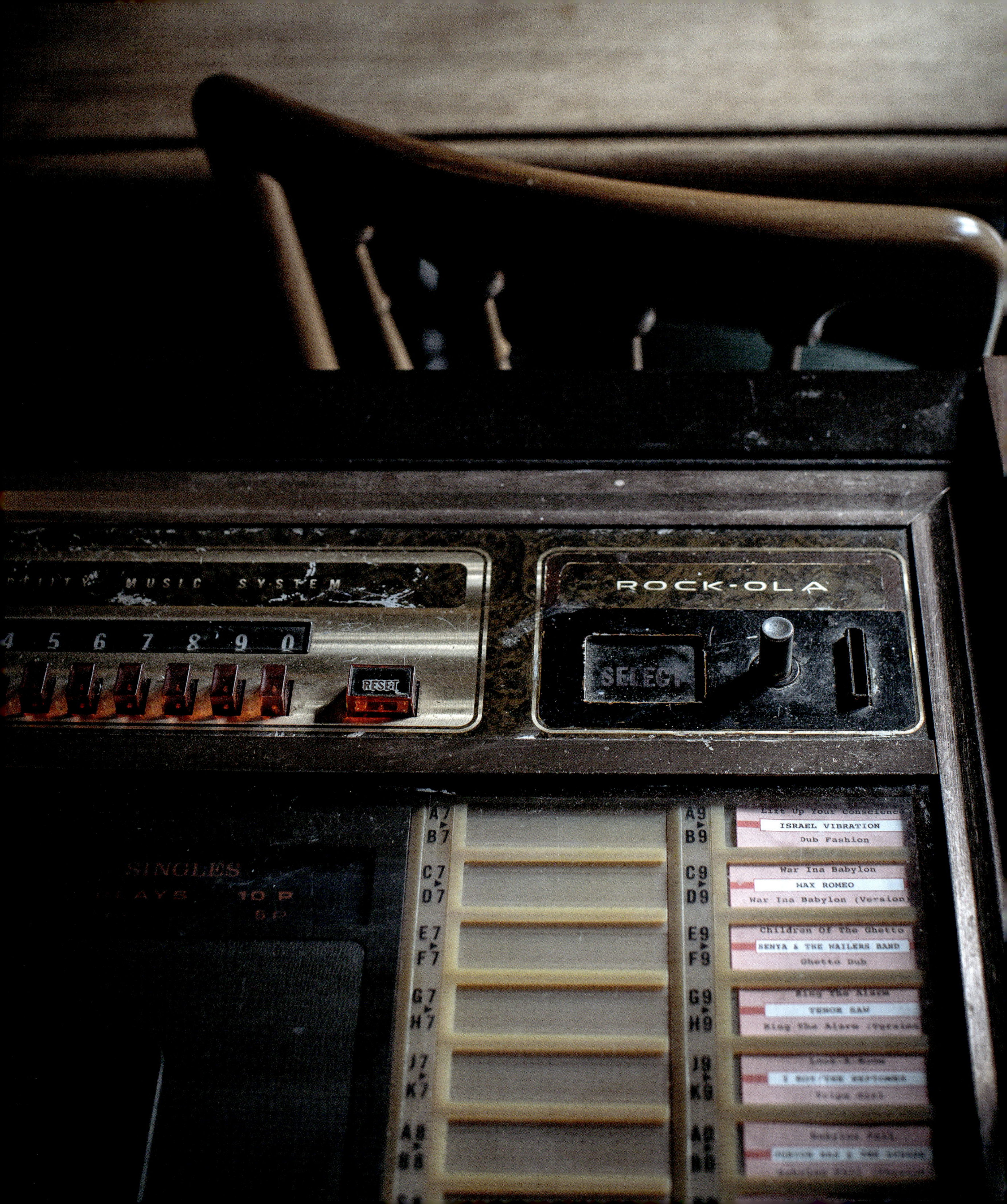
MUSIC SYSTEM
4 5 6 7 8 9 0
RESET
ROCK-OLA
SELECT
SINGLES
10 P
A7 B7
C7 D7
E7 F7
G7 H7
J7 K7
A9 B9
Lift Up Your Conscience
ISRAEL VIBRATION
Dub Fashion
C9 D9
War Ina Babylon
MAX ROMEO
War Ina Babylon (Version)
E9 F9
Children Of The Ghetto
SENYA & THE WAILERS BAND
Ghetto Dub
G9 H9
J9 K9

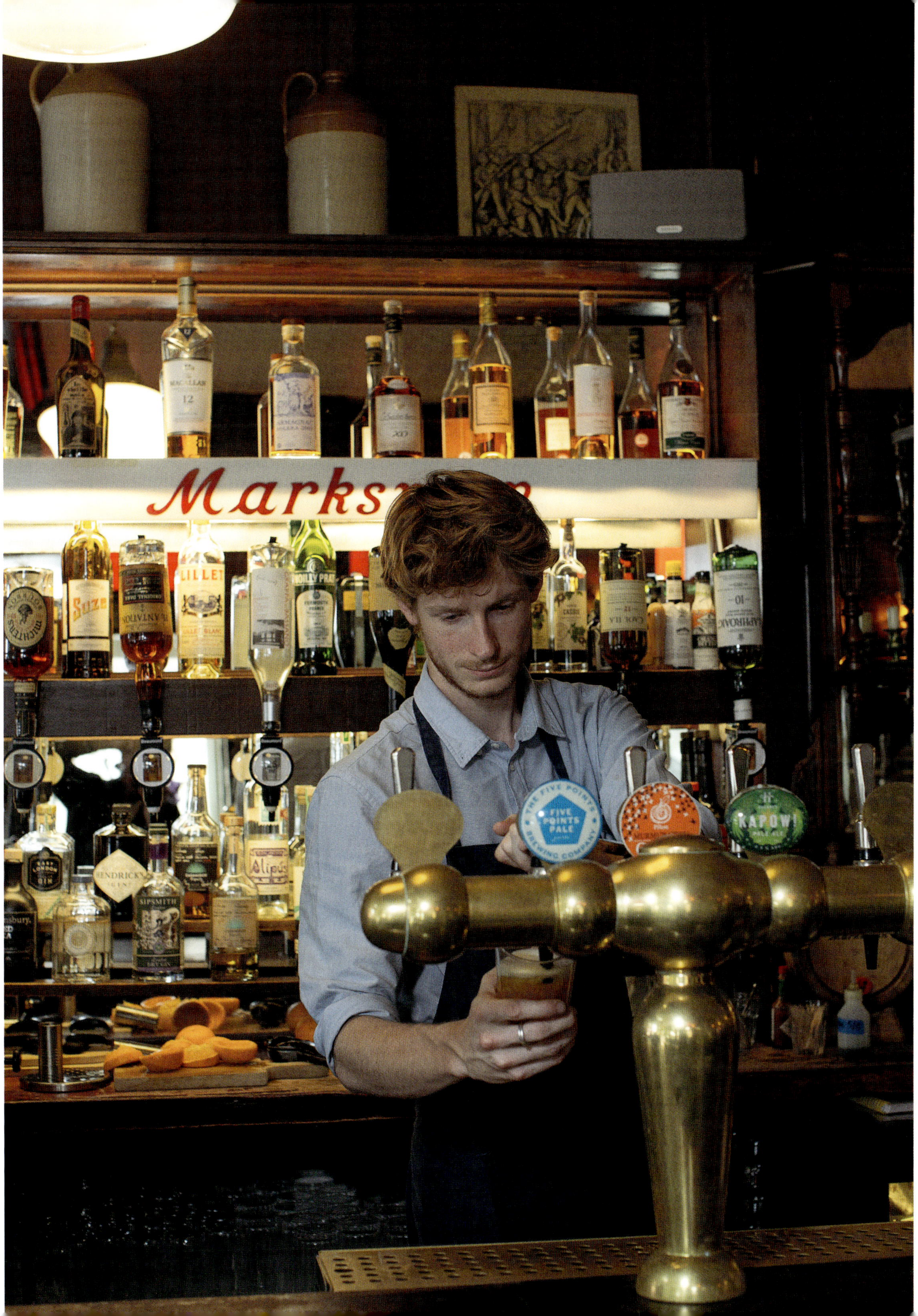

"THE BAR IS THE BEATING HEART"

THE GOLDEN HEART

110 COMMERCIAL ST, LONDON

Sandra Esquilant is enumerating all the qualities you need to be a good landlady. "You have to like people," she says, with a broad Cockney twang. "You have to have an eye for bad people. And you have to be hardworking, oh my God." She takes a sip of her coffee. "But luckily, I like hard work."

Esquilant has displayed all these qualities and more during her forty-five years of stewardship of The Golden Heart, her pub on a busy intersection in Spitalfields, that buzzy part of London where the City towers abut the East End terraces. "She's a local legend and the pub's held many a legendary party," says Timothy Everest, a tailor and former neighbour of The Golden Heart. The U-shaped bar – all Victorian stained glass and no-nonsense bench seating – is pretty serene today, but look closer and you'll see that it's studded with what Esquilant, who was born "just five minutes down the road", describes as "things that mean a lot to me because this place is my life and my front room." There are Catholic statues, a light-up Buddha, and a photo of Queen Elizabeth II, described by locals as "Sandra's presiding deities". There's a sign reading "Sine Labore Nihil" – "Nothing Without Labour" – above the bar. There are Damien Hirst-esque mini-diamond skulls nestling among the toby jugs, plus cut-outs of artist neighbours Gilbert & George in the window, and a work by Tracey Emin, another former neighbour, high on a wall, that spells out "Fucking Beautiful" in white neon, all a reminder of the mid-90s days when The Golden Heart became the in-house boozer for the Young British Artist crowd. (A photograph of a grinning Emin – another presiding deity, perhaps – hangs next to an Eagle Ale sign.) And behind the bar is a hula hoop, ready to be pressed into service for whenever the septuagenarian Esquilant feels moved to perform her party piece. "I would always hula-hoop at parties when everyone was smoking and dancing and singing, and I still do it now," she shrugs. "I mean, if you can't have a bit of fun..."

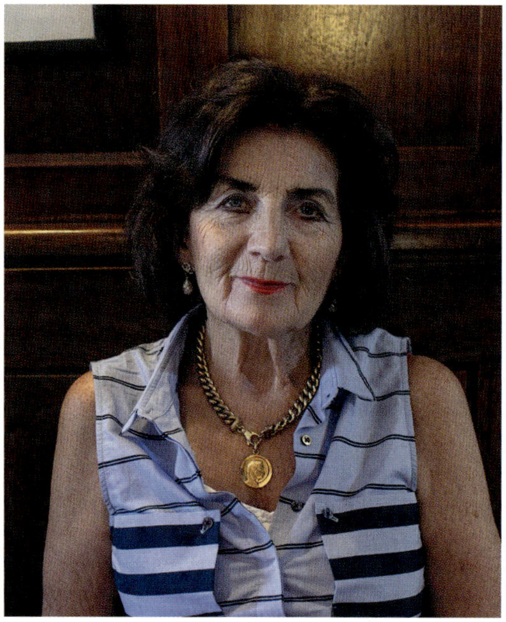

The history of Esquilant's time at The Golden Heart is woven into the history of this corner of London. She and her husband Dennis took it over in the late 1970s – "I didn't want a pub any more than I wanted to fly in an aeroplane", she says, "but I walked in the door and fell in love with it" – when its twenty-four-hour license meant it served pre-breakfast pints to the porters from Spitalfields fruit and veg market and clocked-off night-shifters from the nearby Truman brewery, and the area was full of Jewish tailor shops and Catholic retreats. "It was another world," says Esquilant, who fondly remembers regulars such as Big Keith, who obligingly lived up to his name by devouring nineteen pies in the pub's pie-and-mash-eating competition, and Old Rose, "a wonderful Jewish lady who'd sit at the same table every night and nick everyone's cigarettes."

The Golden Heart suffered with the loss of the market, the closure of the brewery, and Dennis' death – "sometimes we'd have a single customer per day", says Esquilant, "and I worked it all on my own, because I couldn't afford staff" – but gained a new lease of life when the run-down area was adopted by a new generation of artists and creatives. Now Esquilant found herself playing den mother to the likes of Sarah Lucas and Tracey Emin, The Libertines' Pete Doherty, and the bon vivant and restaurateur Fergus Henderson, who opened a branch of St John a few doors down. "I love them dearly," she says. "We had such good times. And that's what a pub should be, the heart of the community."

That's what The Golden Heart continues to be, with Esquilant's daughters now presiding at the bar alongside her – "women are better at running a pub, just as they're better at everything," she says – and curious sightseers now joining the seasoned regulars at Esquilant's own storied shrine. "Retirement?" she sniffs. "They'll have to carry me out of here. I think finding this place was my destiny. And it's not over yet."

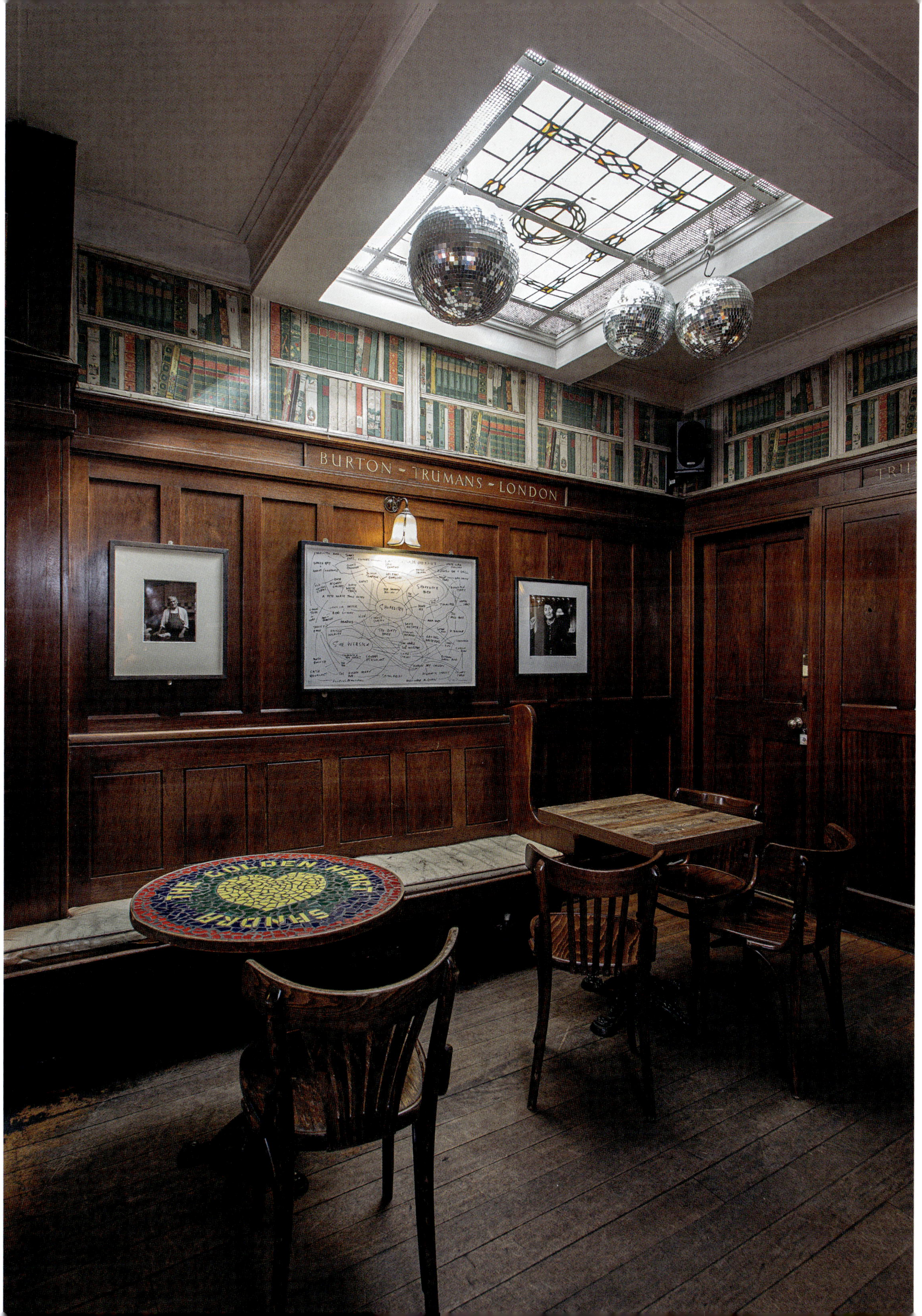
BURTON ~ TRUMANS ~ LONDON
THE GOLDEN HEART
TRUMANS

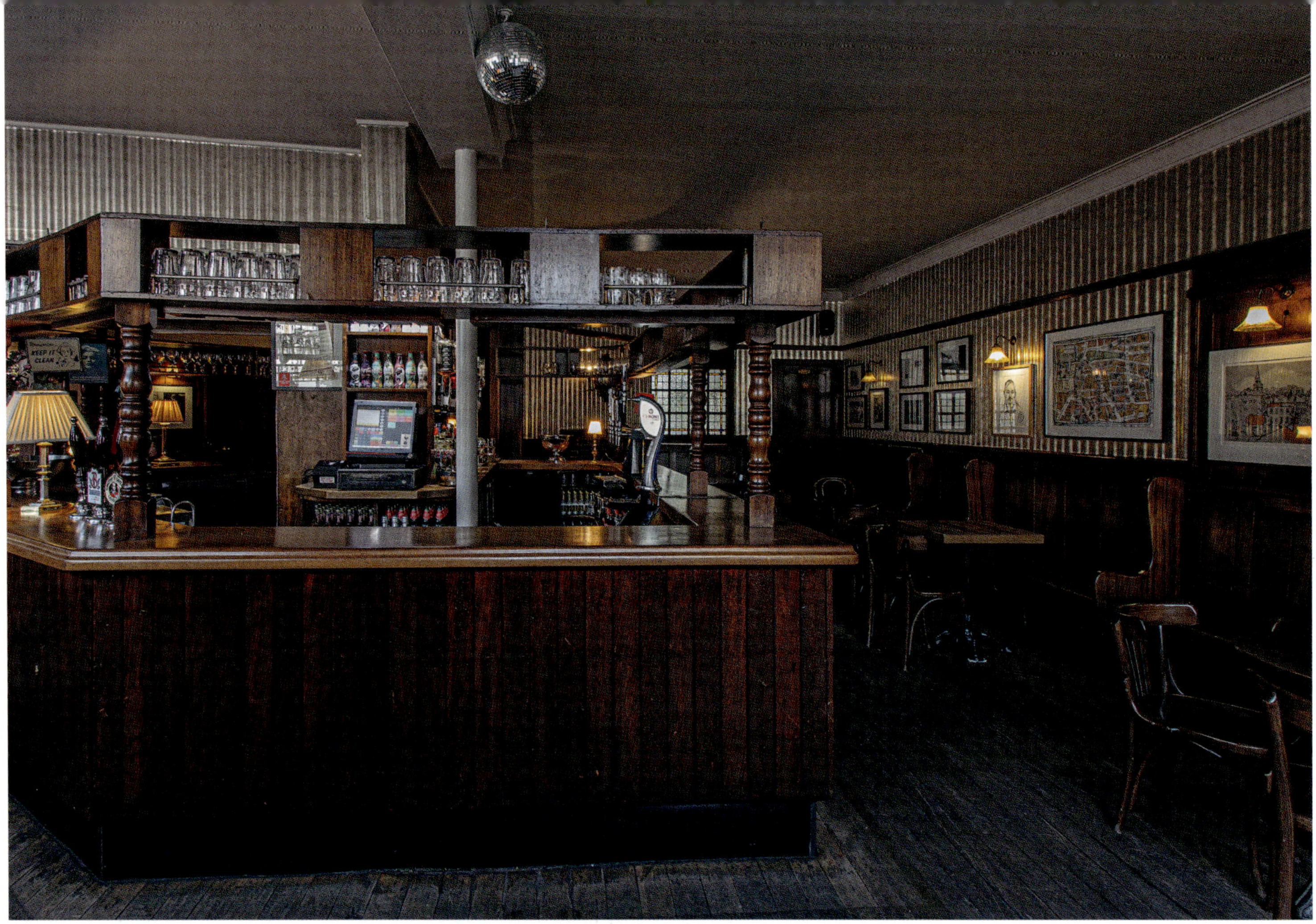

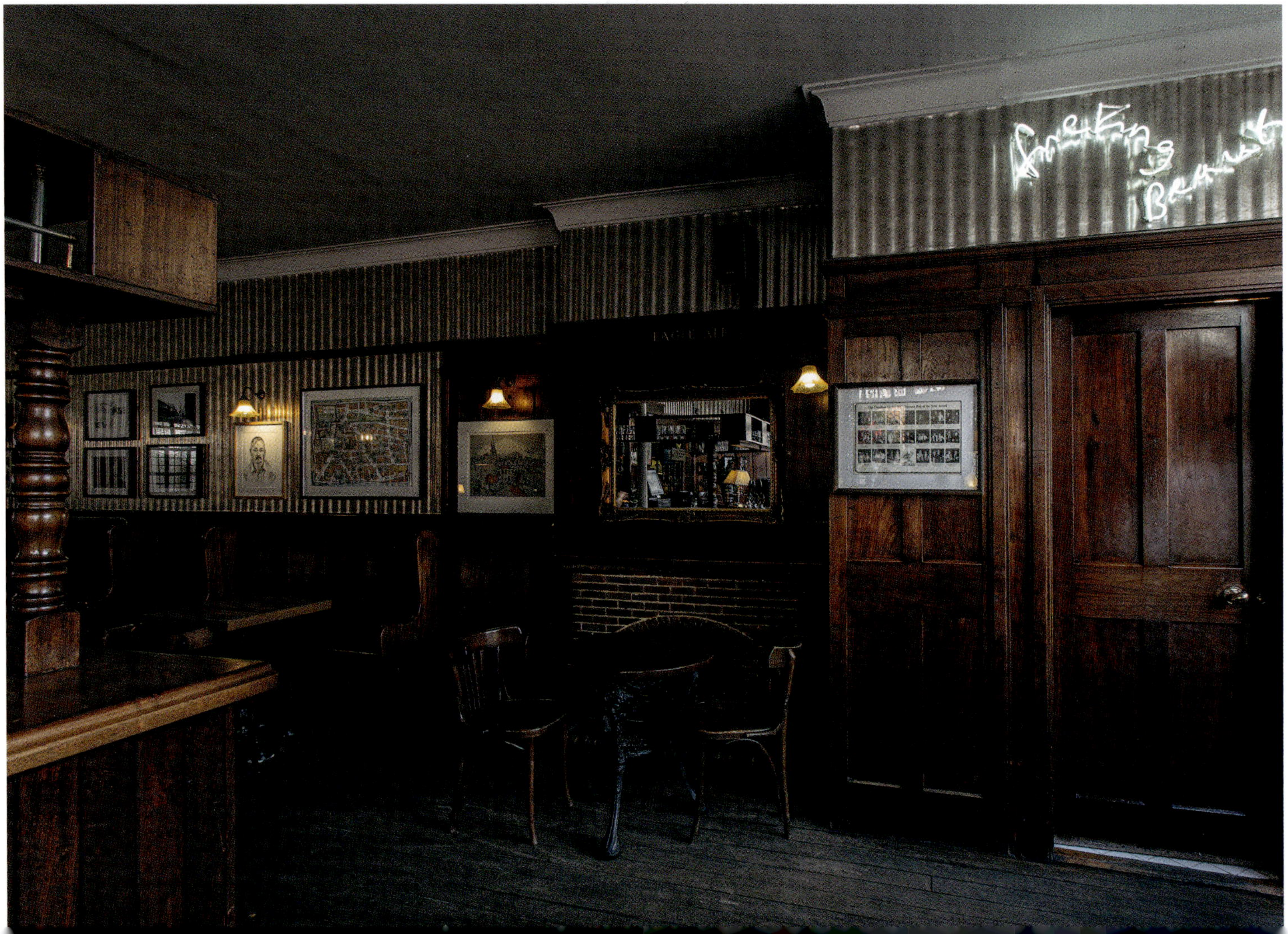

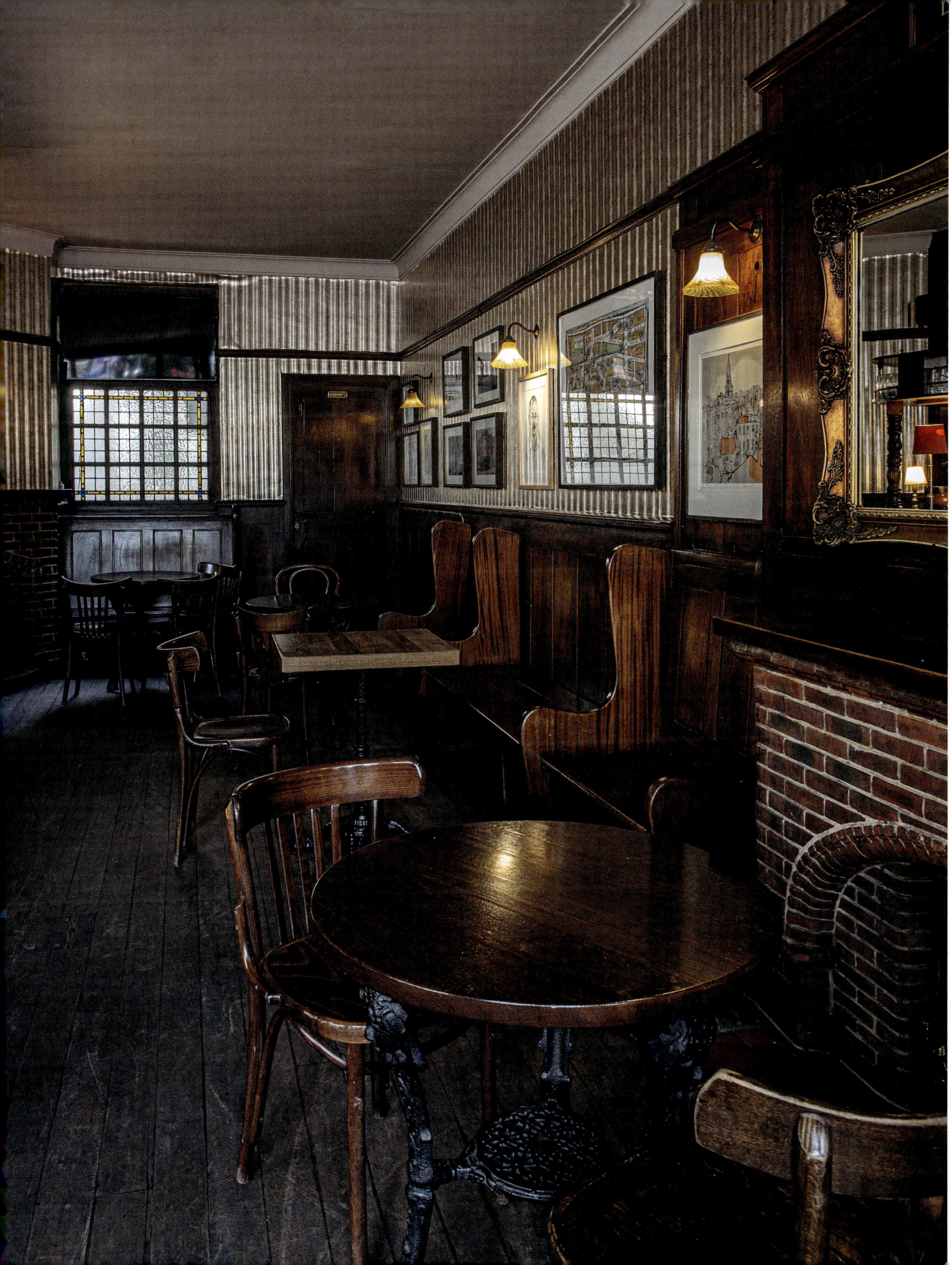

"I WALKED IN THE DOOR AND FELL IN LOVE WITH IT"

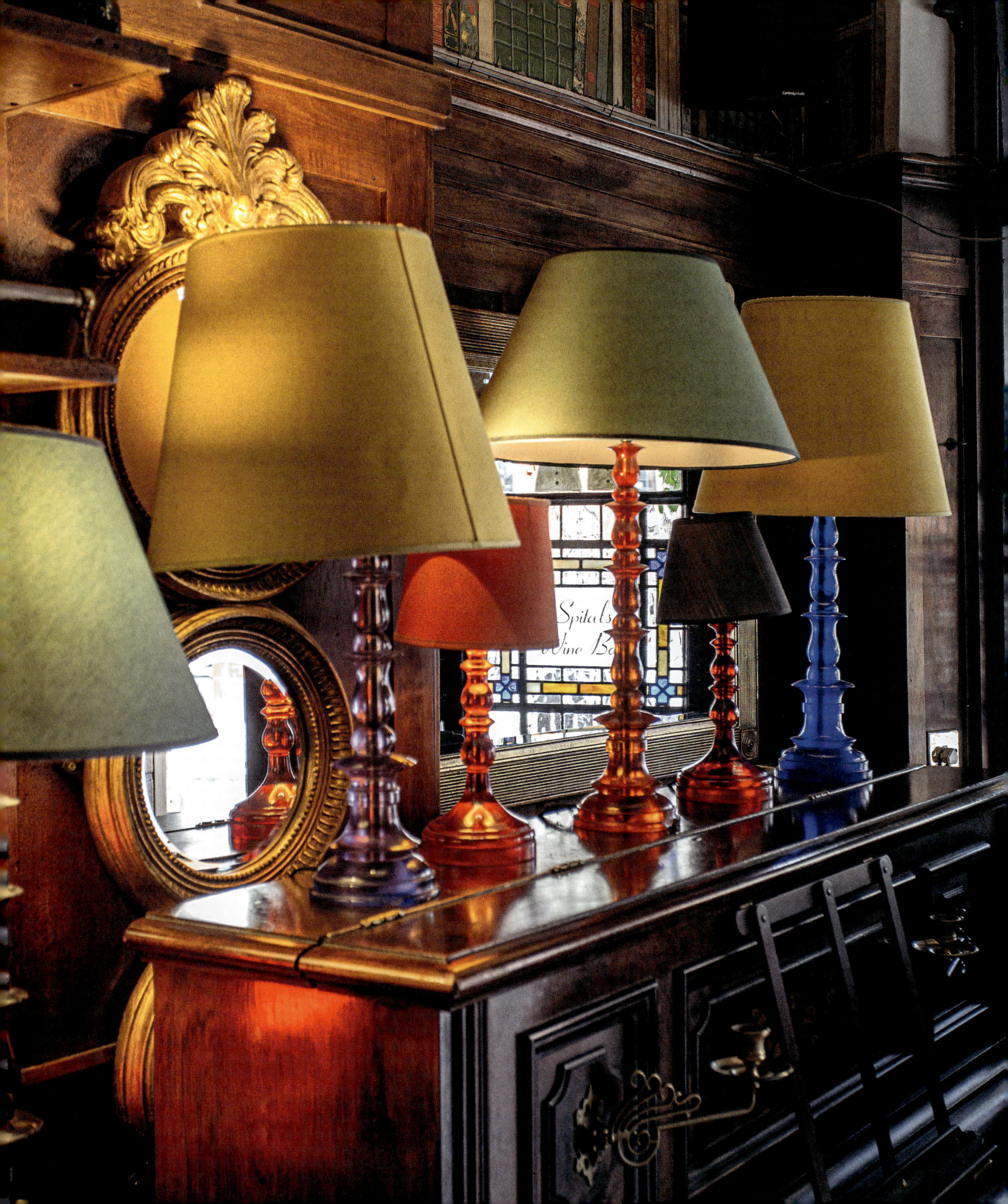

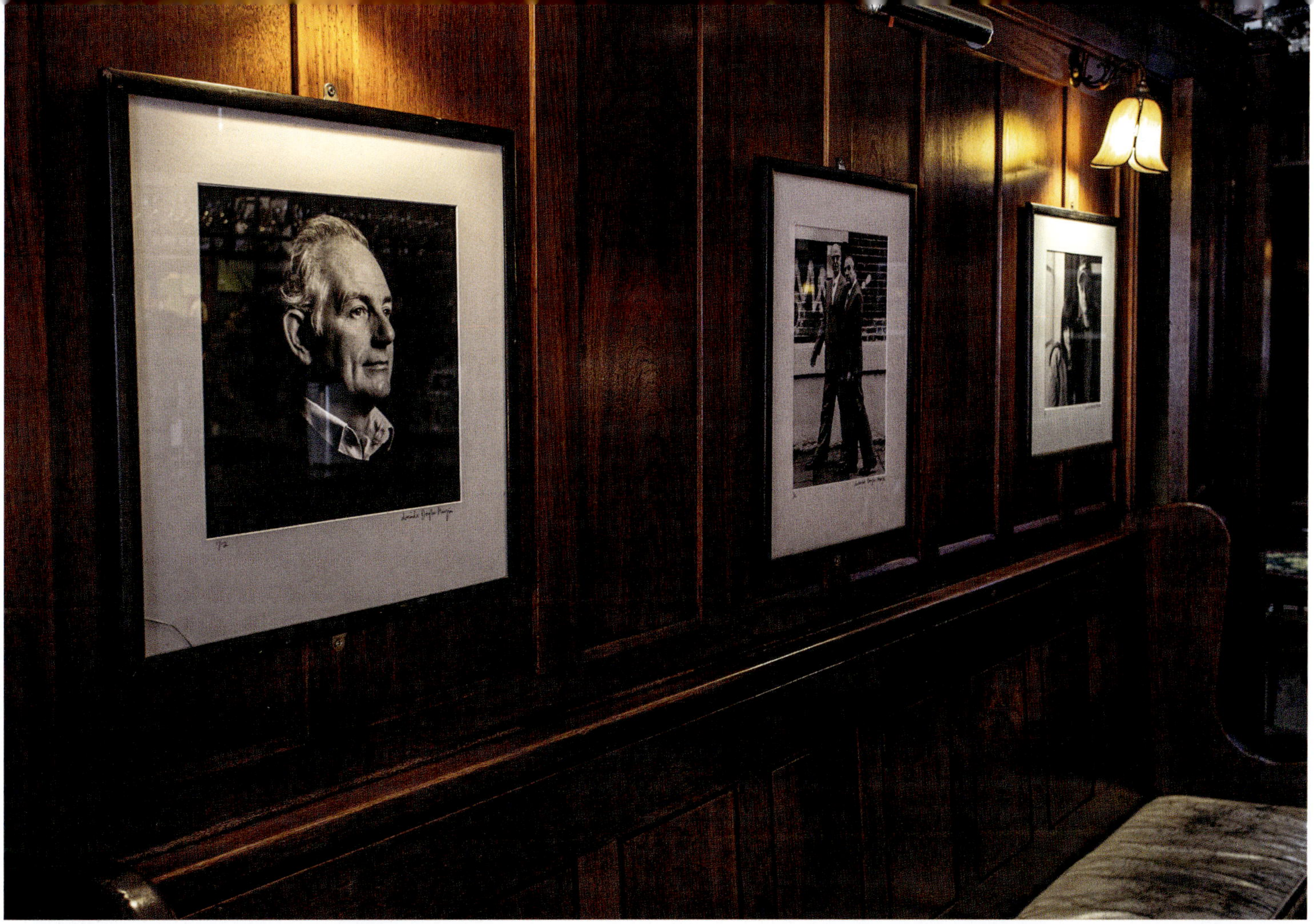

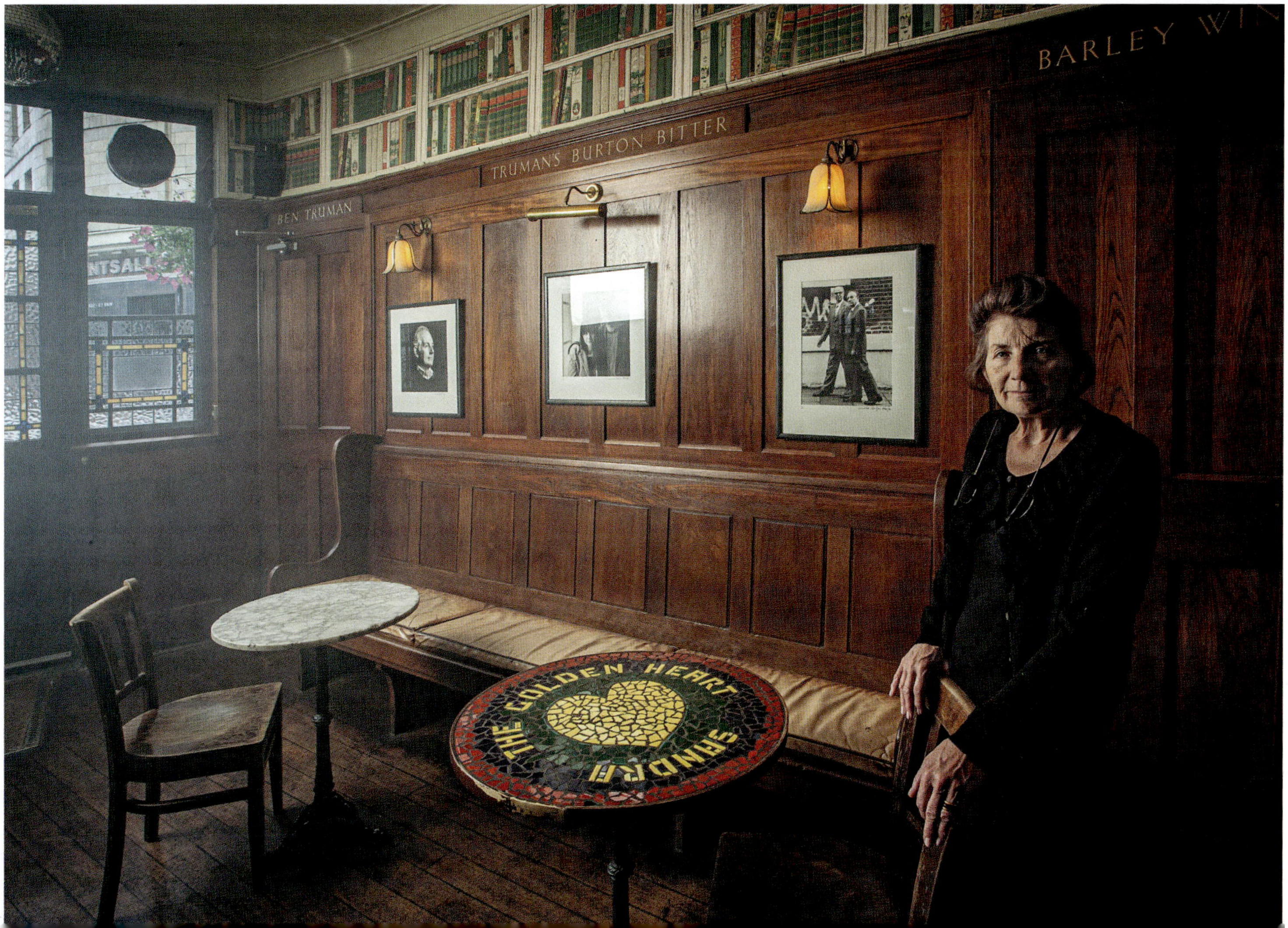
BARLEY
TRUMAN'S BURTON BITTER
BEN TRUMAN
THE GOLDEN HEART
SANDRA

PRINCESS LOUISE

208 HIGH HOLBORN, LONDON

The Princess Louise is an object lesson in not judging a book by its cover. You might scurry past its exterior, facing out on to a slightly overlooked part of Bloomsbury, on your way to the British Museum or the Inns of Court just beyond Holborn tube station, without paying much heed to the brown paintwork or the less-than-scintillating signage. However, the art nouveau swirl of the windows and the elaborate carvings on the pillars give just a hint of what lies within.

Push back the door and prepare to have your mind blown, because the interior of the Princess Louise – named, appropriately, for the sixth child of Queen Victoria, regarded as her most beautiful daughter, and a talented artist and sculptor – is the apotheosis of the Victorian gin palace, a rococo riot of etched glass, verdant tilework, Portland stone columns, authentically tarnished engraved gilt mirrors, gleaming brass, vibrant mosaics, pearl-drop lamps, and an ornate crimson and gold ceiling teeming with curlicues. The formidable island bar is surrounded by a series of separate enclosed snugs, housing up to eight people and divided by mahogany "snob screens" – originally intended to enable middle-class drinkers to be effectively walled off from their working-class counterparts, but now ensuring privacy, as well as many WhatsApp messages between straggling members of any party to clarify which particular nook they need to aim for. A more expansive back room features a roaring fireplace and a stained-glass skylight, along with windows depicting the arts, including music – a subtle reference, to those in the know, that the Princess Louise has played a small part in the history of English folk and protest song, with the Ballad & Blues Club, one of the earliest English folk clubs run by the singer-songwriter and folk song collector Ewan MacColl and his wife, the American folk singer Peggy Seeger, first established in the upstairs dining and function room at the end of the 1950s. It's tempting to imagine the hardscrabble ballads and caustic sea shanties echoing incongruously through these palatial surroundings, which are now Grade II listed, right down to the reassuringly monumental marble urinals.

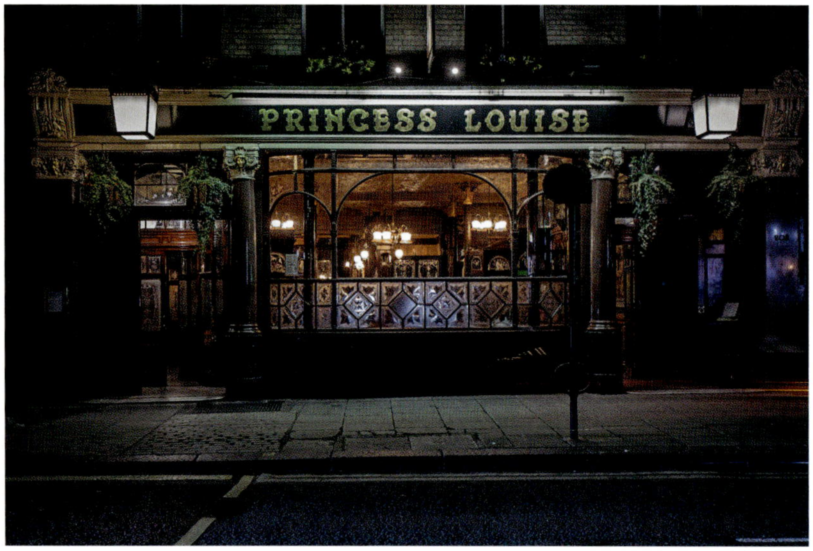

The snob screens, finely etched with a comprehensive selection of flora Britannica, have proved a big draw for the Princess Louise since their reinstatement in 2007 (it went on to win a Refurbished Pub of the Year award the following year). "It gives the place a very unique vibe," says one regular. "The spaces are almost like confessionals; you can imagine all kinds of plots being hatched and secrets being spilled in them. But you have to get here early if you want to bag one. They're incredibly popular." And while there's no typical Louise drinker, the central location pulls in visitors keen to unwind after a trawl round the British Museum, as well as office workers, lawyers from the nearby chambers at the Inns of Court, and students of the no-adornment-too-elaborate school of Victorian décor.

The original Princess Louise apparently enjoyed a smoke, dabbled with nude painting, and allegedly had a string of affairs. At her namesake, the first is a definite no-no, and the second would require some logistical planning and not a little brazenness. But you could easily imagine the third taking place, along with those plots and disclosures, within the seclusion of a snob screen or two. That's the unique pull of the Princess Louise – in its lustrous environs, everything gets heightened to the level of Victorian melodrama.

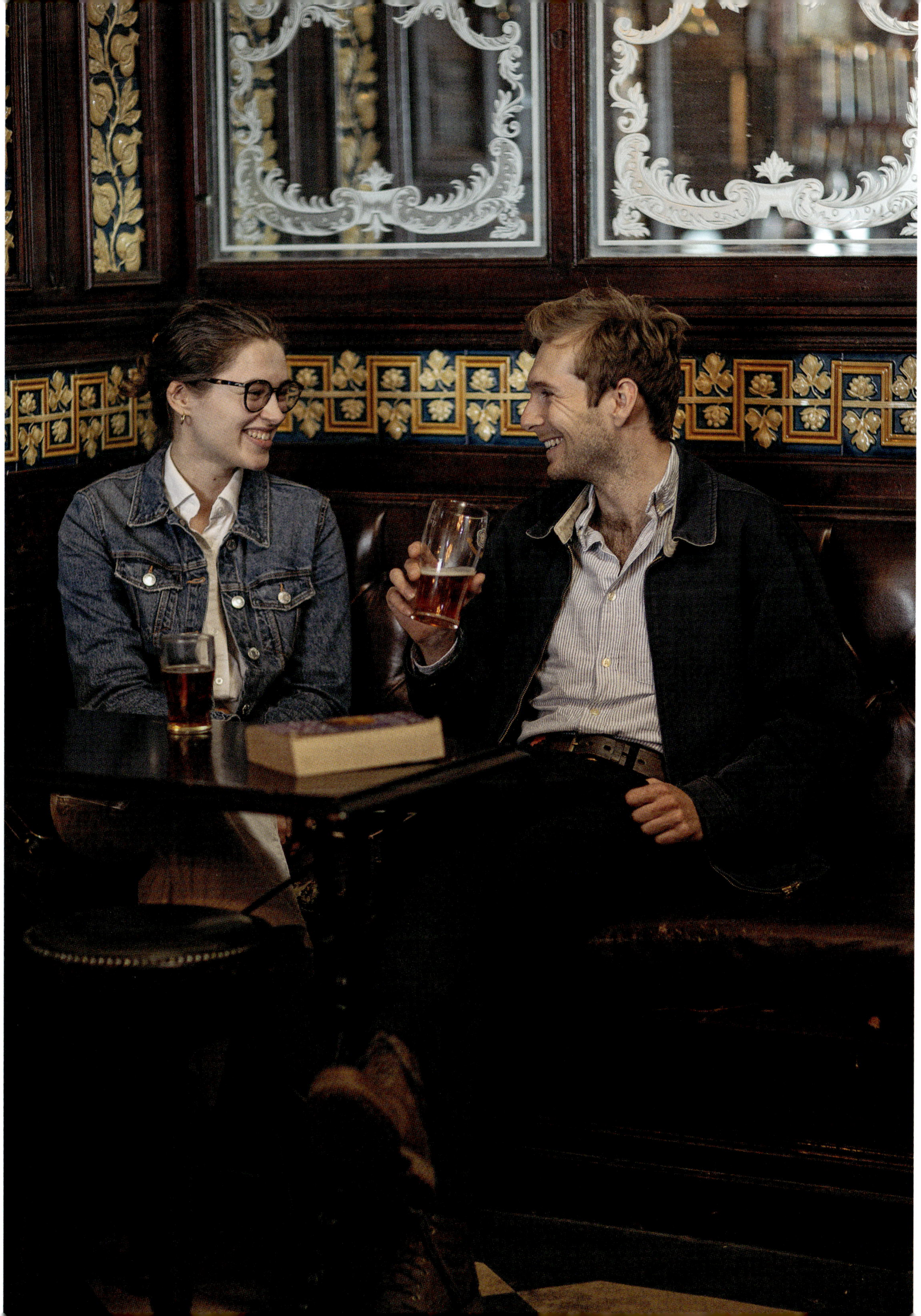

"THE SPACES ARE ALMOST LIKE CONFESSIONALS"

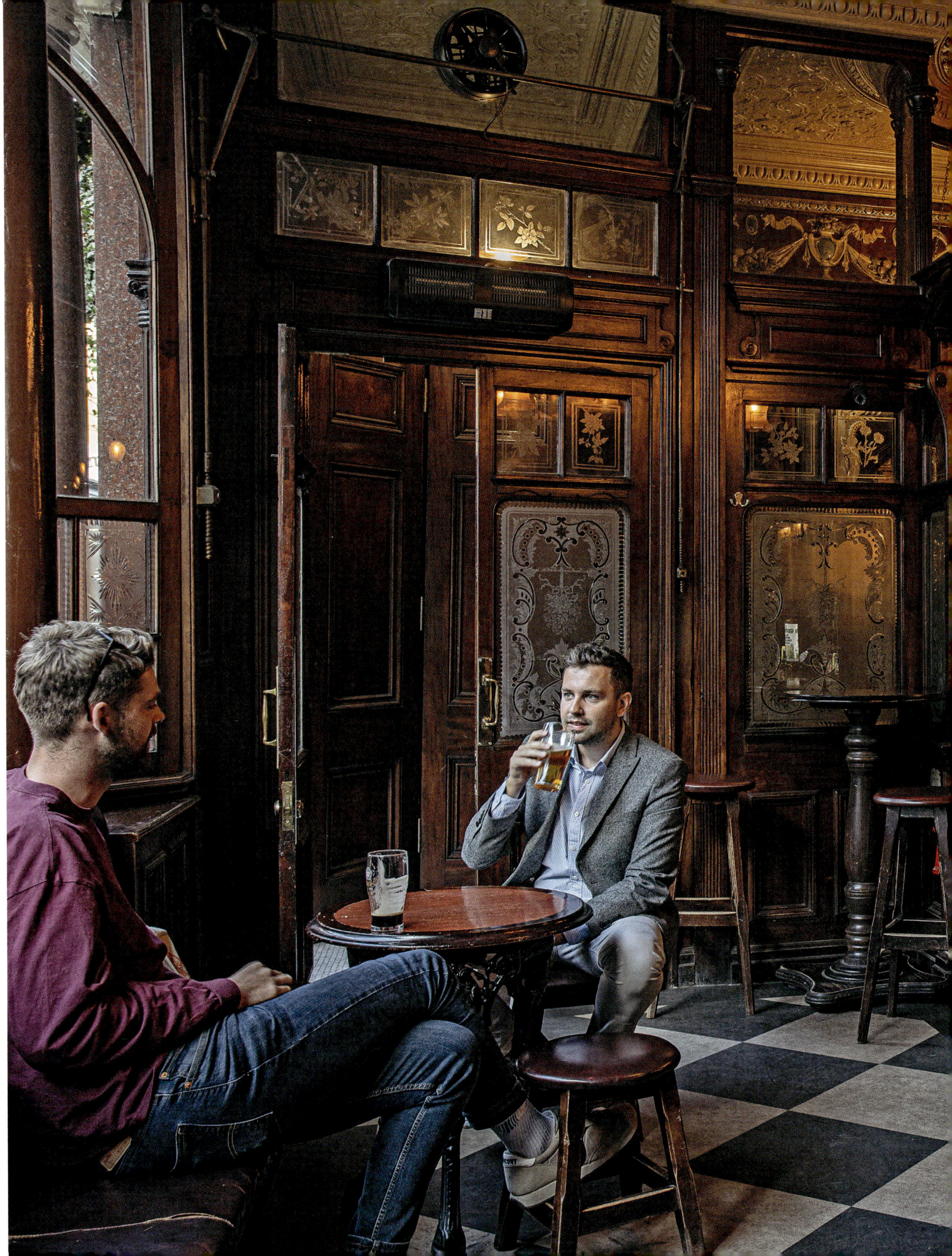

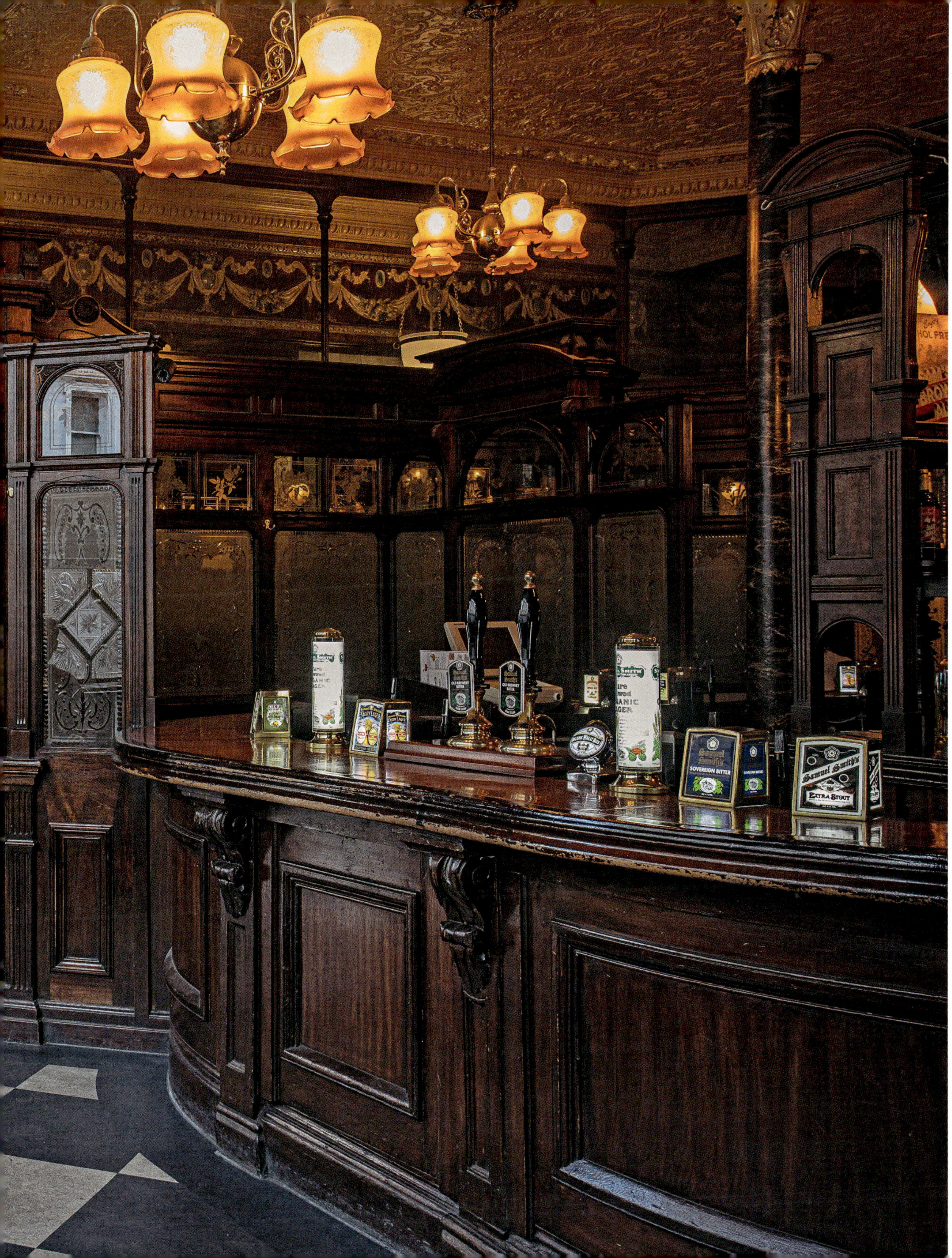

THE “FORMIDABLE” ISLAND BAR

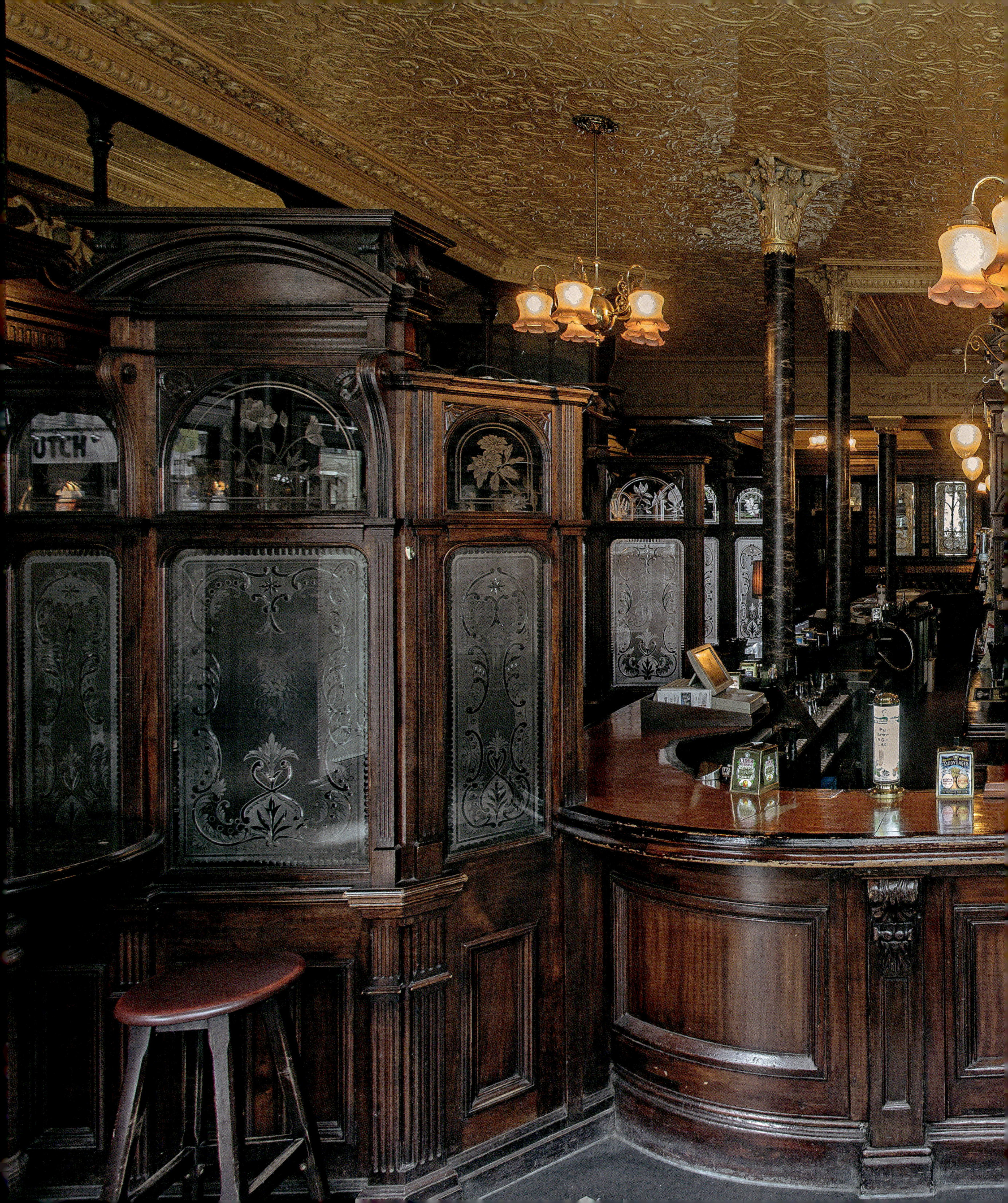
TADDY LAGER

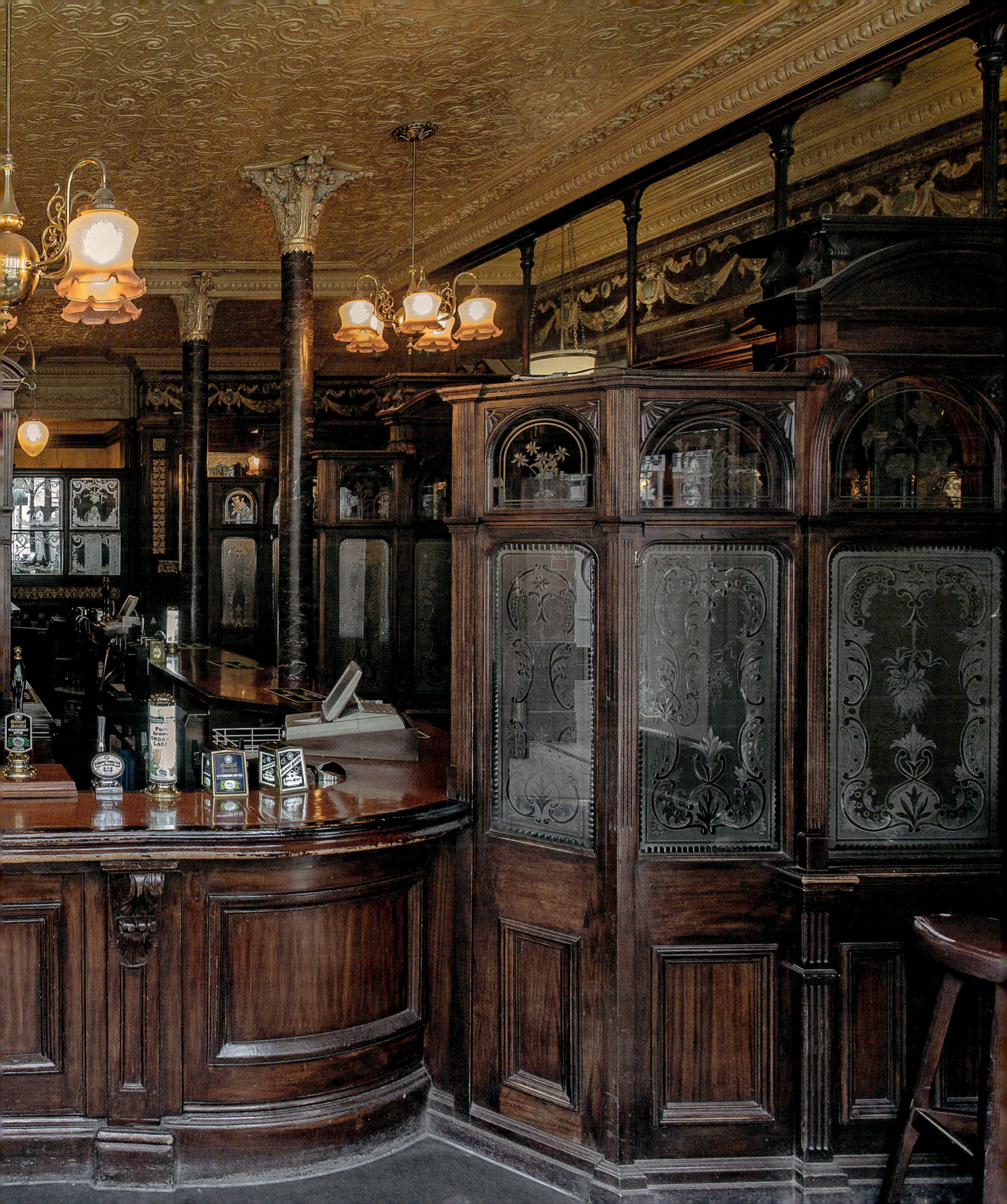

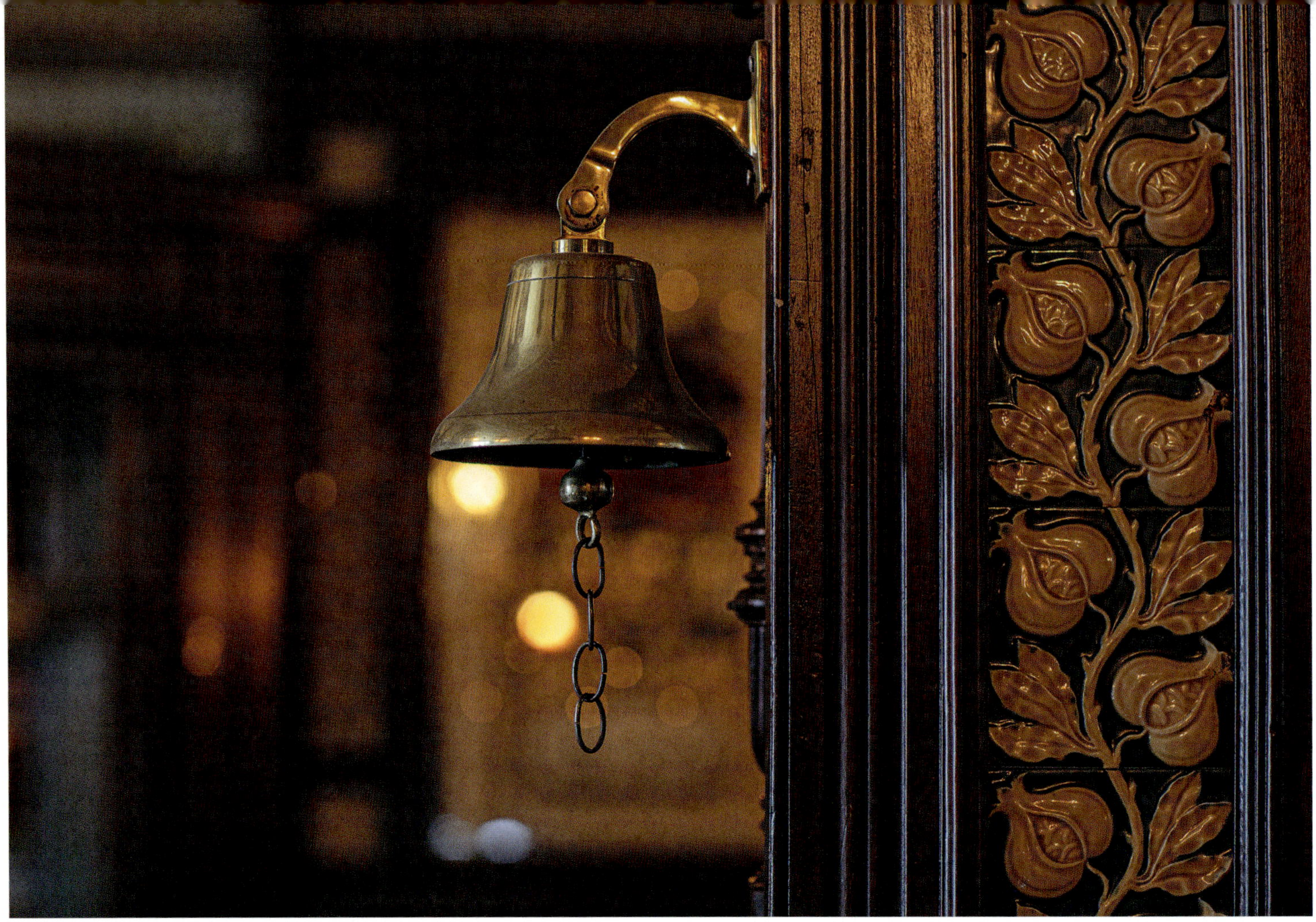

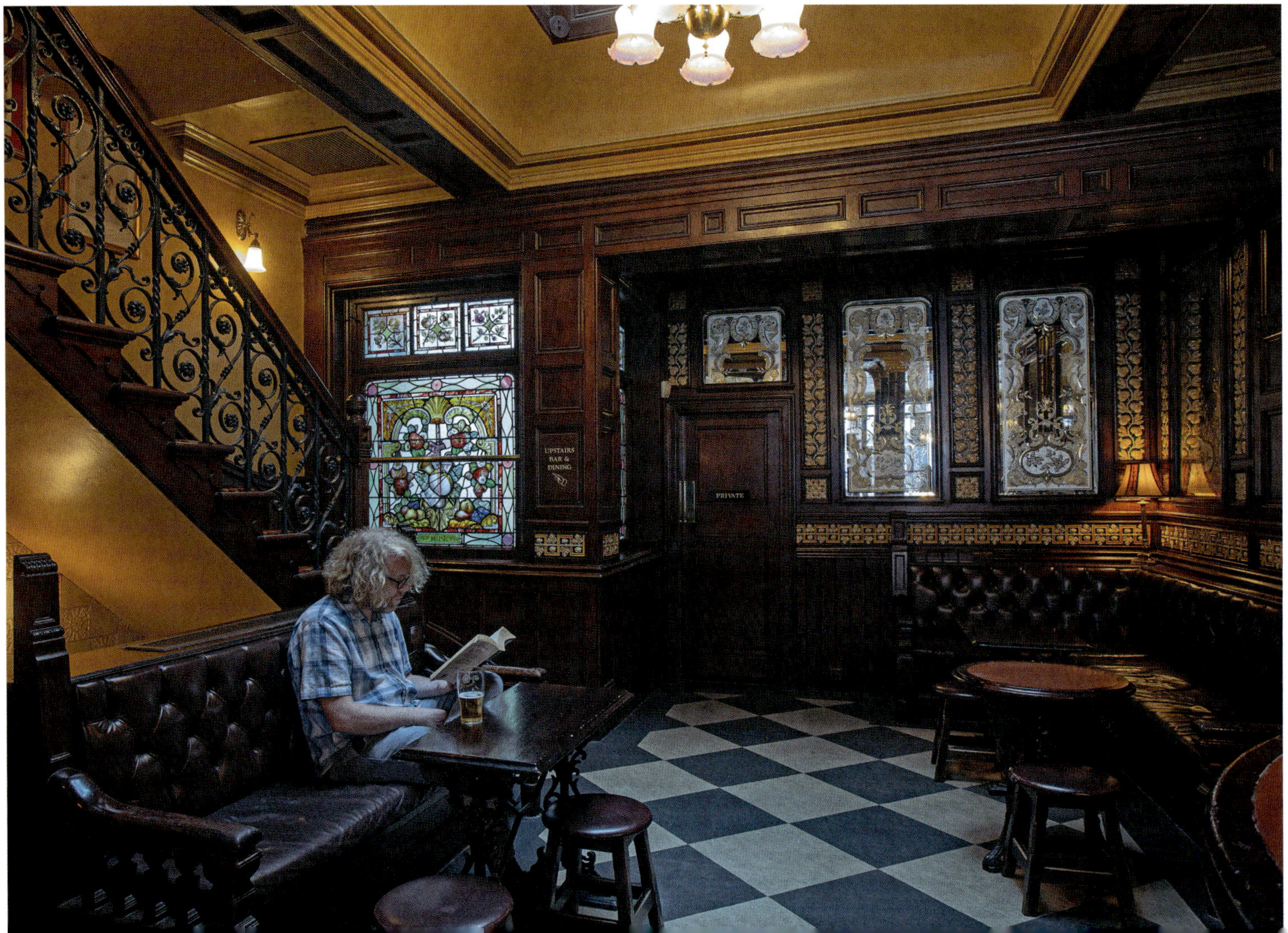
UPSTAIRS
BAR &
DINING
PRIVATE

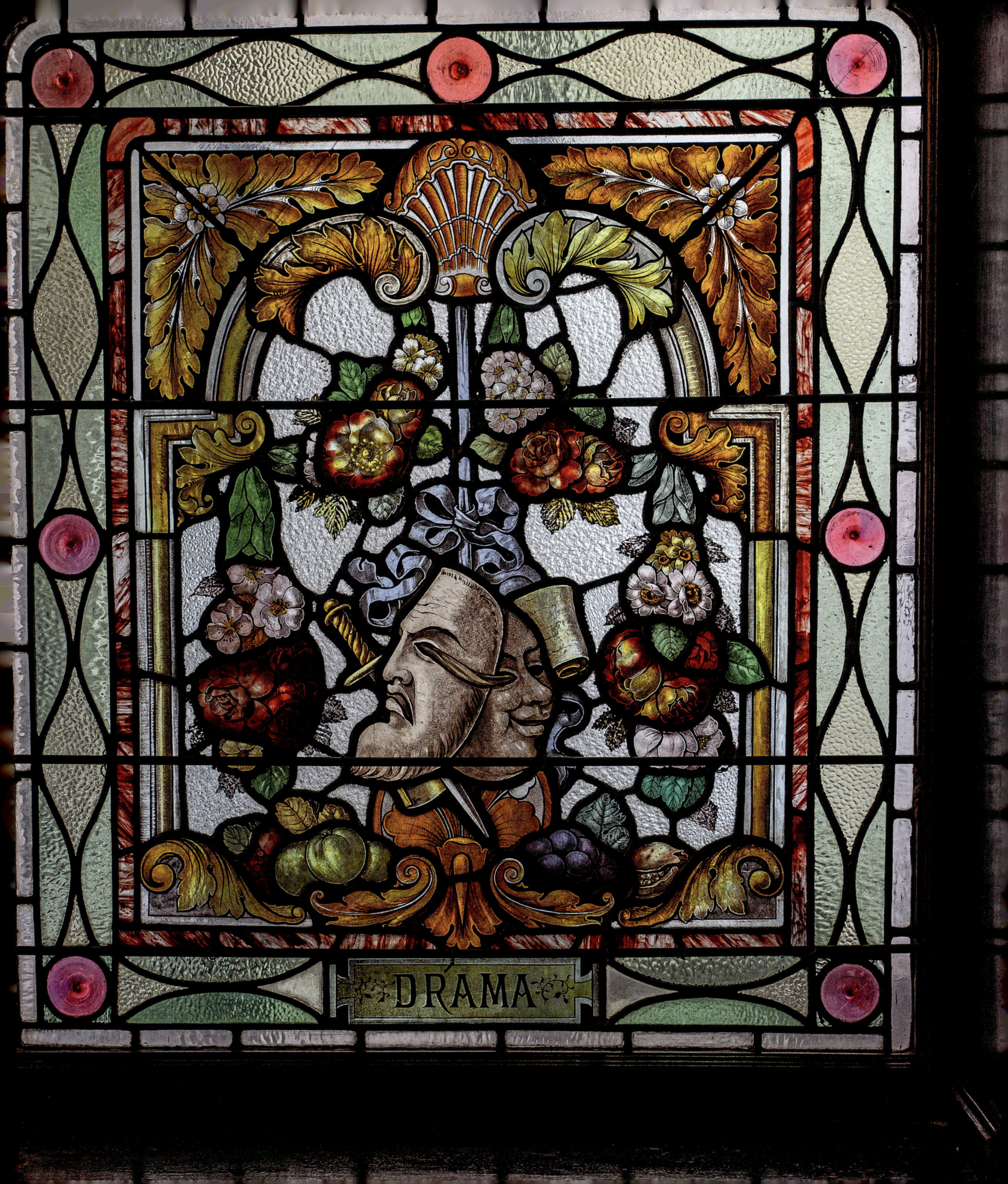
DRAMA

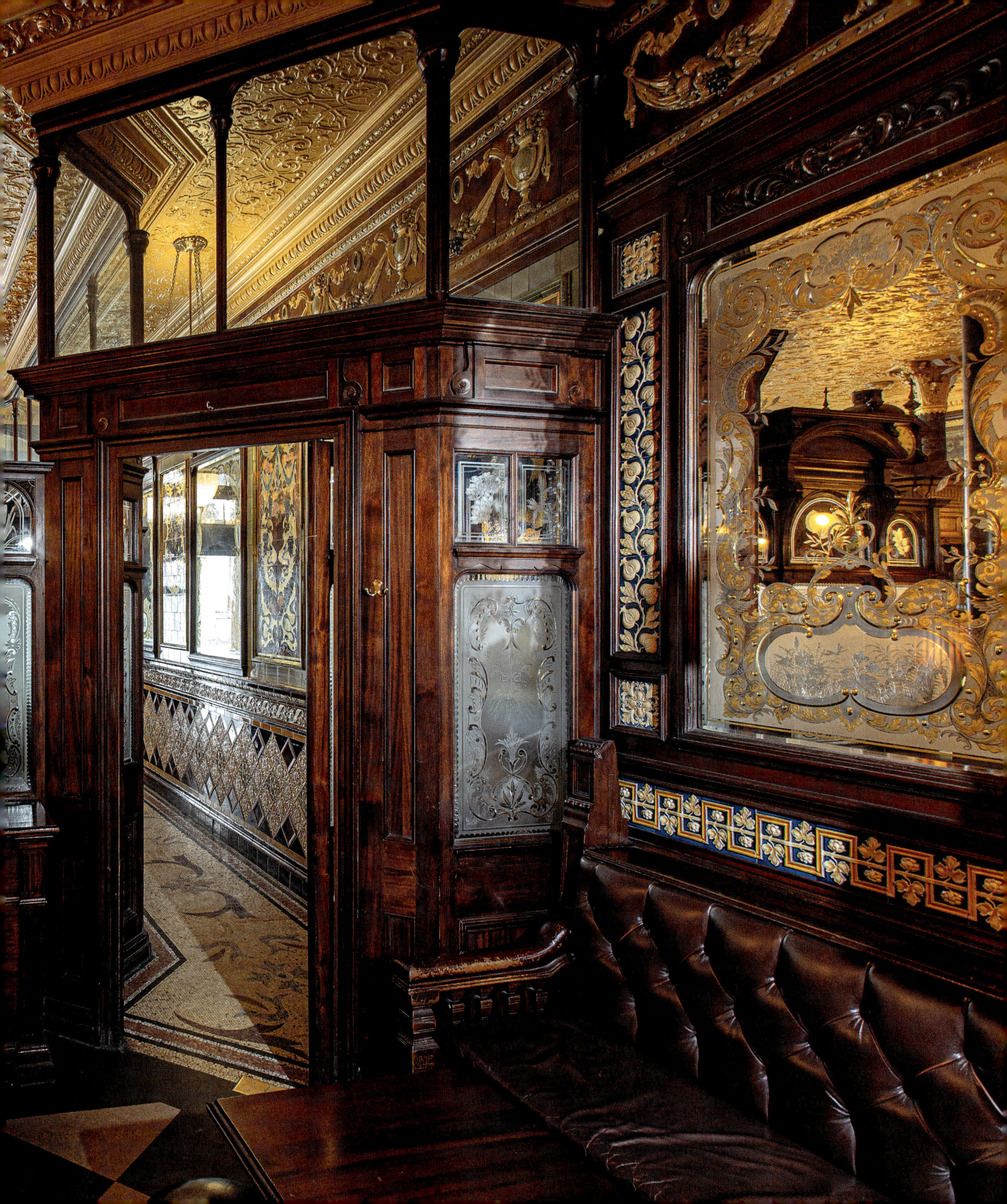

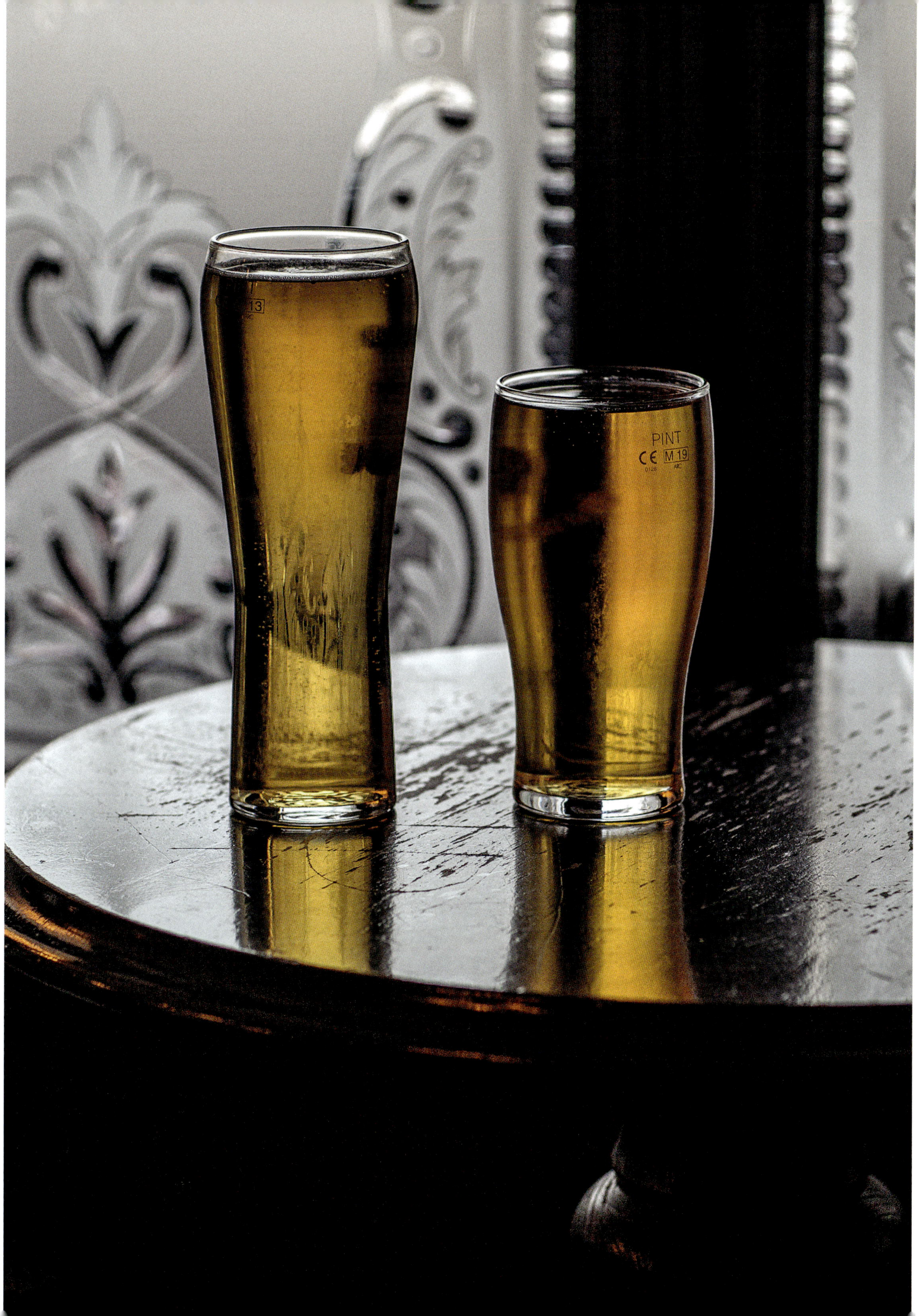
PINT
CE M 19

THE DOG AND DUCK

18 BATEMAN ST, LONDON

"Two legs good, four drinks better" may not quite be the maxim chanted by the livestock at the end of George Orwell's political allegory *Animal Farm*; but it might well have seemed more apt to the author as he made his way to The Dog and Duck in London's Soho in the mid-1940s to celebrate the novel's choice for the American Book of the Month Club.

Soho is not short of literary-lush legends; there's barely a hostelry in the area that doesn't claim that Dylan Thomas, say, once toppled off one of its barstools. Orwell's presence here can be confirmed, however; he was apparently keen to sample some of the 135-proof absinthe the owner had somehow obtained (the pub has returned the favour by naming the upstairs bar/dining room after him). But you don't need the allure of a mind-blowing anise-flavoured spirit to enjoy the delights of The Dog and Duck, built on the site of the Duke of Monmouth's house in 1734 and festooned in Victorian splendour, from the mahogany panelling and etched advertising mirrors lining the walls to the mosaics and tiles depicting the titular creatures in a dog-eat-duck kind of way that Orwell, master of the unflinching narrative, would surely have appreciated. Other famous visitors have included John Constable (who lived round the corner), Dante Gabriel Rosetti (who lived just across Oxford Street), and, more latterly, Madonna. Whether she joined the media-centric crowd's habitual overspill from the compact and bijou bar into the street hasn't been recorded; but if she managed to bag a coveted spot in the understairs snug, with the twinkling chandeliers overhead adding to the general air of affable bonhomie, she may have found herself paraphrasing another well-known *Animal Farm* line, in tribute to her surroundings. Namely, that all pubs are equal, but some pubs are more equal than others.

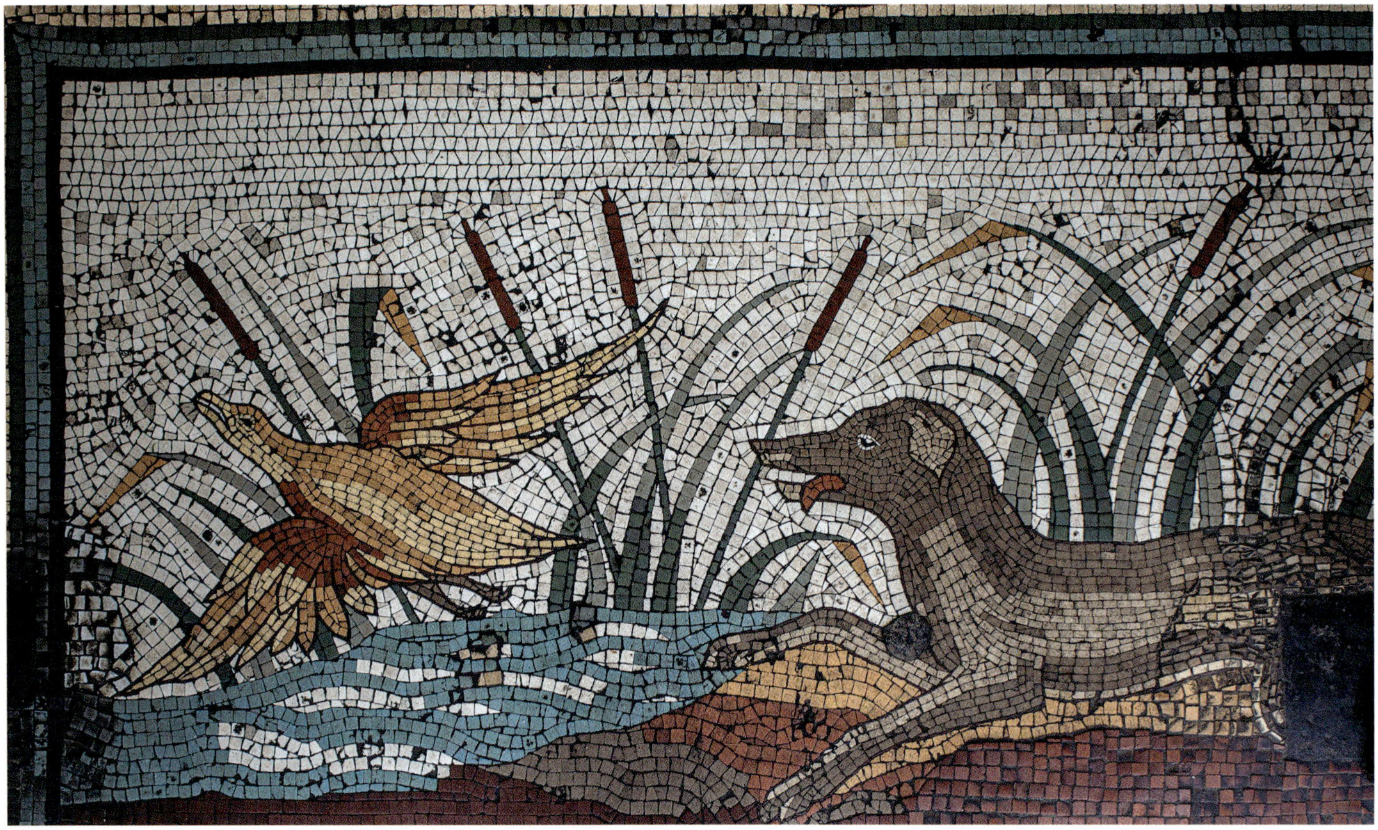

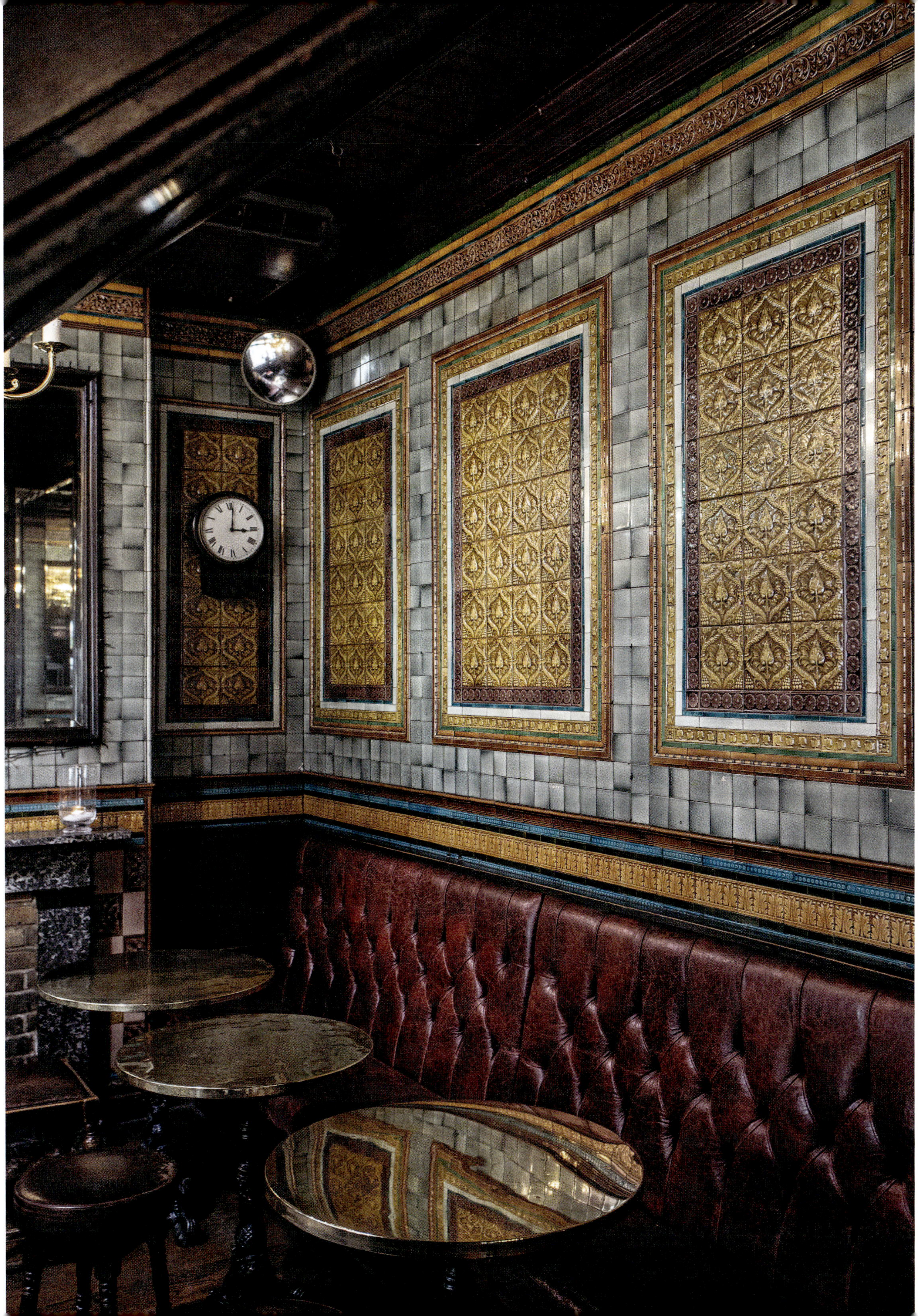

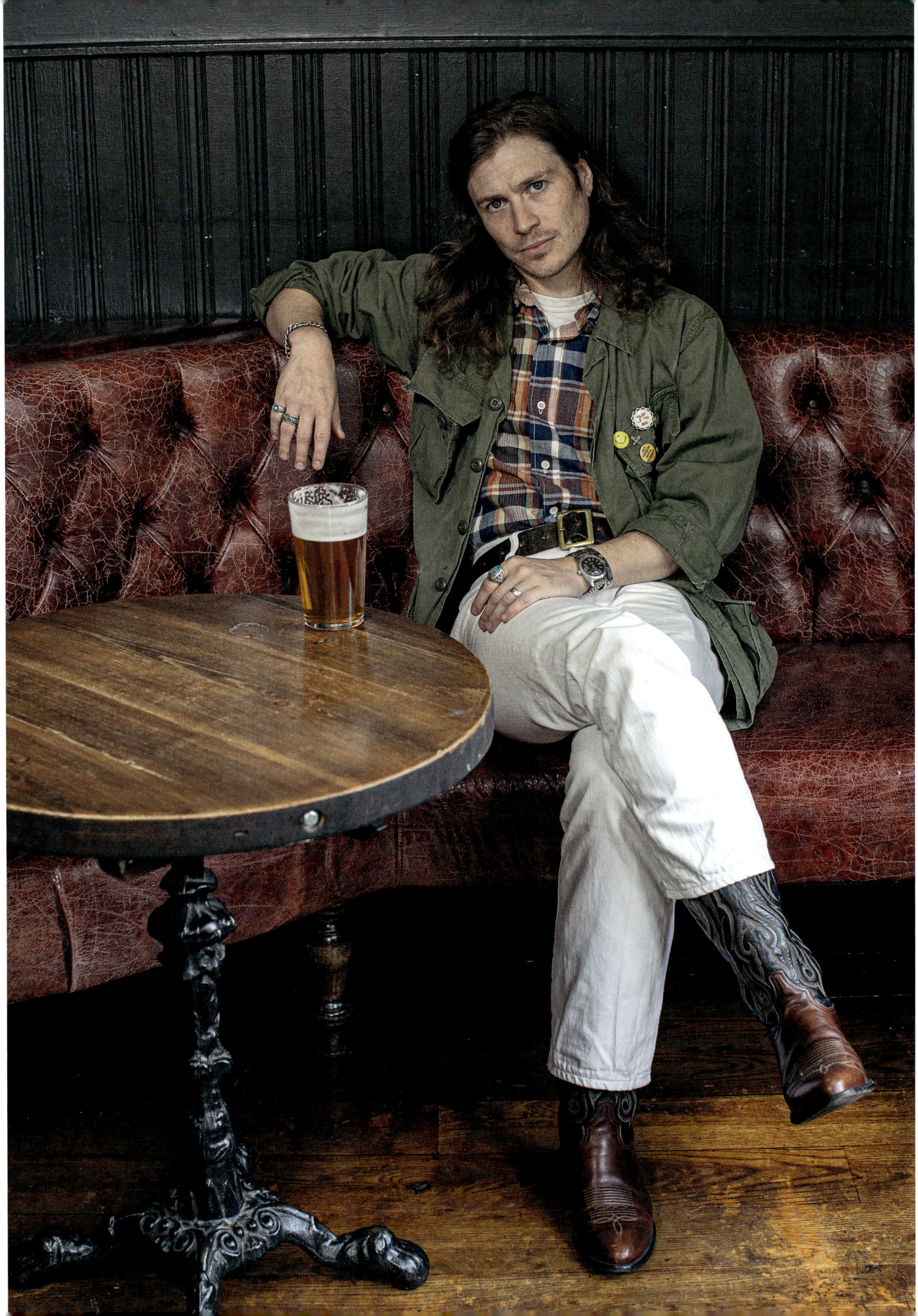

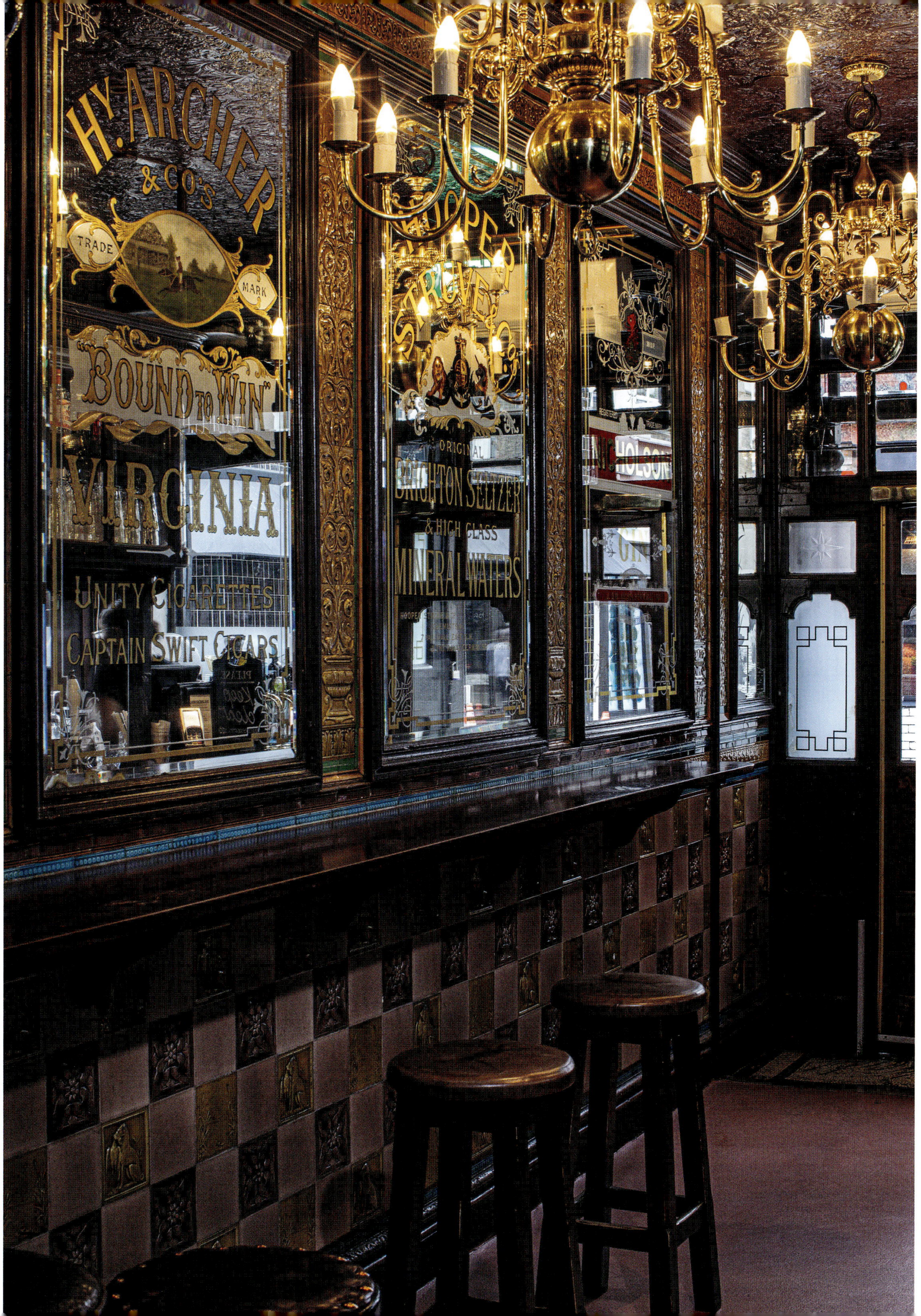
HY. ARCHER
& CO'S
TRADE
MARK
BOUND TO WIN
VIRGINIA
UNITY CIGARETTES
CAPTAIN SWIFT CIGARS
ORIGINAL
BRIGHTON SELTZER
& HIGH CLASS
MINERAL WATERS

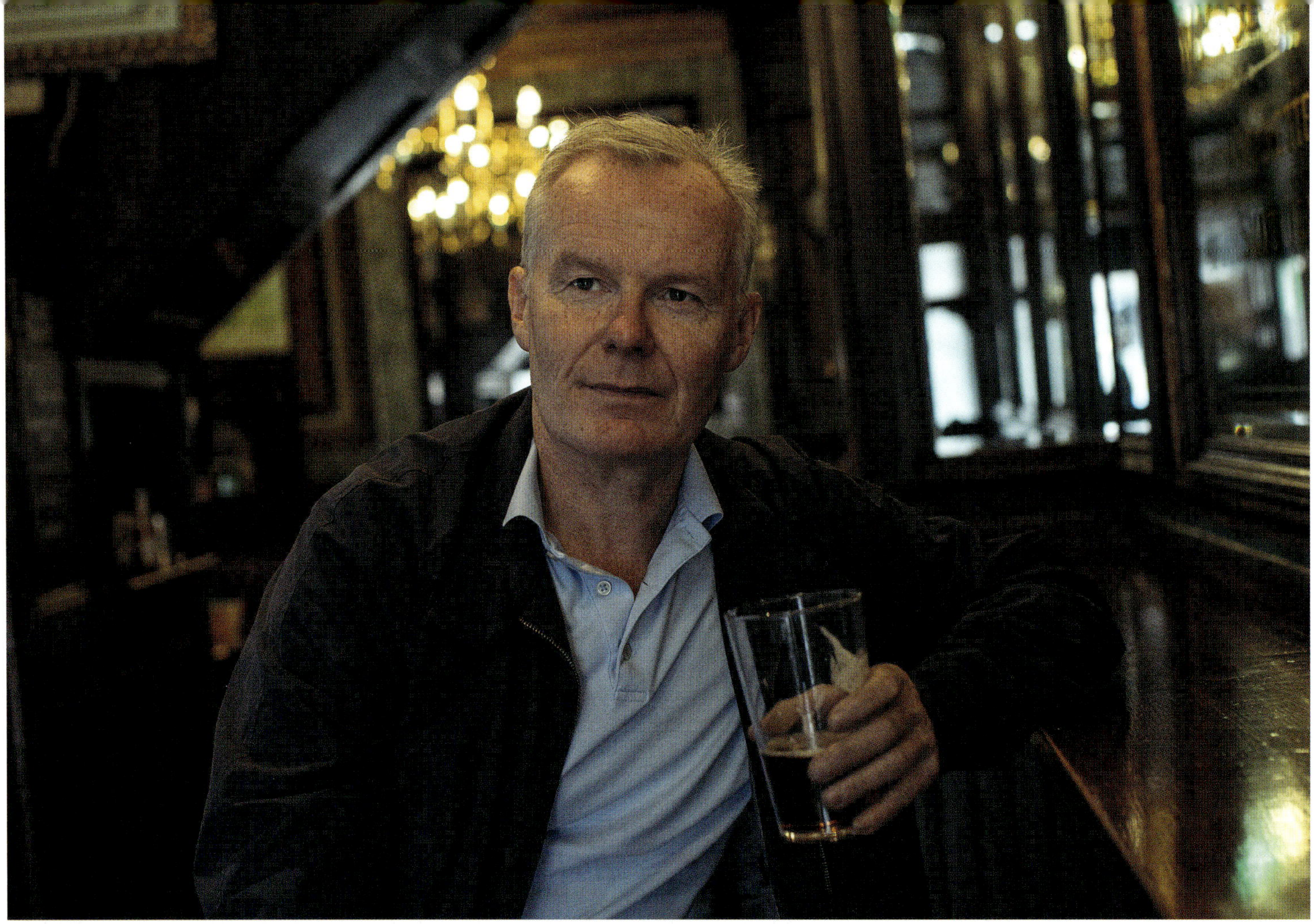

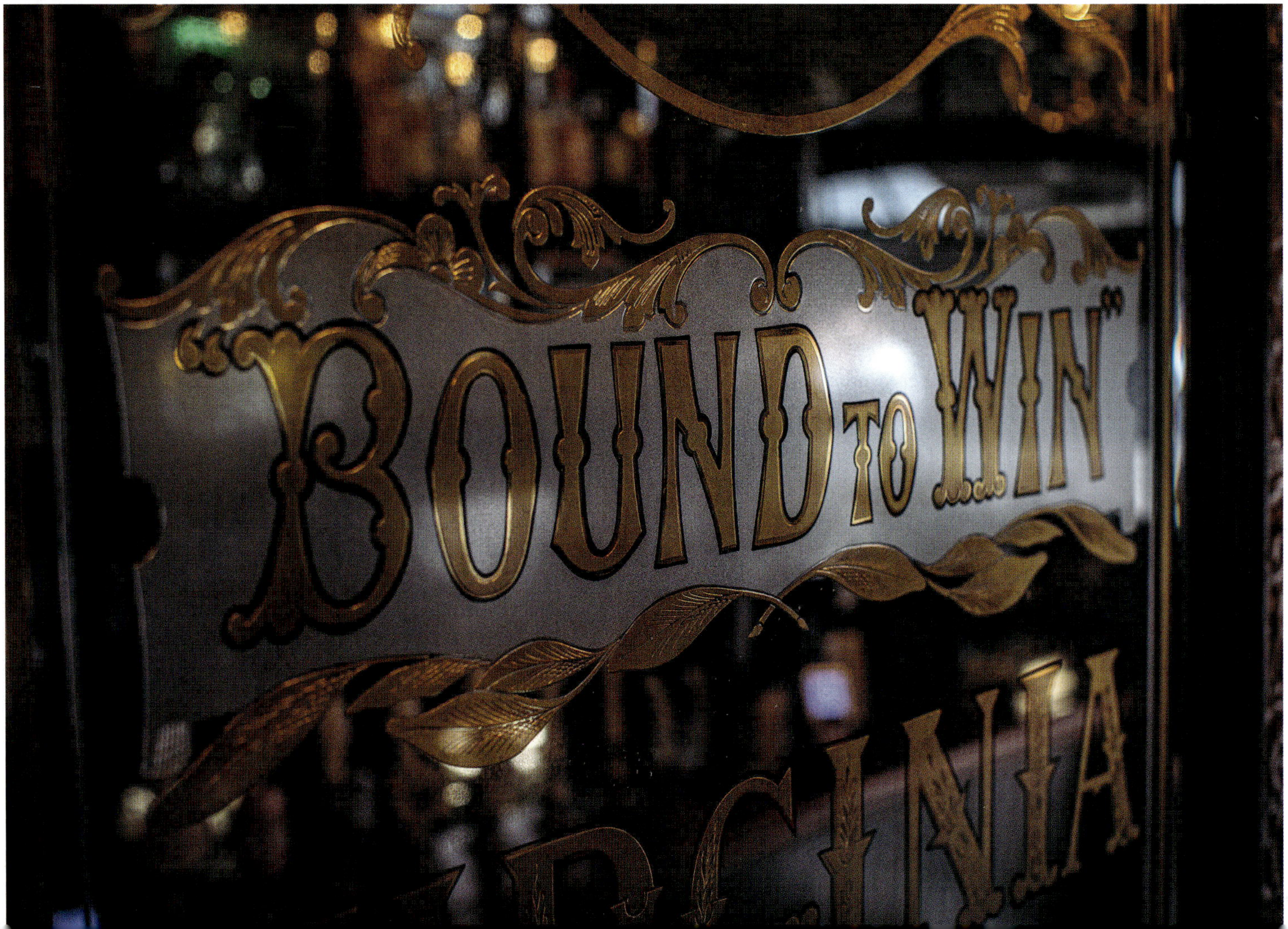
"BOUND TO WIN"

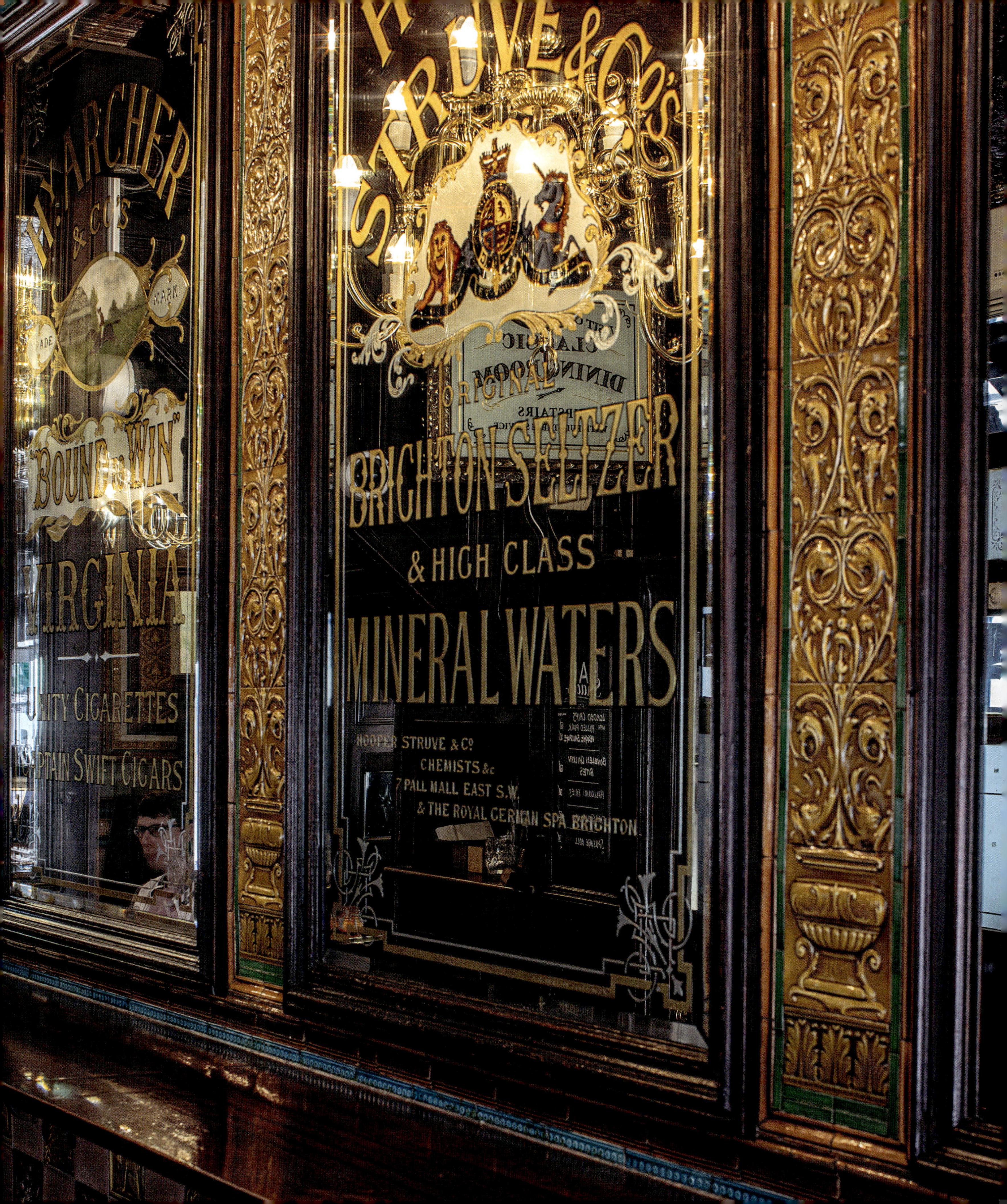

ARCHER
& CO'S
TRADE
MARK
"BOUND TO WIN"
VIRGINIA
CIGARETTES
SWIFT CIGARS
STRUVE & CO'S
BRIGHTON SELTZER
& HIGH CLASS
MINERAL WATERS
HOOPER STRUVE & Co
CHEMISTS &c
7 PALL MALL EAST S.W.
& THE ROYAL GERMAN SPA BRIGHTON

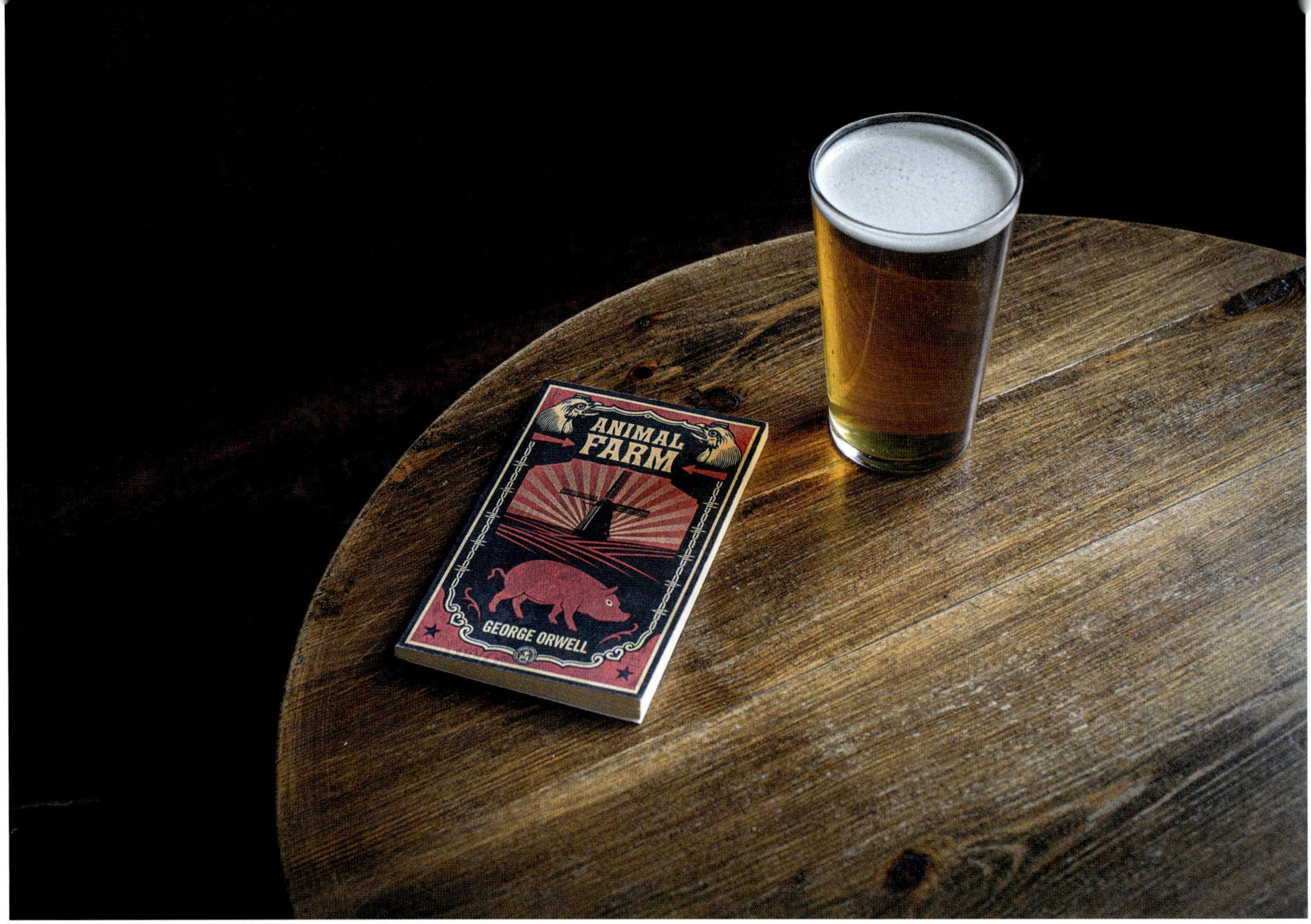
ANIMAL
FARM
GEORGE ORWELL

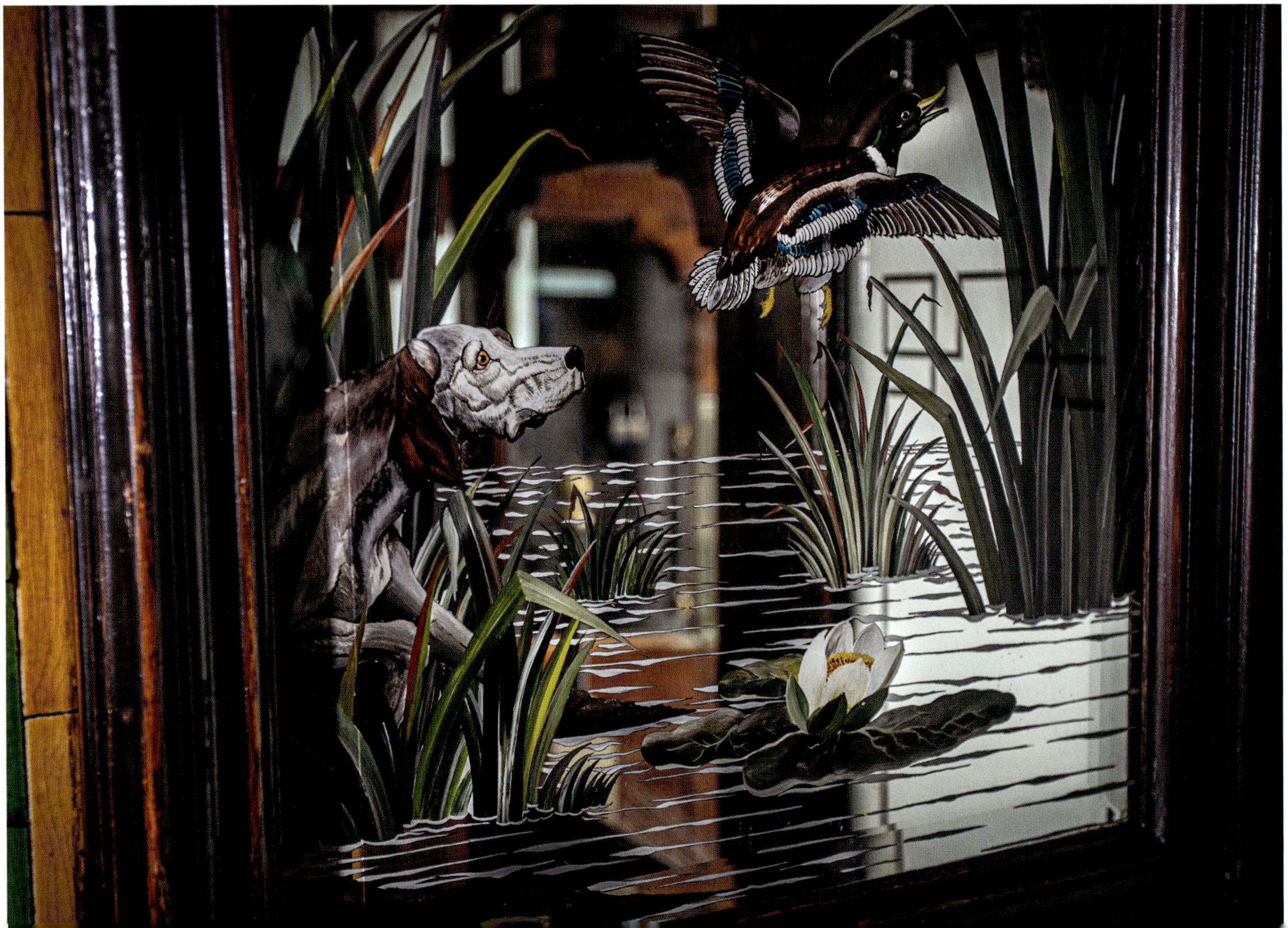

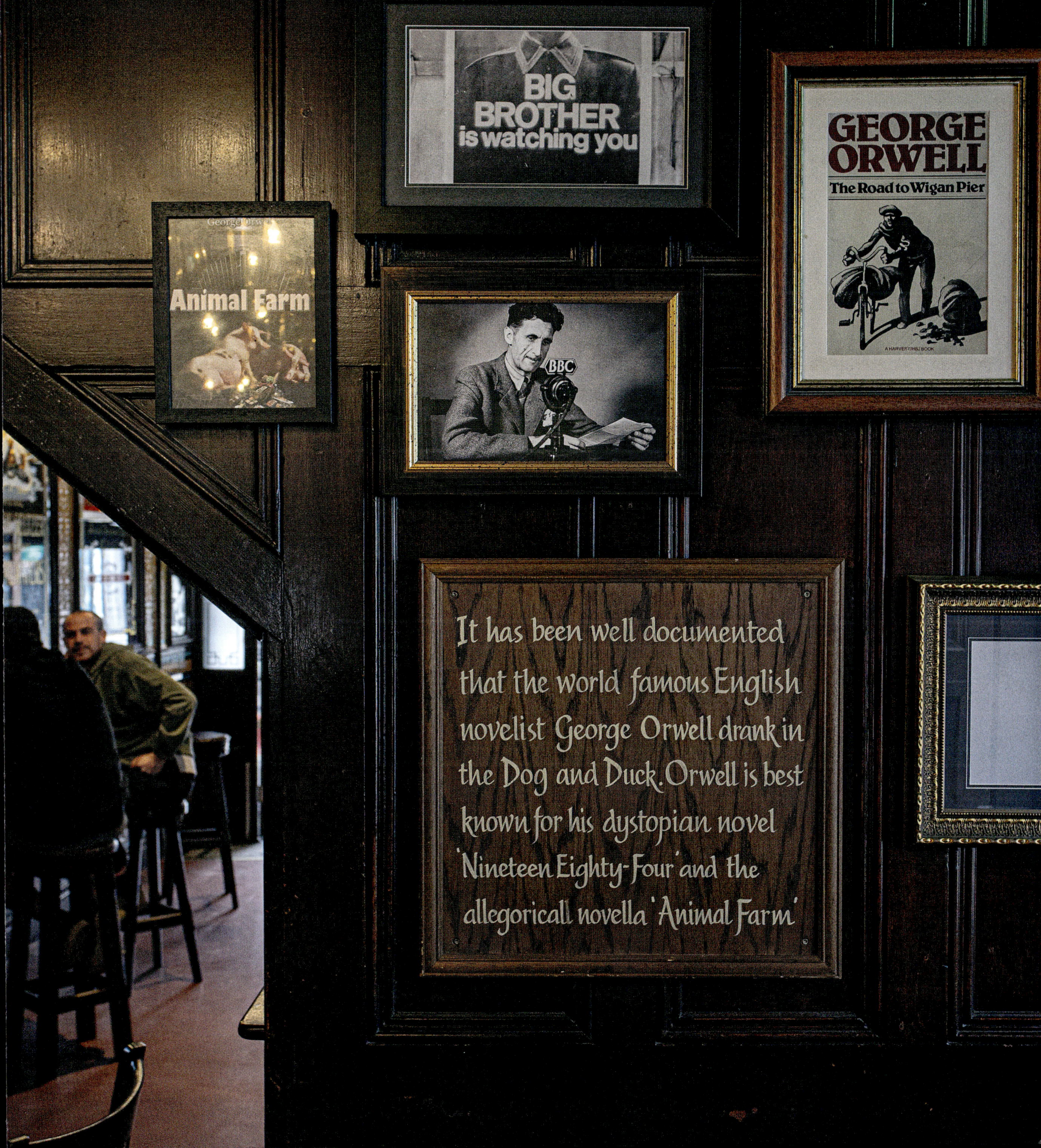
BIG
BROTHER
is watching you
GEORGE
ORWELL
The Road to Wigan Pier
Animal Farm
BBC
It has been well documented
that the world famous English
novelist George Orwell drank in
the Dog and Duck. Orwell is best
known for his dystopian novel
'Nineteen Eighty-Four' and the
allegoricall novella 'Animal Farm'

THE BLACKFRIAR

174 QUEEN VICTORIA STREET, LONDON

The first thing to say about The Blackfriar is that it's a theme pub – in the most spectacular and giddily eccentric sense. Yes, it faces off against the shiny glass and steel façade of Blackfriars station, its Flatiron Building-style wedge shape a relic of the days when it was surrounded by tapering alleyways rather than major arterial roads. And yes, the building, completed at the start of the 1870s, is built on the site of a thirteenth-century Dominican priory, the order distinguished by their inky habits as well as their fierce opposition to heresy. And yes, a large stone friar stands sentinel above the doorway, looming Buddha-like above an art nouveau mosaic promising "Brandies". But it's inside that the fun really starts.

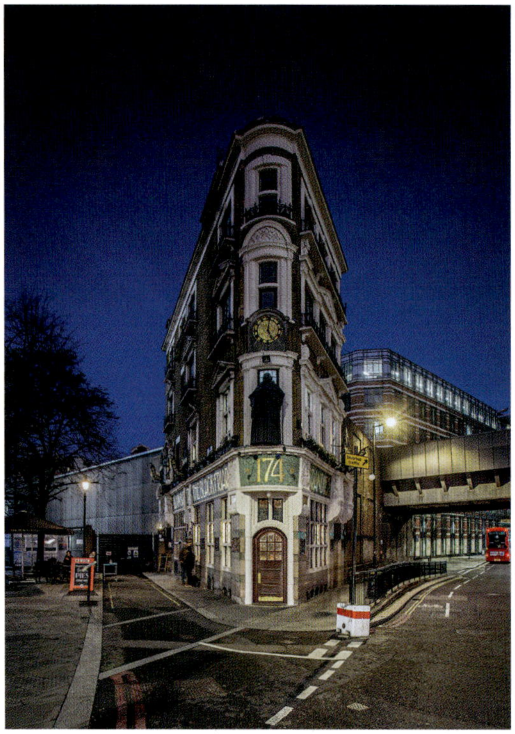

Because here are more friars – dozens of them, in sculptures, mosaics, metal reliefs and stained glass, a Gesamtkunstwerk that surely constitutes London's most singular pub interior. You'll notice immediately that these particular brothers seem to have formed a breakaway sect – the Order, perhaps, of Overindulgence. Above the marble bar, in a tableau entitled "Tomorrow will be Friday", they're seen gathering fish and eels for the ensuing pescatarian dinner (with a bird hopping at their sandalled heels, ready for discarded heads and/or guts). Over the arched entrance to a smaller room is another group scene, "Saturday Afternoon", again full of pre-banquet prep (boiling eggs, harvesting grapes, clutching pumpkins).

The alcove within, however, is The Blackfriar's real showstopper; a windowless space with a barrel-vaulted gold mosaic ceiling, lined with marble and alabaster. "It's like a Byzantine chapel designed for Croesus, or maybe Donald Trump," says one regular, and, indeed, some of the axioms emblazoned on the cornices – "Silence is golden", "Wisdom is rare", "Finery is Foolery" – only seem to get more apposite as the decades pass. Here are more friars, doing the weekly wash ("Don't advertise, tell a gossip"), and pushing a trussed pig in a wheelbarrow ("A Good Thing is Soon Snatched Up"), along with illustrations of nursery rhymes and Aesop's fables, and a group of squatting devils representing Literature, Painting, Music and Drama. Finally, a sleeping monk surrounded by fairies, executed in mother-of-pearl and semi-precious stones, is labelled "Contentment Surpasses Riches" – a debatable argument, but one that regulars are increasingly susceptible to after successive Holy Negroni cocktails (featuring Dom Benedictine, of course).

The Blackfriar's startling bling came courtesy of the architect Herbert Fuller-Clark and the sculptor and Royal Academician Henry Poole, who were given carte blanche to remodel the pub in the 1900s by then landlord Alfred Pettitt (the golden grotto began life, incredibly, as a separate snack bar under the railway). Both men were acolytes of the Arts and Crafts Movement, and it's clear on this evidence that they thoroughly embraced its elevation of high-quality materials and hand-craftsmanship, and its idiosyncratic approach to design. "It's a stunning space, but somehow it feels homely," says another regular. "There's something about nursing a pint or tucking into a Sunday roast under all these carousing friars that makes you want to sit back and settle in."

The Blackfriar's survival hasn't always been assured in a city with a mania for demolition; it was due to be pulled down in the 1960s to make way for a new road, but a pressure group of powerful literary figures, led by the future poet laureate Sir John Betjeman, saved it from the wrecking ball. Now Grade II listed, successive generations can take their ease among the ever-gambolling friars. "Seize occasion" exhorts another slogan on the walls, beneath a boozing brother. Good advice – to miss this place would not only be regrettable. It would amount to heresy.

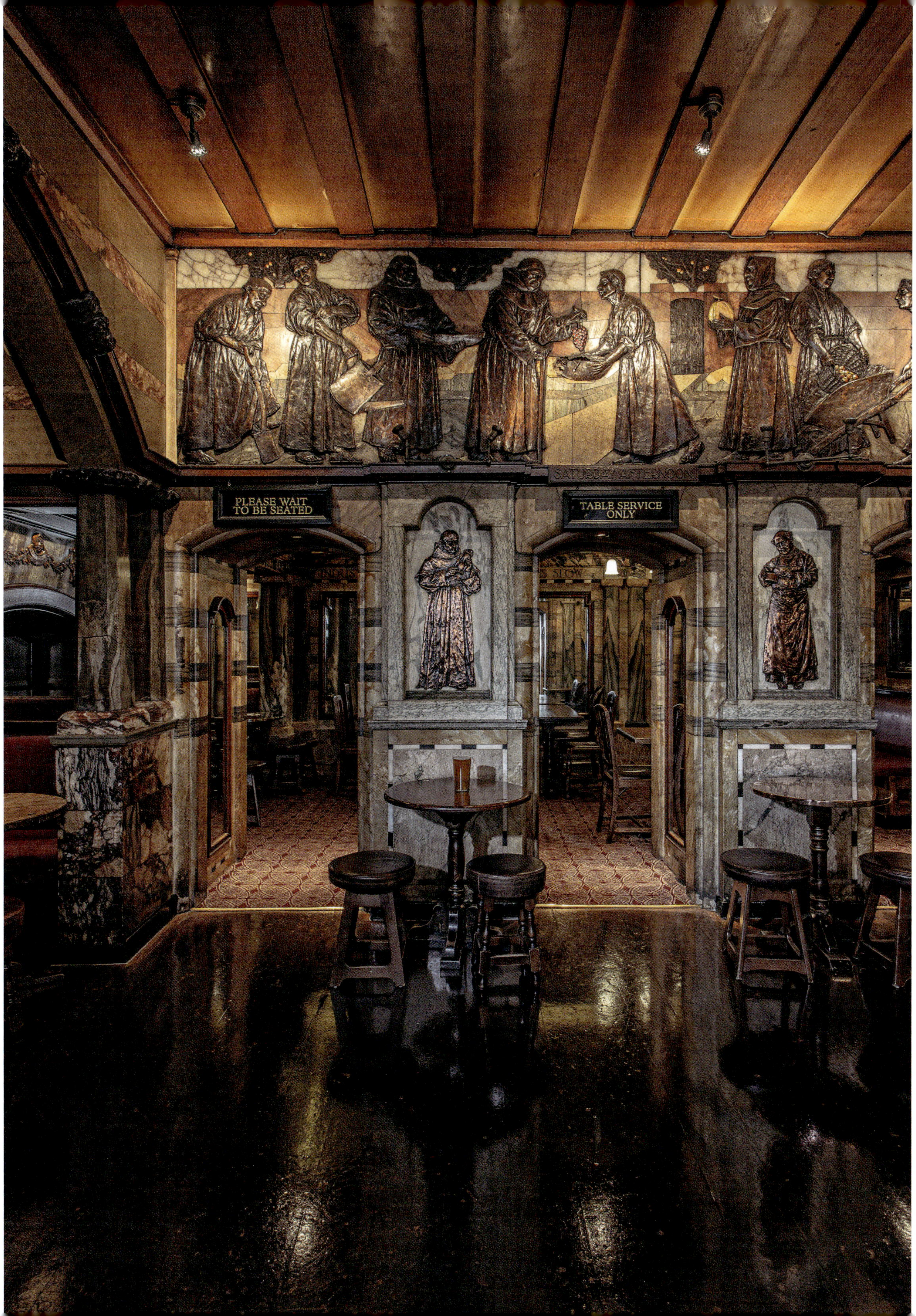
SATURDAY AFTERNOON
PLEASE WAIT
TO BE SEATED
TABLE SERVICE
ONLY

"IT'S A STUNNING SPACE ..."

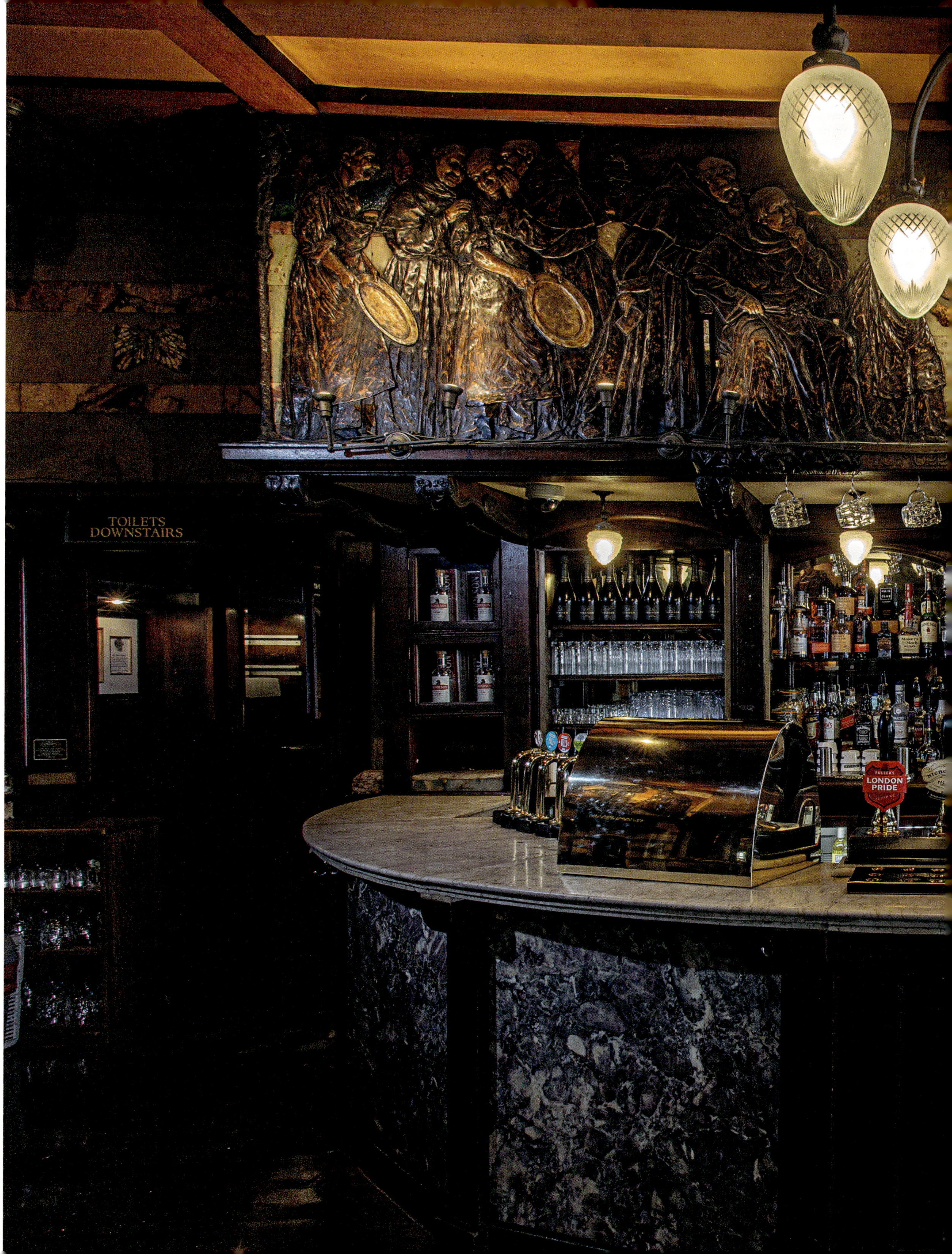

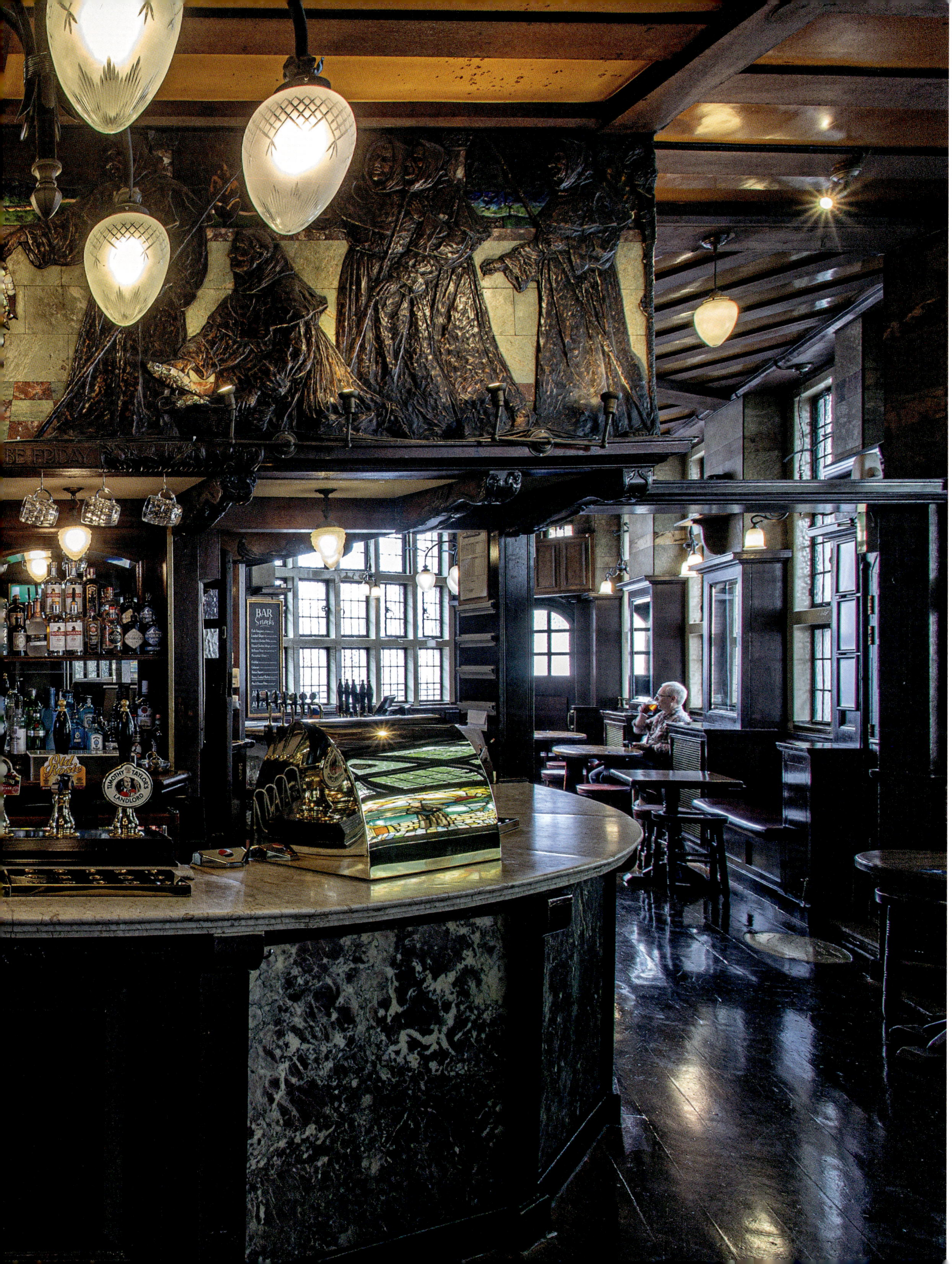

"... BUT SOMEHOW IT FEELS HOMELY"

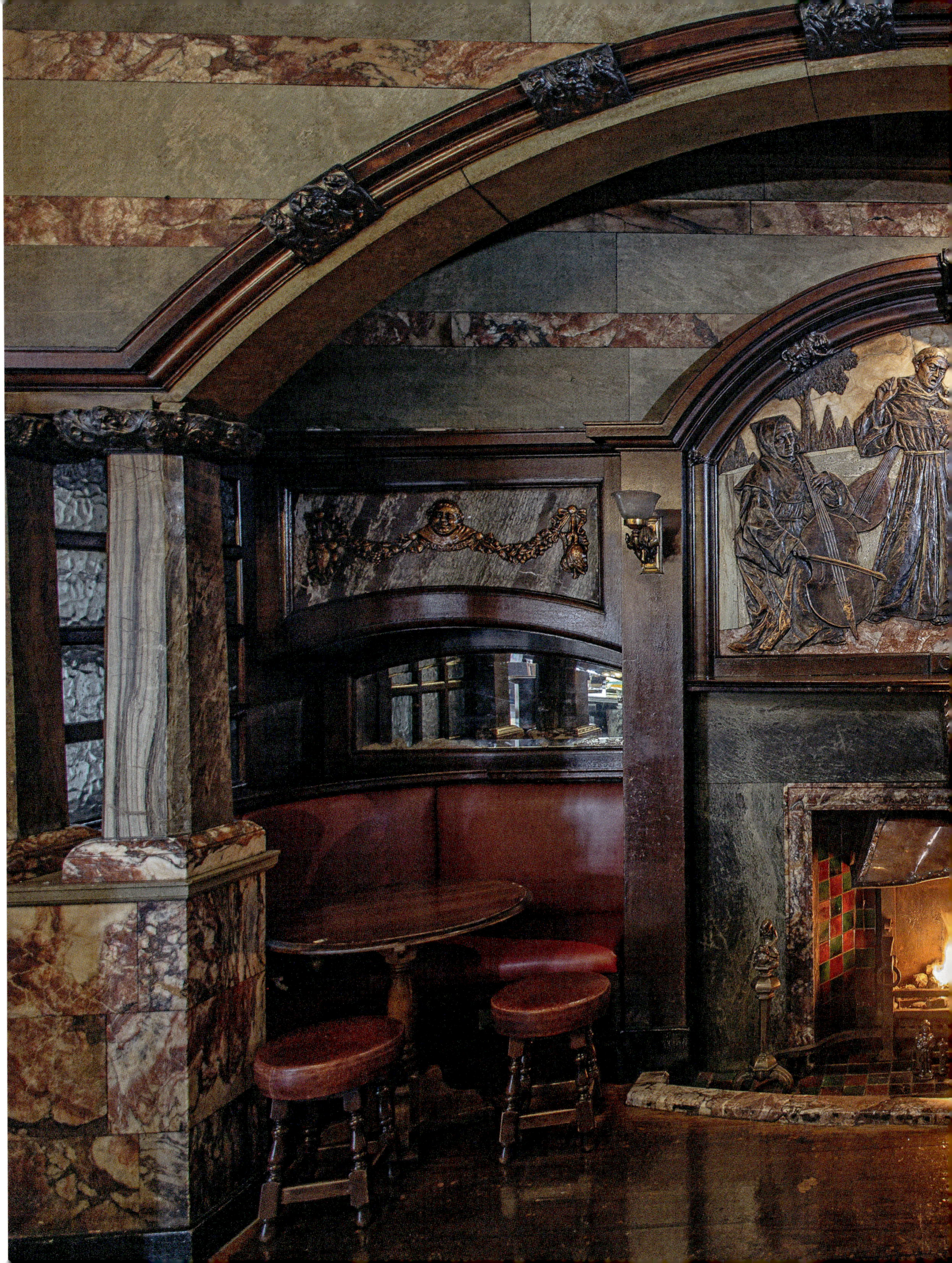

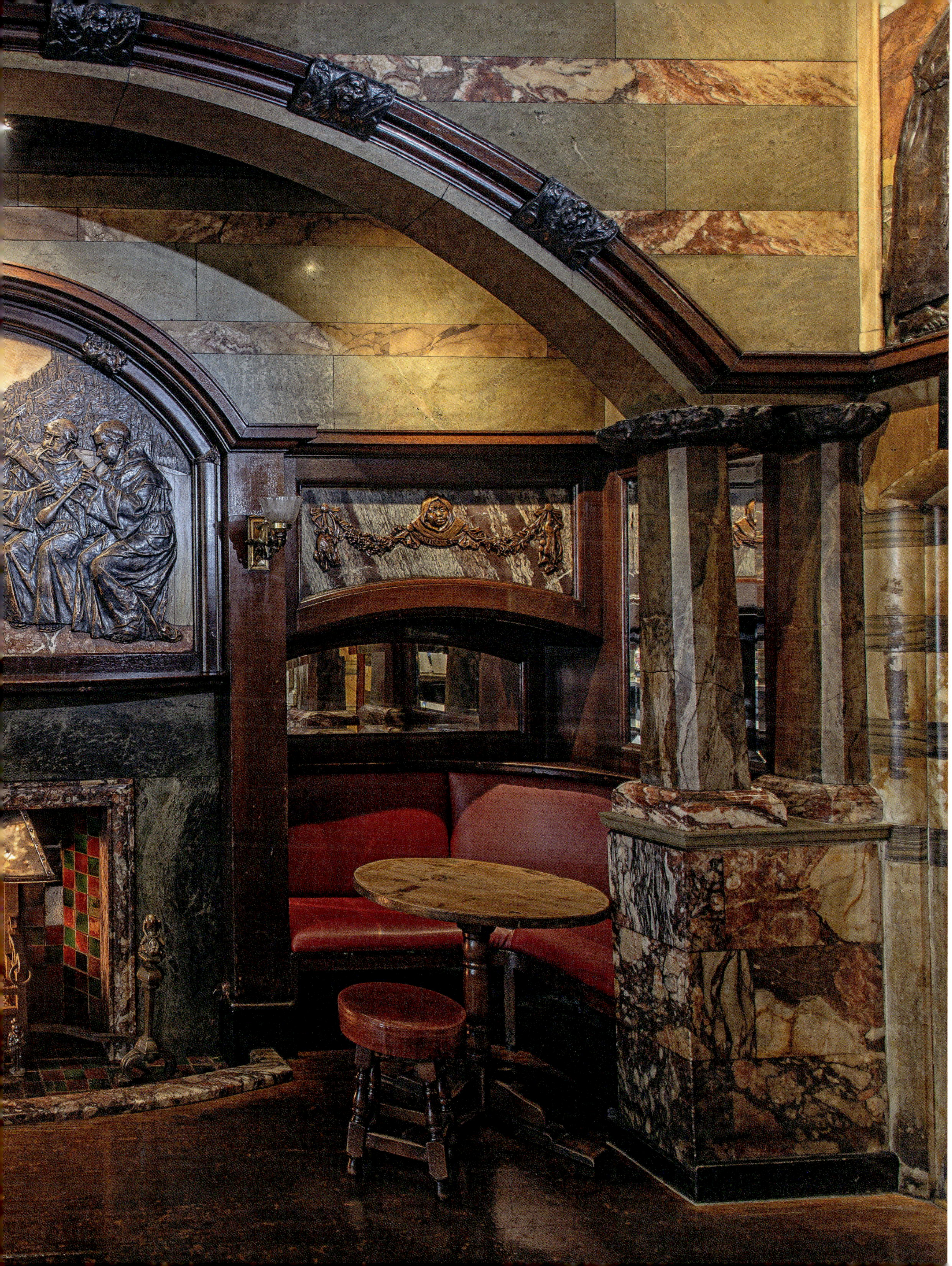

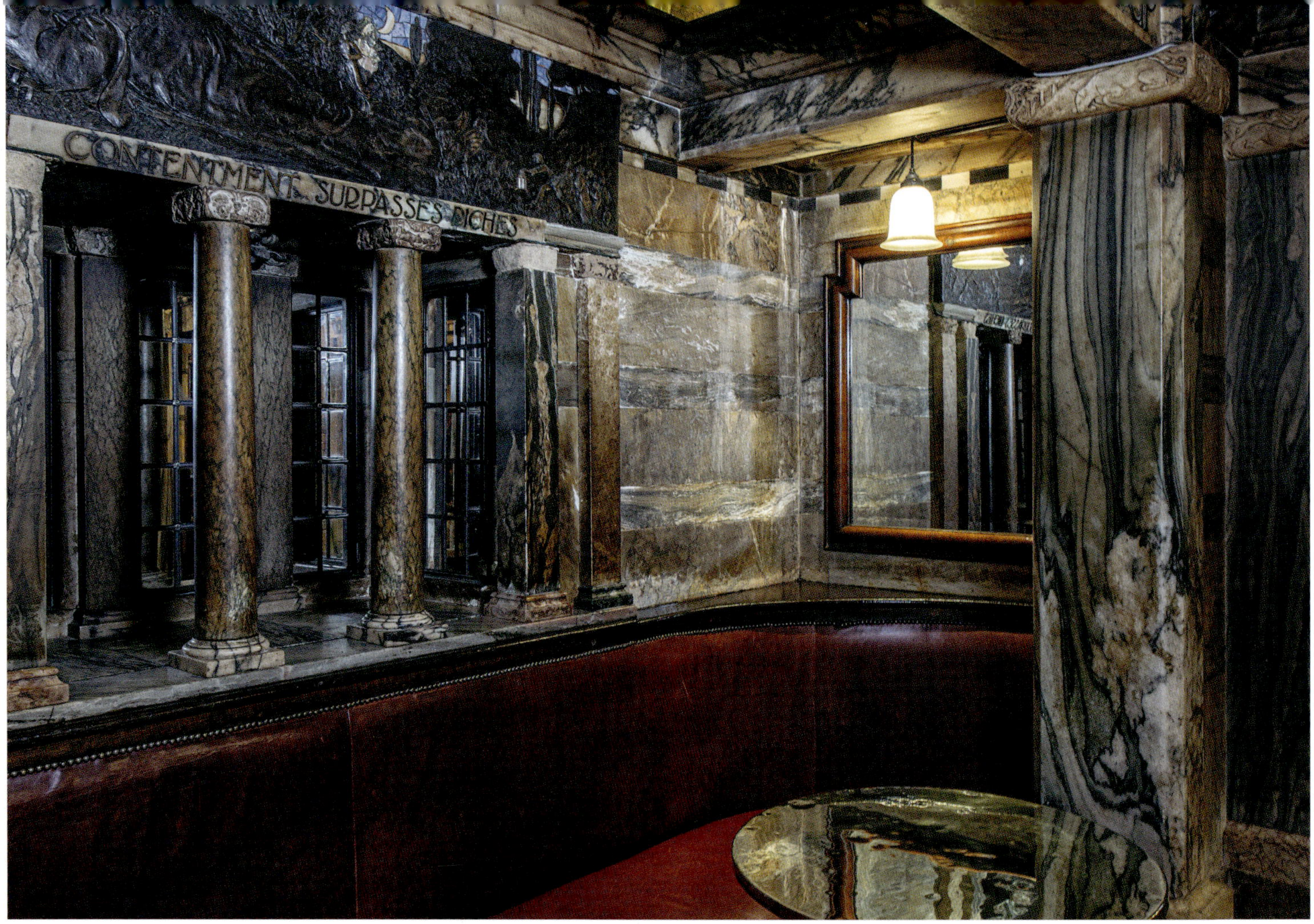
CONTENTMENT SURPASSES RICHES

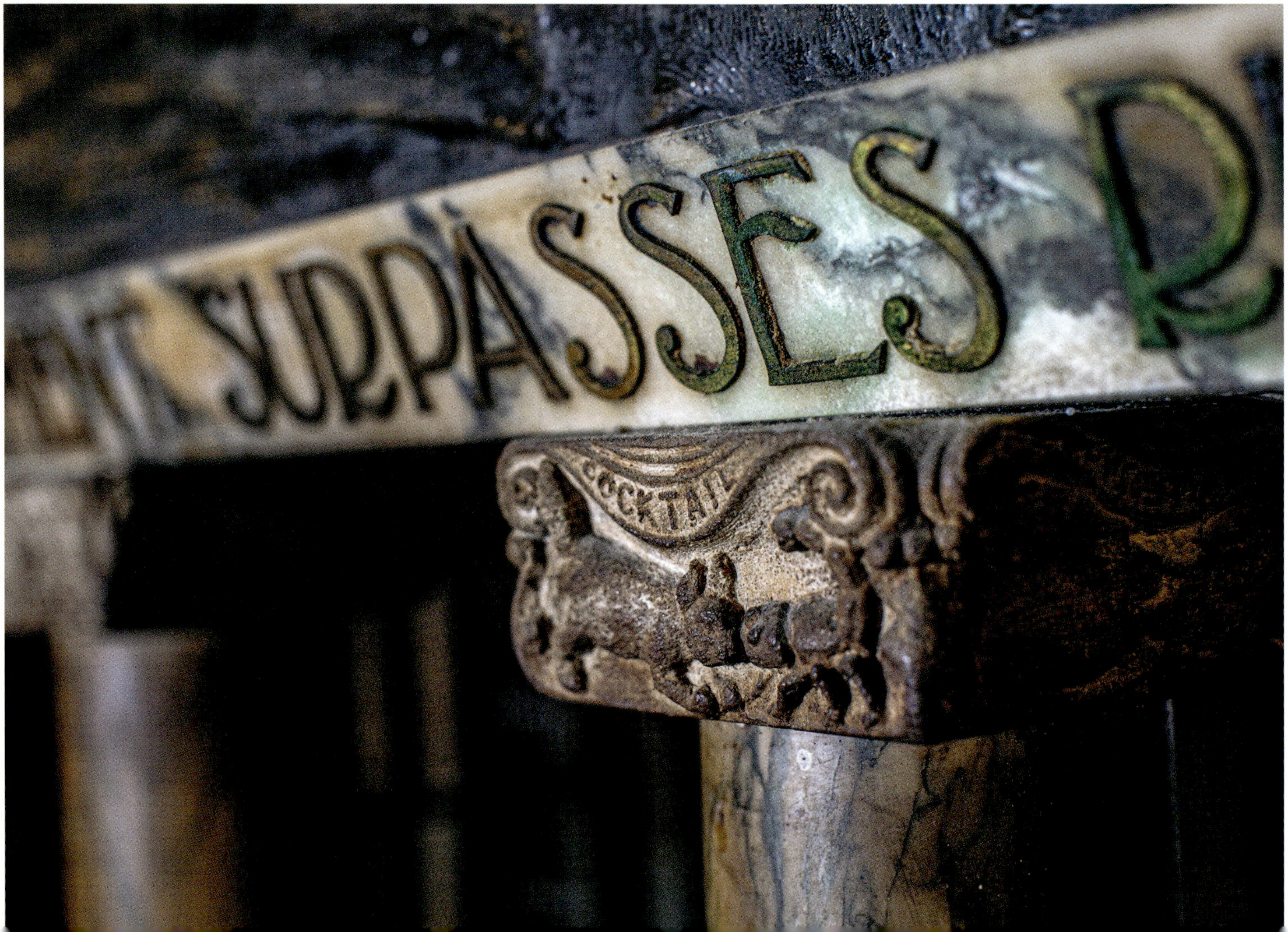
SURPASSES
COCKTAIL

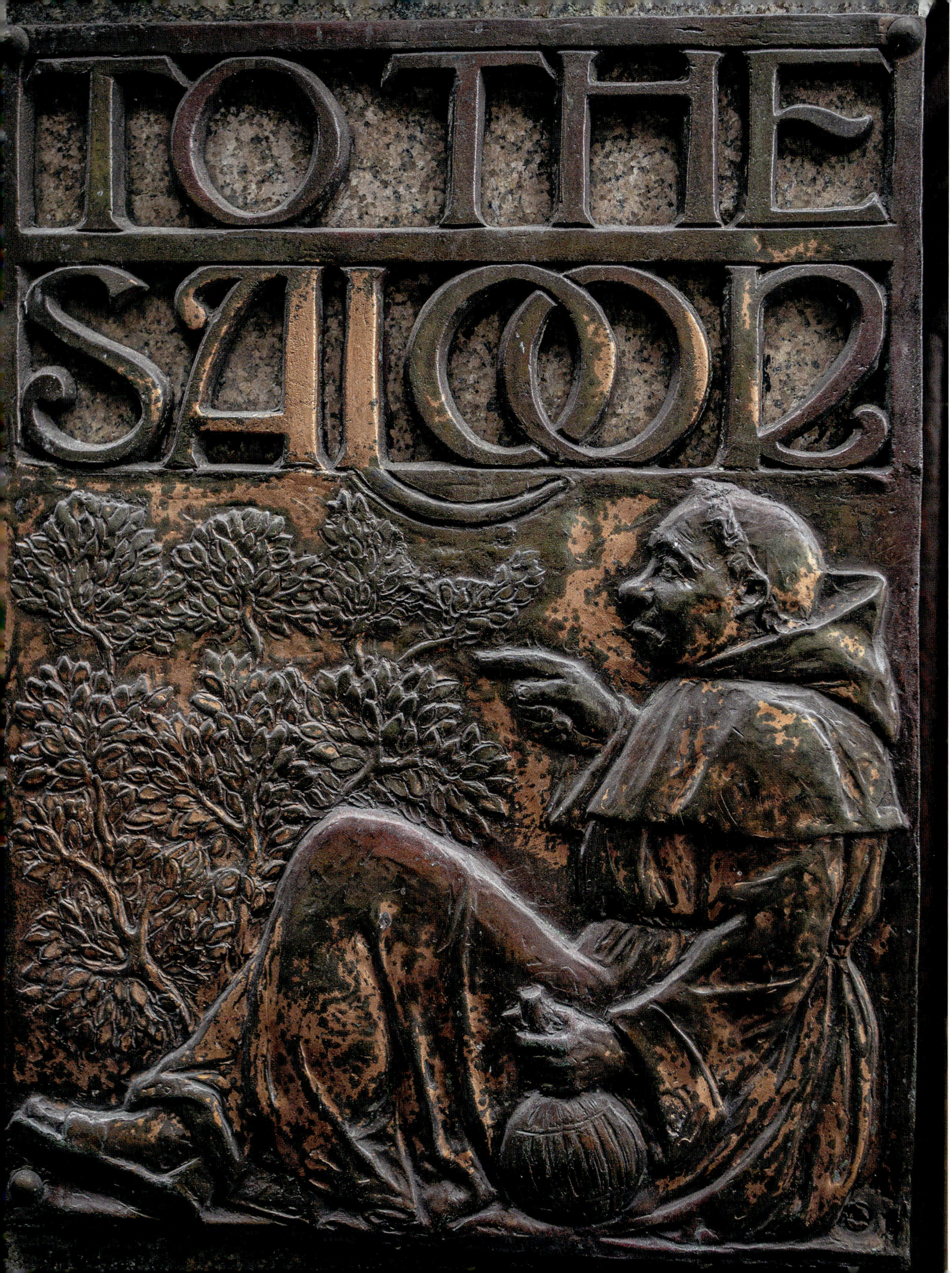
TO THE
SALOON

THE FOX & PHEASANT

1 BILLING RD, CHELSEA, LONDON

There are surely few celebrity pub owners who can boast that they installed their own urinals; but then, as James Blunt confirms with a grin, he's "a hands-on sort of person".

We're sitting in the airy dining conservatory of the seventeenth-century coaching inn in west London that the singer-songwriter bought a few years ago. The Fox & Pheasant is set in The Billings, an area of postcard-pretty cottages whose neighbourhood enclave feel is only enhanced by the metal barrier that separates them from Fulham Road. Urinals aside – sturdy, floor-length Kohler porcelain numbers, thanks for asking – signs of Blunt's proprietary interest are few and subtle: the stuffed fox that presides over one of the pub's three roaring fires wears a pith helmet, alluding to his previous life as a captain in a cavalry regiment (Blunt's, that is, not the fox's); and the cocktail menu includes You're Beautiful, named in honour of the imperishable date-night earworm that catapulted Blunt to million-selling superstar status (it's a suitably starry-eyed mixture of gin, grapefruit juice and elderflower). There are no framed portraits of Blunt, or jukeboxes heavy on his back catalogue; "though", he says, with the gift for self-deprecation that's gained him two million Twitter followers, "we threaten to put on 'You're Beautiful' at closing time each night just to clear people out."

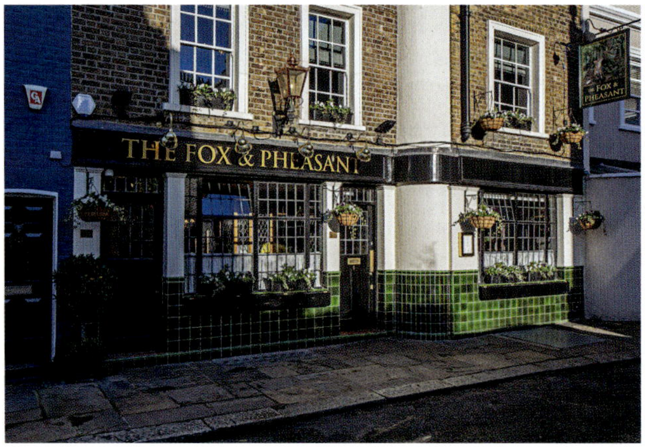

It wouldn't always have required such drastic action to make people flee the place. Not so long ago, The Fox & Pheasant was a raucous football boozer – Chelsea's Stamford Bridge ground is just a lobbed pint glass away – with sticky tables, a concrete smoking area and a thick coat of brown paint on every surface. It was also Blunt's local. "It was so run down and tired that we called it The Fox & Unpleasant," he says. "Then I was on the town with an estate agent friend and he told me it was for sale. I'd had around four pints already, so I just said right, I'll take it."

Blunt threw himself into the work of renovation, wielding a sander, obsessing over cornicing, and sourcing green Victorian tiles for the pub's façade to replace the dingy brown ones. The outdoor area was transformed into an orangery-style dining room with a retractable glass roof and a resident olive tree; the upstairs flat was converted into a private dining room that seats twenty-two. Blunt assembled a crack corps of staff – "they give this place the energy, the character, and the warmth" – led by manager Toby Milne and chef Toby Bee. The main bar, with its wood panelling and stained-glass, alongside the bottle-green leather armchairs, log burners, and prints of hunting and fishing scenes and wading birds, has a winningly bucolic, country-pub-comes-to-town vibe. Playing music and running a pub have many similarities, Blunt adds: "Music brings people of all nationalities, classes, religions, races, ages, and sexual persuasions together, and pubs can do the same thing. I wanted this place to be everybody's second living room."

The broad church thing seems to be working out for The Fox & Pheasant's new incarnation. The Chelsea fans have retained their loyalty on match days – "they said, look, make sure this is still a place for us, and I respect that," says Blunt – while families and locals also now appreciate the modern English pub grub menu – lamb and mint pie, sea bream with cauliflower, eggs every which way at brunch, and the hugely popular Sunday roasts – and the regulars can settle in with a Scotch Egg and a pint of Fox & Fez, specially brewed for the pub by Trumans. You may not spot any of Blunt's famous friends – Harry and Meghan, say, or Ed Sheeran, godfather to Blunt's eldest son (who, coincidentally, has a pub of his own), but there's every chance you'll see Blunt, with wife Sofia and children in tow, engaging in what he calls his "royal walkabout". "I like saying hi, thanks for coming, how's the food, that kind of thing," he says. "I'm happy to have been able to save this place, but I'm merely its current custodian." And he's already thinking of the succession: "Maybe my kids can take it over one day. I can think of no better gift to hand on than your own pub."

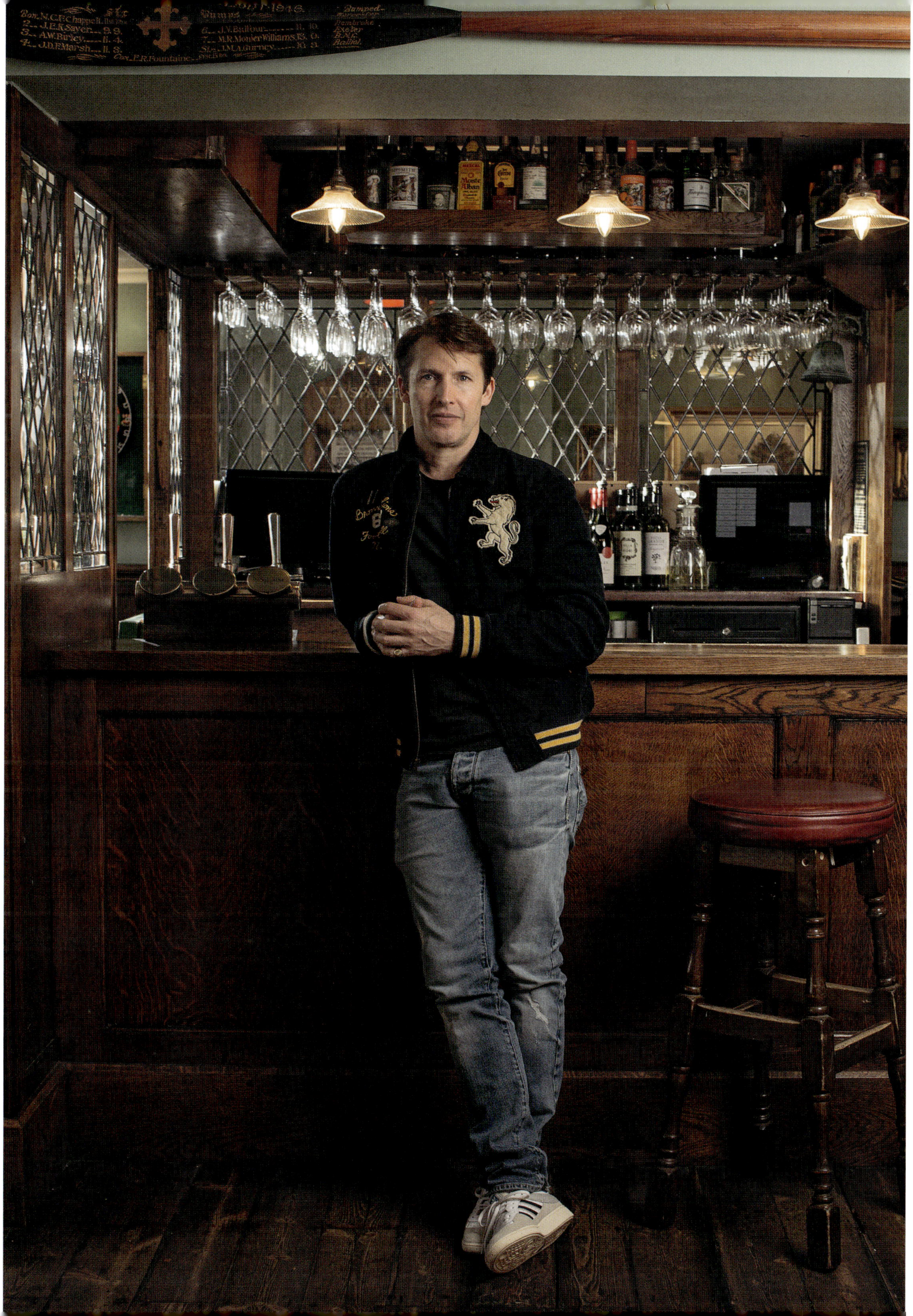

"MY MAIN JOB WAS TO MAKE THIS PLACE BEAUTIFUL"

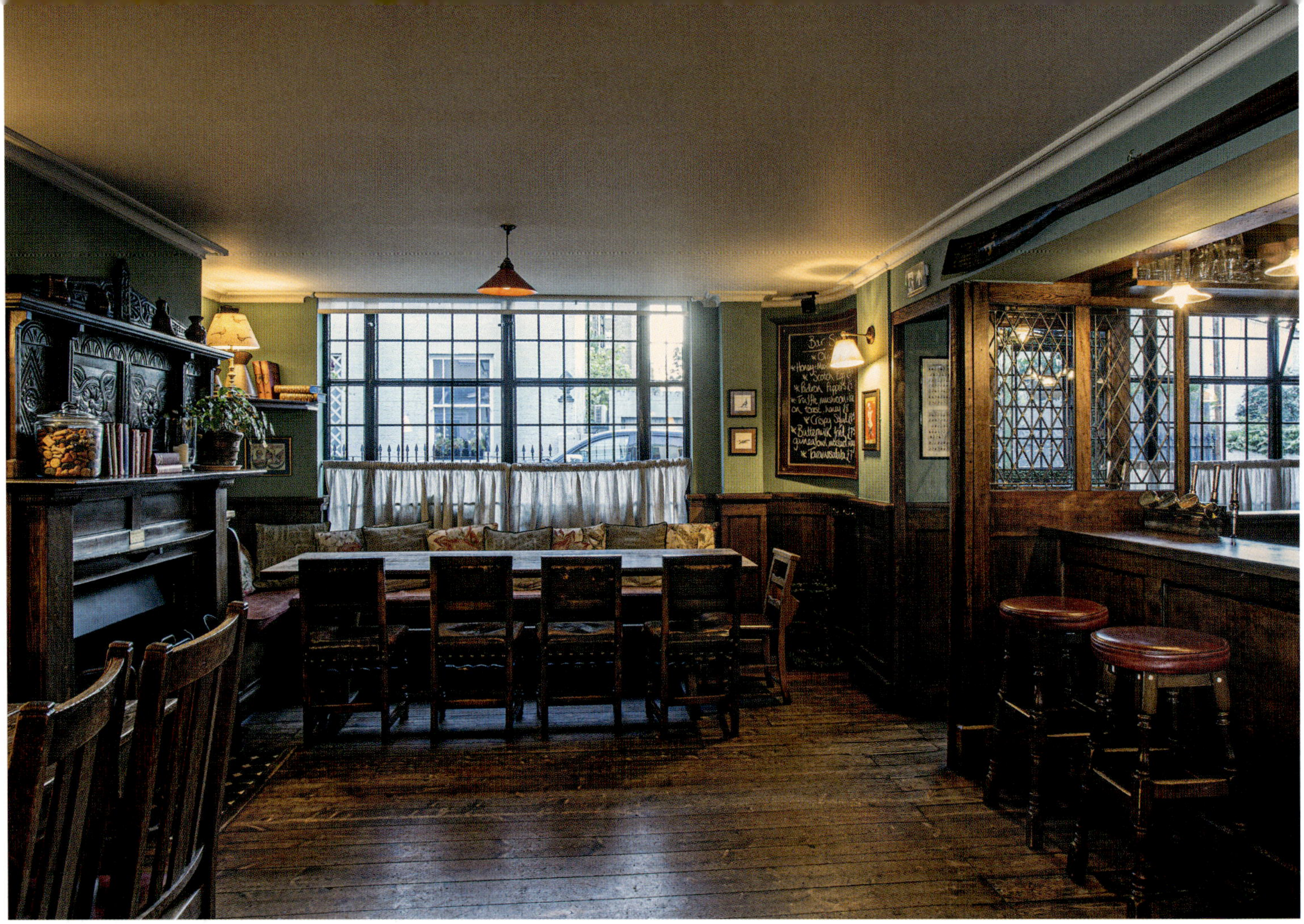

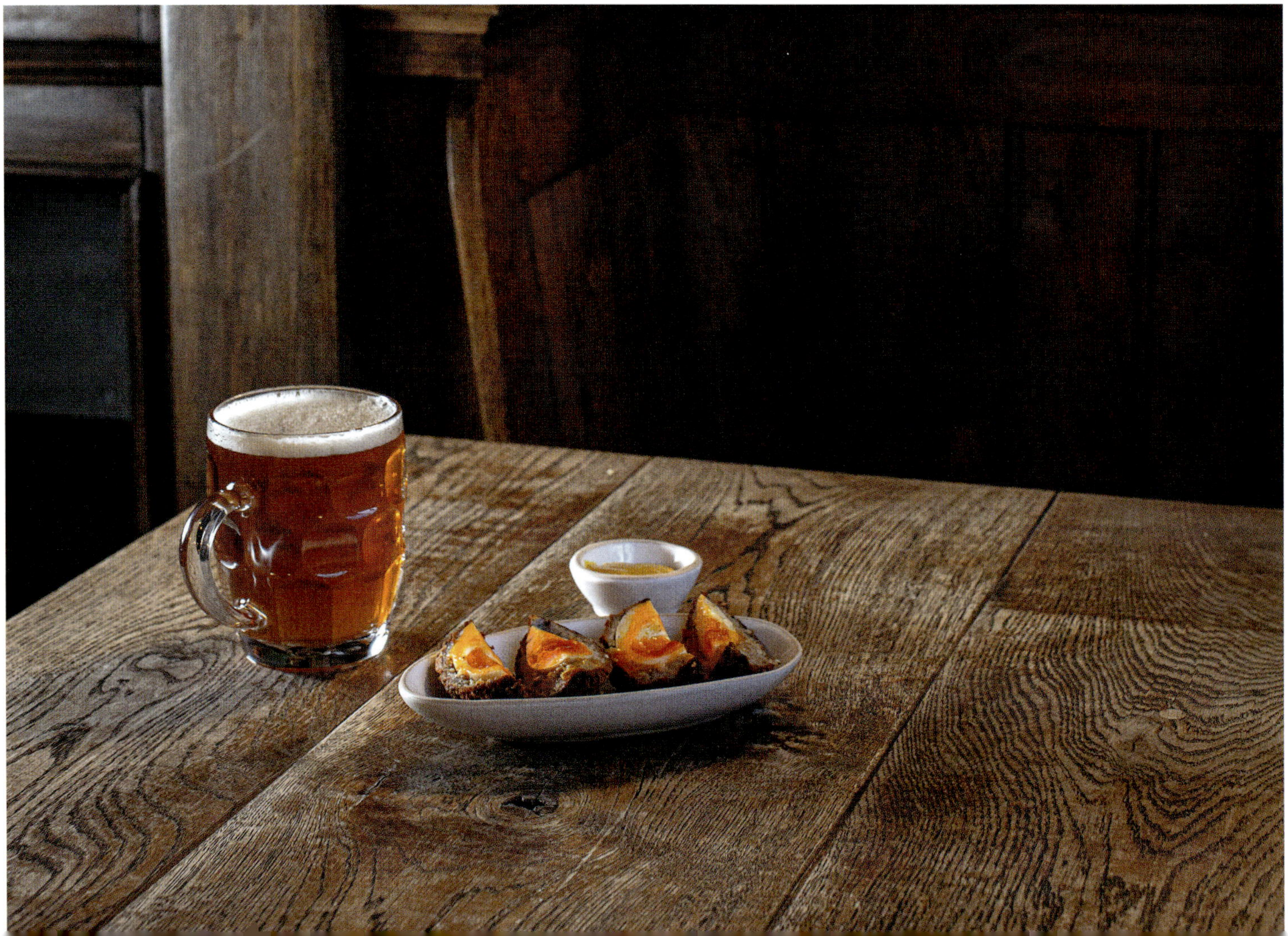

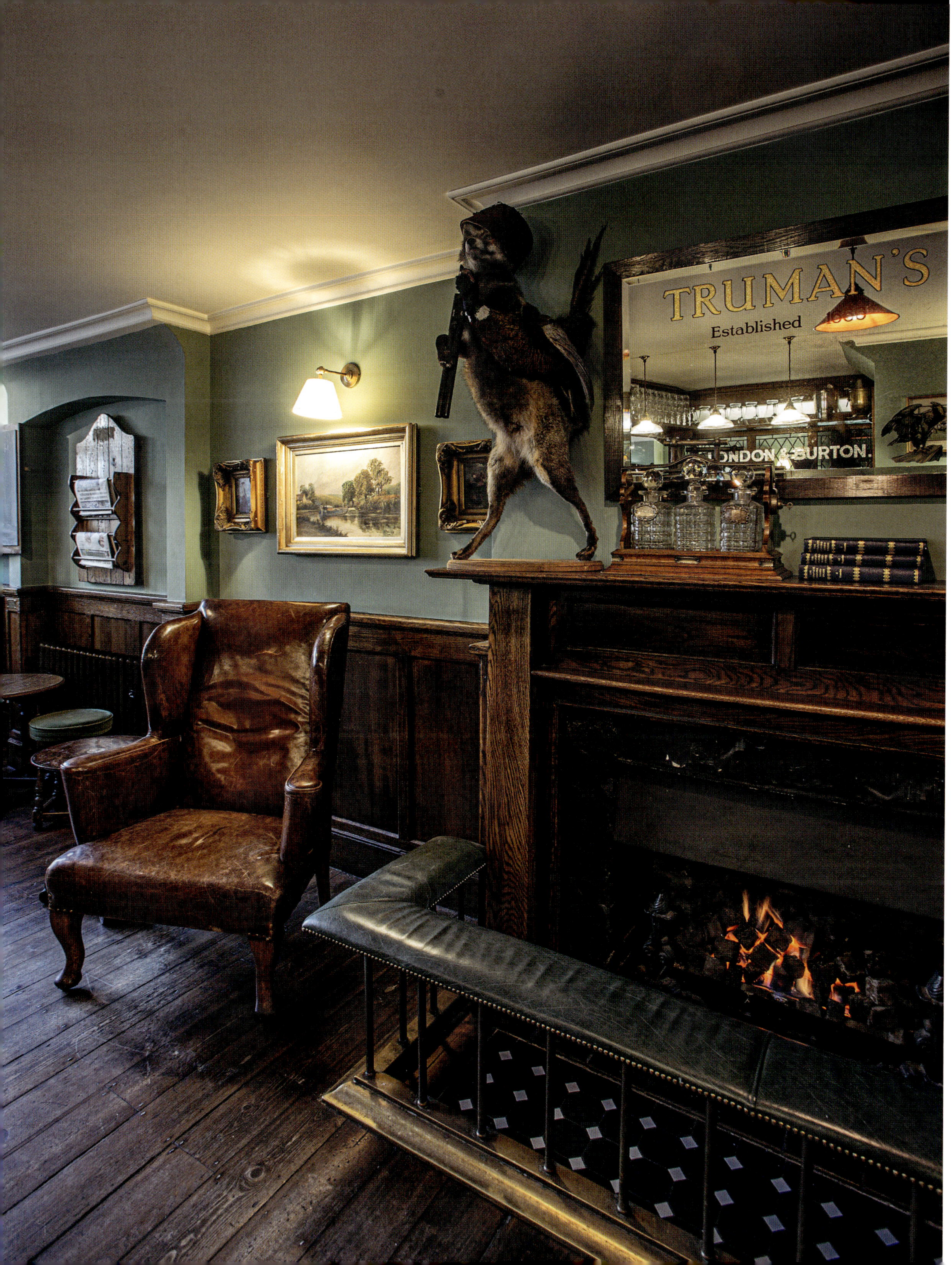

"A COUNTRY-PUB-IN-TOWN KIND OF VIBE"

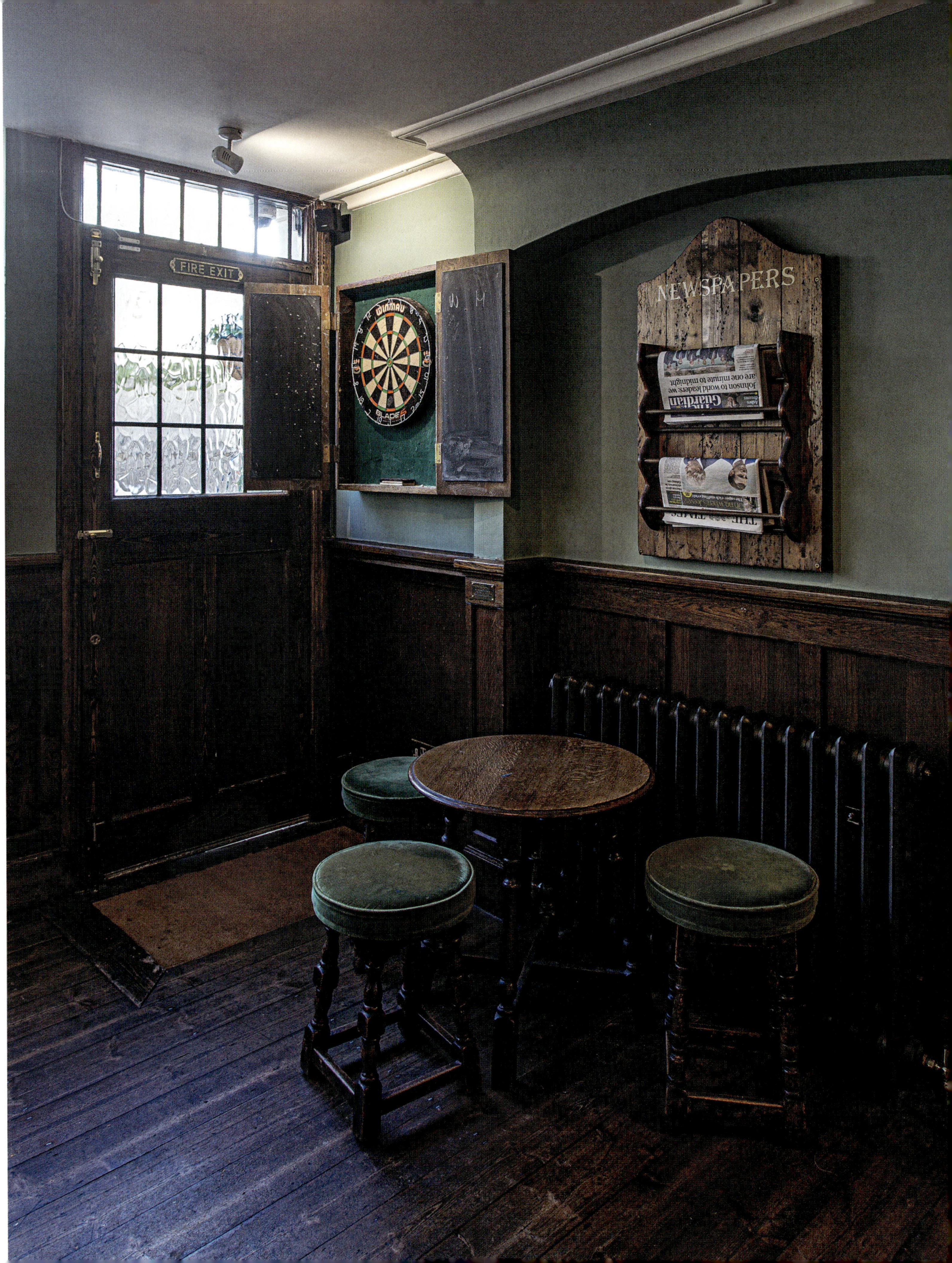
FIRE EXIT
NEWSPAPERS

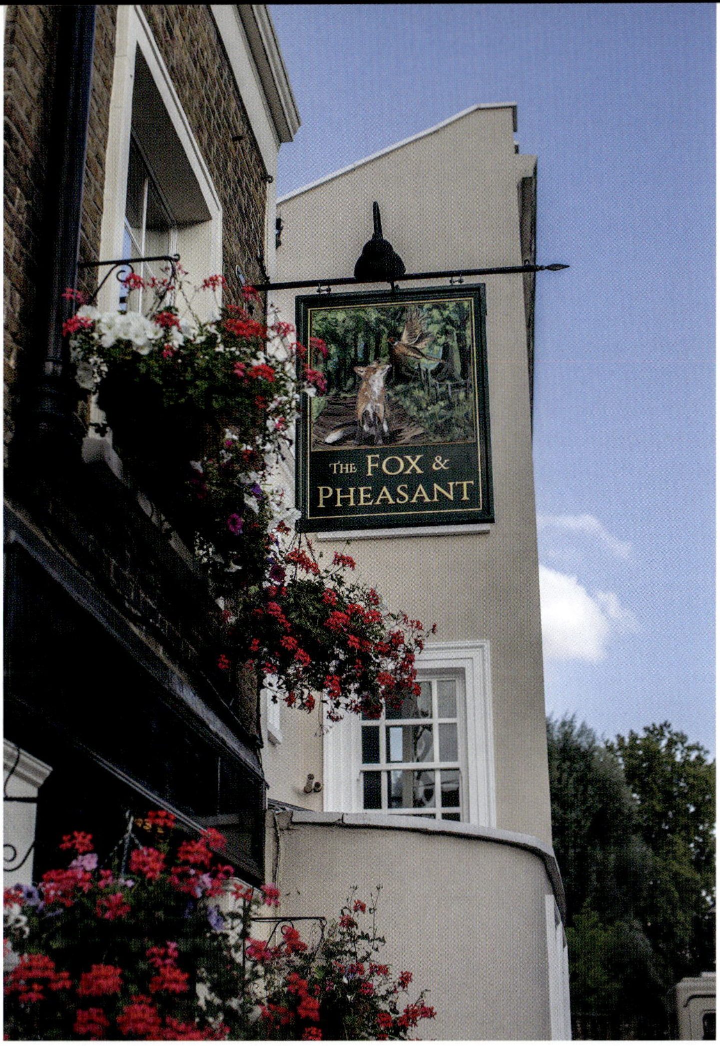

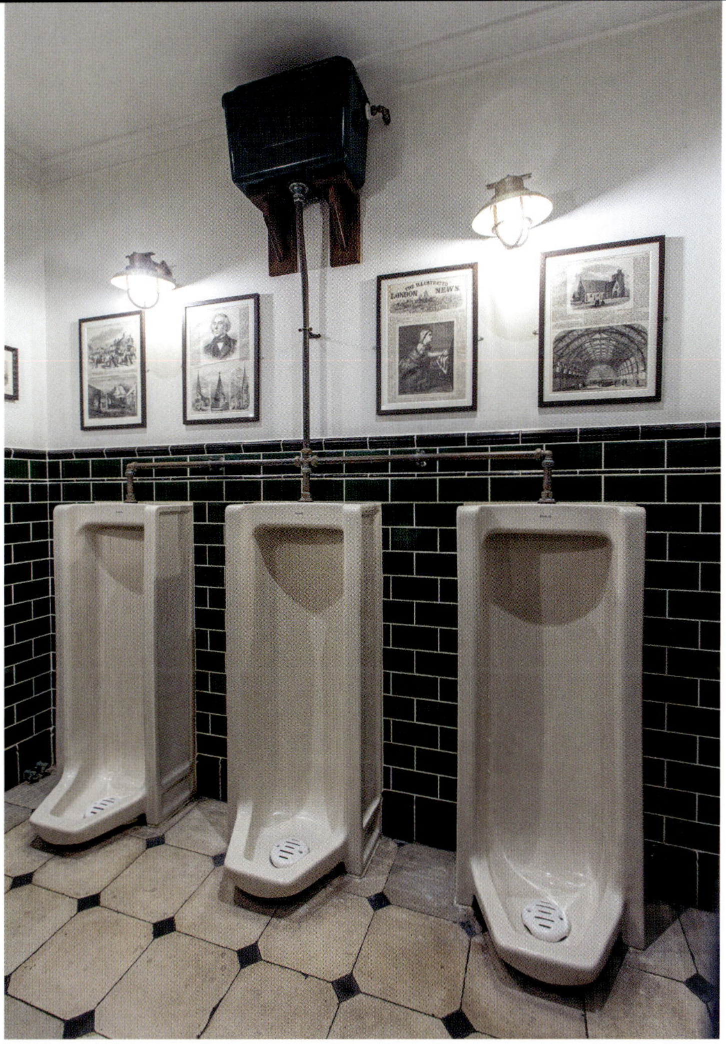

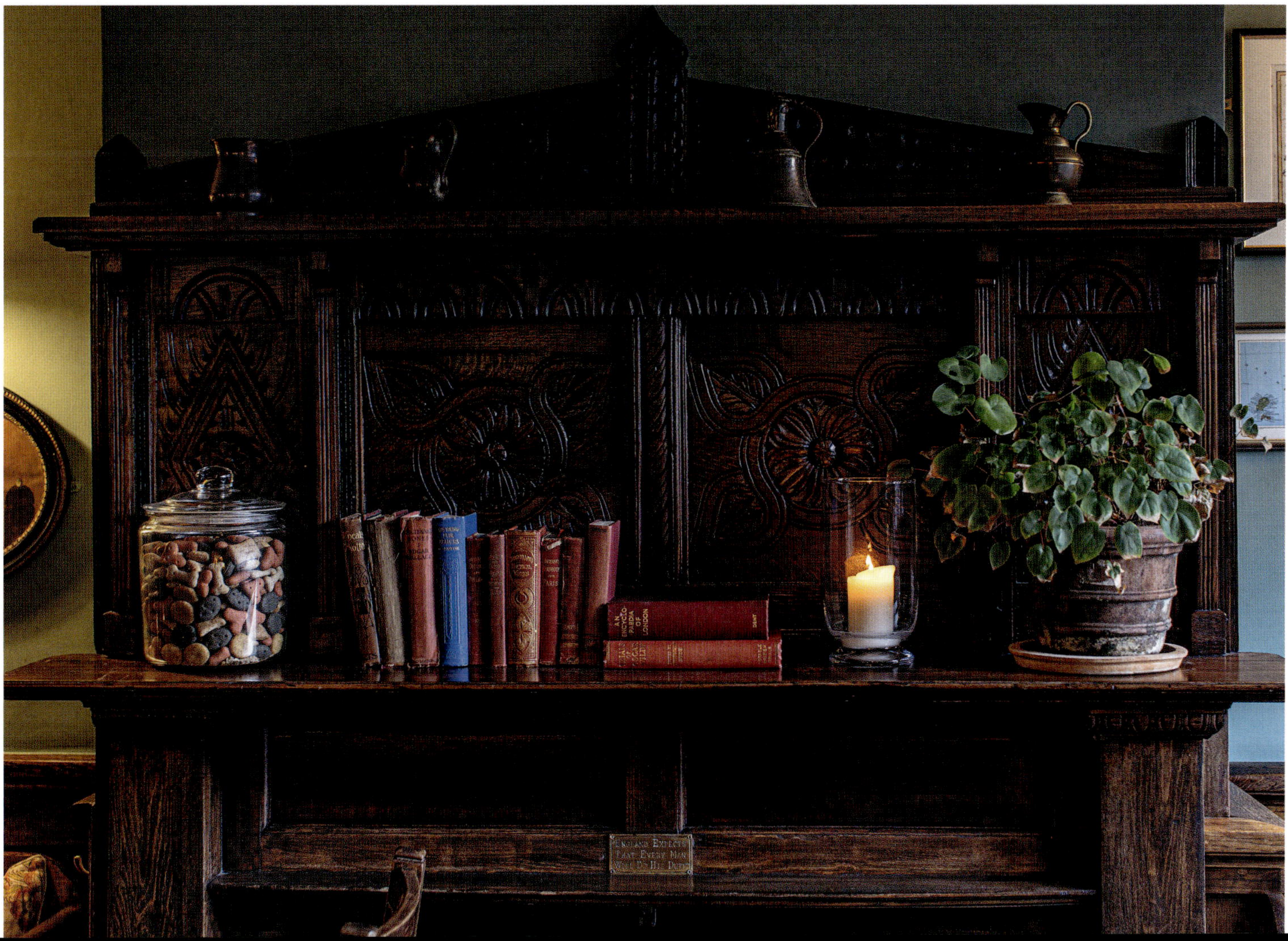

"THERE'S NO POINT DOING IT UNLESS YOU REALLY GET STUCK IN"

THE DUBLIN CASTLE

94 PARKWAY, CAMDEN, LONDON

Henry Conlon is recalling the first time that a certain band ventured into his family pub and asked if they could gig there. "They were 17–18-year-old kids," he says. "My dad said to them, can you play a bit of jazz? They were like, yeah, we can do that. It was a blag, of course. But they packed the place out for six weeks with all these ska kids. Then they got on *Top of the Pops*." He grins. "They moved on, but they'd put us on the map by then."

The pub is The Dublin Castle, situated in that part of Camden Town that's halfway between the buzz of the street markets and the more rarefied environs of Primrose Hill and Regent's Park. The band is Madness, now a beloved British institution, much like The Dublin Castle itself. A black Music Heritage Award plaque, given to venues that have played a crucial role in creating music history, adorns its façade. The red-painted and poster-plastered interior, along with the 200-capacity backroom venue, is as Guinness-steeped and authentically scuffed as any mosh-pitting indie kid could wish. There are scrawled testimonials from the likes of Suggs ("Long may you reign!") and Amy Winehouse ("Thanks for letting me behind the bar – I need the tips"). There are murals of Blur and Supergrass, reflecting the pub's early championing of Britpop (Coldplay and The Libertines also played some of their formative gigs here). And the list of coming attractions – could Twatville be the new Coldplay, or Screamin' Irene the heirs to Blur? – proves that, over forty years after Madness first walked through the doors, The Dublin Castle is still stoking the live music coals at least five nights a week. "You can't beat the feeling of the music pumping through your body, and getting all hot and sweaty," says Conlon. And, he adds, maybe catching someone's eye across the dancefloor who turns out to be the love of your life (a pillar by the bar is known as "The Tinder Column" because of the amount of first dates who arrange to meet up there).

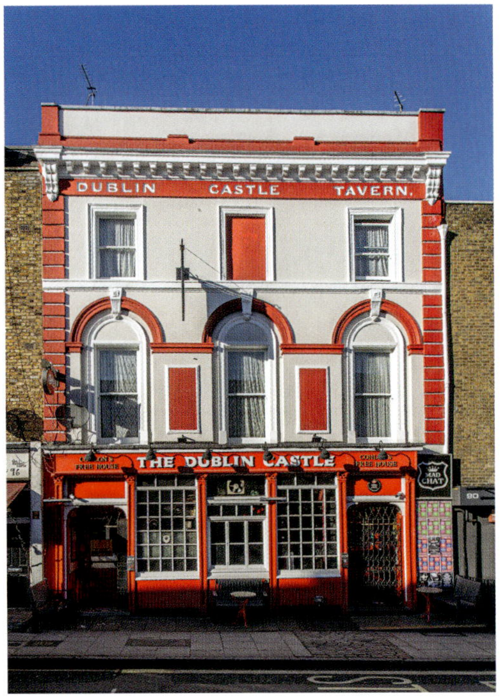

The Dublin Castle opened in 1856 to serve the Irish community of "navvies" who were building the nearby railway (the English, Welsh and Scots labourers all had their own venues, in an effort to prevent sectarian skirmishes). The pub's music tradition grew out of its original patrons' weekend ceilidhs; the Madness connection meant it ended up catering to the ska-punk contingent among Camden's many musical tribes. "It's very difficult to get barred from here, but it can get quite interesting at times," says Conlon. He recalls the night that a trench-coated couple came in, removed their outerwear to reveal their naked bodies, and clambered onto one of the bar tabletops to indulge in a short but energetic bout of congress ("everyone else just carried on drinking – I mean what else could you do?"). Or the time when Amy Winehouse, who lived nearby and treated the pub as her local, was accosted at the jukebox by a somewhat inebriated man celebrating his stag party, and, irritated by his attentions, "smacked him in the chops". Or the time when thrashcore band Cradle of Filth carried a coffin through the pub, out of which popped a topless woman who sprayed the audience with fake blood. On such occasions, says Conlon, his octogenarian mother Peggy, who still lives above the premises, has the perfect response: "She gets her holy water out and starts spraying the place, saying her Hail Marys."

The Dublin Castle may be hallowed ground, in many senses, but it's not resting on its laurels; Conlon points out that it's now holding queer nights like Club Smiler and Sunday afternoon "ska dances" alongside the gigs. "We're not everyone's cup of tea," he concedes. "But when the jukebox is going, the vibe's rocking, and the Guinness is flowing, it's good times here." As Madness themselves said, apropos of 'Our House' but with equal relevance to the pub that remains their alma mater: "There's always something happening, and it's usually quite loud."

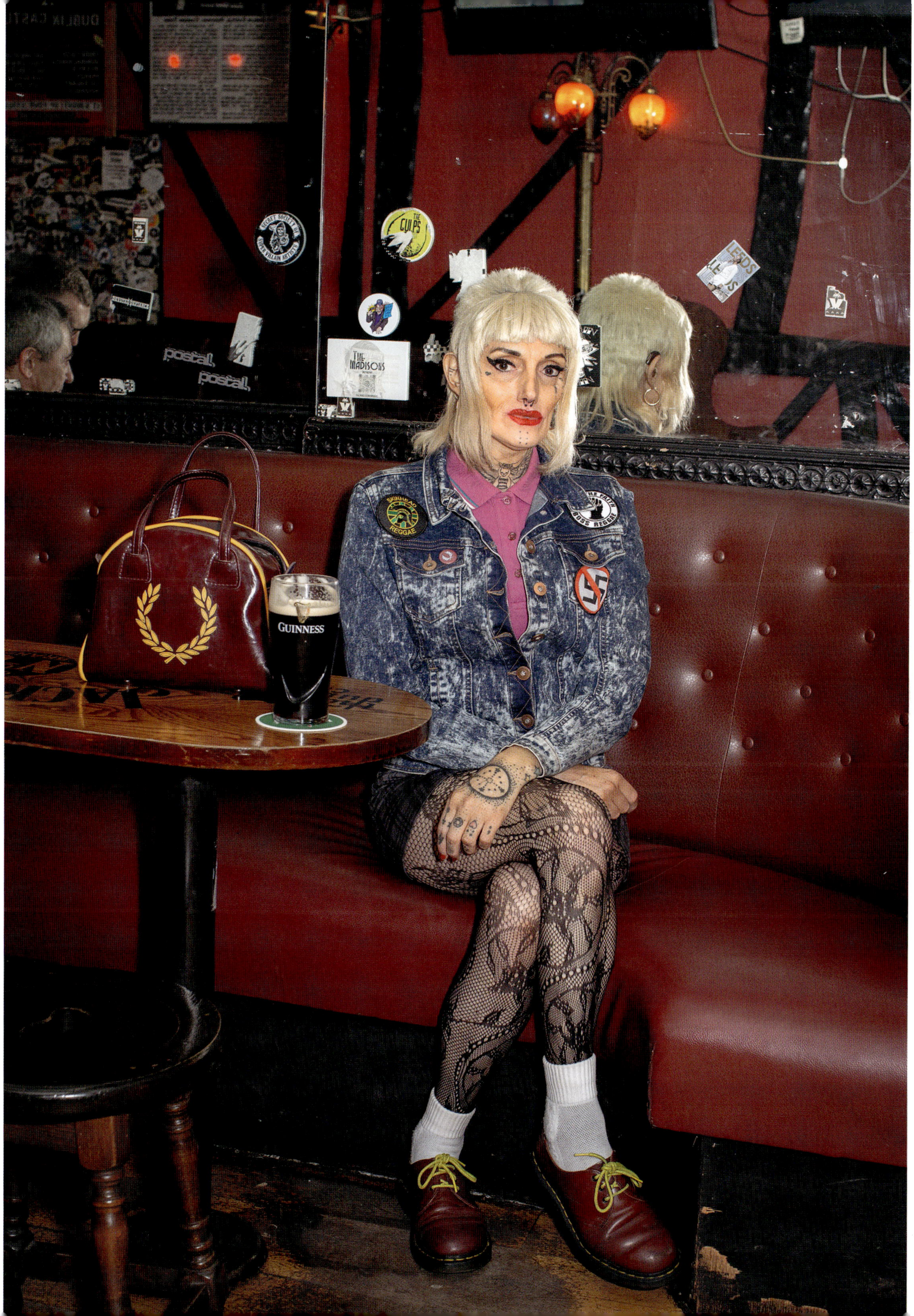

"IT'S A PLACE WHERE YOU CAN BE YOURSELF"

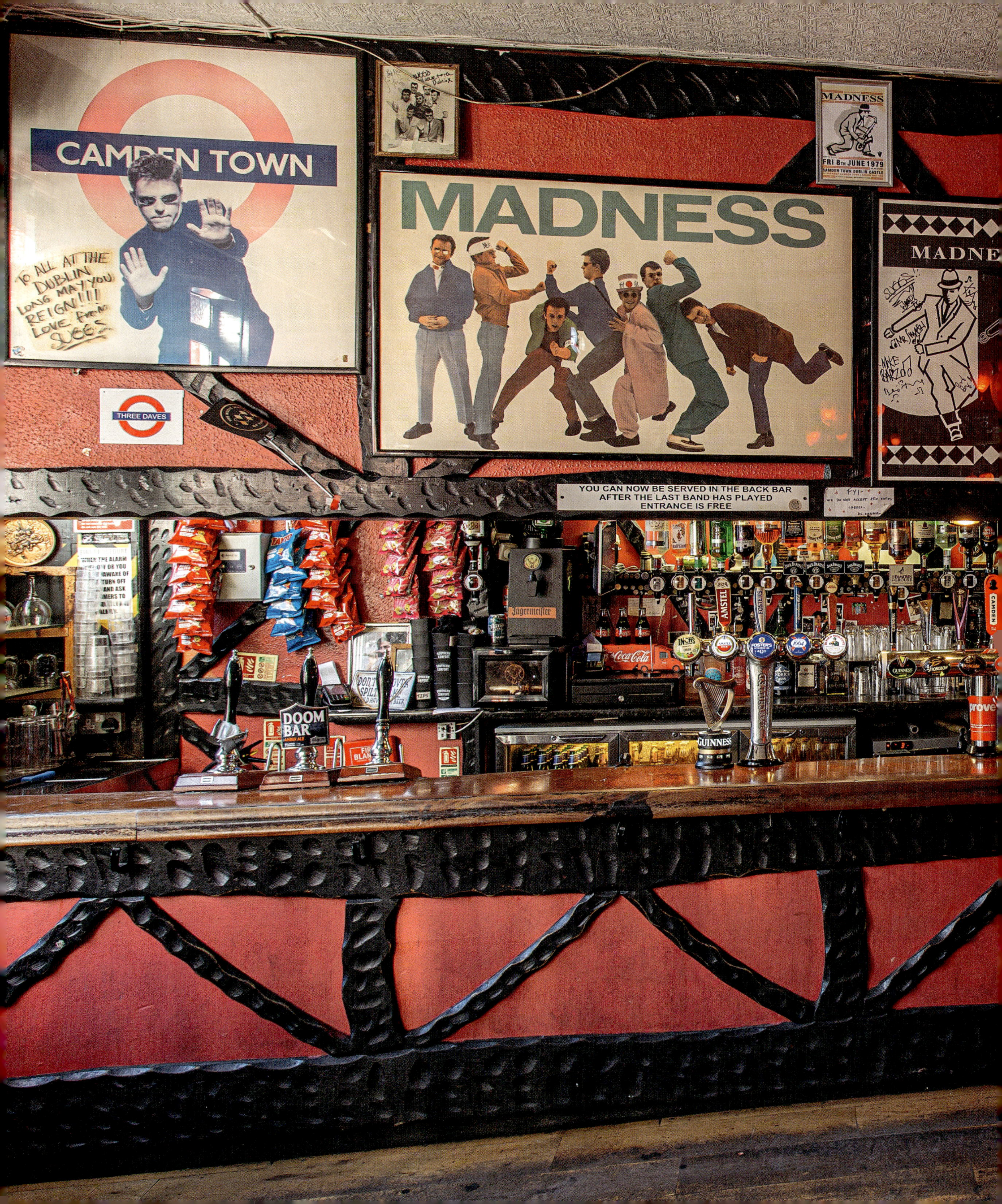
CAMDEN TOWN
To all at the Dublin long may you reign!!! Love from Suggs
MADNESS
MADNESS
FRI 8th JUNE 1979
CAMDEN TOWN DUBLIN CASTLE
MADNE
THREE DAVES
YOU CAN NOW BE SERVED IN THE BACK BAR
AFTER THE LAST BAND HAS PLAYED
ENTRANCE IS FREE
Jägermeister
AMSTEL
Coca-Cola
DOOM BAR
GUINNESS

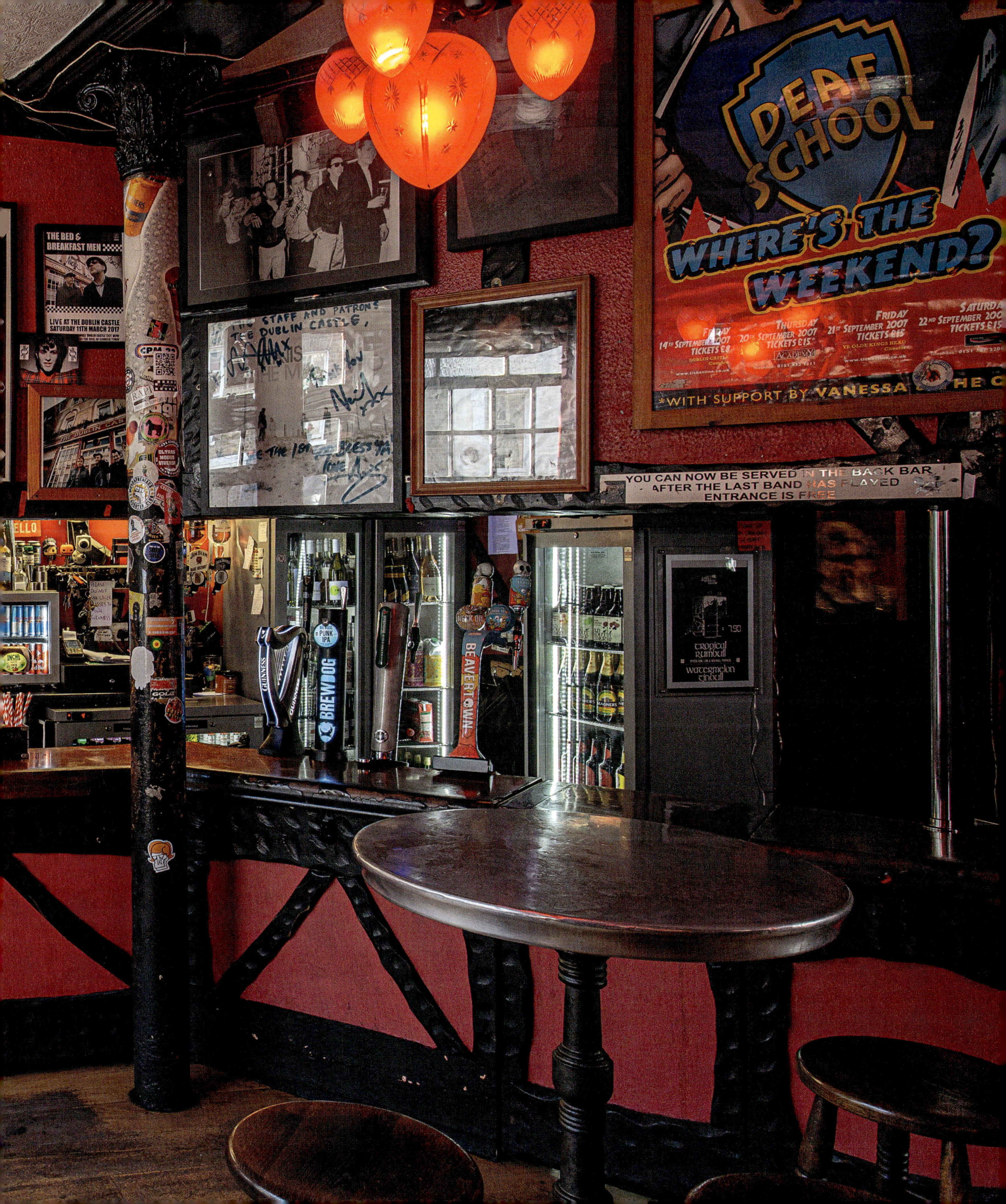
DEAF SCHOOL
WHERE'S THE WEEKEND?
*WITH SUPPORT BY VANESSA
THE BED & BREAKFAST MEN
LIVE AT THE DUBLIN CASTLE SATURDAY 11TH MARCH 2017
YOU CAN NOW BE SERVED IN THE BACK BAR
AFTER THE LAST BAND HAS PLAYED
ENTRANCE IS FREE
PUNK IPA
BREWDOG
BEAVERTOWN

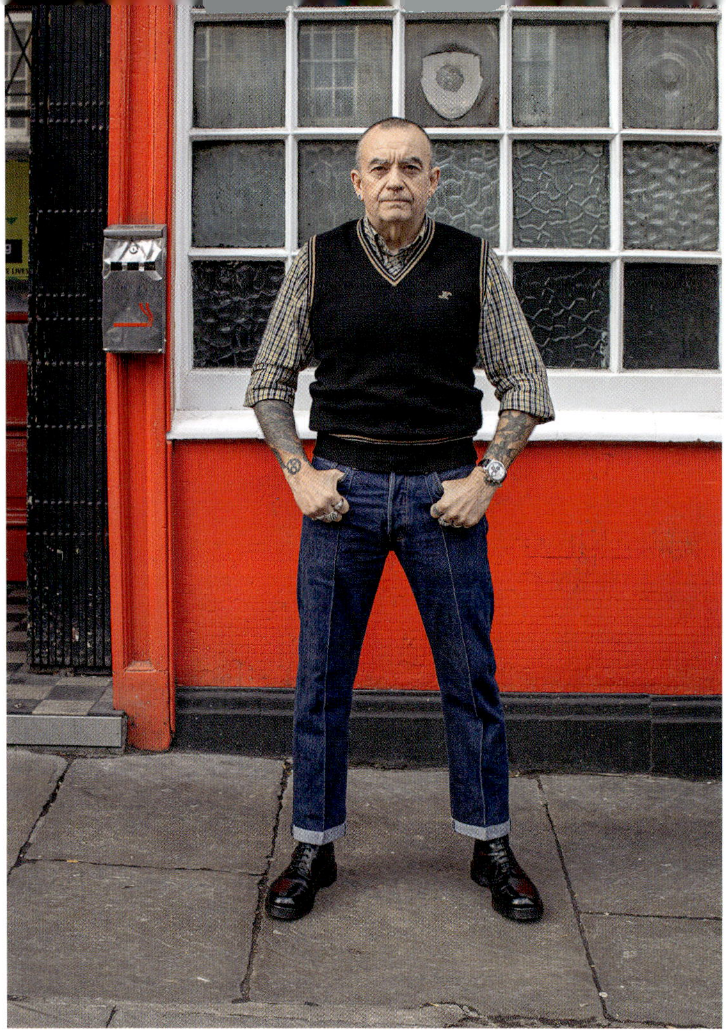

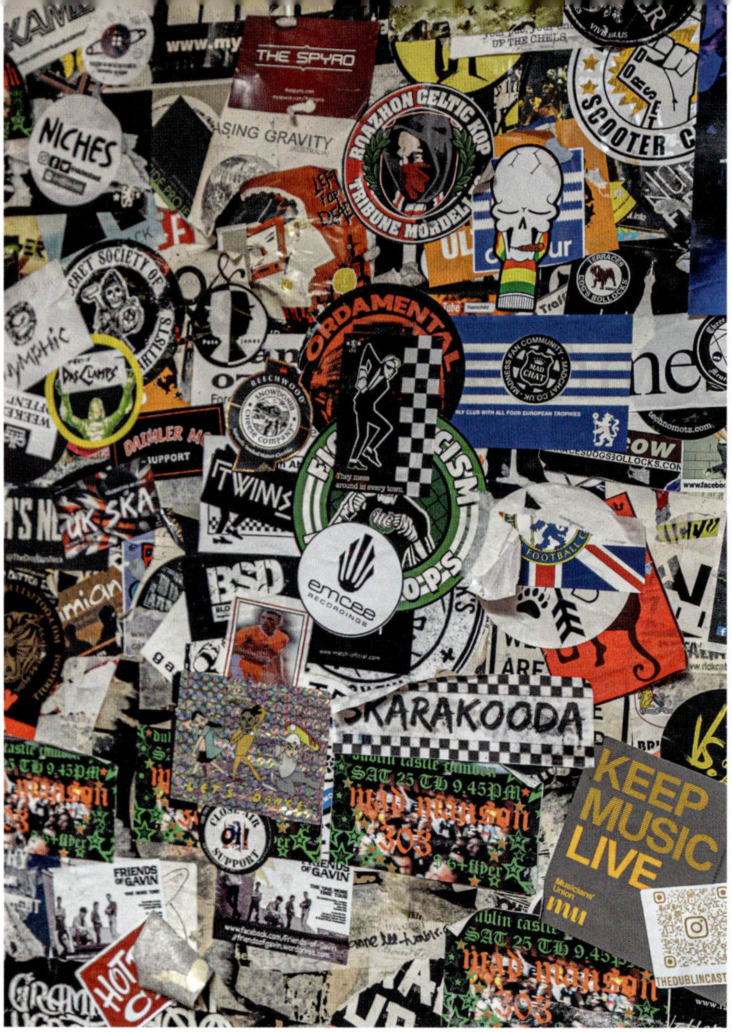
THE SPYRO
NICHES
SCOOTER
SKARAKOODA
KEEP MUSIC LIVE
FRIENDS OF GAVIN
emcee RECORDINGS

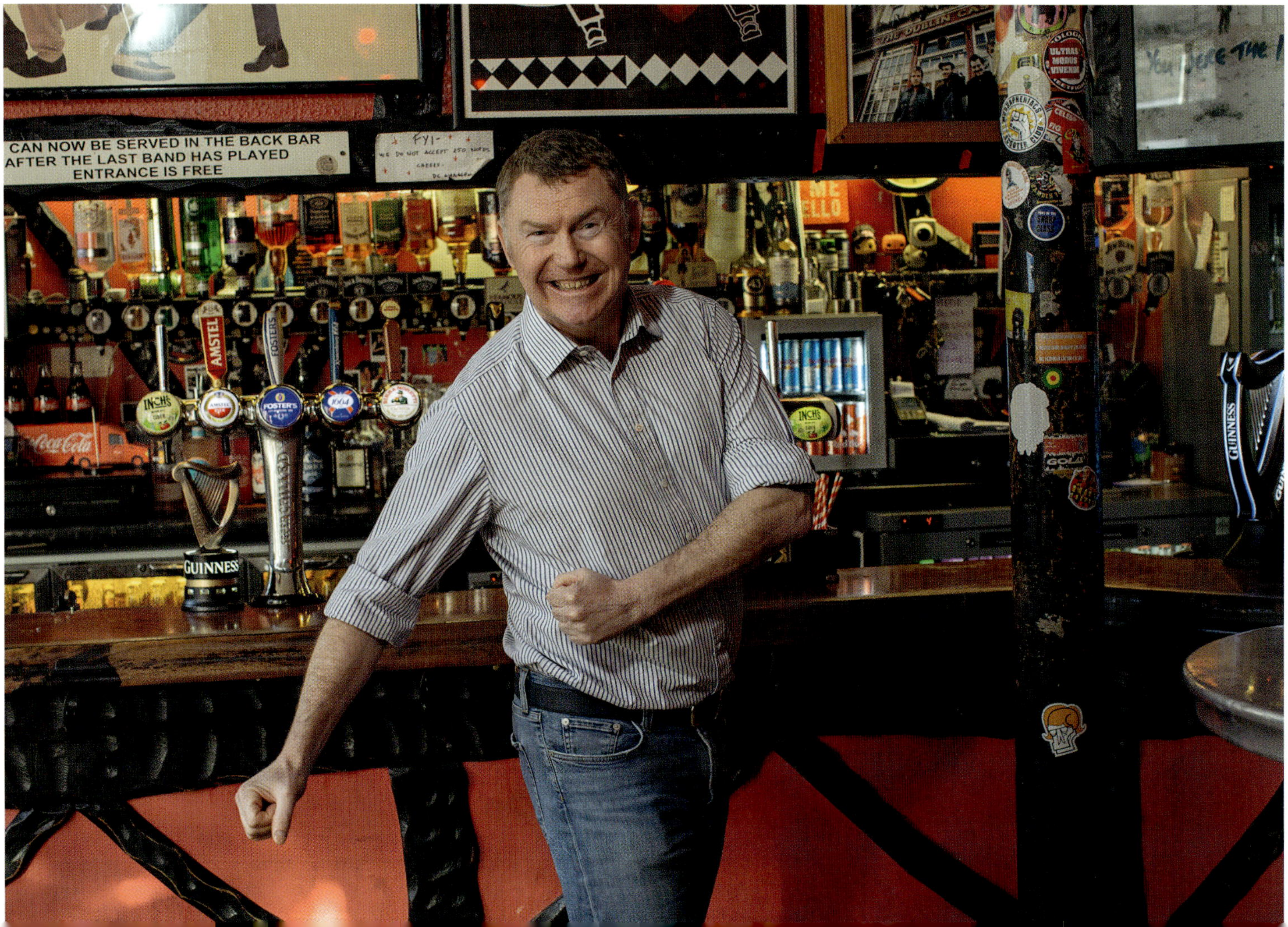
CAN NOW BE SERVED IN THE BACK BAR
AFTER THE LAST BAND HAS PLAYED
ENTRANCE IS FREE
AMSTEL
FOSTER'S
GUINNESS
Coca-Cola

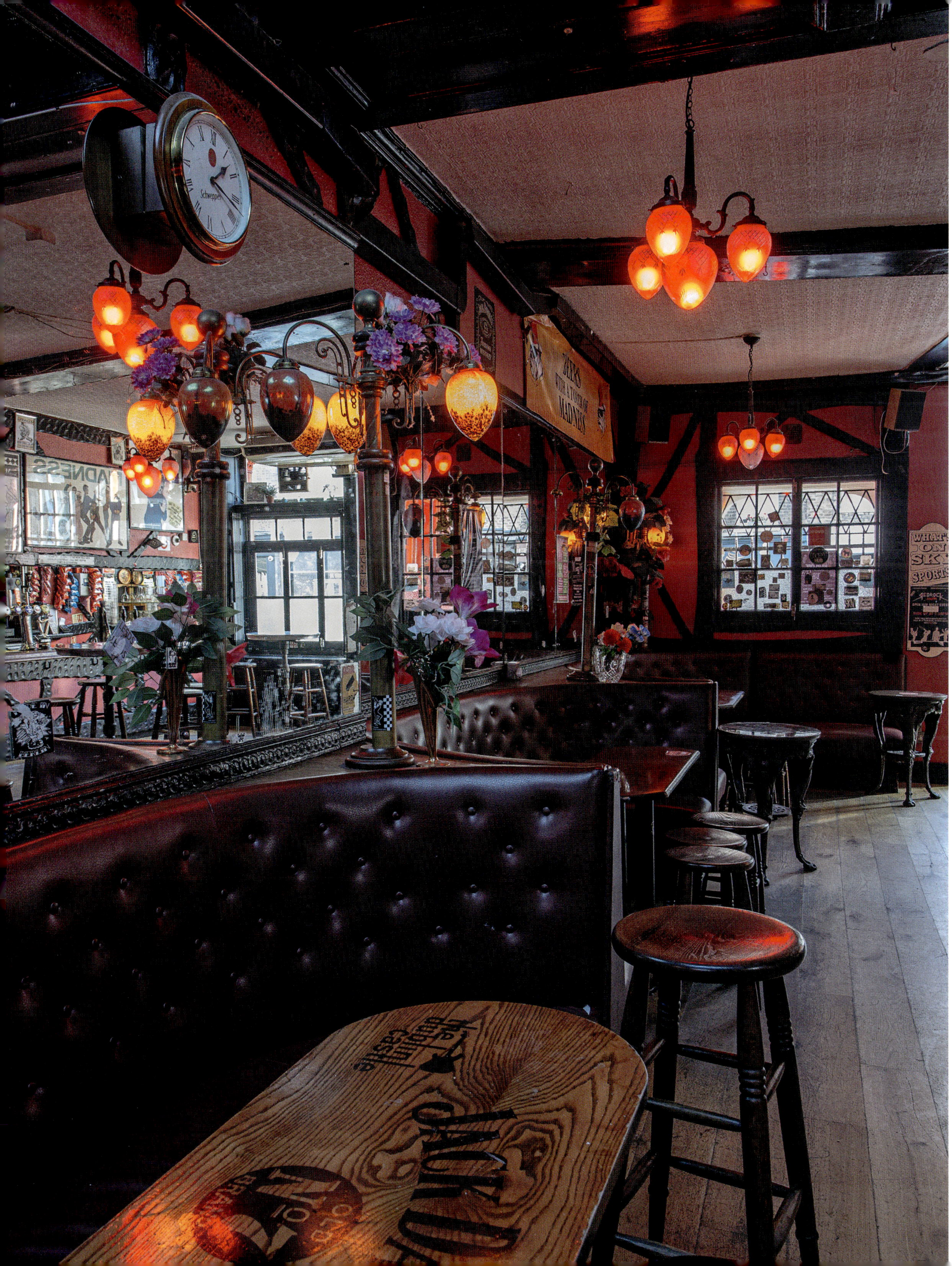

"IT'S STILL A SOCIAL HUB, A SCENE FOR THE KIDS"

THE PALM TREE

127 GROVE RD, BOW, LONDON

Some pubs are great survivors. While change occurs at dizzying speed all around them, they doggedly and defiantly remain true to themselves. There probably isn't a better example in England of this tenacious tendency than The Palm Tree, in London's East End. If you had trained a time-lapse camera on the pub from 1977 to the present day, the footage would show the surrounding streets of Georgian terraces vanishing under wrecking balls to create the Mile End Eco-Park, with the pub left in splendid isolation, facing off against a rising phalanx of cookie-cutter apartment blocks across the Regent's Canal.

Why 1977? That was the year that the pub was taken over by East End couple Val and Alf Barrett, and the place has been pretty much preserved in aspic ever since. Witness the remarkable interior: an oval-shaped wooden bar, dazzling gold wallpaper, a psychedelic carpet, and red velour curtains. The front bar is hung with photos of old-school tuxedoed crooners and thrilled celebrity visitors ("The Palm Tree is a real oasis," writes actor John Hannah, who's pictured, fittingly, on a camel), and the back bar is chock-full of Alf's sporting trophies and boxing memorabilia, including studies of 1970s giants like Henry Cooper and John Conteh. There's a heavyweight cash register (The Palm Tree doesn't take cards, and the unwary are directed to a cash machine at a convenience store about a half-mile away, though a sign does reassure punters that "we now sell spirits in metric sizes"), and the whole pub is perennially bathed in a whisky-warm orange glow. Alf credits Val, who unfortunately passed away a few years ago, with the pub's singular look: "She knew how she wanted it and she took to it like a fish to water," he says. "She was fantastic, a real perfectionist."

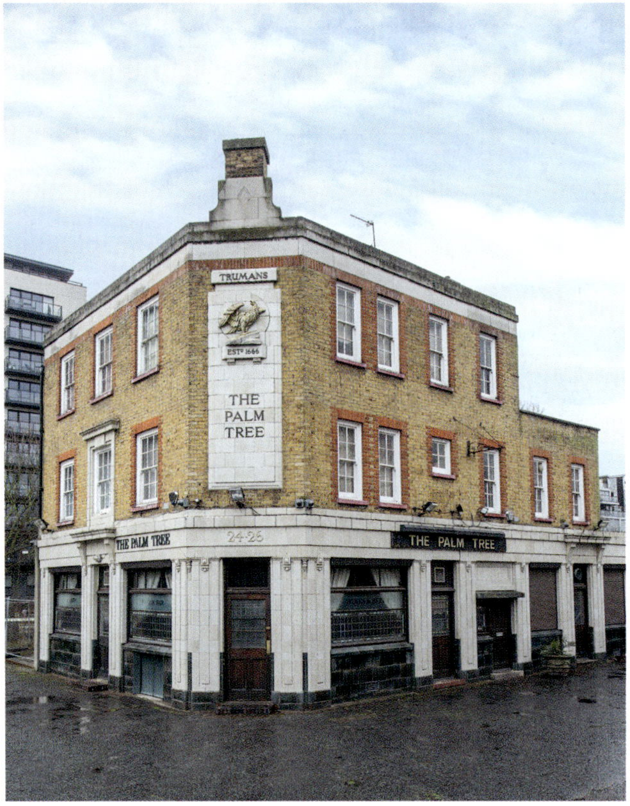

Alf now presides with his daughter Kerrie, and eschews contemporary pub gimmickry – steak nights, quizzes, filament bulbs, that kind of thing – for some well-honed routines (The till? "It went in the canal, but it didn't sink – it's got a float in it." The beer? "It's fresh – it's piped in from the canal"), and anecdotes about fierce East End matriarchs demanding gin and tonics from flustered police rookies who've come to break up lock-ins, and cheeky-chappie market porters trying to offload surplus pig's trotters on the nonplussed clientele ("It wasn't that it was bad – it was offal."). These days, arty Hackney locals and curious tourists cherish the pub's time-capsule quality, while no less than three proprietors of the Queen Vic, the ur-Cockney hostelry in the BBC's long-running soap *EastEnders* – Mike Read, Barbara Windsor and Danny Dyer – have pulled up a stool at Alf's bar, perhaps in order to see how it's done.

As if all that weren't already enough to gain The Palm Tree a prominent spot on UNESCO's intangible cultural heritage preservation list, there's also the weekend jazz sessions that have taken place on its tiny front-bar stage for the past four decades. Impromptu musical gatherings and singalongs were once de rigueur in East End hostelries; today, the likes of Helen, an octogenarian singer who once lived next door to notorious East End gangsters the Kray Twins (Alf: "And they were frightened of her!") and 94-year-old Jack, who used to play piano for Second World War icon Dame Vera Lynn, keep the flame alive with their renditions of Cole Porter and Irving Berlin standards. It's all tinged with bittersweet nostalgia, of course, but, like The Palm Tree itself, it remains spirited and vital. Long may it stand tall.

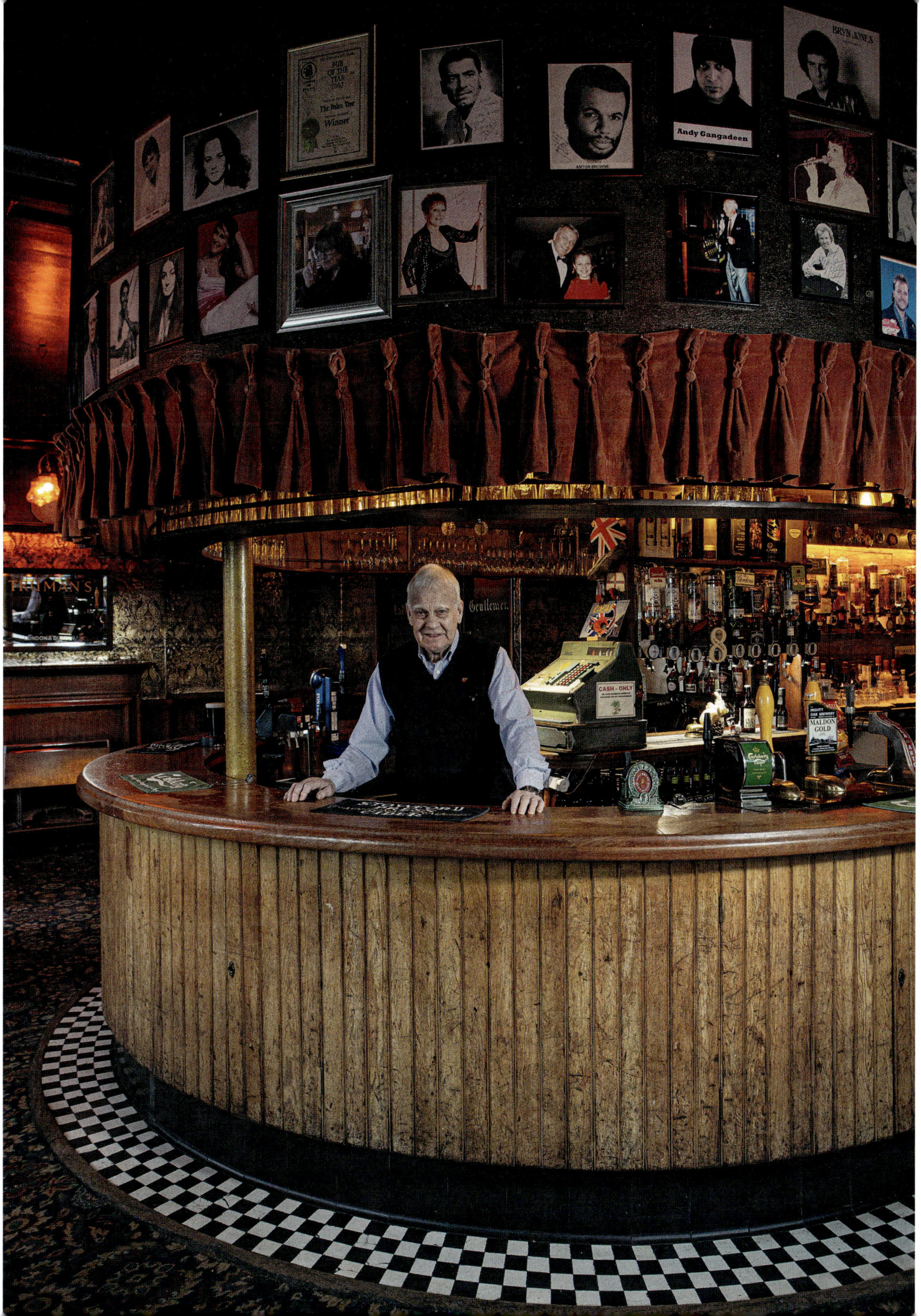

"A REMARKABLE SURVIVOR IN A BLITZED-OUT STREET"

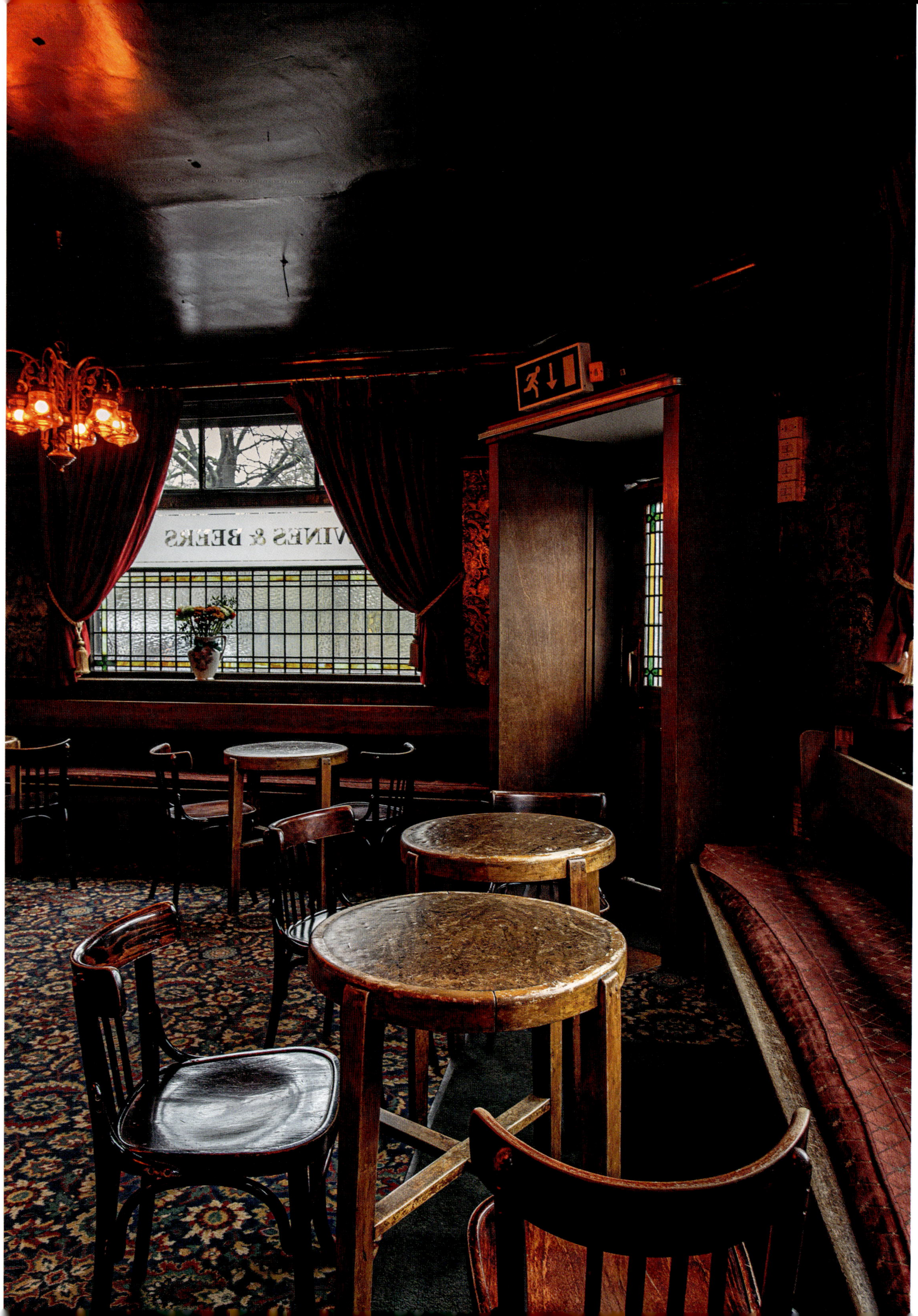

"IT'S LIKE STEPPING BACK IN TIME ..."

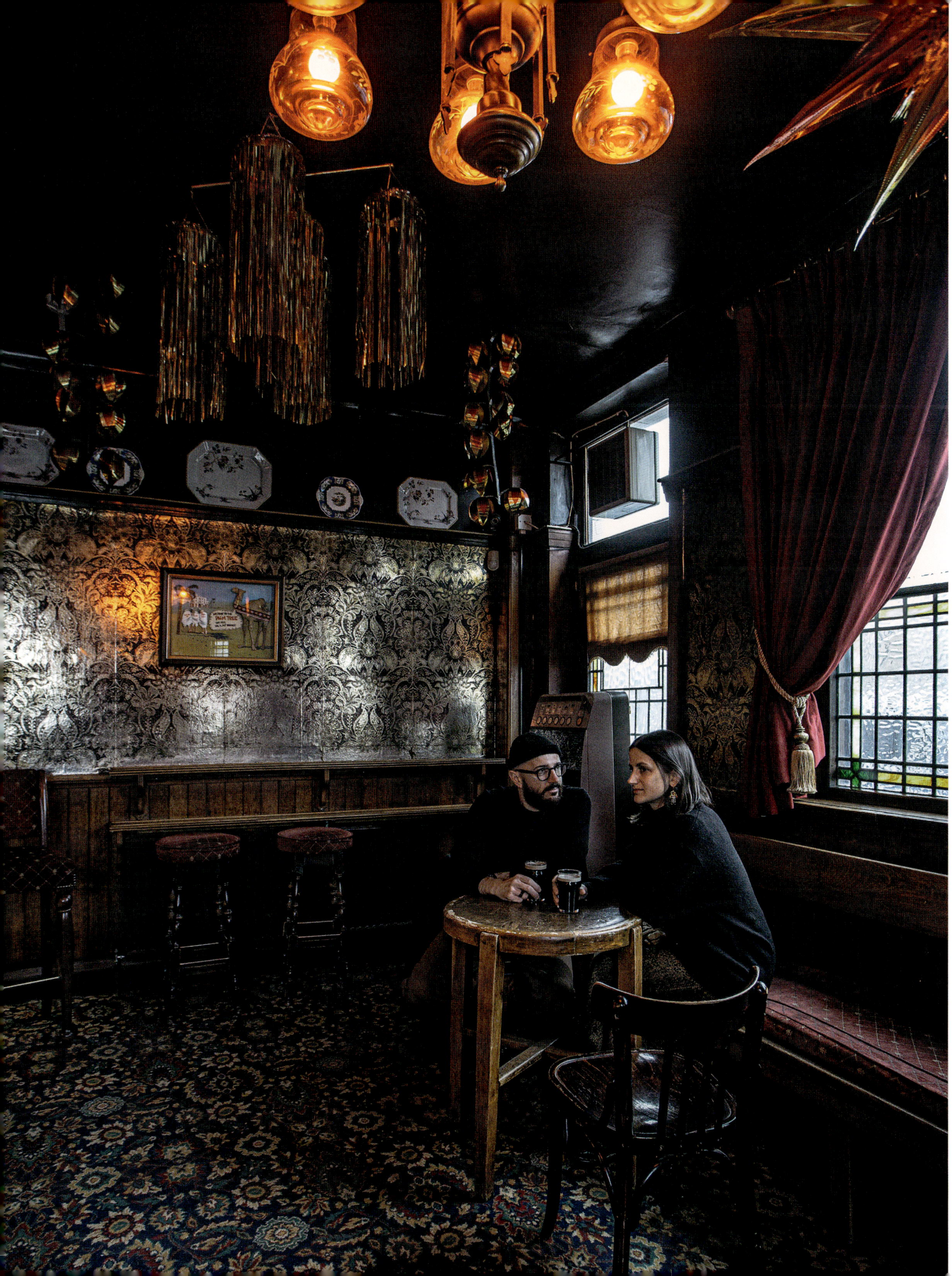

"… IT'S A FLAVOUR OF THE OLD EAST END."

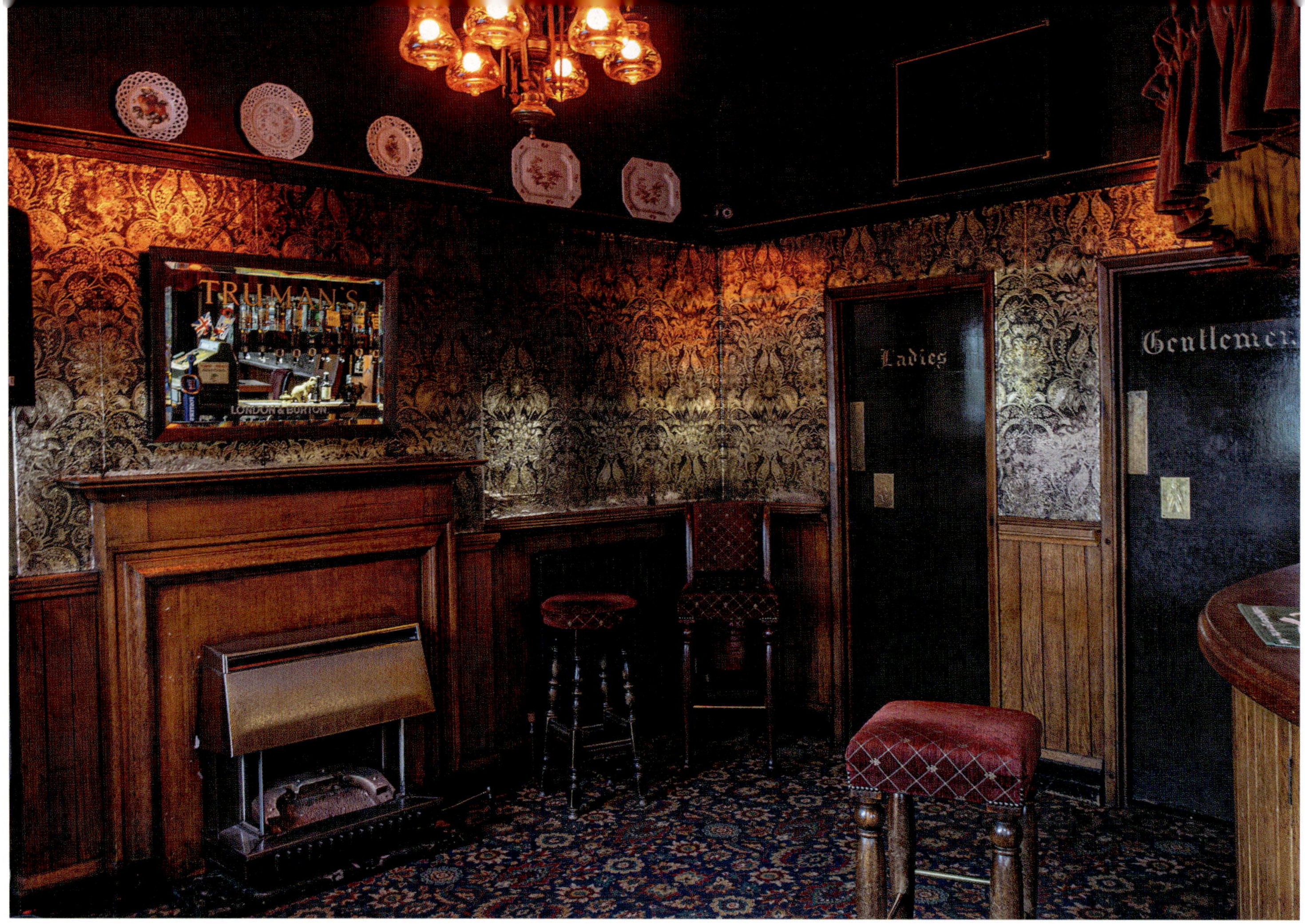
TRUMAN'S
LONDON & BURTON
Ladies
Gentlemen

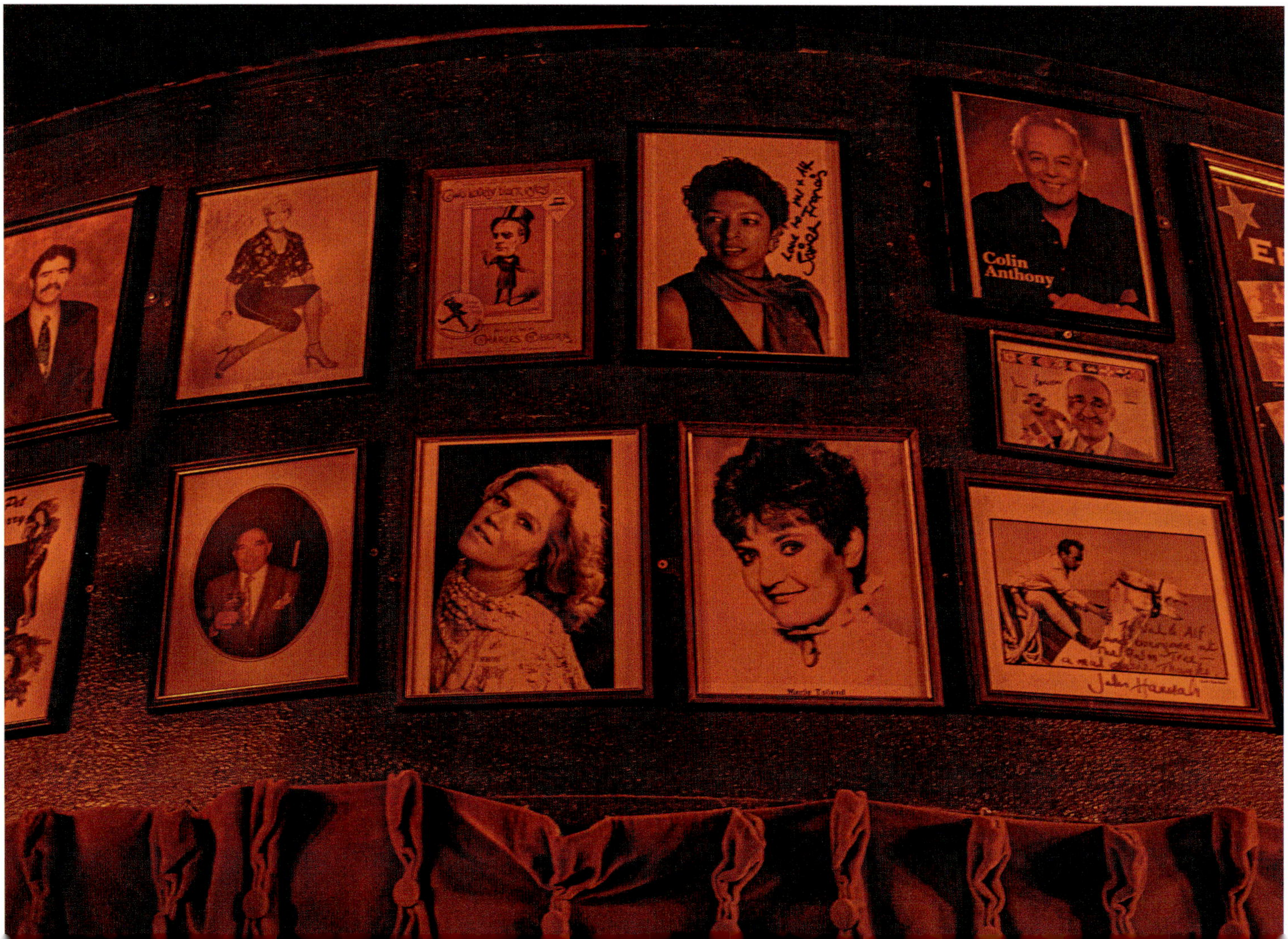
Colin
Anthony

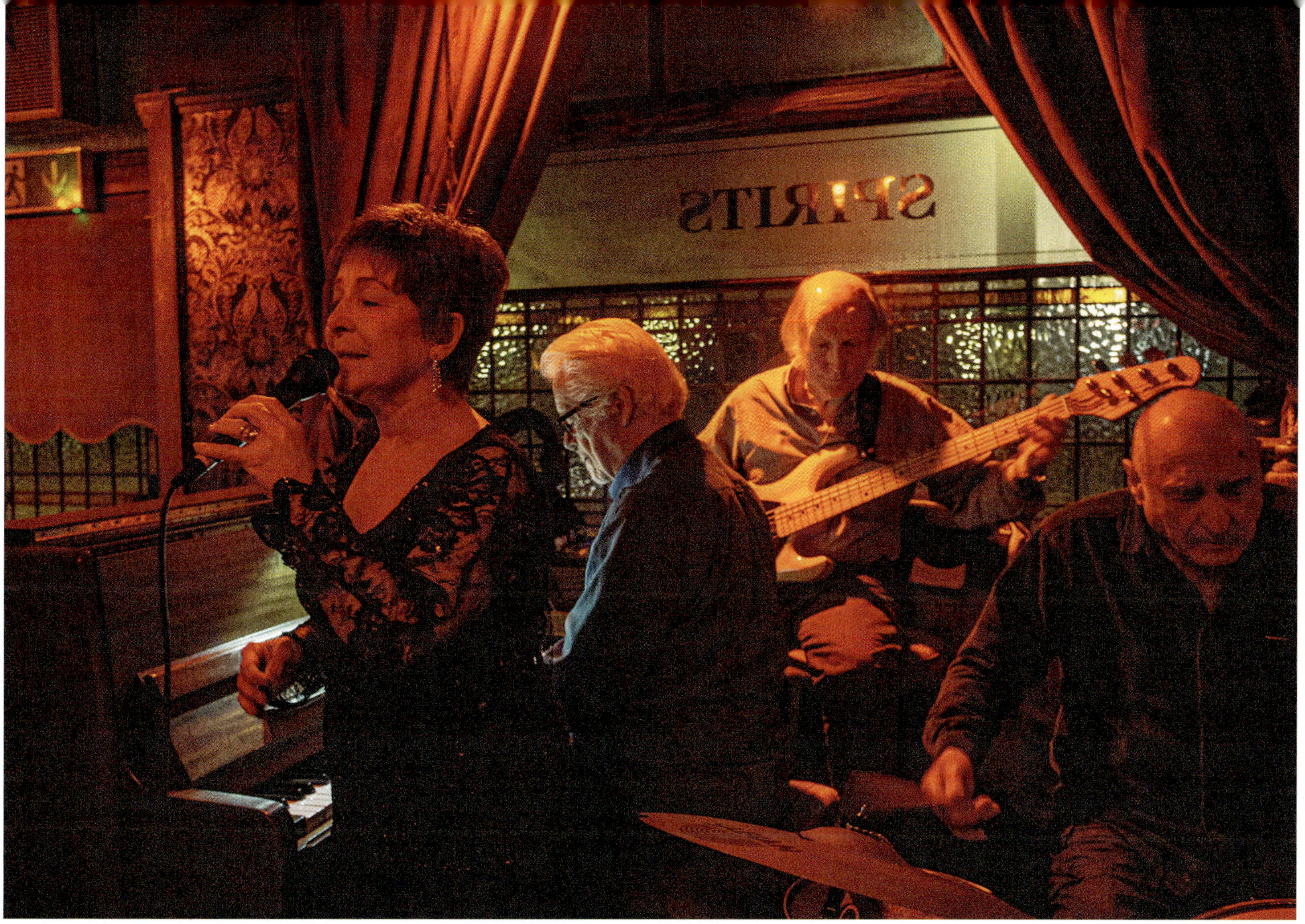

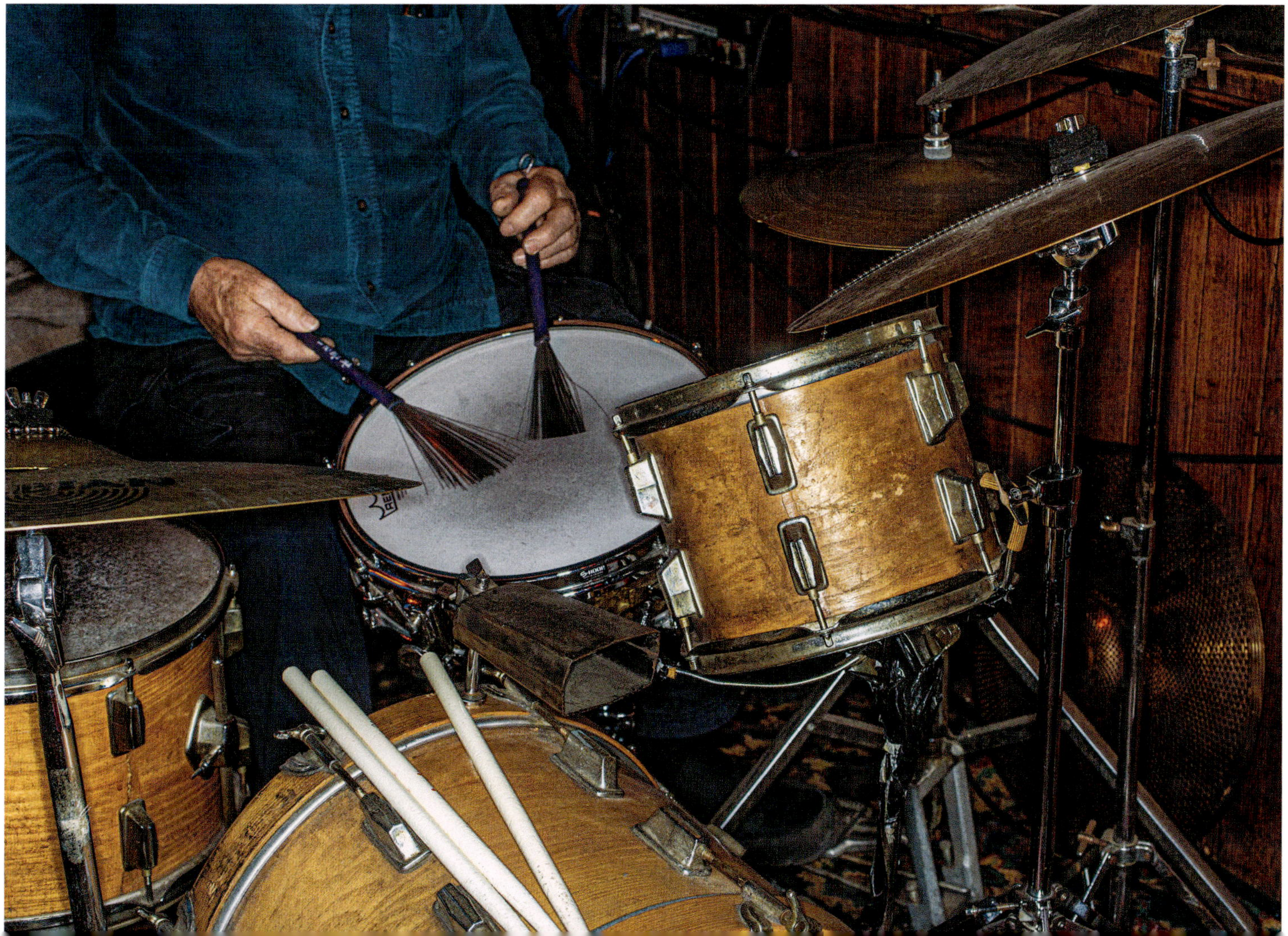

"THE PUBS ROUND HERE WERE ALWAYS FULL OF MUSIC"

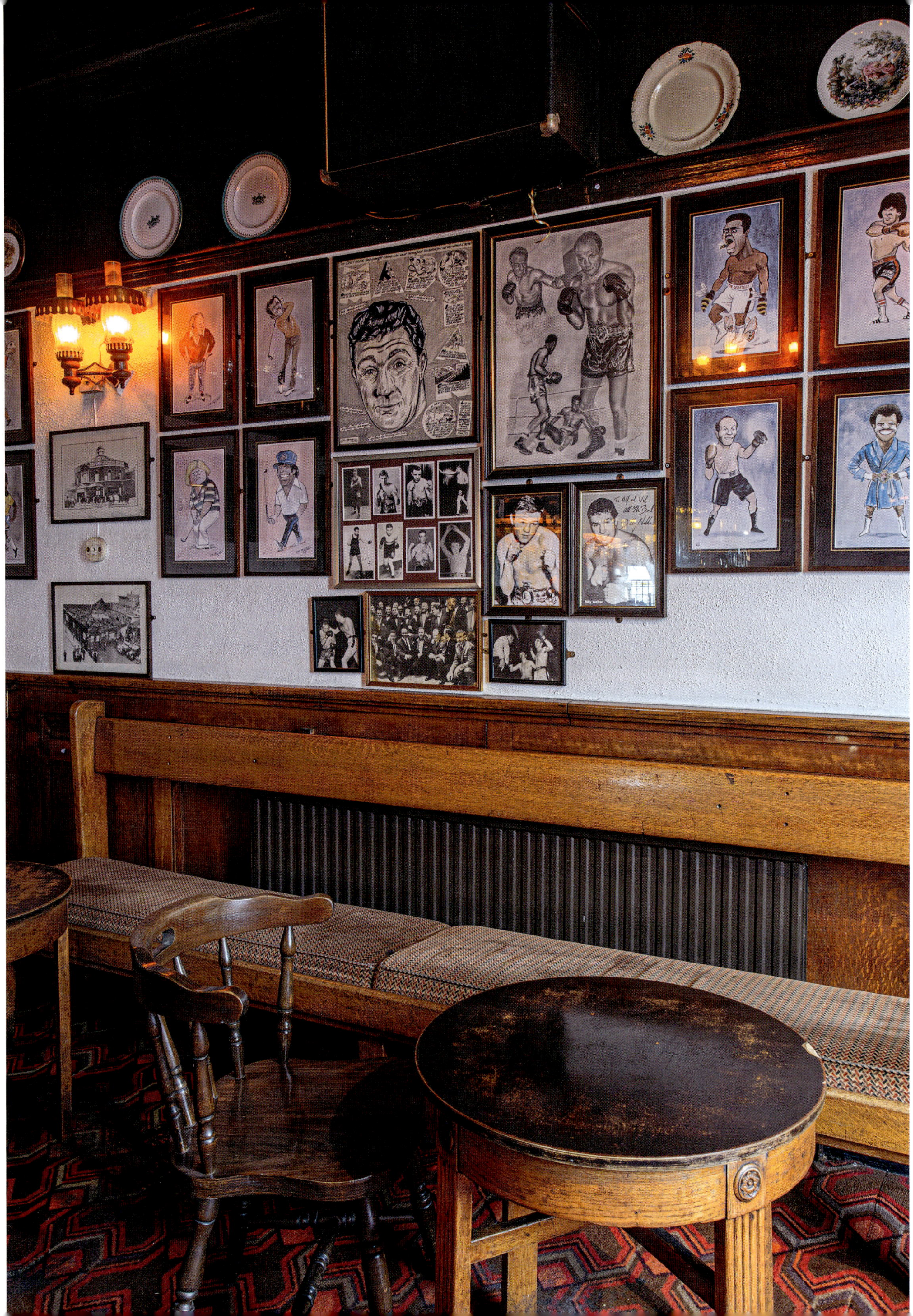

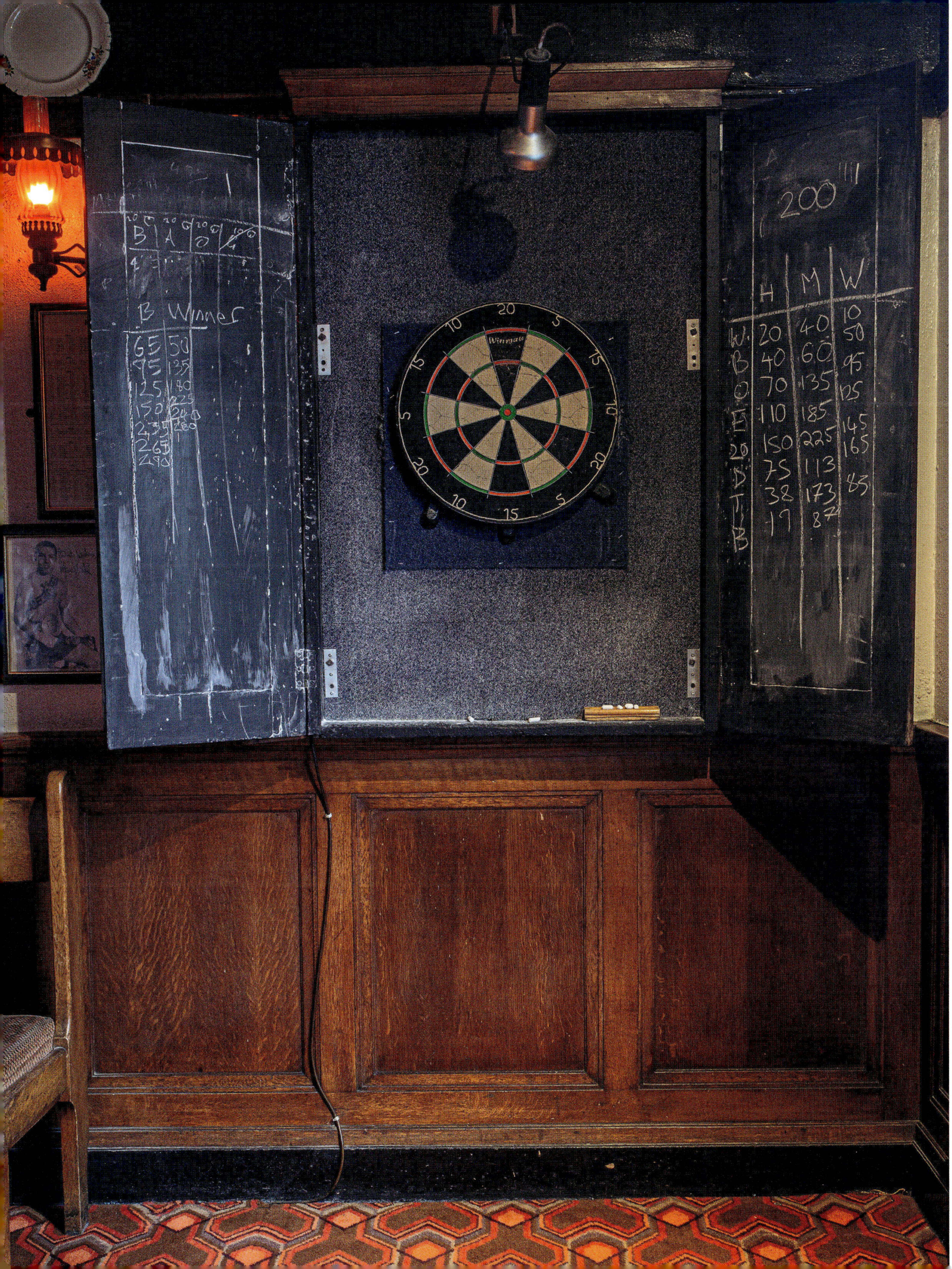

"WE'RE STILL HERE BECAUSE WE'RE THE REAL DEAL"

THE FRENCH HOUSE

49 DEAN ST, LONDON

Just to the left of The French House's creatively cluttered bar, you'll find a drawing of a woman whose Bond girl va-va-voom style is only enhanced by the large python draped around her midriff, next to the scrawled legend: "Between the crisis and the catastrophe, there is always time for a glass of champagne."

The slogan comes courtesy of the late Daniel Farson, the legendary writer, photographer and Soho habitue; and the woman depicted is Lesley Lewis, only the third publican in The French House's 130-year history. The python, alas, is long gone. It dates from Lewis's previous life as a cabaret artiste, but this diverting artwork seems to sum up the unique place that "The French" occupies in the hearts of its legions of regulars. While old Soho watering holes like The Colony Room and The Spice of Life have either shuttered or become shadows of their former selves, The French, with its let's-face-the-music-and-dance ethos, its battered glamour, and its whiff of the burlesque, continues to conjure the rakish, arty-boho air that the area was once a byword for, from the photos of the household gods adorning the walls – Francis Bacon and Lucian Freud of course, but also George Melly, Samuel Beckett, Tommy Cooper and the artist Maggi Hambling, with her trademark ciggie and death-ray glare – to the crush of their contemporary equivalents, fresh from the theatre or the skatepark or the editing suite or the studio. "This place is the centre of the universe," calls out a man cradling a miniature dachshund, as a double G&T is whisked to his table. "Why would you want to be anywhere else?"

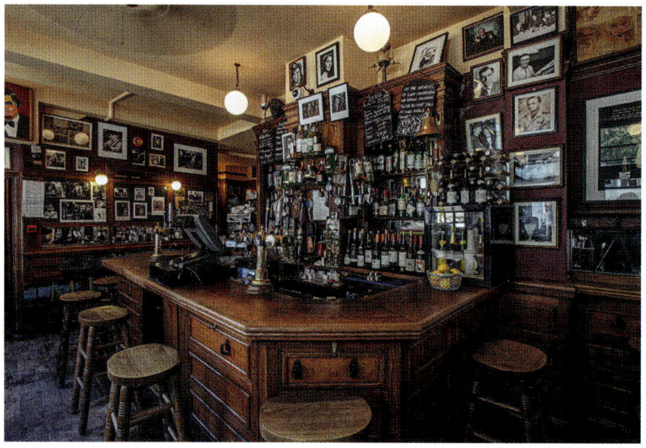

Many have asked themselves the same question, from The French's earliest days, when it was known as the York Minster and run by a Belgian named Victor Berlemont (a brawl in the 1920s between French sailors smashing pint glasses over each other's heads led to a unique house policy of serving only half-pints of beer, while the exiled Charles de Gaulle is said to have written part of his famous 1940 radio speech, rallying his fellow citizens against the Vichy regime, in the upstairs bar), through the 1950s and 1960s when Victor's son Gaston took the reins, armed with a formidable walrus moustache and an increasingly infamous clientele. Brendan Behan would sing and dance for the assembled company when sufficiently lubricated, while Dylan Thomas accidentally left an early manuscript of *Under Milk Wood* under his chair after a night of carousing.

Lewis arrived in 1989, five years after the pub bowed to the inevitable and rechristened itself after its long-standing nickname. Some things have changed – the windows, unopened since the 1960s, now admit the heady Soho air; the first-floor bar became a dining room, currently presided over by Neil Borthwick, a Gordon Ramsay protégé – but The French retains its freewheeling ambience, due in no small part to Lewis herself, who lives upstairs and personally throws open the doors at 12.01 to welcome the eager supplicants hungry for human connection. She can often be found at the bar, chatting with storied regulars like Rose Peter (named for his favourite shade of wine) who travels in every day from distant Walthamstow, or 93-year-old Dotty, a former actress whose favoured tipple is a pint of gin and tonic (accompanied by her refrain "ice to the top darling, ice to the top"), while the floor is run by what one reviewer called "a brigade of fierce, funny women in perpetual motion" who know each regular by name, along with their drink of choice and, perhaps most importantly, exactly when to refill it.

"I look on The French as a sort of village pub, and the staff and regulars as family," says Lewis. "A big city can be a lonely place, so you need somewhere to relax, be yourself and leave the world behind. You know, there are times when you're sat at the bar, having a lovely chat, the afternoon light is streaming in, there's a nice buzz in the room, and you think, oh yes, all is well with the world."

To which the only response is surely: *plus de champagne, s'il vous plait.*

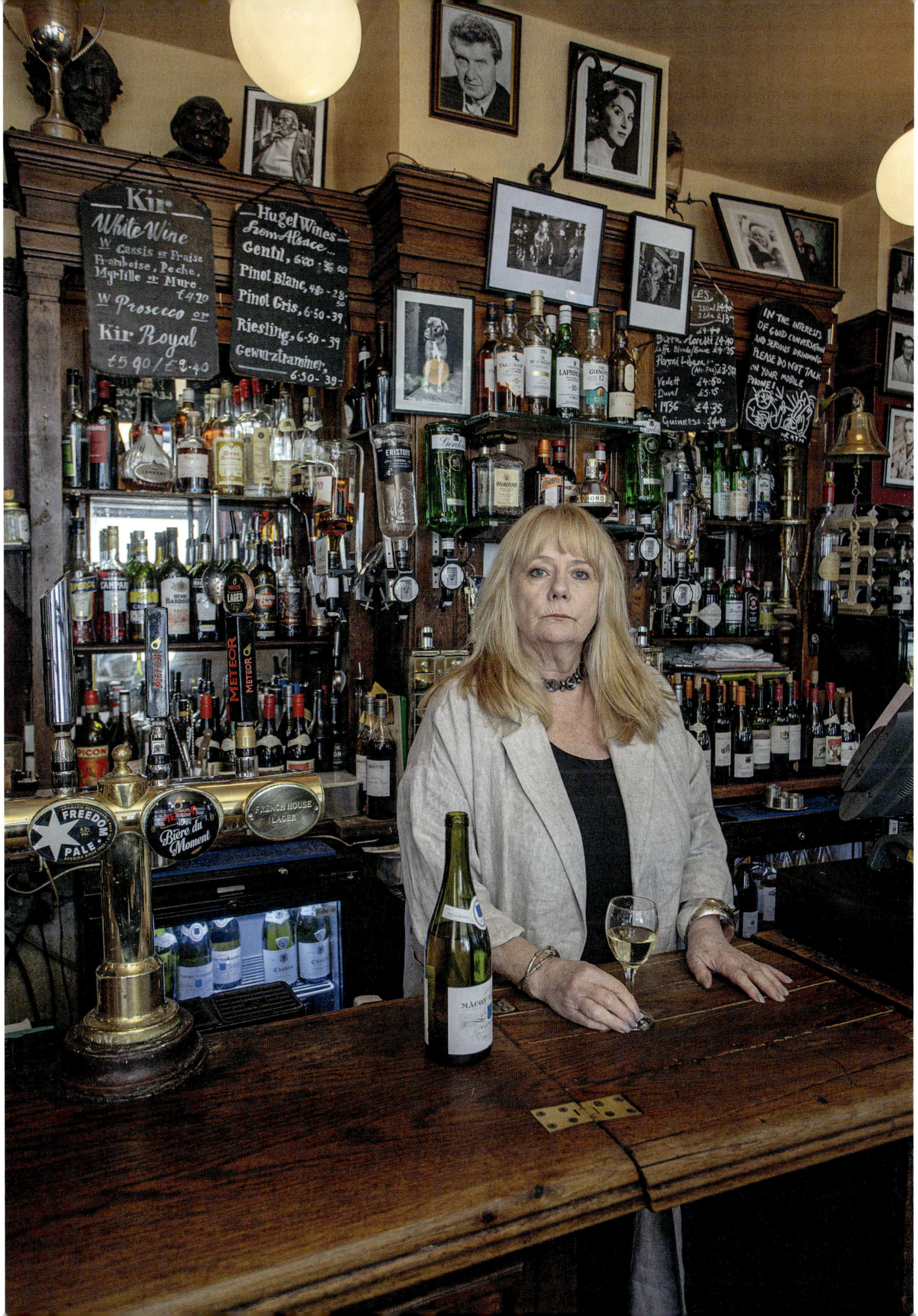

"I'M PART THERAPIST, PART AGONY AUNT, PART HOSTESS"

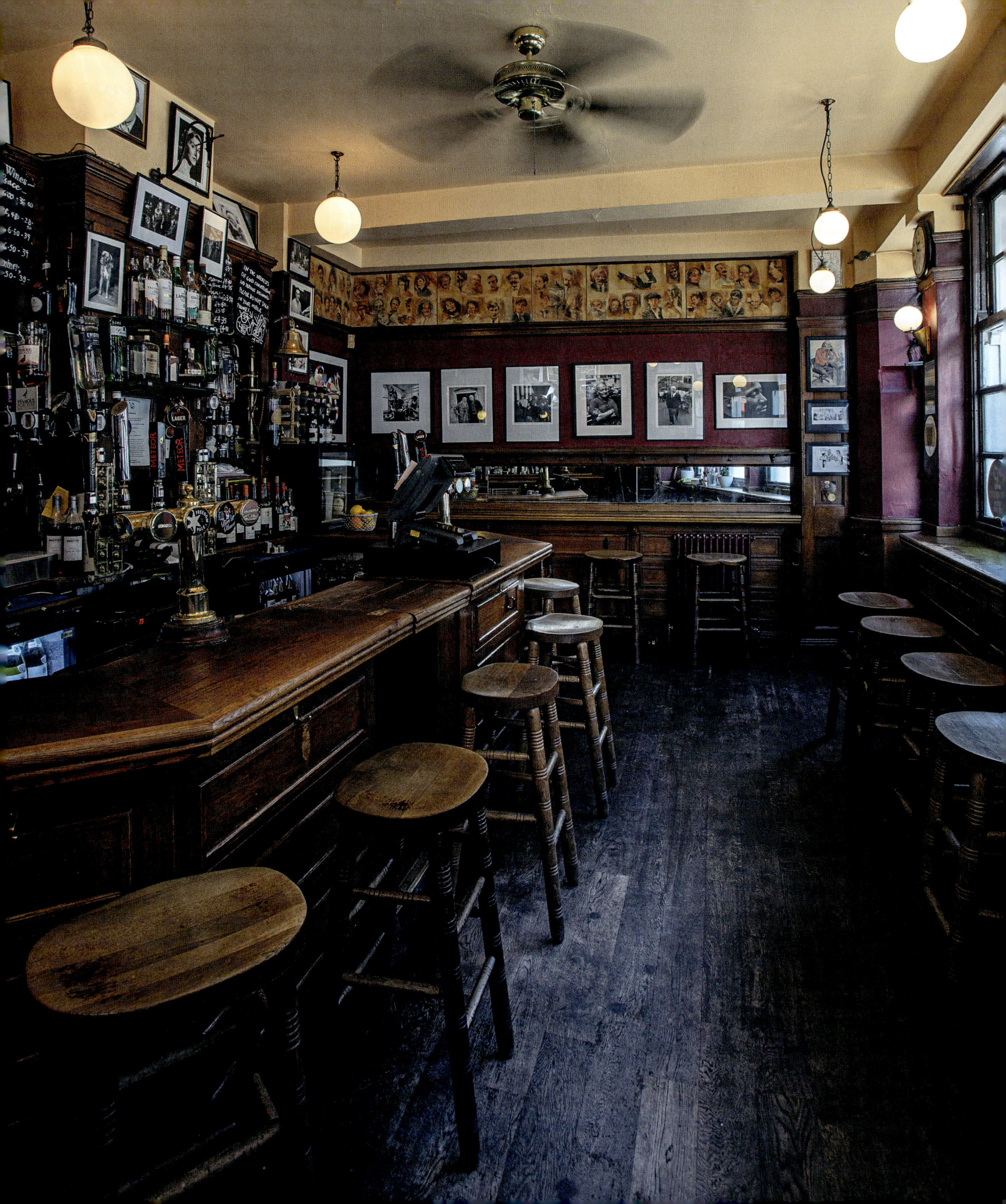
LAGER
METEOR
METEOR

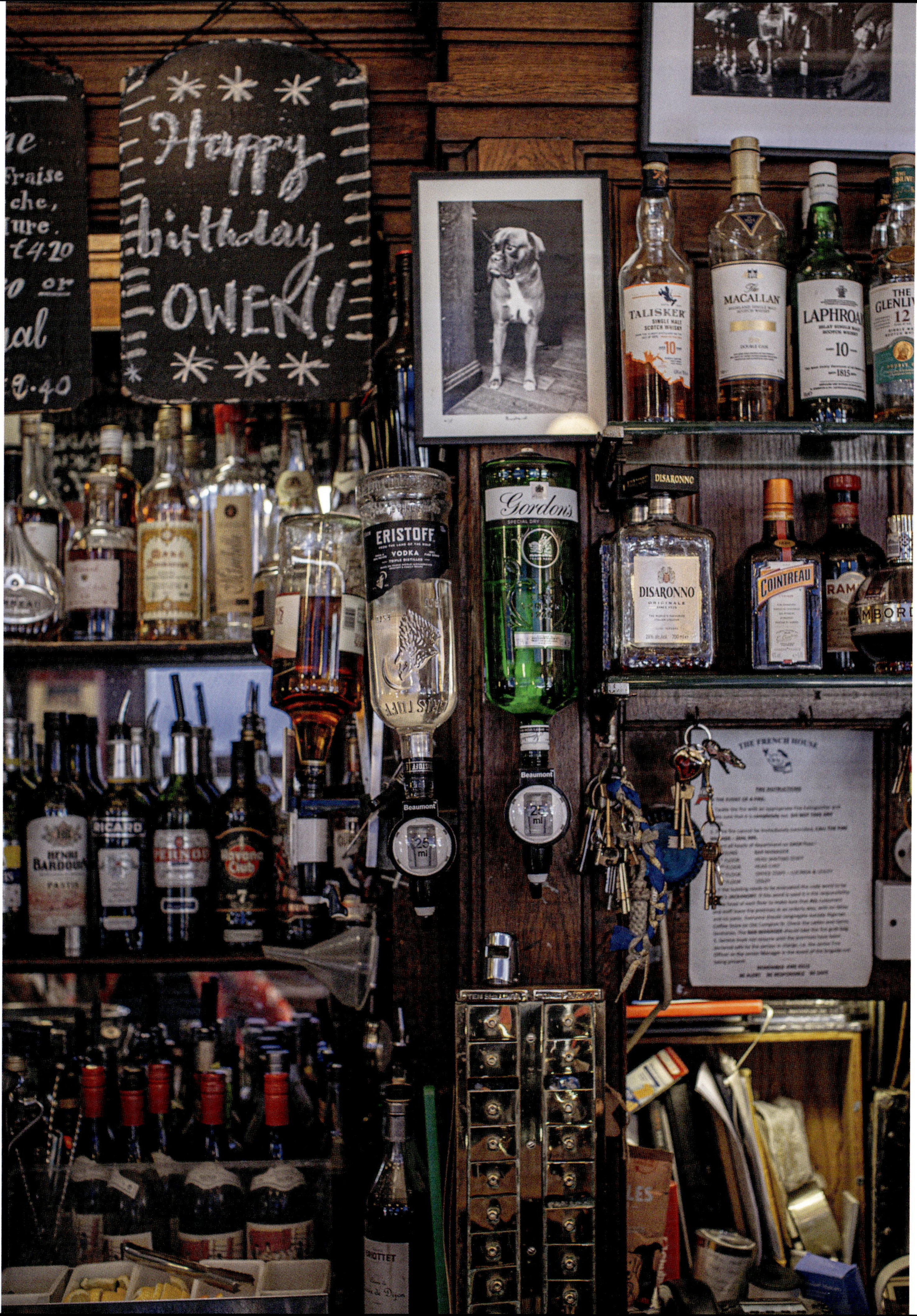

"A SPIRITUAL HOME FOR ARTISTS AND WRITERS"

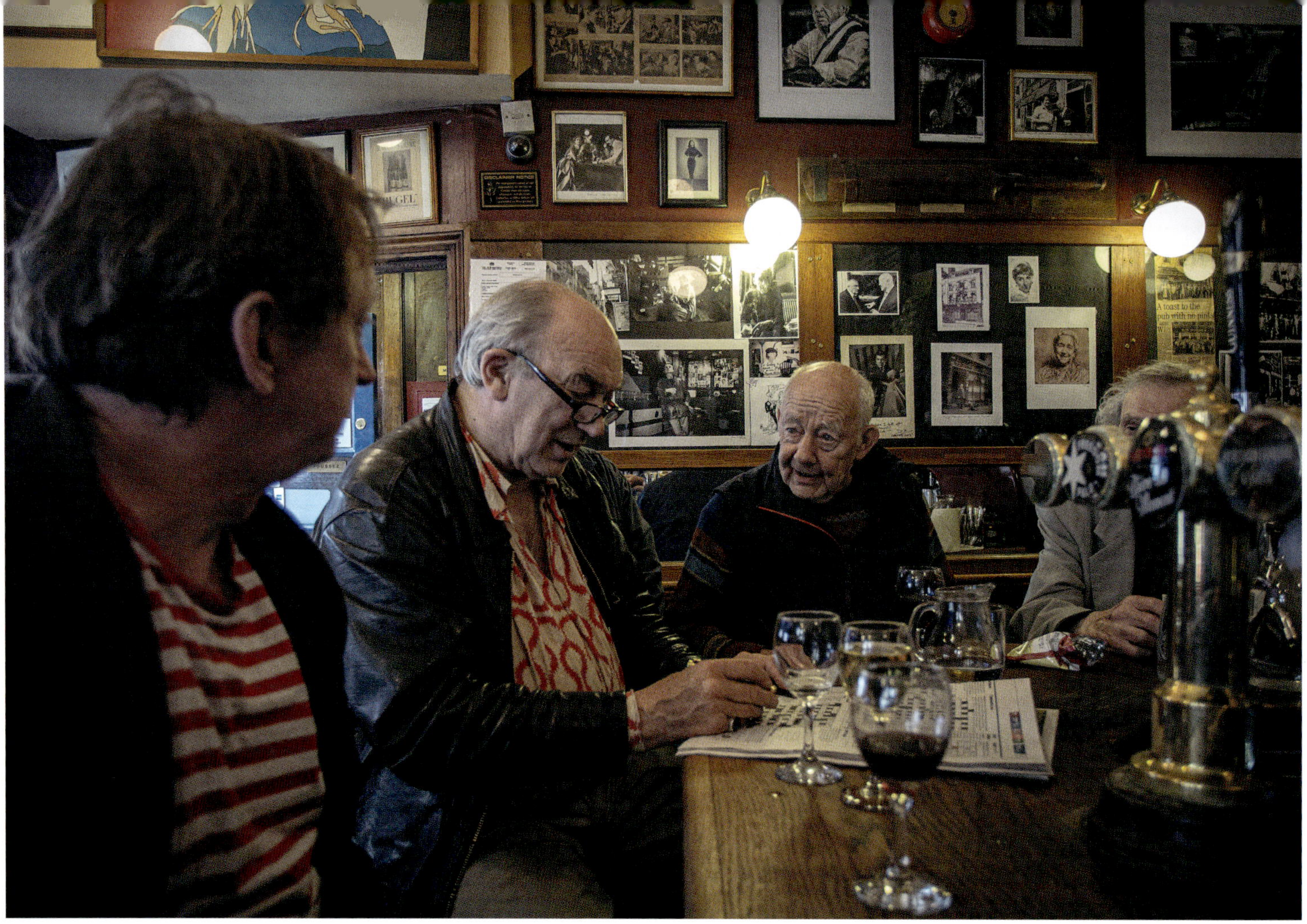

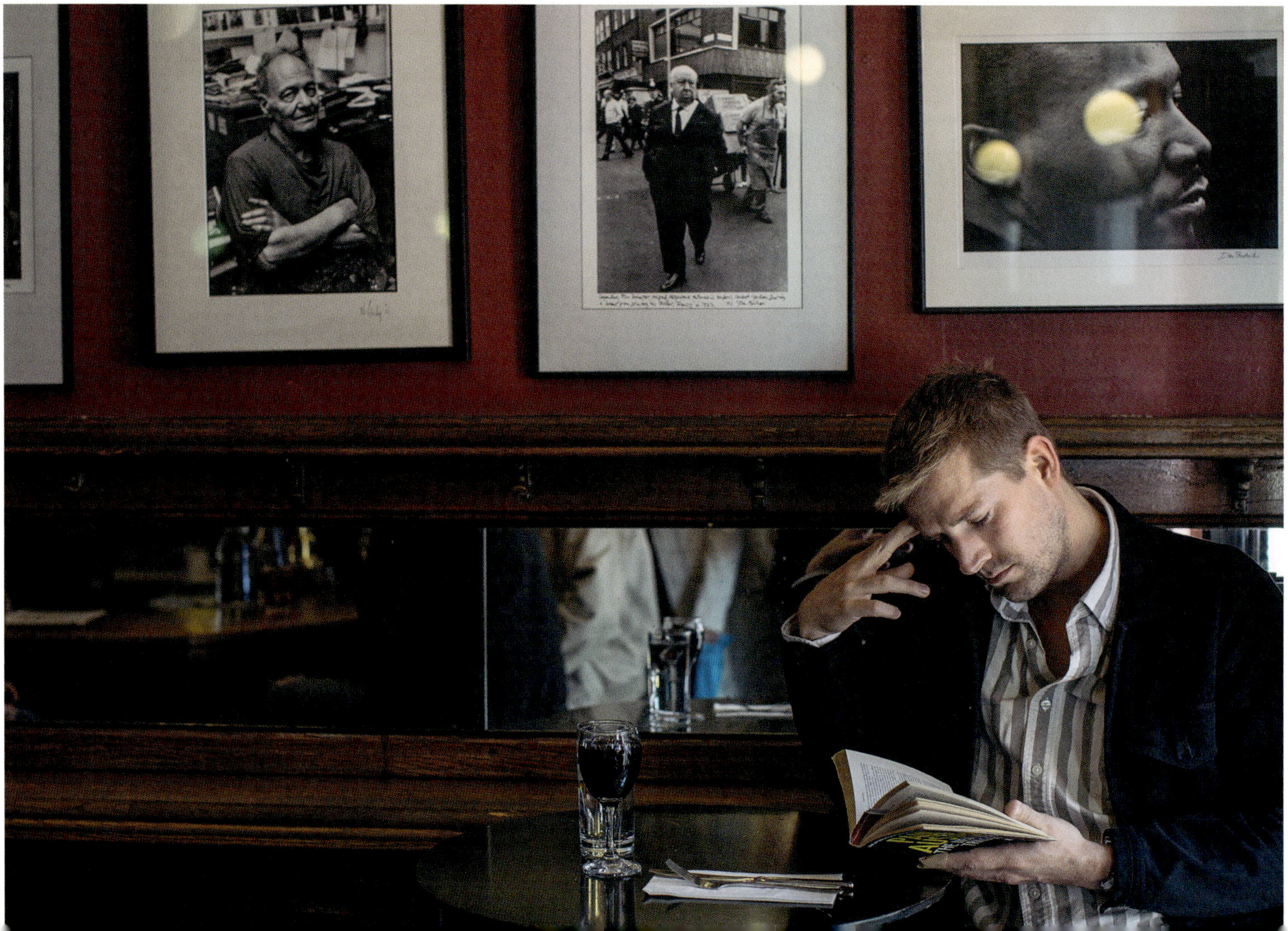

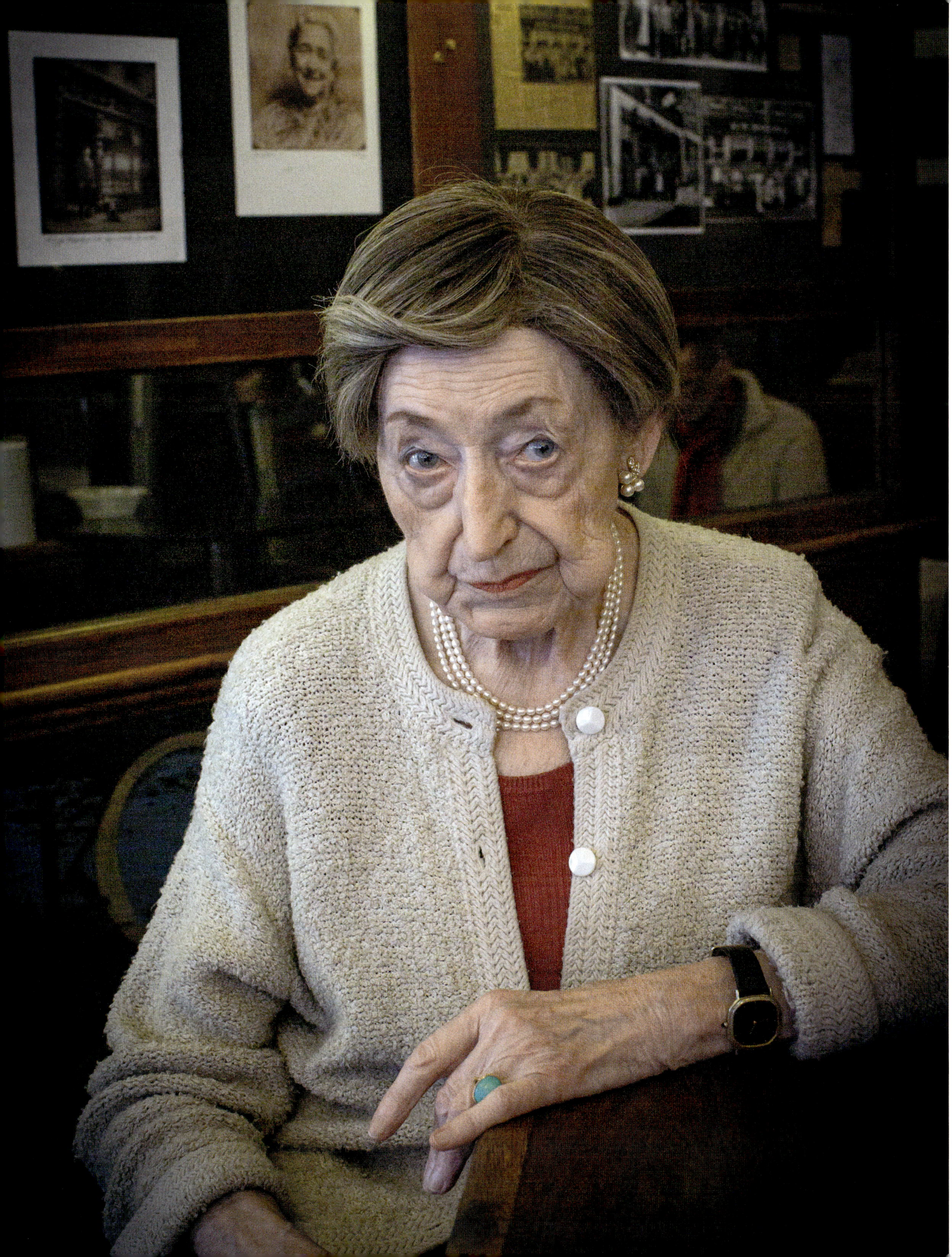

BEAVERTOWN CORNER PIN

732 HIGH RD, LONDON

"I got stuck on the Smog Rocket" isn't a phrase you hear every day, but it's not uncommon in the Corner Pin, the North London pub run by the acclaimed microbrewer Beavertown, where someone will be referencing the fact that their attempted "taster flight" of the brewery's finest, available on draught – the light and zingy Neck Oil, say, or the tropical fruit fizz of Gamma Ray – has hit some turbulence owing to their partiality to a particular tipple, in this case a smoky brew apparently inspired by "industrial old London".

Beavertown has gone from crafty start-up to supermarket staple in a matter of years, and the Corner Pin, directly opposite the Spurs stadium in Tottenham and opened in 2021, is their first bricks-and-mortar boozer. It's an area they've already put their stamp on – the brewery is nearby, in a 29,000-square-foot former light-bulb factory, and they have a taproom within White Hart Lane – and, even in the shadow of the mothership-like stadium, it's hard to miss the Corner Pin, decked out as it is in Beavertown's primary-coloured cartoon livery; a distinctive branding that Nick Dwyer, Beavertown's creative director, has said is "built on skeletons, skulls and weird shit exploding". "It always gets a reaction," says Ashley Crane, assistant manager at the Corner Pin. "Some people think we're a sweetshop, some people think we're the Nickelodeon Channel."

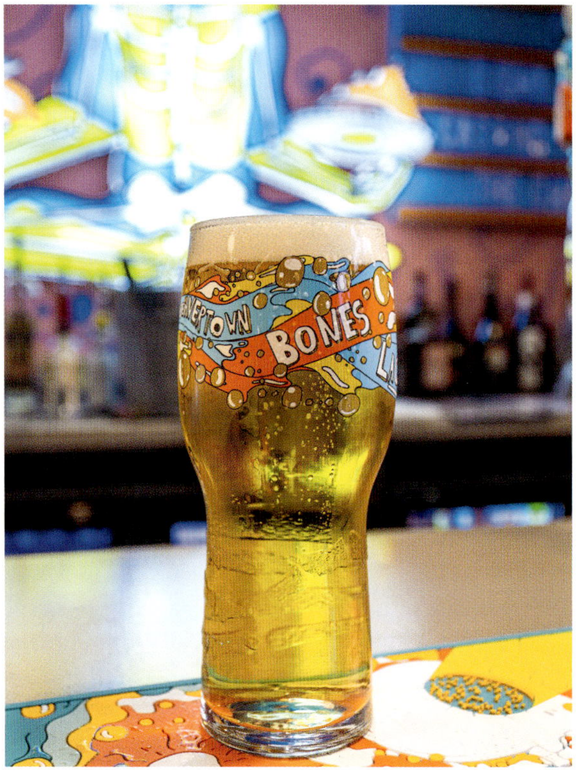

Inside, there are hints of the traditional tavern that's stood on the site since the 1970s – half-panelled walls, mini-strip wall lights – which have been incorporated into Beavertown's psychedelic-steampunk scheme; the lights illuminate fevered renderings of erupting volcanoes and *Mars Attacks*-style aliens wielding ray guns, while the walls are papered in a skull-and-bones pattern which gets so many approbatory comments that it may yet end up on the growing list of Beavertown merch. There are groovily retro arcade machines – a Pac-Man and an Avengers pinball – and modern flourishes such as cycle parking (in the expansive beer garden, with its own bar, at the rear). There's also a food menu, designed to complement the beer's tasting notes, which includes firecracker hot wings, a Nitro stout-battered fish and chips, and a dry-aged burger with all the oozy trimmings. "We want this to be a place where people can hang out," says Crane.

On a chilled weekday afternoon, there are a bunch of people doing just that, from curious Spurs tourists who've just had their photos taken with a cut-out Harry Kane or Emerson Royal to intrepid hipsters congratulating themselves on making the leap from Bethnal Green, a full nine stops down the Overground line. There's an affable buzz as people sip from their Beavertown-branded glasses and Tottenham denizens amble by on the High Road. However, Crane and his team are quick to point out the stark contrast between days like today and match days, when two of the greatest English obsessions – football and beer – come together, in the manner of one of the Corner Pin's erupting volcanoes. The roads are closed off, mounted police are patrolling, the air crackles with the surging emotions of 63,000 fans, and the Corner Pin is mobbed, with punters spilling out onto the pavement and the staff entering a kind of pump-action fugue state. It's then that, according to one of the Corner Pin's regulars, a perfect symbiosis between product and consumer can be achieved: "The beer gets you going," he says. "I only need to have a couple of pints and it feels like my lungs are drunk." Smog Rocket snafus aside, there could be no higher praise for the state of ferment that Beavertown's finest can engender.

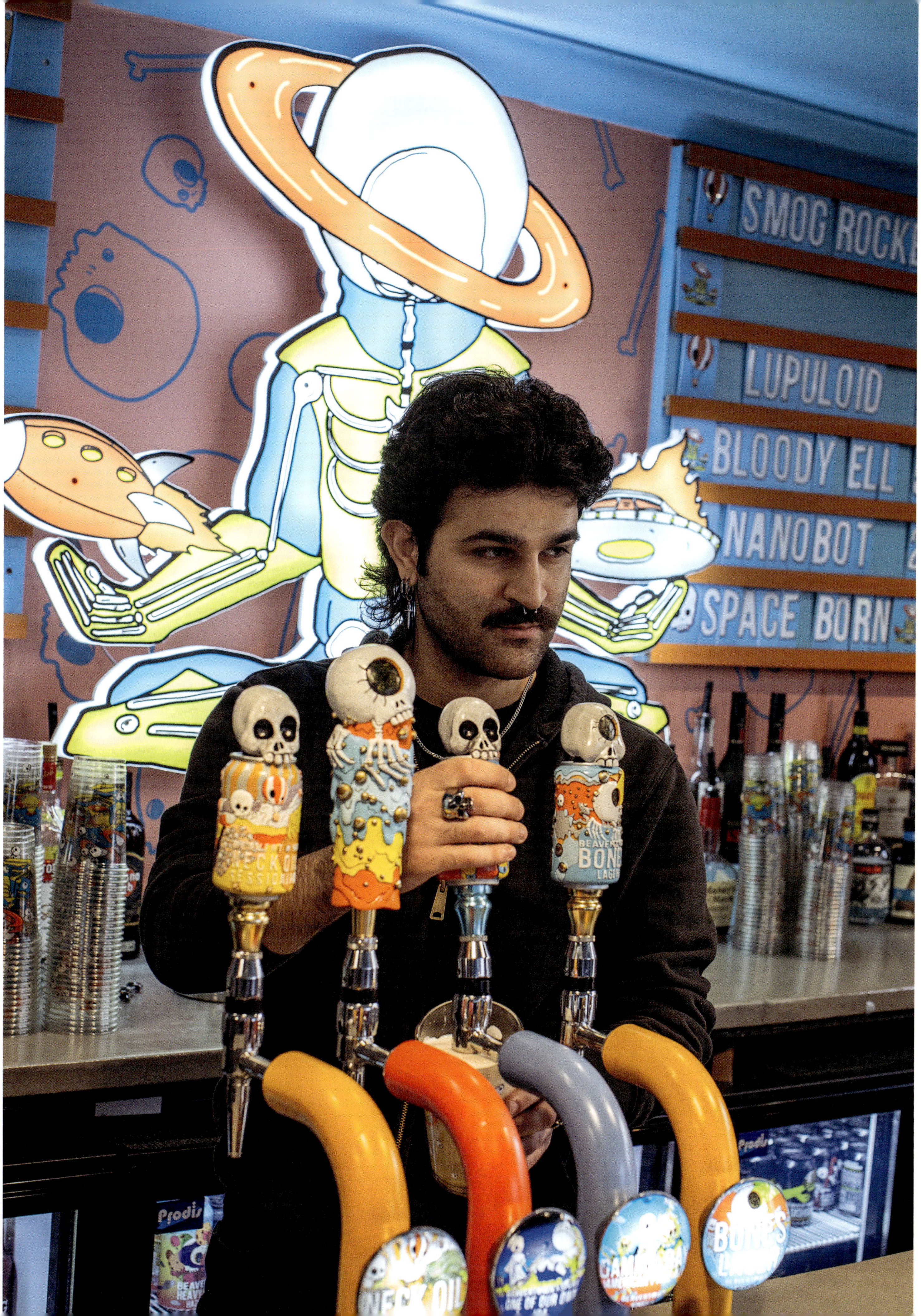

"SOME PEOPLE THINK WE'RE A SWEETSHOP"

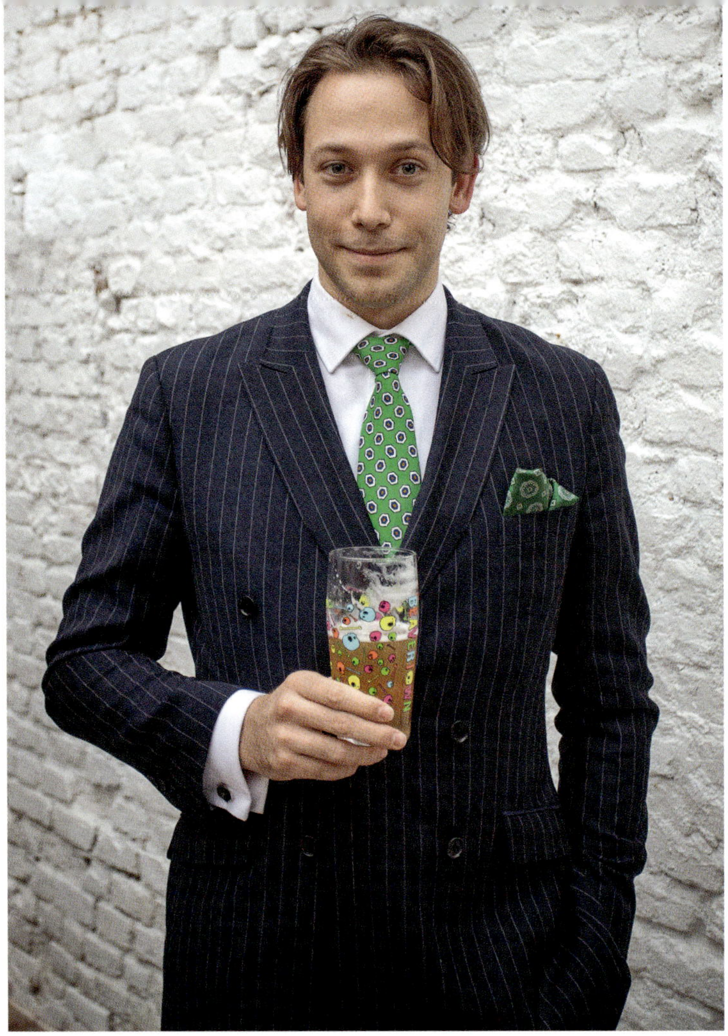

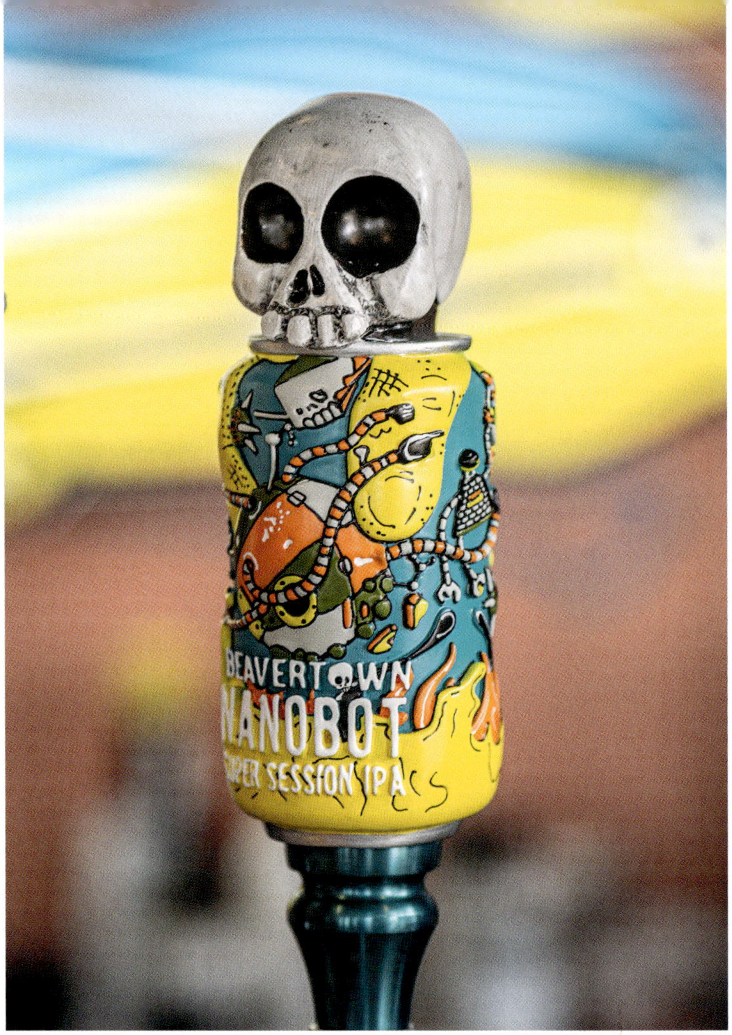
BEAVERTOWN
NANOBOT
SESSION IPA

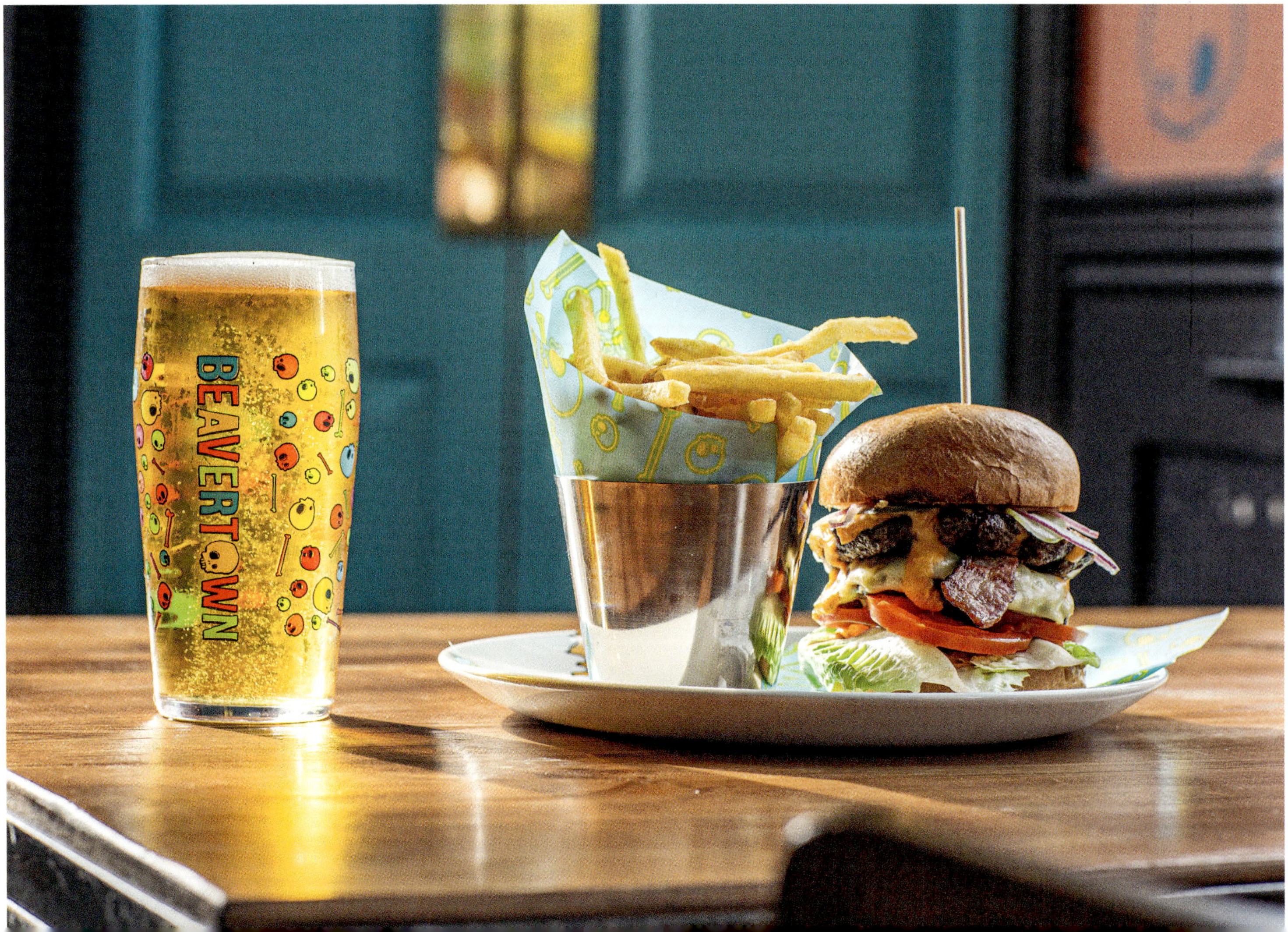
BEAVERTOWN

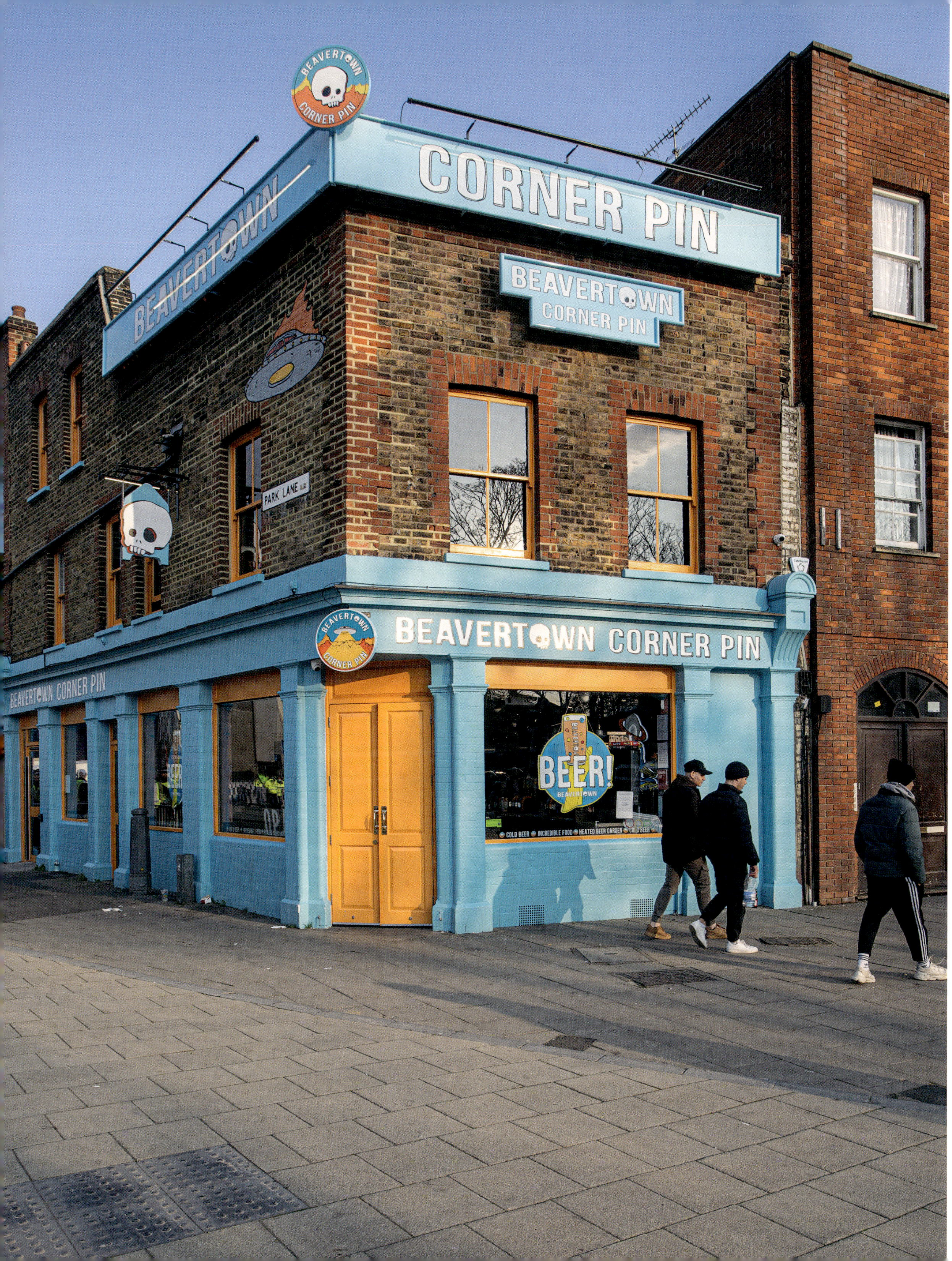

PRIMARY-COLOURED CARTOON LIVERY

ROYAL VAUXHALL TAVERN

372 KENNINGTON LN, LONDON

You wouldn't expect to find the gateway to Nirvana clinging to the edge of a major roundabout in South London; but then, the Royal Vauxhall Tavern has spent over 150 years upholding two joyous and imperishable British pub traditions – music hall and drag. Built on the site of the original Vauxhall Pleasure Gardens – a place, as its name suggests, where Londoners came to indulge their drunken, and maybe even somewhat debauched, fancies – the RVT is a beloved cross-dressing cabaret institution, and the UK's first building to be listed in recognition of its importance to LGBTQI+ community history. Drag legends like "blonde bombsite" Lily Savage (the alter ego of Paul O'Grady, who went on to present prime-time British TV shows) got their start here; and the rumour that Diana, Princess of Wales, once snuck in dressed as a man in the company of Freddie Mercury, has only grown stronger over the years, despite – or perhaps because of – the persistent denials. On an otherwise fairly prosaic Monday night, motorists might be momentarily distracted by the sight of, say, a man in a dress-and-hat ensemble designed to look like a crumpled-up Ferrero Rocher box, sipping a cocktail in the pub's outdoor overspill area; but this is simply the RVT staging a drag competition to find the stars of tomorrow – in other words, doing its time-honoured sequinned-and-lip-syncing thing.

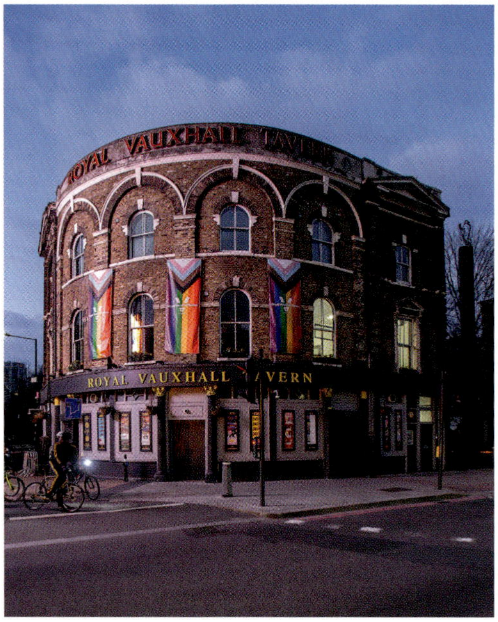

"When you enter the Royal Vauxhall Tavern, it brings to mind the inner workings of a carousel," wrote the comedian Elf Lyons, in a tribute on the Londonist website: "High beams, red and gold interior, decorated with the bright dancing movements of the disco lights above and the oscillating gaggle of the great and the good in sweaty gay abandon below." The kidney-shaped bar, compact and bijou, is perennially packed, though, as Lyons says, "'packed' suggests discomfort, while even at the busiest of times, you only ever feel cuddled at the RVT." The contestants – including Shar Cooterie, in the Ferrero Rocher rig, and Wet Mess, whose takedown of alpha masculinity involves sporting a Formula 1 jumpsuit and stuffed utility belt and lip-syncing to Jeremy Clarkson voiceovers – perform on the tiny apron stage, under the watchful eye of the evening's host, Me the Drag Queen (who kicks things off with a sync-perfect rendering of 'As If We Never Said Goodbye', Norma Desmond's big number from the *Sunset Boulevard* musical) and a panel of judges offering both practical advice ("I would have quite liked a butt-packer"), and sisterly bigging-up ("You give such great lip"). The whooping, hollering audience, meanwhile, have come as various glammed-up versions of their best selves, whether that's 1980s New Romantics, 1940s screen sirens, or moustachioed harlequins. "To me, this is a sacred space," says Mona, a fine art student who, like the rest of her cohort, has donned bunny ears for the occasion (leopard-skin, in her case). "So much of London is commodified and commercial. This is a space for the new, the daring, and the subversive. It's still got that punk attitude, which is so important."

Many tonight also stress the importance of the RVT's continuing survival in the face of so many of London's dedicated LGBTQI+ pubs closing down – victims both of London's spiralling property values and the migration of much of queer life to the internet – and of the gentrification of Vauxhall itself. The building was sold to property developers in 2014, but the community campaign group RVT Future was formed to defend its continued use as a site of LGBTQI+ community and culture – something its Grade II listing will help with. "This place has always welcomed the different and the defiant with open arms," says Son of a Tutu, a British-Nigerian drag queen and one of the evening's judges. "It would be unthinkable not to have it here." Sentiments later echoed by Me the Drag Queen, after a tearful Wet Mess is crowned the contest's winner, and the last of the panstick is coming off: "This place has so much heritage, but it's still got some edge. And that's why we love it."

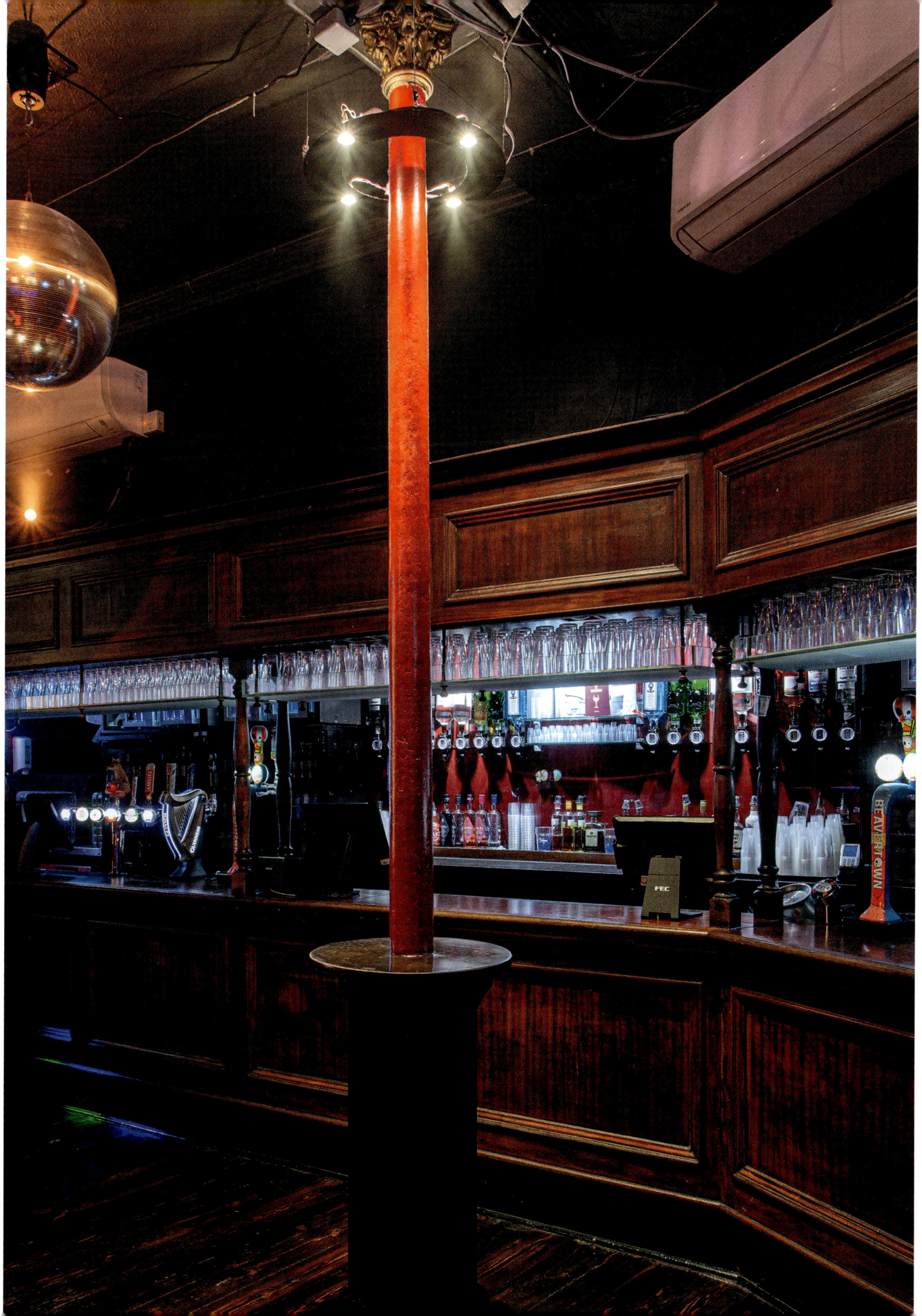

"THE INNER WORKINGS OF A CAROUSEL"

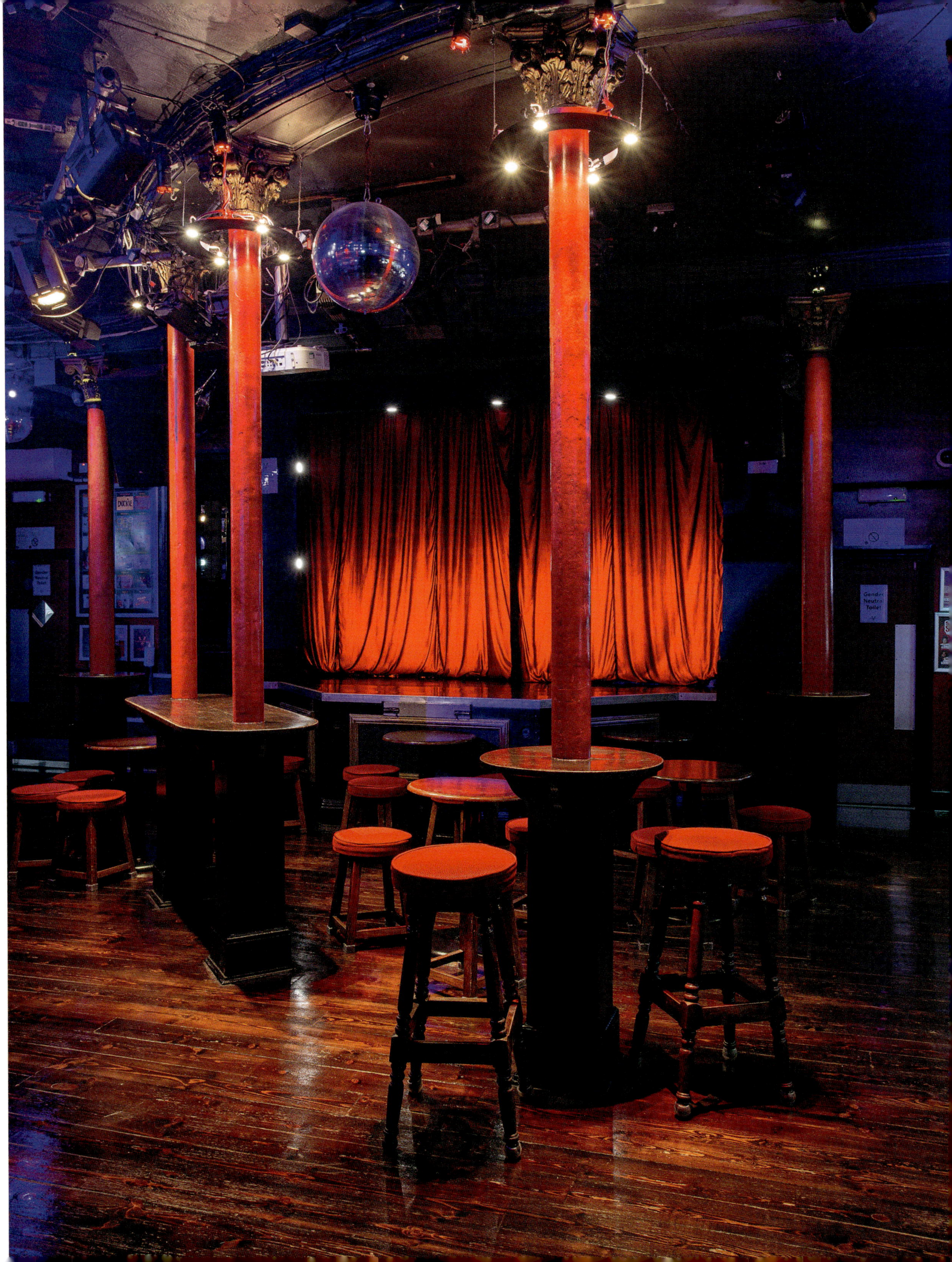
Gender Neutral Toilet

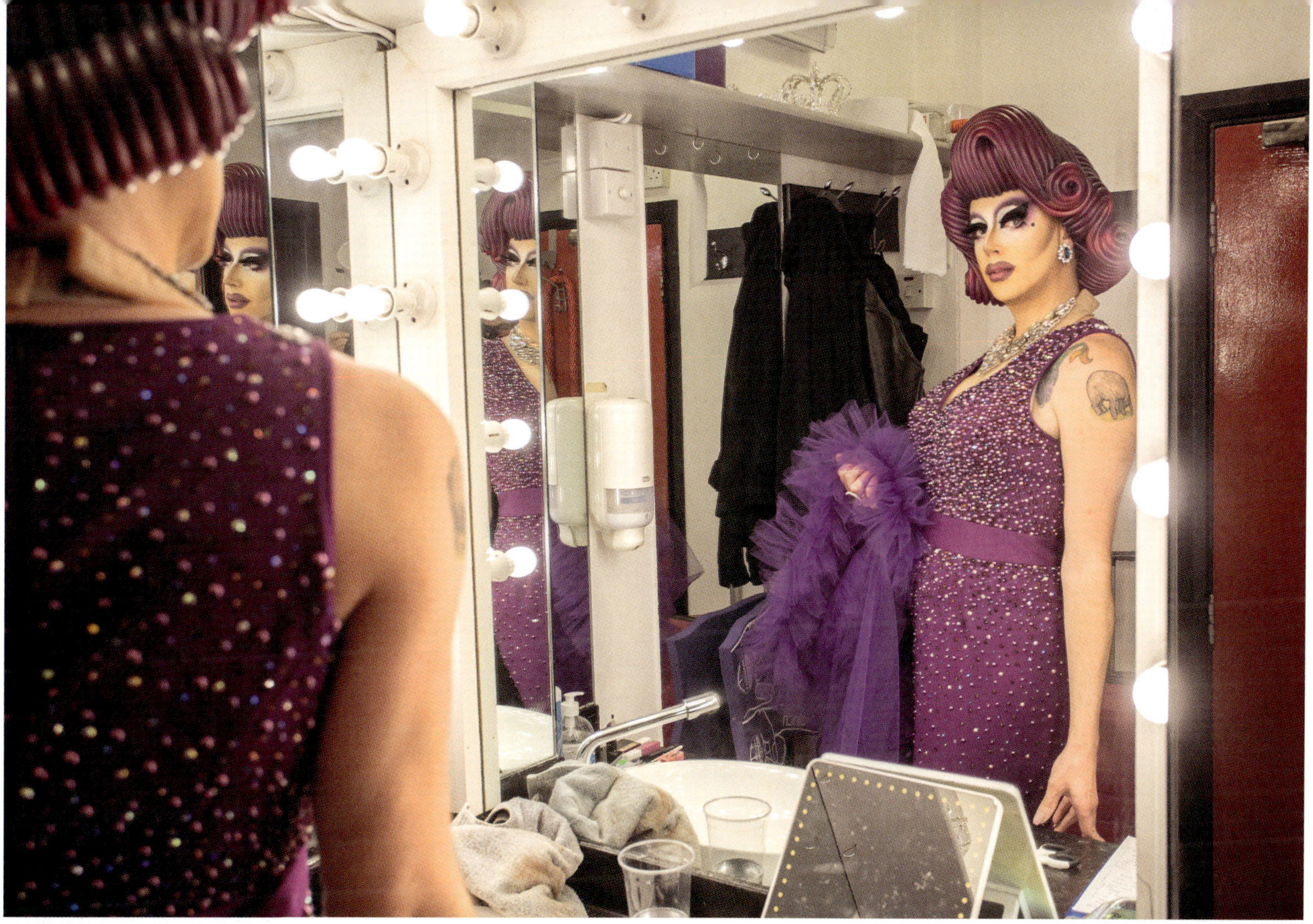

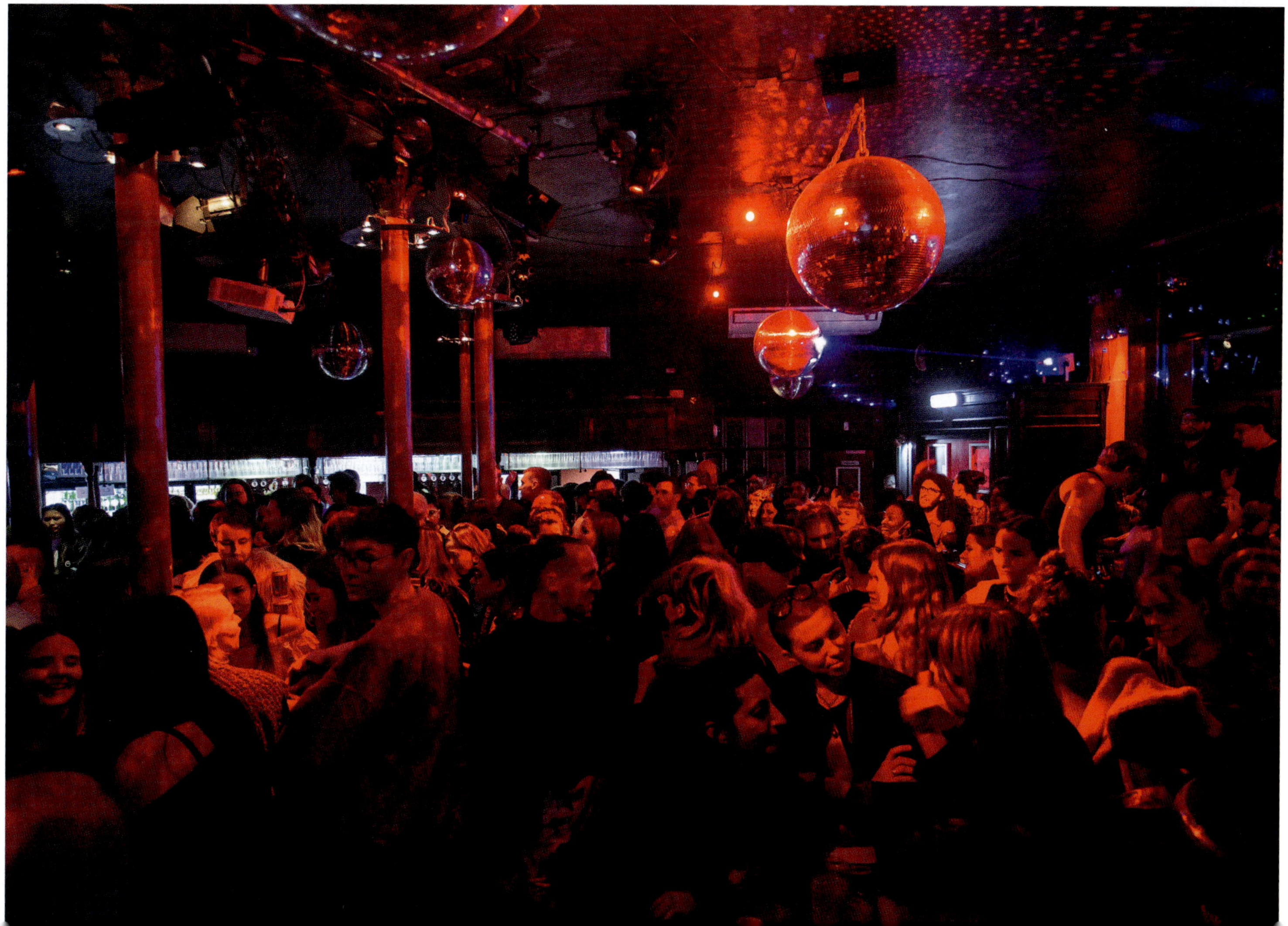

"IT'S STILL GOT SOME EDGE – AND THAT'S WHY WE LOVE IT"

THE BUTCHER'S TAP AND GRILL

15 SPITTAL ST, MARLOW

Tom Kerridge is, by his own admission, a driven man. The super-chef and TV presenter presides over a mini-empire of restaurants, cookbooks, brand ambassadorships and collaborations with the likes of British Airways (for whom he devised an on-board menu). But at heart, he stresses, he's a pub man: "I love their democratic nature and their accessibility." And, he adds, they're the best fit for his personality: "I'm a big fat bald bloke with a regional accent that smiles a lot on the telly. I think people know that lack of pretension will be reflected in any space of mine."

Such is Kerridge's fealty to pubs that he owns no less than three of them, all in the pretty Thames-side town of Marlow, an hour or so west of London. Kerridge has thought a lot about the changing place of the pub in British life – a previous TV series of his, *Saving Britain's Pubs*, addressed the fact that, from 2000 to 2019, pub numbers in the UK declined by 13,600, or 22 per cent, a trend only exacerbated by the pandemic – and his brace of establishments in Marlow deploy the Kerridge trademarks ("flavour-driven cooking", irreproachable British ingredients, a homely buzz) to point a number of possible ways forward. "Pubs have to change what they're offering," he says. "You can now get so much brilliant stuff – wine, beer, a Deliveroo – brought straight to your home, so if pubs are going to survive as social spaces, they have to make sure they've got everything – great food, good wine, coffee in the morning, wi-fi, amazing staff – to get you there, and keep you coming back."

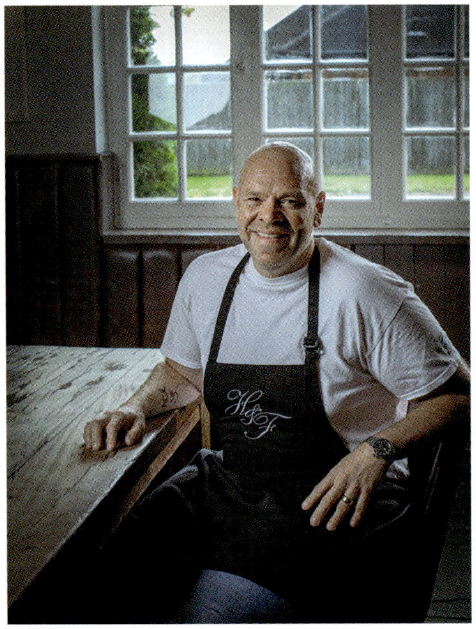

The Butcher's Tap and Grill may represent the biggest step change that Kerridge is offering in his own pub portfolio. Visitors are greeted by a delicious aroma of grilling meat and a cabinet of choice cuts backed by a vitrine of hanging haunches that's part Francis Bacon, part Damien Hirst (Kerridge's wife Beth, a sculptor, oversees the décor in all his businesses). The idea behind this all-day drop-in butchery-pub mash-up is that you can pick your joint after consultation with a butcher-chef – a côte de boeuf, say, or an increasingly popular bavette – and have it prepared to your liking on-site and served with fries and sides. Needless to say, the meats are impeccably sourced (Dovecote beef, Blythburgh pork), the drinks accentuate the crafty and local (Marlow's own Rebellion beer), and the ambience is suitably replete, whether you're going the full chateaubriand or just popping by for a pint. "We get such a wide range of people," says Jamie May, head chef at the BT, "from families for early dinner to date-nighters, post-work suits, and people who just want drinks or to stay and graze all day."

Kerridge's other two Marlow offerings are proving equally winning. The Coach, opened in 2014, has a Michelin star and comes across as a loose, funky pub/diner hybrid, with its long U-shaped aluminium bar and leather-curtained booths; its small plates, available throughout the day, include an already legendary pulled pork burger, and its weekend brunches are considerably enlivened by the likes of honey-glazed bacon bagels. The Hand & Flowers, meanwhile, is the jewel in Kerridge's crown. The only pub in the world to hold two Michelin stars, it exudes old-school market-town-hostelry charm – inglenook fireplaces, exposed beams – but the pearl-drop chandeliers, attached rooms and hum of intent activity all indicate a showpiece venue, as do the £80 sirloin steaks, the £25 puddings, including a chocolate and ale cake, and the fact that the whole place is perennially booked out weeks in advance. "Two stars means you're getting the very best in terms of energy, effort and quality," says Kerridge. "At the same time, you don't have to rise to meet expectations. It's a pub ethos – we make everyone welcome."

That, of course, is also the Kerridge ethos, and the chief lesson his Marlow testbed might teach other pubs. "Try harder, aim higher, go the extra mile," he says. "There isn't anyone who doesn't appreciate that."

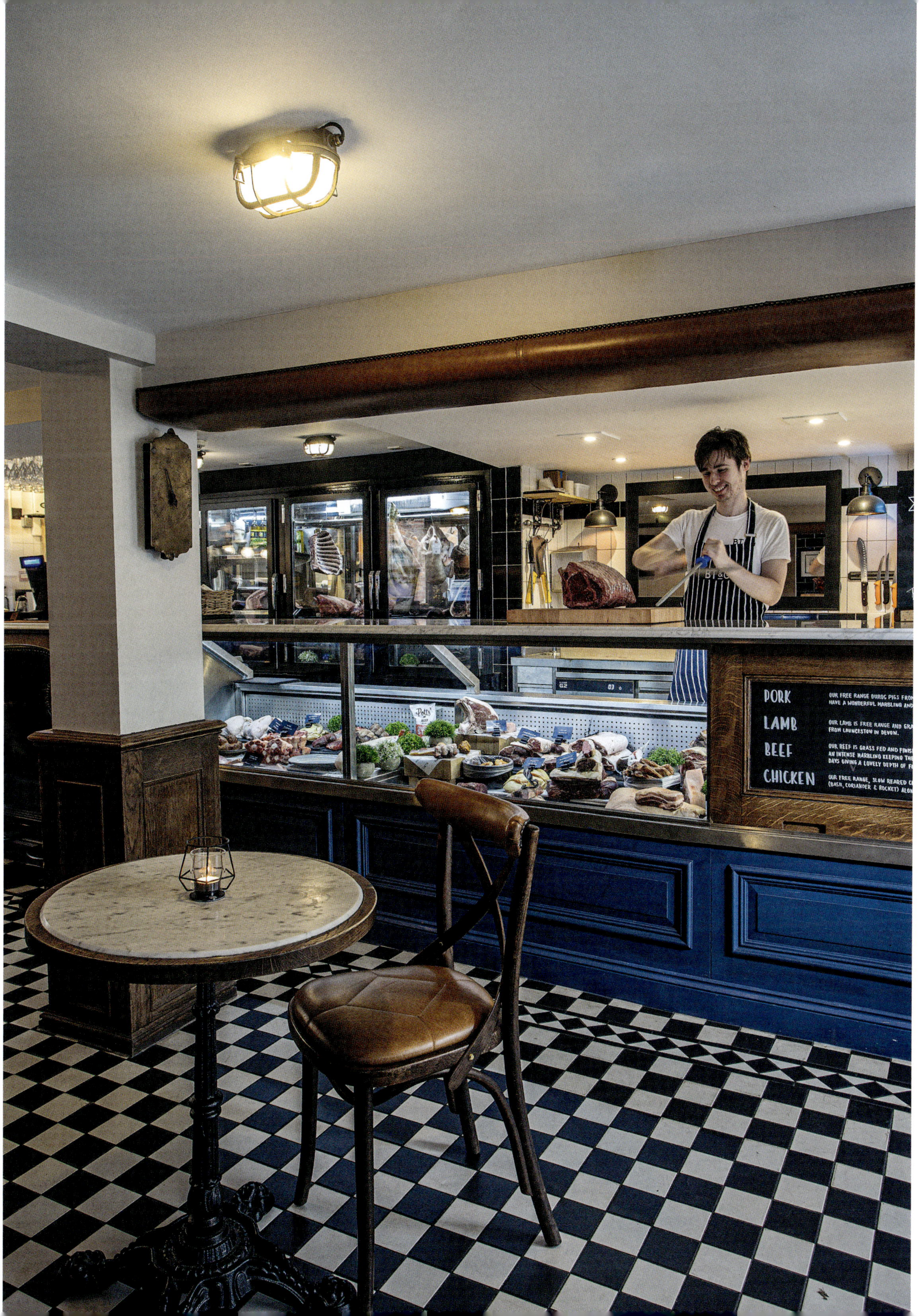
PORK
LAMB
BEEF
CHICKEN

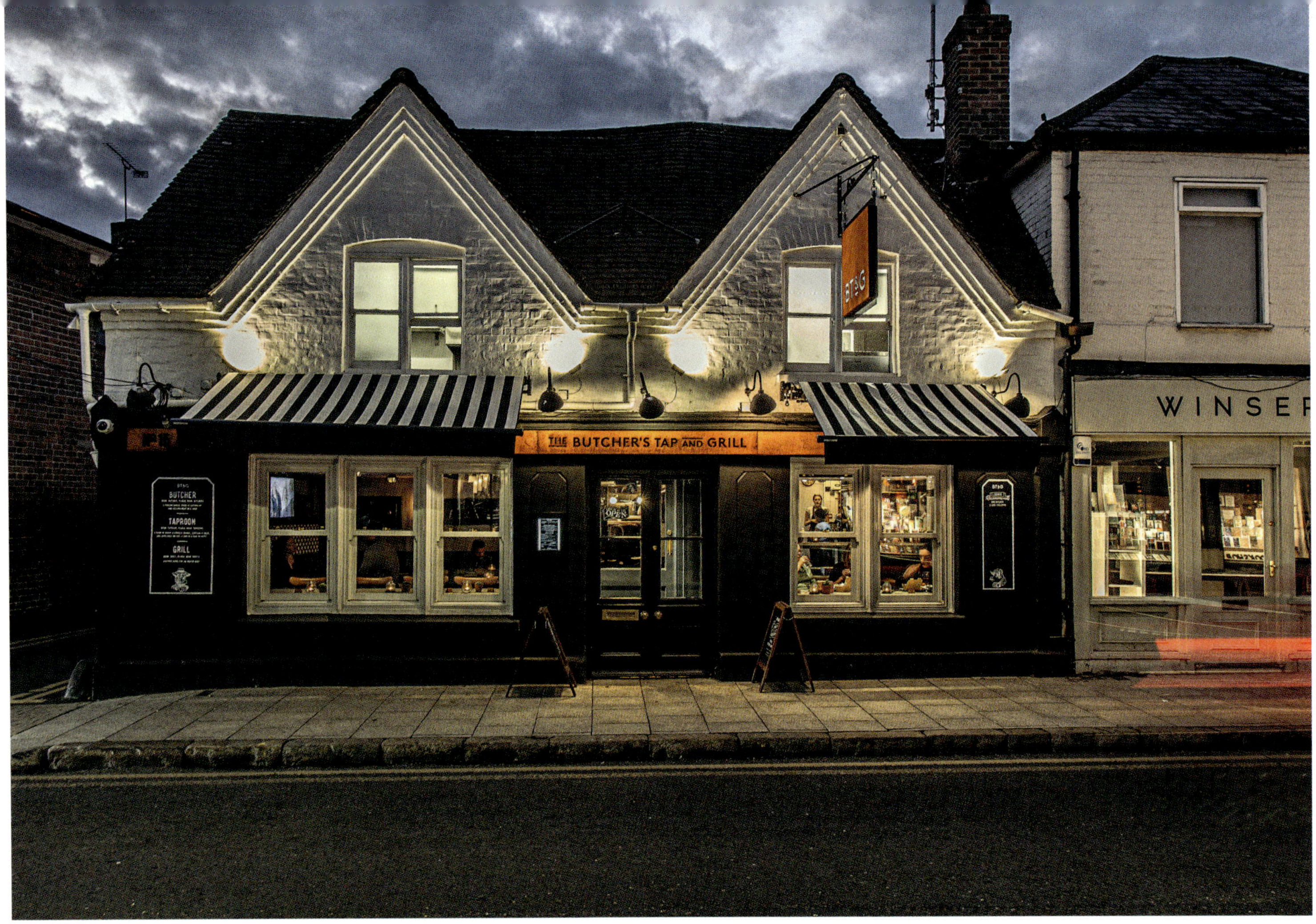

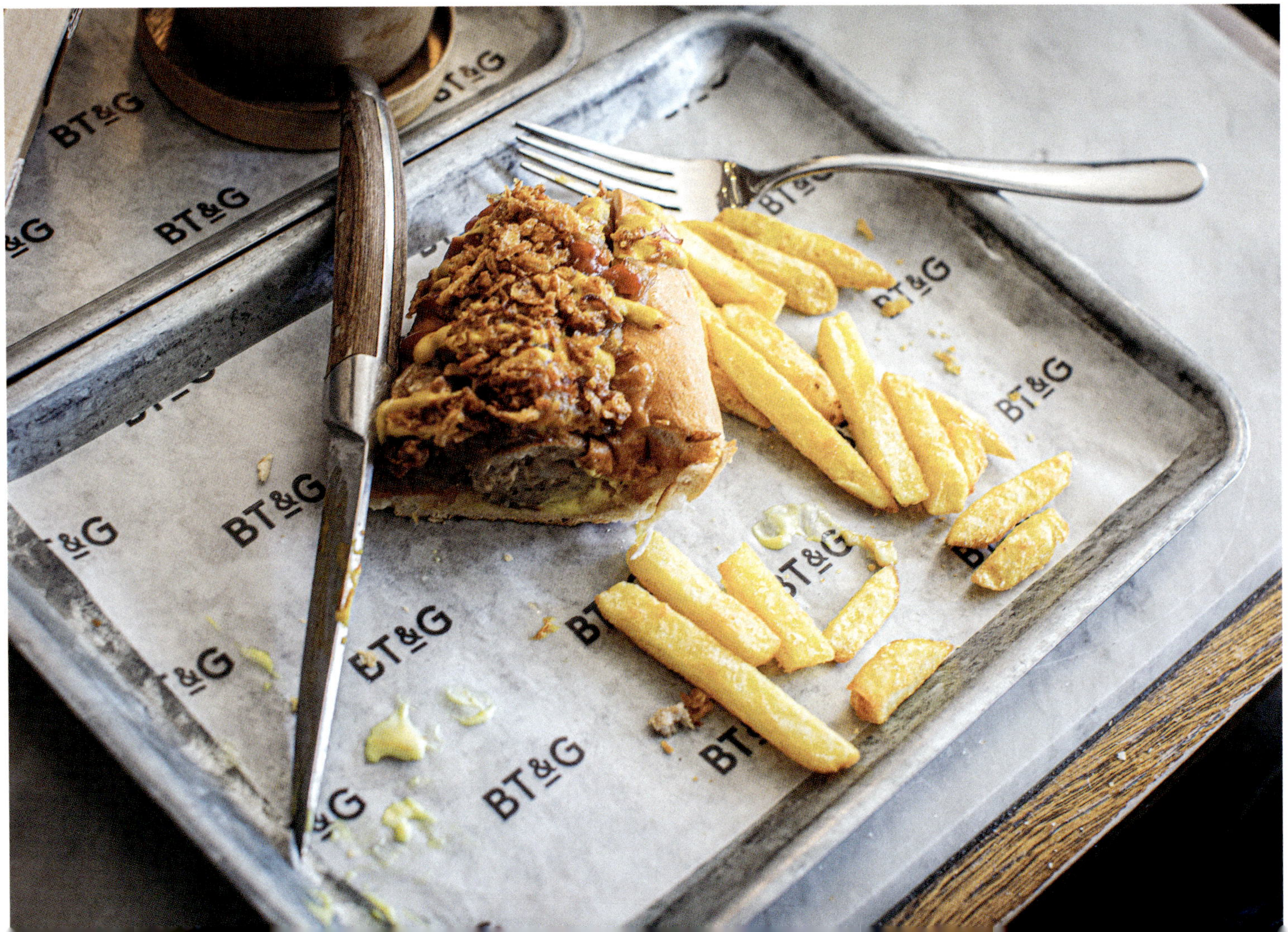

"FOR DRINKS, OR GRAZING, OR SERIOUS DINING"

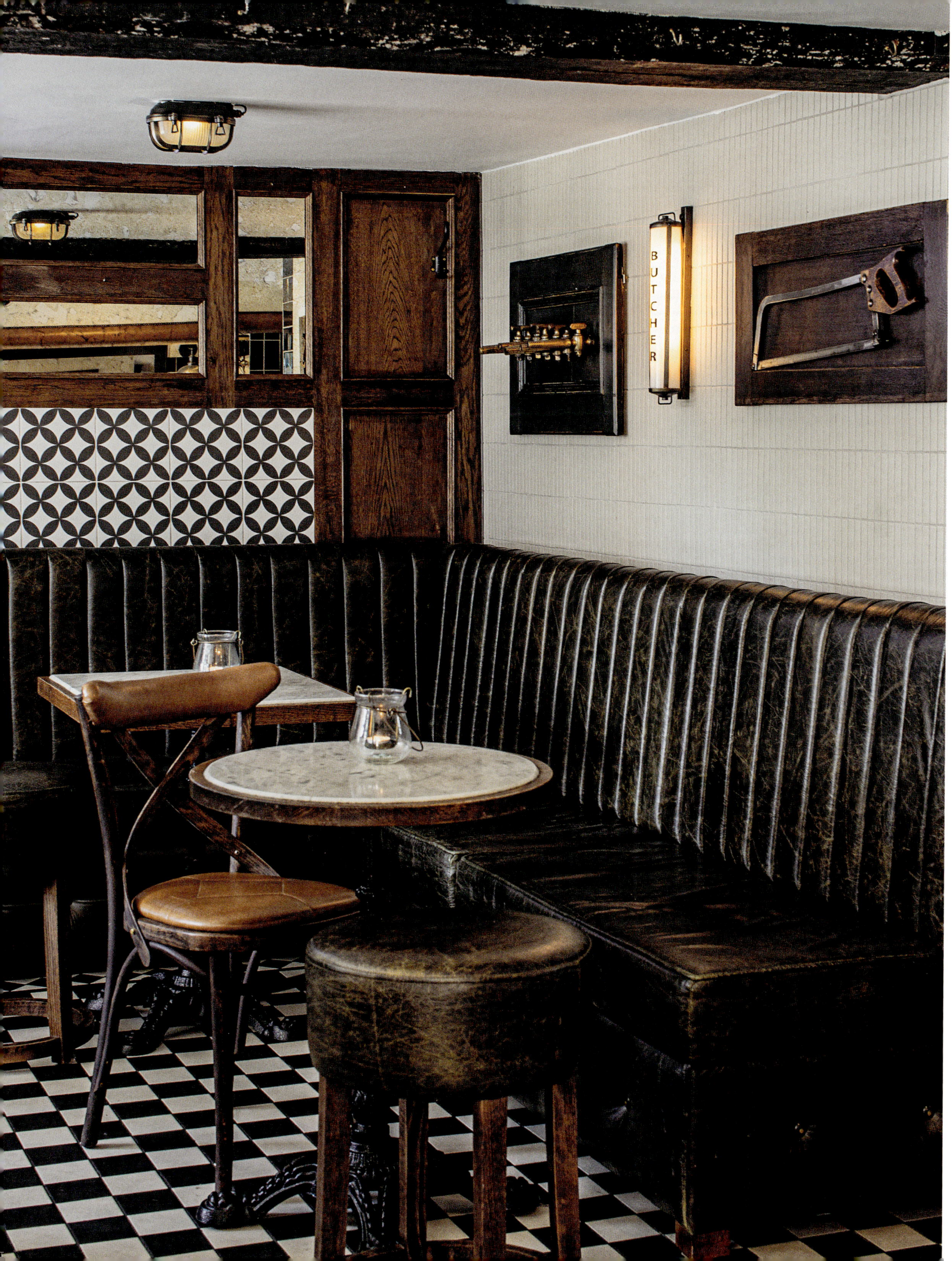

"THE BEST PUBS OFFER THE BEST WELCOME"

THE CROWN

64-66 ALL SAINTS' ST, HASTINGS

"If you are asked why you favour a particular public house, it would seem natural to put the beer first," wrote George Orwell, in his celebrated essay 'The Moon Under Water', "but the thing that most appeals to me ... is what people call its 'atmosphere'."

Orwell was laying out his vision of what an English pub should be, but for many of its patrons, The Crown, in Hastings, comes as close as anywhere to his Platonic ideal of the welcoming local. It boasts many of the features Orwell hymned – grained woodwork, cast-iron fireplaces, a roaring winter hearth, plenty of elbow room, staff who know their customers by name – and a few he wouldn't have conceived of, such as a knitting circle that meets regularly in the snug. The beer is more than passable – lots of local pump action from the likes of the Romney Marsh Brewery – but the atmosphere, buzzy at peak times and bucolic at others, is the chief draw. "We always wanted it to be a pub for everybody," says the landlady Tess Eaton.

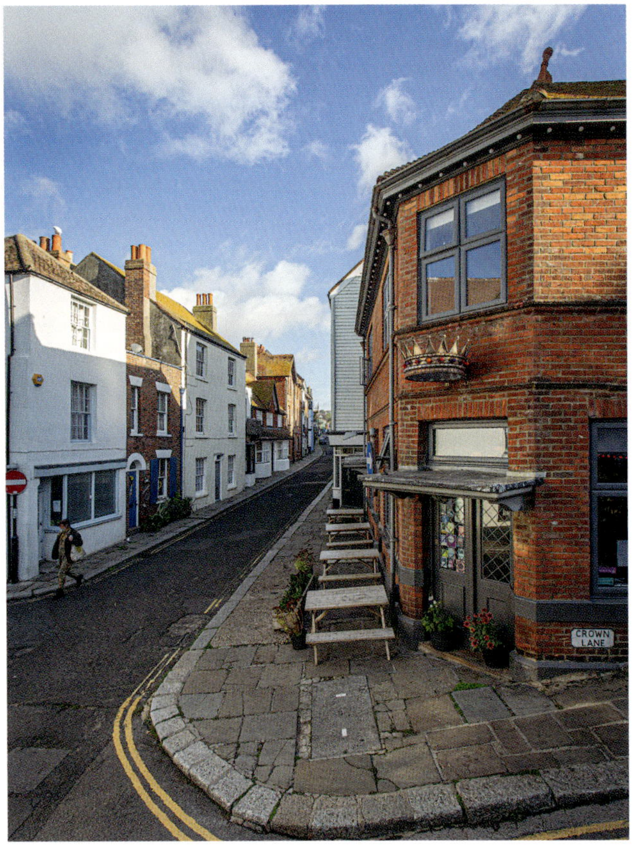

"But with a focus on interesting local producers and suppliers," says her partner Andrew Swan. "Hastings is a town of creatives, and, being independent, we could act as a showcase for them."

"We've held gardening clubs, wreath-making workshops, cider festivals, you name it," says Eaton. "We never wanted to limit ourselves."

Little wonder that The Crown has won numerous awards, including Best Place to Drink in the UK from the prestigious *Observer Food Monthly*, or that it attracts such a diverse crowd. It sits at the end of the much-Instagrammed All Saints Street, between the picturesque jumble of Hastings Old Town and the seafront. Dyed-in-the-wool locals – fishermen, foragers – hold court alongside more recent arrivistes deemed DFLs (Down from London), plus curious gourmands and casual drinkers. They all sense that Eaton and Swan have gone the extra mile in everything from their handmade tables (courtesy of Hastings & Bexhill Wood Recycling) to their painstakingly sourced and seasonal menu (their much-prized fish finger sandwich utilises all local ingredients, from the fish and the oil and eggs in the mayonnaise to the beer in the batter), and the extensive selection of local beers, ciders and spirits. The art on the walls is covetable stuff, courtesy of the town's not inconsiderable tally of artists; even the fresh-cut flowers decorating the tables are from Eaton's mother's garden. Some regulars have received the ultimate accolade of having a drink named after them (try the Eric, a piquant combination of ginger beer and shandy). "There's a real warmth about the place," says Lisa, who calls in "a few times a week" from her house around the corner. "I can come here on my own and feel totally at ease and totally looked after."

There's been a pub on this site since 1758, but The Crown had been boarded up for two years when Eaton and Swan, refugees from marketing and structural engineering respectively, stumbled across it while touring the UK in their camper van. From their "secret" opening in July 2014, which attracted some two hundred people, including a mariachi band and a contingent of piratically costumed locals (Hastings is big on pirates), they've assiduously created their own neighbourhood hub; to paraphrase Orwell, you'll come for the beer (or the wine, or the roast haddock), and you'll stay for the conversation.

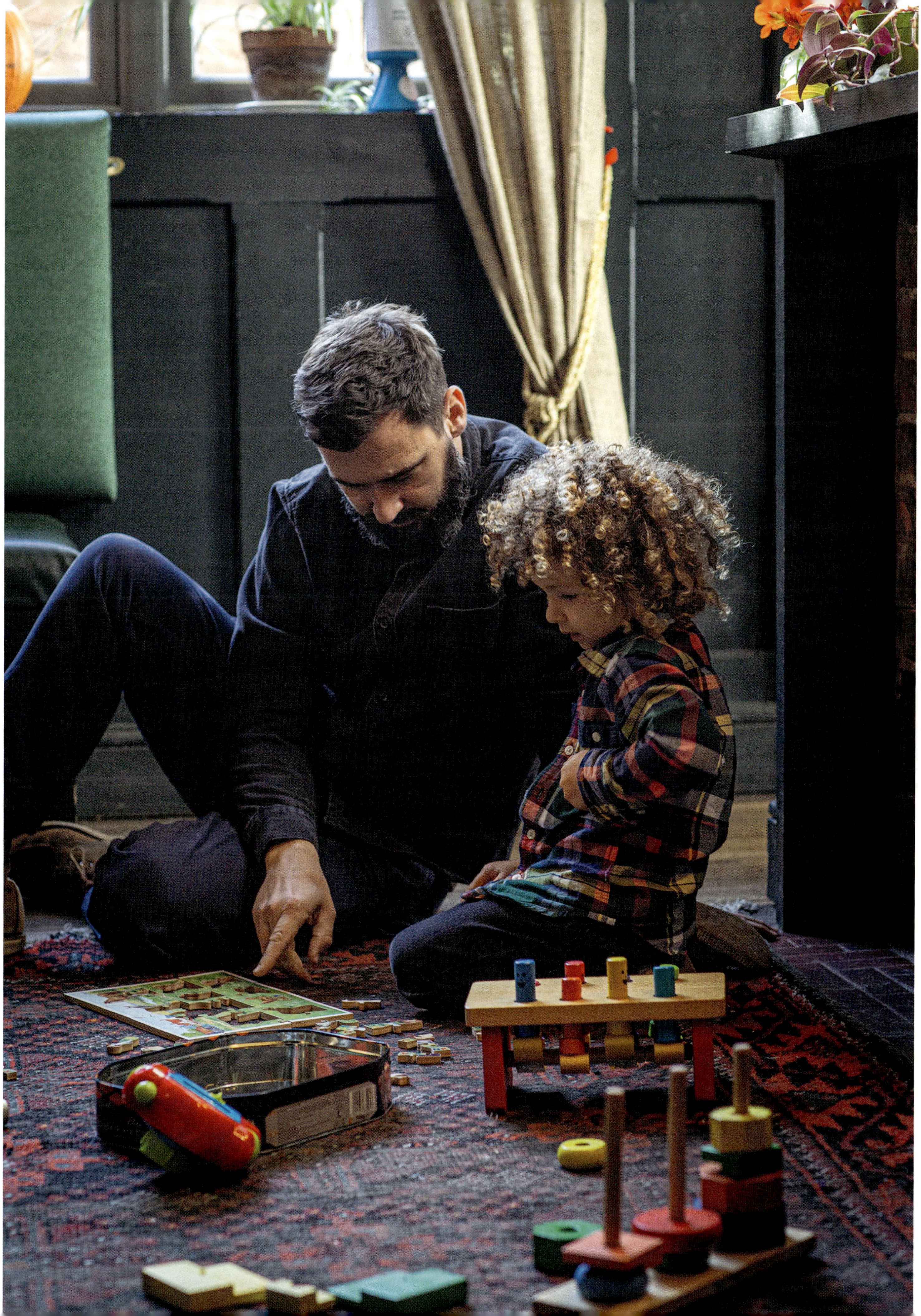

"THERE'S A REAL WARMTH ABOUT THE PLACE"

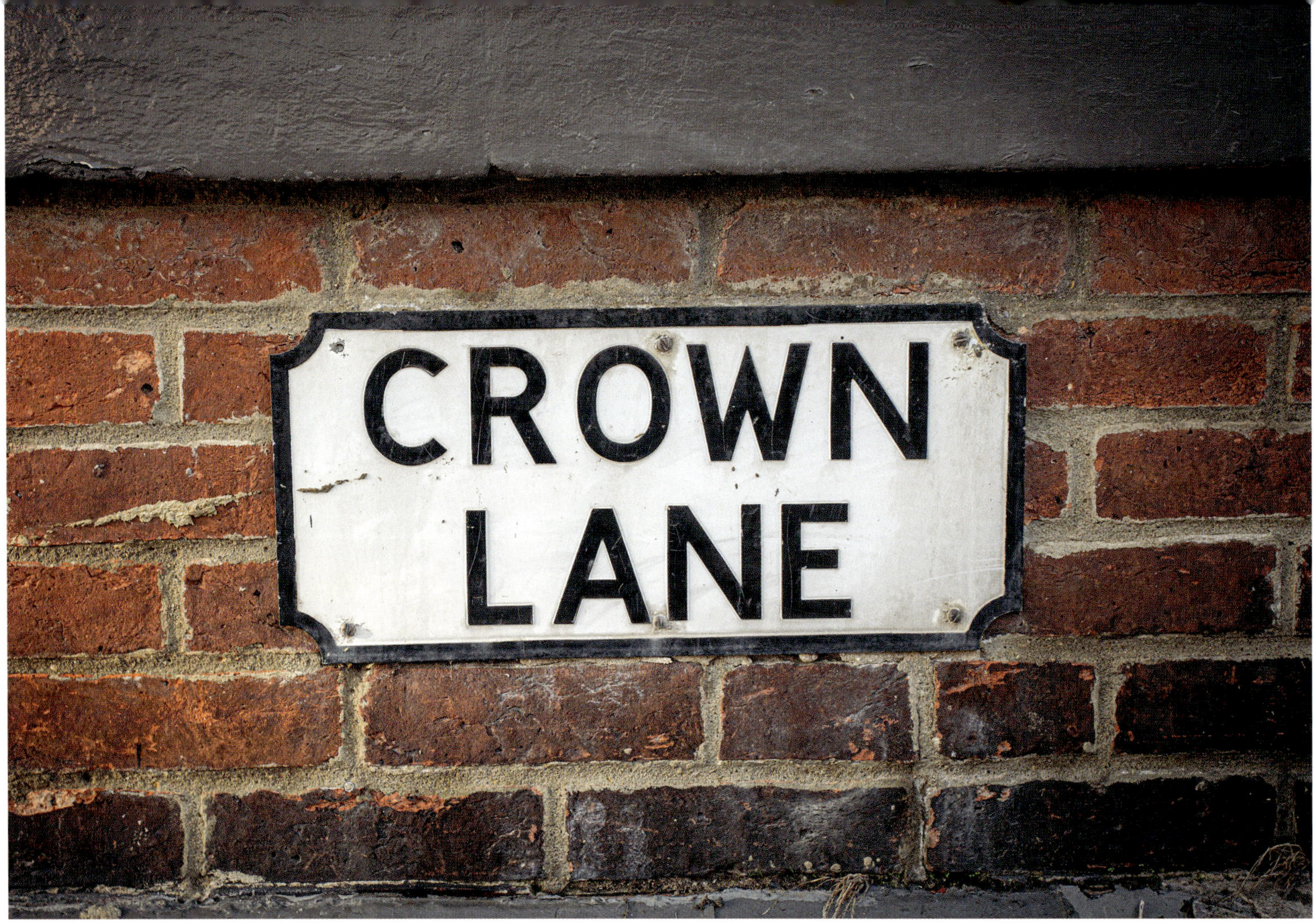
CROWN
LANE

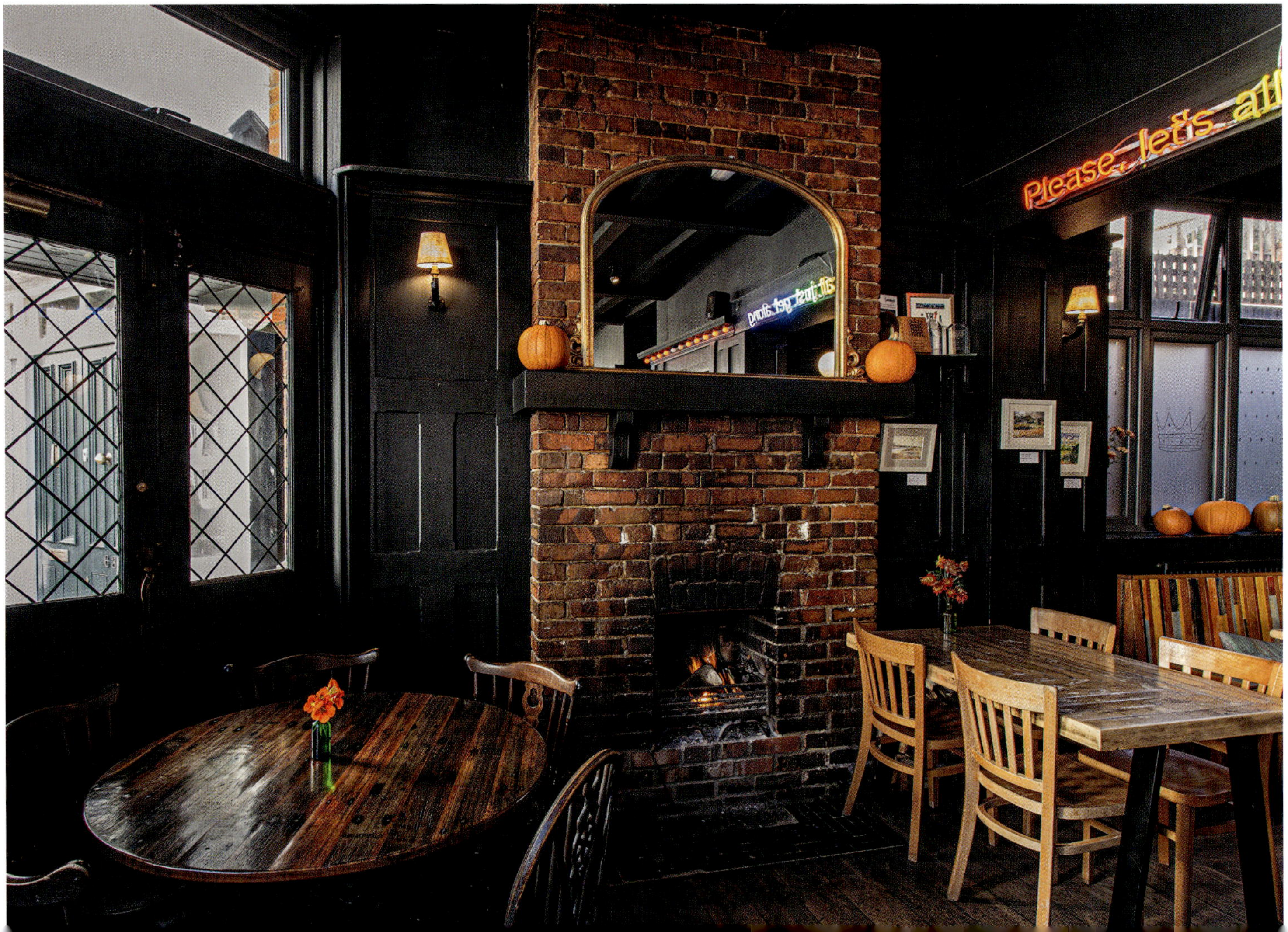
Please, let's

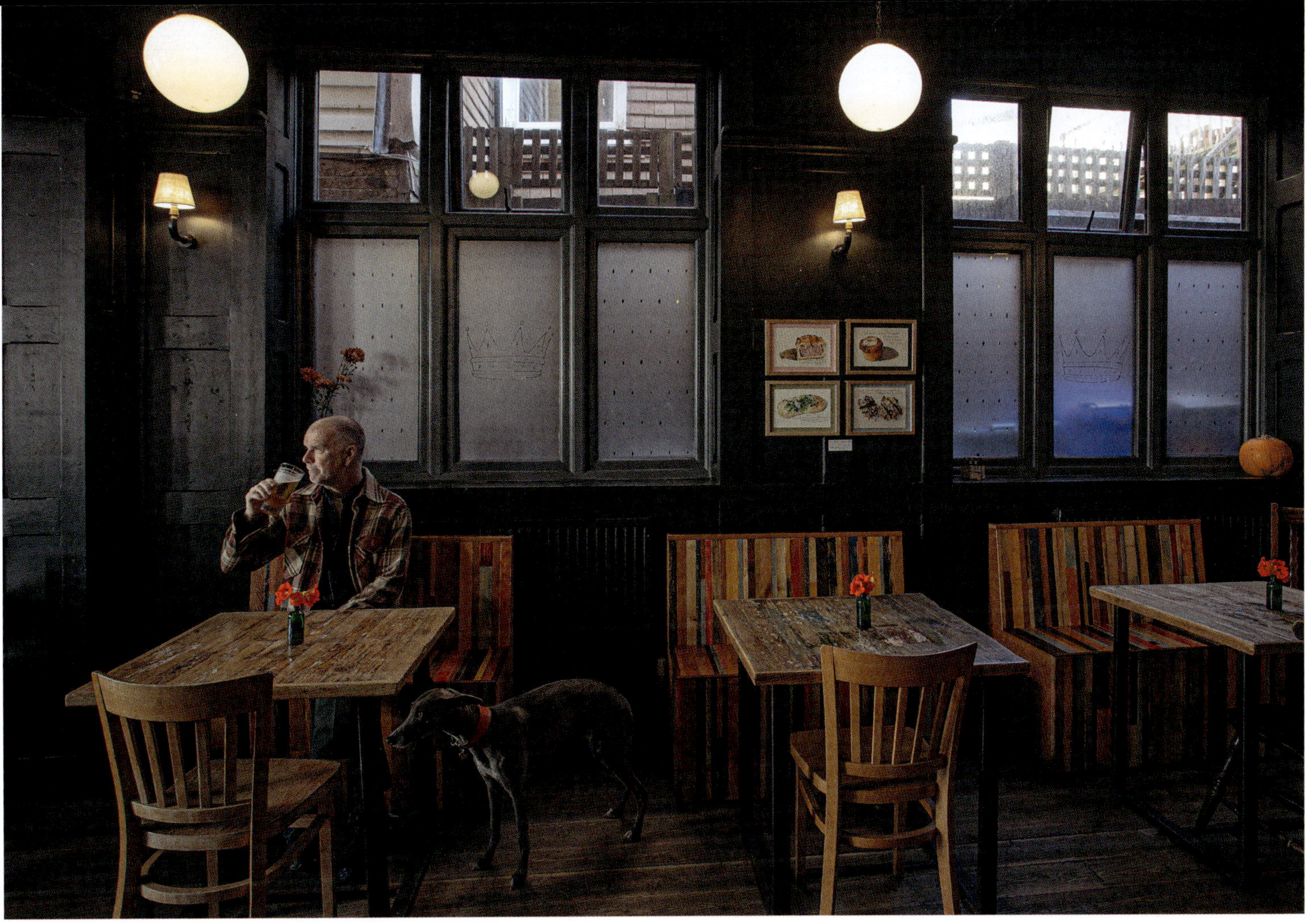

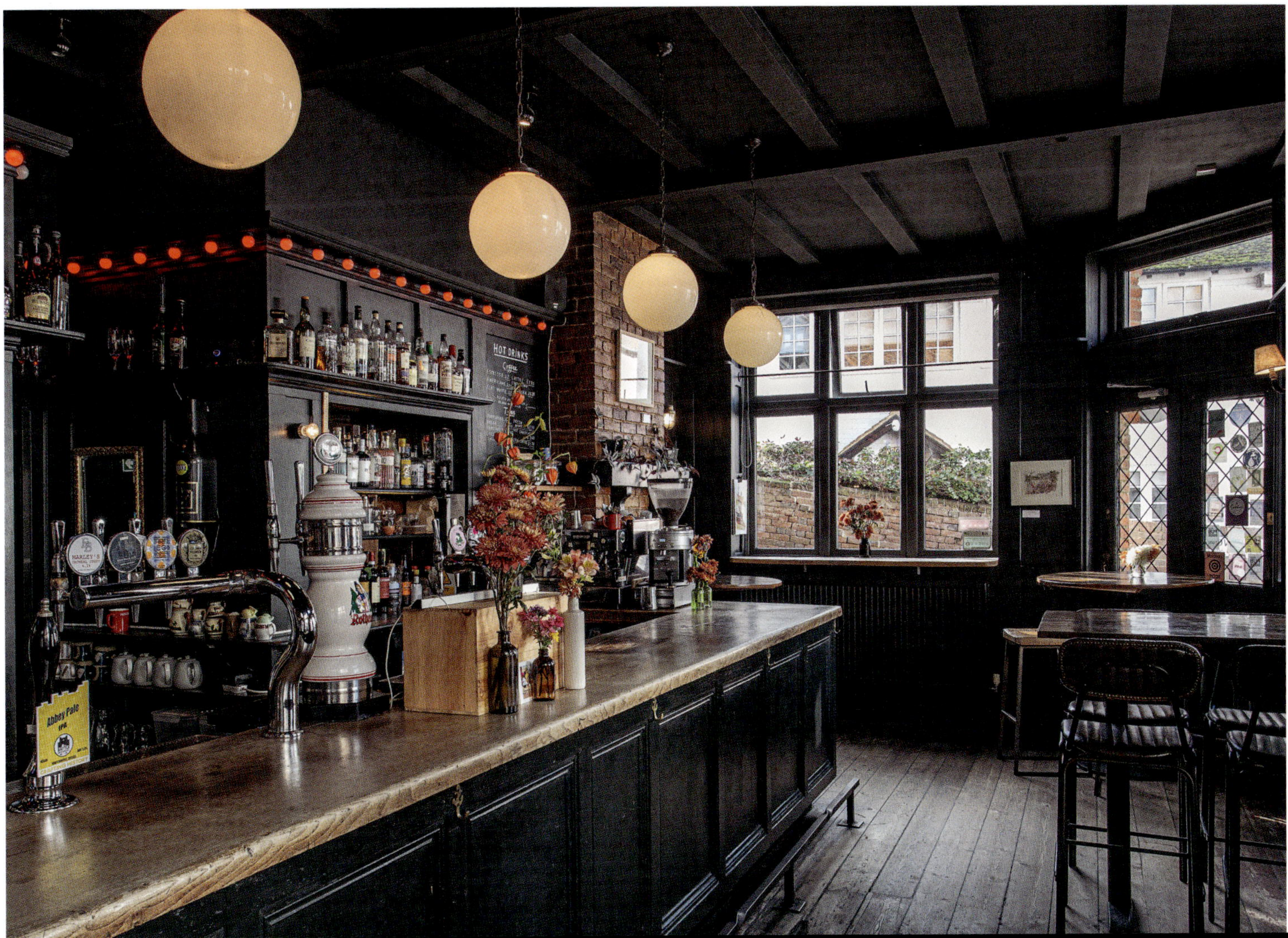

"… WE NEVER WANTED TO LIMIT OURSELVES."

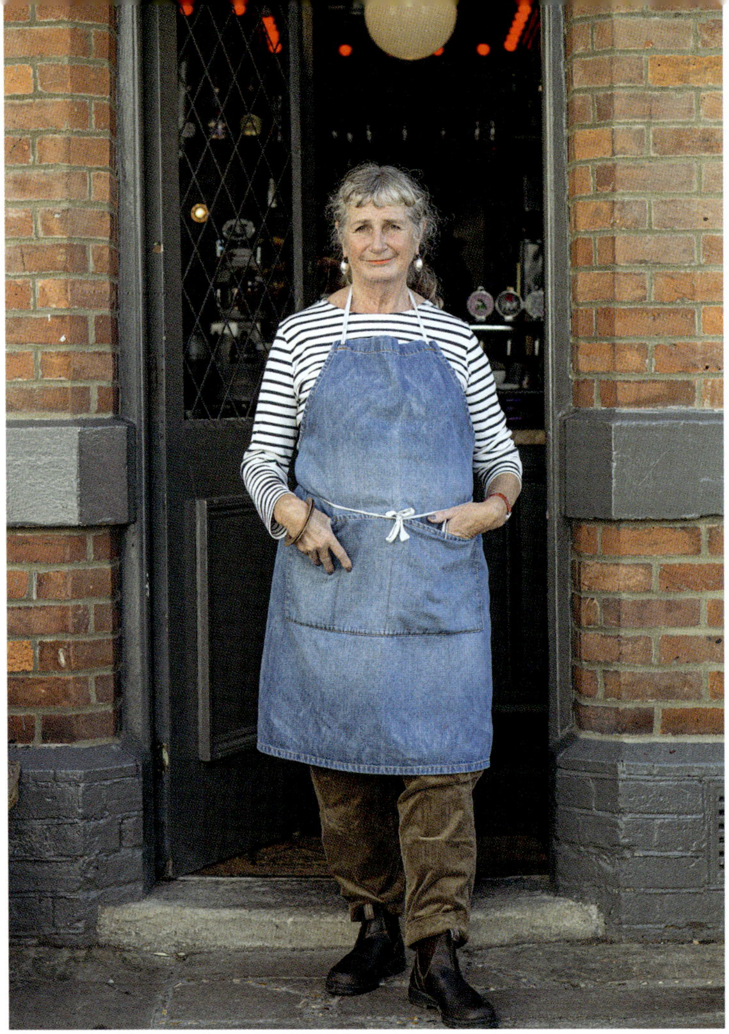

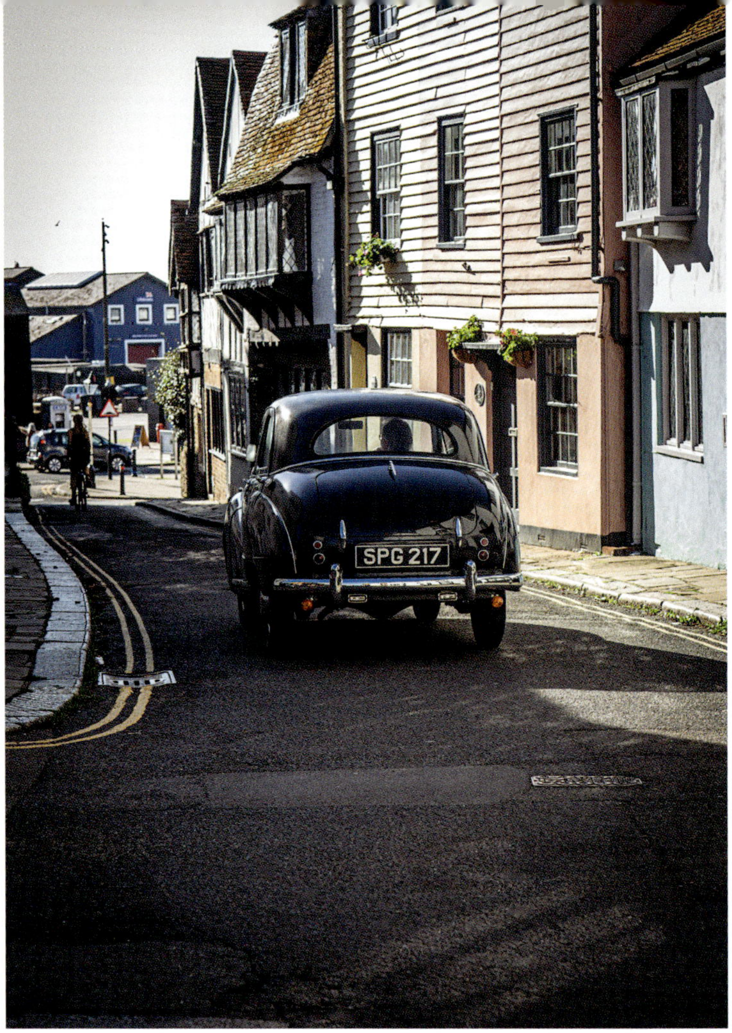
SPG 217

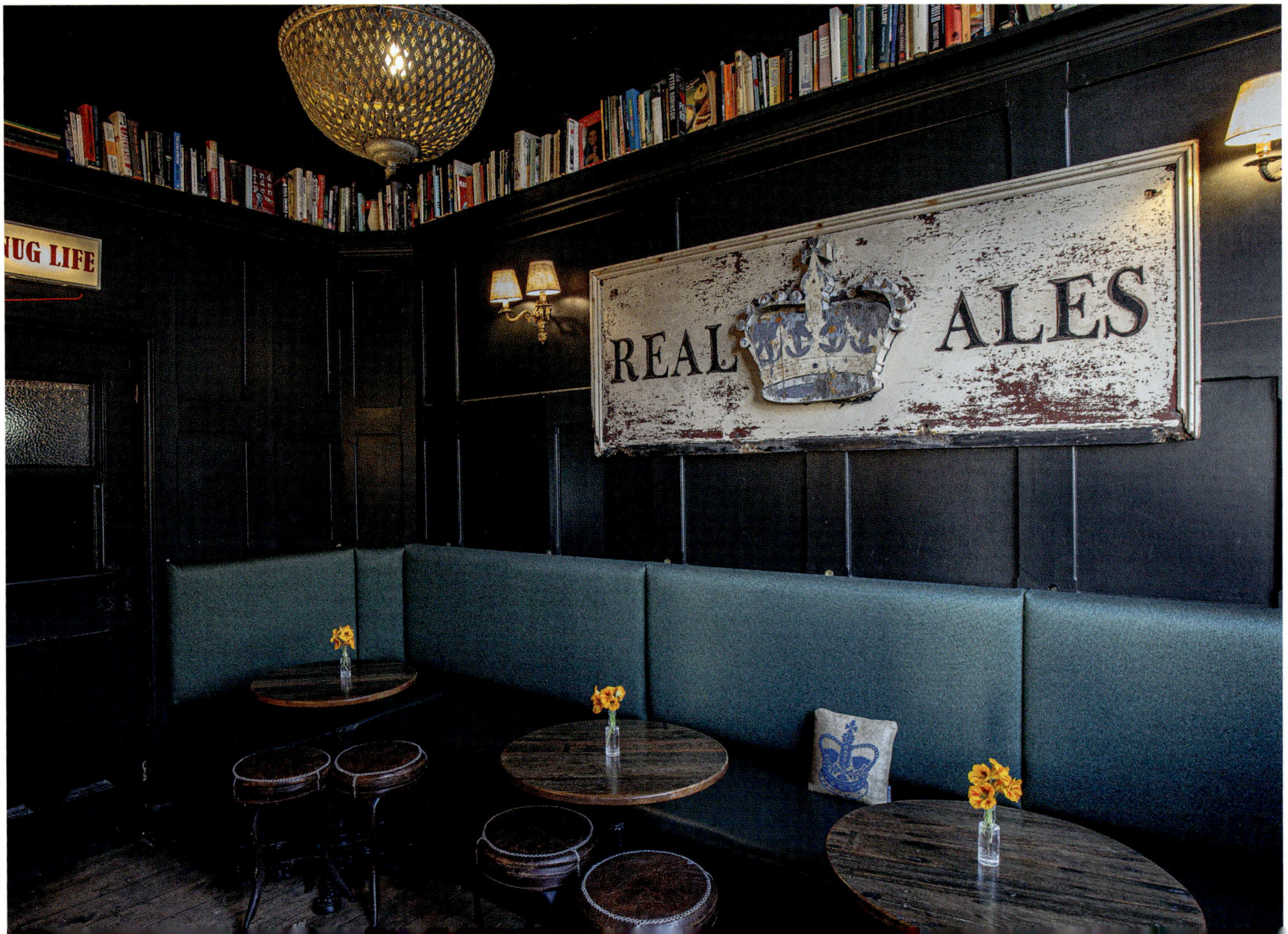
REAL ALES

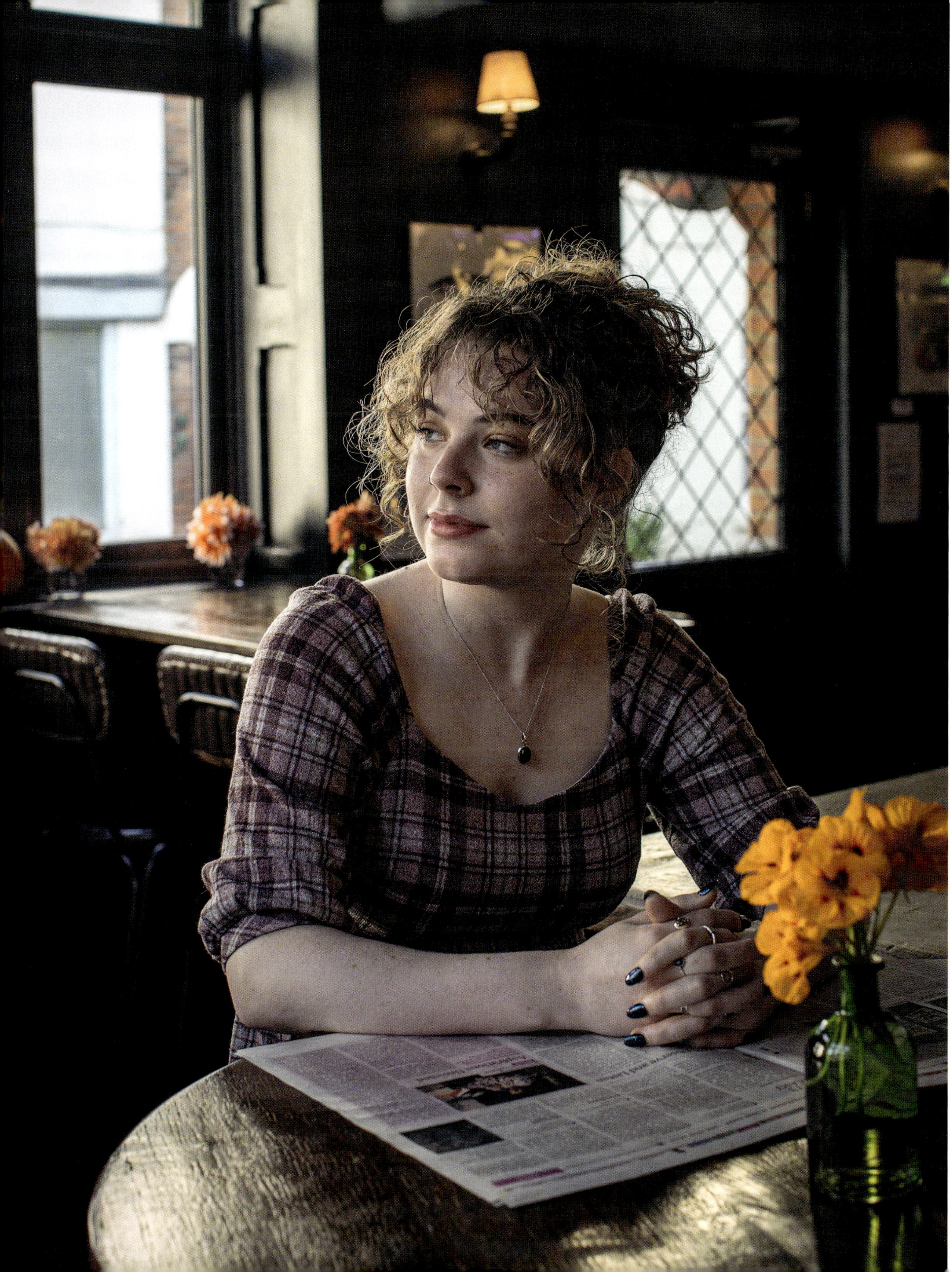

"YOU FEEL TOTALLY AT EASE"

THE FALKLAND ARMS

19-21 THE GREEN, GREAT TEW, CHIPPING NORTON

The meaning of "bucolic", according to the *Merriam-Webster Dictionary*, is "pleasing or picturesque in natural simplicity", or "idyllic", and it's certainly a fitting word for Great Tew in Oxfordshire, a hamlet in the heart of the Cotswolds. A jumble of ridiculously pretty cottages cluster round a village green; it's a riot of thatched roofs, yew hedges, pollarded beeches and handmade "Slow – Kittens" road signs. And at the centre of it all is the sixteenth-century Falkland Arms, perhaps the quintessential English village pub.

Spend a little time here, and you'll become aware of how this part of England has become a rural retreat for the one per cent. The chirrup of robins and the clop of horses' hooves now mingle with the purr of Land Rover Defenders driven by Hunter-wellied hedge-funders; the manor house on the adjacent hill, currently undergoing a multimillion-pound refit, is owned by Rupert Murdoch and Jerry Hall; and the 3,500-acre Great Tew estate which the pub backs onto, once the property of Lord Falkland (who gave his name to the islands), now belongs to property tycoon Nicholas Johnston, a friend of the former prime minister (and near neighbour) David Cameron. The pub has certainly not remained unaffected by this – "The Beckhams were in recently", says manager Andy, "we had Sir Patrick Stewart in last night, and Simon Cowell's a regular" – but, he adds, whoever walks in, however elevated their status, will find the same things on offer: "Great beer, great service and a sense of familiarity."

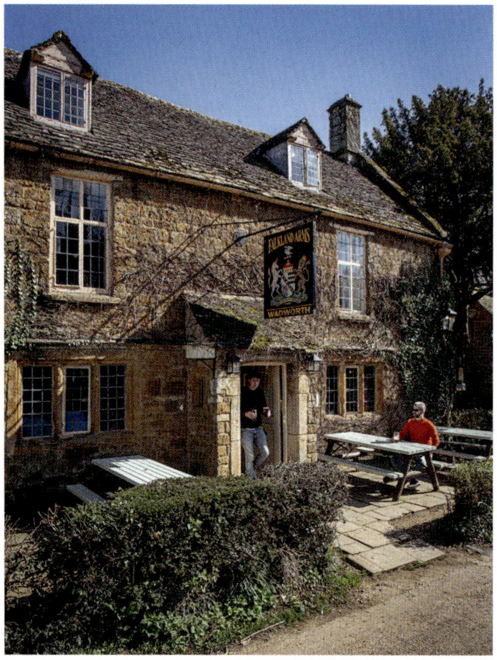

The first is pretty much covered by a selection of casks from Wiltshire's Wadworth brewery; the second by Andy's team, who are preparing to welcome a lunchtime crowd of regulars, tourists, bikers, walkers and maybe a showbiz colossus or two. The third is provided by the archetypal country-pub interior; five-hundred-year-old flagstone floors, max headroom-style beams that support a cornucopia of hanging mugs and jugs (there were more than three hundred the last time anyone had the energy to count, though Andy concedes a few have been lost to involuntary headbutts), a prodigious fireplace complete with little stools and built-in niches where farmers once toasted themselves after a hard morning's harrowing, and piles of horse blankets in case anyone fancies a bit of postprandial snuggling. There's no music, no fruit machines and no TVs; instead, there's rambling roses round the door, a view of the ancient village school across the lane through the mullioned windows, and an ambience as timeless as the ancient grandfather clock in the corner, which stopped at some point between the sixteenth century and the twenty-first (until relatively recently, you could even still purchase snuff from behind the bar). Not that The Falkland Arms is resting on its venerable laurels; the top-notch menu features rebooted takes on pub staples (the "Henry" burger, named for the founder of the Wadworth brewery, comes with an IPA onion relish), alongside cheffy additions – Jerusalem artichokes with crispy sage, Asian-inflected grazing boards – that should leave even the most jaded multiplatformed media mogul feeling replete, and plans are well in hand to transform the generous beer garden at the rear into a grass arena for alfresco cocktails and barbecue broiling.

On a sunny afternoon, with an outside seat and an amber ale both bagged, The Falkland Arms feels like it's at the very heart of England, both in terms of ancient traditions – some thatchers are working on a roof a few doors down, and a small army of landscapers are attending to the garden of a fashion maven in the adjacent house – and modern obsessions ("There's now an entire ecosystem around mobile banking," a woman assures her companion over two glasses of chardonnay at the next table). It's bucolic, certainly; but it's somehow very Cotswold-contemporary too.

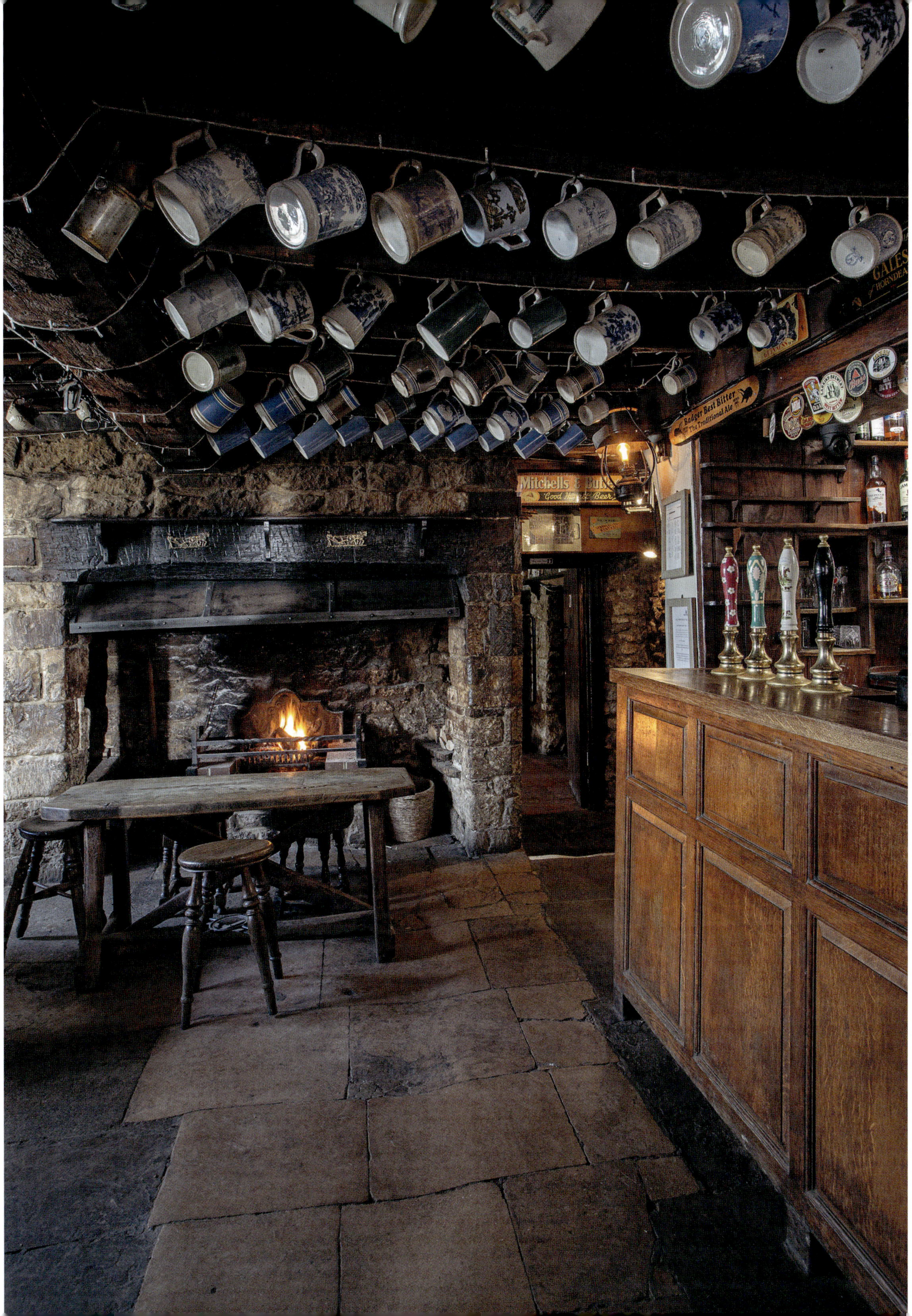
Badger Best Bitter
The Traditional Ale
Mitchells

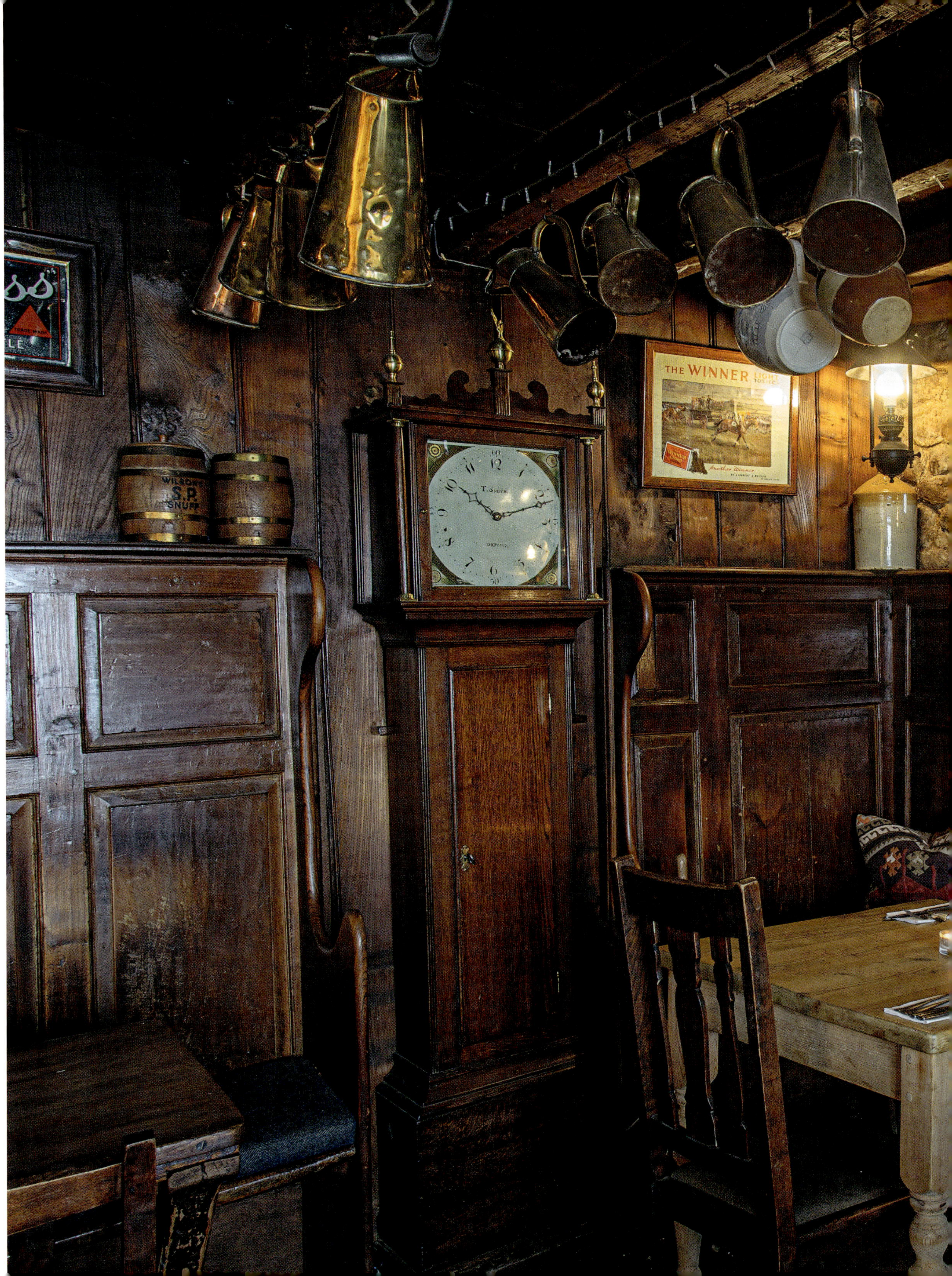
THE WINNER
S.P.
SNUFF

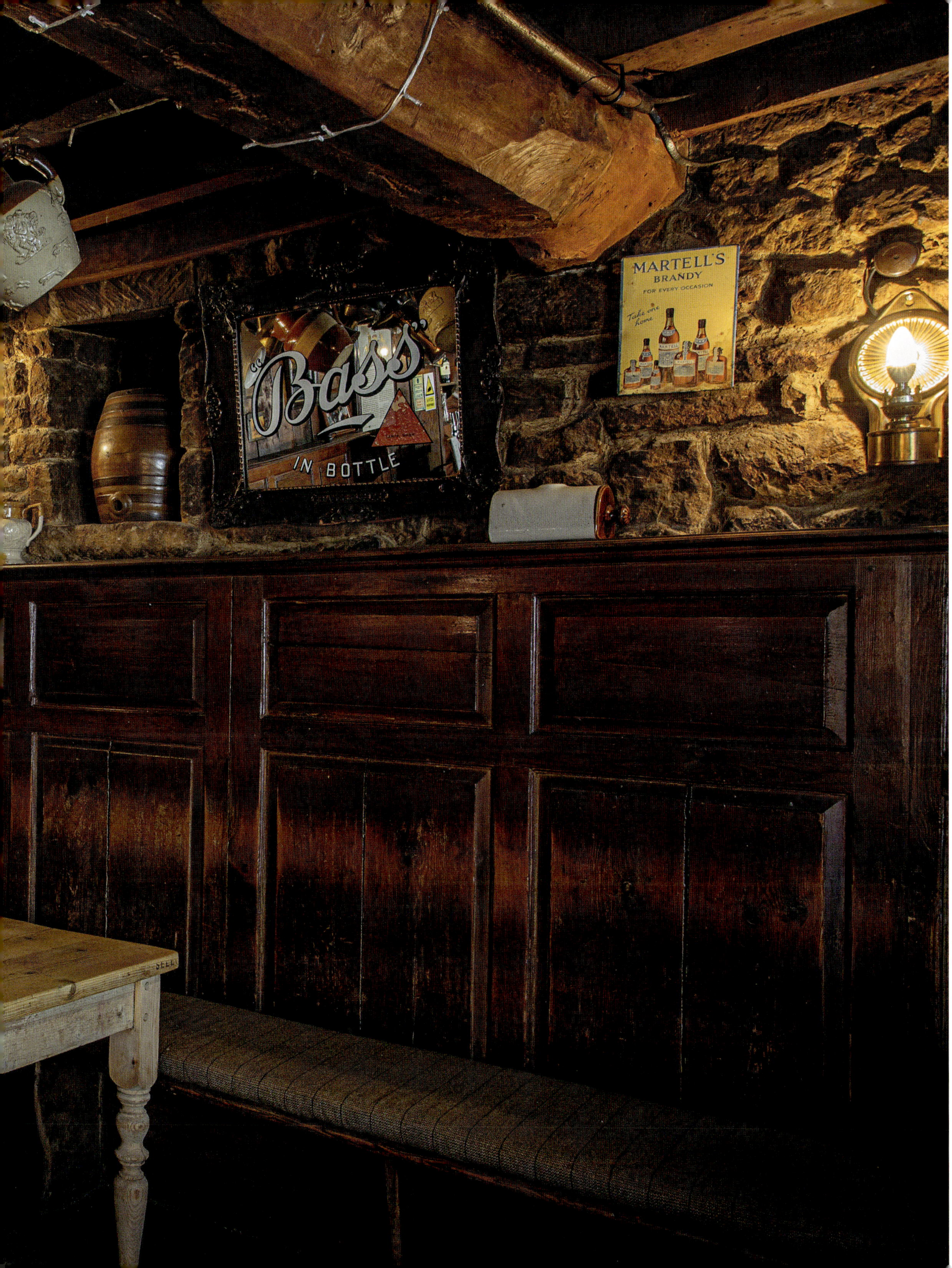
Bass
IN BOTTLE
MARTELL'S
BRANDY
FOR EVERY OCCASION
Take one home

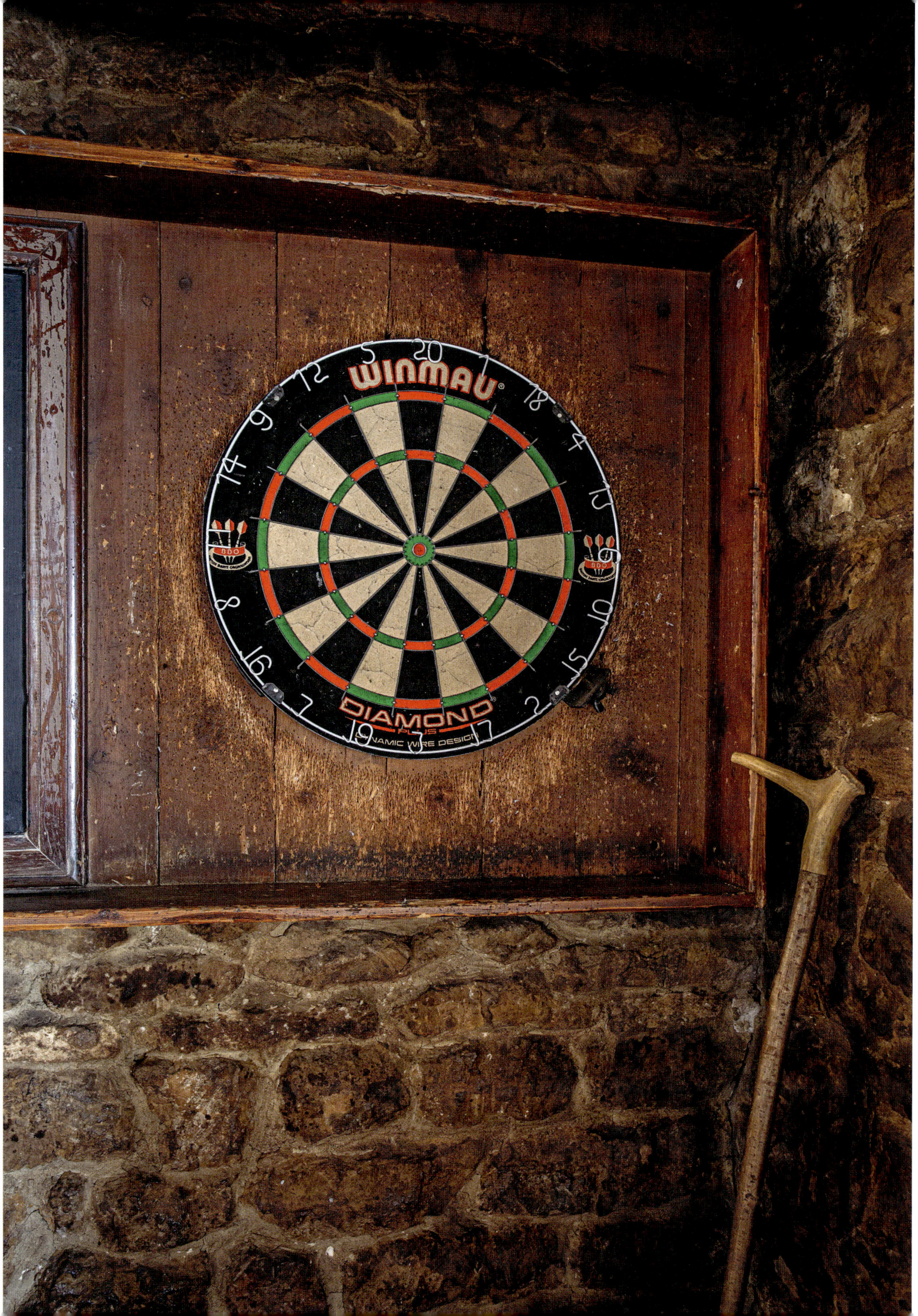
WINMAU
DIAMOND

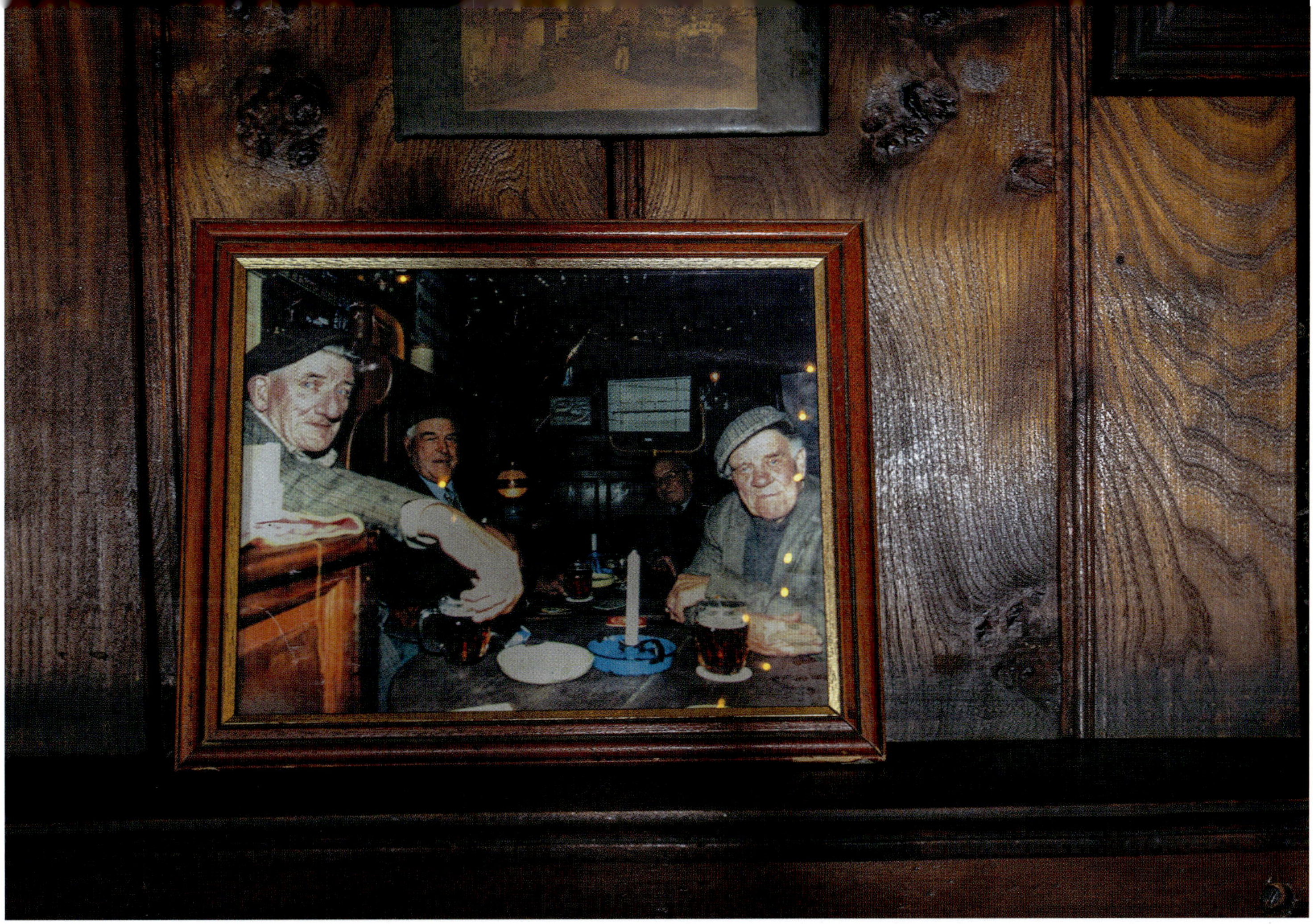

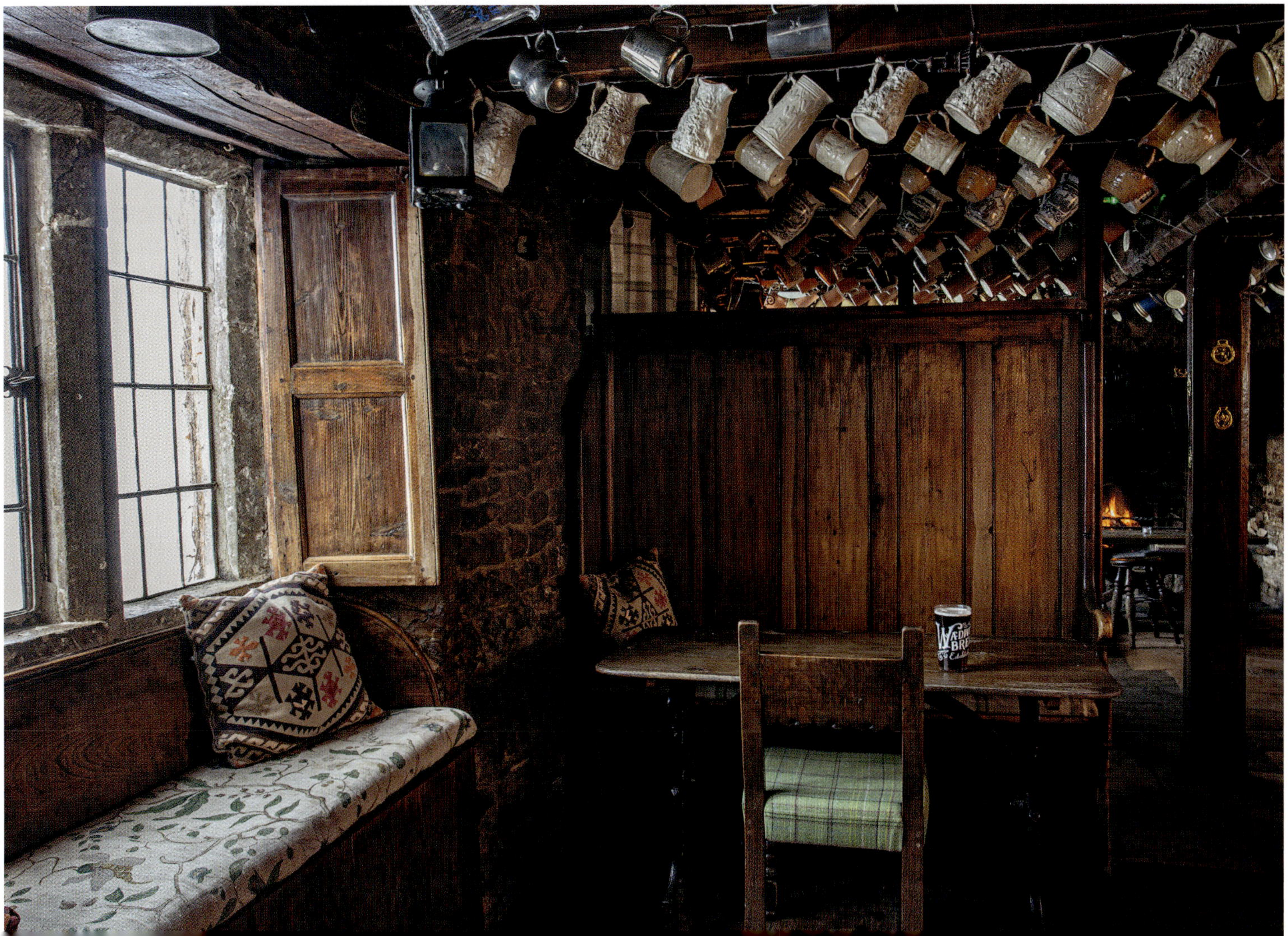

HAUNCH OF VENISON

1 MINSTER ST, SALISBURY

What does seven hundred years of history look like? In the case of Haunch of Venison, a timber-framed "noted house for wines and spirits" that has stood on its site in Salisbury's Minster Street since 1320, it's a winning jumble of bars, a smattering of relics and myths, and a requisite complement of ghosts.

The sepia-toned days-of-yore ambience is set by a pair of compact bars on the ground floor; the wood-panelled Horsebox, a former "ladies snug", would actually just about accommodate a full-grown equine within its walls (and the photo of Winston Churchill and Dwight D. Eisenhower on the wall references the legend that the pair plotted the D-Day landings here in 1944), while the House of Commons, with its bench seating and roaring hearth, is the place where today's regulars, such as Jim Beam John and Half and Half Jim, maintain the age-old tradition of putting the world to rights. The bar boasts one of the few remaining pewter countertops in England, along with seven gravity-fed spirit taps dating back to 1909, though the prominent "Live eels" sign thankfully only promises rather than delivers. Upstairs, the House of Lords bar features a mummified hand housed in a former bread oven by the inglenook, said to be forcibly excised from a punter, christened the Demented Whist Player, after he was caught cheating during the titular card game sometime in the eighteenth-century (it's actually a replica; the original was stolen before being "handed in" to the police, and now resides in the Salisbury Museum). The top-floor restaurant, with its wealth of exposed beams and massive stone fireplace, looks onto St Thomas' Church (at the back, reflecting the fact that the building originally served as the church house) and the fourteenth-century Gothic Poultry Cross (at the front). It's also the place, according to owners Ilia and Anastasia Klekovkin, where a wealth of paranormal activity is served up alongside the venison sausages and casseroles, with reports of skittering chairs and shattering candleholders (all, frustratingly, occurring just out of CCTV reach). It could be the work of the Demented Whist Player (presumably wielding his remaining hand), or of the two female ghosts said to haunt the place; a mother looking for her lost son, and a forlorn denizen of the brothel that used to trade within the pub's premises. Given all this, it's brave of the Klekovkins to open up the "secret" bar, a tiny and crepuscular space under the restaurant with its own concealed entrance, just once a year – on Hallowe'en. But spooks and inebriated trick-or-treaters are not the only example of culture shock that the couple, natives of Nizhny Novgorod, have had to adjust to; there's also the concepts of lunchtime drinking ("we don't have that in Russia; here, a pint at midday is apparently perfectly acceptable"), and "pub golf", a five iron-themed pub crawl ("they're all dressed in golf shorts – in the middle of winter!")

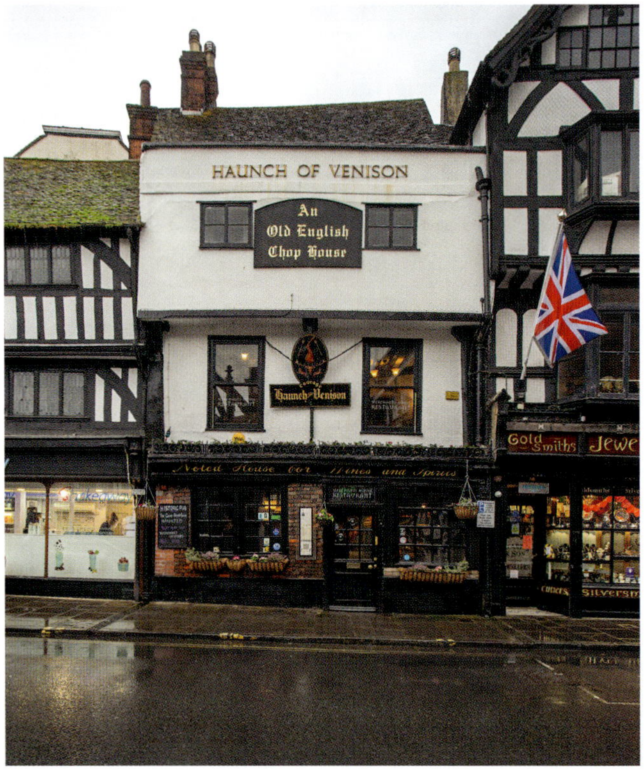

It's a tribute to their Anglophilia that, golf shorts notwithstanding, Ilia and Anastasia are still enamoured of the "romance" of the Haunch of Venison. "I love it when people come in here and their eyes go really wide, because we were the same," says Ilia.

"It's great to have the sense of history here and to see the way people care about it," adds Anastasia. "In Russia it's much easier to simply pull things down. We'd like to keep this place just the way it is, so that future generations can enjoy it." The next seven centuries start here.

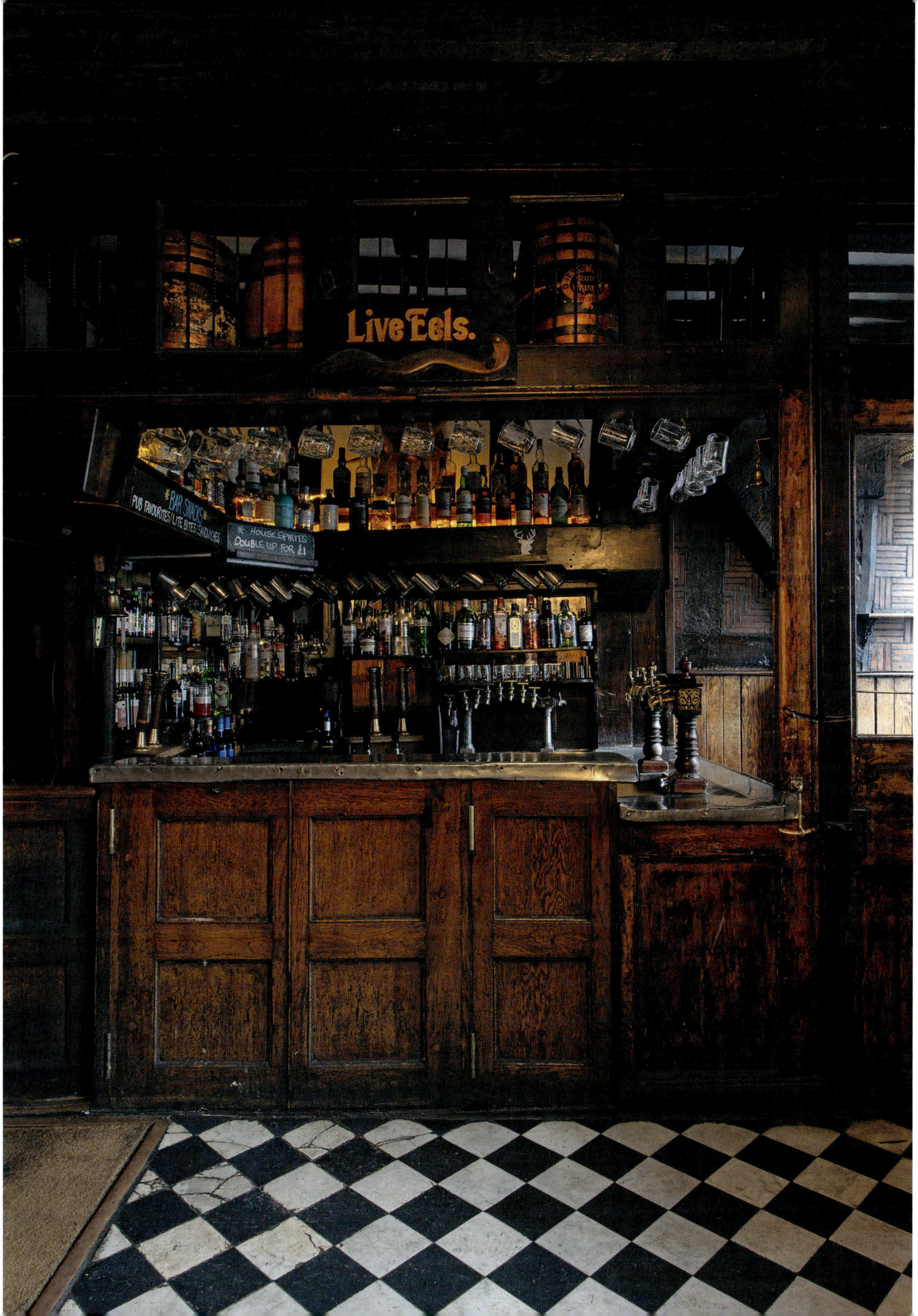

"WE WALKED IN HERE AND FELL IN LOVE"

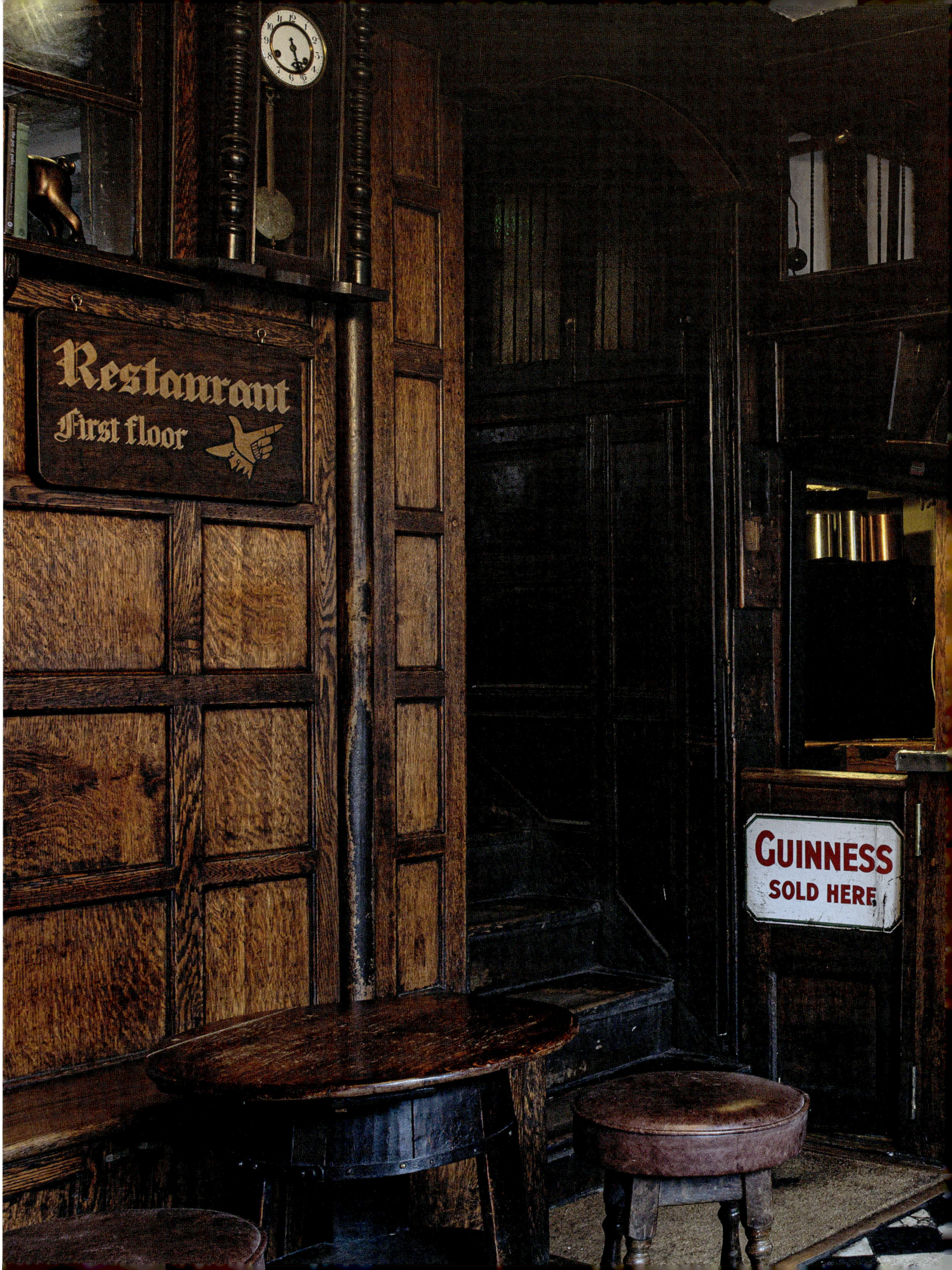
Restaurant
First floor
GUINNESS
SOLD HERE

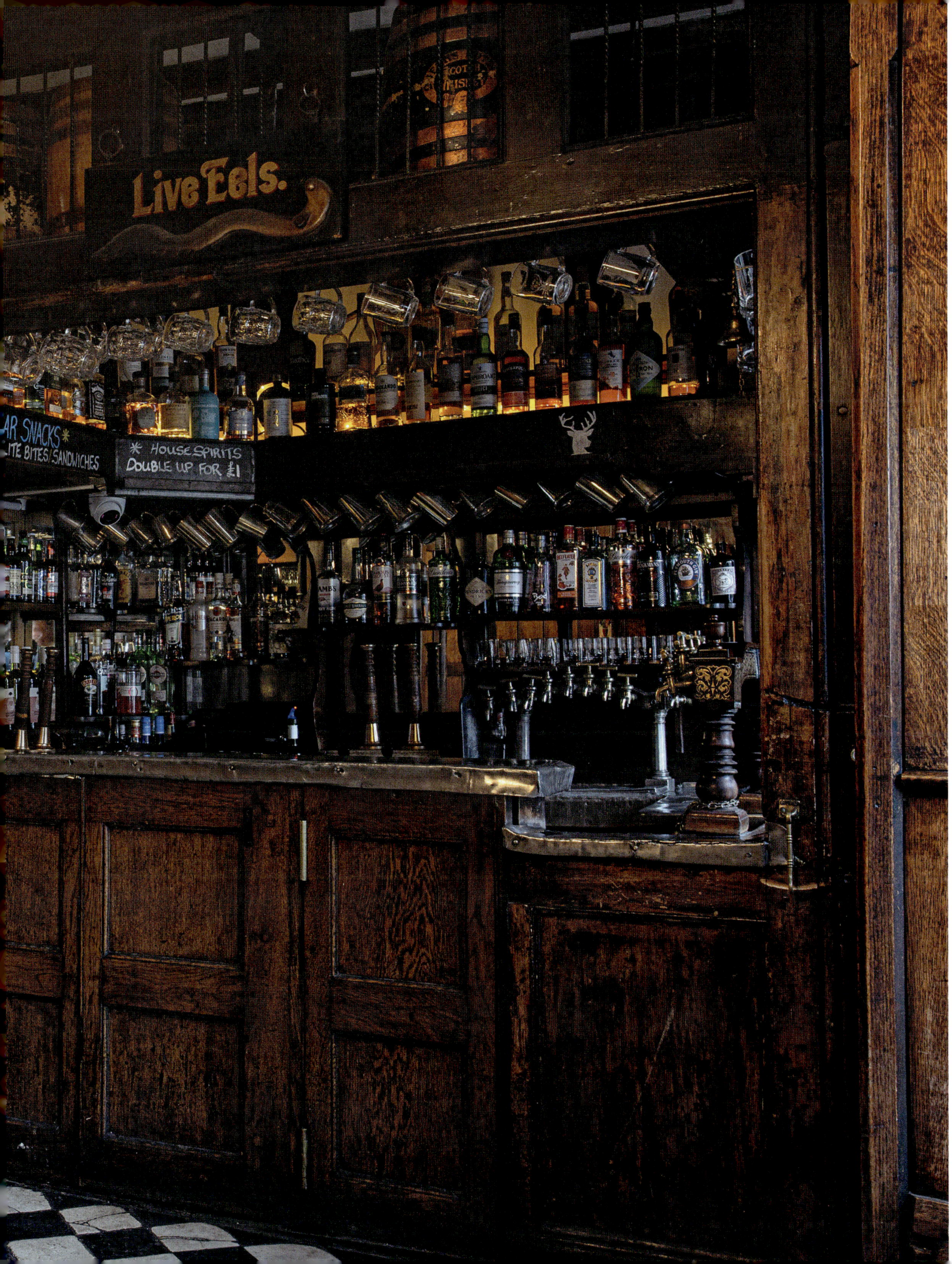

"... PEOPLE REALLY CARE ABOUT IT"

"THE PLACE IS ALIVE WITH SPIRITS"

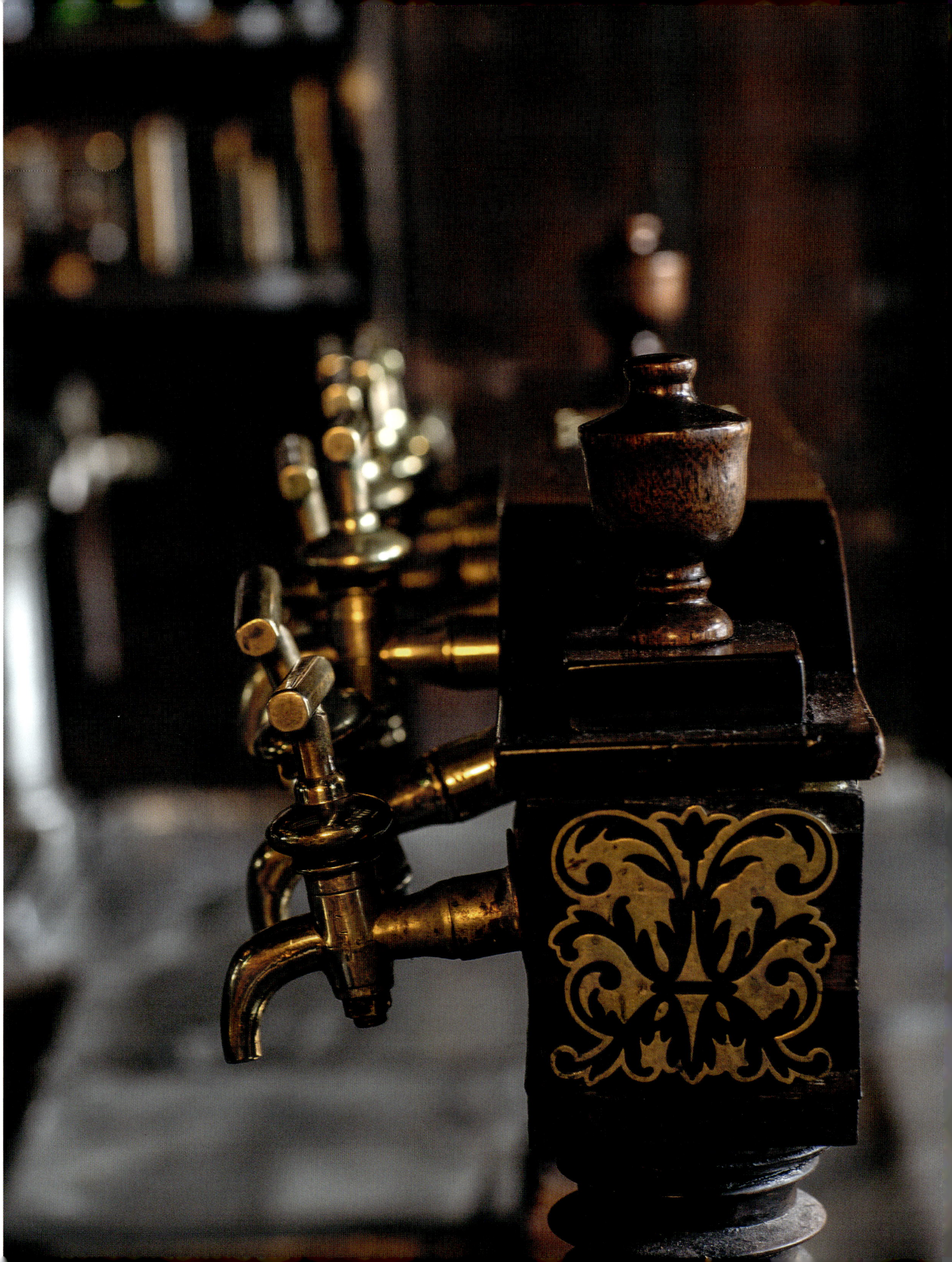

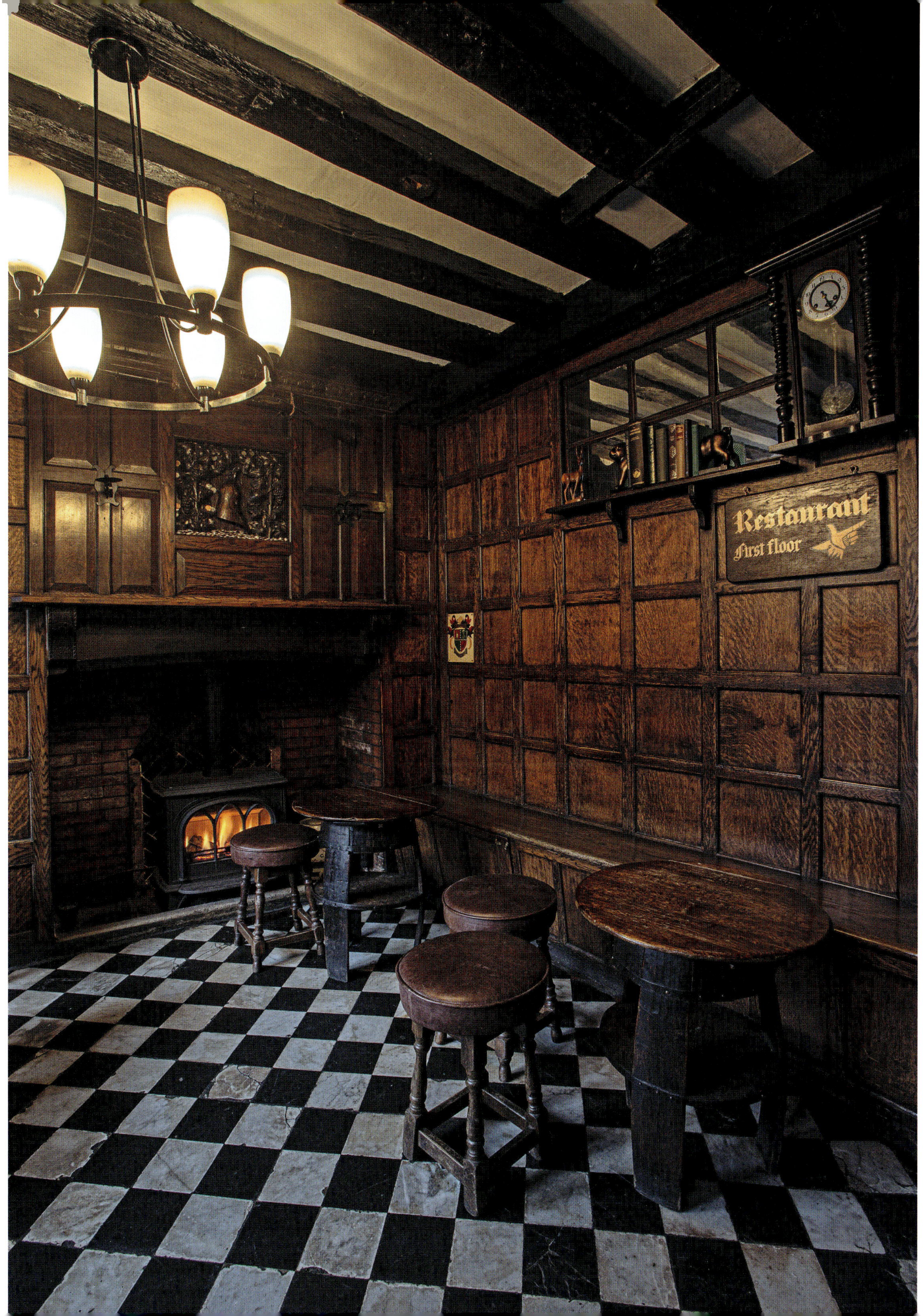

"THE FIRES ARE ALIGHT ALL THROUGH THE WINTER"

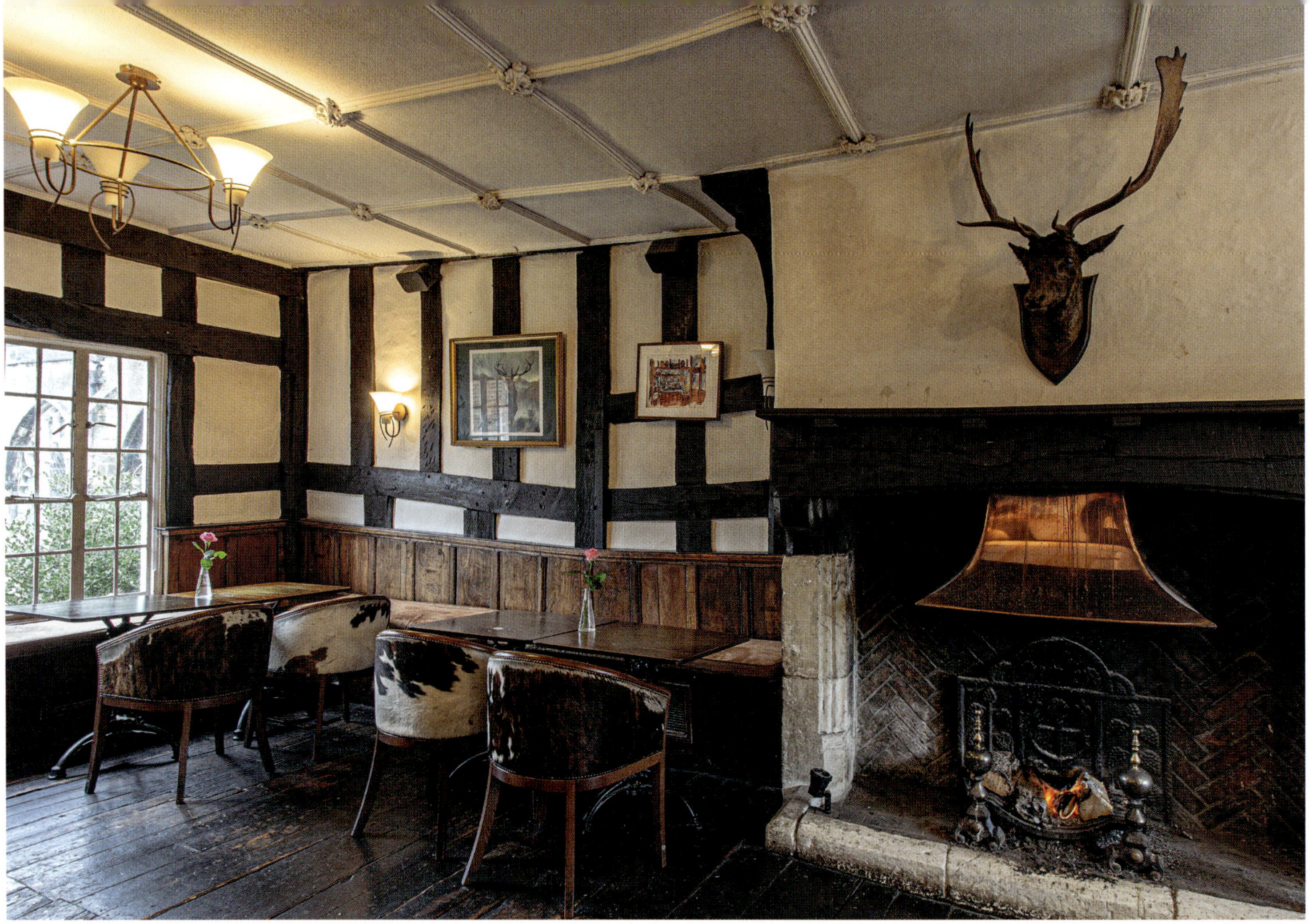

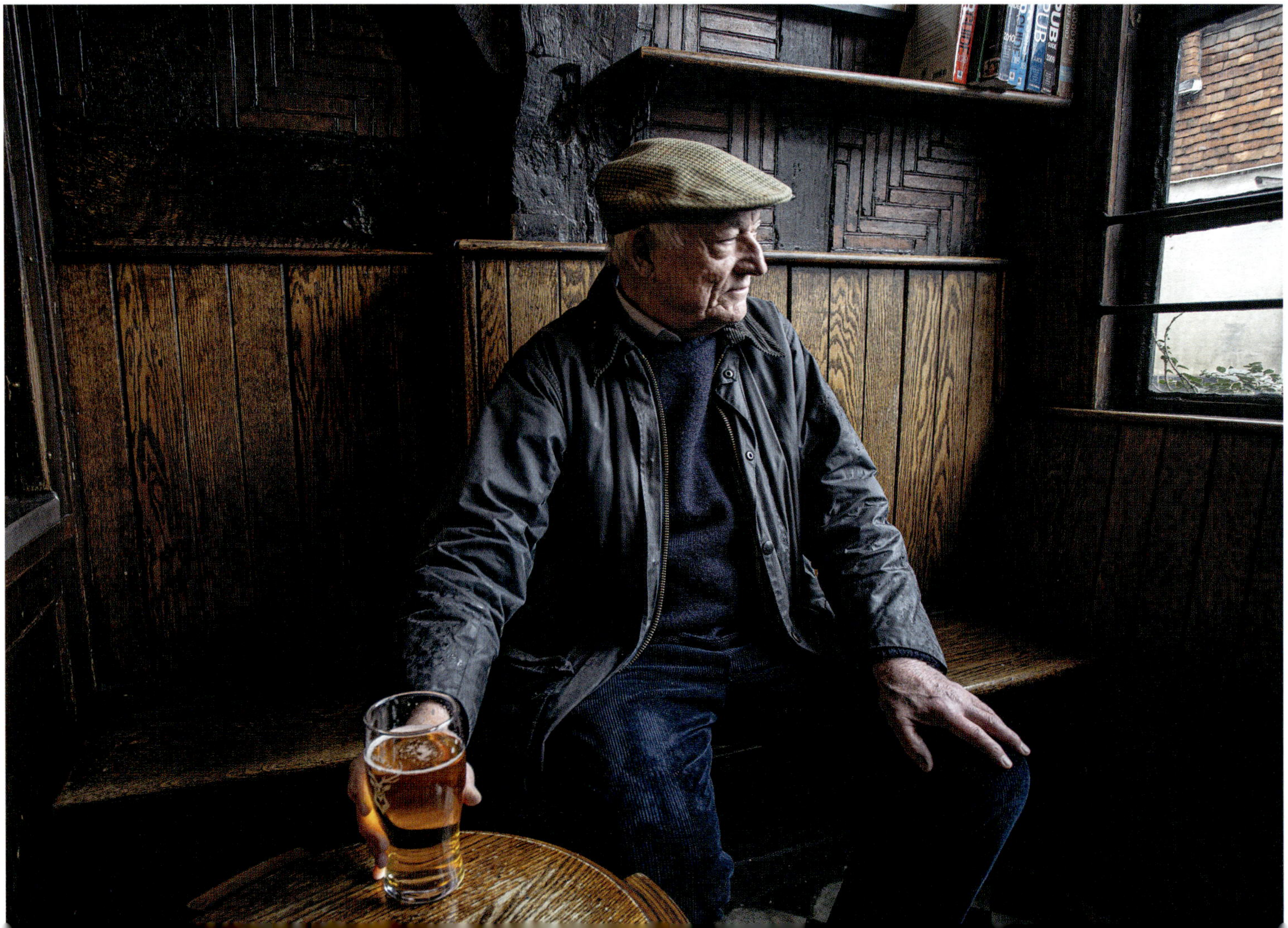

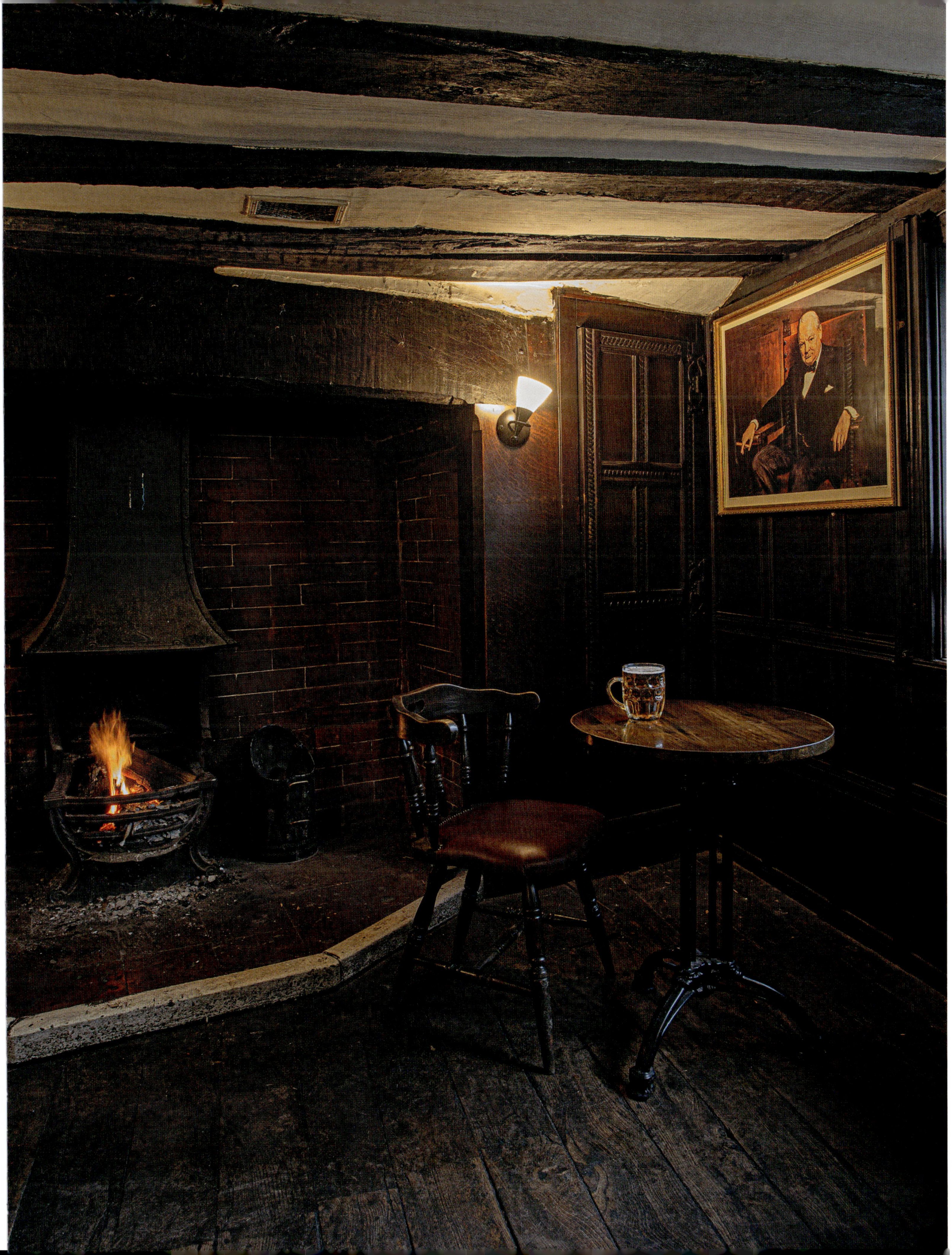

"THERE ARE SO MANY STORIES WITHIN THESE WALLS ..."

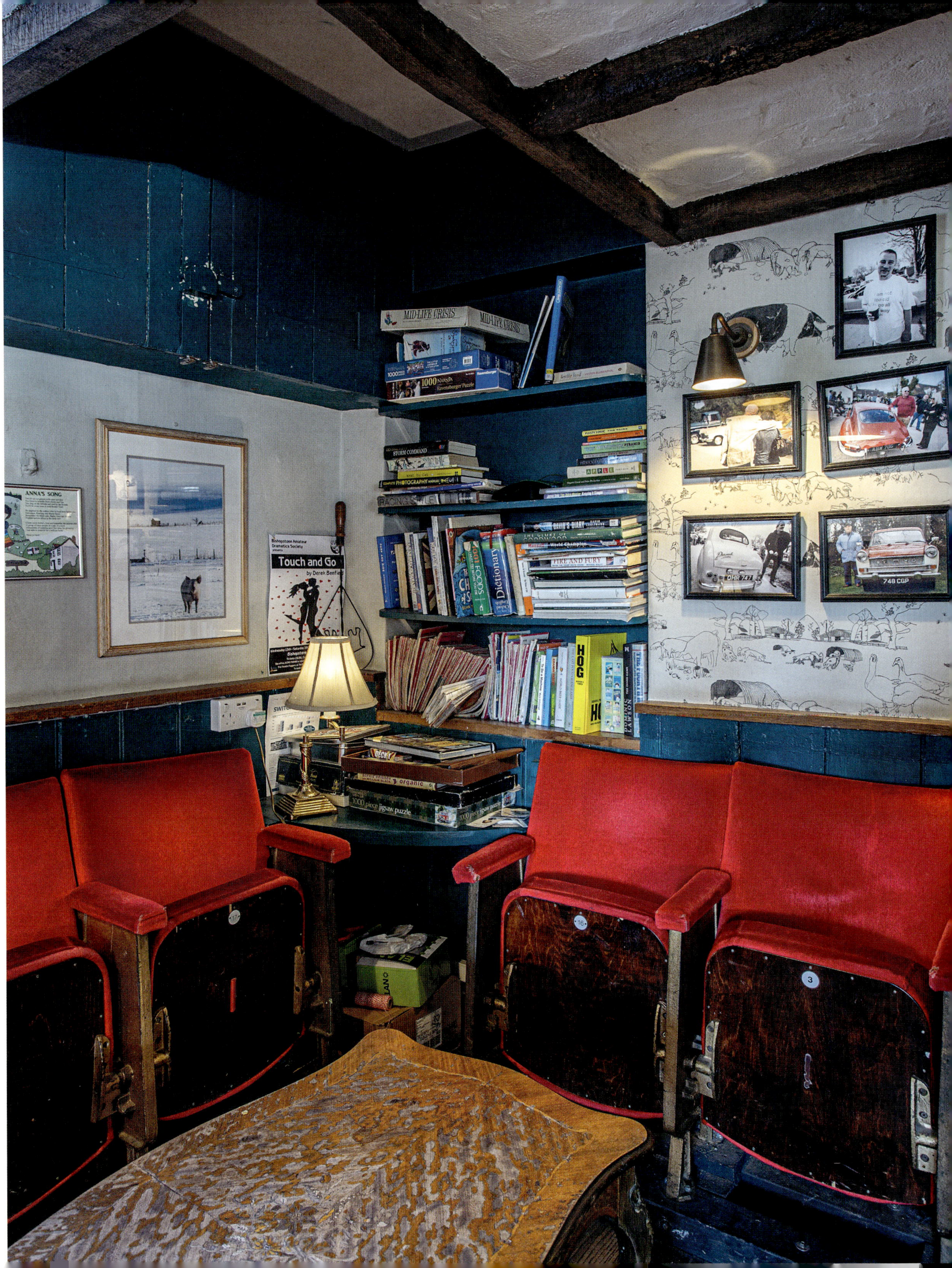
ANNA'S SONG
Touch and Go
by Derek Benfield
MID-LIFE CRISIS
1000
Dictionary
HOG
748 CGP

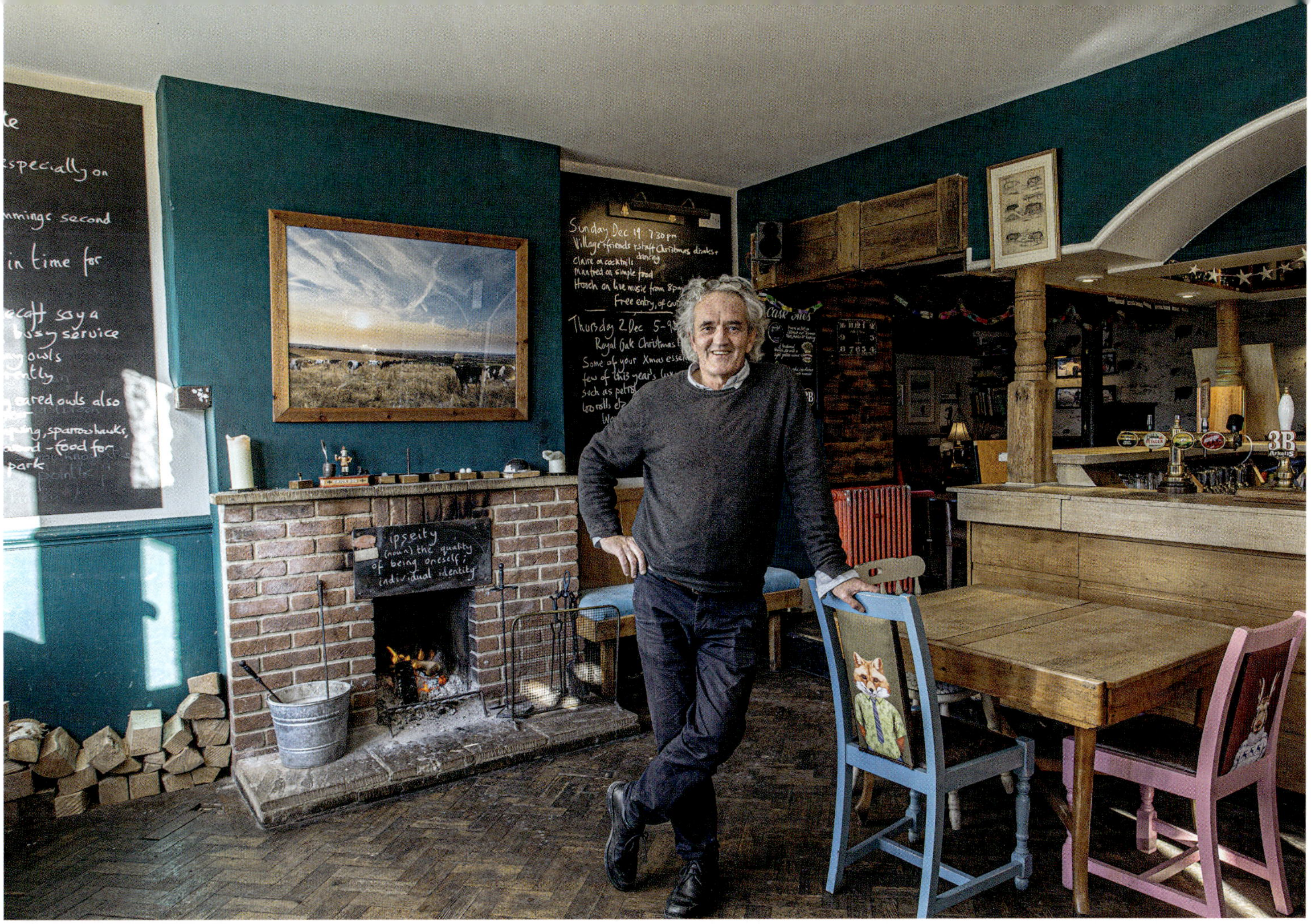

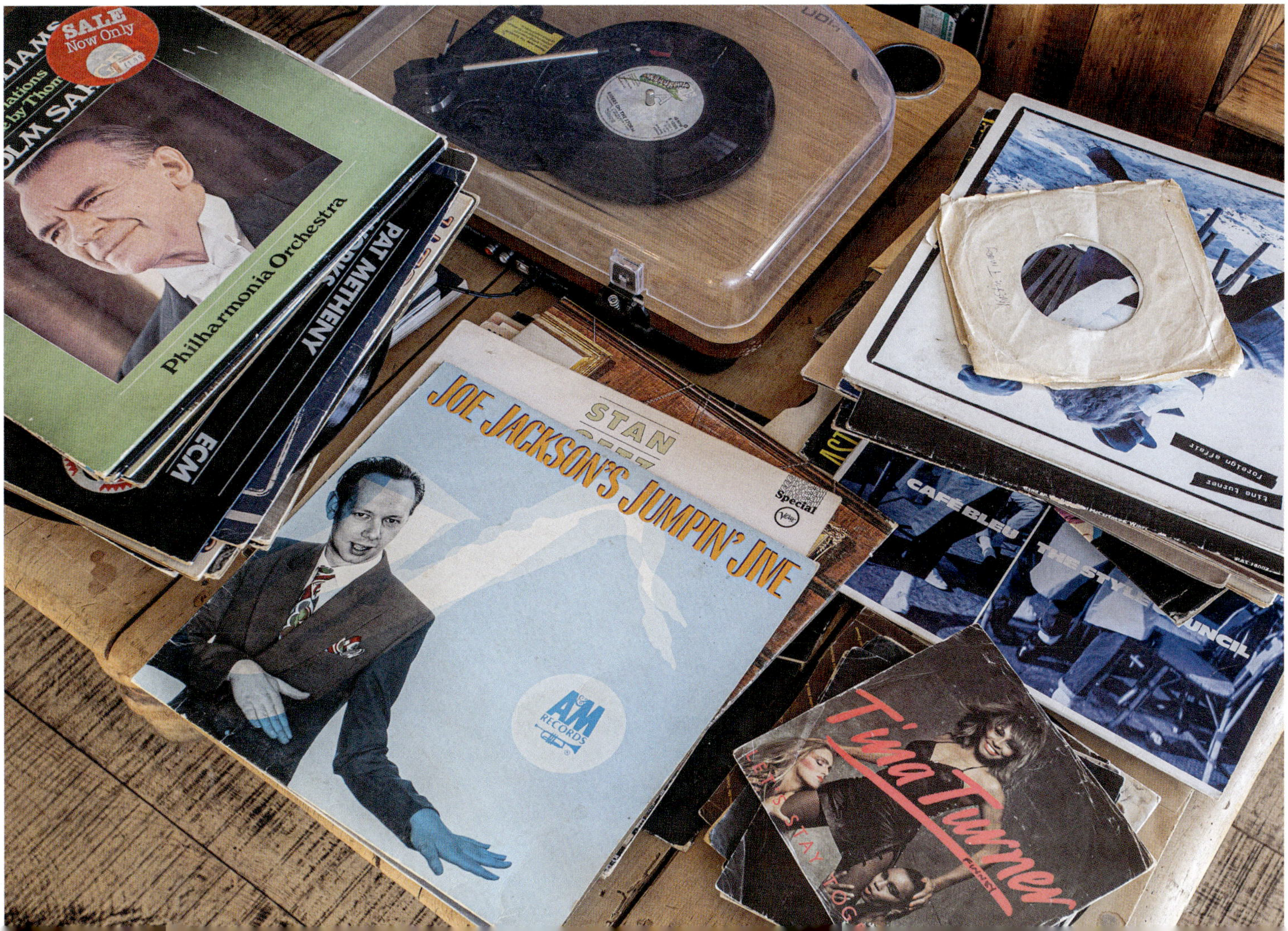

"WARM, GENEROUS, A LITTLE BIT IRREVERENT"

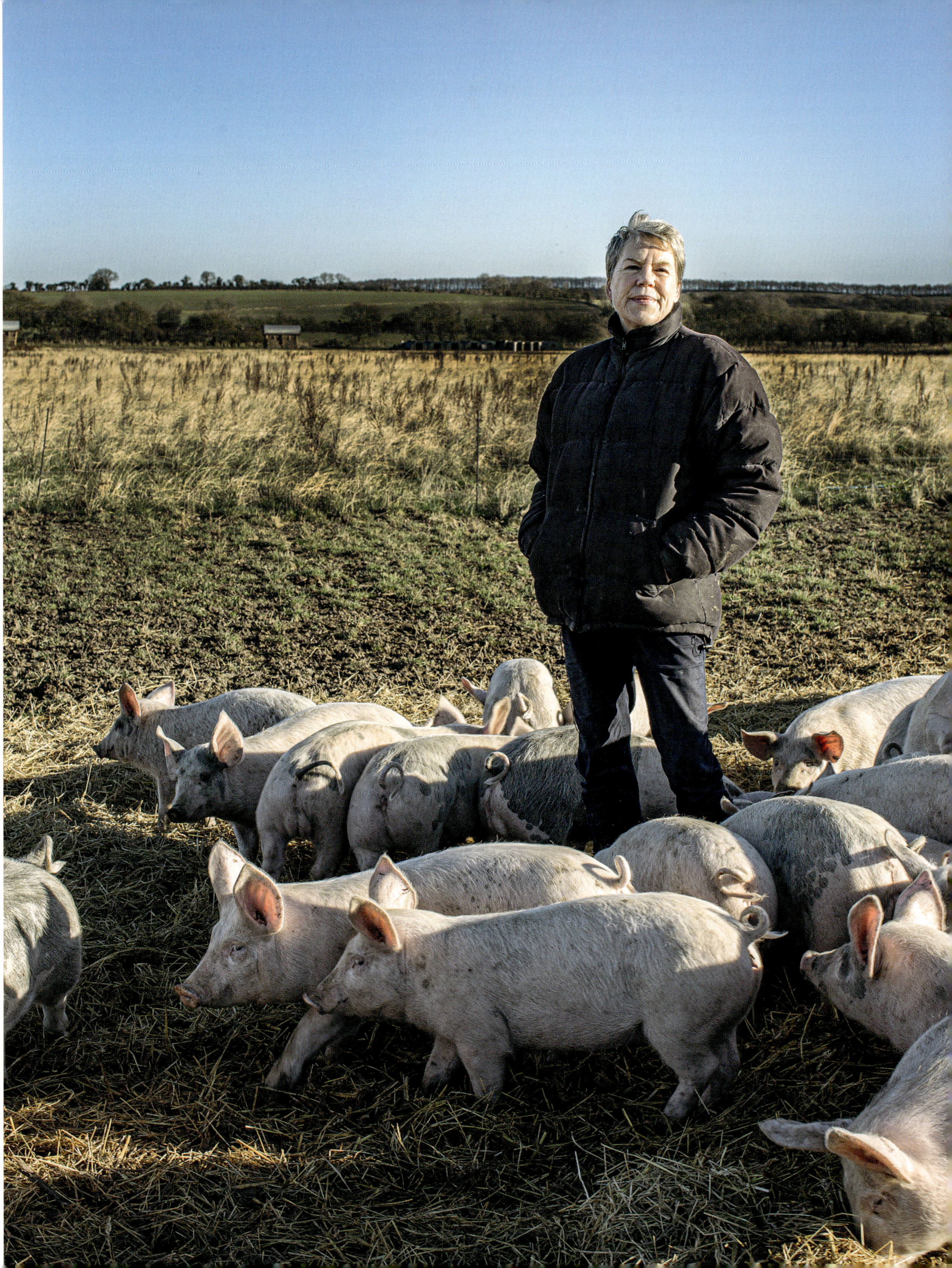

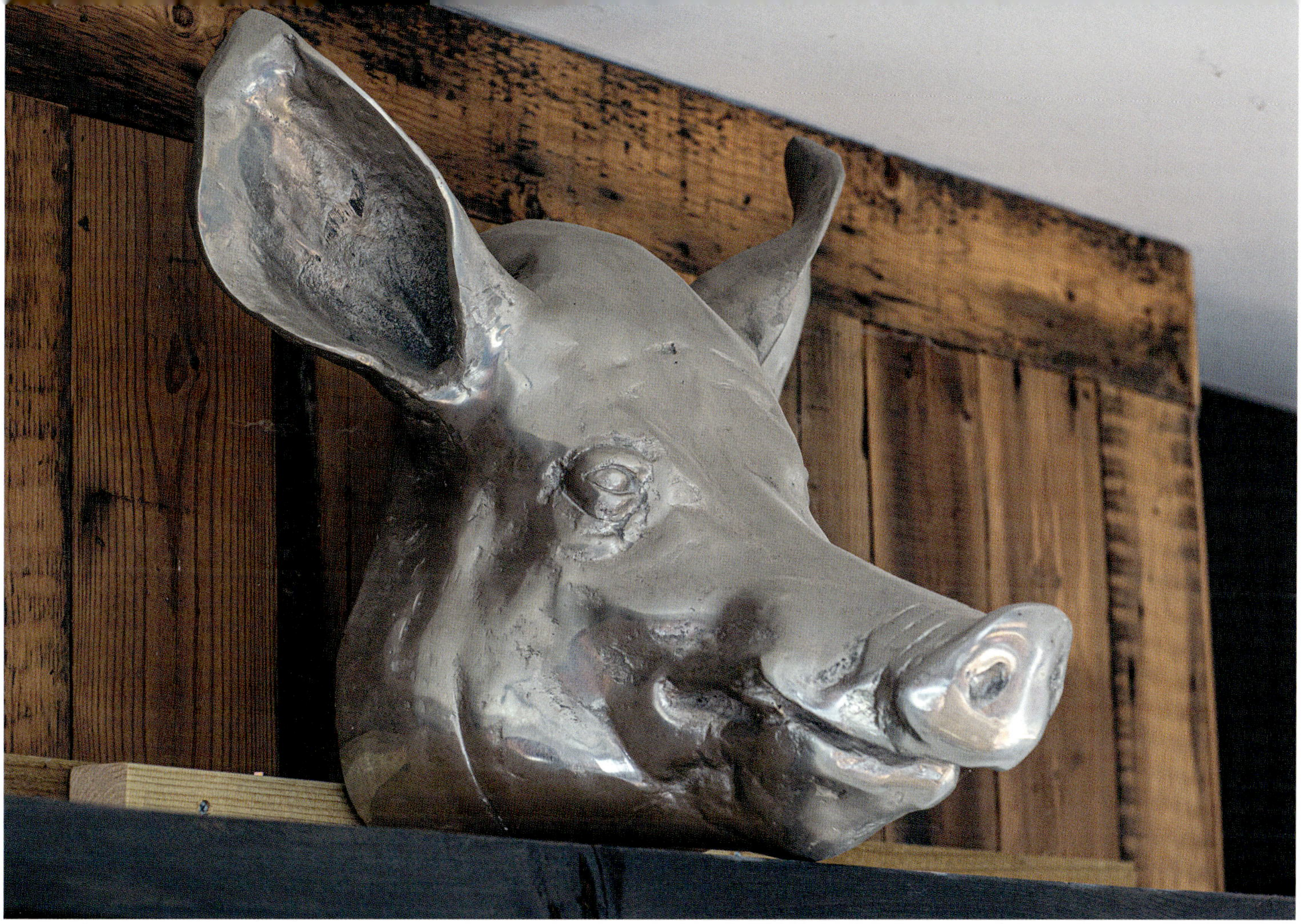

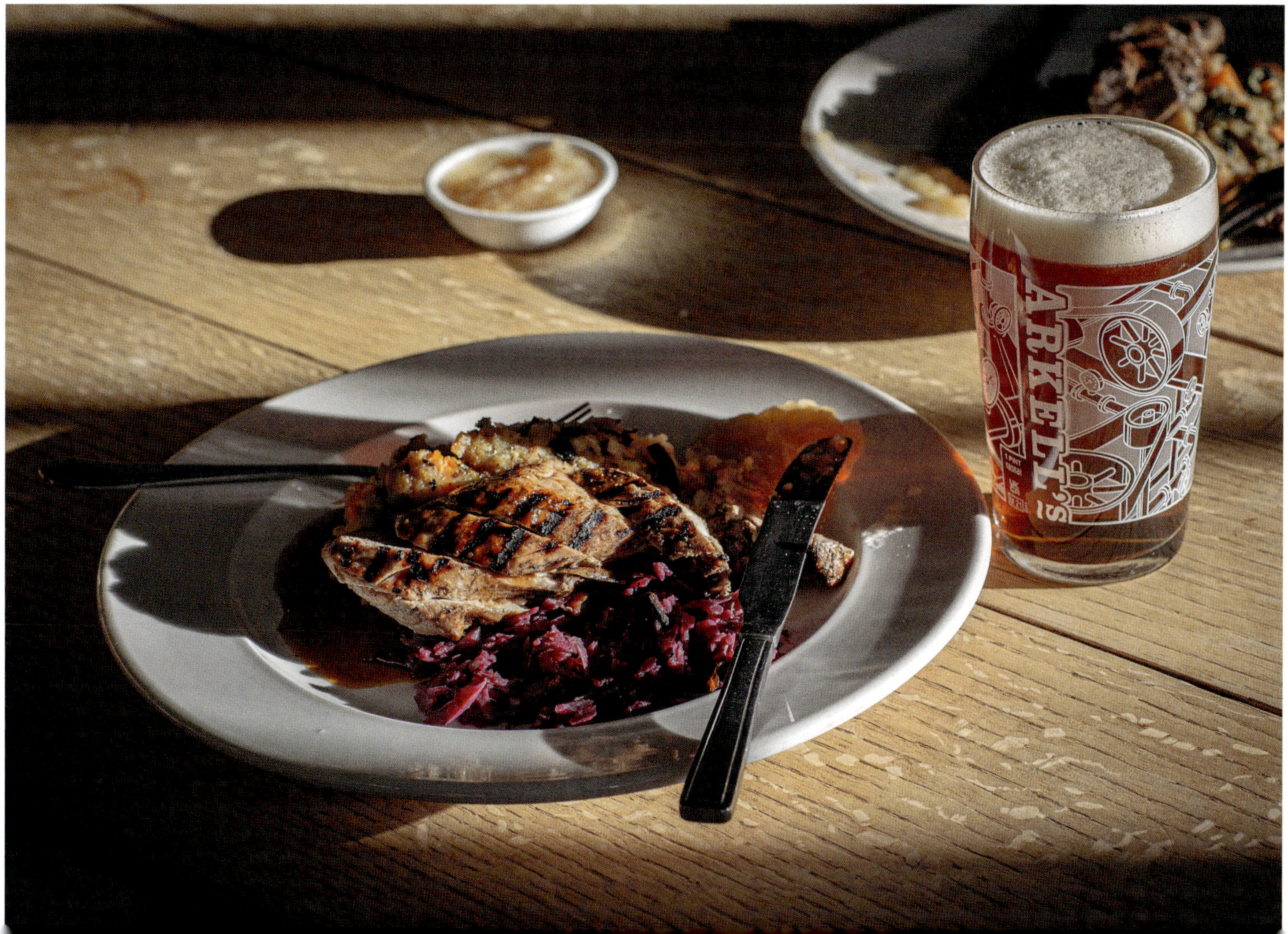

"IT FEELS LIKE A KIND OF MIRACLE"

TOLCARNE INN

9 TOLCARNE TERRACE, NEWLYN, PENZANCE

Ben Tunnicliffe is sitting in the bright Cornish sunshine, explaining why a pub is the best fit for his particular brand of cooking: "It takes away from the pomp and ceremony," he says. "I like things to be simple and rustic, no airs and graces. It might look unassuming from the outside, but you'll find there's something a bit special going on inside."

This is undoubtedly the case with Tunnicliffe's Tolcarne Inn, just inside the harbour wall in the fishing port and artists' colony of Newlyn, in Cornwall's far west. The building is undeniably modest, with its whitewashed walls and sun-trap courtyard, though a lintel above the door with the date of construction – 1717 – means it has been welcoming miners, seafarers and painters for more than three centuries. Now, it's also attracting foodies, in particular seafood lovers, which is Tunnicliffe's speciality: "There are fifty-three varieties of fish landed here, so I get to put all kinds of specials on my chalkboard," he says. "Like weaver fish, for example – you wouldn't think of cooking it, you just think of standing on the bloody thing and getting stung. But it's delicious."

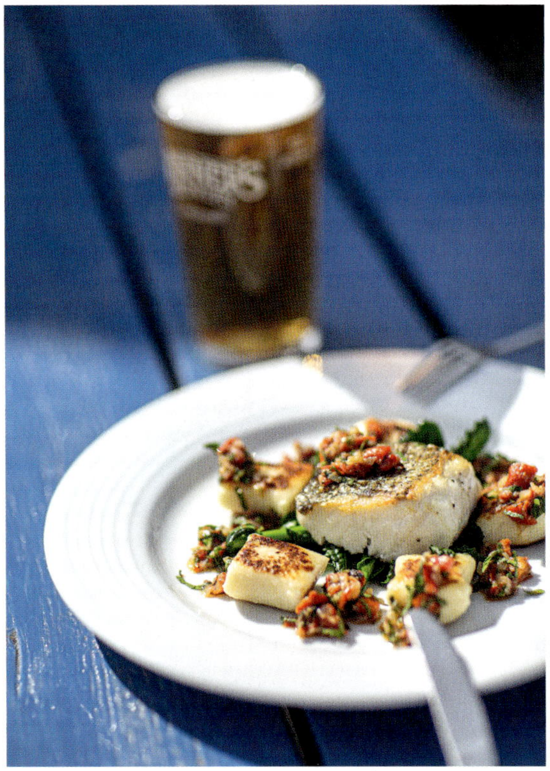

Remarkably, there was no fruits de mer-oriented venue in Newlyn before Bournemouth-born Tunnicliffe took the reins at the Tolcarne in 2012. He'd previously earned one of Cornwall's first Michelin stars at The Abbey in nearby Penzance in the early 2000s, but found the experience ambivalent at best. "I never set out to get a star, and people's perception became a problem; that who they think you think you are thing," he says. Tunnicliffe's language is as salty as the Atlantic, which we can hear gently lapping at the beach on the other side of the wall; he talks about "not dicking around with the ingredients", and creating "something that tastes the bollocks" – and the Tolcarne reflects his straightforward, honest earthiness. "I don't want people to feel uncomfortable, I want them to relax," he says. "Foams and syringes and molecular gastronomy isn't cooking to me, it's theatre, or chemistry. I'm simply trying to put a smile on people's faces."

Tunnicliffe achieves this with the help of "the amazing produce I have to draw on". Today, the gentle breeze carries a brackish aroma, along with a deep-sea undertow from the nearby fish market. He has two daily suppliers from the latter (he's also licensed to buy directly from the boats, though he rarely has time to make it to the quayside), and by mid-morning the catch is being prepped along with the bar – all whitewashed beams, plaid banquettes, a crackling wood burner, and watercolours depicting some of the house favourites (mussels, crab, gurnard). At lunchtime, the kitchen is in full cry ("two mussels, one monkfish!") and diners are making appropriately appreciative noises over the likes of whole lemon sole with crushed Cornish earlies and brown shrimp butter; spiced monkfish with hummus, pomegranate dressing and dukkah; or hake, pancetta and fagioli bean stew, washed down with Cornish beers including Lushington's and, fittingly, Offshore pilsner. "We have a solid core of regulars here, as well as the seasonal influx of visitors," says Tunnicliffe. "Newlyn has managed to retain that sense of community, while other places have simply become hollowed out with holiday homes. It's always a conundrum for places like ours, because we need both to stay sustainable."

For now, as the sun does its circuit and the prospect of a vanilla crème brûlée looms, there are fewer places one would rather be; there are smiles all round, including from Tunnicliffe, emerging, in his apron, from another session of de-scaling and expectation-exceeding. "Job done," he says.

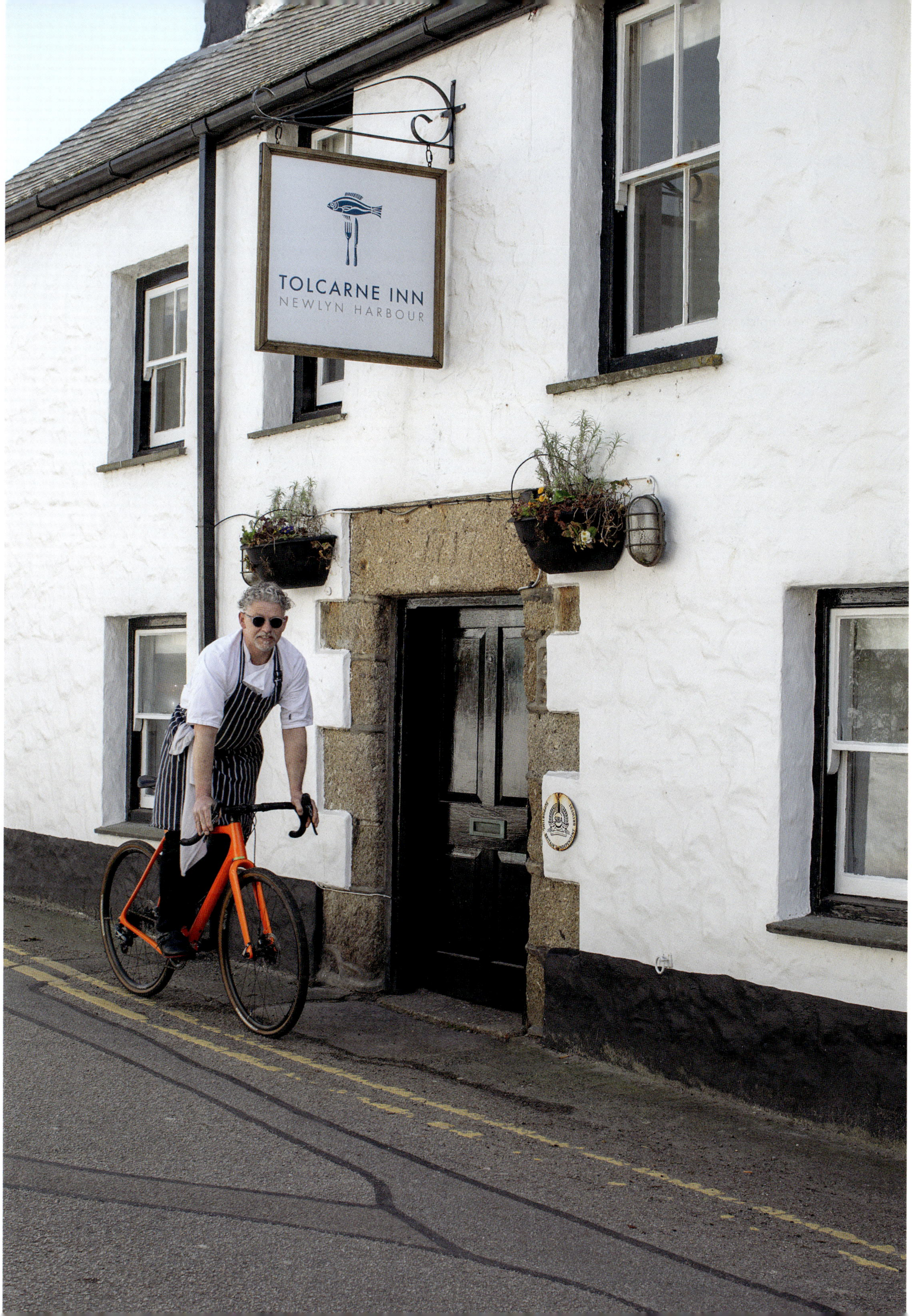

"UNASSUMING FROM THE OUTSIDE, SOMETHING SPECIAL INSIDE"

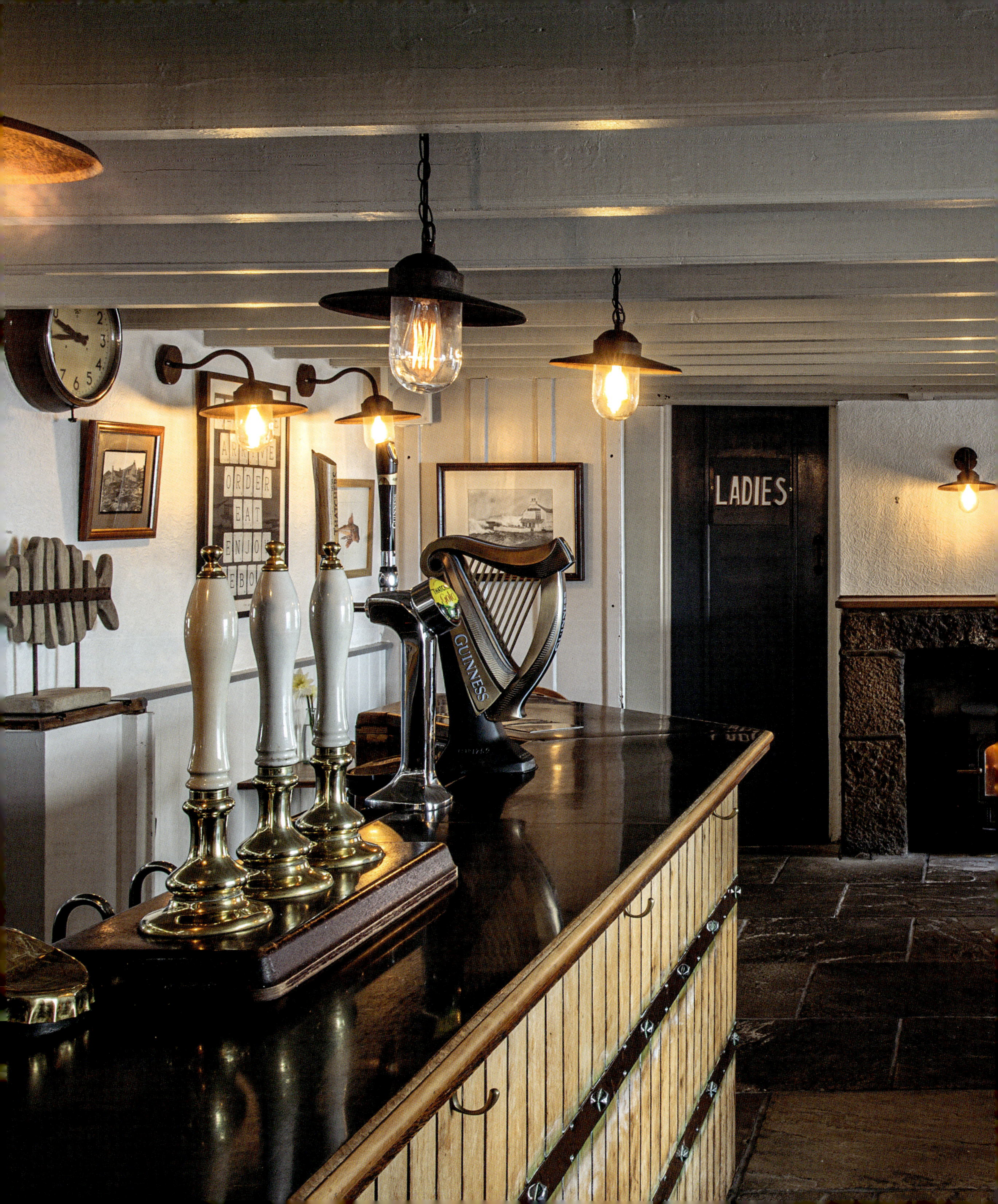
ARRIVE
ORDER
EAT
GUINNESS
LADIES

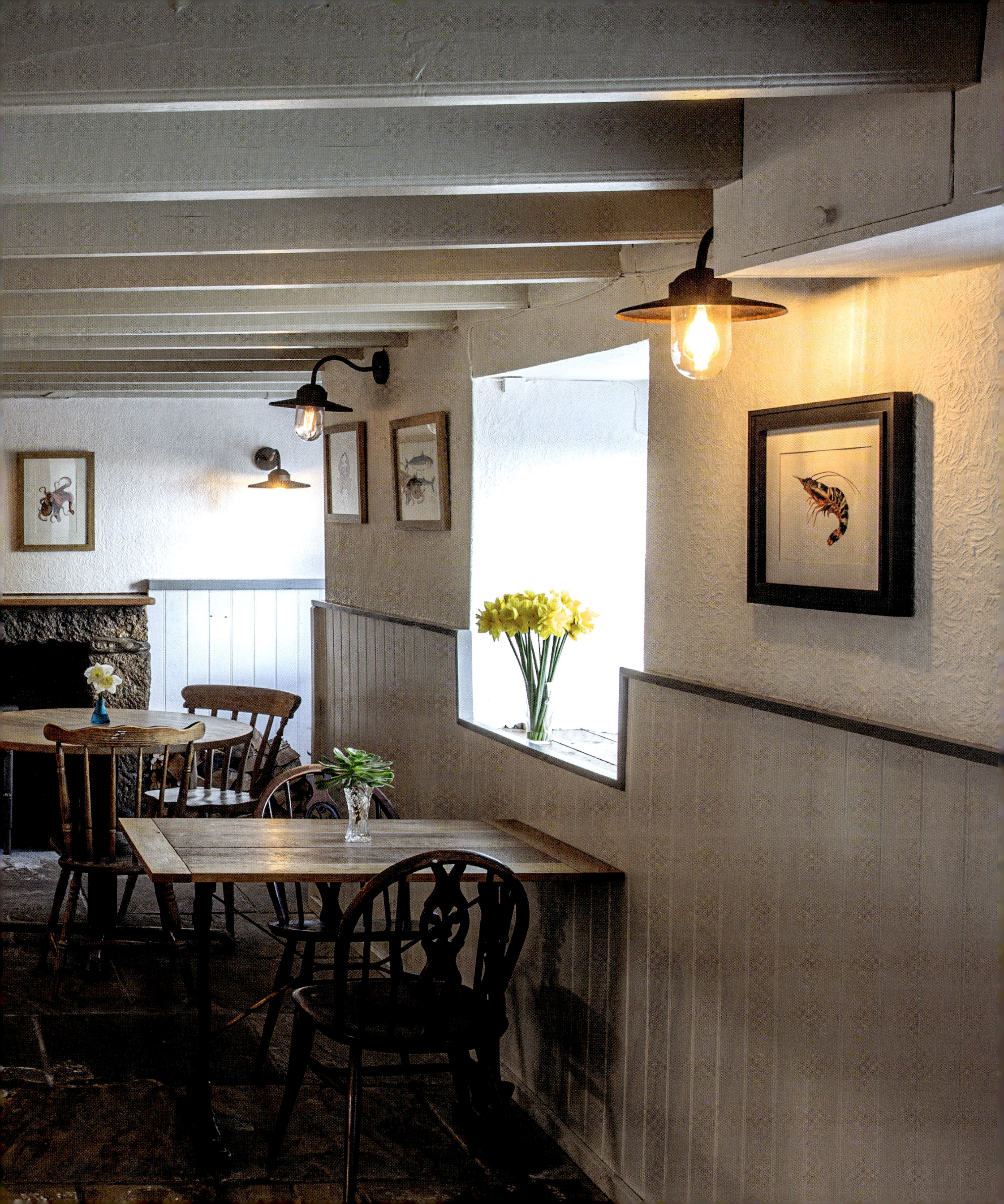

THE BLUE ANCHOR

50 COINAGEHALL ST, HELSTON

Younger generations tend to think they invented all the fun stuff – sex, for example, or shopping, or microbrewing. So it might give the craft-bearded, small-batch mash-tunners of Shoreditch pause for thought to realise that there's a pub in the market town of Helston, near Cornwall's south coast, that's been malting, milling and fermenting its own ale for close on six hundred years.

The Blue Anchor certainly looks the venerable part. Fulsomely thatched, and crouching between the surrounding buildings, it's thought to have begun life as a monk's rest house around 1400, and was then converted into a tavern sometime in the mid-sixteenth century. Inside, its compact rooms open off a flagstone alleyway, worn to a concave sheen by centuries of footfall. The cramped bar is festooned with tankards and bedecked with hand pulls; walk through to the back and you'll find a jumble of outbuildings including an expansive outdoor area, a still-functioning eighteenth-century skittle alley, and, up a flight of stone steps and through a door marked "brewery", landlord Ben Stone, keeping a close eye on his copper. "This is where the magic happens," he says.

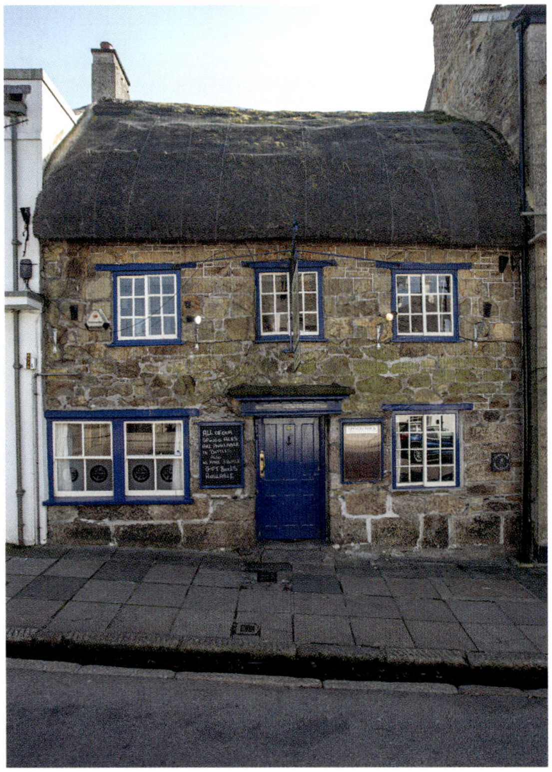

Stone recently assumed the pub's reins from his parents, Simon and Kim (resolutely unfazed by the fact that, among his predecessors in the eighteenth and nineteenth centuries, one was stabbed to death, one fell to his death in The Blue Anchor's well, and yet a third hung himself in the skittle alley). The magic he's referring to is Spingo, the pub's signature ale. Possibly originally brewed by those chillaxing monks – the history books fall silent on this point – it's definitely potent (Stone points out that the name comes from the Old English slang word "stingo", meaning "strong ale"), with its various iterations, including Jubilee ("smooth, Indian pale, complex hop") and Special ("smooth, defined, dark reddish, well hopped") coming in north of 5%, and up to 6.6%, when the more mainstream British beers commonly sit closer to 4%. But it's Middle ("smooth, reddish, lightly hopped") that is the crowd-pleaser, The Blue Anchor's 'Stairway to Heaven' or 'Bohemian Rhapsody'. It was first brewed to welcome home soldiers returning from the First World War, and if anything could have temporarily deferred memories of the trenches, this juicy, malty confection, rich with dried fruit and plum, with a light peppering of bitterness and a lingering nutty aftertaste, would have been it. On Flora Day, Helston's spring festival, Stone needs to brew sixty kegs of Middle at eighty-two litres each to meet popular demand; no wonder it's exalted in a poem hung in the back bar ("you'll be singing one moment and snoring the next"), or that its fans, including beer pilgrims from Germany, Japan and the United States, as well as locals, talk reverently of "being Spingo'd".

"A lot of people say it's a happy beer," offers Stone during a break from his labours, and, indeed, there's a general hum of contentment coming from the smattering of regulars (and a Japanese visitor) as they take their leisurely lunchtime sips (The Blue Anchor stopped doing food after plates and cups started flying, unassisted, off tables and shelves – perhaps a warning from the spirits of those long-gone landlords not to put any spin on the Spingo). There's a sweet smell of fermentation in the air, and a few drunken wasps are jerkily buzzing about – it seems that they, too, have been Spingo'd. The Blue Anchor hosts beer festivals, and Middle and its peers are now available online, but the heart of it all remains the unassuming brewery. "It's strange to think that the essential processes haven't changed in all this time," says Stone. "It feels like I'm the custodian of a long and noble tradition."

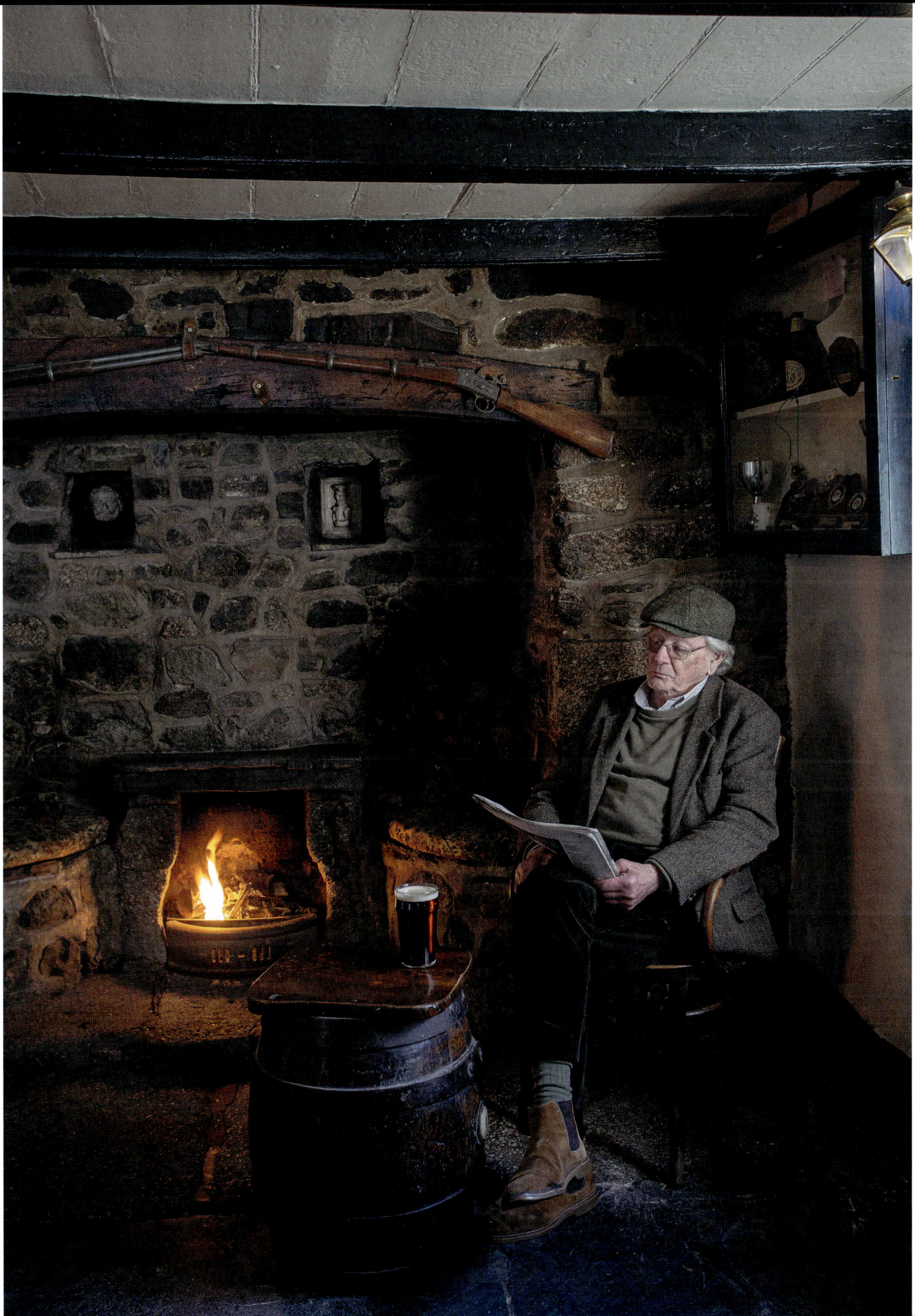

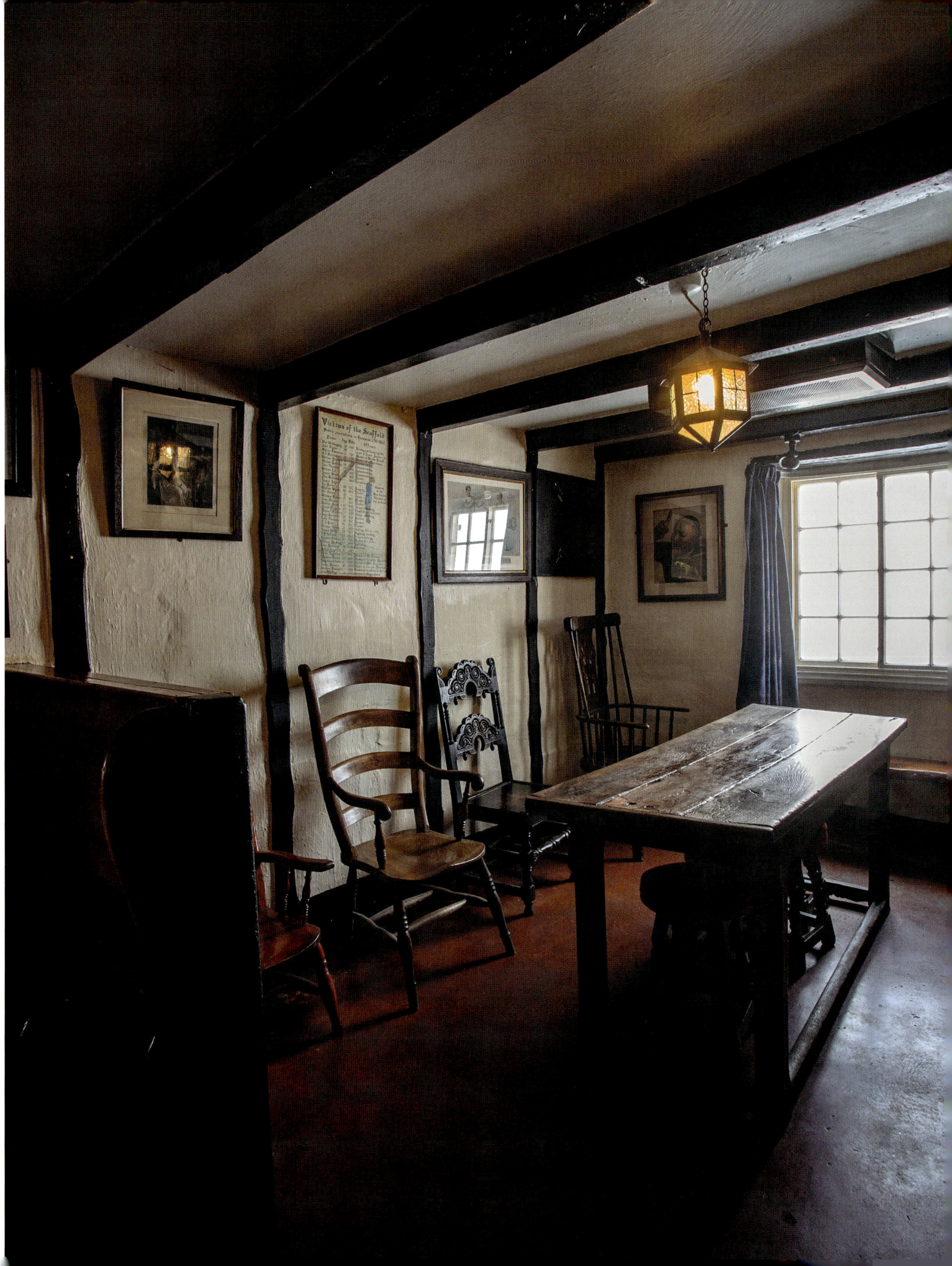
Victims of the Scaffold

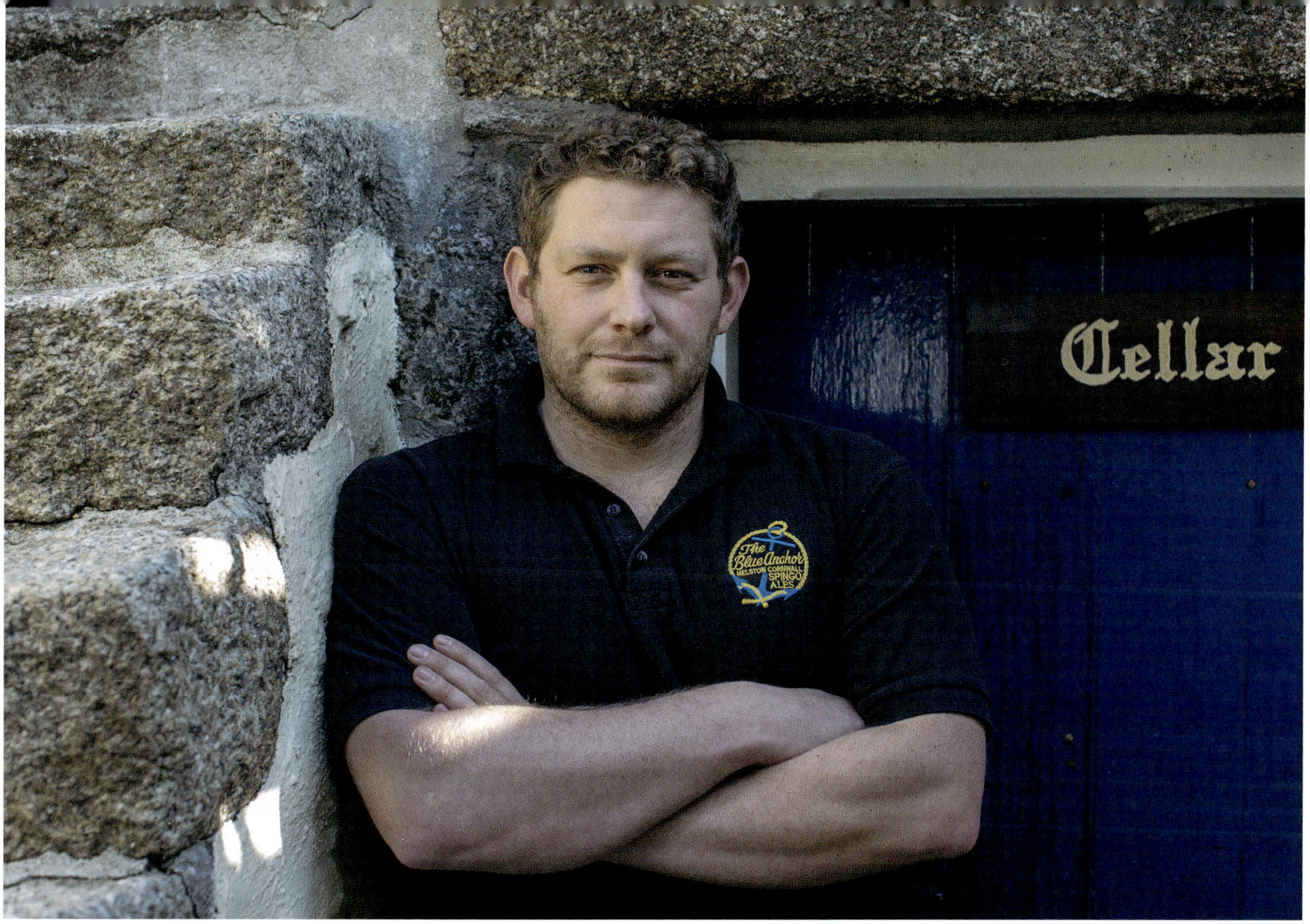

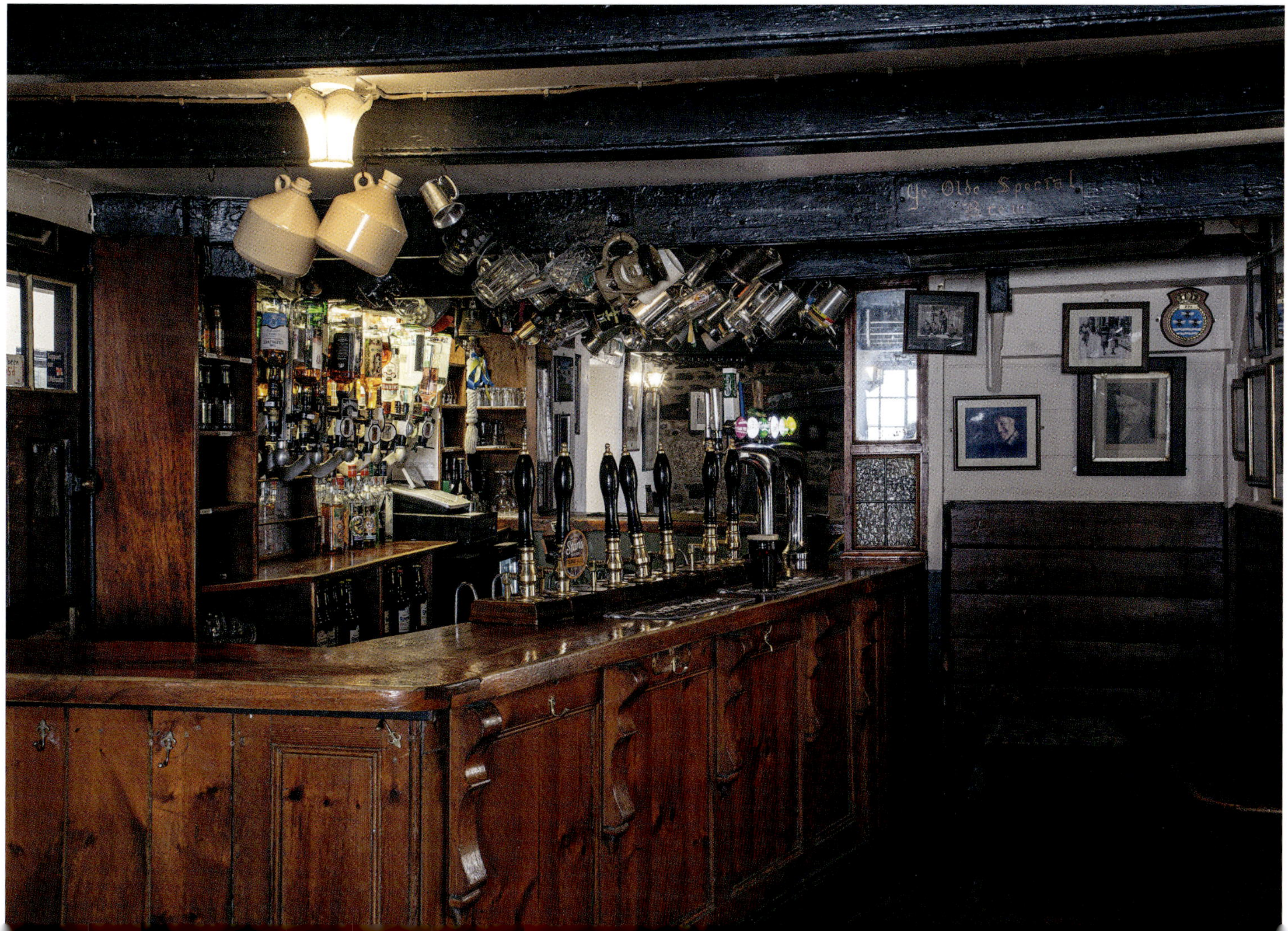

"IT'S ABOUT MAKING PEOPLE HAPPY IN A VERY BASIC WAY"

"THE BIGGEST DRAW FOR ME WAS THE SENSE OF FAMILY …"

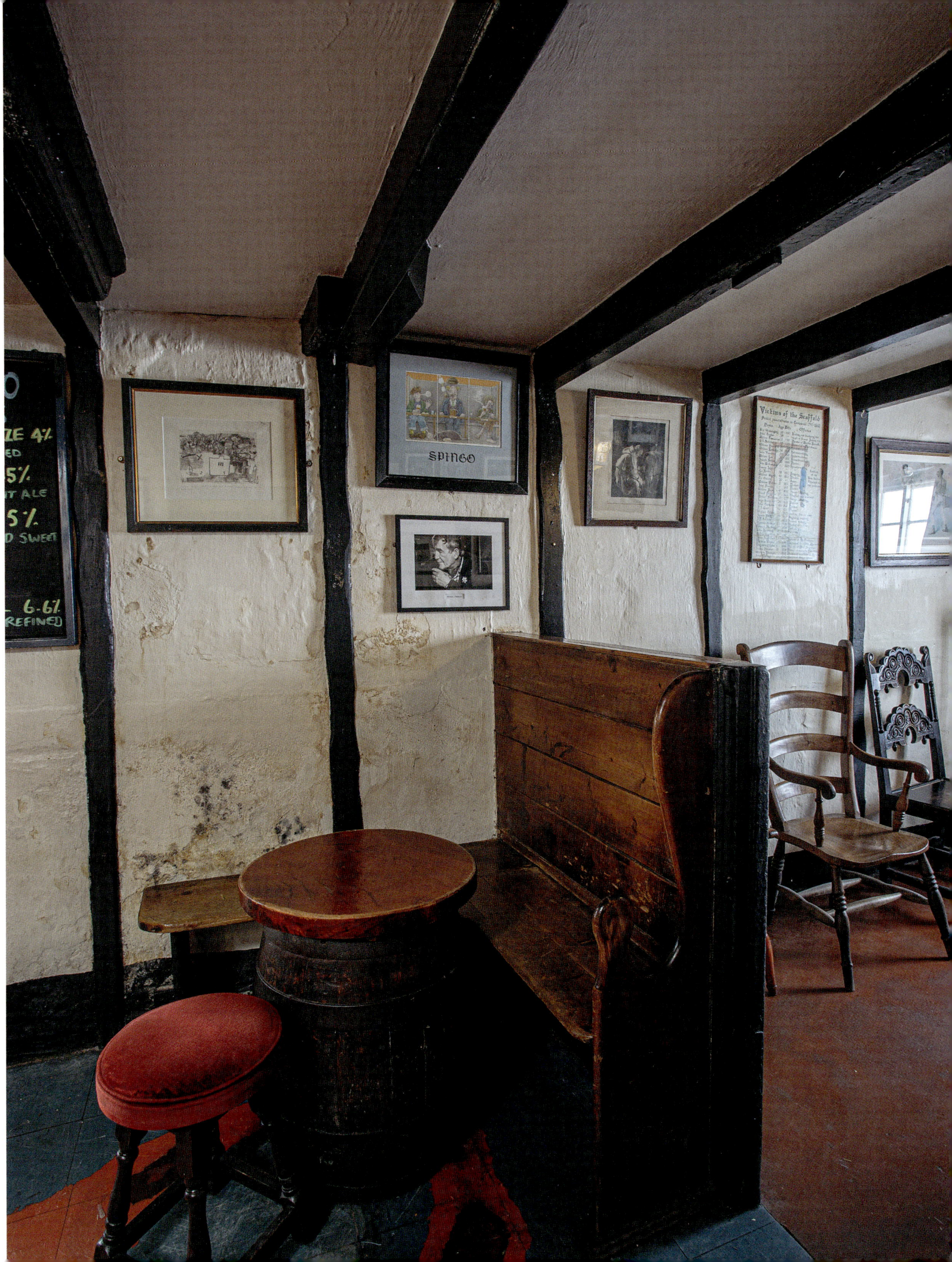

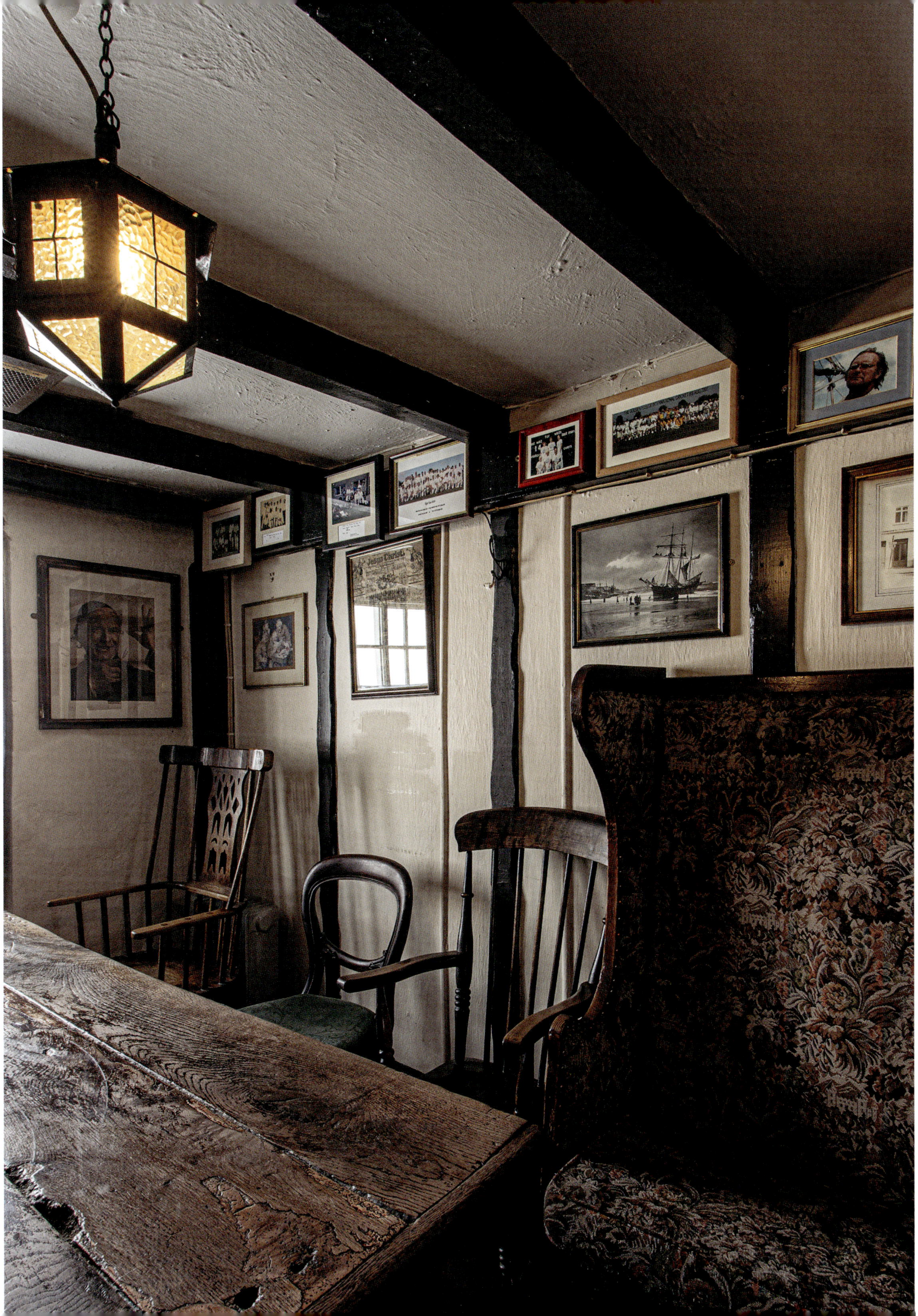

"… MAKING SURE EVERYONE'S LOOKED AFTER PROPERLY"

THE FARMERS ARMS

WOOLFARDISWORTHY, BIDEFORD

"I'm sentimental about places," says Michael Birch. "I feel a lot of connection to them."

For many people, this would simply equate to a warm, fuzzy feeling; for Birch, who made an early dot-com fortune when selling his pioneering social-networking site Bebo in 2008, it means something more practical, at least in the case of Woolsery, a village tucked into the rolling North Devon hills, where his grandmother was born and where he spent his childhood summers. By the mid-2010s it had declined from best-kept village status to a place where both the pub and the nearby Manor hotel and restaurant lay derelict. Birch bought both, then added the chippie, the village shop, a number of cottages and a couple of outlying farms to his portfolio; today "the Woolsery project" employs more than seventy people, and The Farmers Arms, reopened in 2019, is a showcase for the talent he's brought to bear on the regeneration of the village. "I used to go there when I was younger, and I met my wife Xochi in a bar, so I know a pub's value as a social space," he says. "We wanted to do it right, and do it well."

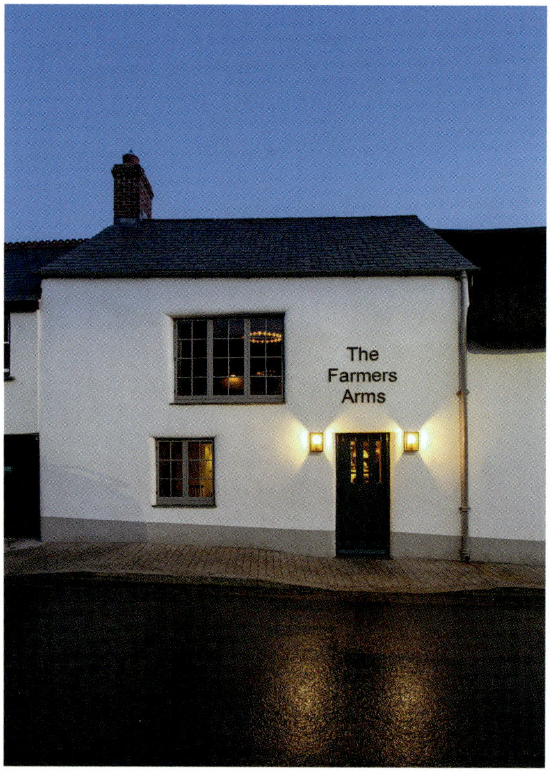

The old Farmers had a somewhat forbidding reputation – "I heard about the old owner hitting people with pool cues and chasing them down the street, like something out of the Wild West," says Woolsery project manager Emily Harmon – which only serves to point up the contrast of its new incarnation, perhaps best described as haute hunting lodge; two massive bulls' heads look down on stripped-back pale grey plasterwork and exposed stone, with Chesterfields and banquettes clad in jazzy plaids, and Victorian portraits mingling with a hologram of David Bowie demonstrating his tai chi technique (the toilets are labelled "bays" and "maids", a tribute to Old North Devon patois). "It's a blend of old and new, time-honoured and modern," says Harmon. "Michael and Xochi are obsessed with things being comfortable, but you also have new takes on tradition, like the contemporary pewter plates that hark back to old tankards."

Similarly, the food, under the aegis of chef Ian Webber, reinvigorates a raft of pub standards. Thus, you can sample a Birch Farm Hogget, with courgette, tomato and lavender; a Monkfish and Scallop Fishcake (with a poached Birch Farm egg); or – the biggest revelation to California-born Harmon – a raft of steamed puddings and custards. "Our inspiration is, what would you have seen on the menu of a coaching inn back in the day?" says Harmon. "So it's roasted meats from the farm, and vegetables from the garden, and we build on those with different textures and flavours." There are also complementary local beers like Tarka (named for Henry Williamson's fictional otter, who plashed about in the nearby River Torridge), and – another nod to the local dialect – Proper Ansome. "We support local makers and suppliers, and make a lot of things ourselves, and people were really receptive and embracing of the fact that we don't do the marquee brands," says Harmon. "That's been the thing that's made me happiest – that people are open to what we're doing here."

The Farmers now attracts visitors from across the region, as well as maintaining a solid core of regulars, including the village choir (after practice) and the skittles team (after fixtures). So how does building real communities compare to building virtual ones? "I'm not a great believer in the latter any more," says Birch. "I feel like the village is the ultimate community, a microcosm of society as a whole. And there are certain institutions that help bind that community together, the pub foremost among them. I'm thrilled to see the Farmers back at the heart of Woolsery, and I hope we've given it another hundred-year lease of life."

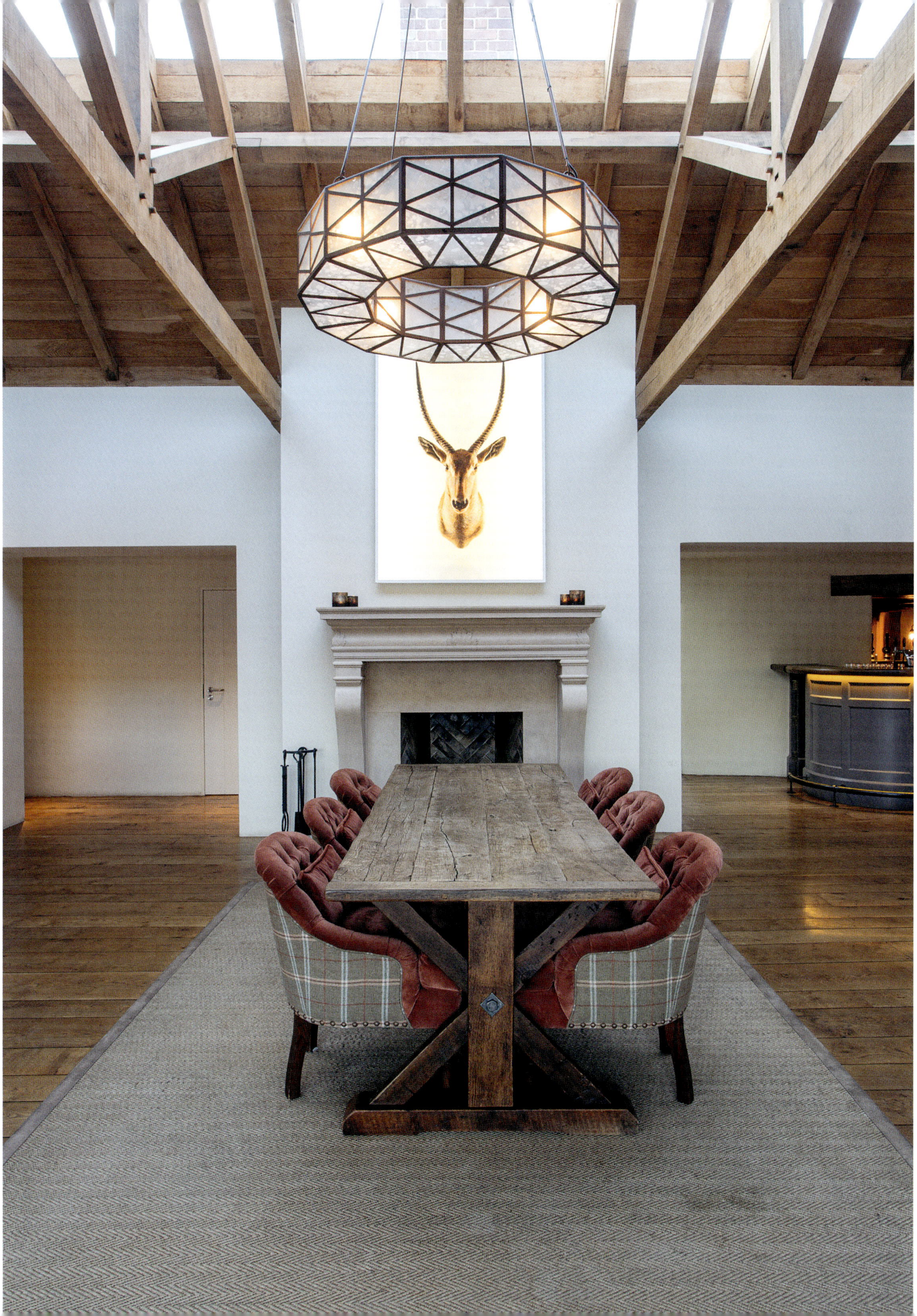

"PUBS ARE CRITICAL TO THE LIFE OF A VILLAGE"

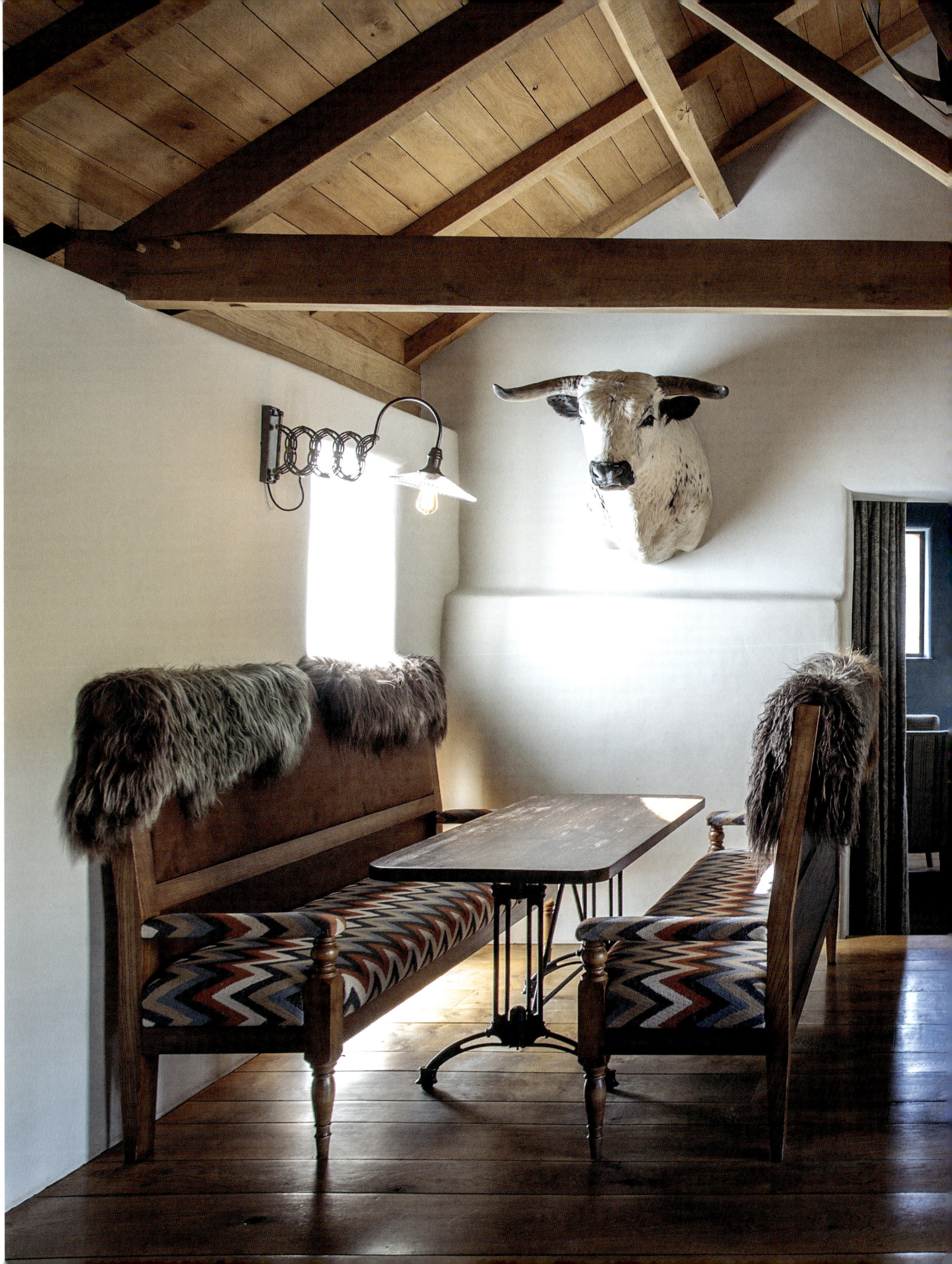

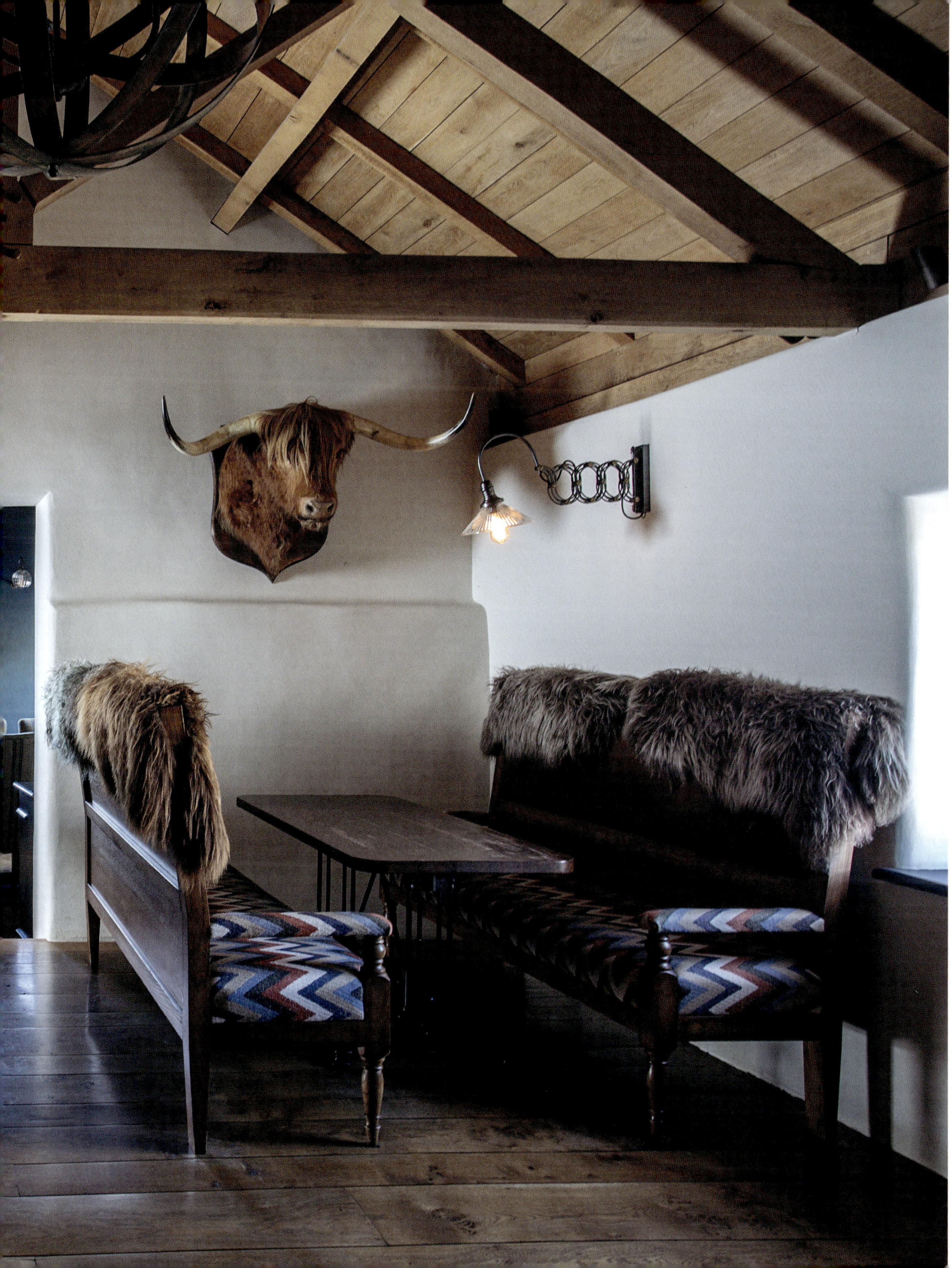

"... A MIX OF MODERN AND TRADITIONAL"

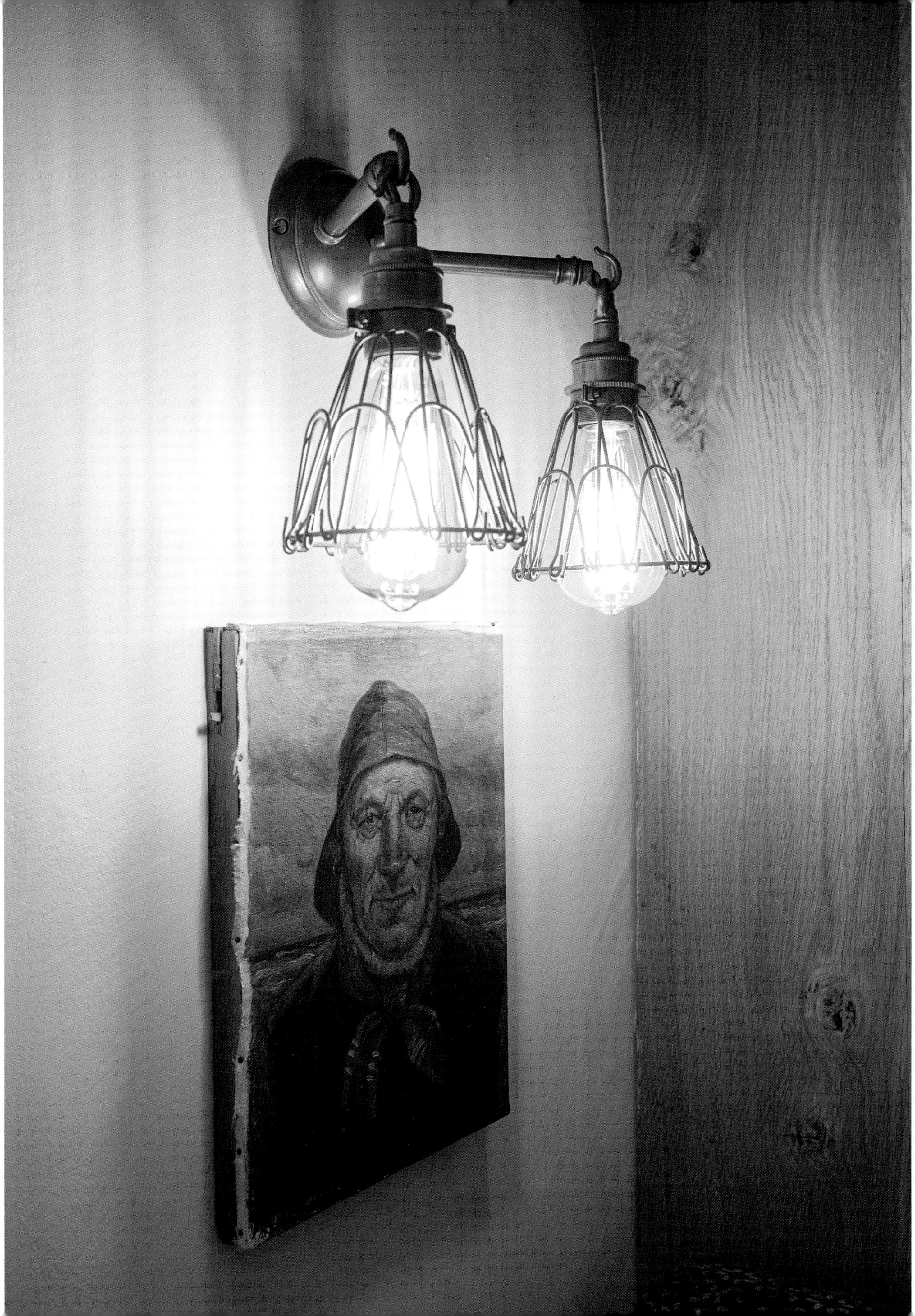

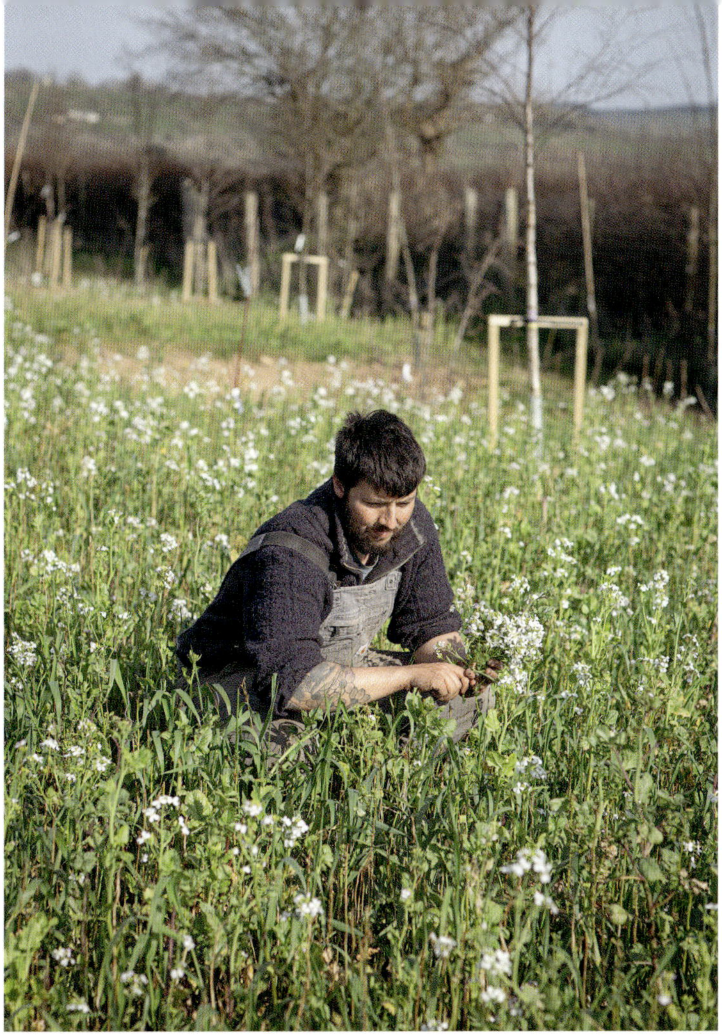

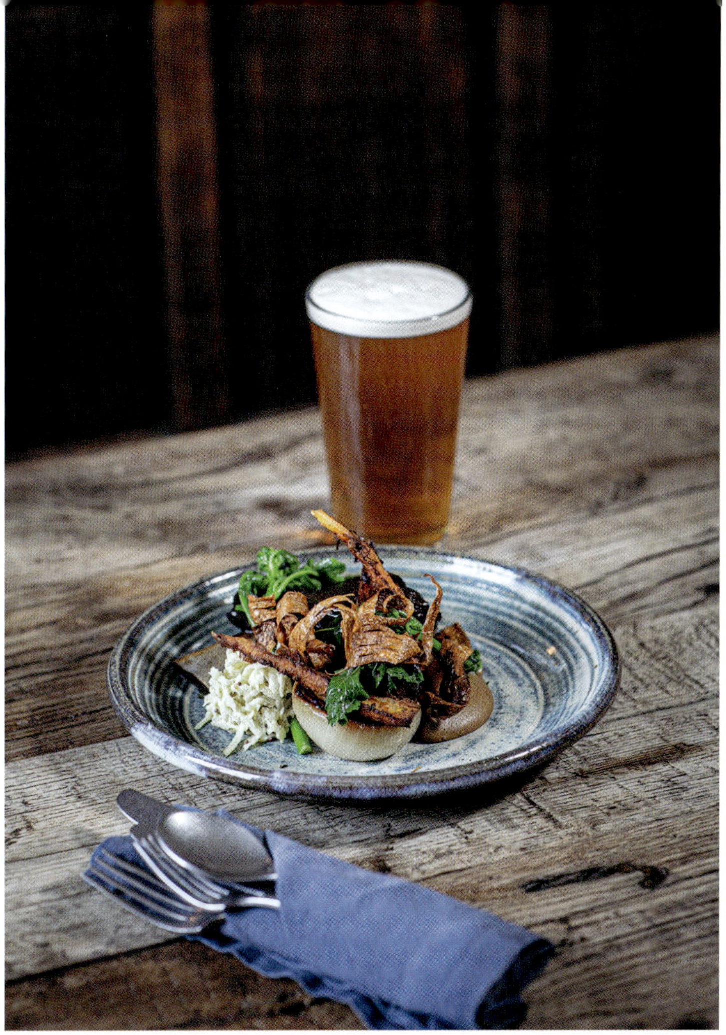

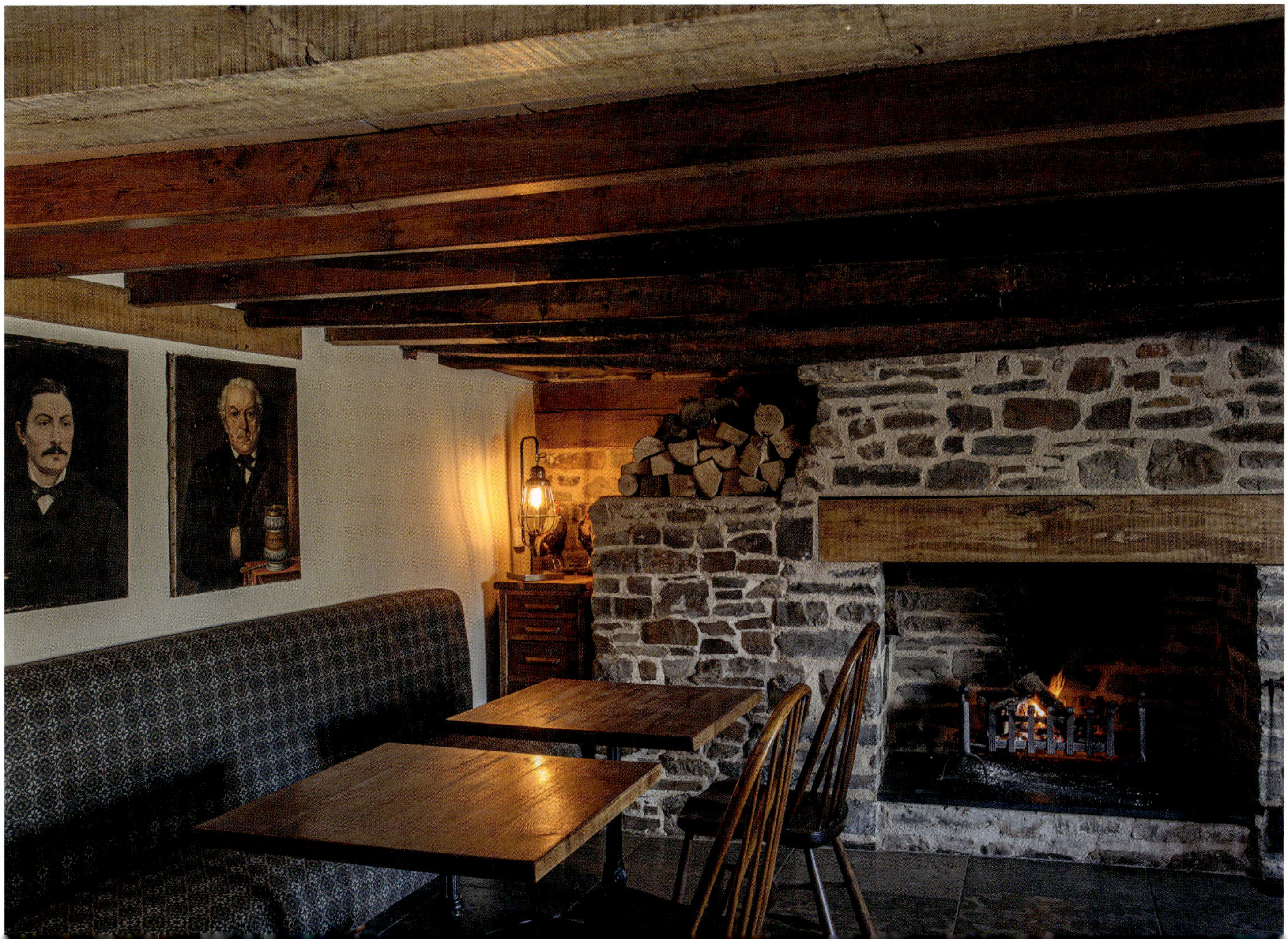

"IT'S LIKE A COMMUNITY, WITH EVERYONE BRINGING THEIR OWN PASSION"

THE BAG OF NAILS

141 ST GEORGE'S RD, HOTWELLS, BRISTOL

In The Bag of Nails, a corner pub in Bristol midway between the leafy heights of Clifton and the hum of the city centre, "herding cats" isn't a metaphor, or even an analogy – it's an imperative. "Come here Philomena, Wolfgang, don't do that, Absinthe, how many times do I have to tell you," calls out landlord Luke Daniels, as the pub's pride of felines – there are fifteen in all, living here alongside the real ales – slink around his legs, or bed down in repurposed soft-drink boxes.

Daniels has the flowing beard of an Old Testament prophet, and, indeed, the forbearance of Job – at least when it comes to his four-legged charges. Did he find them, or did they find him? "The former," he says. "I got the first cat, Malcolm, when I took over here around ten years ago. Then we got a little black lady cat, Beresford, and they got on like a house on fire." One thing inevitably led to another, and, several litters later, their progeny free-range around the premises, led by Malcolm's son Big George, who's living up to his appellation by engulfing a mini-chaise on the bar. Daniels thinks cats and pubs are a good mix: "Unlike dogs, they don't drink beer. And they don't make a noise."

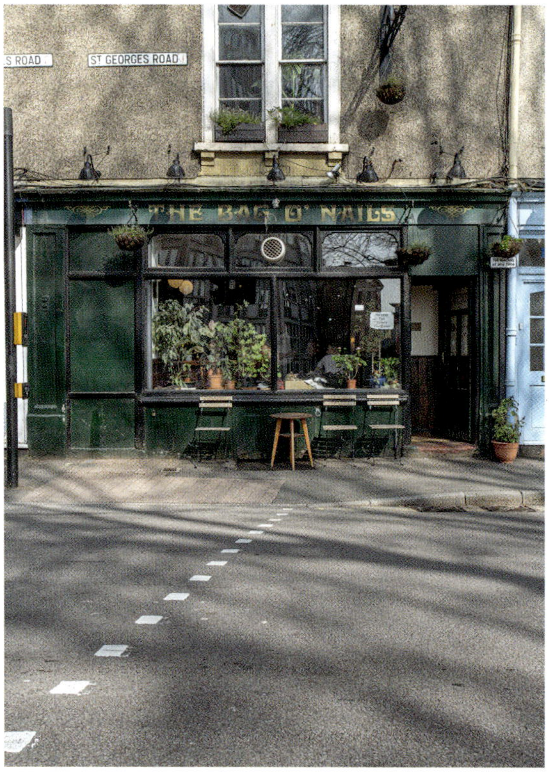

The Bag of Nails has a mellow, if not whimsical, vibe; in the parlour-like main bar, spider plants and mini-galleries of cat portraits and poems submitted by regulars (and yes, the temptation to rhyme "fur" with "purr" has proved impossible to resist) happily commingle with wallpaper featuring stylized fashion divas ("Isn't it great?" says Daniels; "I got it for a song when the shop was closing down") and a turntable that spins selections from Daniels' vinyl collection – today, Queen's *Jazz* album, which prompts an impromptu singalong to the knotty 'Bicycle Race'. Looming over the room, however, is a chalkboard list of Daniels' house rules. Some are axiomatic, including the first, which is a little too Anglo-Saxon to be reprinted here, but can be paraphrased as "no idiots"; others seem rather random (#19: "Keith Moon was the best"); and others, perplexing at first, make perfect sense when Daniels elucidates them: "No snogging because no-one needs to see that. No judo because the floor's not very good. And no 'Stairway to Heaven' because, well, I think we can all agree it's been done to death, can't we?" It's Rule #8 – "Babies and Toddlers Must be Stored in the Cellar" – that's caused the most controversy, however. "And that's the one that's actually backed by law, because the license says we can't have any children under 14 in here," protests Daniels. "But people get so angry about it."

An idiosyncratic establishment will attract a like-minded clientele, and Daniels has welcomed everyone from Bookshop Ben, who ran the world's least profitable emporium and ended up working behind the bar, to a delegation from Tokyo, who'd seen an item on "the British cat pub" on Japanese TV. For all, Daniels provides the two things he feels a pub should offer – "fun, whether I'm playing up the grumpy landlord caricature or dancing on the bar, and pub serendipity, where you get talking to people you never thought you'd meet. Last night we were in here chatting with a microbiologist about RNA and DNA."

There's a third great attraction, of course; the pub as the preserve – indeed, the haven – of the great English eccentric. "Well, I can tell you this place hasn't been focus-grouped – Luna, what are you doing? You've done a pee on my shopping and now you're sniffing it like it's the most exciting thing in the world – sorry, where were we?" says a distracted Daniels. Where were we? In a place where it seems that it's not just the cats who've found a welcoming refuge.

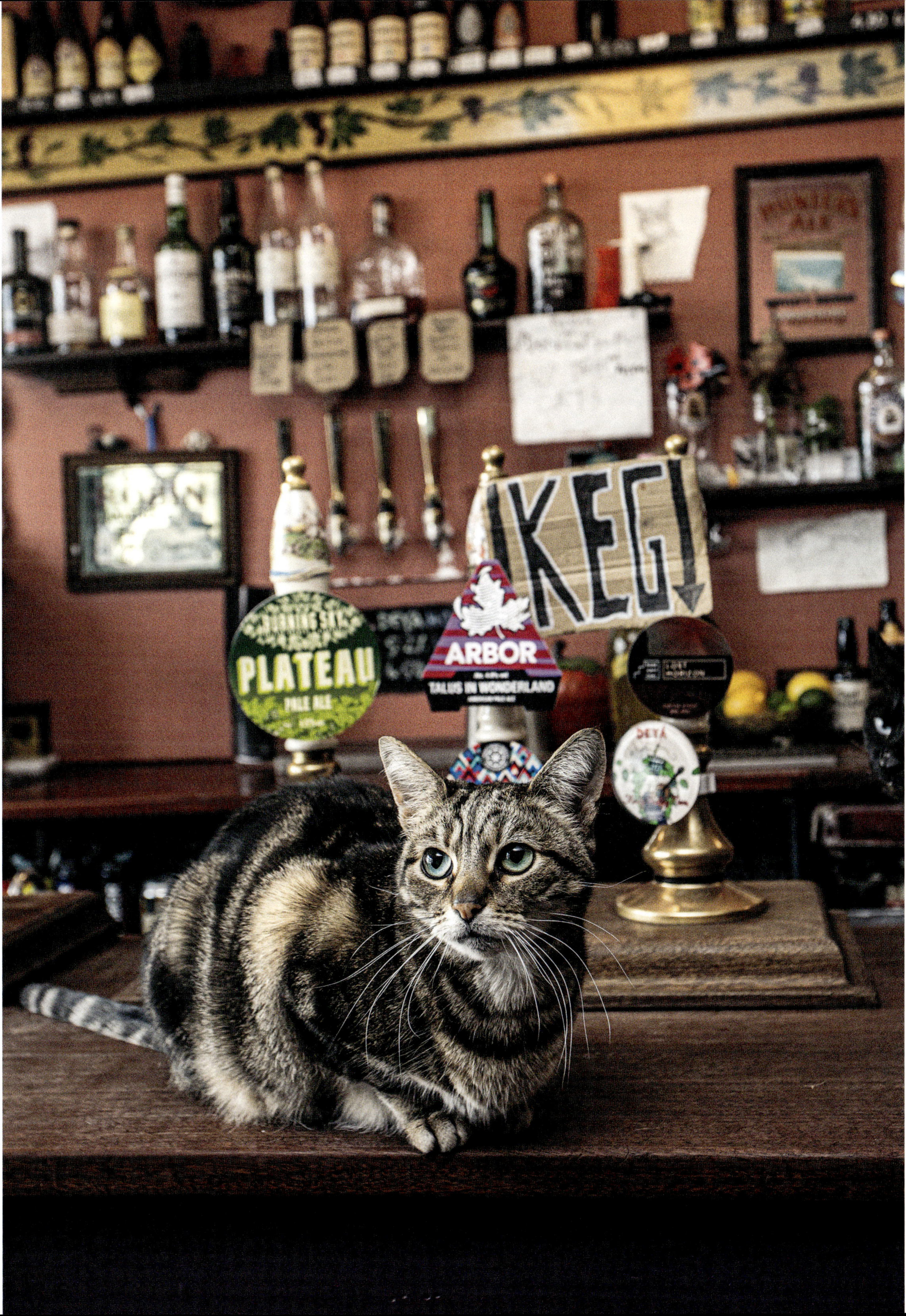

"UNLIKE DOGS, CATS DON'T DRINK BEER"

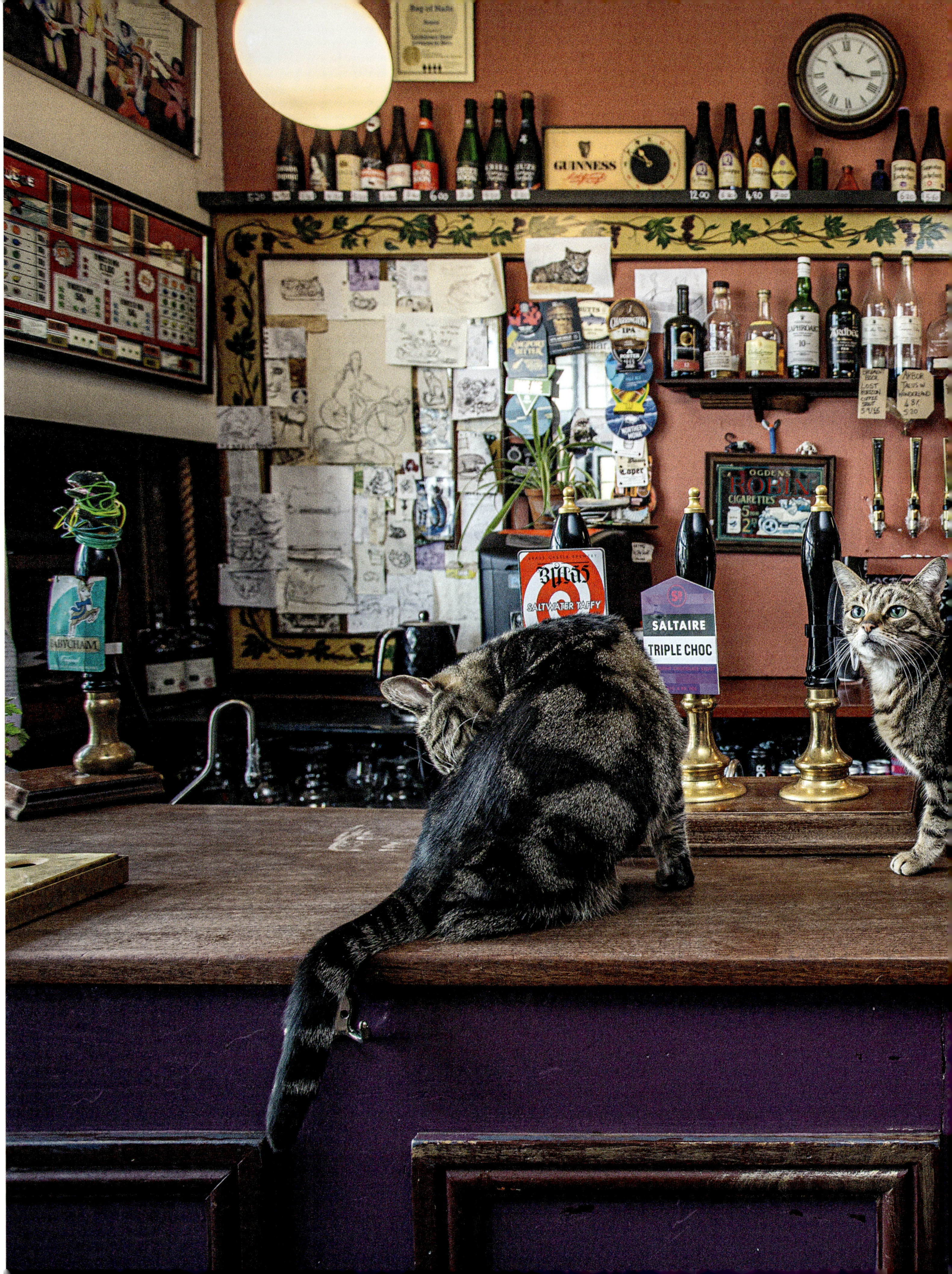
GUINNESS
SALTWATER TAFFY
SALTAIRE
TRIPLE CHOC
OGDENS
ROBIN
CIGARETTES
BABYCHAM

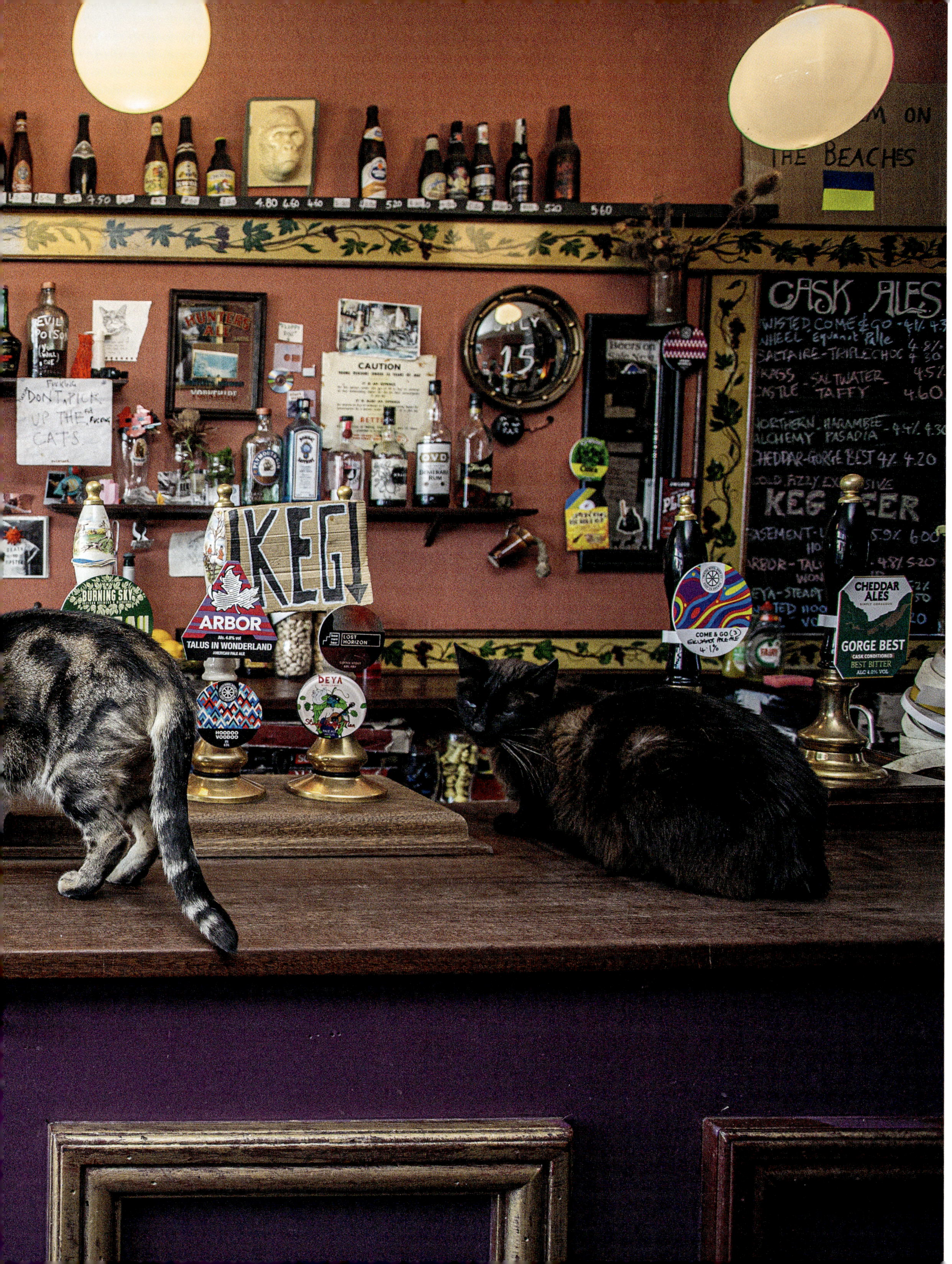
THE BEACHES
CASK ALES
SALTAIRE - TRIPLE CHOC
SALTWATER TAFFY
NORTHERN ALCHEMY
HARAMBEE PASADIA
CHEDDAR-GORGE BEST 4% 4.20
KEG
CAUTION
DON'T PICK UP THE CATS
KEG
BURNING SKY
ARBOR
TALUS IN WONDERLAND
AMERICAN PALE ALE
LOST HORIZON
DEYA
HOODOO VOODOO
CHEDDAR ALES
GORGE BEST
CASK CONDITIONED
BEST BITTER

“IT'S VERY FRONT ROOM-Y AND RELAXED”

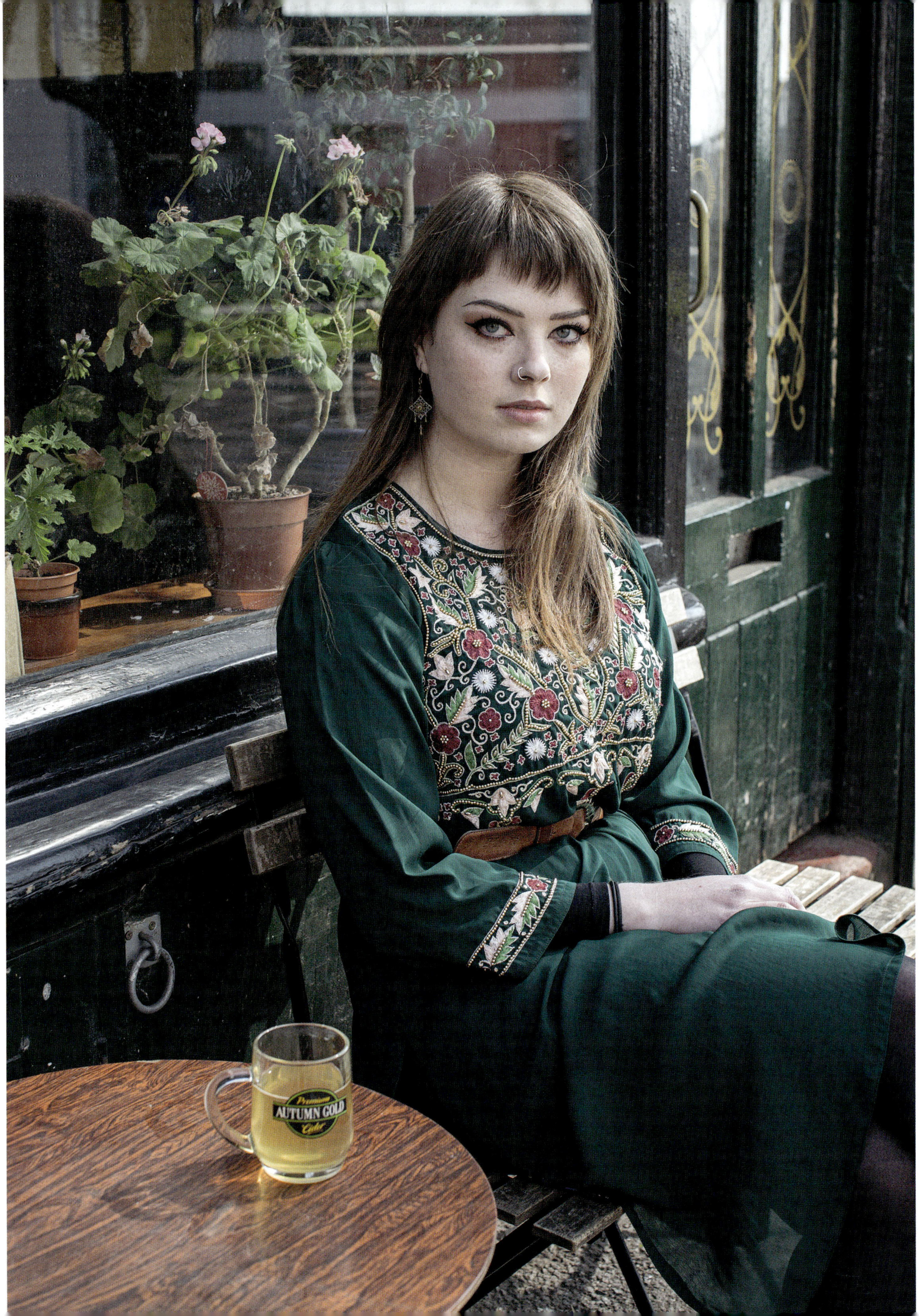

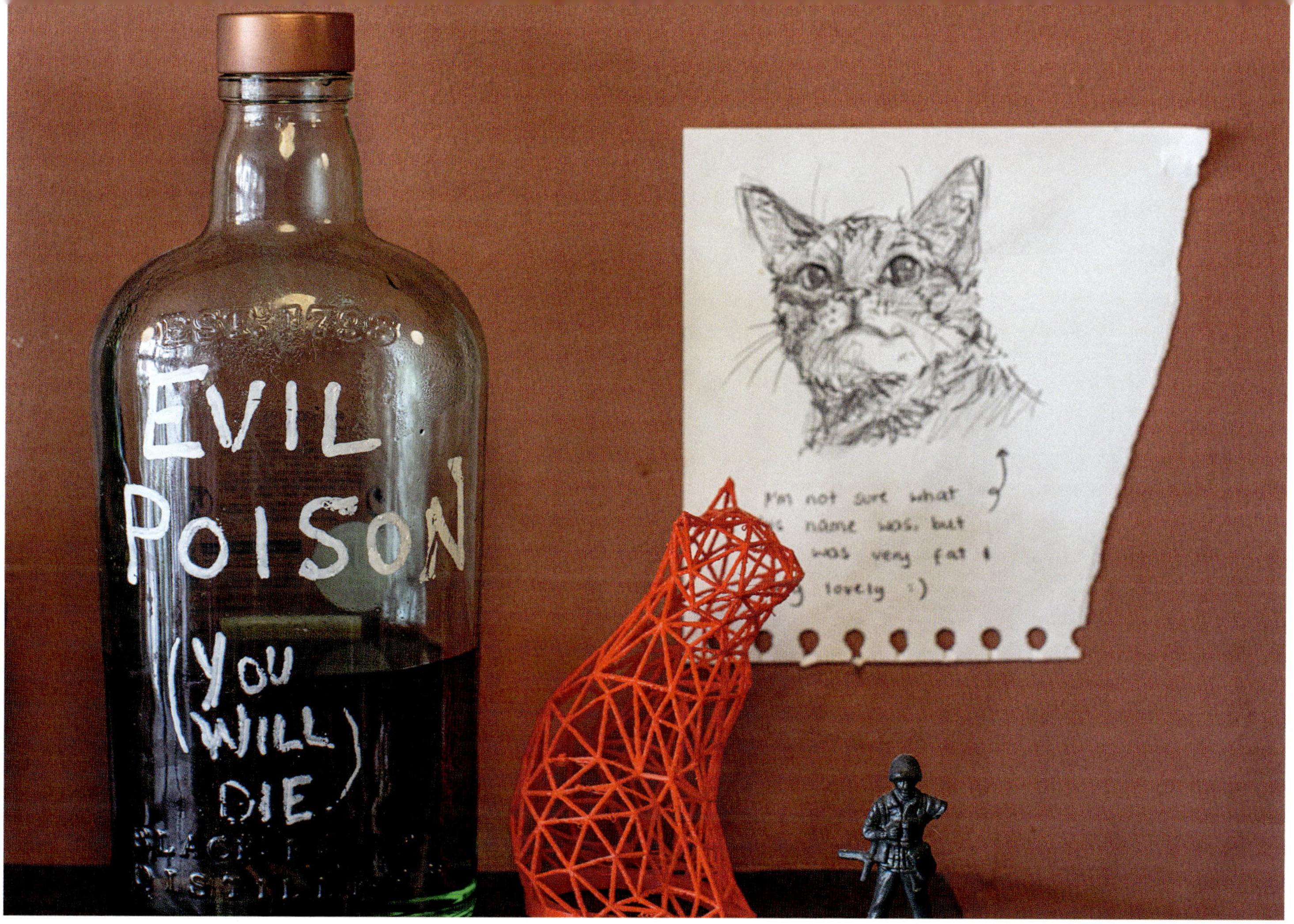

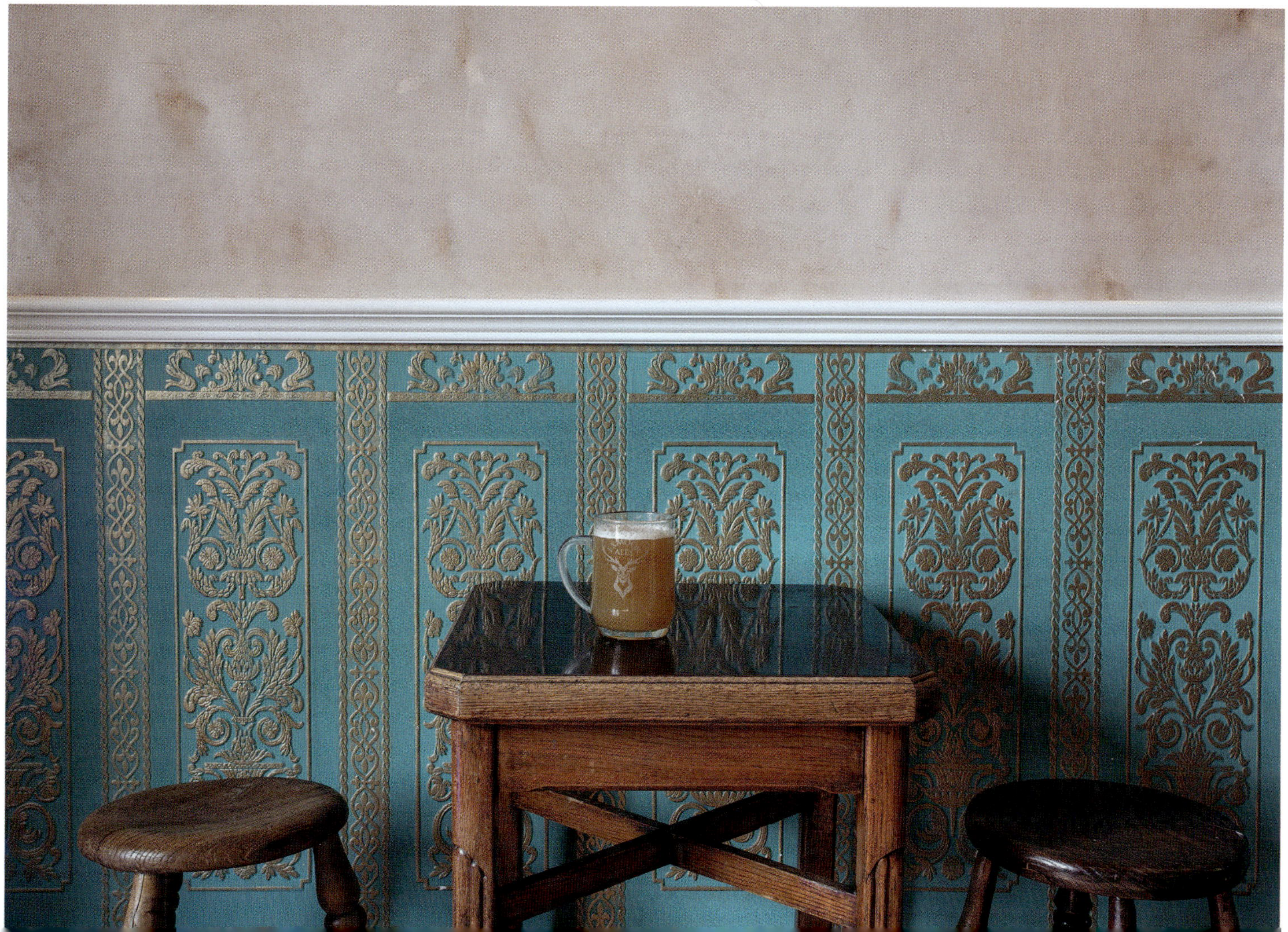

"A PLACE WHERE IDIOSYNCRASY IS CHERISHED"

“CROSS THIS PORTAL AND YOU'RE IN ANOTHER PLACE”

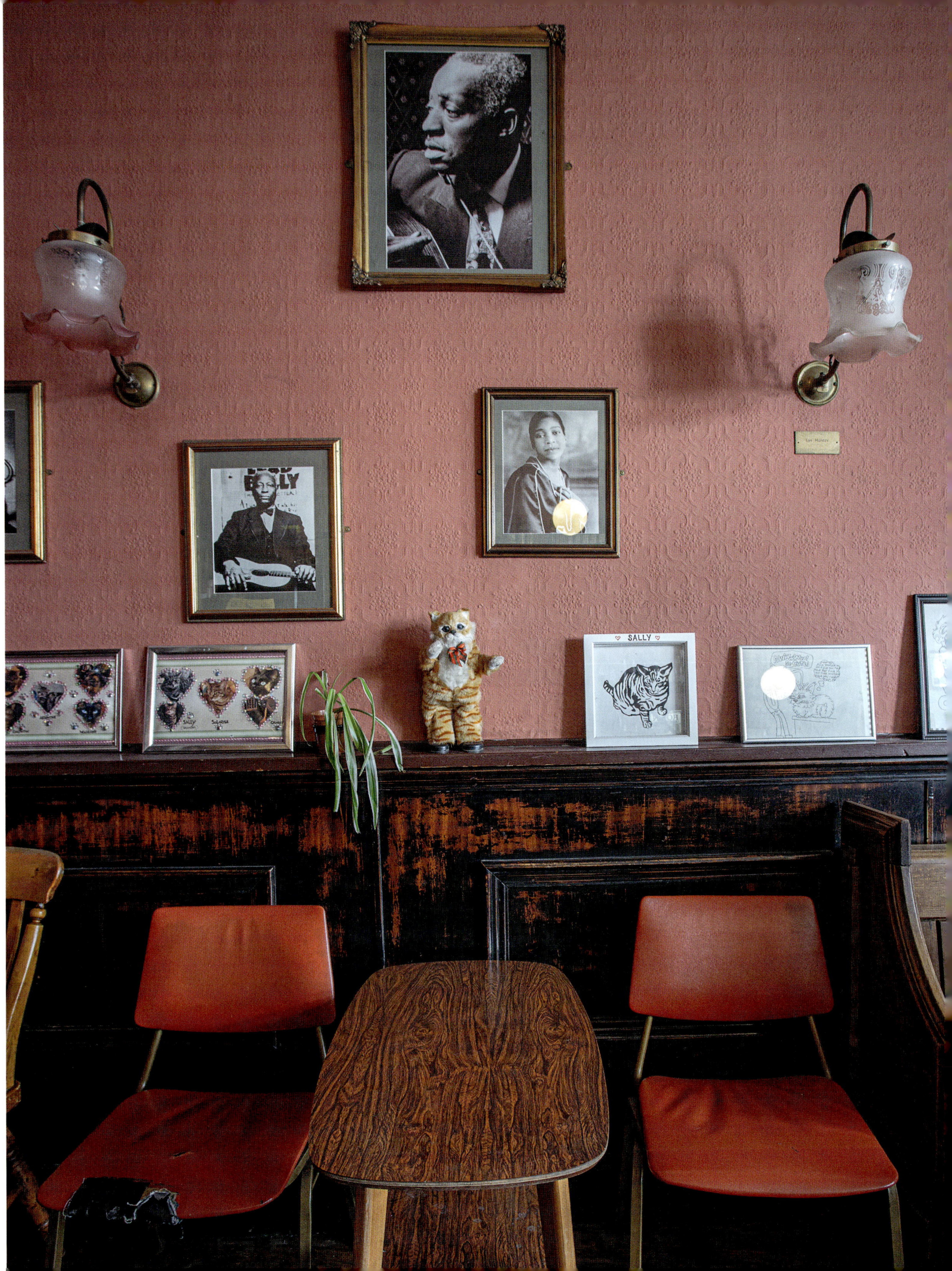

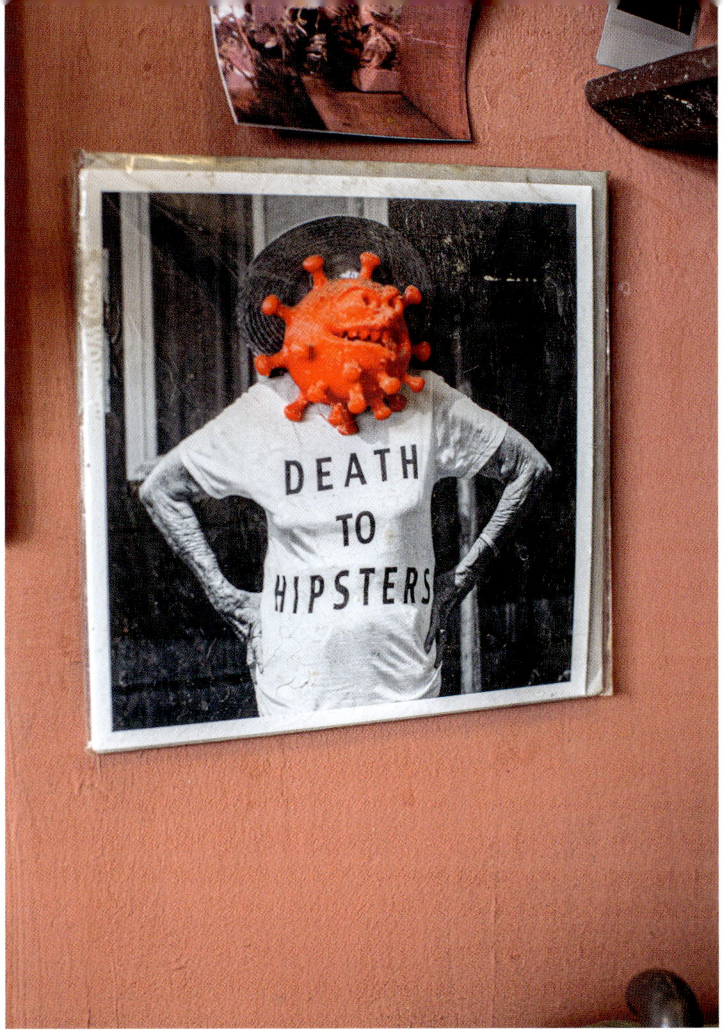

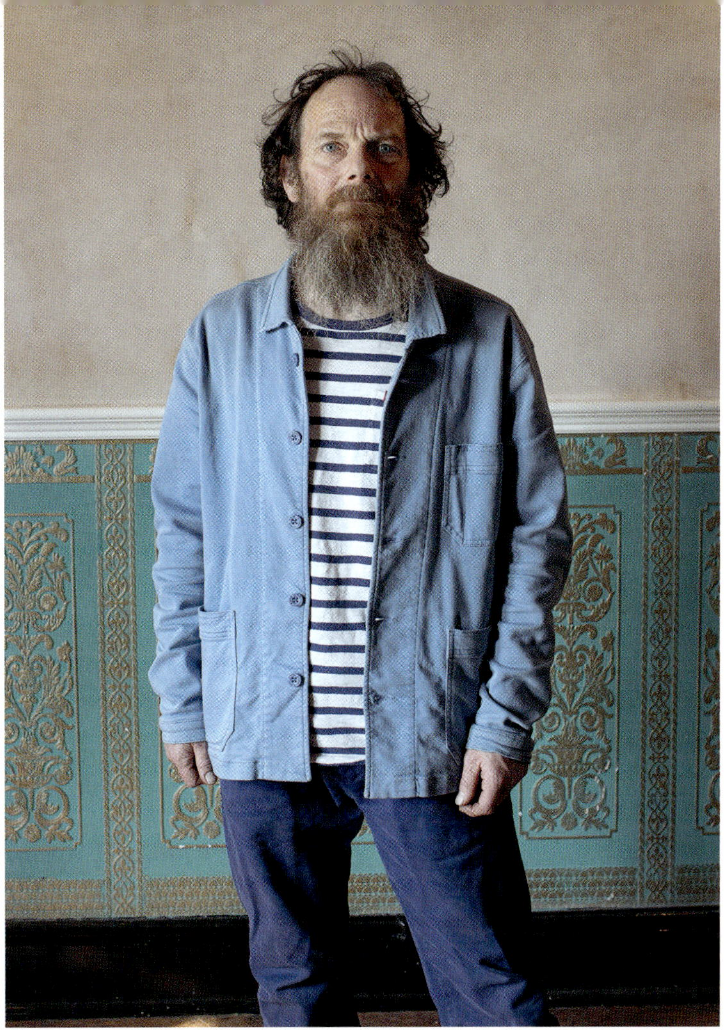

"I BELIEVE THIS IS THE PERFECT PUB"

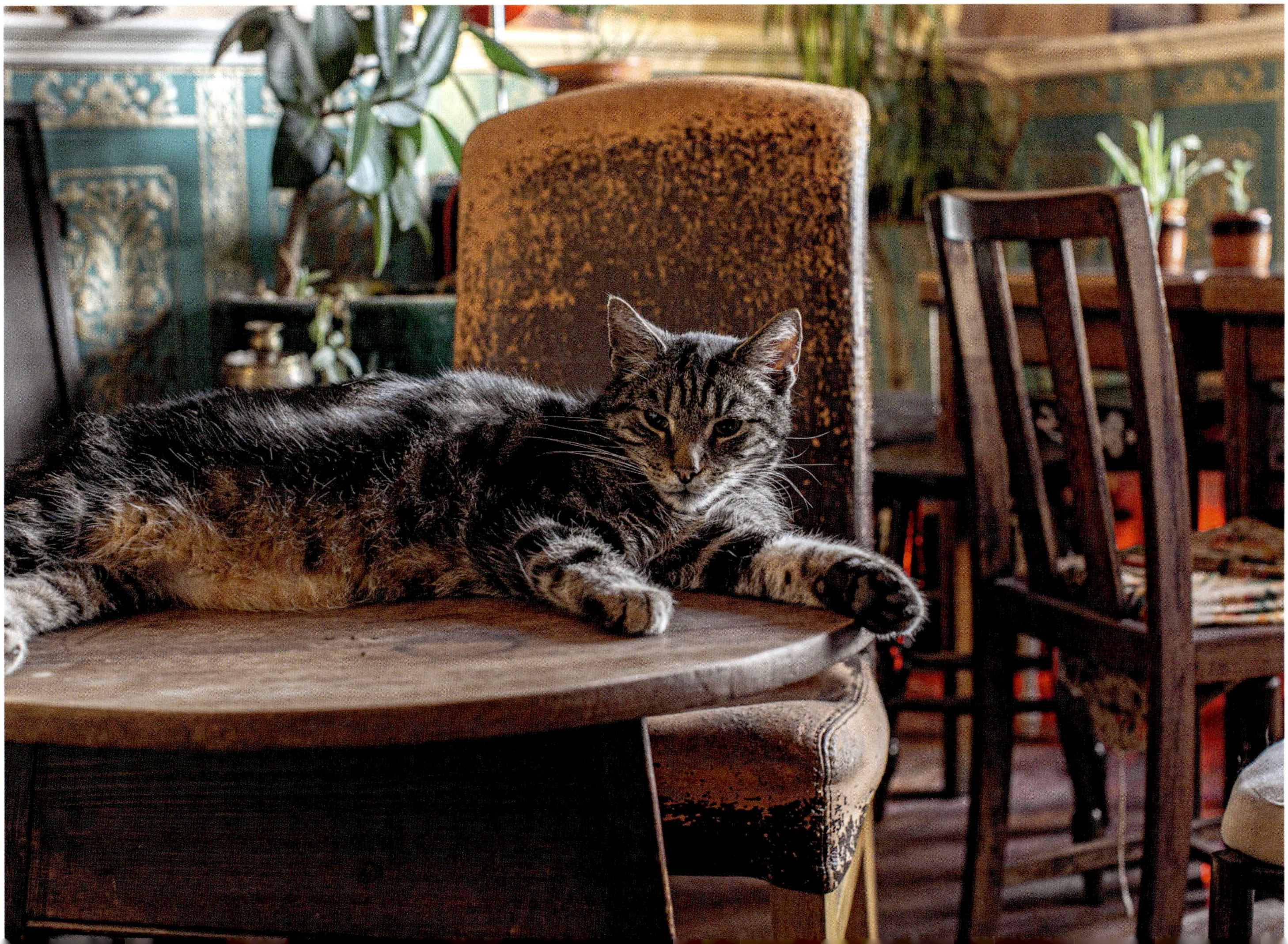

PHILHARMONIC DINING ROOMS

36 HOPE ST, LIVERPOOL

There can be few pubs where you'll regularly find a line of ladies waiting to be admitted to the gents. But then there are few gents – and, indeed, few pubs – like Liverpool's Philharmonic Dining Rooms. The allure of the rose-pink faux-marble 1890s "Rouge Royale" urinals, amid a riot of glinting mosaics, is all of a piece (yes, we said "piece") with a place lauded by heritage body Historic England as "a cathedral among pubs" and "the pinnacle of the gin palace".

"The Phil" more than lives up to the hype; it's a phantasmagoria of High Victoriana, from its turreted, gabled and oriel-windowed castle-like exterior (courtesy of architect Walter W. Thomas) and its extraordinary art nouveau wrought-iron and copper entrance gates by designer Henry Bloomfield Bare, decorated with female heads, garlands and the legend *pacem amo* (I love peace), to an interior that puts a melange of imposing styles – Gothic, classical, Jacobean, Romanesque, Scots baronial – into a giant blender, and tops it off with a healthy dollop of Scouse irreverence; the two snugs have been christened Brahms and Liszt, which has the dual merit of giving the ongoing musical theme a Romantic twist, while alluding to the Cockney rhyming slang for a state of severe inebriation.

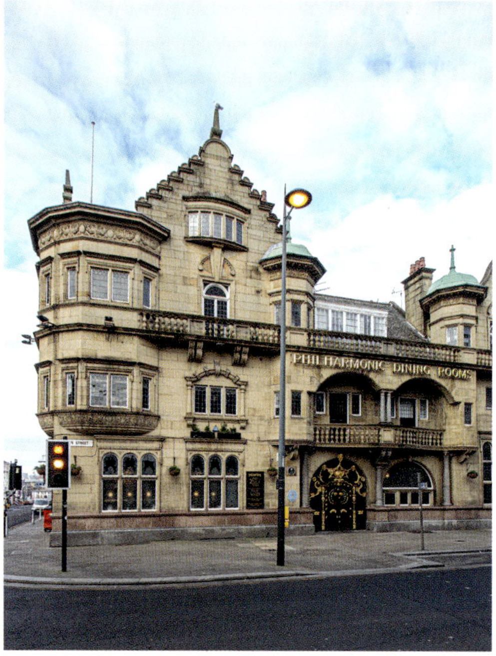

The Phil was built between 1898 and 1900 by the brewery chief Robert Cain, as an extravagant manifestation of Liverpool's importance as a centre of maritime trade. Its listing was raised to Grade I in 2020 – the first purpose-built Victorian pub in England to gain the status. Looking round, your eye slides off opulent detail after detail as if you were scrolling through a procession of heritage-nerd Pinterest pages, from the main bar lobby, with its Corinthian pilasters and rich mosaic detailing, to the saloon, with its decorative wooden partitions, and the cavernous Grande Lounge, originally built as a billiard room, with its mullioned windows, copper panels depicting New Brighton seafront, and carved ceiling friezes of the Crowning of Apollo. Oh, and did we mention the stunning stained-glass renderings of the likes of Lord Kitchener and St Cecilia, patroness of music, alongside Longfellow quotes ("music is the universal language of mankind")? "You know what we say about this place?" says manager Eamonn Lavin, as he prepares to open up. "It's part hostelry, part Hogwarts."

The Phil has its own indelible connections with Liverpool's own boy wizards. It's not far from both the former Liverpool College of Art building, where John Lennon briefly studied, and the former Liverpool Institute for Boys building, the school that Paul McCartney and George Harrison attended; plans for world domination were undoubtedly hatched in the lounges by the nascent Beatles. Lennon would go on to say that the principal price of fame was "no longer being able to have a pint in the Phil," while McCartney returned in 2018 to play an impromptu gig in the Grande Lounge for James Corden's US TV show. Troupes of musicians still cross Hope Street from the Philharmonic Hall for a post-rehearsal snifter, and, says Lavin, it's played host to everyone from Welsh choirs to Coldplay tribute acts. "The place was built around music, and I think it's important that the connection continues," he says. "The difference between this place and other Grade I listed places is that you can come in, sit down, have a drink, and interact with it. I can assure you that it's as unpretentious as a place that looks like this can be."

A recent weekday lunchtime visit bears him out; there are regulars chowing down on toad in the hole in the Liszt lounge, a coach party or two getting their fill of the panels and plasterwork, and a steady stream of people, um, interacting with the legendary urinals. "It's amazing that it's survived, right?" says one impressed punter. "Long may it reign." It feels appropriate, in this cathedral among pubs, to whisper: amen to that.

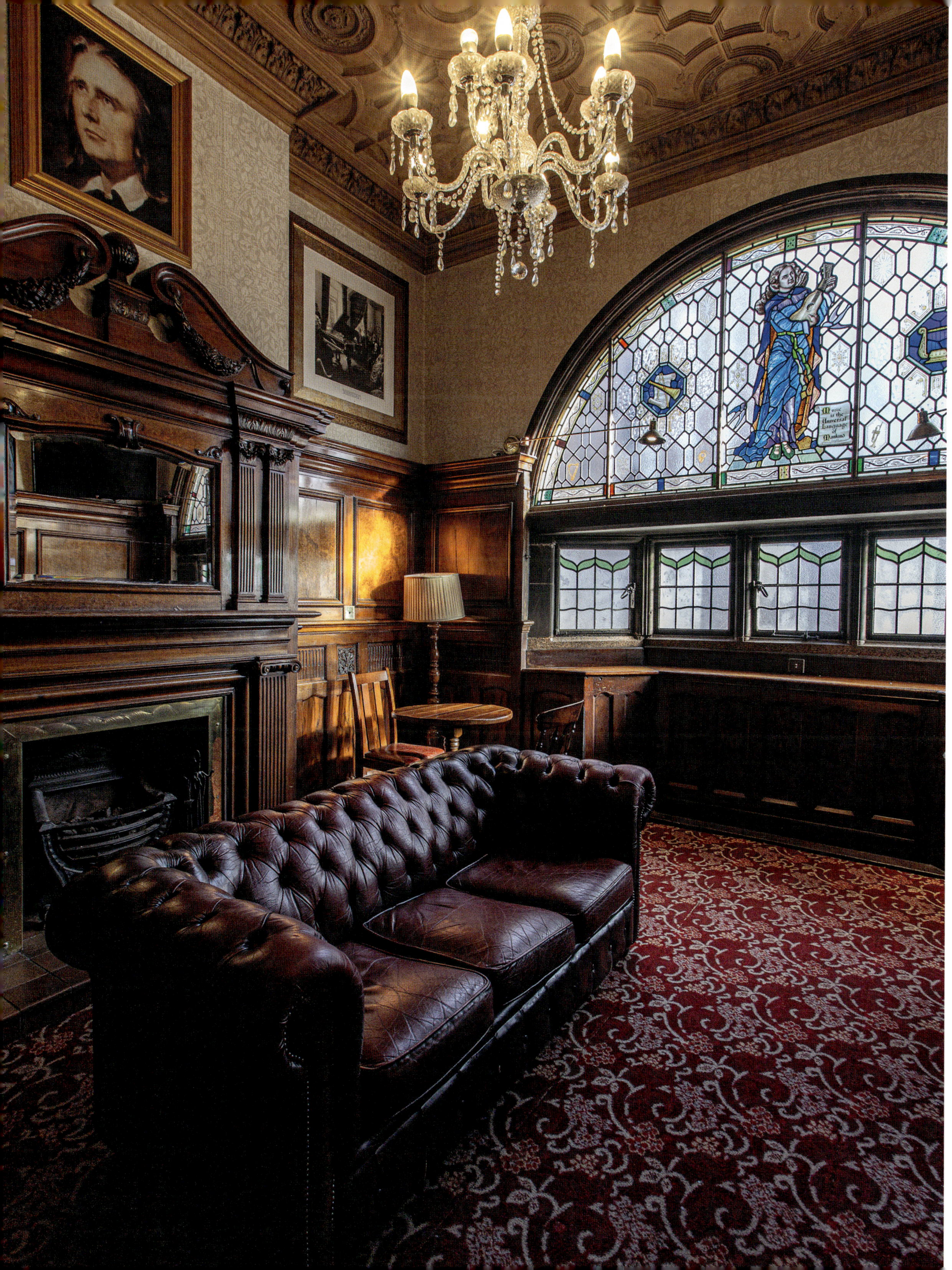
Music
is the
Universal
Language
of
Mankind

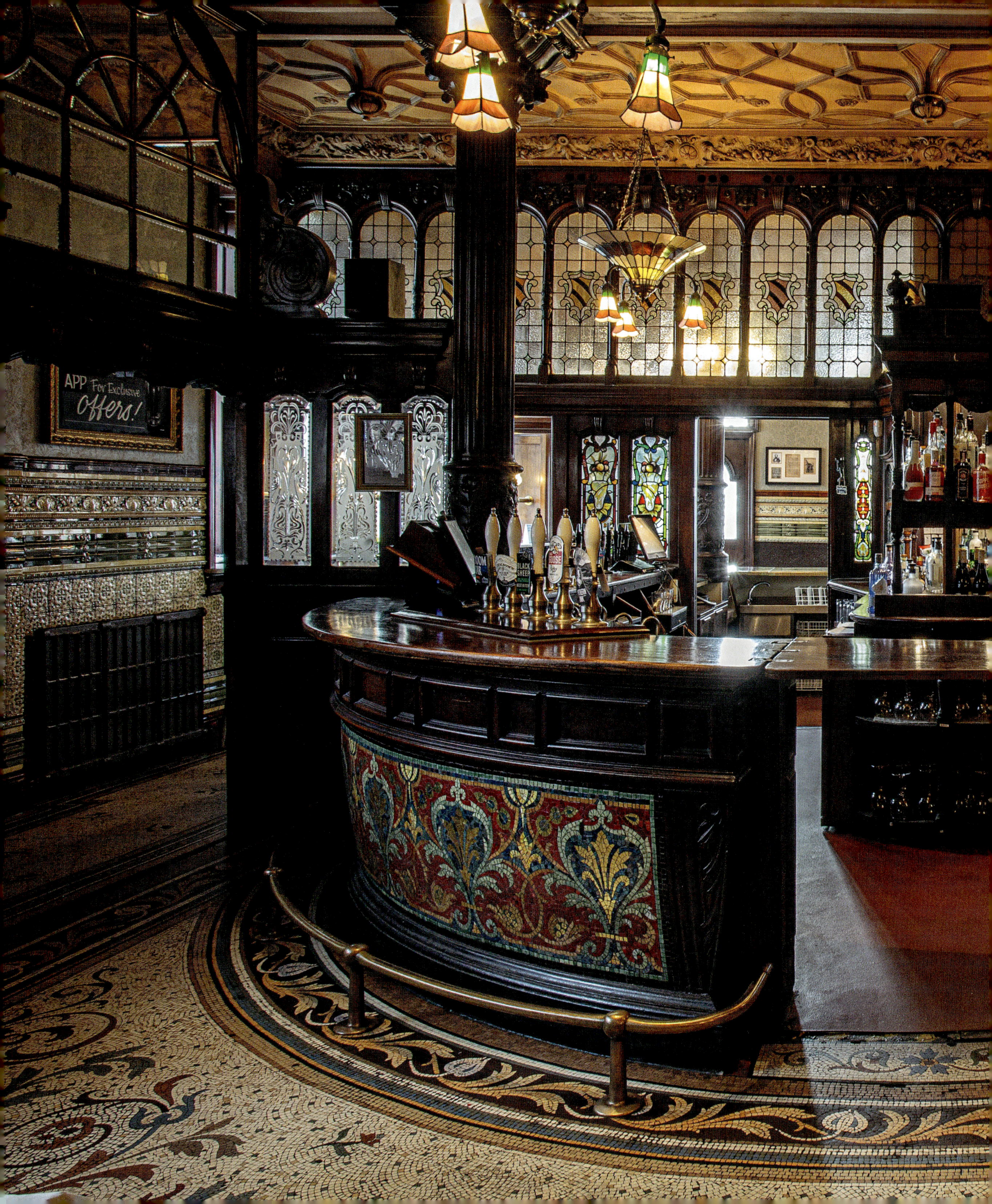
APP For Exclusive
Offers!

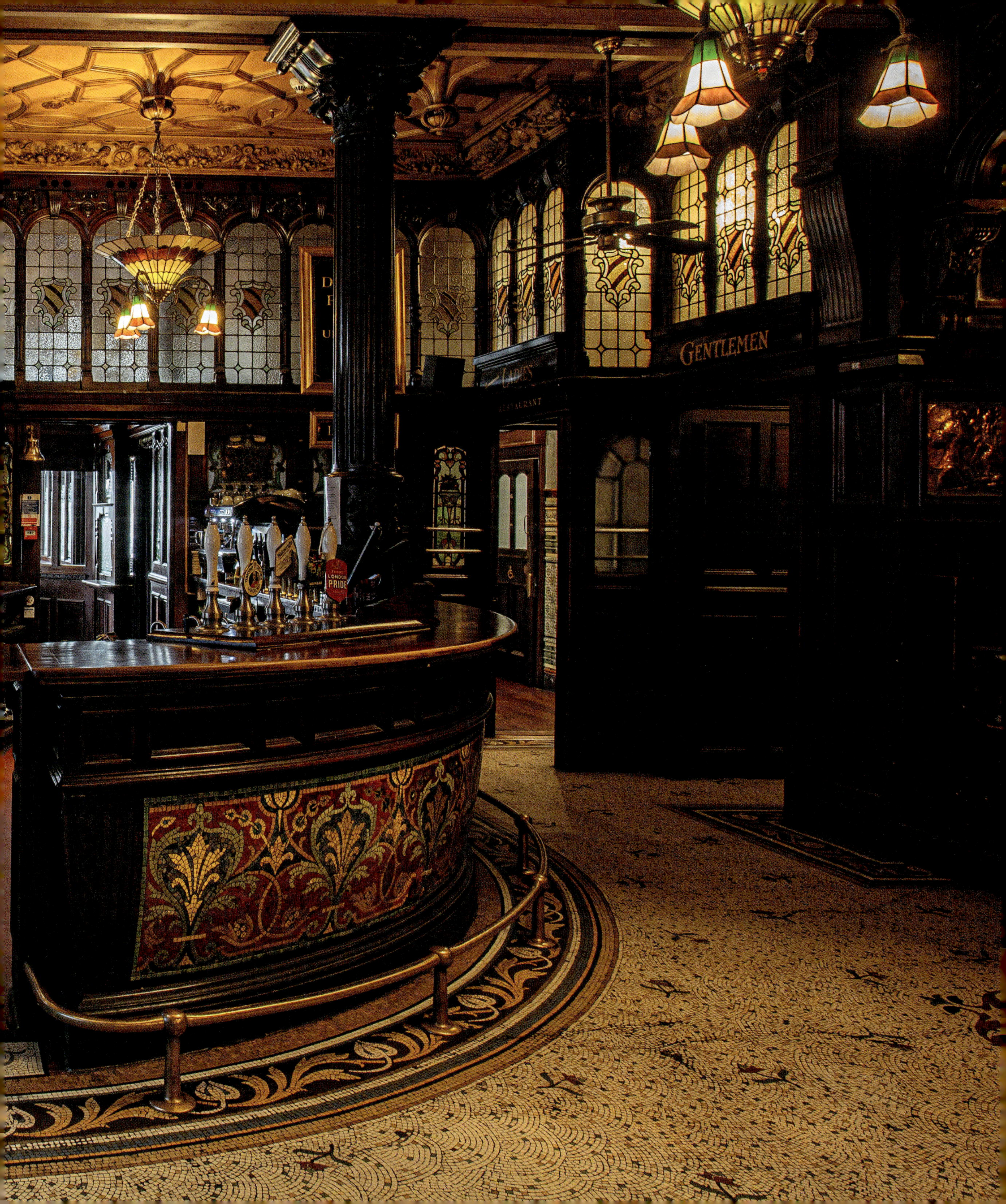
GENTLEMEN
LADIES
LONDON PRIDE

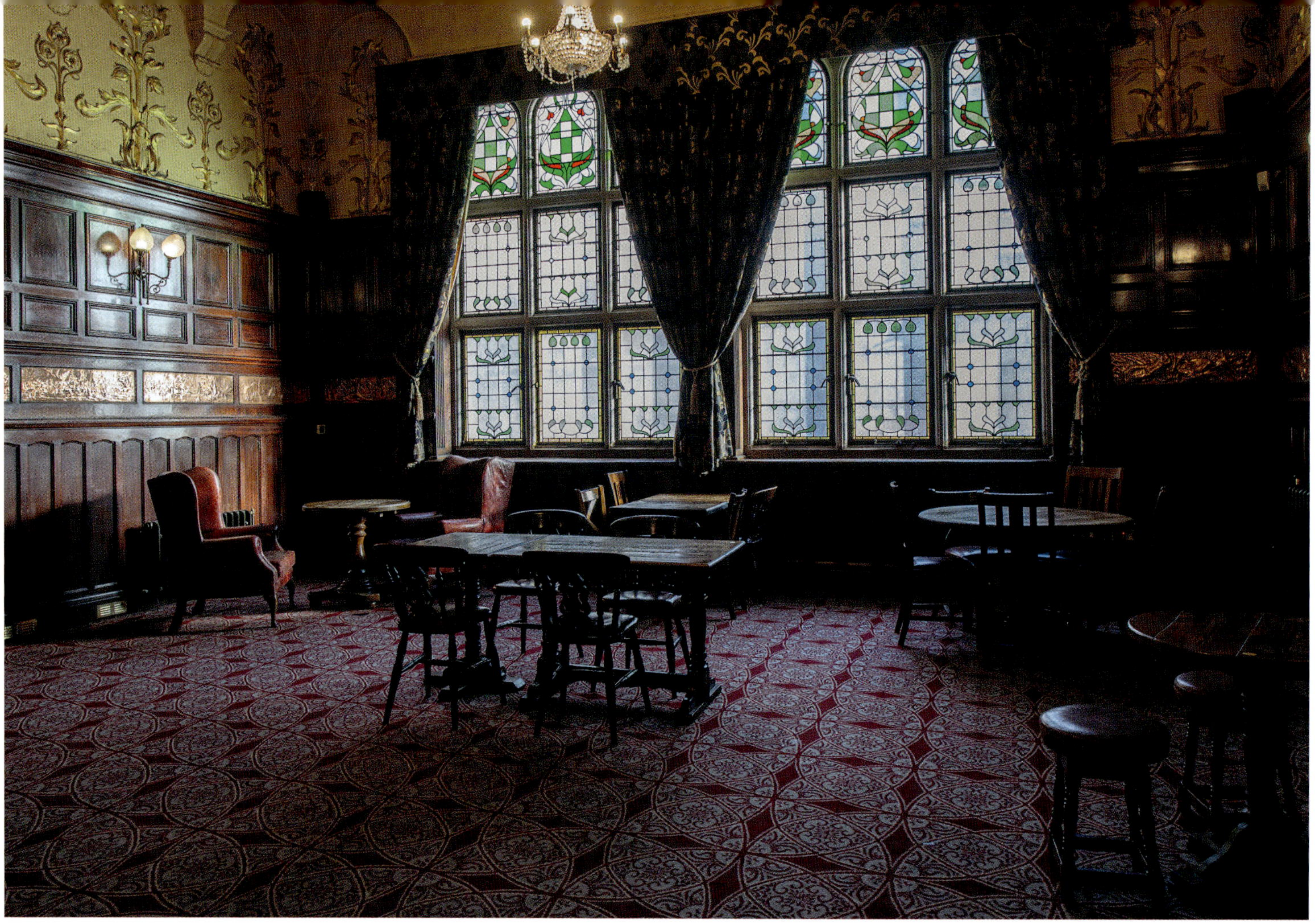

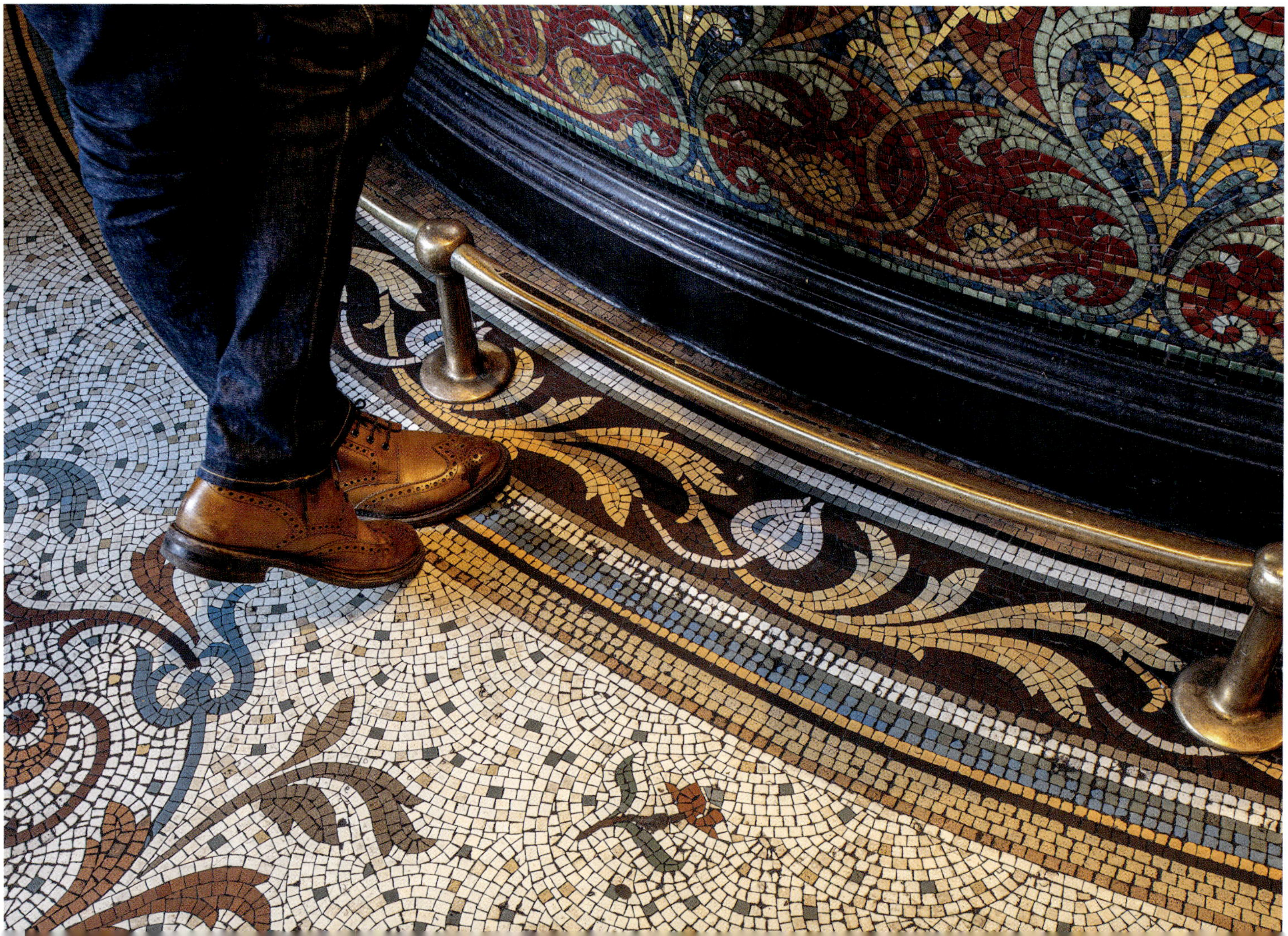

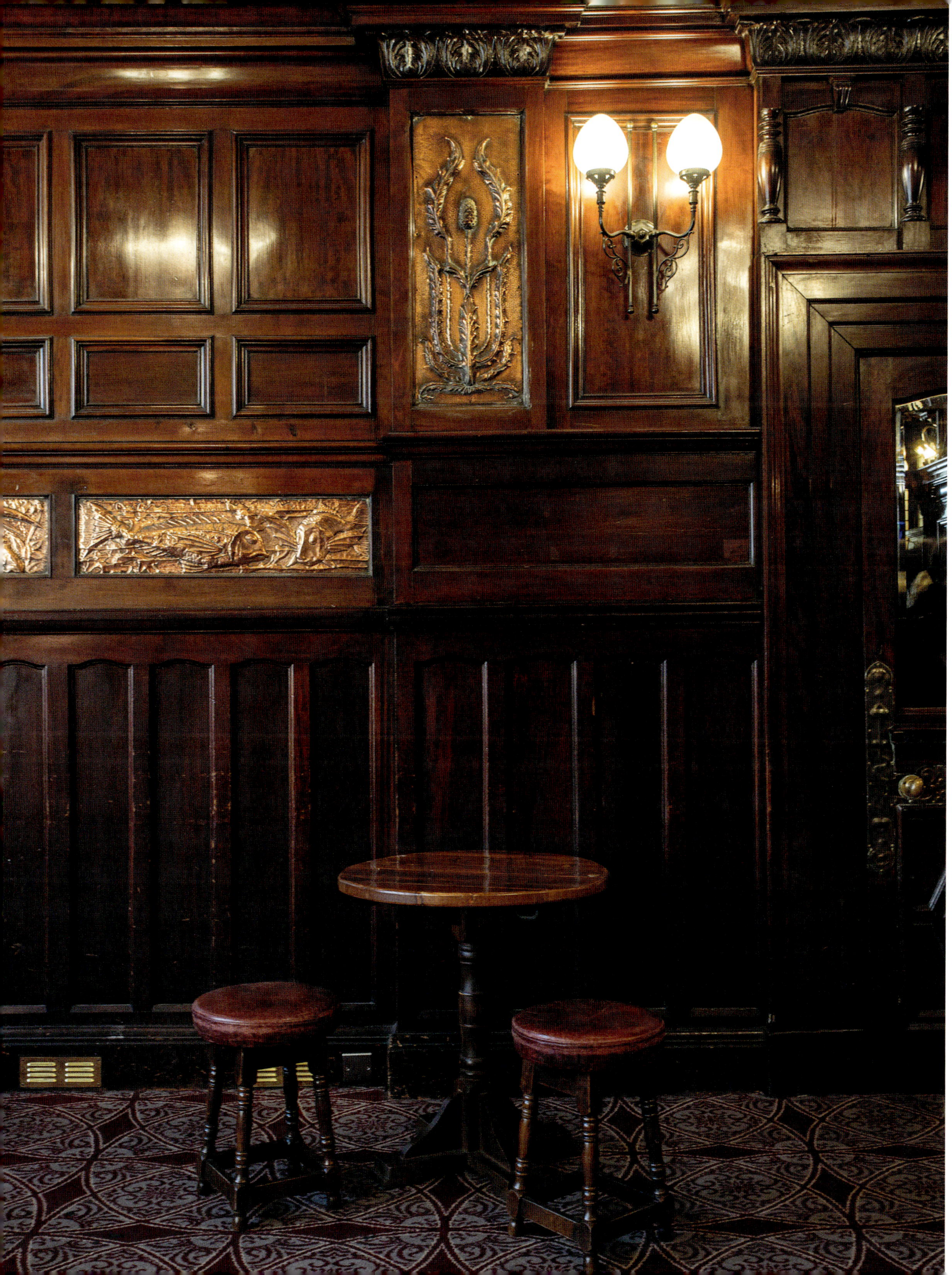

"PART HOSTELRY, PART HOGWARTS"

THE BRITON'S PROTECTION

50 GREAT BRIDGEWATER ST, MANCHESTER

In one of the rear lounges of The Briton's Protection, amid the old-school bell pushes and 1930s fireplaces, manager Alan Hudd is elaborating on its singular place in Manchester history. "You'll get a group of lads coming in, mid-twenties or so", he says, "and they'll pull out a piece of dog-eared paper, which turns out to be their great-granddad's pub trail from his stag do, and we'll be at the centre of it." He smiles wryly. "And we're almost invariably the last place that's still here. It's like they've come to bear witness to a living monument."

All around The Briton's Protection, on the corner of a busy junction in the heart of the city centre, are echoes of Manchester's more recent epochs; across the road is the Hacienda apartment complex, a towering slab on the former site of the legendary club, while a windswept plaza further on has been christened Tony Wilson Place, after the late TV presenter and Factory Records boss who did so much to thrust Manchester to creative centre stage. But the Brit, or the BP, as it's known to locals, harks back beyond acid house and even post-punk; to 1795, in fact, when its regulars were at the mercy of recruiters for the Napoleonic Wars. Meanwhile, a series of murals in the corridor connecting the front bar and back rooms commemorate the infamous Peterloo Massacre of 1819, where the king's sabre-wielding militia brutally cut down a crowd of pro-democracy demonstrators, all within glass-lobbing reach of the BP's front door.

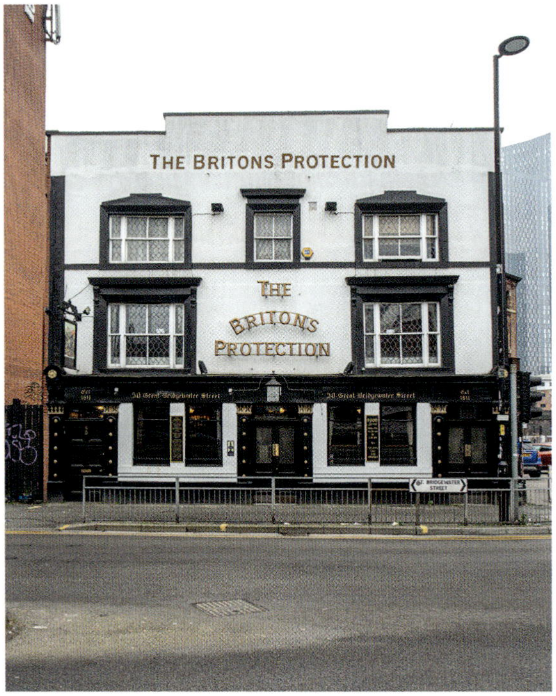

Today, Hudd and his staff preside over a meticulously preserved 1930s interior – six rooms, mahogany bar, red and gold moulded ceiling – that attracts its share of heritage buffs, including a Victorian tile appreciation group who came to ooh and aah over its resplendent tortoiseshell-brown exemplars. But the BP, as Hudd says, is far from a museum piece; it's a cherished holdout and bolthole for those seeking refuge from the steel and glass behemoths and repurposed warehousing that have come to dominate modern Manchester. "It feels like we've got an authentic taste of the old city here," says Hudd, "an escape from all the party pubs with their identikit industrial look and banging music. This place is all about sitting, drinking and chatting."

That's a winning combo for a wide variety of regulars and BP diehards, from the after-work crowds and the Friday night rugby teams to the musicians taking a rehearsal break from the adjacent Bridgewater Hall and the Manchester United fans on match days. As well as mainstays like Guinness Terry – "I get his pint ready as soon as I see him coming," says Hudd – there's Elbow's Guy Garvey, who usually pops in when he's in town, and Vivienne Westwood, who settled in one evening with a glass of rosé. Even the famously abstemious Morrissey was occasionally spotted in one of the snugs, back in the day, nursing a Carling Black Label. As well as its five cask ales, the BP is famed for its exhaustive whisky collection – over 300 at the last count, from the Jim Beams and Johnnie Walkers to the highly acclaimed and vanishingly scarce Middleton Very Rare. A recent lunchtime saw its fair share of both pump and lowball action, a mellow buzz, football lore being traded at the bar ("they begged Ferguson not to run 4-2-4, but you can't tell managers anything"), and the arrival of a man named Neil, a Mancunian native, who was making his first visit to the BP. "I've seen it from the tram so often," he says. "I've actually been meaning to come and check out the place for about forty-five years."

"We get that a lot," laughs Alan Hudd. Empires may rise and fall, and industries may come and go, but, after two and a quarter centuries, The Briton's Protection continues to valiantly uphold its duty of care.

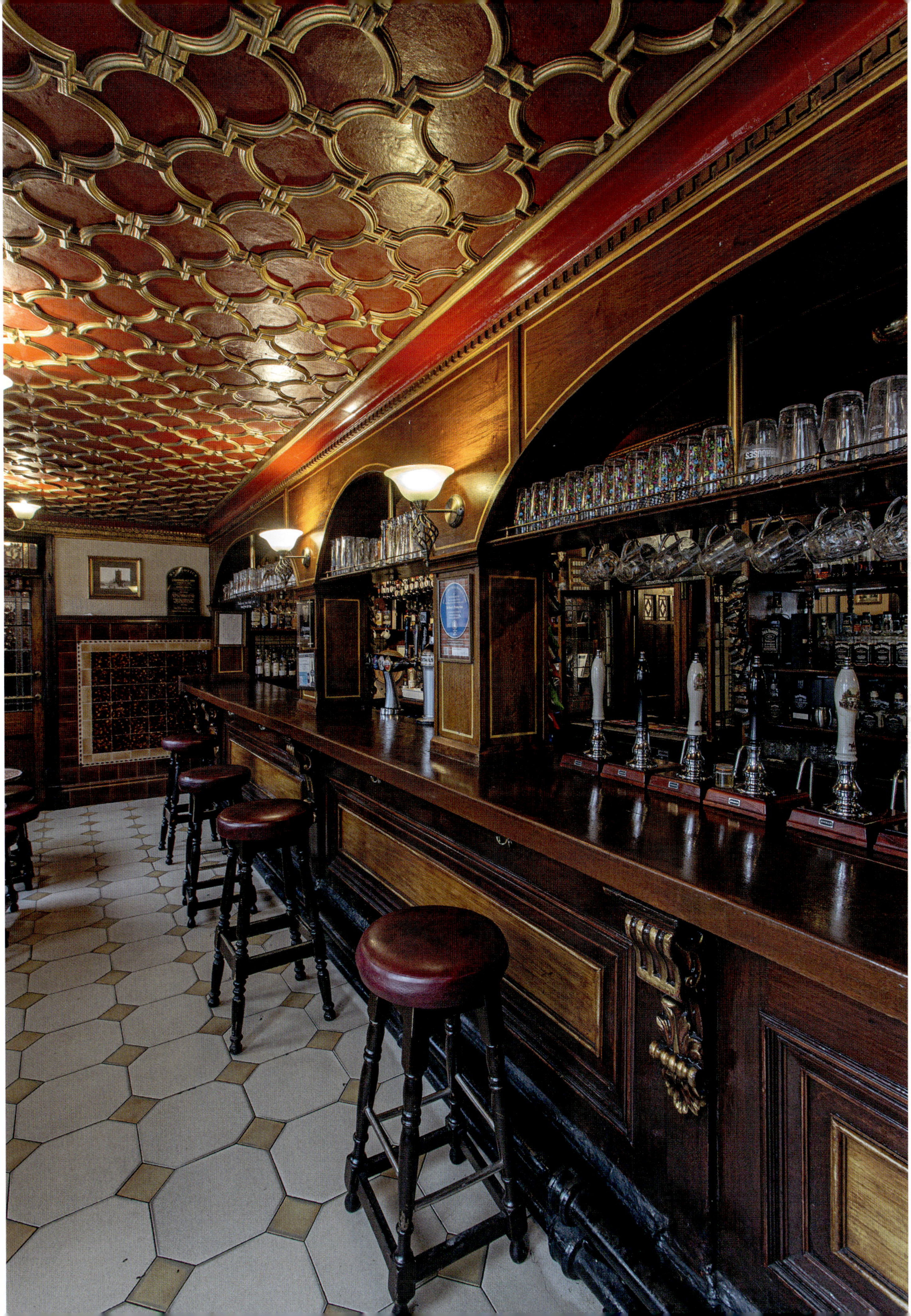

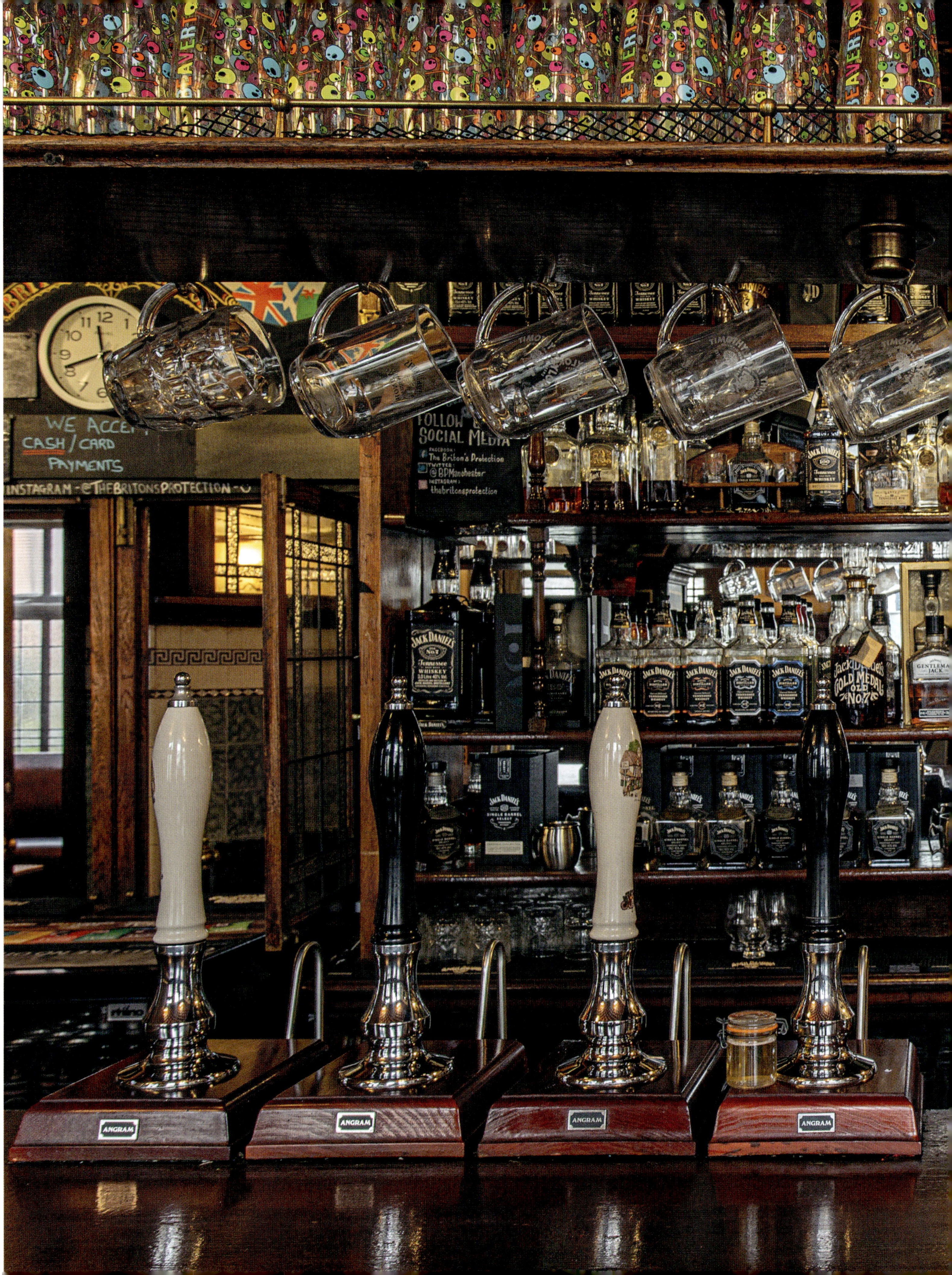
WE ACCE
CASH / CARD
PAYMENTS
INSTAGRAM - @THEBRITONSPROTECTION
FOLLOW
SOCIAL MEDIA
The Briton's Protection
@BPManchester
thebritonsprotection
JACK DANIEL'S
GOLD MEDAL
ANGRAM
ANGRAM
ANGRAM
ANGRAM

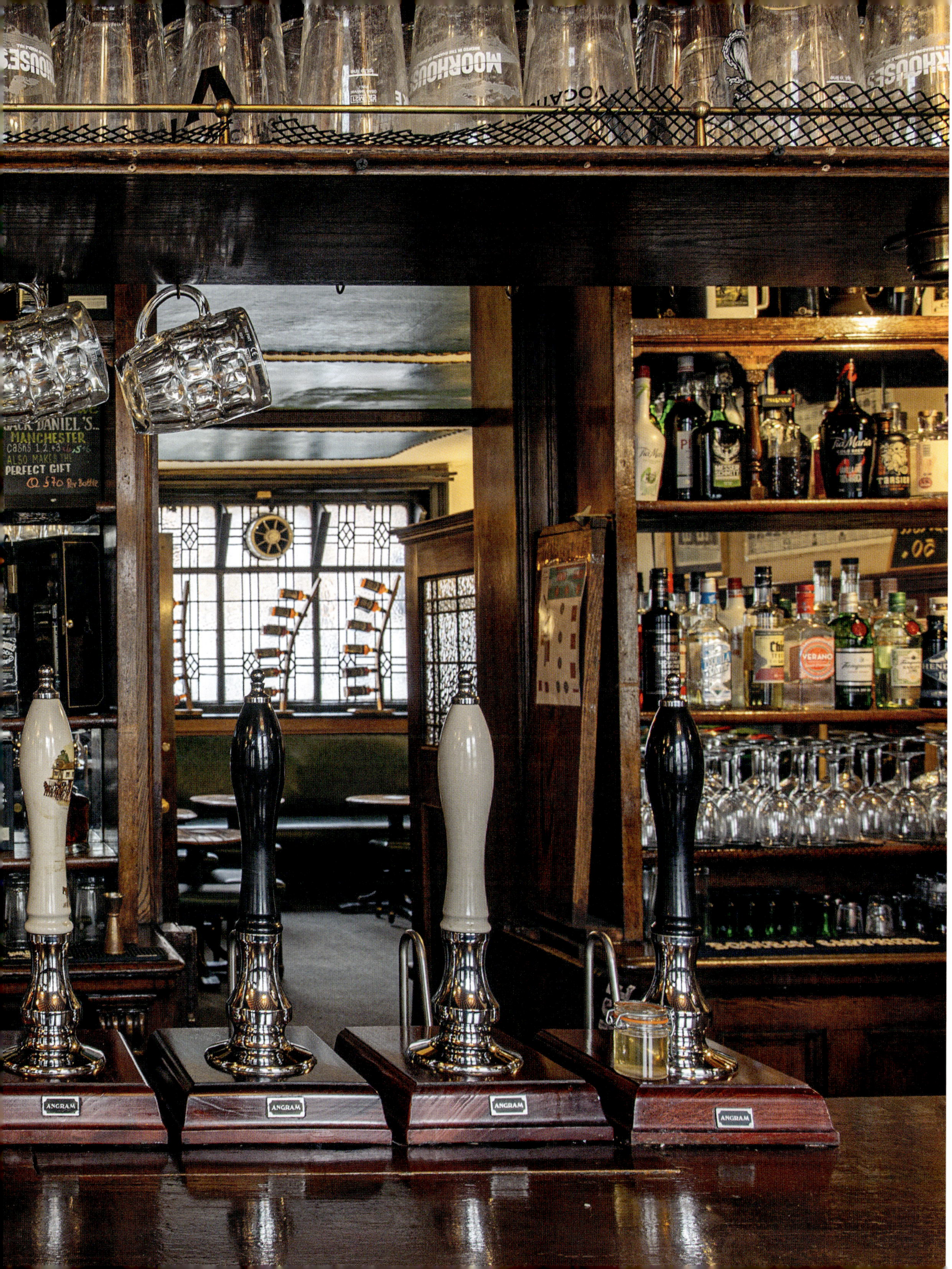

"… IT'S ABOUT SITTING, DRINKING AND CHATTING"

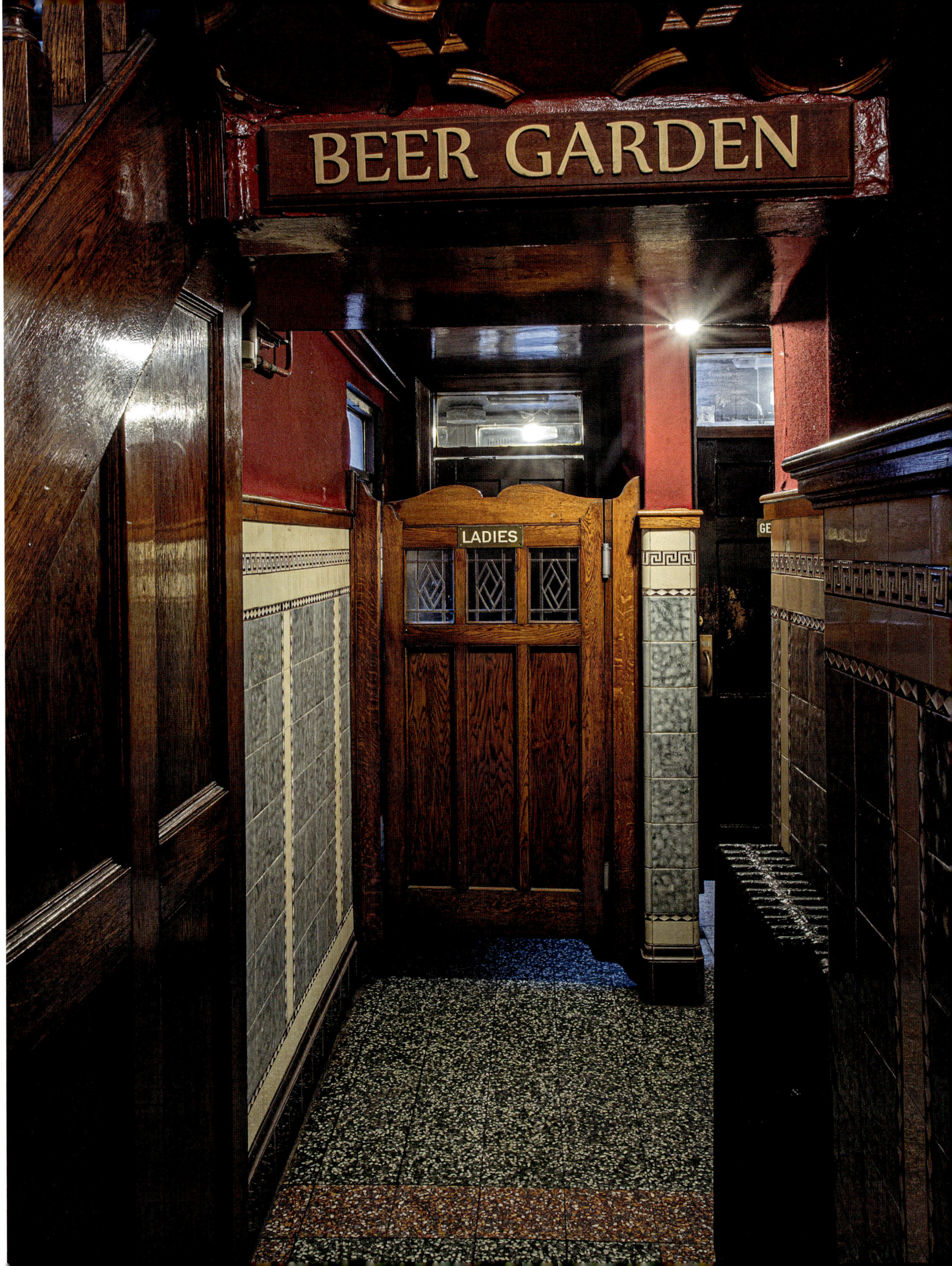
BEER GARDEN
LADIES

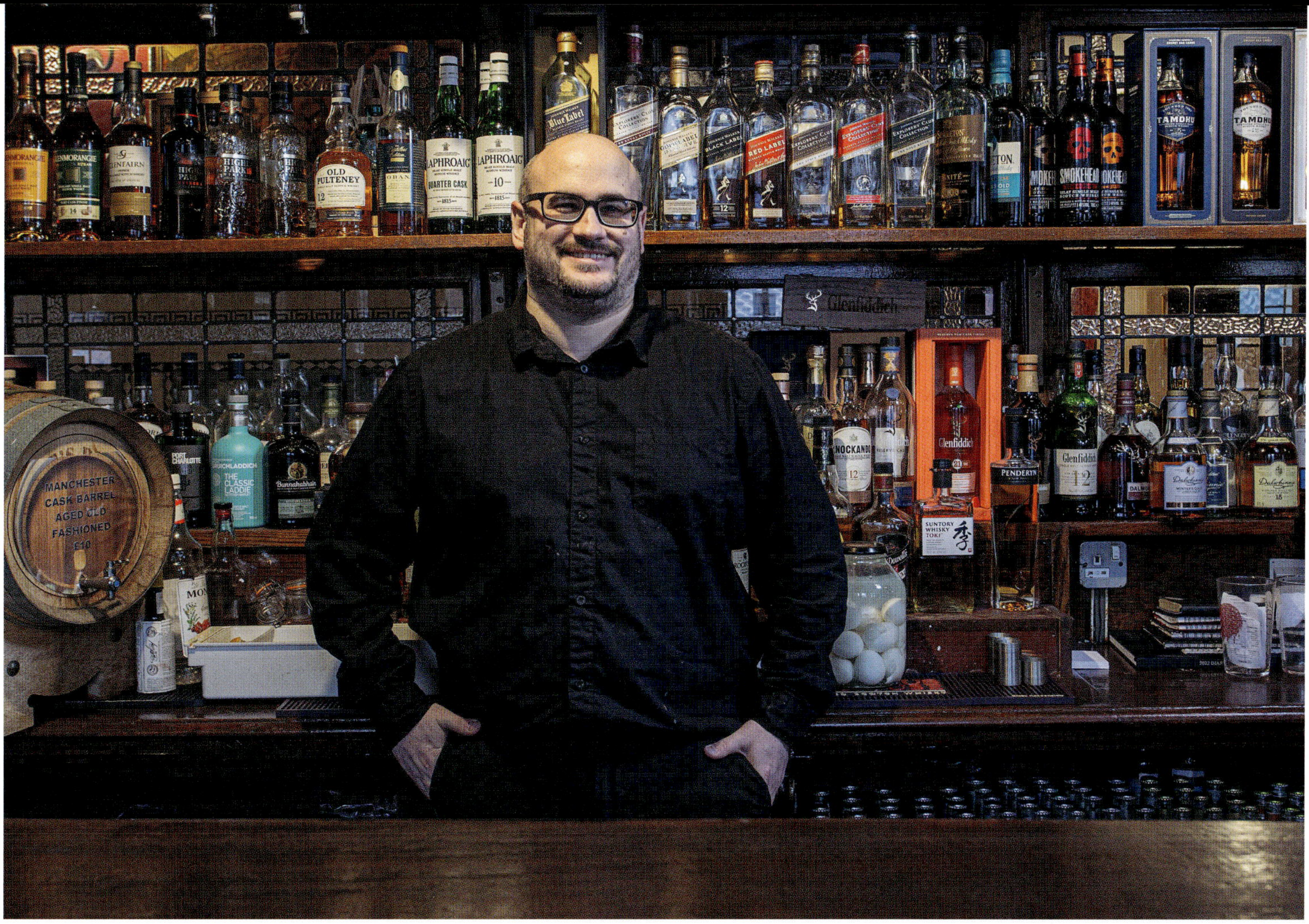

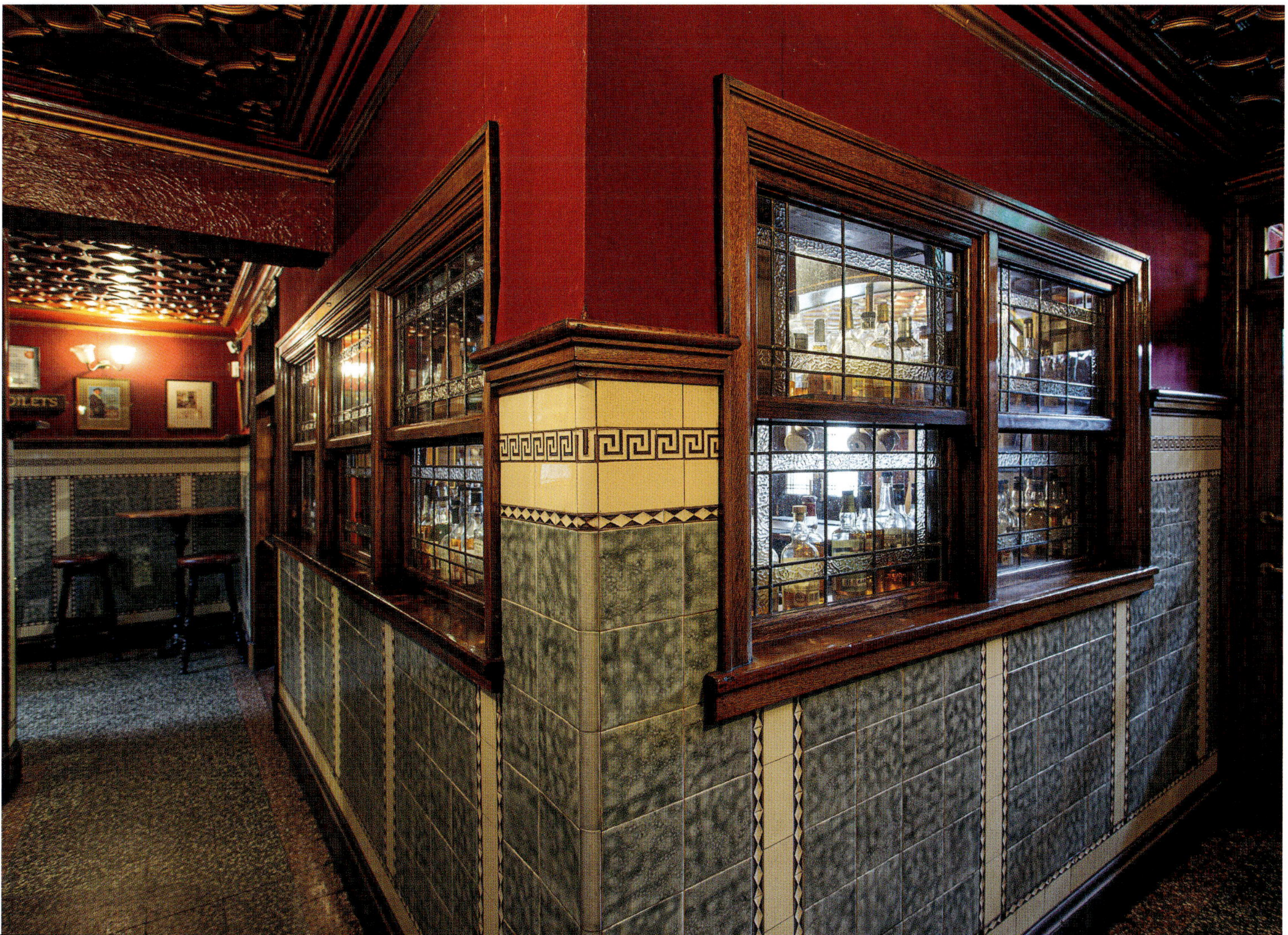

"THE WHISKY'S A PASSION FOR ME"

PEVERIL OF THE PEAK

127 GREAT BRIDGEWATER ST, MANCHESTER

There's a sign on the wall of the billiard room in Peveril of the Peak which reads thus: "A publican must be a democrat, an autocrat, an acrobat and a doormat."

Over the course of a half-century of running the pub – one of Manchester's finest and most distinctive – Nancy Swanick has doubtless found herself playing a version of the first three roles; but no one could ever accuse her of resembling the fourth. During her long tenure, Swanick – now in her nineties, and thought to be Britain's oldest serving landlady – has restored the pub to its Victorian glory from the strip-lit, white-painted, timber-clad dive she inherited in 1971; prevented city planners from taking the wrecking ball to it and brewery officials from transforming it into a plastic palm tree-adorned "sports bar"; welcomed everyone from Steve Coogan to Robbie Coltrane and the Gallagher brothers (as the photos dotting the walls attest); and raised her three sons in the flat above, where she still lives. "Nancy's mantra has always been to keep it simple," says Nadim Hammad, the pub's manager. "It's remarkable that she's managed to maintain that down the decades."

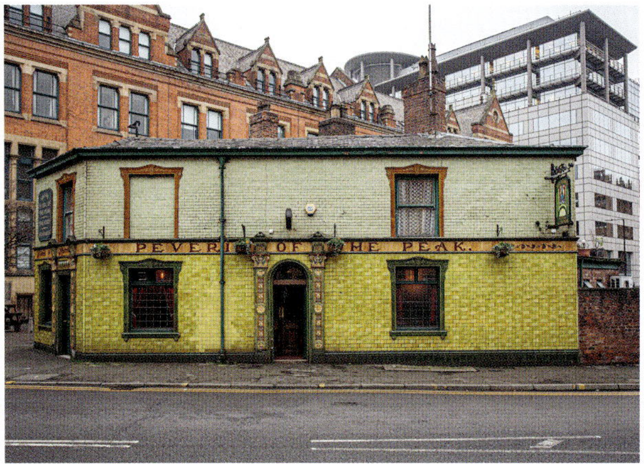

But then, "the Pev" is a pretty remarkable pub. Named after a stagecoach that once ran between Manchester and London, or possibly a Walter Scott novel – people seem hazy on this point, which, after all, is many pints in the past – it's a vision in green, with its vivid tile-clad exterior. That alone would be enough to justify its Grade II listing, but the interior, with its three rooms and dog-leg corridor, could be a time capsule from the 1830s, when the Pev first opened: more tiles, stained glass, florid art nouveau detailing, cast-iron fireplaces, and leaded panels. Even the table football set is an antique, dating from the 1950s; it was once patronised by a visiting Eric Cantona, but he was hopelessly outclassed by a regular known as Tony Soccerballs. "He must be in his late seventies", says Hammad, "and he's been coming here for more than forty years."

Mr Soccerballs is just one of the members of the extended family that Nancy Swanick has welcomed to the Pev (her husband Tommy, a one-time foundry foreman, died of cancer in 1981). When she arrived, the pub was still trying to live down its reputation as a brothel for GIs during the Second World War, and post-work punch-ups were the dismaying norm. "But she just had this way of dealing with troublemakers," says Hammad. "Grown men would be reduced to little boys when she scolded them. People learnt that this was a place you respected. She set the tone. A lot of modern places are a bit soulless, but she invested the Pev with real heart."

Today, the crowd at the Pev is a testament to Swanick's inclusive ethos. There are students, office workers, football fans (it now opens every Saturday, and not, as formerly, only when Manchester United were playing at home), the occasional Scandinavian stag party, and regulars like Vox, a Norwegian émigré who brings her knitting to the bar. "It's a real mix, and it's the atmosphere, the authenticity of the place, that people love," says Hammad.

The atmosphere-authenticity thing is in full swing on one of the Pev's regular evenings of folk music, presided over by the veteran guitarist and unofficial Bard of the North Mike Harding. Banjos are plucked, fiddles are sawed, tin whistles are trilled, beards are stroked, feet are stamped, pints are supped, talk is somehow very Mancunian ("some scallywag stole my back wheel..."), and the city's faces, both fresh and venerable, are present and correct (visitor, to a tousle-haired, elfin-faced guy: "Are you a rock star?" Elfin-faced guy: "Not yet."). Nancy hasn't made an appearance – her arthritis increasingly prevents her descending the stairs – but, says Hammad, you can bet that she'll be listening up above, revelling in the bonhomie, and imbibing the buoyancy of a place that she has fashioned after her own indomitable spirit.

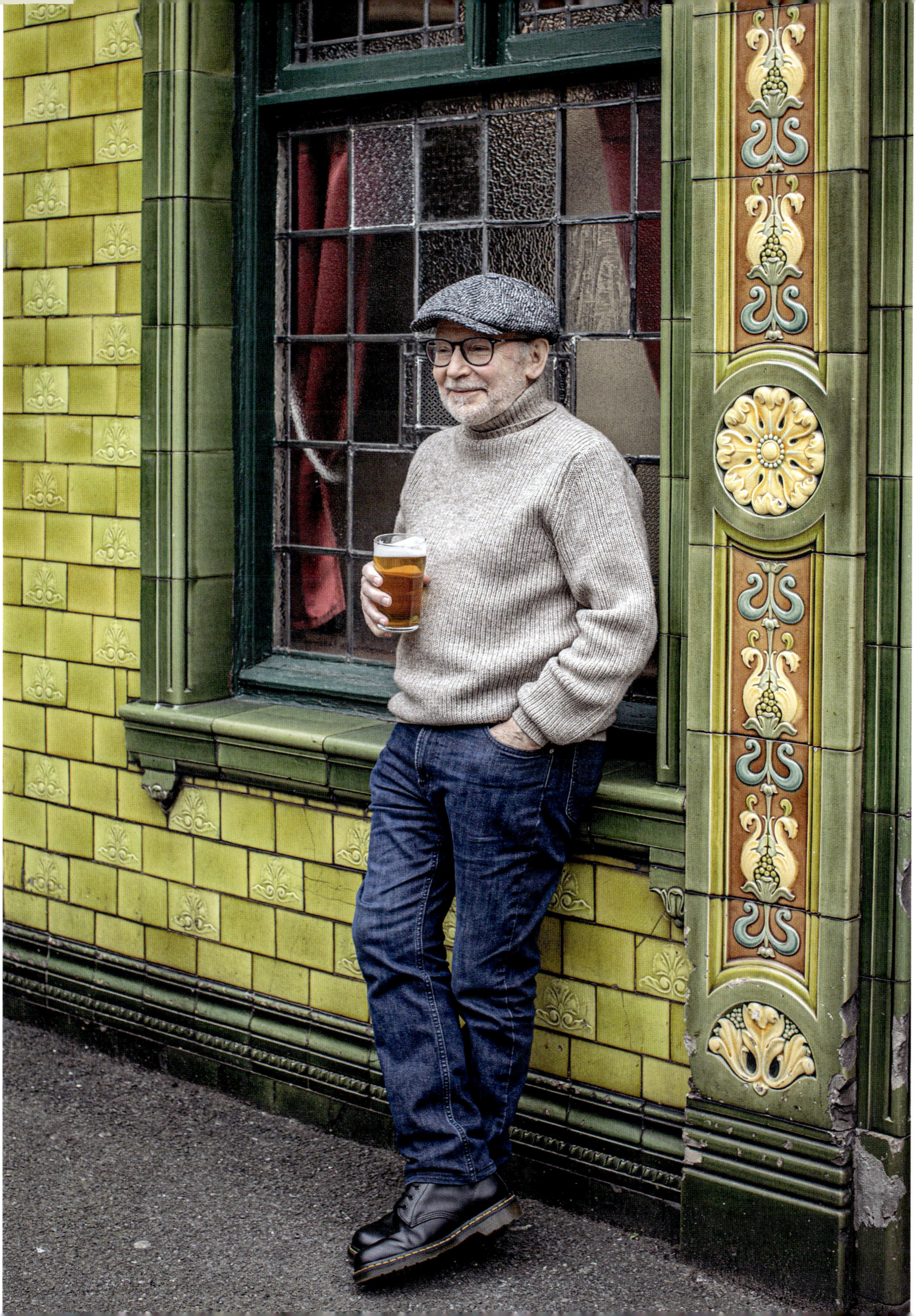

"A REAL MIX, A GREAT ATMOSPHERE"

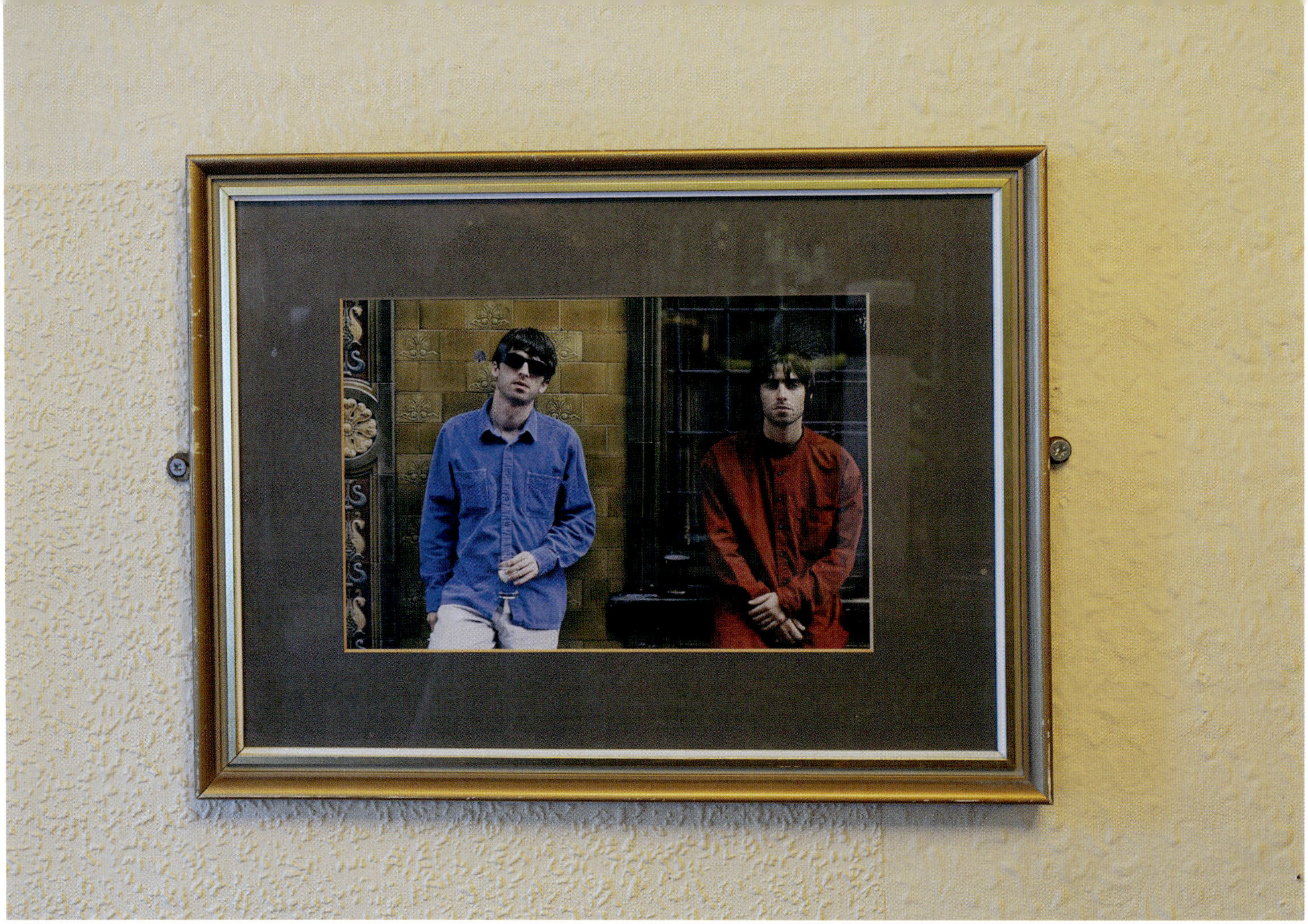

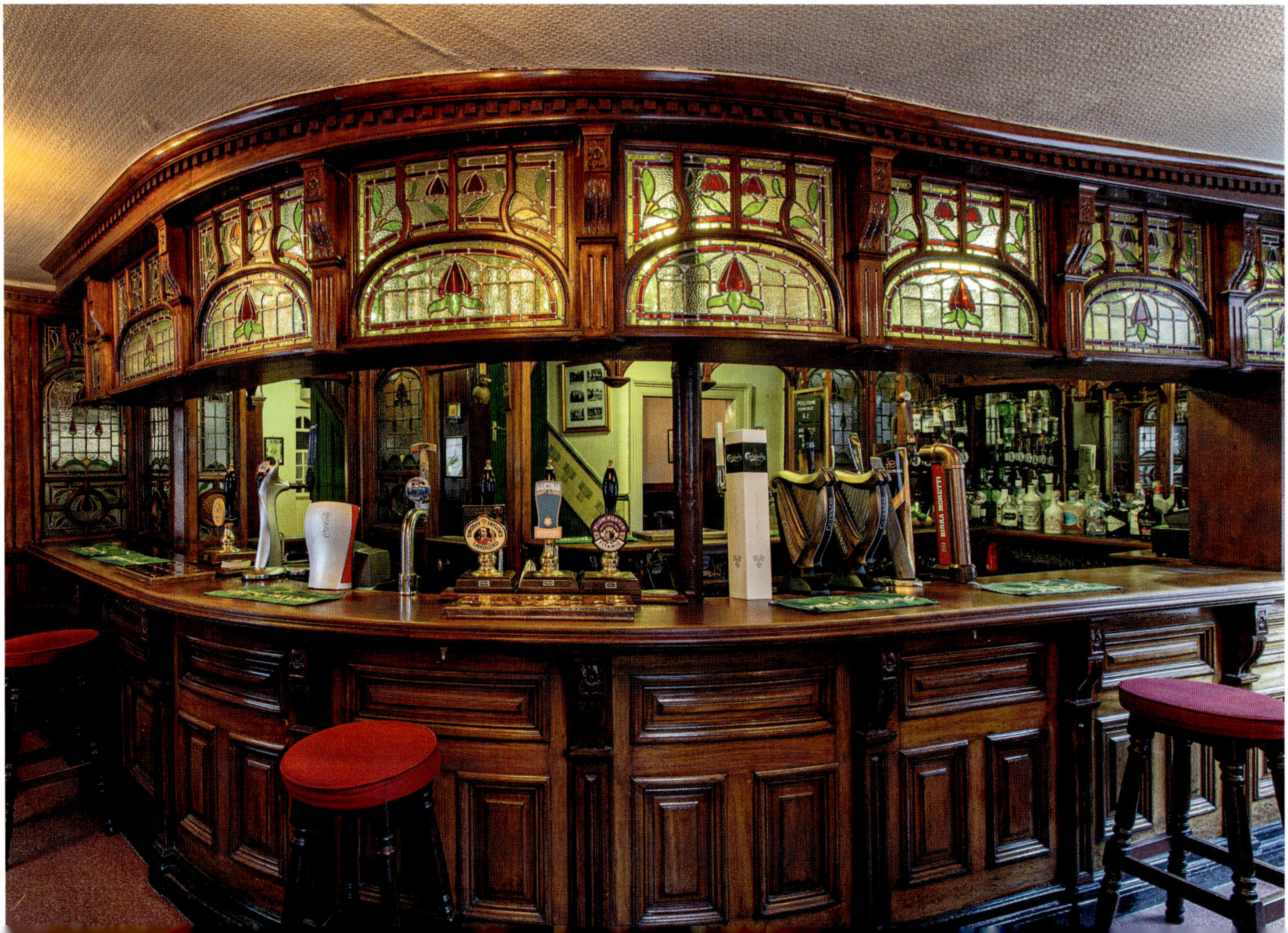
BIRRA MORETTI

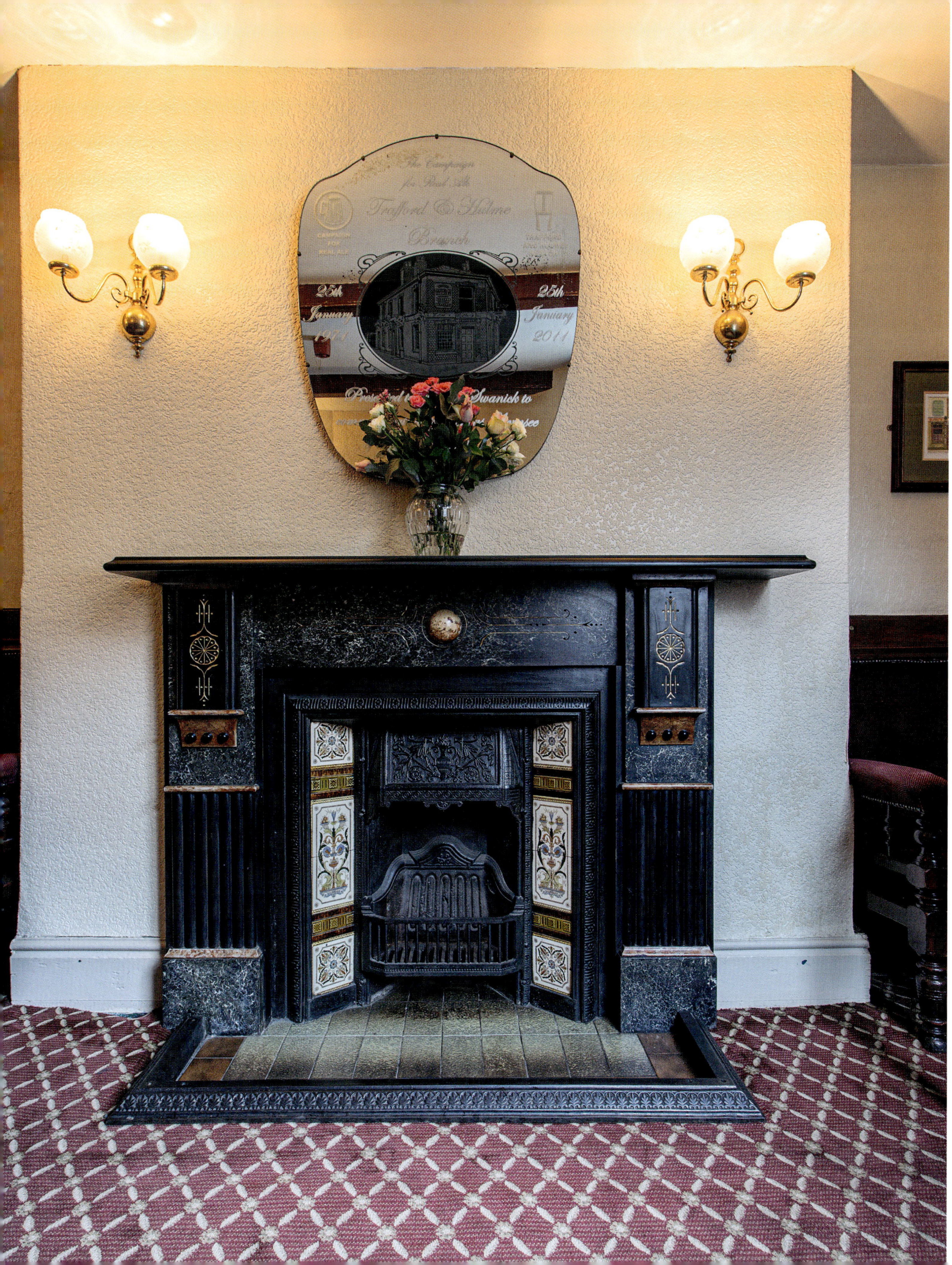

Trafford & Hulme
Branch
CAMPAIGN FOR REAL ALE
25th January
25th January 2011
Swanick to

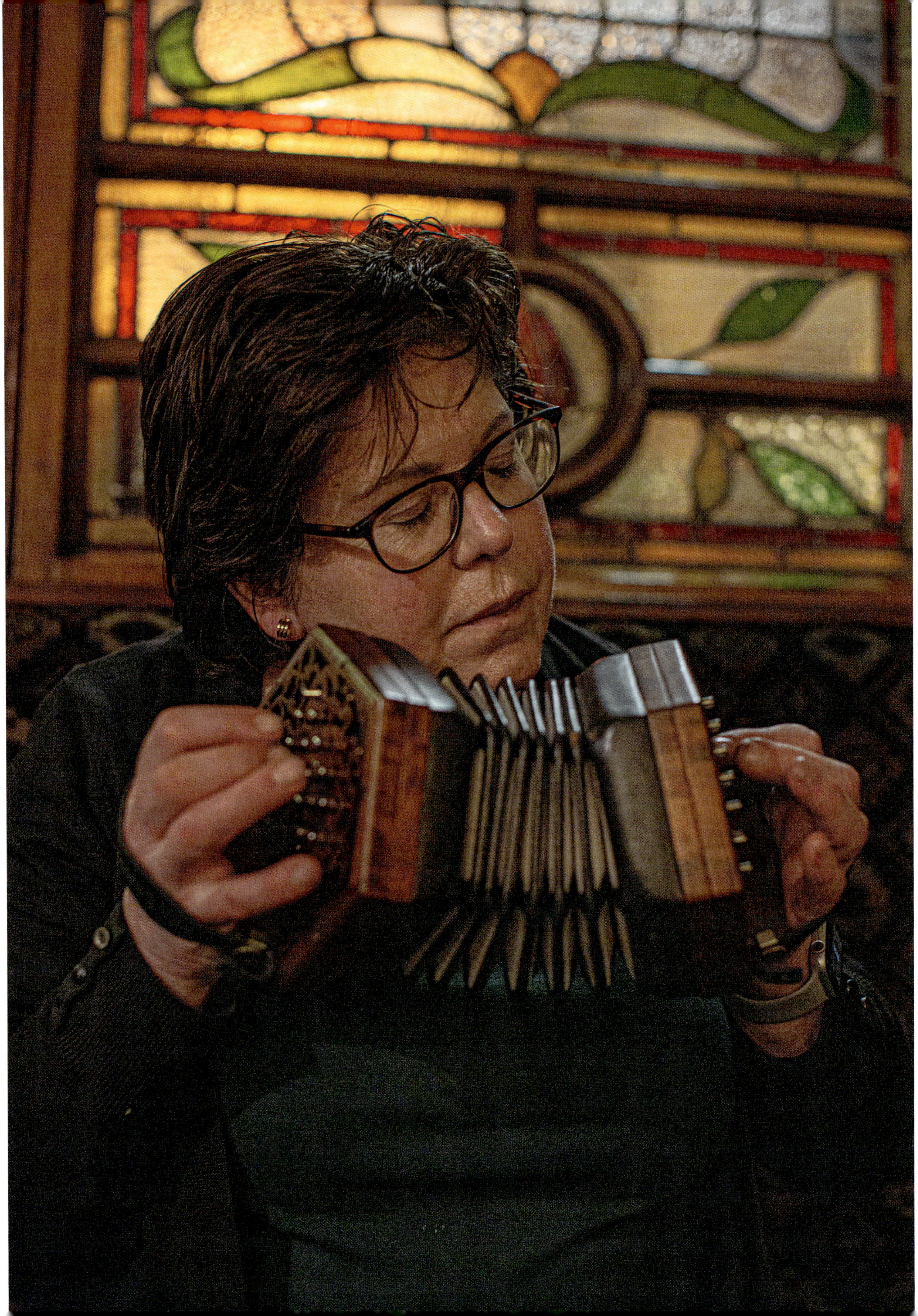

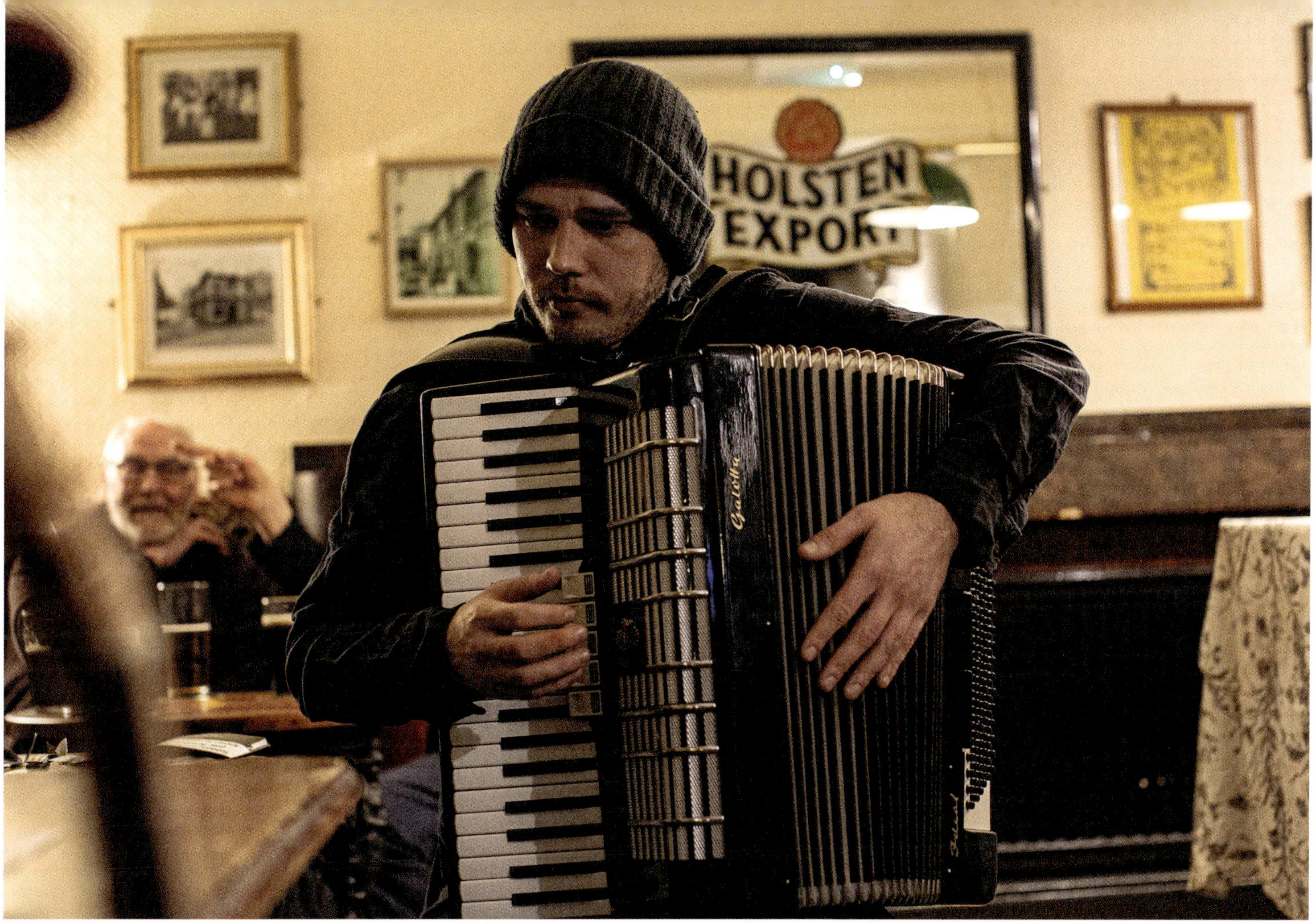

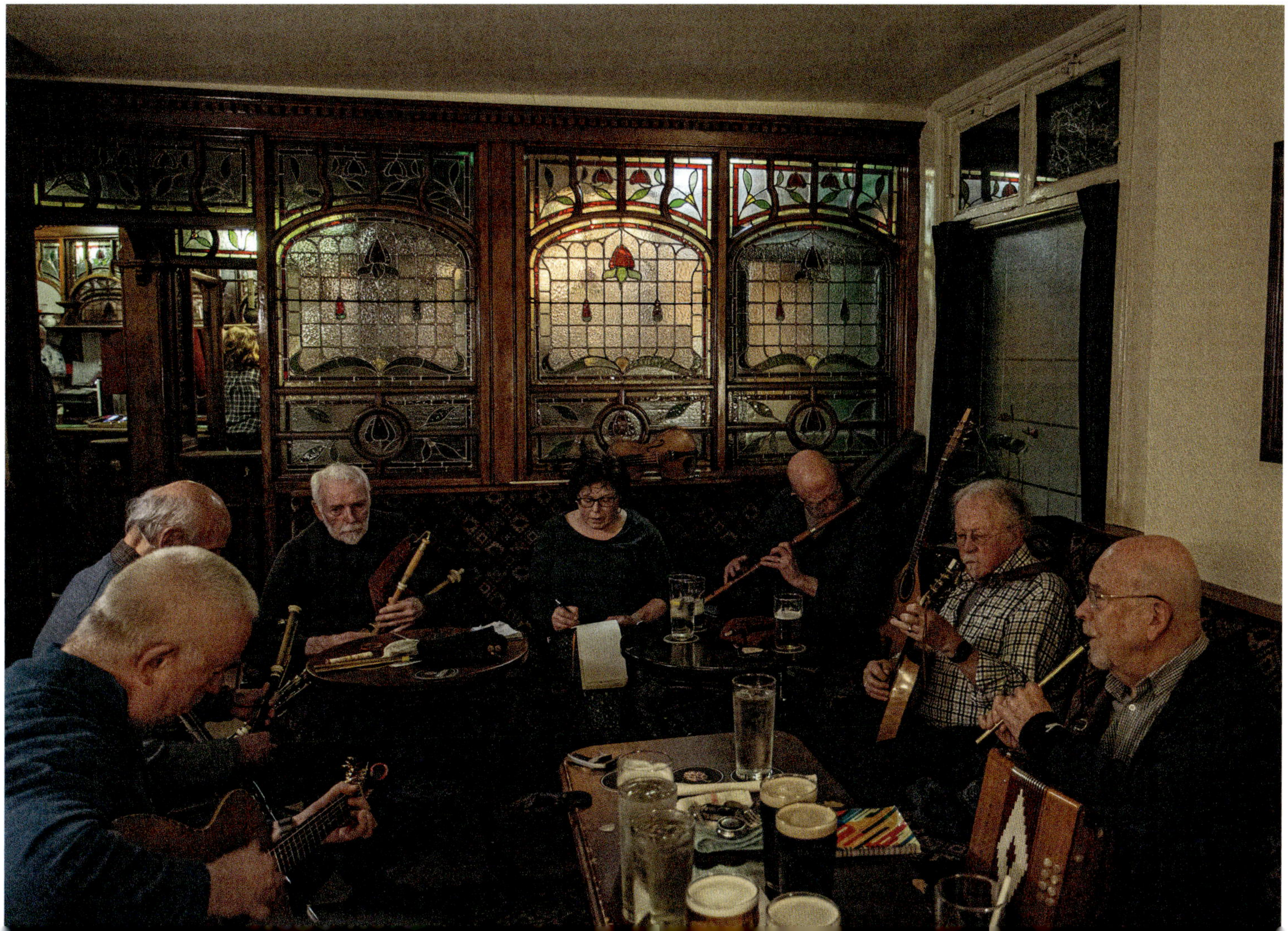

"IT'S IMPORTANT TO HONOUR OUR HERITAGE"

“UNSPOILT INTERIOR FEATURES ARE RARE ...”

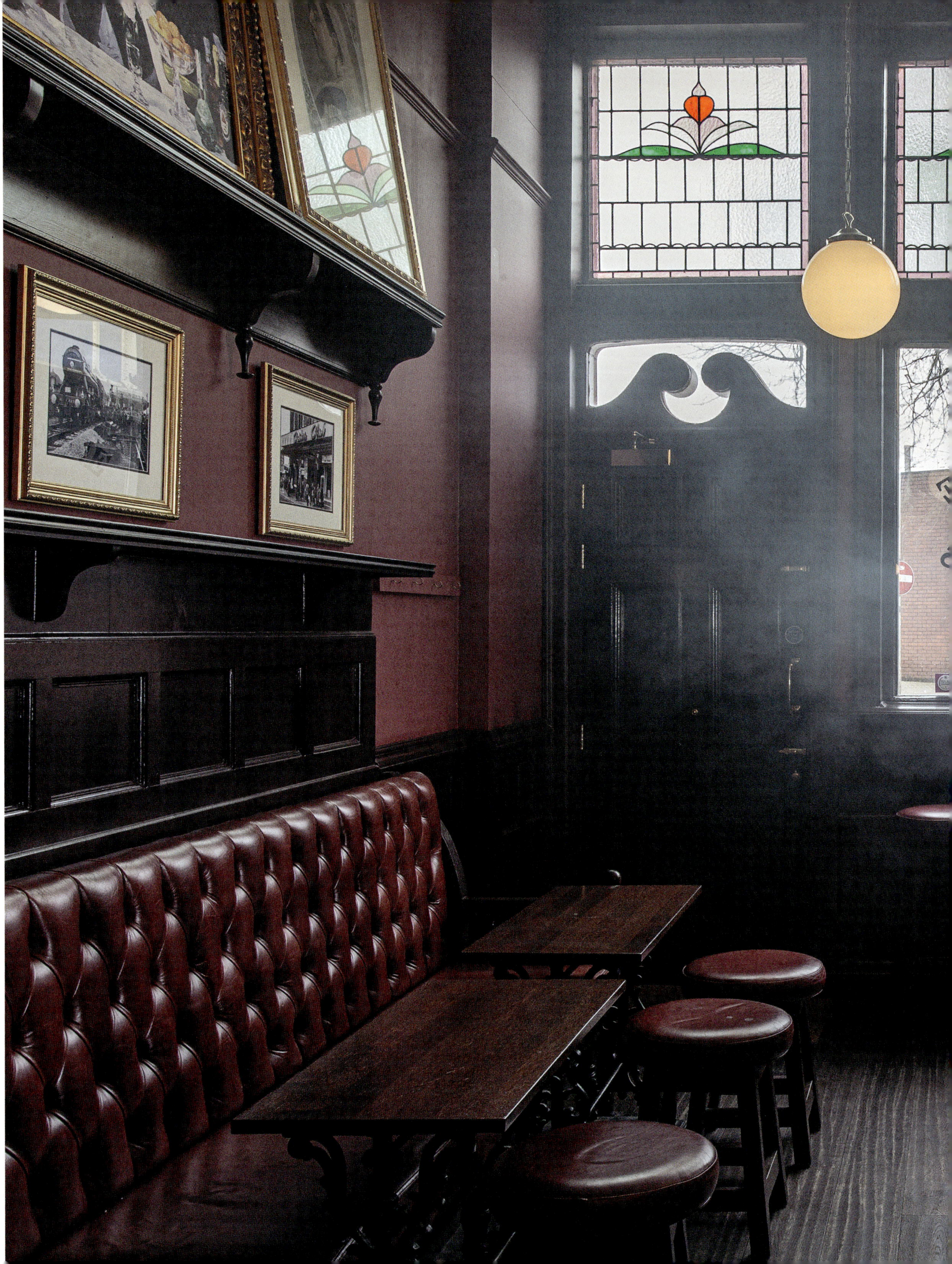

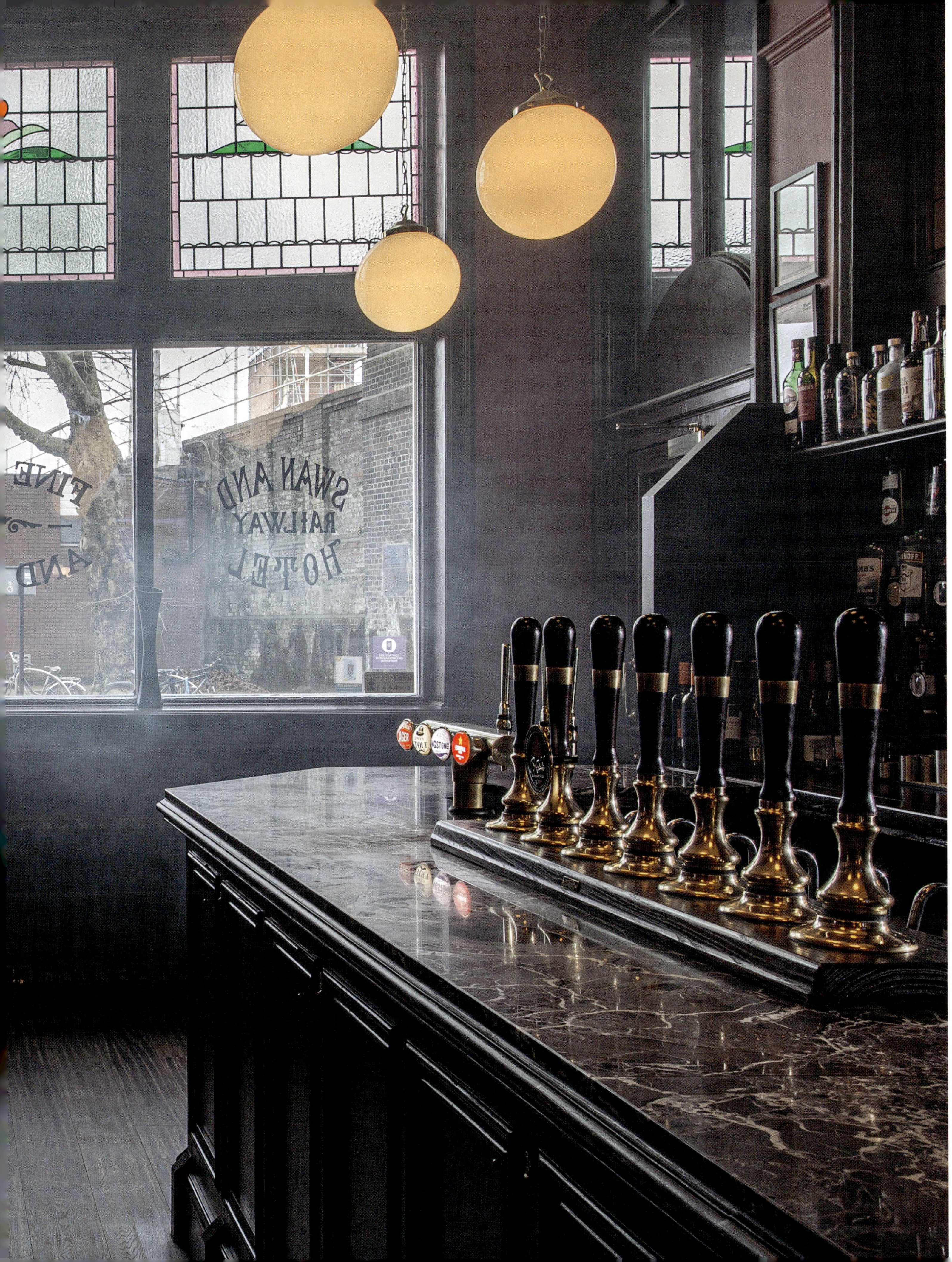

"... THERE ARE SO FEW THAT HAVEN'T BEEN MESSED WITH"

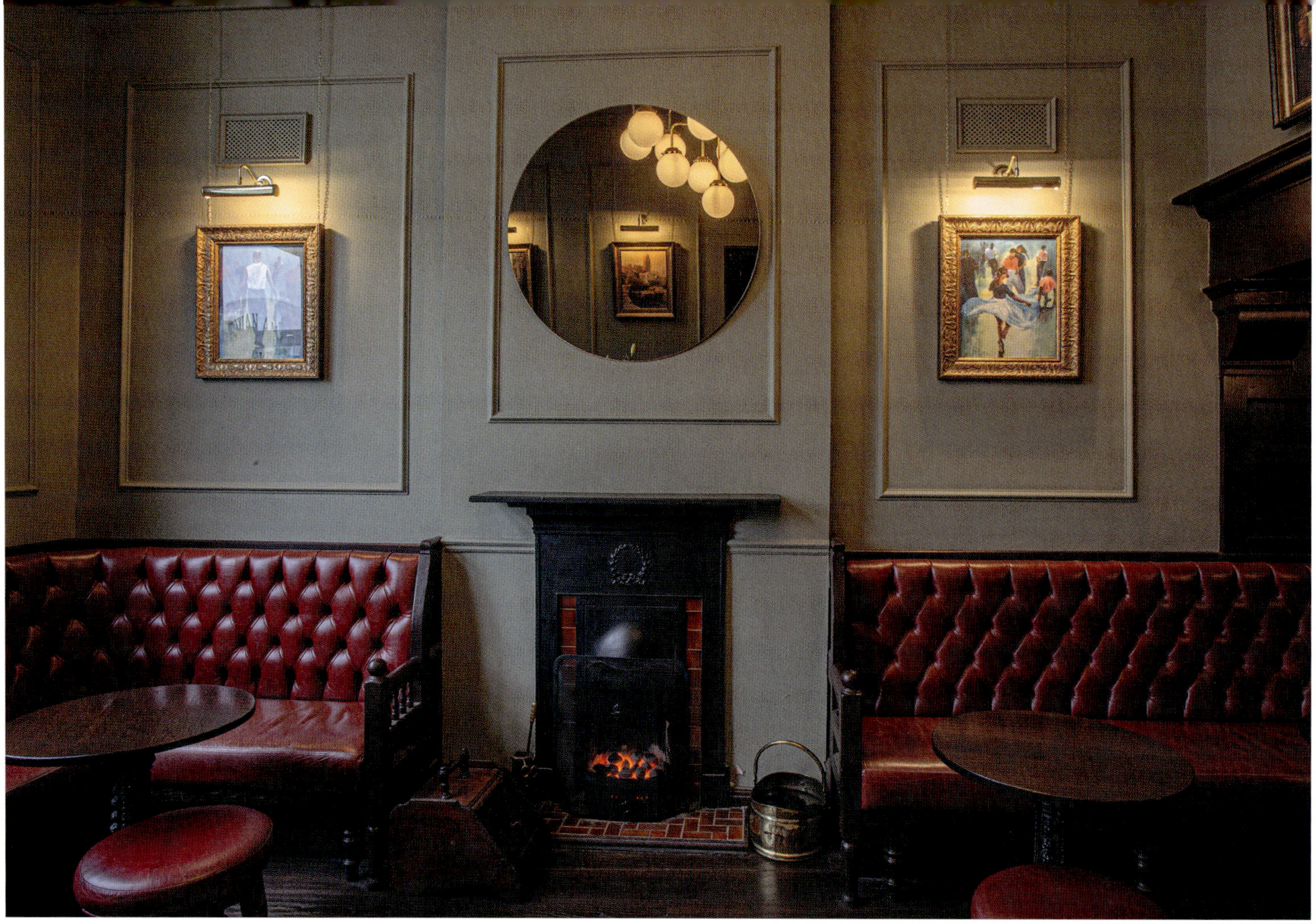

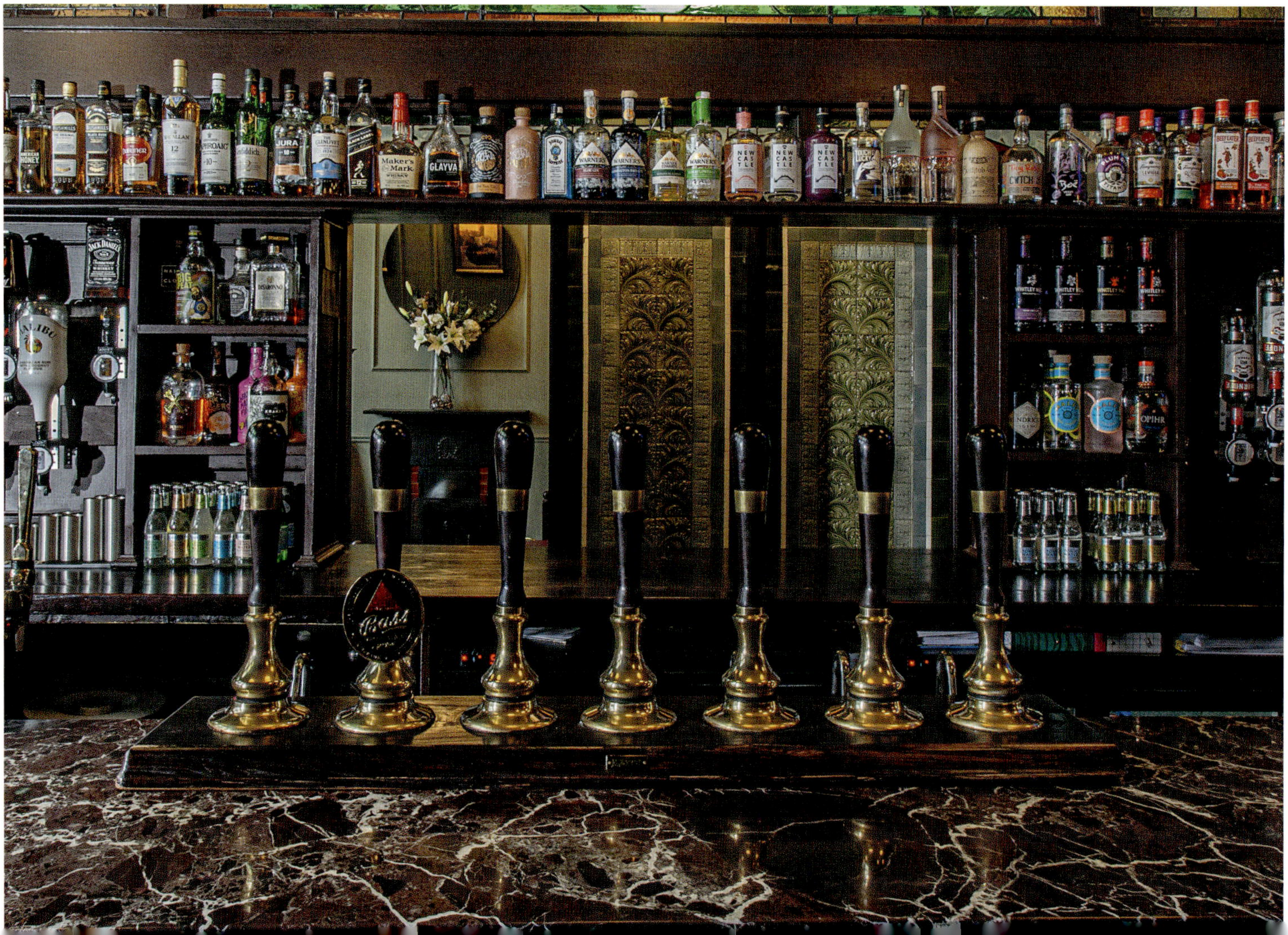
Maker's Mark
GLAYVA
Bass

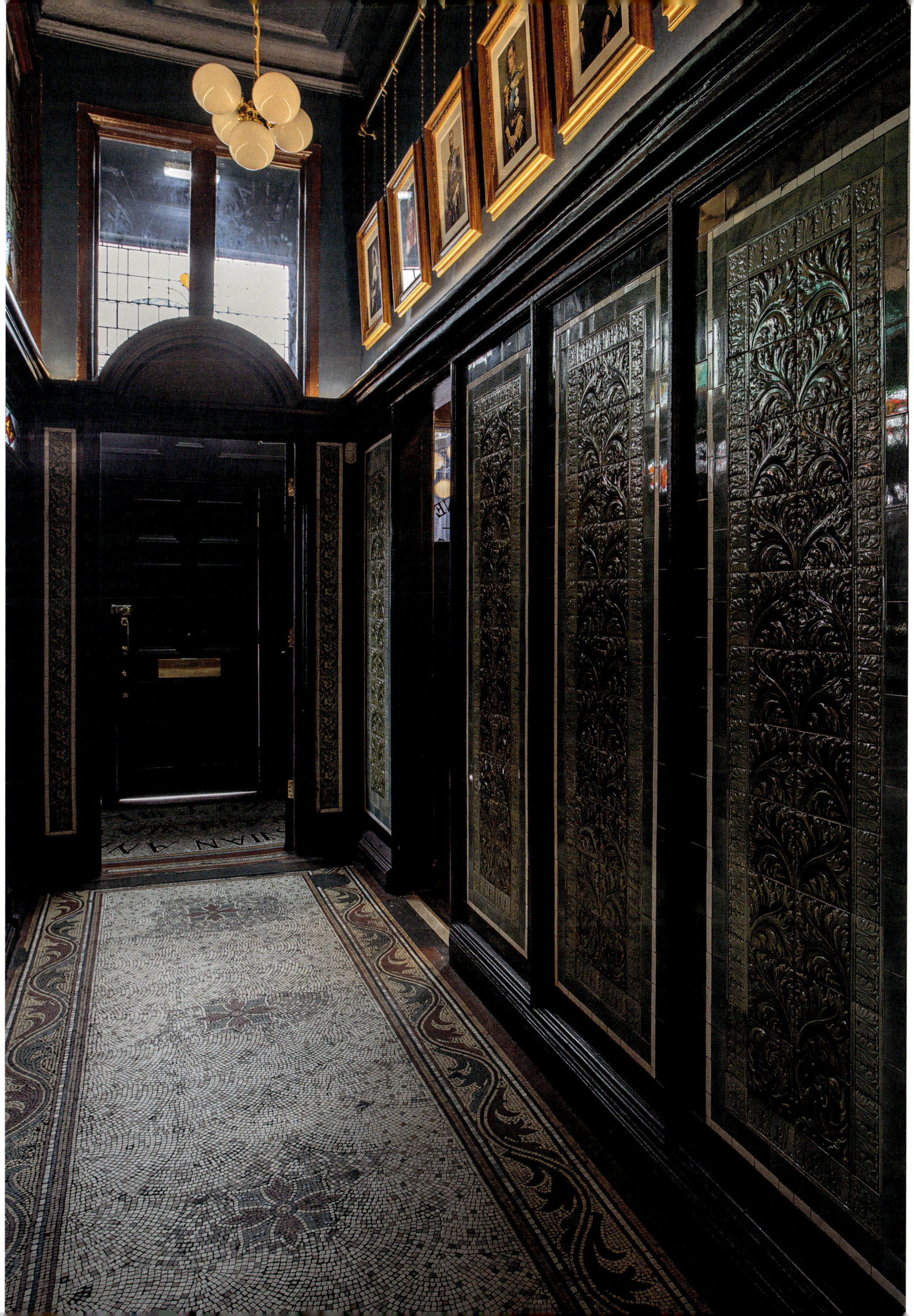

"THE STYLE AND FEEL IS TIMELESS"

"WE'VE ONLY GOT FIVE TABLES TO FILL HERE ..."

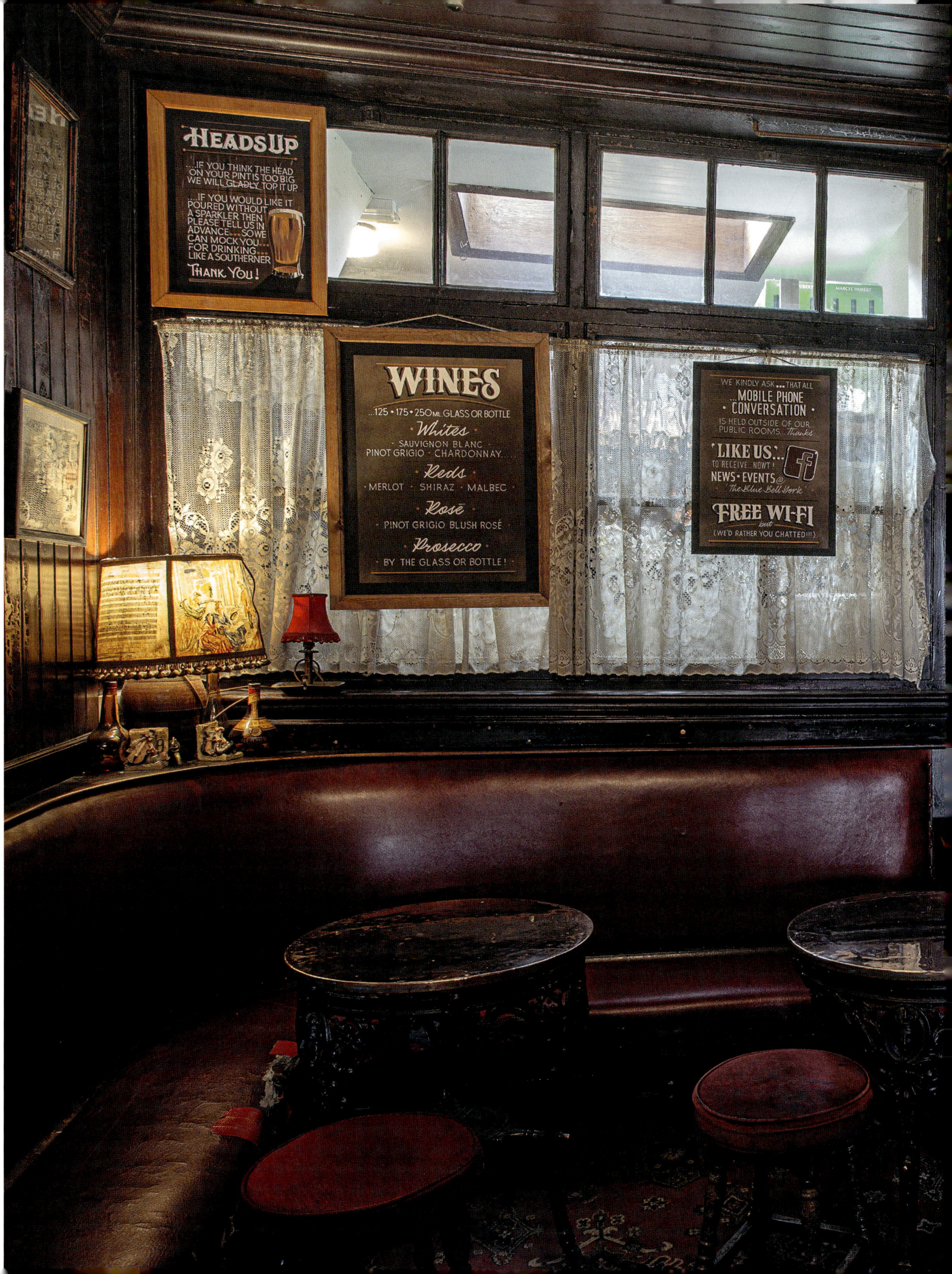

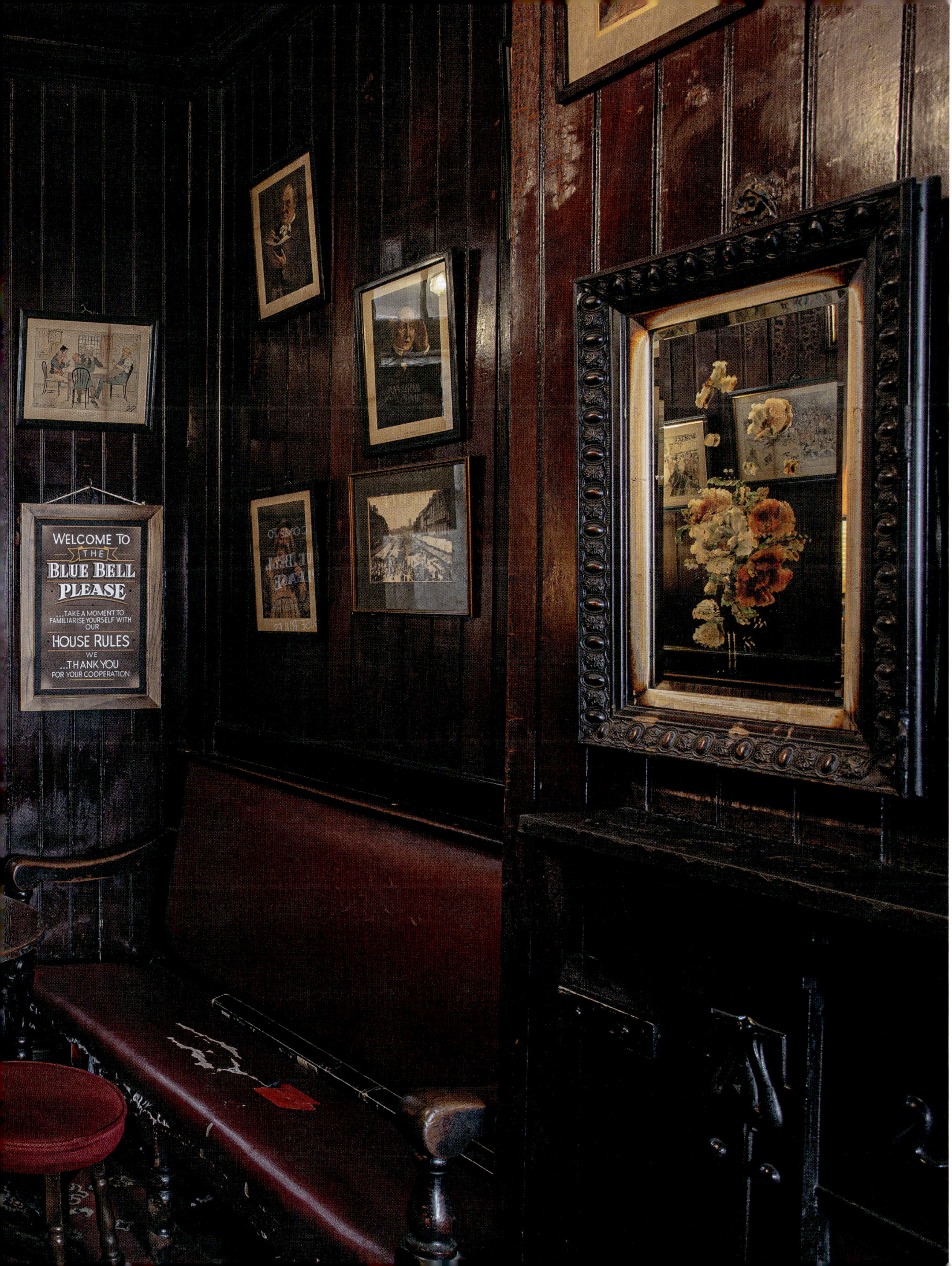

"... PEOPLE STRIKE UP CONVERSATIONS, MAKE FRIENDS"

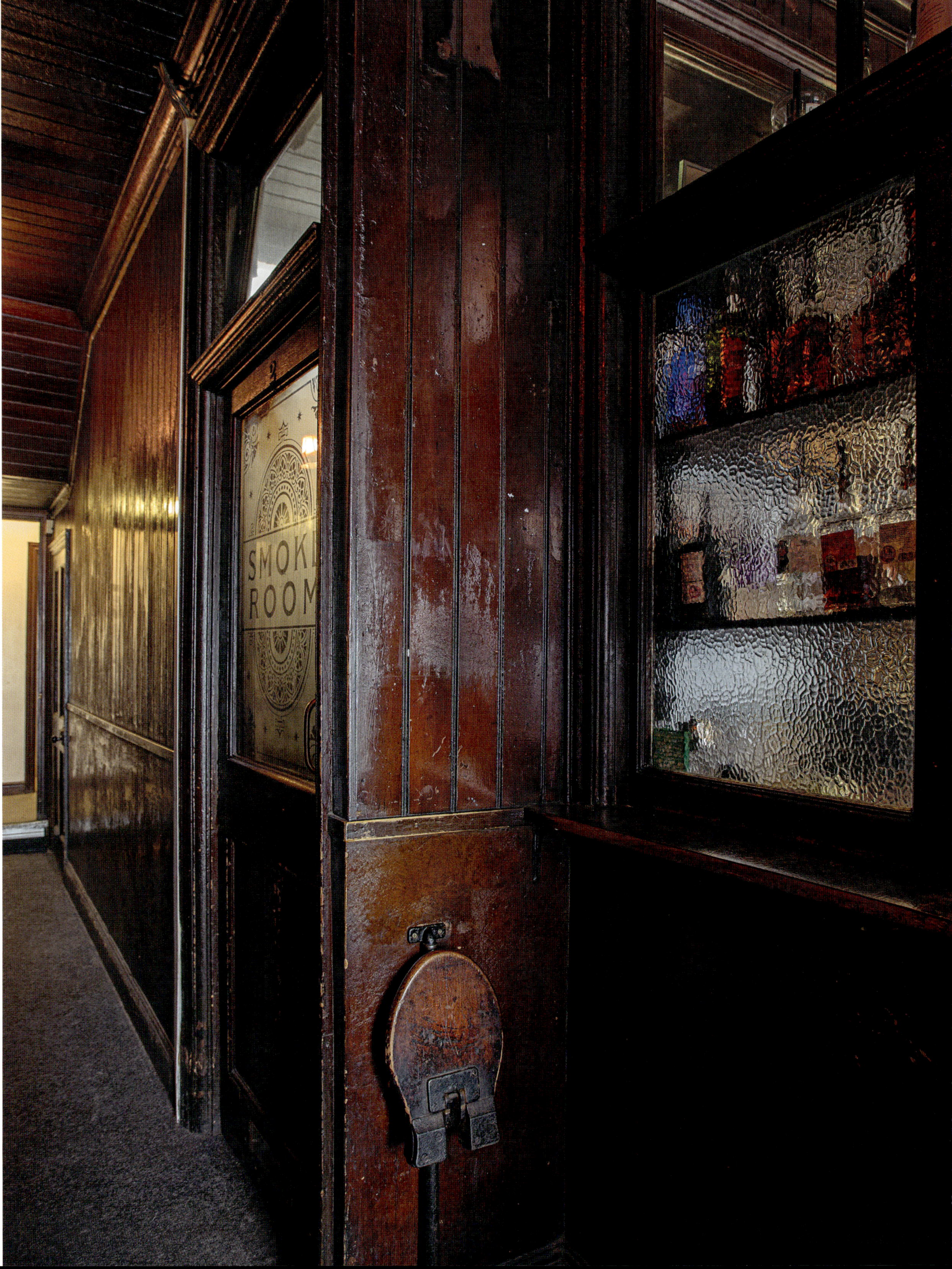
ROOM

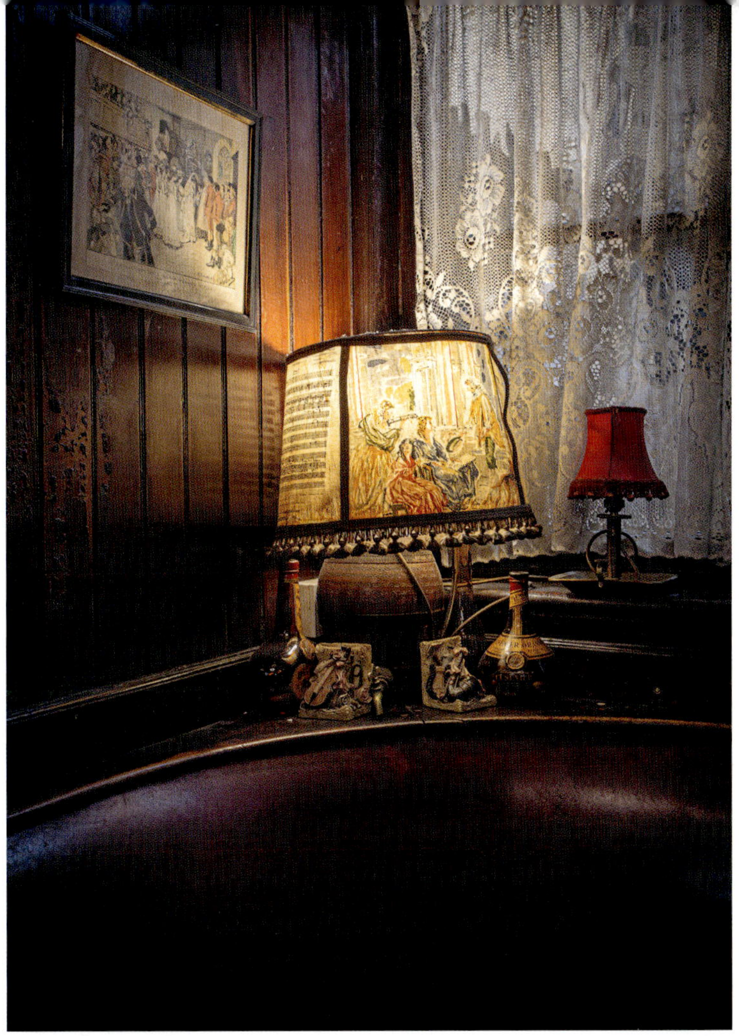

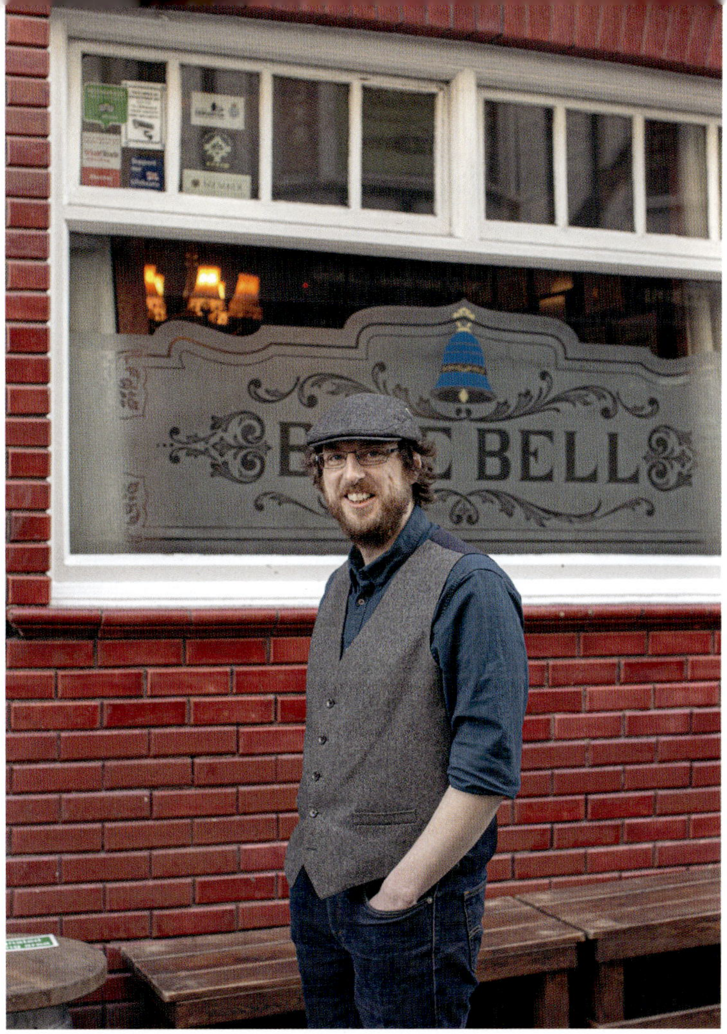

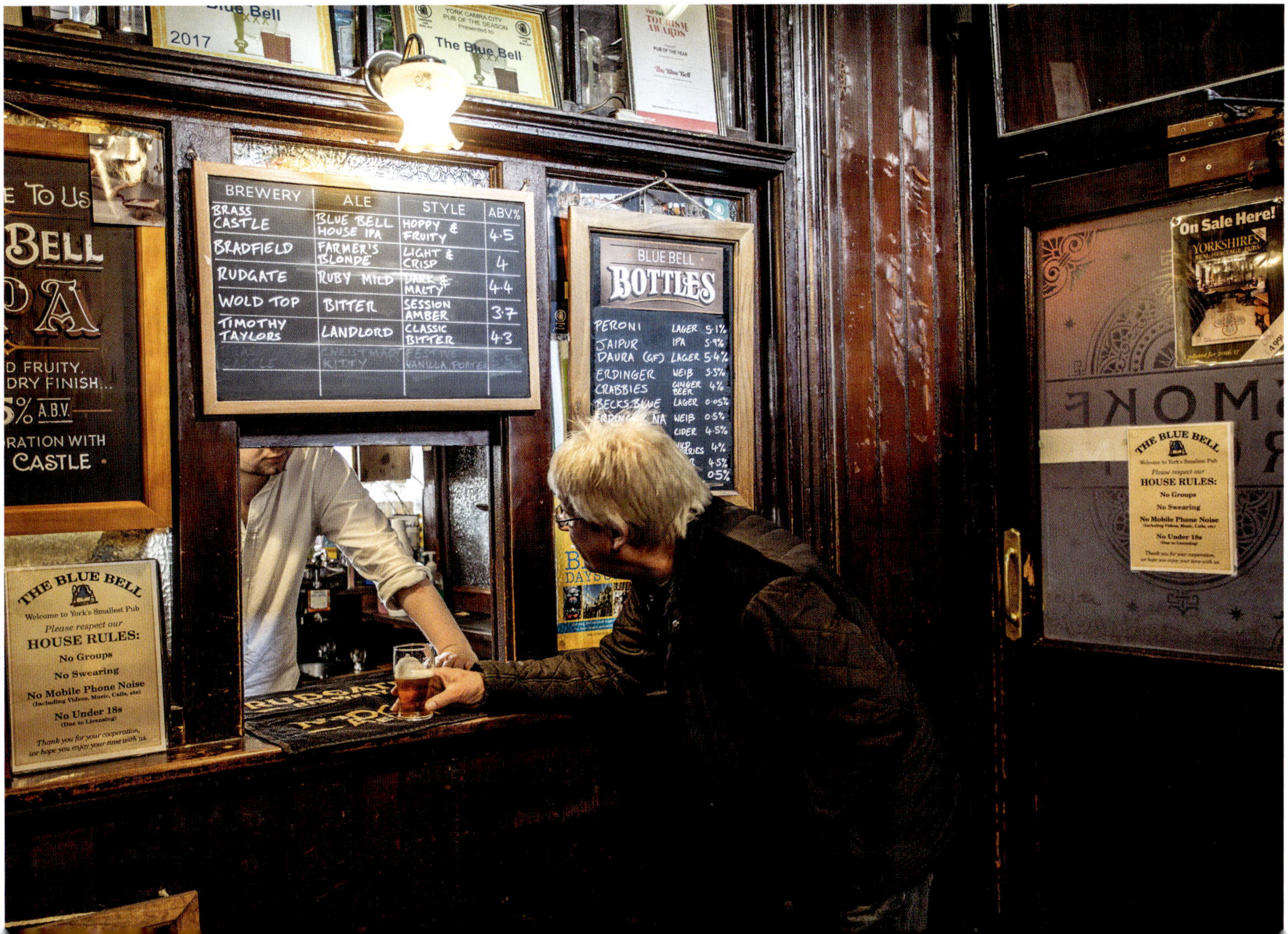

"IT'S LIKE BEING ON STAGE BEHIND THE BAR"

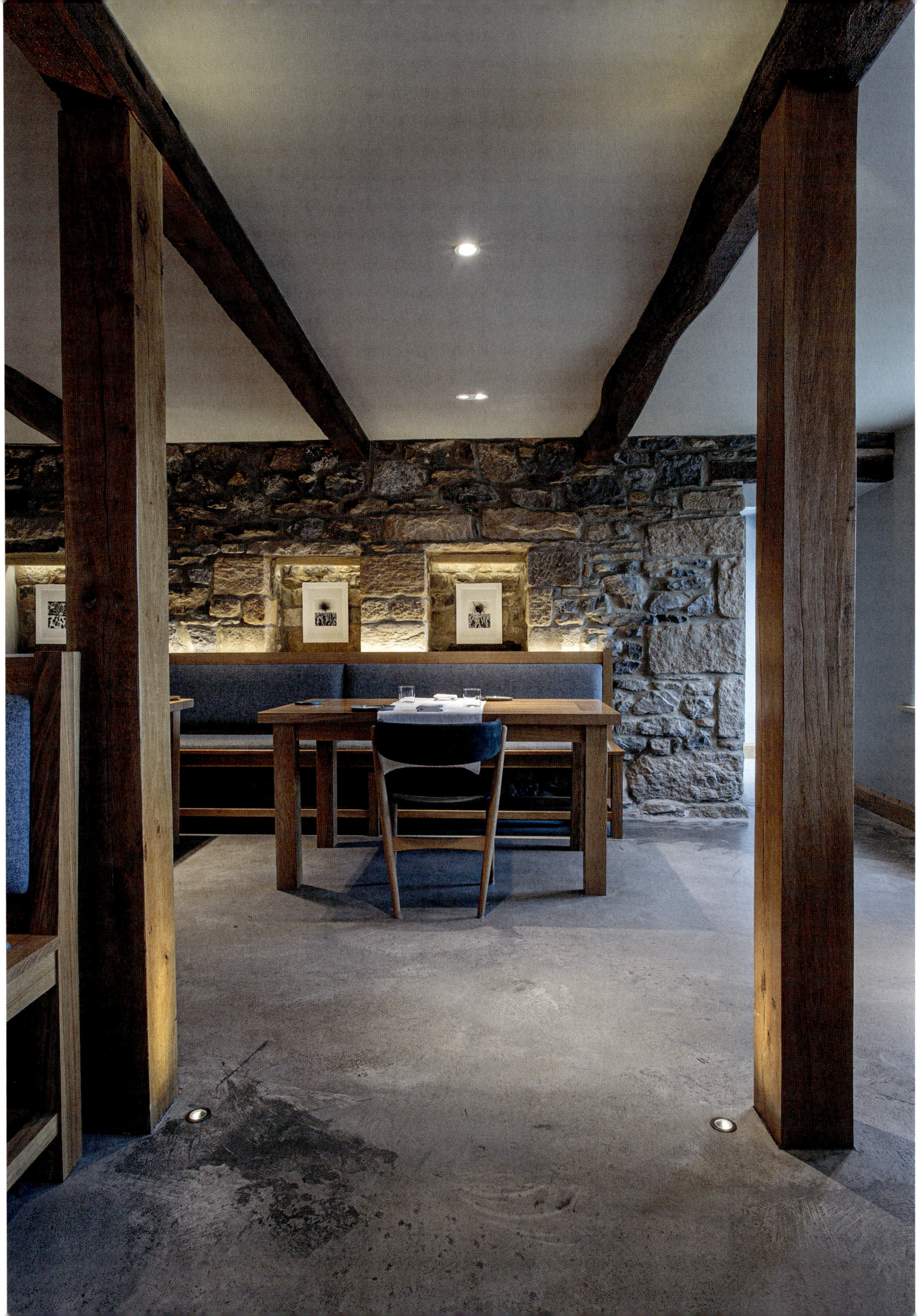

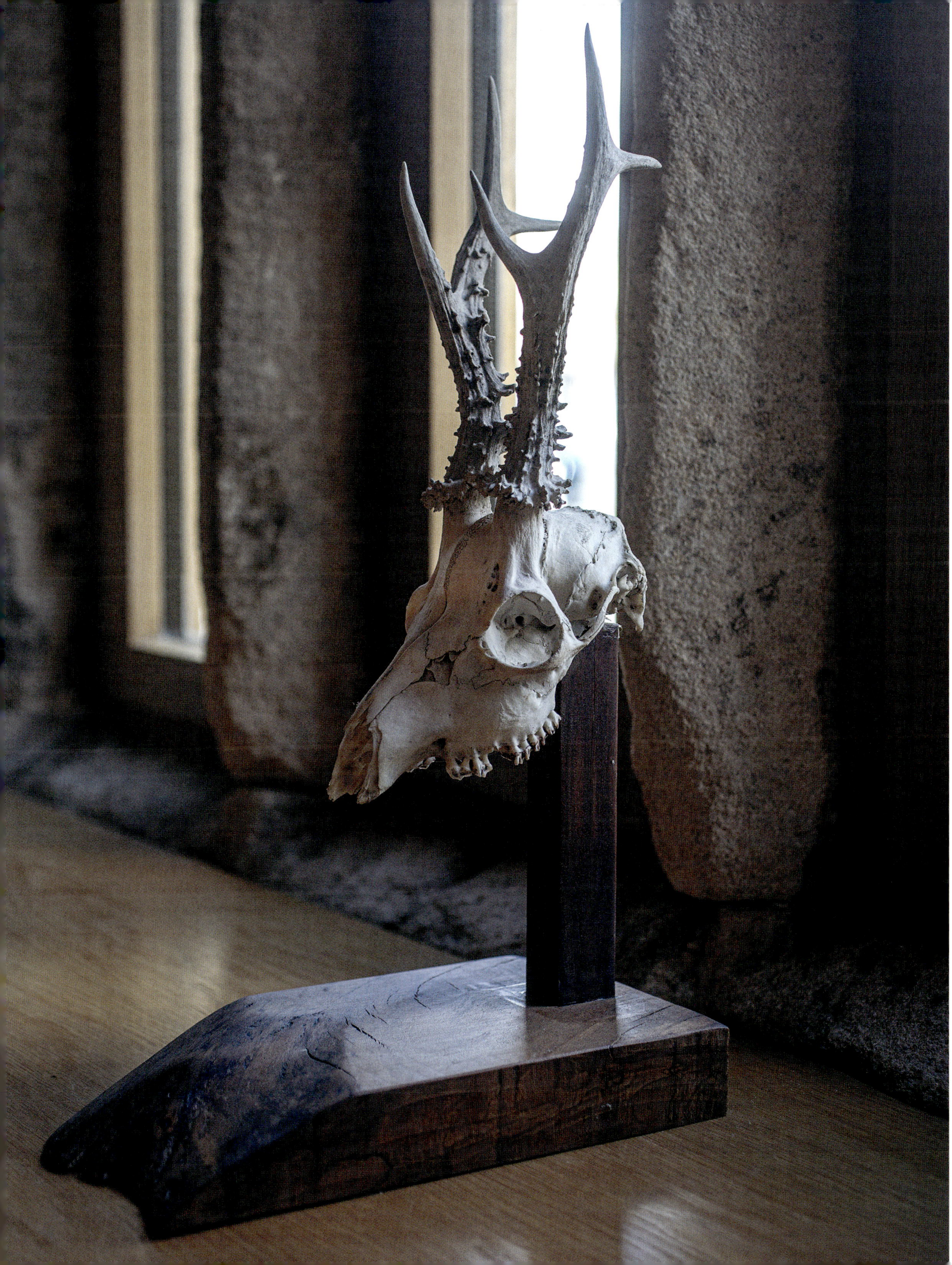

"CAN WE SAY HAUTE RUSTIC?"

"IT'S QUALITY, PREMIUM, HANDMADE STUFF"

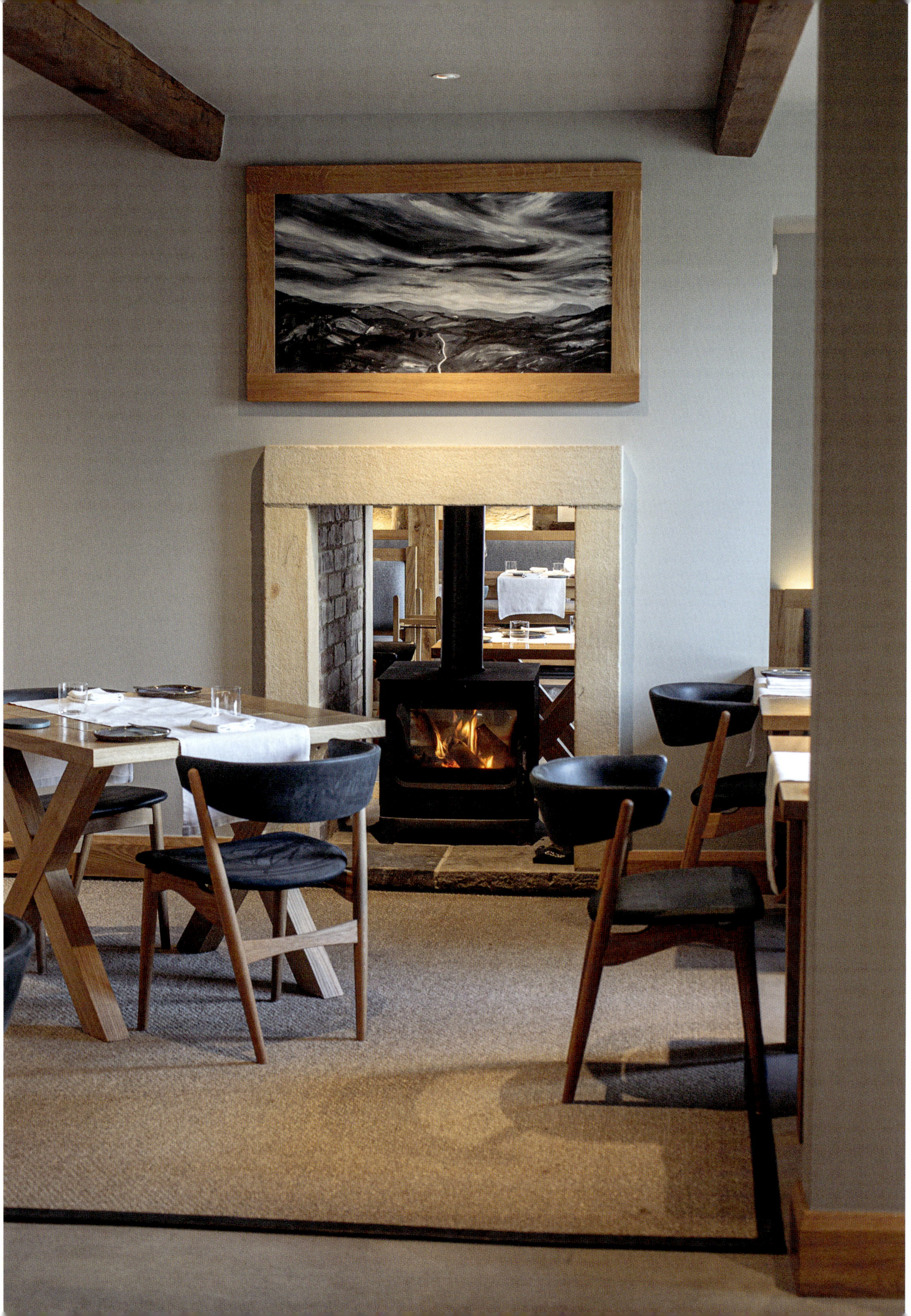

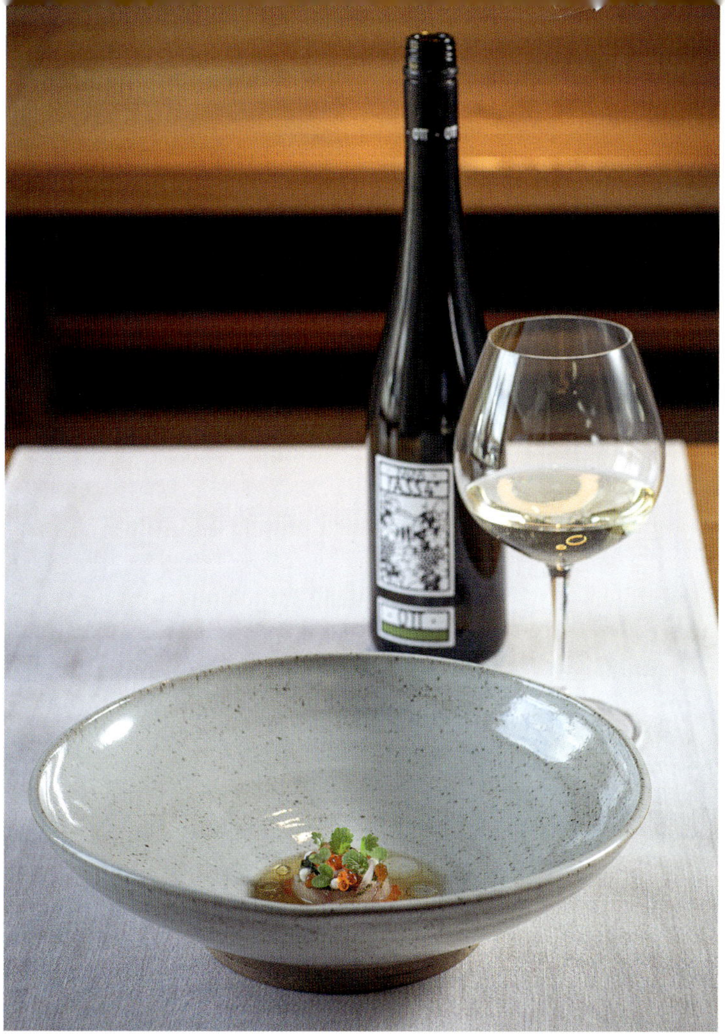

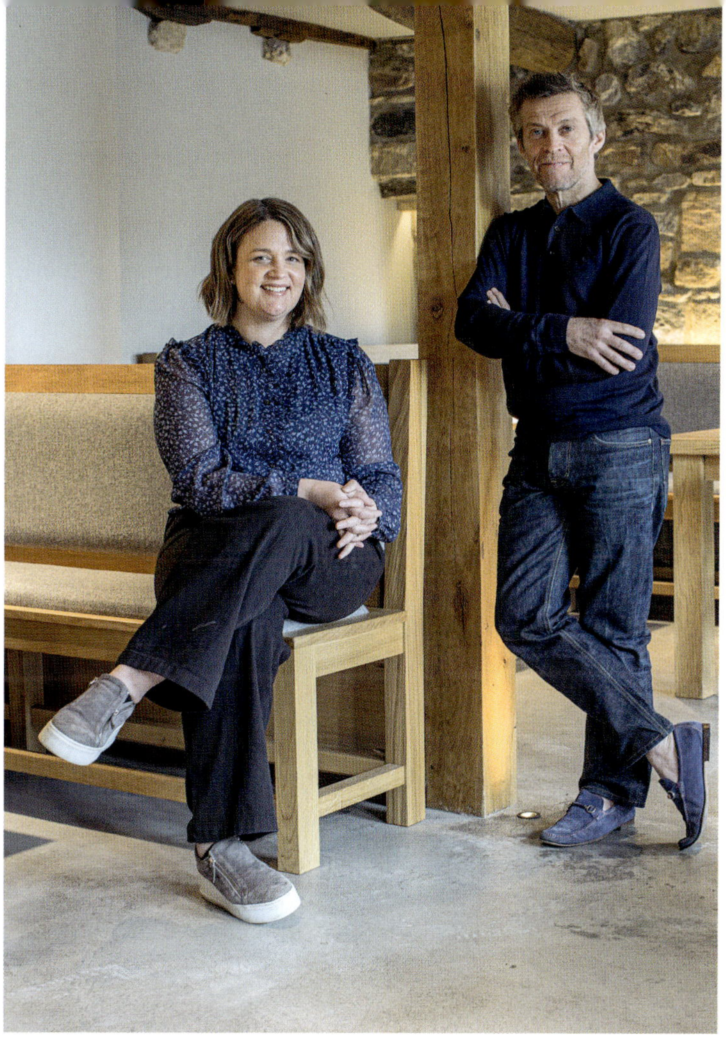

"I WANTED TO PUSH THE FOOD BEYOND PUB GRUB"

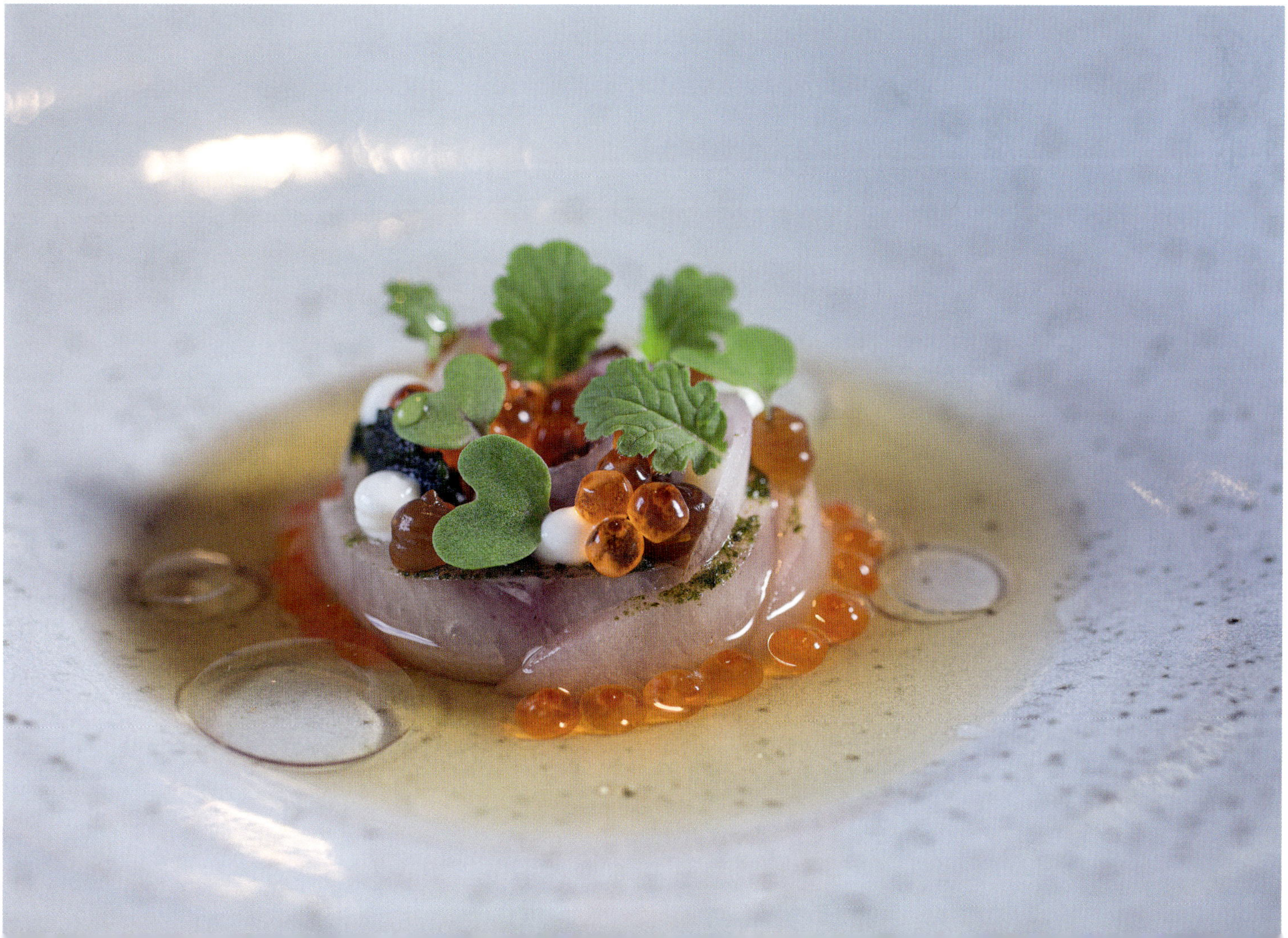

WHITELOCK'S ALE HOUSE

TURK'S HEAD YARD, LEEDS

If you want to find "the very heart of Leeds", as the former poet laureate Sir John Betjeman once described Whitelock's Ale House, you have to know where to look. The pub, first established in 1715, is tucked away down a tiny blind alley between a couple of standard-issue shopfronts in the city centre; trust in Google Maps and you'll step out of the corporate contemporary and into what amounts to pub Narnia, with the element of secrecy even adding a Prohibition-esque frisson.

Whitelock's, however, is no subterranean speakeasy. It's built into a row of Georgian working men's cottages – the sign for an engraver's is still emblazoned above one of the doors – and faces onto a long, narrow yard, which becomes an al fresco social hub in summer. The Edwardian interior, also compact – an Olympic long jumper could probably make a podium-worthy leap from the farthest end of the rangy mahogany bar to the kitchen serving hatch on the other side of the saloon – has been largely untouched over its three-hundred-year lifespan, from the bar itself with its ceramic tiles and windows of etched and stained glass, proclaiming its status as "Whitelock's First City Luncheon Bar", to the homely fireplace and the original cast-iron table bases with the pub's name adorning them – an early example of branding. It was reportedly the first building in Leeds to have electric lighting and an electric clock installed, sometime around the turn of the twentieth century, and it's been known to attract the great and the good; Prince George, later Duke of Kent, entertained a party in a curtained-off section of the saloon in the 1920s, an era when liveried doormen enforced a dinner-jacketed dress code and women weren't allowed at the bar. In the 1960s and 1970s it became the watering hole of choice for literary greats – including local boy and *Billy Liar* author Keith Waterhouse and hobbit maestro J.R.R.Tolkien – and acting colossi such as Peter O'Toole (the nearby presence of the City Varieties theatre means that it still gets a fair smattering of thespians). It's also endured its share of "colourful" custodians, including a landlord who presided over an electrified meat counter and apparently took sadistic delight in watching the unwary step up and experience a literal shock, and a landlady whose frigid demeanour earned her the soubriquet of "Ice Queen".

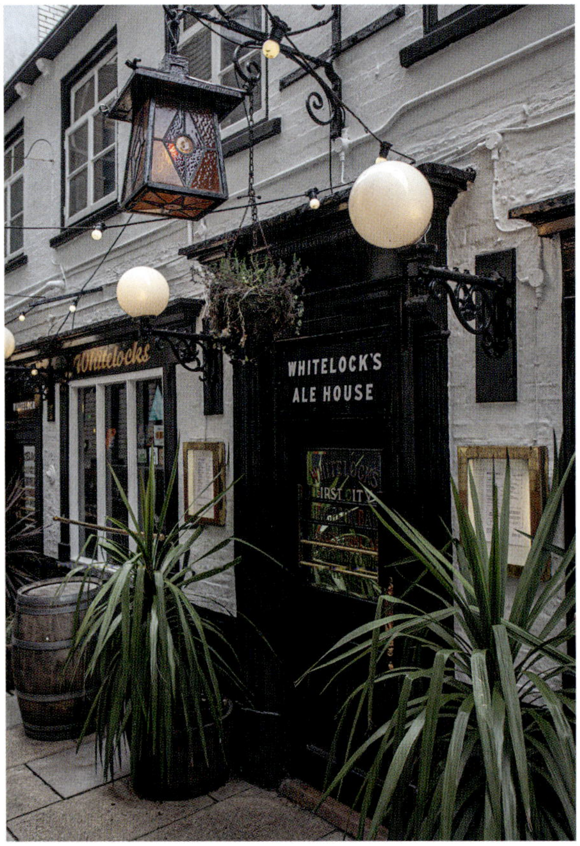

Today, the only buzz is coming from a packed midweek "luncheon" crowd, and the ice is assuming its rightful place – thunking into a generous tumbler of G&T. Whitelock's might be heading into its fourth century, but it's still looking sprightly. "We have regulars who've been coming for decades, including a guy who shows up at eleven o'clock every day," says manager Beth Templeton. "We get locals, tourists, shoppers and young hipsters who like to think they've discovered the place. They love the authenticity of it." They also love the range of Yorkshire brews old and new, including Anthology, Ilkley, and the hoppy, citrusy Kirkstall; the above-and-beyond pub grub, including a chive gnocchi and a spiced cauliflower steak; and the northern-centric soundtrack (if we must have music in a pub, at least let it be 'Hit The North' by The Fall and 'Tinseltown in the Rain' by The Blue Nile). "We get so many people saying 'I met my husband here', or 'I had my first pint here', whether that was legal or illegal," says Templeton. "I think what Betjeman said about it absolutely hits the nail on the head." The heart of Leeds is still the one to beat.

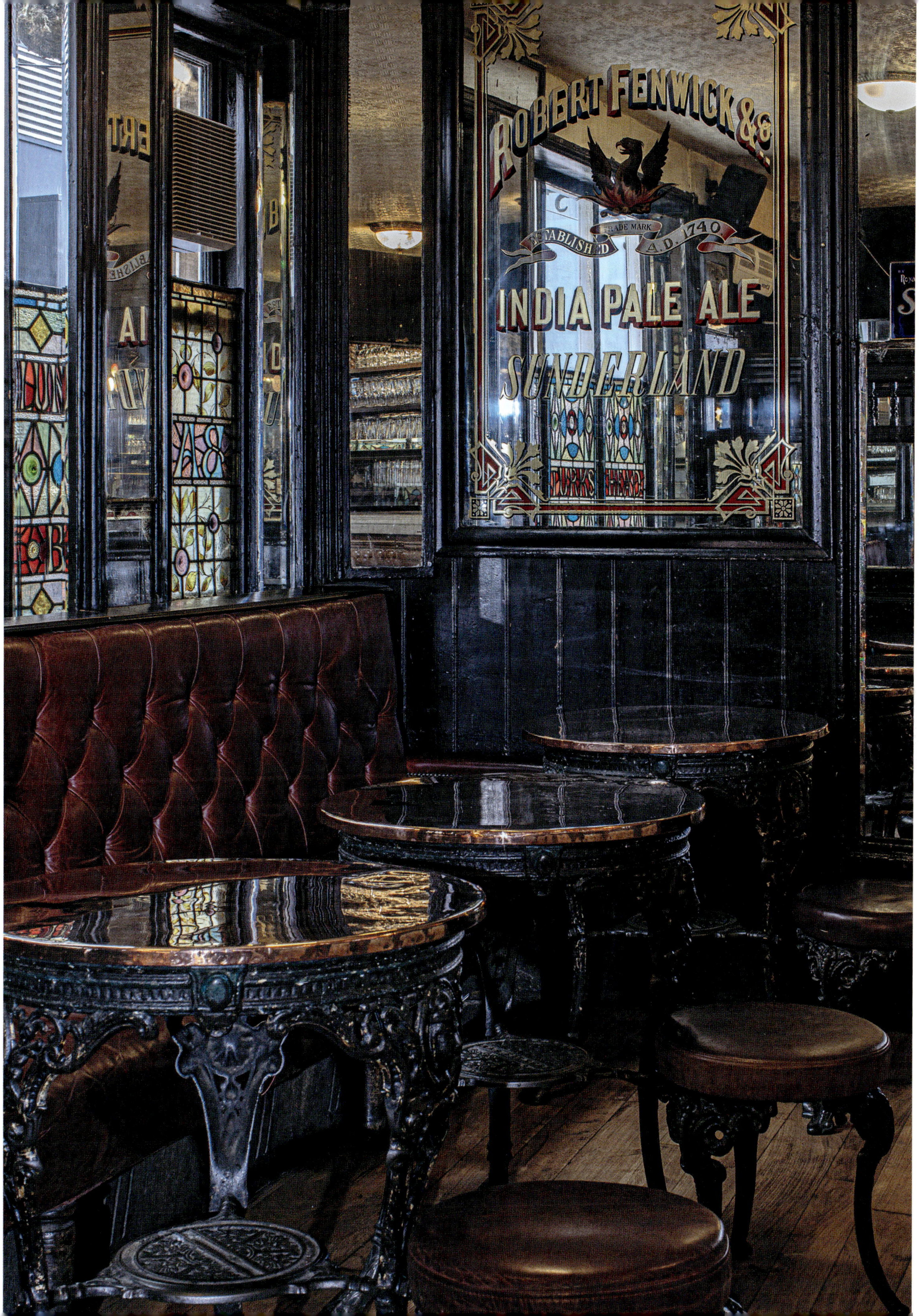
ROBERT FENWICK & Co.
TRADE MARK
ESTABLISHED A.D. 1740
INDIA PALE ALE
SUNDERLAND

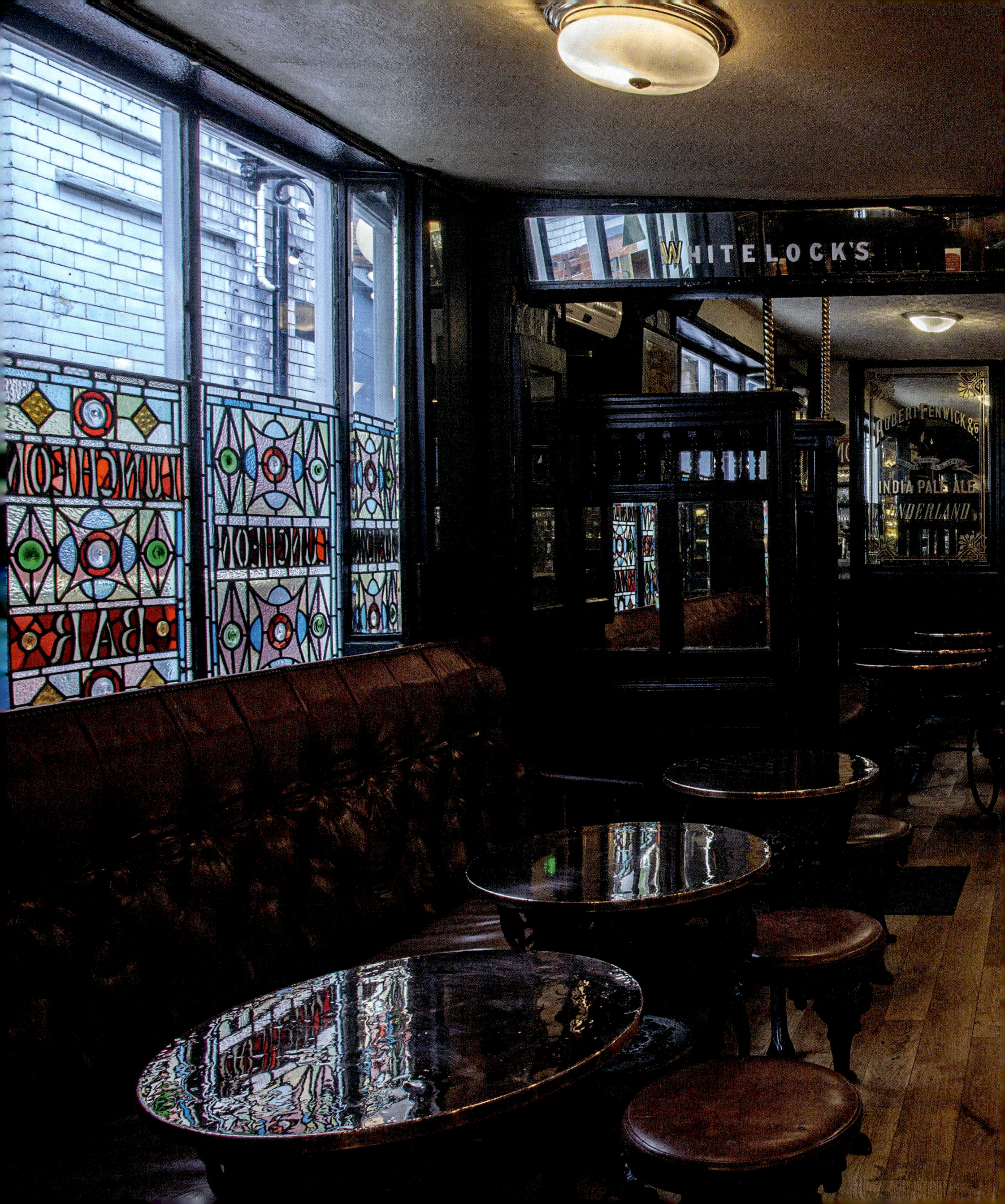
WHITELOCK'S
ROBERT FENWICK & Co
INDIA PALE ALE
SUNDERLAND

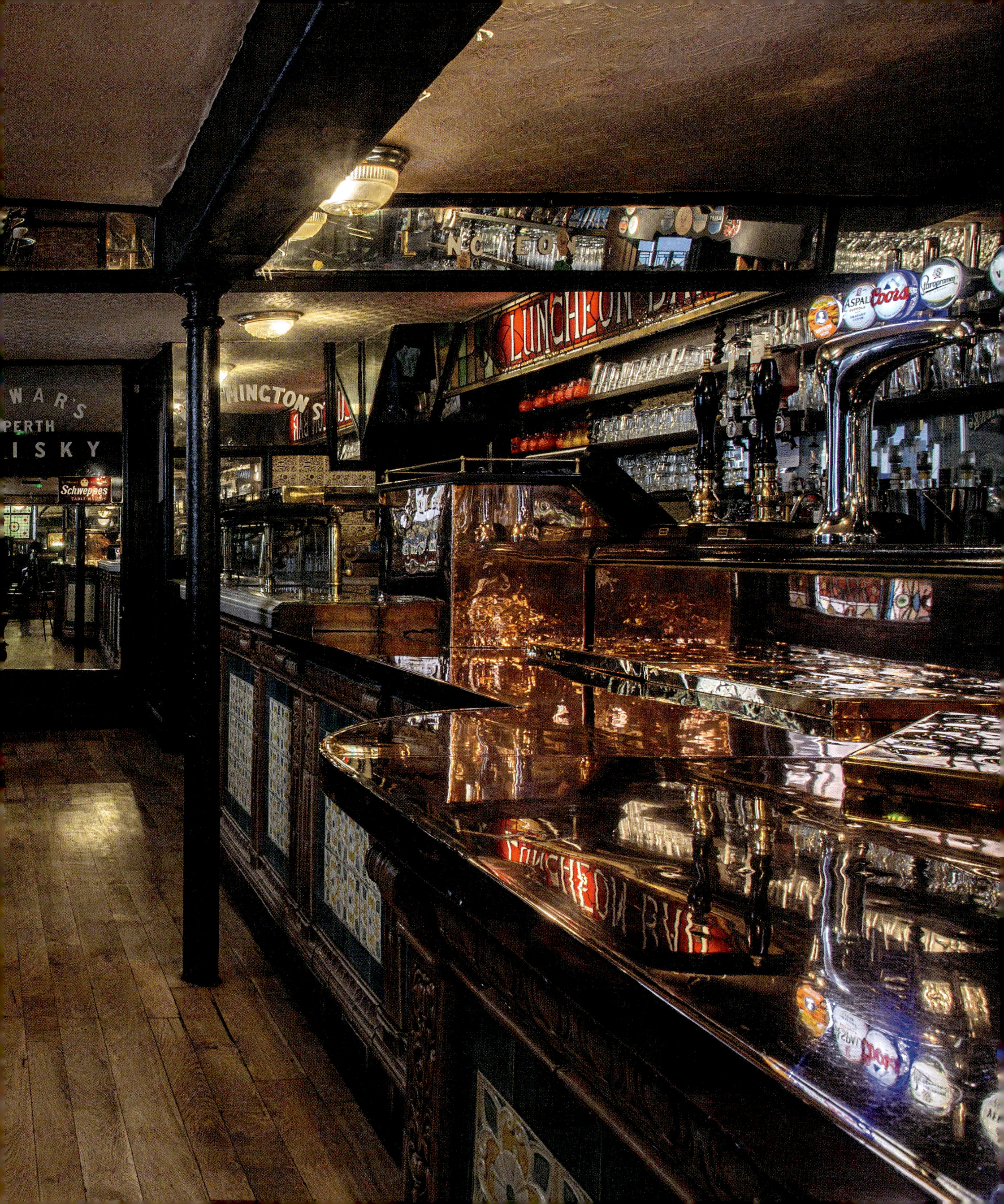
LUNCHEON
PERTH
Schweppes
Coors

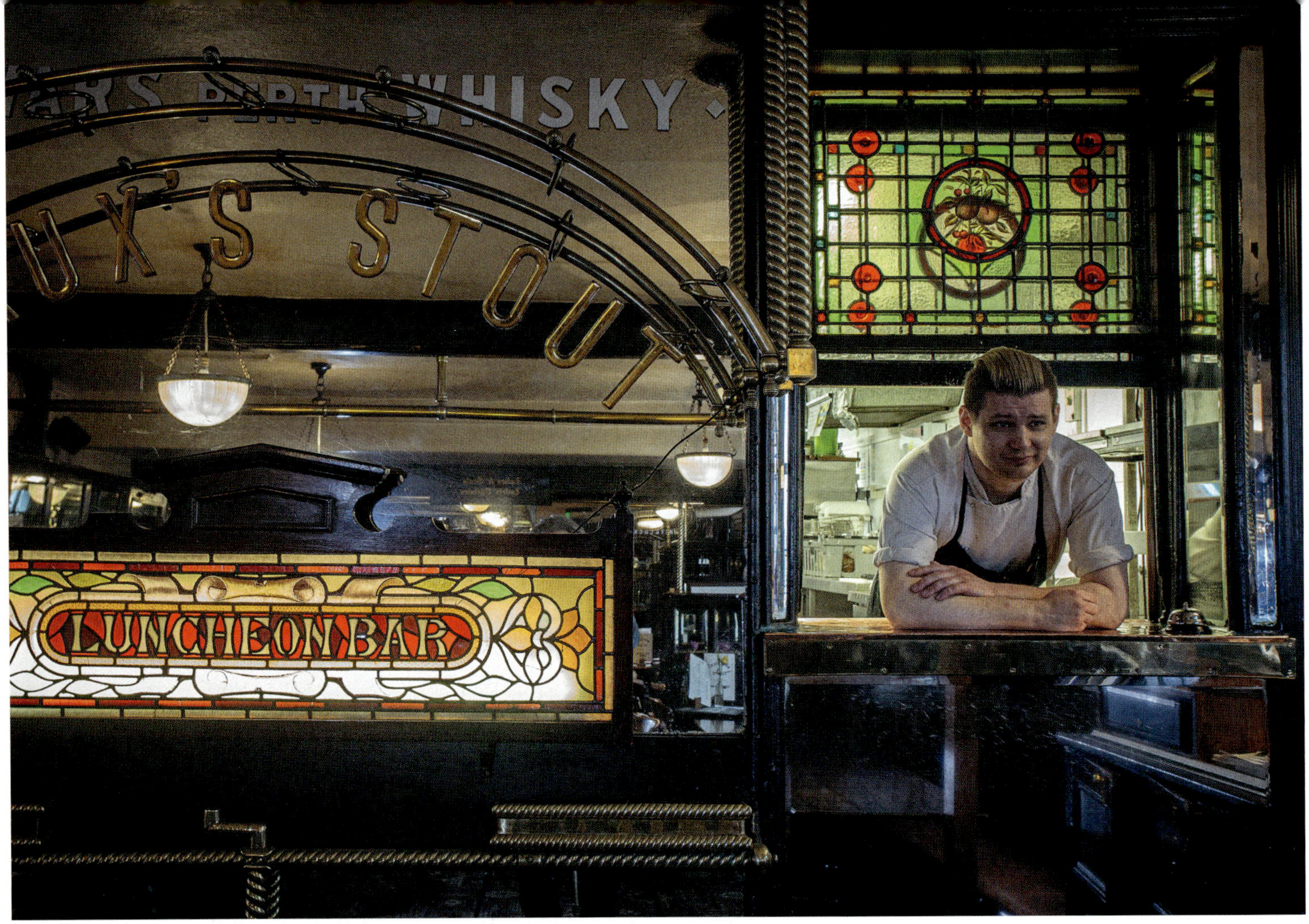
WHISKY
LUNCHEON BAR

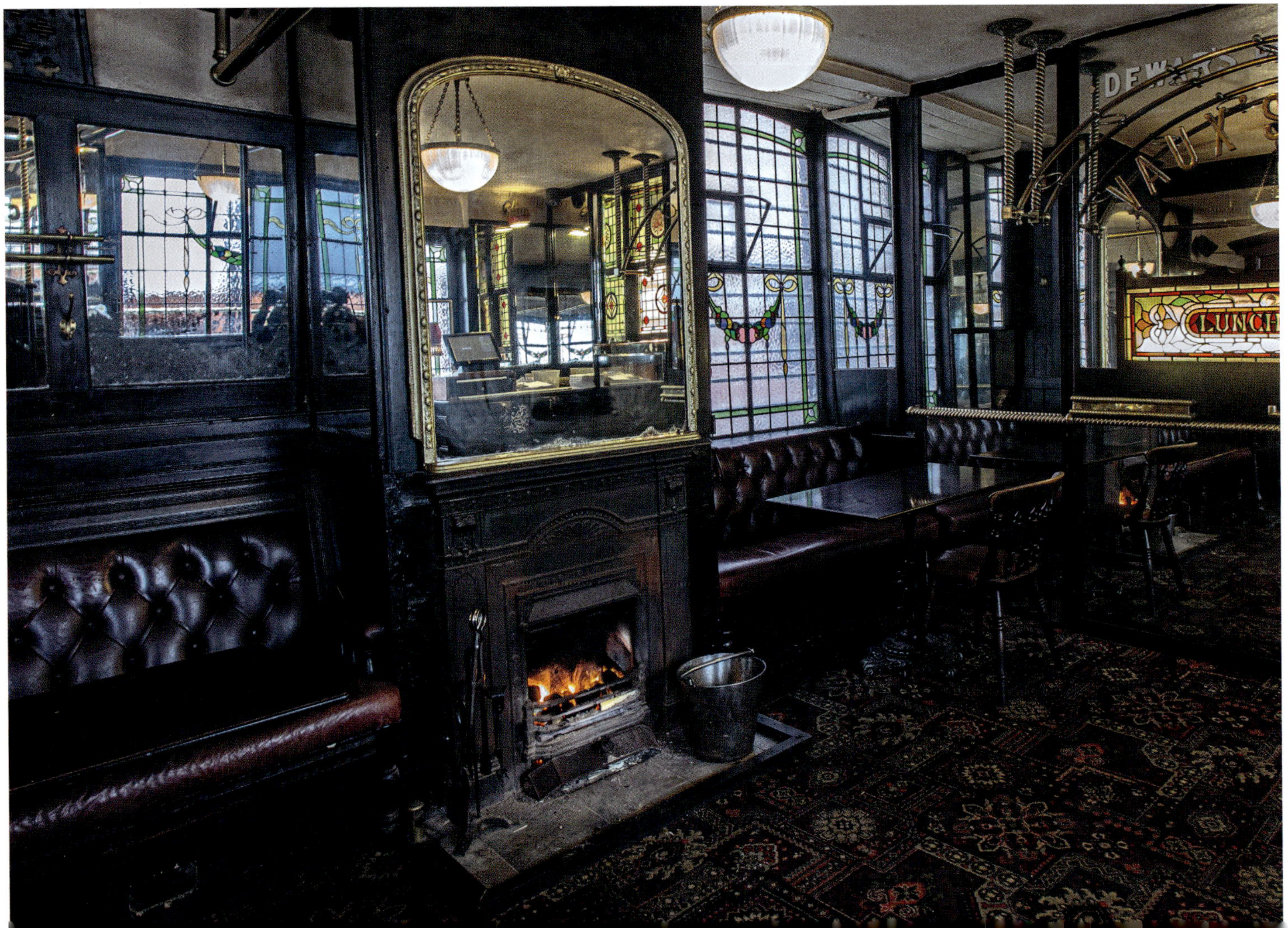

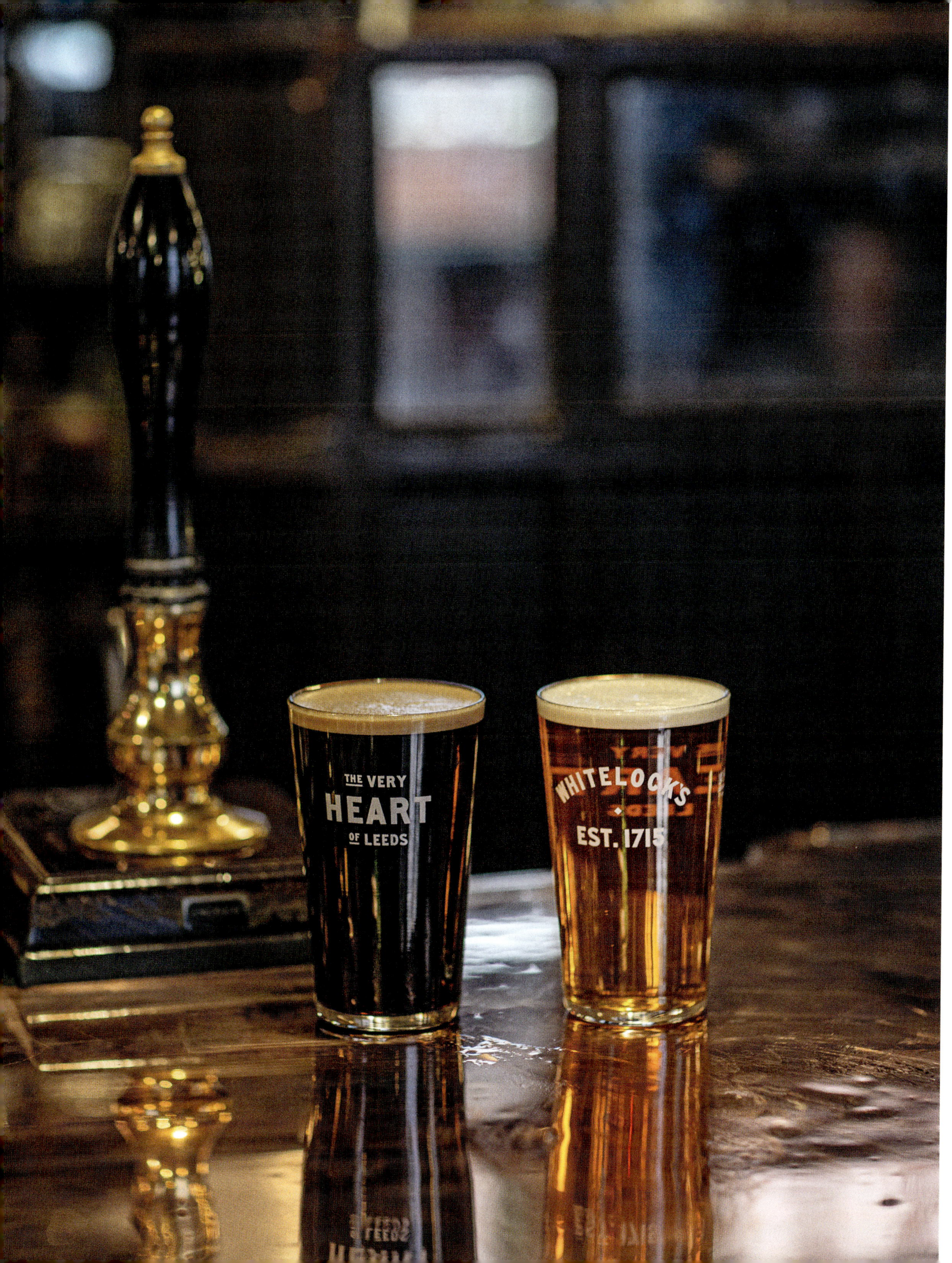

"SO MANY PEOPLE SAY THEY HAD THEIR FIRST PINT HERE"

CROWN POSADA

31 SIDE, NEWCASTLE UPON TYNE

The longer a pub sticks around, the more legends tend to accrue to it; but often, the reality behind those legends can be even more compelling. Take Newcastle's Crown Posada, an ornate 1880s gem on Newcastle's Quayside, flanking the river Tyne, that was recently restored to its late Victorian glory by new owners the Ladhar Group. Are its resplendent stained-glass windows – of a lady pouring a drink, and a gentleman receiving it – the work of celebrated Pre-Raphaelite artist Edward Burne-Jones? No, but they're thought to be "inspired" by the windows that he did indeed create for the Cathedral, just up the road, with the woman representing Hebe, the Greek cup-bearer to the gods, and the gentleman representing the unknown artist himself. And was the "posada" (Spanish for "resting place" or "inn") appended by a Spanish sea captain who bought the pub for his Tyneside mistress? No – this story was apparently completely fabricated by a landlady called Christine in the 1980s, "on a slow day" – but it was added to attract the Spanish sailors who would hove into port, many of whom would "accidentally" leave their caps behind, giving them an excuse to return. "They'd be stashed in their droves above the bar," says Andy Nicholson. "We still have half a dozen or so."

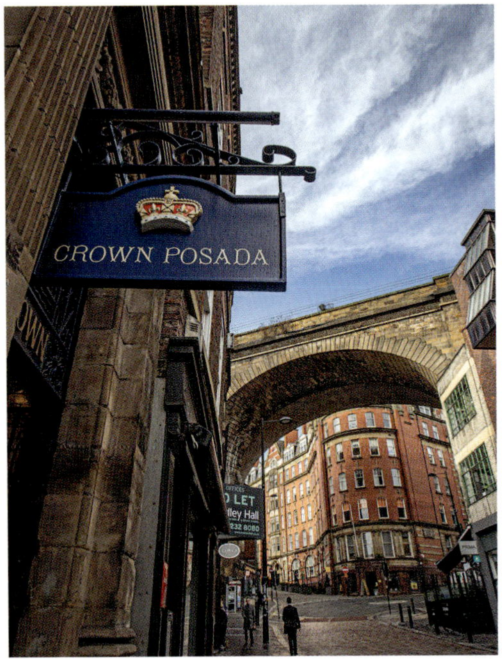

Nicholson is the former bar manager and unofficial historian of the Posada, which he describes as "an oasis of calm on the quayside". It's certainly stately, with its recessed and moulded ceiling, mahogany fittings and long, narrow footprint; sandwiched between the alleys where goods were shunted from shore to market, it once hummed with mariners and merchants. "The snug was the VIP section, where the ship's captains and their business contacts would retreat for a bit of privacy," says Nicholson, who further speculates that "ladies of the night" may have formed part of the wheeler-dealering.

Thankfully, there's no such torrid trade being enacted in today's Posada, which, thanks to Nicholson and his successors' enlightened inventory – "I'm a cellarman by trade, and what the Posada does best is good beer," he says – attracts everyone from retired gents and barristers to local office workers, students and a groovier crowd who might go for the craft beers – the local and spectacularly bittersweet Jakehead IPA, say, or an Imperial raspberry stout with hints of liquorice and chocolate – or the flavoured gins and potent rums. It seems that, whatever their persuasion, the average Posada punter loves to be spoiled for choice, and there should be something among the array that should satisfy even the most outre of tastes, while helping spark the art of civilised conversation at the communal bar. "If a dialogue gets going between people," says Nicholson, "the bar staff should help conduct it as if the punters were an orchestra, keeping it flowing, making connections."

There are further touches that add a homespun air to the Posada's haute Victoriana. A gallery of caricatures of old regulars, created by an artist who worked upstairs in the 1980s, adorns one wall; only one, Tony the Fish, is still alive (and if you want to know why another of the sitters has subsequently had an Elastoplast appended to his forehead, maybe one of the staff can enlighten you – the story is a little too torrid to go into here). Meanwhile, a 1950s gramophone at the end of the bar spins a selection of vinyl, maybe some jazz and Johnny Cash during the day, with some Beatles, Stones and Who later, and then, who knows, maybe even a bit of fist-pumping Van Halen as the evening draws on. The albums have all been donated by regulars, giving them a second life. "It's a kind of romantic idea, to me, that it gives people an emotional connection to the pub," says Nicholson, "because they leave a little bit of themselves behind, much like those sailors did with their caps." And with the generous investment lavished on the Posada by its new owners – shiny parquet flooring, a new cellar and revamped bar systems – it looks like it'll be offering "a cold pint and a warm welcome" for some time to come, along with a memory to cherish and a story to inspire.

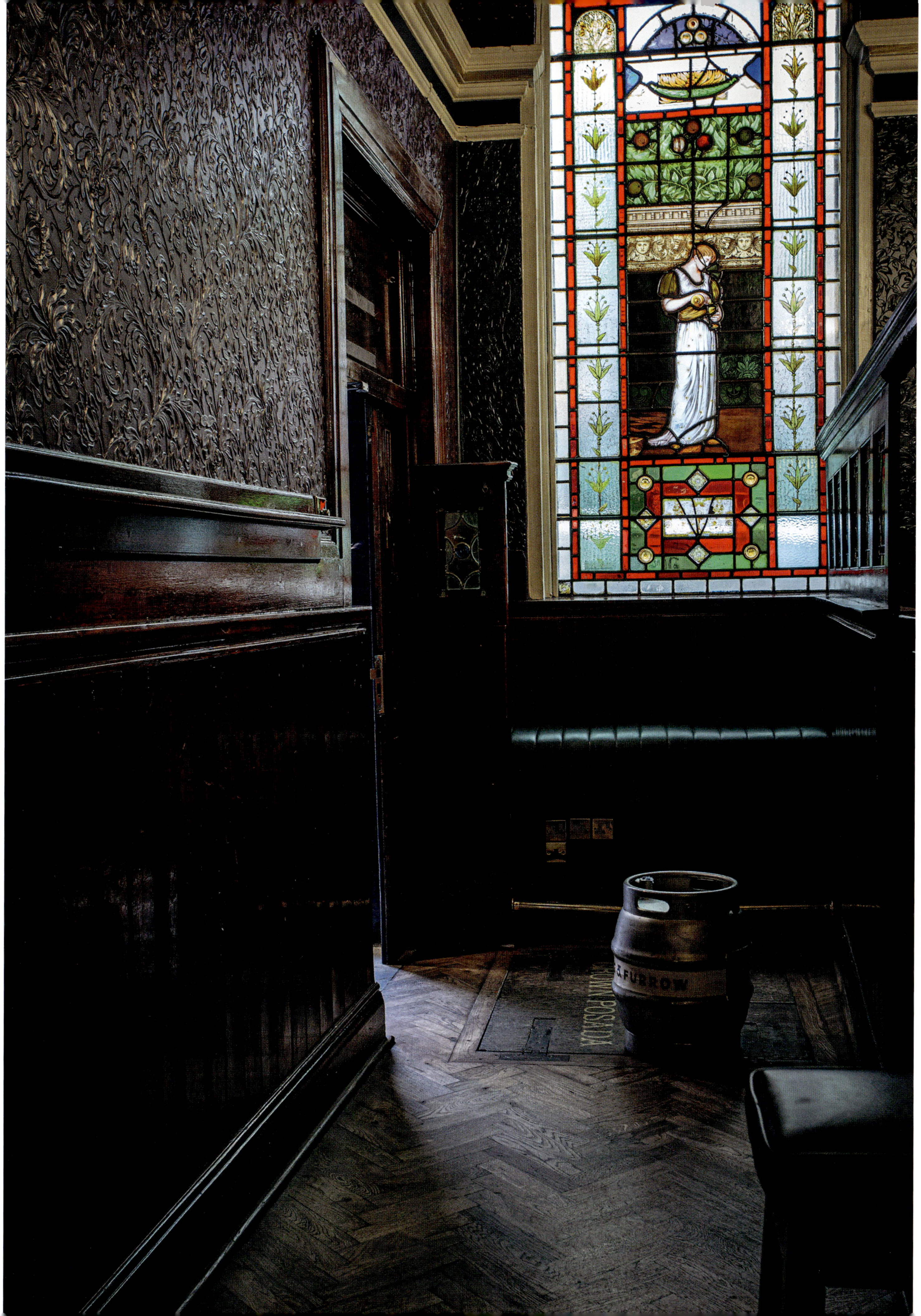

"AN OASIS OF CALM ON THE QUAYSIDE"

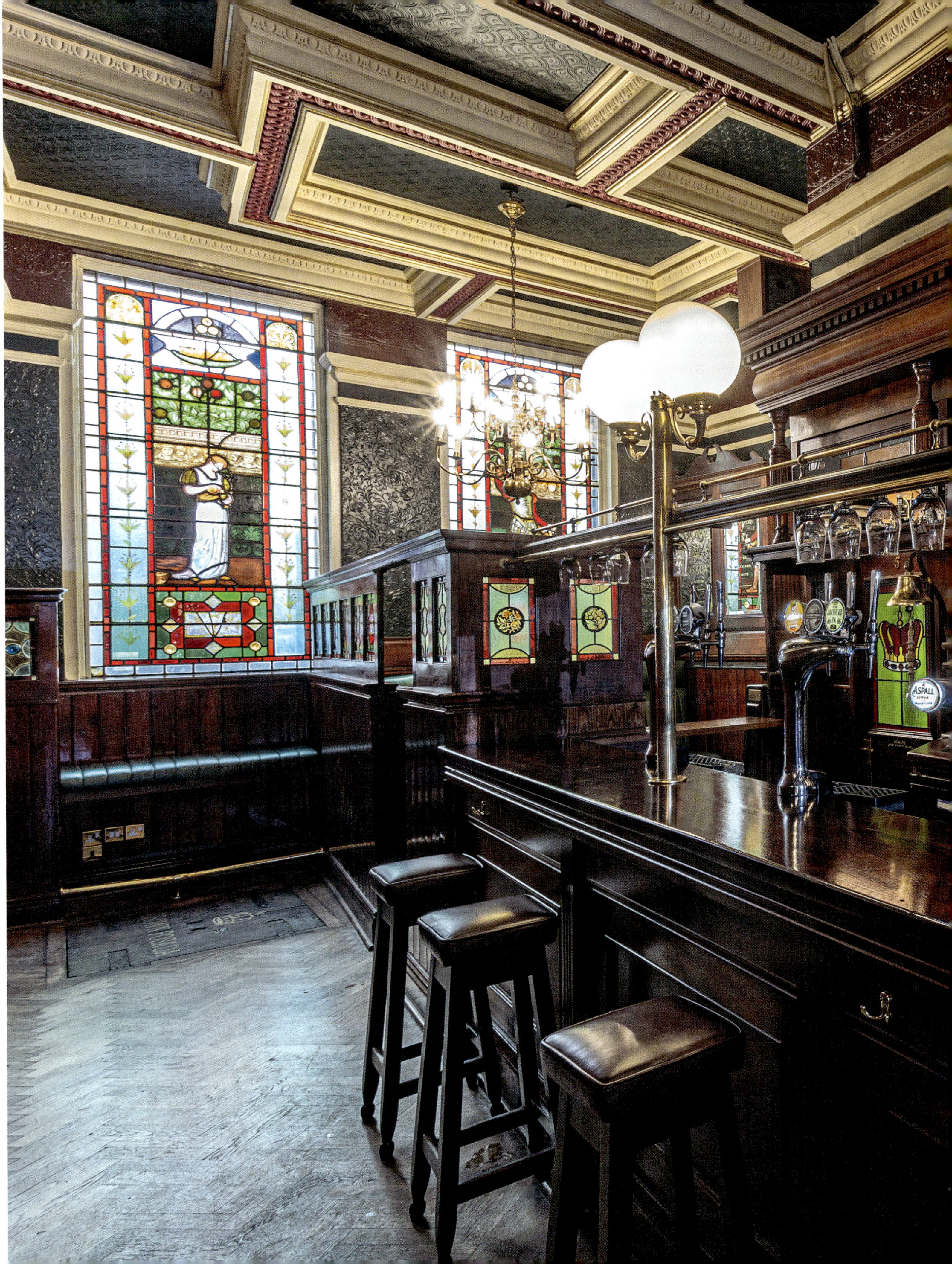
ASPALL

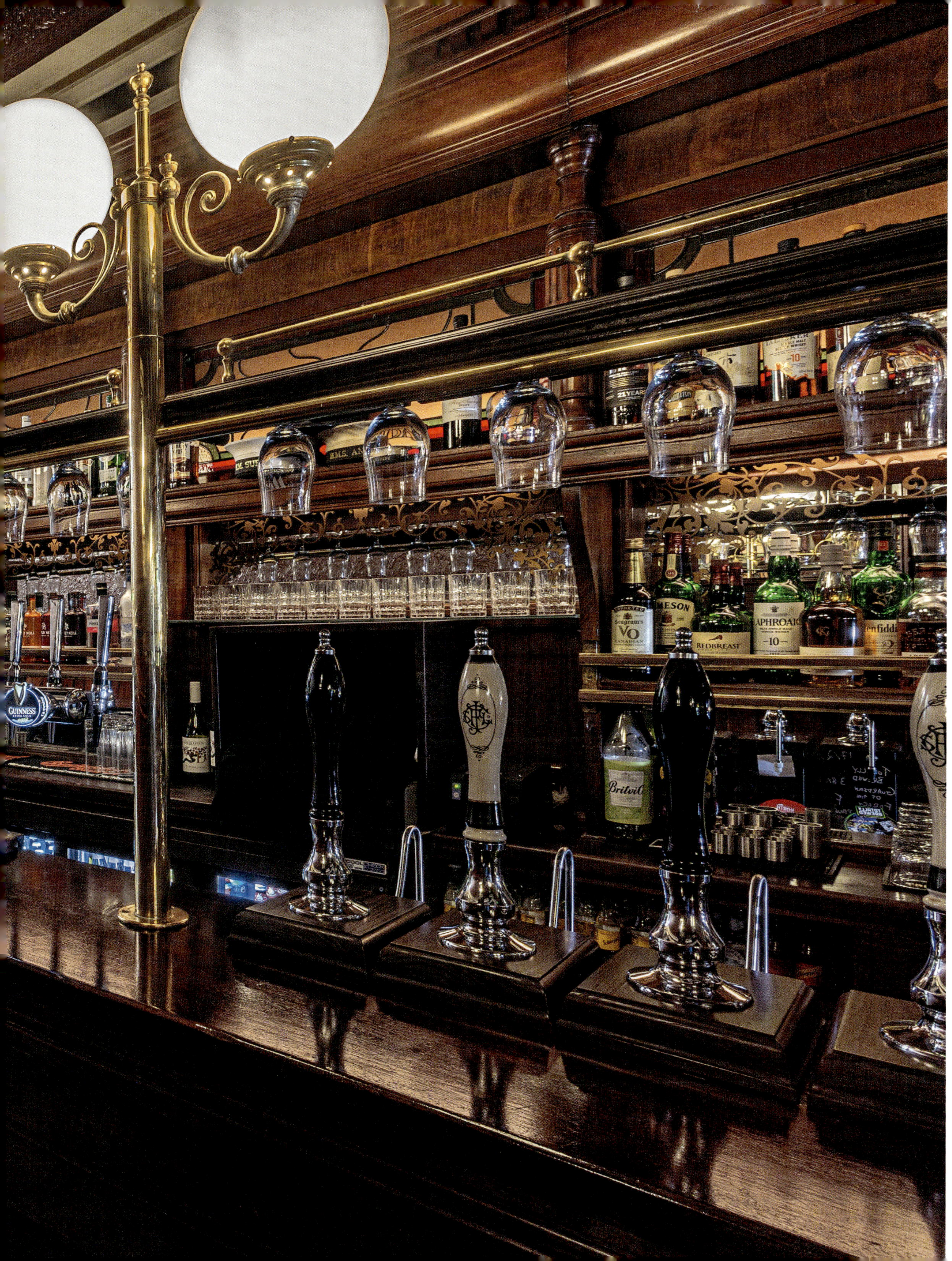

"… IT'S MY JOB TO CONDUCT THE CONVERSATIONS"

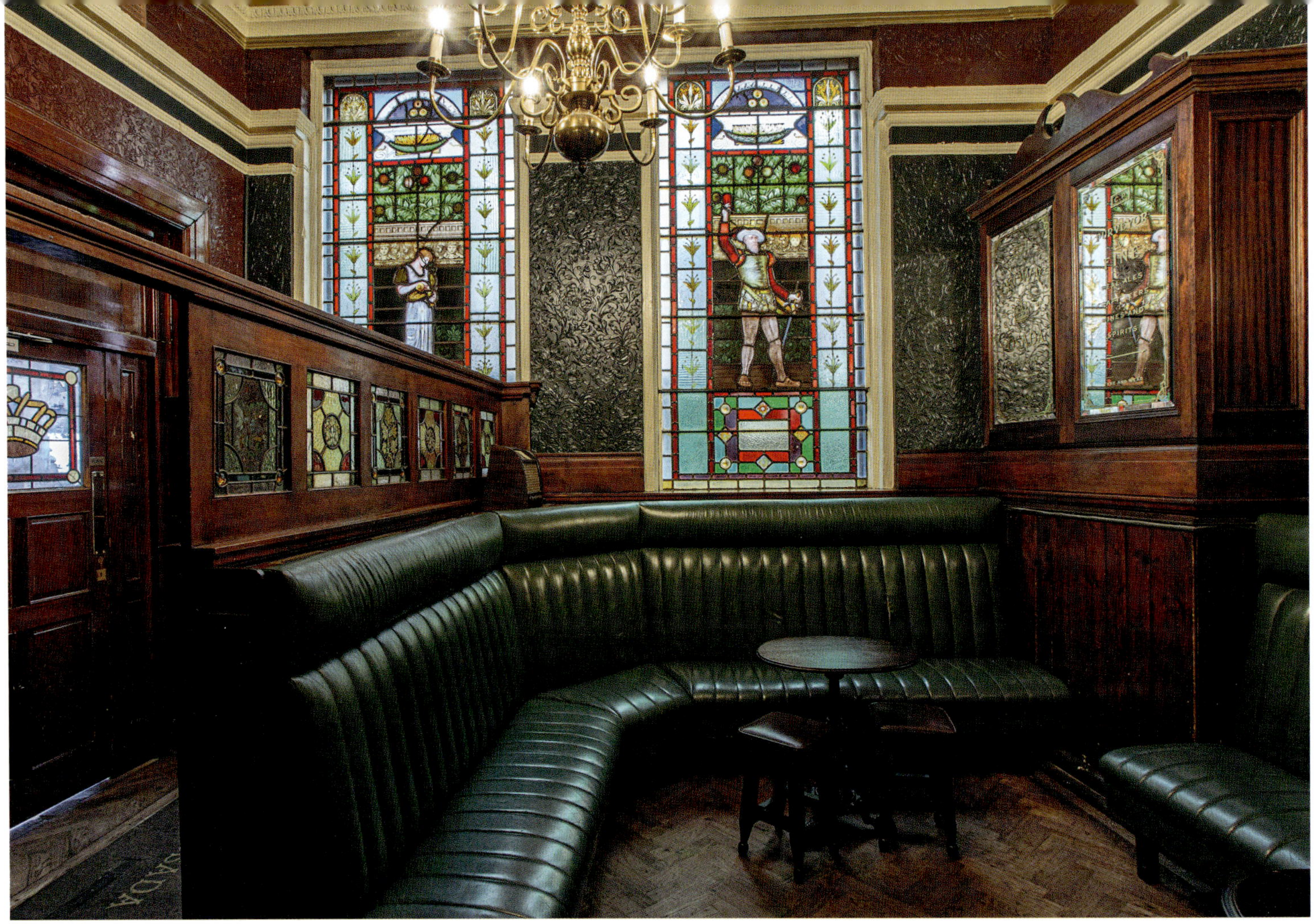

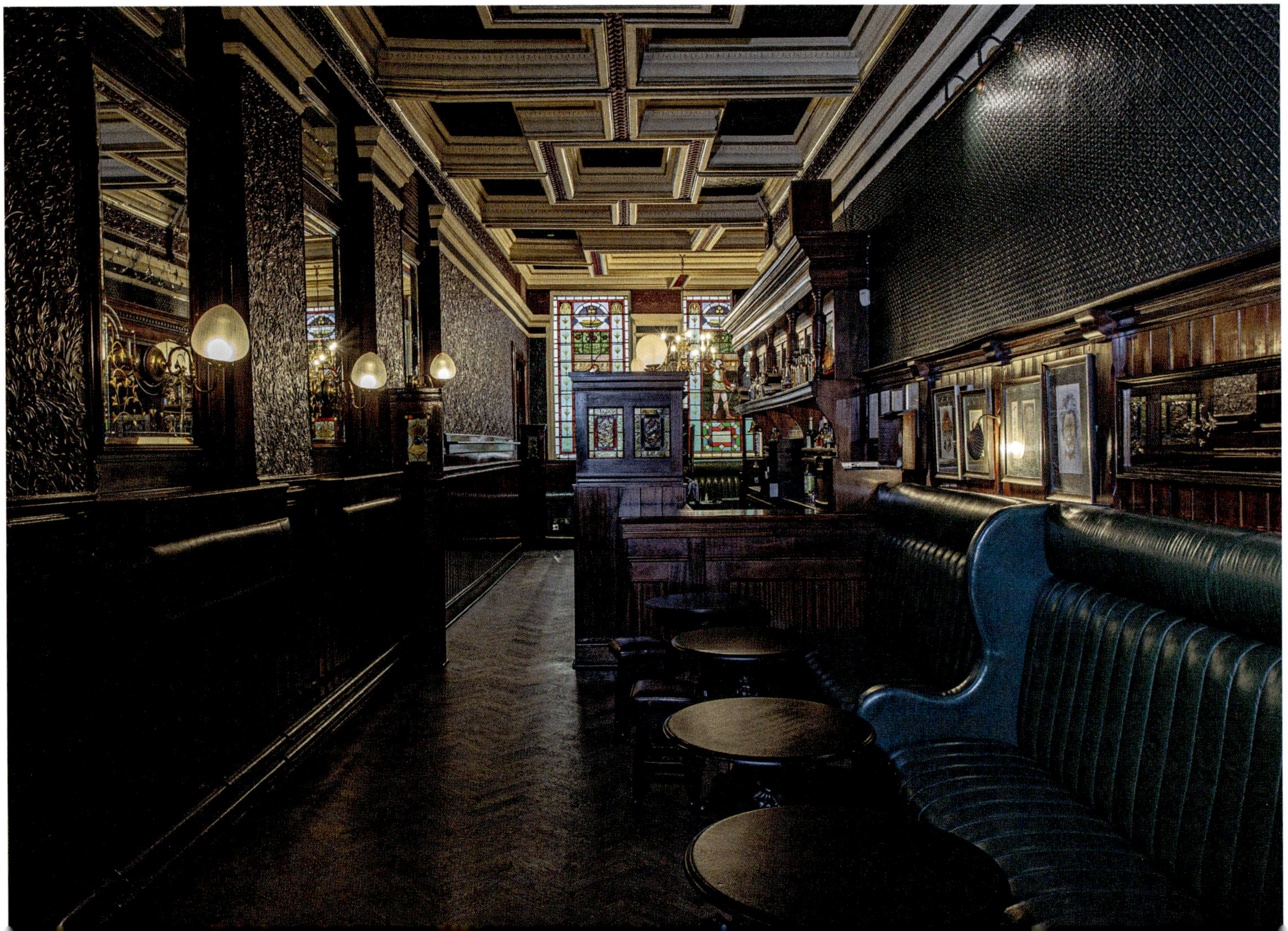

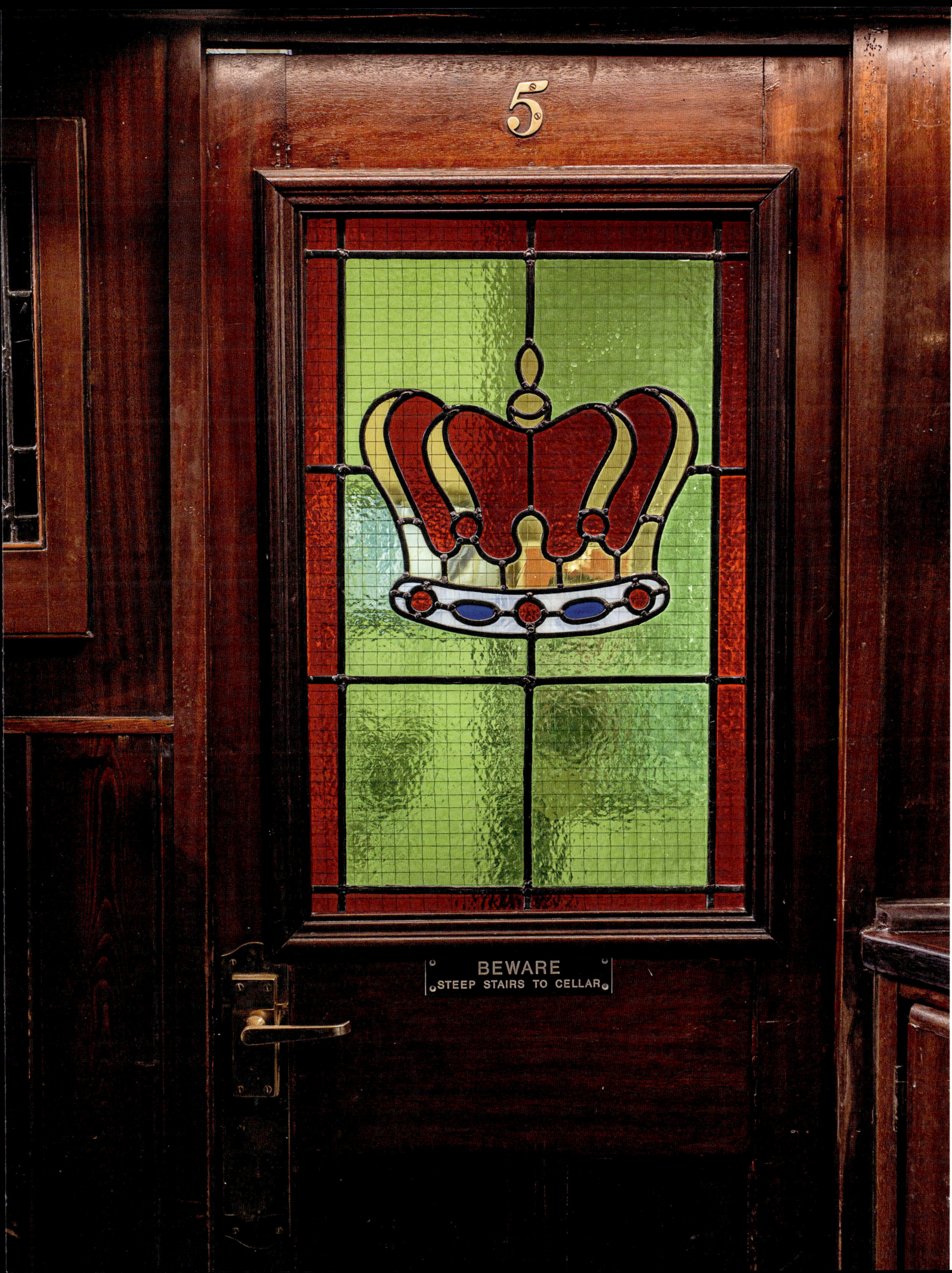
5
BEWARE
STEEP STAIRS TO CELLAR

WHITE HORSE INN, aka NELLIES

22 HENGATE, BEVERLEY

"A lot of people think it's a museum," says one of the regulars of the White Horse Inn, and you can see what he means. This Yorkshire institution, in the stately county town of Beverley, was originally a seventeenth-century coaching inn – it still has a stable yard designed to accommodate seventy horses – and, over the centuries, it's evolved into a warren of idiosyncratic rooms – the Ladies' Parlour, the Linen Press Room, the Scullery – with tobacco-stained walls, pitched wooden floors, gas lighting, ornate mirrors, and a series of cast-iron fireplaces and open ranges that, when all ablaze, set the fire alarms jangling at such a pitch that they drown out the peal of the bells from nearby Beverley Minster. No wonder the short-cased wall clock in the main bar, hopelessly outgunned, chimes at random times, and in random configurations. It's easy to picture the place thronging with farmers, ruddy of complexion, clay pipes bobbing in the corners of their mouths as they discussed livestock vicissitudes, after a hard morning's haggling at the cattle market. Their modern equivalents may have spent the morning browsing stalls laden with vegan sausage rolls and handmade lip scrubs rather than pens packed with beasts of the field, but, at around midday, as the doors open, familiar cries can be heard ("stout please"), favourite tables are bagged, newspapers are spread out, pints are nursed, and dry-as-dust Yorkshire witticisms are exchanged – "the eternal Yorkshire verities", as another regular says.

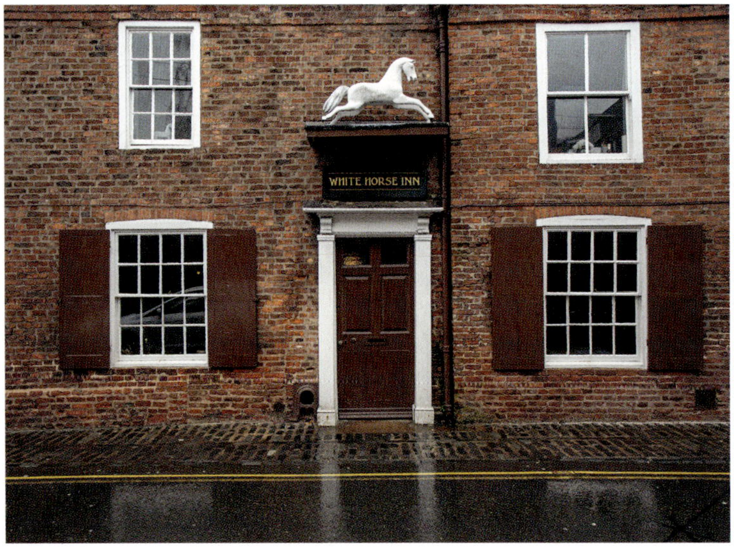

As you enter the pub – under the figure of a carved wooden horse, supported on brackets – you're confronted by a sign in the flagstone passage, above the tongue-and-groove walls and bar hatch: "Nellie Collinson Licenced Retailer Spirits Liqueurs Wines Spirits Ale Porter & Tobacco to be Consumed on the Premises". This refers to the fact that the pub was in the tenure of the Collinson family from 1892, and in 1927 their patriarch Francis Collinson purchased it from the church. Five spinster sisters and two brothers were involved in running the place, but in 1952 the redoubtable Miss Nellie took sole charge and remained at the helm for nearly a quarter of a century, hence the pub's popular nickname. Vintage photos show a figure as stout as the beers she served from a humble table – the main bar was only installed with the takeover of the pub by the Samuel Smith Brewery in 1976 – and with a somewhat forbidding cast. "She was like a sort of mother figure," recalls Ian, one of the regulars ("yes, like Joan Crawford", says another, sotto voce), "but she took a dim view of what she considered inappropriate behaviour." When pressed to elaborate on what constituted the latter for Miss Nellie, he says "Well, you know, kissing and cuddling, stuff like that."

Miss Nellie would be gratified to see that there's no hanky-panky going on today (indeed, this being a Sam Smith's pub, it would simply join the list of the brewery's other prohibitions – no mobile phones, no swearing, no food, etc. – though the second injunction is blithely ignored by all concerned and the third is circumvented by the smuggling-in of some samizdat sausage rolls). Another regular, John, laments the brewery's further embargo on music, as the place used to resound to jigs and reels on folk music nights and singalongs round the now banished upright piano, "despite all the bum notes I used to hit". Nevertheless, he says, Nellie's fully deserves its accolade – recently bestowed upon it by food writer Tom Parker-Bowles and wine aficionado Olly Smith – as one of the cosiest Pubs in Britain: "It's a gem," he says. "Yes, in many ways it's stuck in a time warp – but, when the fire's going and the beer's flowing, you wouldn't want to be stuck anywhere else."

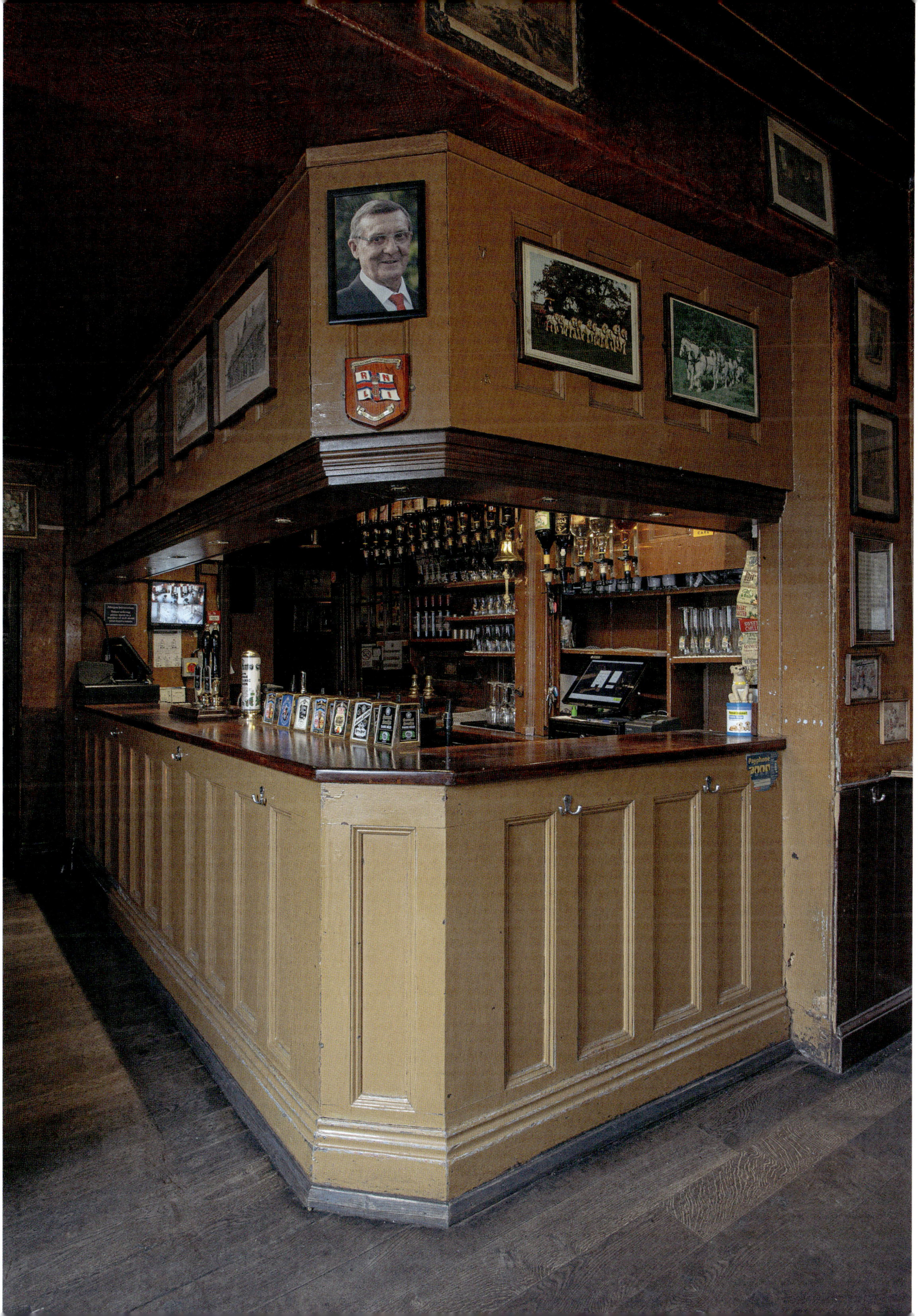

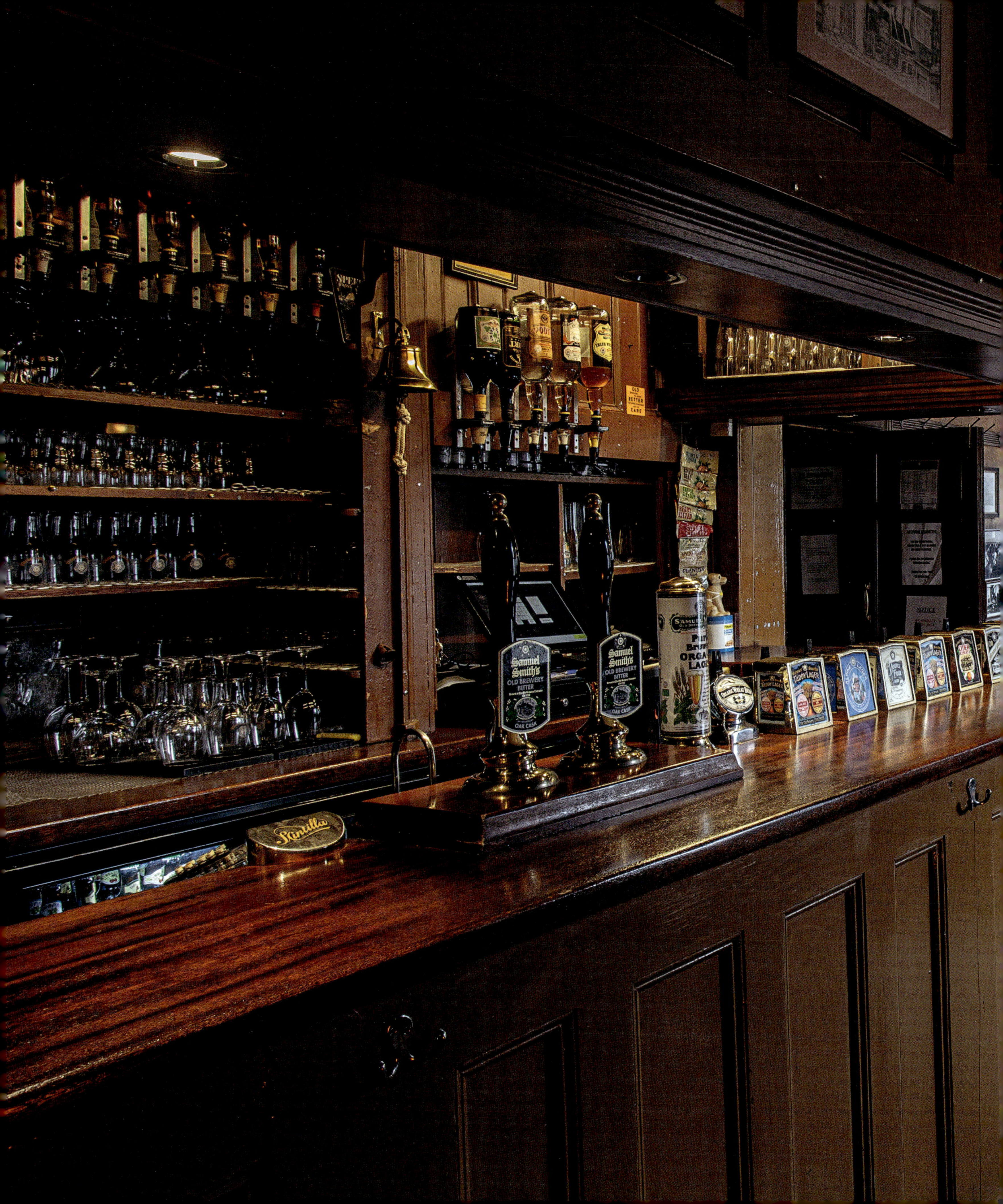
Samuel Smith's
OLD BREWERY
BITTER
OAK CASK
Samuel Smith's
OLD BREWERY
BITTER
OAK CASK
TADDY LAGER

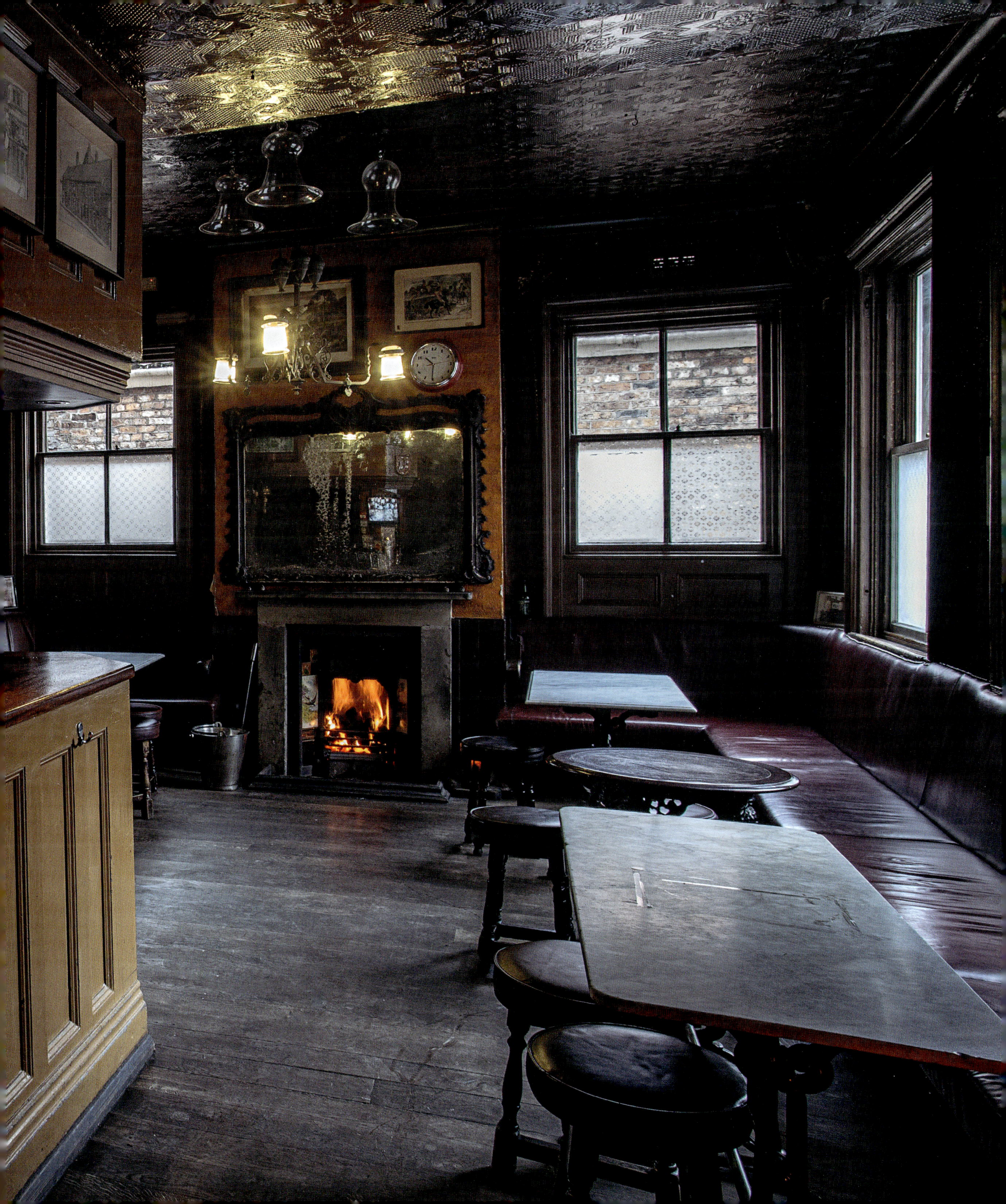

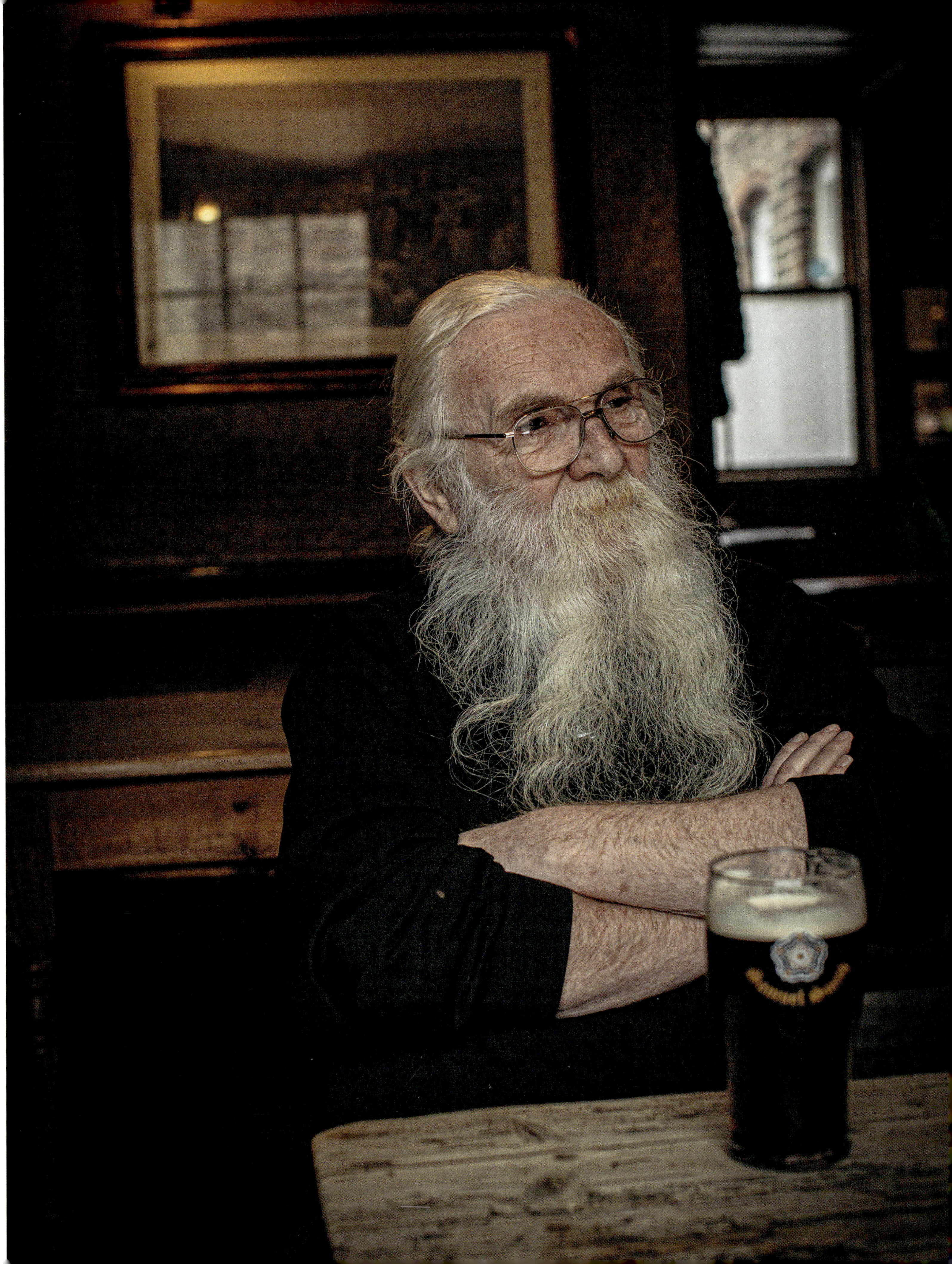

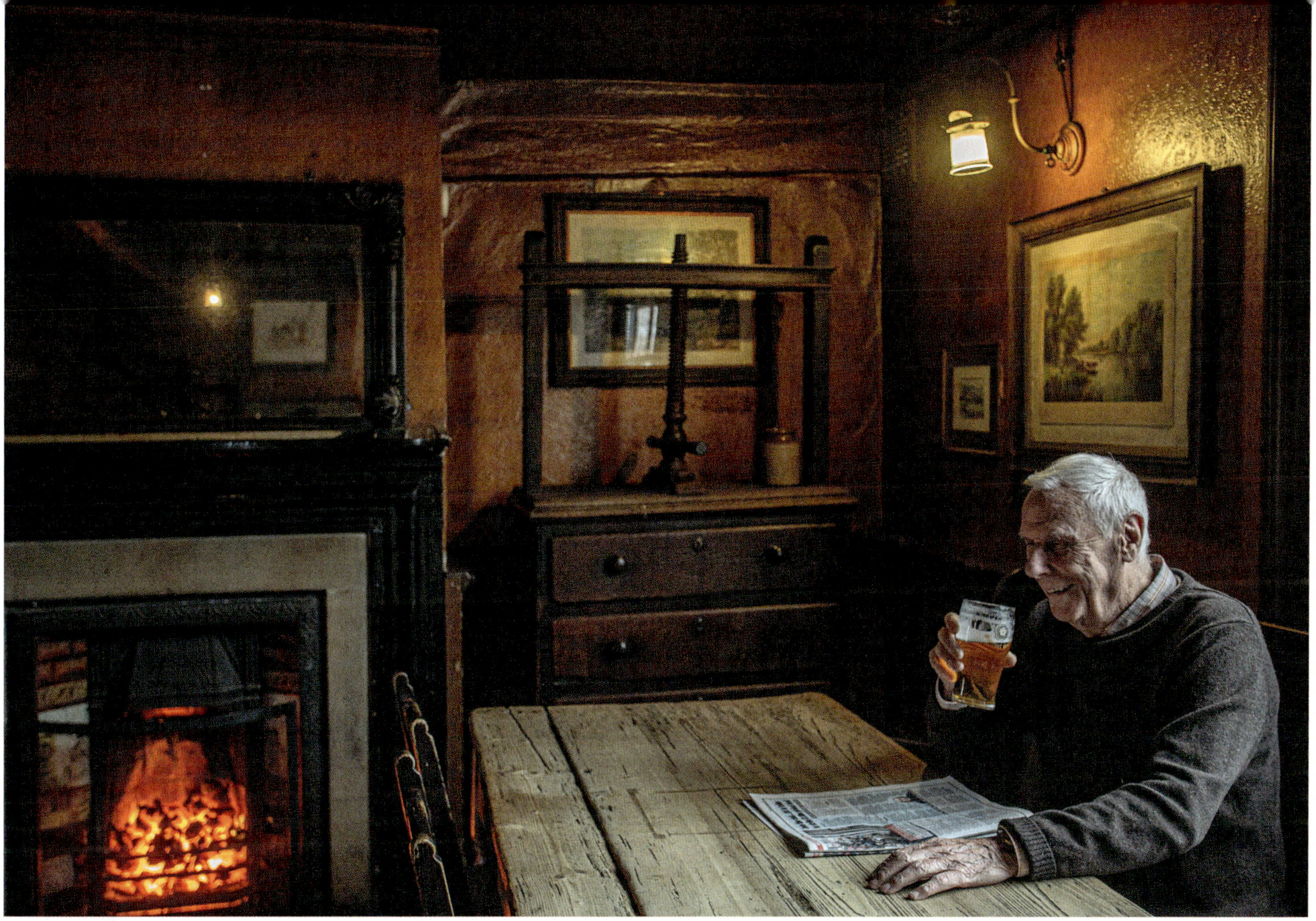

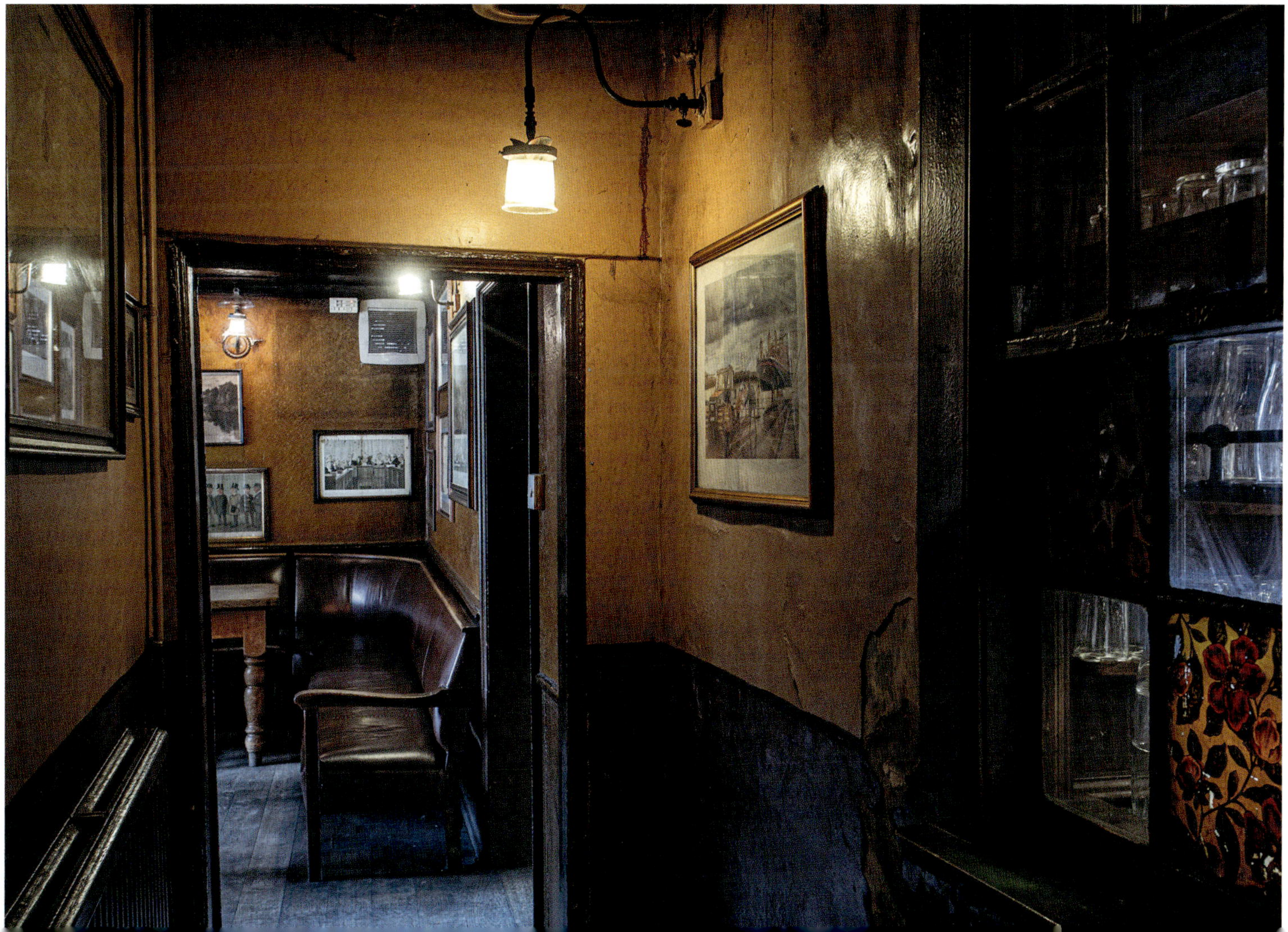

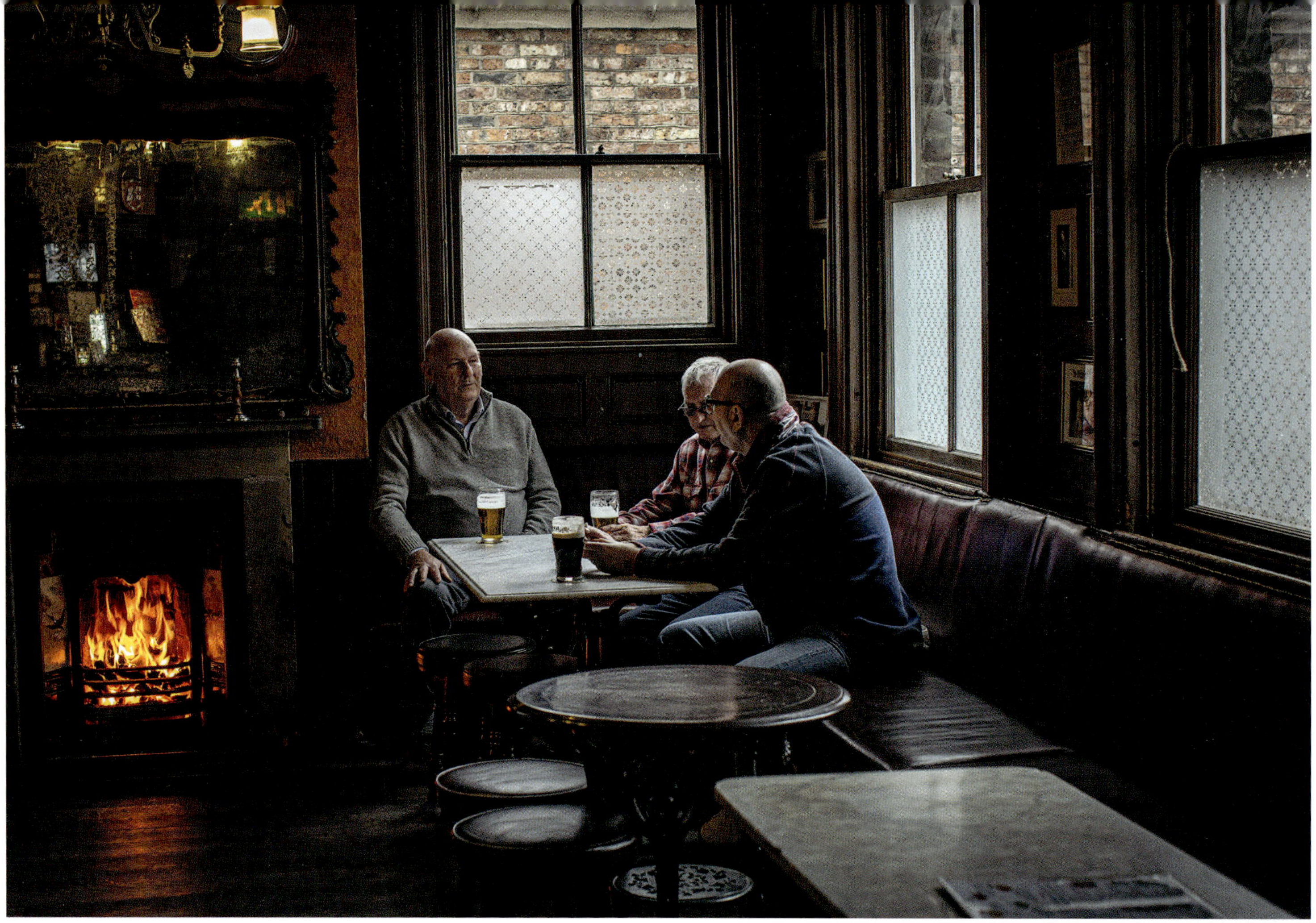

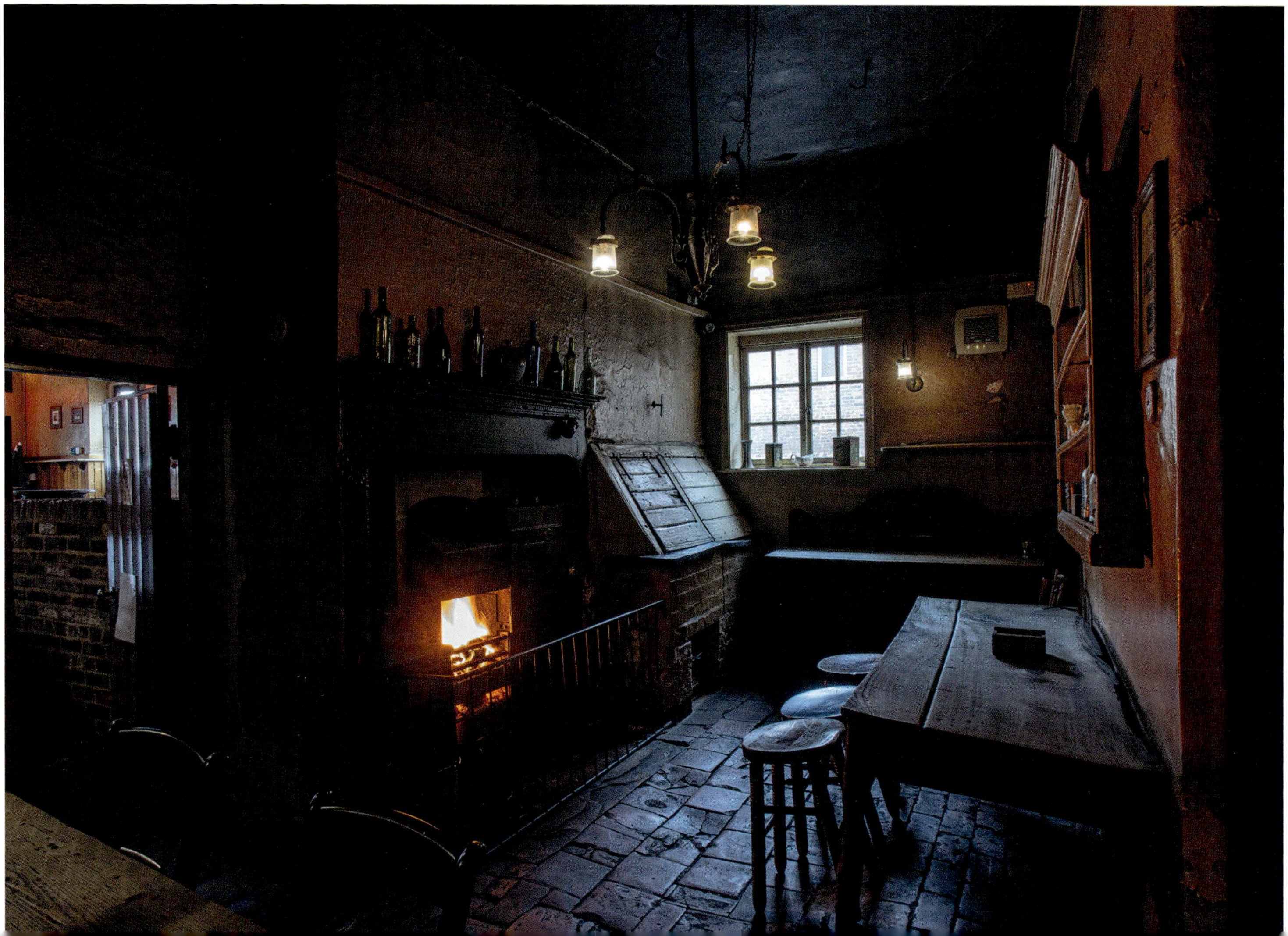

"IN MANY WAYS IT'S STUCK IN A TIME WARP ..."

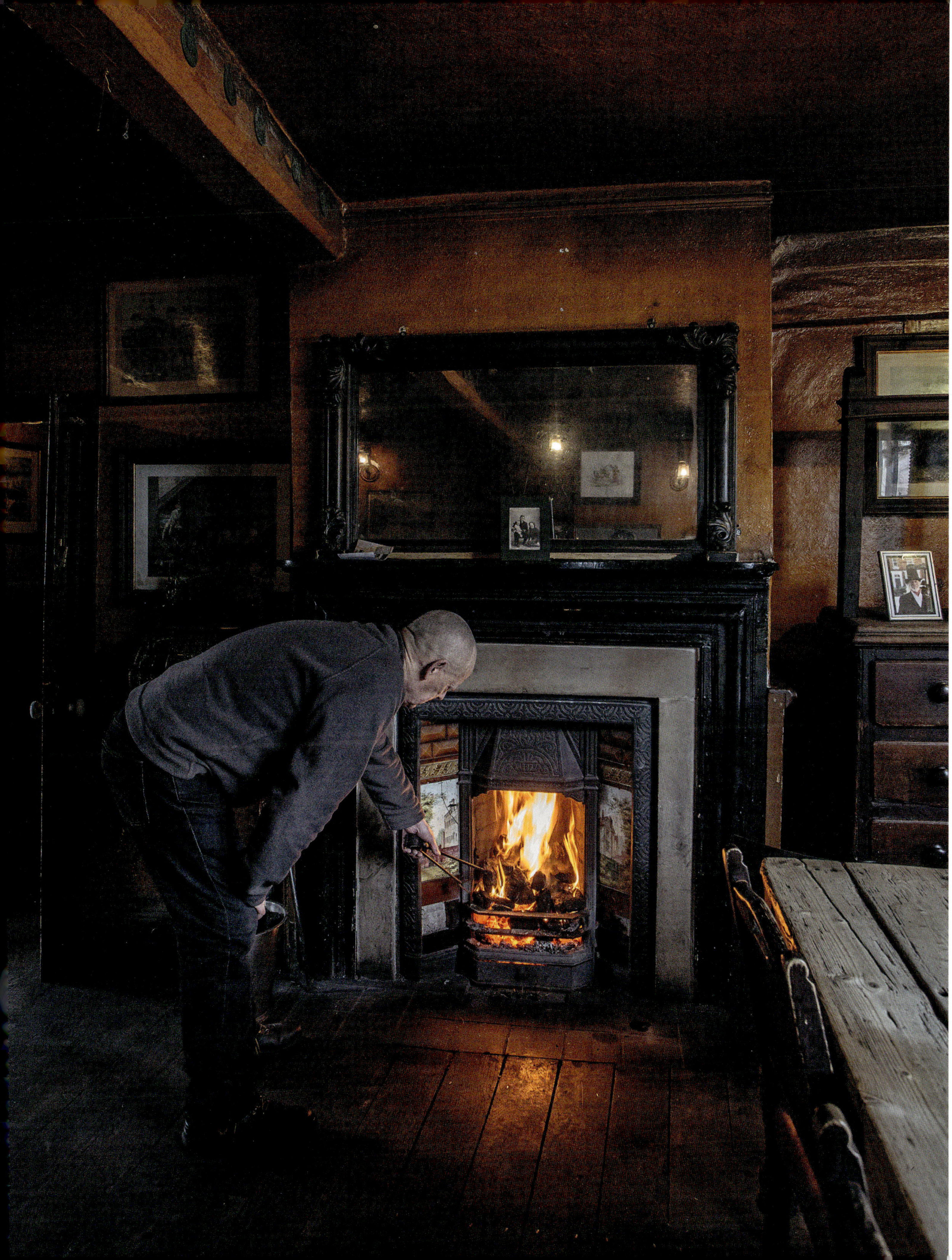

"... BUT IS THERE A BETTER PLACE TO BE STUCK?"

HORST A. FRIEDRICHS

Internationally renowned photographer Horst A. Friedrichs was born in Frankfurt in 1966. He studied photography in Munich and has worked for a number of noteworthy publications including *National Geographic, The New York Times* and *The Observer*, taking portraits of everyone from Robbie Williams, Peter Gabriel and Tony Blair to Bill Gates and Stephen Hawking. Though he made a name for himself with commercial work, it is his long-term book projects, documenting subcultures and architecture, that bring out his fierce and excitable passion. From the Sufis in Pakistan to the Mods and Rockers of the British underground, Horst has spent decades digging into these scenes and cultures and capturing their fascinating characters. He has published numerous books including the bestselling *Cycle Style, I'm One: 21st Century Mods, Or Glory: 21st Century Rockers, Drive Style, Denim Style, Coffee Style, Best of British* and *Bookstores* (all by Prestel). He is currently based in London.

STUART HUSBAND

Stuart is a Hastings-based journalist whose work has appeared in *Monocle, The Telegraph, The Observer, The Sunday Times* and *The Independent*. He is the author of *Bookstores* with Horst A. Friedrichs.

ACKNOWLEDGEMENTS

This book could not have been realised without the enthusiasm and support of the following people: Johanna and Michael Wignall, The Angel at Hetton; Lilly and Luke Daniels, The Bag of Nails; Katie Bone, Calven, Jake, Beavertown Corner Pin; Simon, Kim and Ben, The Blue Anchor; John Pybus, The Blue Bell; Sean Atkinson, The Boleyn Tavern; Nick Lawrie, British Beer and Pub Association; Alan Hudd, The Briton's Protection; Laura Hadfield and Tom Kerridge, The Butcher's Tap and Grill; Tess and Andrew, The Crown; Andrew Nicholson and Chris Foster, Crown Posada; Maria, The Dog and Duck; Henry Conlon, The Dublin Castle; Andy's team, The Falkland Arms; Michael and Xochi Birch, Emily Harmon and Charlie Heath, The Farmers Arms; James Blunt and Toby Milne, The Fox & Pheasant; Lesley Lewis, The French House; Sandra Esquilant, The Golden Heart; Kinga Cholewka, The Guinea Grill; Ivor Braka and Stuart and Simone Tattersall, The Gunton Arms; Ilia and Anastasia Klekovkin, Haunch of Venison; Tom Harris and Jon Rotheram, Marksman Public House; Humairaa Tedds, Mitchells & Butlers Brewery; Alf and Kerrie, The Palm Tree; Nadim Hammad, Peveril of the Peak; Eamonn Lavin, Philharmonic Dining Rooms; Mr Vasile, Princess Louise; Helen and Tim, Royal Oak; Dave Cross and James Lindsay, Royal Vauxhall Tavern; Linda Stuart, Samuel Smith Brewery; John Brearley, The Swan & Railway; Ben Tunnicliffe, Tolcarne Inn; Sara Cornfoot, White Horse Inn; Beth Templeton, Whitelock's Ale House; Neil Warren, Ye Olde Cheshire Cheese.

Thank you to all the participants who gave generously of their time, especially Nick Appleton, Lee Broom, Ben Chamberlain, Patrick Carroll, Diana, Dotty, Erika, Bernard Freeland, Stella Friedrichs, John Hansford, Phil James from & SONS, Maria Chiara and Stefano, Me The Drag Queen, Mike Harding Folk Show, Stuart Minshaw, John O'Conner, Sam and Grace, Jasper Selwyn Sharpe and Denis Whiteside.

My publisher Prestel has made this a great experience and a deeply satisfying creative undertaking, thanks to the efforts of my editor Curt Holtz and the contributions of Jonathan Fox, Ryn Gardner, Andrew Hansen, Corinna Pickart, Christian Rieker, Sabine Schmid, Will Westall and Pia Werner.

A special thanks to my wife Adriana and my two daughters Greta and Zoe, for their love, faith and inspiration.

I would also like to thank the author Stuart Husband for your words and the way you have woven them together. You are the best! And creative director Lars Harmsen who created the book's design, for his generous work, tremendous enthusiasm and never-ending creativity. The input from both of you during the making of this book, and your enduring friendship, are invaluable to me. I would also like to thank the art director Alexander Staudt.

Cheers!

Horst A. Friedrichs, London, 2022